NATIONAL ACADEMIES *Sciences Engineering Medicine*

NATIONAL ACADEMIES PRESS
Washington, DC

Understanding the Aging Workforce

Defining a Research Agenda

Susan T. Fiske and Tara Becker, *Editors*

Committee on Understanding the Aging Workforce
and Employment at Older Ages

Committee on Population

Committee on National Statistics

Division of Behavioral and Social Sciences and
Education

Consensus Study Report

NATIONAL ACADEMIES PRESS 500 Fifth Street, NW Washington, DC 20001

This activity was supported by contracts between the National Academy of Sciences and The Alfred P. Sloan Foundation (G-2019-12542), with additional support from the National Academy of Sciences W.K. Kellogg Foundation Fund. Any opinions, findings, conclusions, or recommendations expressed in this publication do not necessarily reflect the views of any organization or agency that provided support for the project.

International Standard Book Number-13: 978-0-309-49387-1
International Standard Book Number-10: 0-309-49387-0
Digital Object Identifier: https://doi.org/10.17226/26173
Library of Congress Control Number: 2022946343

Additional copies of this publication are available from the National Academies Press, 500 Fifth Street, NW, Keck 360, Washington, DC 20001; (800) 624-6242 or (202) 334-3313; http://www.nap.edu.

Copyright 2022 by the National Academy of Sciences. National Academies of Sciences, Engineering, and Medicine and National Academies Press and the graphical logos for each are all trademarks of the National Academy of Sciences. All rights reserved.

Printed in the United States of America.

Suggested citation: National Academies of Sciences, Engineering, and Medicine. 2022. *Understanding the Aging Workforce: Defining a Research Agenda*. Washington, DC: The National Academies Press. https://doi.org/10.17226/26173.

The **National Academy of Sciences** was established in 1863 by an Act of Congress, signed by President Lincoln, as a private, nongovernmental institution to advise the nation on issues related to science and technology. Members are elected by their peers for outstanding contributions to research. Dr. Marcia McNutt is president.

The **National Academy of Engineering** was established in 1964 under the charter of the National Academy of Sciences to bring the practices of engineering to advising the nation. Members are elected by their peers for extraordinary contributions to engineering. Dr. John L. Anderson is president.

The **National Academy of Medicine** (formerly the Institute of Medicine) was established in 1970 under the charter of the National Academy of Sciences to advise the nation on medical and health issues. Members are elected by their peers for distinguished contributions to medicine and health. Dr. Victor J. Dzau is president.

The three Academies work together as the **National Academies of Sciences, Engineering, and Medicine** to provide independent, objective analysis and advice to the nation and conduct other activities to solve complex problems and inform public policy decisions. The National Academies also encourage education and research, recognize outstanding contributions to knowledge, and increase public understanding in matters of science, engineering, and medicine.

Learn more about the National Academies of Sciences, Engineering, and Medicine at **www.nationalacademies.org**.

Consensus Study Reports published by the National Academies of Sciences, Engineering, and Medicine document the evidence-based consensus on the study's statement of task by an authoring committee of experts. Reports typically include findings, conclusions, and recommendations based on information gathered by the committee and the committee's deliberations. Each report has been subjected to a rigorous and independent peer-review process and it represents the position of the National Academies on the statement of task.

Proceedings published by the National Academies of Sciences, Engineering, and Medicine chronicle the presentations and discussions at a workshop, symposium, or other event convened by the National Academies. The statements and opinions contained in proceedings are those of the participants and are not endorsed by other participants, the planning committee, or the National Academies.

Rapid Expert Consultations published by the National Academies of Sciences, Engineering, and Medicine are authored by subject-matter experts on narrowly focused topics that can be supported by a body of evidence. The discussions contained in rapid expert consultations are considered those of the authors and do not contain policy recommendations. Rapid expert consultations are reviewed by the institution before release.

For information about other products and activities of the National Academies, please visit www.nationalacademies.org/about/whatwedo.

**COMMITTEE ON UNDERSTANDING THE AGING WORKFORCE
AND EMPLOYMENT AT OLDER AGES**

SUSAN T. FISKE (*Chair*), Princeton University
EMMA AGUILA, Sol Price School of Public Policy, University of Southern California
PETER B. BERG, School of Human Resources and Labor Relations, Michigan State University
AXEL BÖRSCH-SUPAN, Munich Center for the Economics of Aging; Survey of Health, Ageing and Retirement in Europe; Max Planck Institute for Social Law and Social Policy
COURTNEY C. COILE, Wellesley College
ERNEST GONZALES, Silver School of Social Work, New York University
JACQUELYN B. JAMES, Sloan Research Network on Aging & Work, Lynch School of Education, Boston College
PHYLLIS E. MOEN, University of Minnesota
DAVID NEUMARK, Center for Population, Inequality, and Policy, University of California, Irvine
MO WANG, Warrington College of Business, University of Florida

TARA BECKER, *Study Director*
MARY GHITELMAN, *Senior Program Assistant*
MALAY K. MAJMUNDAR, *Director, Committee on Population*

COMMITTEE ON POPULATION

ANNE R. PEBLEY (*Chair*), Department of Community Health Sciences, Department of Sociology, California Center for Population Research, Bixby Center on Population and Reproductive Health, University of California, Los Angeles
EMILY M. AGREE, Department of Sociology and Department of Population, Family, and Reproductive Health, Johns Hopkins University
DEBORAH BALK, Marxe School of Public and International Affairs and CUNY Institute for Demographic Research, Baruch College of the City University of New York
ANN K. BLANC, Social and Behavioral Science Research, Population Council, New York City, *Retired*
COURTNEY C. COILE, Department of Economics, Wellesley College
SONALDE DESAI, Department of Sociology, University of Maryland; Professor and Centre Director, NCAER-National Data Innovation Centre, New Delhi
DANA A. GLEI, Research Consultant, Georgetown University
ROBERT A. HUMMER, Department of Sociology and Carolina Population Center, University of North Carolina at Chapel Hill
HEDWIG (HEDY) LEE, Department of Sociology Washington University in St. Louis
TREVON LOGAN, Department of Economics, The Ohio State University
JENNIFER J. MANLY, Taub Institute for Research on Alzheimer's Disease and the Aging Brain, Department of Neurology, Columbia University
JENNA E. NOBLES, Department of Sociology and the Center for Demography and Ecology, University of Wisconsin–Madison
FERNANDO RIOSMENA, Department of Geography and the Institute of Behavioral Sciences, University of Colorado Boulder
DAVID T. TAKEUCHI, School of Social Work, Department of Sociology, and the Center for the Study of Demography and Ecology, University of Washington

MALAY K. MAJMUNDAR, *Director*

COMMITTEE ON NATIONAL STATISTICS

ROBERT M. GROVES (*Chair*), Office of the Provost, Georgetown University
LAWRENCE D. BOBO, Department of Sociology, Harvard University
ANNE C. CASE, Woodrow Wilson School of Public and International Affairs, Princeton University, *Emerita*
MICK P. COUPER, Institute for Social Research, University of Michigan
JANET M. CURRIE, Woodrow Wilson School of Public and International Affairs, Princeton University
DIANA FARRELL, JPMorgan Chase Institute, Washington, DC
ROBERT GOERGE, Chapin Hall at The University of Chicago
ERICA L. GROSHEN, The ILR School, Cornell University
HILARY HOYNES, Goldman School of Public Policy, University of California, Berkeley
DANIEL KIFER, The Pennsylvania State University
SHARON LOHR, School of Mathematical and Statistical Sciences, Arizona State University, *Emerita*
JEROME P. REITER, Duke University
JUDITH A. SELTZER, University of California, Los Angeles, *Emerita*
C. MATTHEW SNIPP, School of the Humanities and Sciences, Stanford University
ELIZABETH A. STUART, Department of Mental Health, Johns Hopkins Bloomberg School of Public Health
JEANNETTE WING, Data Science Institute, Columbia University

BRIAN A. HARRIS-KOJETIN, *Director*
MELISSA C. CHIU, *Deputy Director*
CONSTANCE F. CITRO, *Senior Scholar*

Preface

The U.S. population is aging and in the decade preceding the COVID-19 pandemic an increasing number of retirement-age adults were remaining in the labor force. The extended working lives of these older adults has the potential to improve their overall health and financial stability, as well as alleviate the economic impact of an older population on public programs, such as Social Security and Medicare. In addition to these economic impacts, their continued presence in the labor force could affect workplace cultures and employer beliefs about the benefits (and drawbacks) of hiring older adults. However, these effects are shaped by disparities in opportunities to work, which expand at older ages, leaving some older adults unable to benefit from labor market changes that enable participation beyond traditional retirement ages. To better understand the impact of these changes, the Alfred P. Sloan Foundation began its Working Longer research program, which sponsored a range of studies on a broad array of topics associated with the social, economic, and policy implications of an aging workforce.

Over the course of a decade, the Working Longer program expanded our knowledge about the extended working lives of older adults. As this program wound down, the Alfred P. Sloan Foundation requested that the National Academies of Sciences, Engineering, and Medicine (the National Academies) undertake a study to evaluate the current status of research on work at older ages, identify key areas for future research, and suggest methodological and data infrastructure needs to move this new research agenda forward. In response to this request, the National Academies appointed the Committee on Understanding the Aging Workforce and Employment at Older Ages (under the standing committees of the Committee on Population and the Committee on National Statistics) to carry out this task. Ten scholars representing a broad array of disciplines—health economics, labor relations, labor economics, organizational psychology, social psychology, sociology, demography, and social work—were included on the committee, which met six times over a ten-month period.

The committee first met in April 2020, during the national economic shutdown imposed by the federal government in response to the COVID-19 pandemic. As a result of the pandemic, this committee became one of the first at the National Academies to shift to an all-remote consensus study model, which introduced new challenges and opportunities for the committee's work. In many ways, these paralleled the pandemic-based challenges and changes that continue to reverberate and shift the structure and nature of work throughout the labor force—including for older workers—as this report goes into publication. The full scope of these changes and their effects on work at older ages remain open questions for future researchers to address.

This report presents an extensive review of a wide-ranging topic and provides a deeper understanding not only of the effects of individual characteristics on work at older ages but also of the effects of current contexts, as well as the ways in which these effects shape and are shaped by the historical workplace, social, economic, and policy contexts in which people live their lives. The first part of this report describes the evolving older workforce and the committee's conceptual model for understanding transitions between work and retirement at older ages. In the second part of the report, the committee reviews the literature covering the effects of individual-level characteristics and workplace, age discrimination, labor market, and social policy contexts on the extended work lives of older adults. Finally, in the third part of the report, the committee summarizes its findings and presents a new research agenda that, if acted upon, will substantially improve our understanding of work at older ages.

This study would not have been possible without the contributions of many people. Special thanks must be extended to members of the study committee, who devoted extensive time, thought, and energy to this endeavor. The committee received useful information and insights from presentations from outside experts at open sessions of committee meetings. We thank Katharine Abraham (University of Maryland), Michele Battisti (University of Glasgow), Tyson Brown (Duke University), Joseph Coughlin (MIT), Sara Czaja (Cornell University), Gwen Fisher (Colorado State University), Eric French (University College London), Mary Gatta (City University of New York), Kendra Jason (University of North Carolina, Charlotte), Laurie McCann (AARP), Kathleen McGarry (University of California, Los Angeles), Olivia Mitchell (University of Pennsylvania), Michael North (New York University), and Ursula Staudinger (Columbia University).

A number of staff members of the National Academies made significant contributions to the report. Mary Ghitelman made sure that committee meetings ran smoothly, and she and Rebecca Krone assisted in preparing the manuscript, and otherwise provided key administrative and logistical support; Kirsten Sampson Snyder managed the report review process; and Malay Majmundar, director of the Committee on Population, and Brian Harris-Kojetin, director of the Committee on National Statistics, provided valuable guidance and oversight. We also thank Marc DeFrancis for his editing of the report.

This Consensus Study Report was reviewed in draft form by individuals chosen for their diverse perspectives and technical expertise. The purpose of this independent review is to provide candid and critical comments that will assist the National Academies of Sciences, Engineering, and Medicine in making each published report as sound as possible and to ensure that it meets the institutional standards for quality, objectivity, evidence, and responsiveness to the study charge. The review comments and draft manuscript remain confidential to protect the integrity of the deliberative process.

We thank the following individuals for their review of this report: Cynthia M. Beall, Department of Anthropology, Case Western Reserve University; Margaret E. Beier, Department of Psychological Sciences, Rice University; Laura L. Carstensen, Department of Psychology, Stanford University; Kène Henkins, Work & Retirement, Netherlands Interdisciplinary Demographic Institute, Ageing, Retirement and the Lifecourse, University Medical Center Groningen, and Sociology of Retirement, Faculty of Social and Behavioural Sciences, University of Amsterdam; Richard Johnson, Program on Retirement Policy, Urban Institute; Eden King, Department of Psychology, George Mason University; Joanna N. Lahey, Public Service and Administration, Texas A&M University; Nancy Morrow-Howell, Harvey A. Friedman Center for Aging, Brown School of Social Work, Washington University in St Louis; and Kathleen Mullen, Center for Disability Research, RAND Corporation.

Although the reviewers listed above provided many constructive comments and suggestions, they were not asked to endorse the conclusions or recommendations of this report nor did they see the final draft before its release. The review of this report was overseen by Mark D. Hayward, Population Research Center, The University of Texas at Austin, and Jonathan S. Skinner, Department of Economics, Dartmouth College. He was responsible for making certain that an independent examination of this report was carried out in accordance with the standards of the National Academies and that all review comments were carefully considered. Responsibility for the final content rests entirely with the authoring committee and the National Academies.

Susan T. Fiske, *Chair*
Tara Becker, *Study Director*
Committee on Understanding the Aging Workforce and Employment at Older Ages

Contents

Summary   **1**

1   **Introduction**   **9**

     Population Context, 9
     Committee Formation and Statement of Task, 10
     Situating Individual-Level Characteristics Within Contexts, 10
     Boundaries on the Scope of the Report, 12
     Understanding Work at Older Ages, 13
     Organization of the Report, 15

PART I

2   **The Emerging Older Workforce**   **19**

     How Trends in Labor Force Participation Are Gendered, 20
     Employment Characteristics of Older Workers, 24
     Work Preferences of Older Workers, 30
     The Changing Composition of the Older Workforce, 33
     Diversity in Labor Force Participation Patterns, 36
     The Initial Effects of COVID-19 on Labor Force Participation
        and Employment, 42
     Trends in Health and Disability, 44
     Conclusion, 50
     Annex, 52

3   **Work and Retirement Pathways**   **59**

     A Conceptual Framework of Work and Retirement Pathways, 59
     Theoretical Mechanisms, 63
     The Proximal Forces that Shape the Work and Retirement Pathways, 66

Disparities and Heterogeneity in Work and Retirement Pathways, 71
Challenges and Future Research Directions, 74
Conclusion, 75

PART II

4 Individual and Social Factors That Influence Employment and Retirement Transitions — 79

Individual Level Resources, 80
Meaning of Work, Satisfaction with Work, and Sense of Purpose, 90
Family and Household Structure, 91
Social Capital, 93
Cross-Cutting Themes of Inequity: A Life Course Perspective, 94
Research Implications, 97

5 Workplace and Job Factors — 99

Theoretical Approaches, 100
Key Practices, 106
Key Factors of Influence, 112
Implications for Future Research, 115
Conclusion, 116

6 Age Discrimination, One Source of Inequality — 117

Introduction, 117
Distinct Features of Ageism, 117
Face-to-Face Ageism: How People View Older Workers, 118
Assessing the Accuracy of Ageist Stereotypes: Cognitive Capability in Later Life, 124
Workplace Age Discrimination and Exclusion: Older Workers' Reported Experience, 127
Age and Job Performance, 131
Age Discrimination in the Labor Market for Older Workers, 135
Conclusions, 138

7 The Labor Market for Older Workers — 141

The Labor Supply of Older Workers, 143
Factors Primarily Affecting the Demand for Older Workers, 144
The Balance Between Labor Supply and Labor Demand, 148
Summary, 153

8 Public Policy — 155

Introduction, 155
Non-Age-Specific Policies That Support Work, 156
Age-Specific Policies That Support Work, 161
Policies to Support the Financial Security of Disabled and Retired Workers, 168
Conclusions, 182

PART III

9   A Research Agenda to Promote Understanding of   **189**
    Employment among Older Workers

    Defining a Research Agenda, 190
    Conclusion, 209

References   **211**

Appendixes   **255**

    A Meeting Agendas, 255
    B Committee Biosketches, 259

Boxes, Figures, and Tables

BOXES

2-1 Measuring Employment and Self-Employment among Older Workers, 33

4-1 COVID-19, 97

5-1 The Effects of COVID-19 on Workplace Practices and Older Workers, 116

6-1 Theories of Ageism's Origins, with Implications for Interventions, 119

8-1 International Social Security (ISS), 173
8-2 The COVID-19 Crisis and Public Policy, 185

9-1 The COVID-19 Pandemic and Work at Older Ages, 208

FIGURES

2-1 The age distribution of employed adults in the U.S. by gender, 2000–2020, 20
2-2 The age distribution of the U.S. population by gender, actual (2000–2020) and projected (2020–2060), 21
2-3 Labor force participation rates (and change in rates) by gender and age group, selected years, 2000–2019, 22
2-4 2019 labor force participation, adults ages 65 and over by country and gender, 23
2-5 Gender difference in labor force participation rates in 2019 by country, 24
2-6 Labor force participation by age, gender, and birth cohort, ages 25–79, 25
2-7 Self-employment in current main job, by age and gender, 2004 and 2019, 31
2-8 Percent of employed adults ages 50 and over working part-time, by age and gender, 2004 and 2019, 34
2-9 Demographic characteristics of the older labor force, ages 50 and over, 2004 vs. 2019, 35
2-10 Labor force participation among adults ages 25 and over by gender and nativity, 2004–2019, 37

xv

2-11   Labor force participation among adults ages 25 and over by age, gender, and race-ethnicity, 2004–2019, 39
2-12   Labor force participation among adults ages 25 and over by age, gender, and educational attainment, 2004 and 2019, 41
2-13   Labor force participation and employment status among adults by gender and age, January 2020–January 2021, 43
2-14   Labor force participation and employment status among men ages 25 and over by race-ethnicity and age, January 2020–January 2021, 45
2-15   Labor force participation and employment status among women ages 25 and over by race-ethnicity and age, January 2020–January 2021, 46
2-16   Percent of U.S. adults reporting their health as fair or poor, by gender and age, 2000–2020, 47
2-17   Percentage of U.S. adults reporting their health as fair or poor, 2019, and change in percentage, 2000 vs. 2019, by gender, age, and education, 48
2-18   Percent of labor force reporting their health as fair or poor, by gender, age, and education, 2000 vs. 2019, 49
2-19   Presence (percent) of a work disability among labor force participants ages 25 and over, 2000–2020, and change in percent, 2000 vs. 2020, 50

3-1   Labor force status among men in the private sector, by year, 1992–2016, 60
3-2   Labor force status among women in the private sector, by year, 1992–2016, 61
3-3   A conceptual framework of work and retirement pathways, 62
3-4   Theory of planned behavior, 64

6-1   Change and predicted change in implicit and explicit attitudes, 2007–2020, 120

7-1   Factors affecting labor demand for and labor supply of older workers, 142
7-2   Mobility rates by age, CPS ASEC (2019), 150

TABLES

2-1   Distribution of Workers across Occupation Groups by Age Group, 2004 vs. 2019, 26
2-2   Occupation Groups with the Highest Percentages of Oldest and Youngest Workers by Gender and Age Group, 2004 vs 2019, 29

Annex Table 2-1 Age Distribution Within Occupation Group Among Men, 2004, 52
Annex Table 2-2 Age Distribution Within Occupation Group Among Men, 2019, 53
Annex Table 2-3 Age Distribution Within Occupation Group Among Women, 2004, 54
Annex Table 2-4 Age Distribution Within Occupation Group Among Women, 2019, 55

3-1   Theoretical Approaches, 63

4-1   Average Social Security Wealth at Age 51–56 by Quintile of Wealth Within Race/Ethnicity, 2016 Dollars, 86
4-2   Income and Wealth Changes by Income Level, 87
4-3   Changes in Median Income by Race and Ethnic Origin and Income Percentile, 1970–2016, 88
4-4   Indicators of Possible Financial Insecurity in Old Age, 89

5-1   Theoretical Approaches, 100
5-2   Age-Related Flexibility Practices Shaping Later Adult Work, 109

6-1	Theories Applied to Ageism in the Workforce, 119	
6-2	Mixed Stereotypes about Older Adults and Older Workers, 122	
6-3	Stereotypes about Older Workers' Health, 124	
6-4	Workplace Age Discrimination Scale (WADS), 128	
6-5	Age and Job Performance Factors, 132	
7-1	Percent Retired Within Age Group, 2012–2017, 144	
8-1	Public Policies Relevant to Older Workers, 156	

Summary

The U.S. population aging is a fact that may have important economic repercussions, including slowing down long-term economic growth and raising the costs of social programs. At the same time, due to medical advancements and public health improvements, the Baby Boom cohort has experienced better health and increasing longevity, compared to earlier cohorts, as its members enter retirement ages. These improvements in health enable many older adults to continue working at older ages. Such higher labor market participation from this older workforce, were it to continue, could soften the potential negative impacts of population aging over the long term on economic growth, the funding of Social Security, and the funding of other social programs. However, these trends in population aging and healthier longevity have occurred amidst a complicating backdrop of growing social diversity and widening economic inequality in which many older adults face constraints on their working and retirement behaviors.

These constraints fall along existing lines defined by social and economic inequalities such as gender, race-ethnicity, immigration status, socioeconomic status, and geographic region. But these disparities do not suddenly emerge as adults approach retirement. Health, financial security, employment, and retirement at older ages are shaped not only by current characteristics but also by the structures of opportunity experienced throughout the life course. The impacts of discrimination and structural inequality experienced in early adulthood and midlife continue to affect the work and retirement opportunities available to older adults. The effects of these inequities accumulate over the life course, affecting health and determining the resources and opportunities available for retiring or reducing employment in later life. Thus, transitions between work and retirement reproduce and reinforce social and economic inequality at older ages, and their effects are further compounded by the additional, well-documented effects of age discrimination.

These forces together have shaped people's preferences for working longer, their expectations about the future, and the constraints on their working at older ages. An aging workforce, extended healthy life expectancy, mounting inequality, new technologies, and heightened economic and job precarity mean work arrangements among older adults are in flux. Instead of viewing full-time retirement as a one-time event and an inevitable end of one's work engagement, growing numbers of older adults sustain various forms of workforce participation, even though retired from their main or career jobs. These patterned shifts challenge the definitions of what it means to work and to retire in the United States as social, economic, technological, and demographic transformations reshape the possibilities and precarities that characterize the later life course among an increasingly diverse and heterogeneous older population.

STATEMENT OF TASK

The Arthur P. Sloan Foundation asked the National Academies of Sciences, Engineering, and Medicine (the National Academies) to produce a consensus study on the aging workforce and employment at older ages. The specific charge to the National Academies was as follows:

> The National Academies of Sciences, Engineering, and Medicine will undertake a study that will review and assess what is known about the aging workforce in the United States, identify gaps in current knowledge and data infrastructure, and make recommendations for future research and data collection efforts. The study will focus on the individual-level human capital and demographic characteristics associated with decisions to continue working at older ages and on the social and structural factors, including workplace policies and conditions, that inhibit or enable employment among older workers.

The National Academies appointed the Committee on Understanding the Aging Workforce and Employment at Older Ages to carry out this task. Ten prominent scholars representing a broad array of disciplines—including economics, psychology, organizational psychology, labor relations, sociology, and social work—were included on the committee. The committee met six times and deliberated over an 18-month period to produce this report.

OVERARCHING FINDINGS AND CONCLUSIONS

The committee's multidisciplinary framework conceptualizes work at older ages as being shaped by an individual's preferences for work and expectations about the future, as well as the constraints on their ability to realize their preferred work relationships. These three dimensions—preferences, expectations, and constraints—are mutually shaped and reinforcing. When the literature on work at older ages is viewed through this conceptual lens, two overarching conclusions emerge.

CONCLUSION I: Older workers' preferences for work and specific work arrangements, their expectations about available work opportunities and financial stability, and the constraints on their work opportunities and behaviors all reflect the impact of both age bias and social and economic inequalities that structure economic opportunity throughout the life course and lead to wide disparities in employment and retirement pathways at older ages.

CONCLUSION II: The experiences of vulnerable older populations, including women; racial and ethnic minorities; immigrants; those with less education, low income, or limited savings and wealth; those living in rural or economically disadvantaged areas; and those with multiple intersecting vulnerabilities remain understudied within the current literature. This limits our understanding of the ways in which inequality in retirement and work opportunities and outcomes contributes to broader social and economic inequality that affects the well-being of older adults.

Considering the diversity of experiences and outcomes within the older worker population, as well as the ways opportunities are shaped by inequality throughout the life course, can provide important research insights—even when research is not explicitly focused on social and economic inequality. Doing so will provide a deeper understanding of the benefits and disadvantages of extending work lives. That in turn can inform the development of policies to enable work at older ages in ways that account for the challenges vulnerable populations face and, thereby, improve their well-being.

DEFINING A RESEARCH AGENDA FOR OLDER WORKERS

The preceding overarching conclusions provide the framework for implementing future research and data collection agendas. The committee's review of the extant literature identified three specific lacunae in existing scholarship, which cut across multiple levels of analysis and are the most promising areas for future research: the relationship between employers and older employees; work and resource inequalities in later adulthood; and the interface between work, health, and caregiving. Each can be summarized as follows:

CONCLUSION 1: Retirement is too often viewed as an overly individualized process of workers stimulated or constrained by macro-level forces. However, other forces shape work and retirement pathways by constraining or increasing older workers' agency in making decisions. These forces include workplace norms, policies, and practices, within the context of the employer-employee relationship.

CONCLUSION 2: Much of the research on older workers focuses on the experiences of socially and economically advantaged workers, because they are more likely to work longer. Historically disadvantaged subgroups are less likely to have control over when, where, and how much to work or the resources and opportunities to enact their preferences for work at older ages. Less is known about how preferences, expectations, and constraints reflect these differences, intersect with age biases, and translate into different employment patterns at older ages and how this contributes to social and economic inequality in later life.

CONCLUSION 3: Although the relationship between physical health and work at older ages has been well established, less is known about other aspects of the relationship between health and work at older ages, such as the role one's own mental health; the health and caregiving needs of family members; and how accommodative practices can enable working longer. Moreover, little is known about how recent declines in health at midlife and younger ages, particularly among those with less education, will affect labor force participation and worker needs for accommodative practices in the future.

A further explication of the key research questions and data collection needs within each of these three areas is described in greater detail below. When considered as a whole, the findings within the report reveal a research agenda that, if enacted, would provide a more comprehensive understanding of the employment experiences of older workers and the constraints that shape their opportunities for work at older ages.

The Employer-Older Employee Relationship

It is critical to more consistently and comprehensively address research questions about the effects of workplace policies and practices. Employers are the crucial link between macro-level public policies and individual-level outcomes among workers. Employers are also the main social actors who translate public policies into organizational practices that set the stage for individual decision-making, including workforce participation and retirement. Workplace practices shape the incentives and opportunities for older workers to remain productive and engaged. Understanding the role of these practices in facilitating longer working lives is crucial during this period of population aging. Important areas for future research include the implementation of workplace policies; policies and practices that affect work and retirement; and the role of age discrimination.

Implementation of Workplace Policies and Practices

Within workplaces, both employer and employee interests shape the employer-employee relationship, but these interests may differ or align. When employees have a say in their work (employee voice), they can influence the types of practices employers implement. Employee voice can be part of independent collective representation that negotiates with employers or when individual employees express their concerns and opinions directly to employers. Greater employee voice at the workplace can be instrumental in expanding work options for older employees, such as through part-time work, remote work, or partial retirement. Moreover, greater employee voice can help reduce inequalities by fostering greater access to practices across ages and historically disadvantaged subgroups. Few researchers account for employer and employee interests and the institutional context in which workplace policies and practices are implemented even though these interests and contexts determine how they are implemented.

When employers introduce new workplace practices that benefit older workers, they can do so in either age-specific or age-neutral ways. Age-specific practices are tailored to older workers and can be useful in meeting their specific needs, but they run the risk of stigmatizing older workers as a "special group" and encouraging discrimination against them. Age-neutral practices are designed for all workers and therefore avoid age-based stigmatization; however, when the needs of older workers differ from those of younger workers, such practices risk losing the effectiveness found in practices specifically designed for older workers. The relative effectiveness of age-specific and age-neutral practices in improving outcomes for older workers has not been adequately examined and additional research is needed to assess the tradeoffs between the costs and benefits of each.

Workplace Policies and Practices That Affect Work and Retirement

Older adults are more likely than younger people to express preferences for specific work conditions, such as flexible work schedules or paid leave, and they report willingness to delay retirement or return to the labor force if such conditions were available. Workplace practices, such as flexible work schedules, the introduction of accommodative technologies and innovations, and worker training programs have been proposed as ways to improve the retention of older workers, but the effectiveness of these practices has not been empirically established.

Flexible work arrangements can involve flexible work hours, time off, or remote work; they can be voluntarily chosen by workers or involuntarily imposed by employers for business reasons. More research is needed to understand the types of flexible arrangements that affect the retention of older workers and the timing of retirement. Similarly, although technology that reduces the physical or cognitive demands of work can make jobs safer—such as by monitoring repetitive tasks, providing lift and positioning technology, or aiding workers' strength—technological innovations can also eliminate the need for some jobs. More research assessing both the positive and negative impacts of technological change and innovation on the employment of older workers is needed. Very little is known about the implementation of enabling technologies in the workplace or whether there are age-based disparities in the impact of technological innovation on job elimination.

Workplace training programs could help mitigate the impact of technological change by improving workers' skills; however, older workers are less likely to use these programs. It is unclear whether this is because older workers are less motivated to pursue these opportunities or because organizations are less likely to offer them to older workers. Moreover, more research is needed to determine whether older-worker–focused training is effective in retaining older workers.

The Role of Age Discrimination

Workplaces are also sites where age discrimination occurs. Workplace age discrimination can occur in many forms, some of which are subtle or complex, presenting significant measurement and methodological challenges. Current research suggests that older workers experience age discrimination in hiring, promotion, performance evaluation, and workplace opportunity and climate; however, the quality of evidence varies with the strongest evidence (presented from audit studies) demonstrating clear discrimination in hiring. High-quality studies are needed to address whether, when, and how discrimination occurs on the job, and these studies need to be conducted with the same rigor as audit studies.

Most on-the-job measures of discriminatory treatment rely on either self-reported attitudes or stereotypical beliefs about older workers or perceived discrimination reported by the target. However, more subtle forms of bias, as well as discrimination that is unseen by the target, are not captured by these measures. Although older workers report being the target of discriminatory behavior and employers and workers often subscribe to negative stereotypical beliefs about older workers, the causal chain of evidence on age discrimination is incomplete because it lacks evidence of coworkers' and managers' reported and observed discriminatory behavior toward older people. These behaviors require further elaboration through innovative studies that produce rigorous evidence.

Beyond interpersonal treatment, age discrimination can operate through organizational culture and practices. However, better conceptual and operational definitions of inclusive organizational policies are needed, as are multilevel models of their antecedents, indicators, and consequences. More research is needed to identify inclusive organizational policies that mitigate against age-related biases entering into decisions at all stages and levels of analysis and to determine whether these policies actually create a more inclusive culture. For example, organizationally determined measures of employee performance and productivity can be biased in ways that negatively affect both formal and informal assessments of older workers' contributions. Productivity is hard to measure, causally ambiguous, sensitive to the level of aggregation, and distinct by job type. The most common measures omit dimensions on which older workers outperform younger workers, possibly resulting in biased assessments of older-worker performance. More research is needed to evaluate how this exclusion affects researcher, supervisor, and peer estimates of worker productivity, workplace performance, and the value of retaining older workers.

Better measures of discrimination and methodologies that can causally establish these relationships are crucial for understanding the impact of age discrimination on the retention of older workers, as well as the impact of discrimination on health. Older workers who report being the targets of discriminatory behaviors and practices are less likely to be satisfied with and to remain in their jobs, and they are also more likely to report that they are in poorer health. However, although reports of discrimination have been linked to job dissatisfaction and negative health outcomes, the causal link has yet to be established. Evidence of causality awaits better designs, because other factors (e.g., depression) could explain both. Research that includes such covariates (e.g., optimism, personality, support, intersectional identities) will likely clarify and isolate the relationships among perceived workplace discrimination, health, and labor force participation.

New Data Collection Strategies

Addressing the research gaps with respect to the workplace practices outlined above requires gathering data about the organizational context and the perspectives of managers and older workers within the employment relationship. The need to situate employee responses to and outcomes of any policy and/or practice within the organizational context underscores the need for longitudinal data that is matched between employers and employees. Most of the existing panel surveys sponsored by the U.S. government focus on sampling individuals or households; such surveys might inquire about participants' work, but contain little about the context of their work or even their industry sector. Representative population-based surveys of U.S. workplaces are designed to ask only limited organizational questions and cannot be linked to data on workers' understanding of, access to, and use of workplace policies and programs. This has meant that research on workplace policies and practices typically must rely on access granted by individual companies or establishments. This access is difficult to negotiate and sustain over time, which results in findings that are unrepresentative and may not be generalizable beyond the organizations studied.

A nationally representative longitudinal panel focused on sampling U.S. workplaces, which also contains multilevel matched data between employers and workers, does not currently exist, but such a panel would be invaluable for advancing research on the role of employers and workplaces on older workers' employment experiences. The costs of developing a new panel survey could be substantial; however, as an alternative, adding questions about age-related and age-neutral practices to existing surveys would be a step in the right direction. Questions about age-related practices such as partial retirement, mixed age/experience teams, training targeting older workers, and workforce age assessments, as well as questions about age-neutral practices such as flexible schedules, the use of ergonomic technology, employee participation, and skills training would be most welcome.

Work and Resource Inequalities in Later Adulthood

Older adults face inequities in employment opportunities and financial resources and stability that constrain their ability to realize their preferred employment relationships. Though they are often measured at a point in time, these inequities build and accumulate throughout the life span. Adults who face limited work opportunities during their prime working years will face a considerable disadvantage in work opportunities and accumulated savings when they reach conventional retirement ages. Though work at older ages can substantially improve the financial security of older adults, particularly those with limited savings and wealth, work opportunities are not always available.

Opportunities to remain in the labor force often reflect underlying economic inequality in opportunity by gender, race-ethnicity, socioeconomic status, and geography. Since those who work longer are disproportionately economically and socially advantaged, extant research on older workers does not always adequately measure or represent the experiences of less advantaged older workers or how those experiences are shaped throughout the life course.

A Life Course Perspective on Inequality

The processes underlying work outcomes at older ages can be understood as the result of a lifetime of experiences that shape opportunity in later life. The processes that structure unequal work and retirement pathways at older ages do not begin at age 50. Research that adopts a life course conceptual lens could promote a better understanding of disparities in later adulthood by underscoring the cumulative impact of the multilayered embeddedness of lives in ongoing biographies and in historical and institutional environments. A fundamental life course theme is that transitions, such as later adult exits from or reentries into paid work, occur within trajectories of experience that give them shape and meaning. By shifting the research focus to how early experiences and contexts influence older workers' current preferences, expectations, and constraints on opportunities for work, a life course perspective could identify how historical structural inequalities continue to affect inequality in work outcomes at older ages.

Individuals are embedded within a context of mutual interdependence within families and social networks, and in temporal and geographic terms they are also embedded within historical and social contexts. Couples often make decisions around retirement timing together, or in light of each partner's preferences. And family situational constraints, such as the need to care for a grandchild or an aging family member, may alter work and retirement preferences and expectations. Contextual embeddedness implies that life transition and developmental trajectories occur under specific circumstances, including historical, policy, organizational, and social contexts. Individuals are embedded within multiple contexts (e.g., households/families, neighborhoods, states, and nations), which they both shape and are shaped by. A better understanding of these interdependent relationships would provide a more complete understanding of the contexts and constraints under which work transitions occur. Failure to consider these contexts may lead scientists to put too much emphasis on the effects of individual characteristics and miss the ways in which these effects are constrained by the contexts in which they are embedded.

Inequality in Work Opportunities

Labor market factors, such as globalization and automation, target specific occupations and locations, affecting work opportunities within some geographic areas or for some classes of workers. The affected workers are often defined by skill level or type, but also by age, gender, and race-ethnicity due to labor market segregation. These changes often reinforce existing economic inequalities, because displaced older workers are less likely to be reemployed. Though research has documented education-based differentials in the effects of automation, globalization, and geographic disparities on employment opportunities, less is known about their specific impact on older workers or about public policies that could mitigate their adverse impact. Though social policies have been introduced to improve economic opportunities of displaced workers (e.g., local or regional economic revitalization or worker retraining or reskilling), little is known about the effectiveness of these policies in engaging older workers and improving the work opportunities available to them nor their comparative impact relative to integrative policies implemented in other countries.

Wide education-based disparities in employment at older ages has meant that much of the research on older workers has focused on economically advantaged workers. However, vulnerable populations, including less-educated workers, racial-ethnic and other minority workers, women, the self-employed, "gig" and informal workers, workers with poor health or disabilities, noncitizen immigrants, and those living in rural areas, all face distinct challenges in continuing to work in later adulthood. These workers are more likely to engage in informal and unstable work, and they are also more likely to experience multiple transitions into and out of the labor force. Current measures of work provide only a limited understanding of the complex employment experiences of low-income older adults, including simultaneous participation in formal- and informal-sector jobs, involuntary job separations leading to early labor force withdrawal, and barriers to work. They do not adequately capture low-income older adults' sources of income, multiple occupations, sporadic jobs, access to healthcare and other labor benefits, and eligibility for and take-up rates of supplemental income support programs.

Social networks and social capital may play an especially important role in identifying employment opportunities for older adults who have more tenuous and less formal contact with the labor market. These social connections inform and enable varied paths between work and retirement. Although social networks play an important role in labor force participation and employment opportunities among younger workers, less is known about how these social mechanisms function with advancing age, as social networks retract, especially when individuals are pressed to retire or if they live in communities with few employment opportunities. National-, state-, and local-level organizations are institutions that can help older adults build social capital. Formal volunteering could expand and strengthen social ties, while also bolstering various dimensions of health. These social and health resources generated and maintained through volunteering might encourage and aid older adult volunteers in transitioning to employment; however, the pathways between paid work, retirement, civic engagement, and returning to the labor market are not fully understood.

Inequality in Financial Security

Financial security is one of the most important considerations workers face in forming preferences and expectations about retiring or continuing to work. Inadequate retirement savings constrains older individuals' retirement decisions. Although there remains considerable debate regarding whether older adults have adequate savings for retirement, there is a consensus that workers today face growing challenges in saving adequately for retirement. Financial security in old age is more tenuous for members of historically disadvantaged groups due to their lower wealth. It is critical to conduct research on lifetime earnings, saving, and wealth accumulation of historically disadvantaged groups, including lower-skilled vulnerable workers with discontinuous work histories and multiple or sporadic jobs, to better understand their pathways to retirement and income security in old age, including the effectiveness of public programs. Social programs play an important role in both income security and employment decisions at older ages, particularly for vulnerable populations, but more research is needed to understand how these programs affect labor force behavior at older ages.

New Data Collection Strategies

Addressing these key issues will require improvements to the current data infrastructure and data analyses. To date, most existing research focuses on individuals' experiences at particular time points, absent the rich insights that multilayered process-based and contextual data could provide. Understanding the ways earlier life experiences shape the resources and options available to older workers will require expanding data collection strategies to incorporate life-history, relational, and contextual data. The ability to document the experiences and challenges of vulnerable populations has been constrained by both the lack of measures that capture the full range of diversity of their work experiences, such as participation in the informal labor sector or in precarious, sporadic, or "gig" work, and the lack of sufficient samples of respondents from these populations in most data sets. Innovative data collection and research strategies could enable a better understanding of the needs of these populations and, therefore, a strengthened ability to address them.

Such an agenda could document how existing institutional and organizational arrangements serve to structure inequalities in later-life work—and nonwork—outcomes. Future research could prioritize the necessary data and analytic methods to document both disparate pathways and their antecedents, keying in on the distinctive work and retirement preferences and experiences of subgroups of older individuals, as well as heterogeneity and disparities within as well as across subgroups. Such scholarship is necessary to understand inequalities in the possibilities for working longer and the need to recast policies and practices at the national, state, and employer levels in ways that facilitate longer working lives.

The Work-Health-Caregiving Interface

While many studies document an association between poor health and retirement, determining the causal effects of health on retirement is challenging due to several factors: the difficulty of determining the appropriate measure of health; the interrelationship between health and other factors associated with retirement; and the subsequent effect of retirement on health. Despite these challenges, a causal relationship between poorer health and retirement has been well established across a wide number of studies. However, the mostly commonly used measures of health in this research are self-reported health status and the presence of a work-limiting disability. These are useful summary measures that are frequently available in survey data, but they are largely focused on physical health. Mental and cognitive health may also be important for continued employment at older ages, but little is known about this relationship.

Though much of the current research on health has focused on the effects of own health on employment, the health and caregiving needs of family members also affect work and retirement decisions. Informal unpaid caregiving also follows identifiable, patterned pathways; that is, the intensity and duration of providing care to family members often conflicts with employment and often leads to part-time work and forced retirement. The interrelationship between caregiving and labor force participation is dynamic and complex as they jointly play out in later life. Differences in the type and intensity of caregiving needs of the recipient as well as likely interaction effects between the health, social, and economic status of the informal caregiver and that of the care receiver add to the complexity of this relationship. There are likely interactions between working conditions, employment policies, and practices shaping resources for caregiving. Fluctuating caregiving demands affect the timing of retirement and other exits from the labor force. These individual, dyadic, and employment dynamics are further shaped by state and federal policies, such as paid family and medical leave. Research has not yet modeled these conjoint later-life course dynamics nor has it shown how they differ across diverse groups of caregivers and care receivers.

These issues take on greater urgency because in recent years, a growing number of adults at midlife and at younger ages have reported poorer health and more chronic health conditions, while mortality has increased. These trends are more pronounced among less educated individuals, resulting in growing disparities in health by educational attainment that have implications for future trends in the employment of older workers. The presence of chronic health conditions may affect labor force participation and the productivity of older workers in current and future cohorts. Poor health can constrain labor supply, forcing some workers into early retirement. Workers in poor health may be less productive, may require disability accommodations, or may generate higher health care costs for employers—or employers may perceive this to be the case even if it is not. All of these factors could result in lower demand for older workers. Understanding the reasons underlying this erosion in the health of younger cohorts trend may provide insights into future trends in work at older ages.

CONCLUSION

Work and retirement decisions are the result of the interrelated effects of individual preferences for work, expectations about the future, and constraints on work behaviors within the larger contexts of social and economic change. In order to fully understand the ways in which individual characteristics affect the experience of work at older ages, their effects must be considered within these broader contexts to understand how they influence individual preferences, expectations, and constraints. But these individual preferences, expectations, and constraints operate within complex systems of social and economic inequality that develop throughout the life course, and thus they may be specific to the historical circumstances in which individuals enter their adulthood and, later, their retirement ages.

We know too little about the well-being of older workers and of those who are not working but may wish to do so under certain conditions, as well as of those who are working despite a preference to retire. For example, too little is known about the micro-level impacts on older adults' work and retirement of large-scale social changes—in technology, the economy, the labor market, and society at large.

Much of what we know about the later work course comes from studies of earlier cohorts, people who confronted very different demographic, technological, social, and economic forces, as well as from different private-sector and public-policy regimes. It would be beneficial for future research to explore contemporary—and changing—experiences of work and retirement and the conditions that are shaping health and well-being.

1

Introduction

POPULATION CONTEXT

Since 2011, members of the Baby Boom cohort have been reaching age 65, and they will continue to do so through 2030. The sheer size of this cohort has meant that as they have aged, they have shifted the age distribution of the country as a whole; by 2030, one-fifth of the U.S. population will be over age 65 (U.S. Census Bureau, 2018). As members of this cohort have entered conventional retirement ages, they have developed new retirement patterns, with more remaining in or returning to the labor force at older ages, leading to higher rates of labor force participation than in previous generations (U.S. Bureau of Labor Statistics, 2020; Goldin and Katz, 2018a; Schramm, 2018). This aging of the U.S. population may have mixed effects, including potential repercussions for the country's long-term economic growth (Maestas et al., 2016) and the stability of U.S. social programs (U.S. Social Security Administration, 2012). However, the higher labor-market participation of this large older workforce could also help to reduce the impact of population aging on economic growth and the funding of Social Security and other social programs over the long term.

Economic Impact on Older Workers

Working at older ages could also improve the economic well-being of older Americans. Delaying retirement has a larger impact on a household's standard of living than saving throughout the life course, particularly when individuals do not begin saving until they are middle-aged or older (Bronshtein et al., 2019). In the United States, many employers have transitioned away from defined-benefit pension plans to retirement savings and investment accounts, and fears of high long-term care and medical costs in later life prevent older Americans from spending down their savings in retirement (Ameriks et al., 2018). In addition to foregoing labor income that they would earn by delaying retirement, early claimants of Social Security trade lower payments in return for early enrollment. Those who claim Social Security at younger ages tend to have lower total incomes in all subsequent years (Card et al., 2014), both because early claiming permanently reduces their monthly Social Security payments and because early claimants tend to have less income from other sources than those who delay.

Although their low savings rate throughout the life course means that working at older ages would disproportionately improve their financial well-being, older adults with lower socioeconomic status (SES) are more likely than other older adults to retire early. This seeming contradiction occurs because these adults face poorer health and job prospects at older ages and are less able to work past standard retirement ages (Munnell, Webb et al., 2018).

In addition, Social Security provides a higher income replacement rate for those in low-SES households (Kahn et al., 2017), reducing the economic impact of leaving the labor force. The health and work opportunity barriers to employment mean that working longer may not be a realistic solution to declines in economic status at older ages for this group (Munnell, Webb et al., 2018), suggesting that working longer is not simply a matter of choice for many Americans. In fact, those who would benefit the most economically from remaining in the labor force often face constraints to participation that reduce both their preference for working longer and the viability of this as an option for improving their economic circumstances (Solem et al., 2014; Szinovacz et al., 2014; Siegrist et al., 2007).

Systemic Disparities

Constraints on work at older ages are not distributed equally throughout the population but fall along existing lines defined by social and economic inequalities such as gender, race-ethnicity, immigration status, socioeconomic status, and geographic region. Health, financial security, employment, and retirement at older ages are shaped not only by current characteristics but also by the opportunity structures experienced throughout the life course (Moen et al., 2020, 2021; Fisher, Chaffee et al., 2016; Warner and Brown, 2011; Brown, 2009). Thus, the impacts of discrimination and structural inequality experienced in early adulthood and midlife continue to affect the work and retirement opportunities available to older adults. The effects of these inequities accumulate over the life course, determining the resources available for retiring or reducing employment in later life (Rothstein, 2017; Brown, 2016). Then, transitions between work and retirement reproduce and reinforce these social and economic inequalities at older ages. How these factors work together to shape work and nonwork in later life has implications for the well-being of older adults.

COMMITTEE FORMATION AND STATEMENT OF TASK

In 2019, the Arthur P. Sloan Foundation asked the National Academies of Sciences, Engineering, and Medicine (the National Academies) to produce a consensus study on the aging workforce and employment at older ages. The specific charge to the National Academies was stated as follows:

> The National Academies of Sciences, Engineering, and Medicine will undertake a study that will review and assess what is known about the aging workforce in the United States, identify gaps in current knowledge and data infrastructure, and make recommendations for future research and data collection efforts. The study will focus on the individual-level human capital and demographic characteristics associated with decisions to continue working at older ages; and on the social and structural factors, including workplace policies and conditions, that inhibit or enable employment among older workers.

The National Academies appointed the Committee on Understanding the Aging Workforce and Employment at Older Ages to carry out this task. Ten prominent scholars representing a broad array of disciplines—including economics, psychology, organizational psychology, labor relations, sociology, and social work—were included on the committee. The committee met virtually, six times over a 10-month period, to produce this report.

SITUATING INDIVIDUAL-LEVEL CHARACTERISTICS WITHIN CONTEXTS

The statement of task calls for a focus on the ways in which individual-level characteristics are associated with work at older ages. However, it is not possible to understand the role of individual-level characteristics without considering their relationship to the contexts in which work occurs.

Some of these characteristics, such as income or wealth, might be measured at the individual level as an individual's earnings or assets, but individuals are often situated within families in which the income and assets are a shared resource. Relatedly, married couples tend to make joint retirement decisions that lead both spouses to retire at close to the same time (Angrisani et al., 2017; Coile, 2015), which leads women, who are generally younger than their spouses, to retire at younger ages (Maestas, 2018). These decisions may be driven by caregiving needs, which are more likely to be shouldered by women. In fact, women are more likely than men to reduce their employment to meet the informal caregiving needs of a spouse, parent, child, or other relative. The gender gap in earnings, which widens with age (Goldin et al., 2017), also means that women remain more dependent on their spouse's earnings to maintain their standard of living. This greater dependence is why women are more likely to increase their labor market participation after the death of a spouse than are men (Fadlon and Nielsen, 2017).

Individual characteristics, such as age, race-ethnicity, and education, can shape opportunities for work as well as the experience of work within workplaces. Workplace policies and job characteristics often play a decisive role in decisions to retire. Preferences for certain job characteristics can change over the life course, and these preferences can affect retirement transitions. For example, older workers place a higher value on non-pecuniary job characteristics than do younger workers (Maestas et al., 2018). Characteristics such as moderate physical activity, sitting, team-based evaluation, schedule flexibility, and work autonomy are disproportionately valued by older workers (Maestas et al., 2018). Those who work longer in their career job or exit their career job for bridge employment tend to work fewer hours, have a flexible schedule, and receive lower hourly wages (Ameriks et al., 2018). Workers employed by employers who are more willing to accommodate a lighter workload for older employees are more likely to remain employed full-time and less likely to retire (Ameriks et al., 2018).

Employers can signal the value they place on retaining older workers through the policies and practices they enact within the workplace. For example, workers who are provided with a health- or disability-related accommodation by their employer are less likely to file for disability and more likely to remain employed than workers who do not receive accommodation (Maestas et al., 2019; Hill et al., 2016). In contrast, employers may weight employee evaluations toward characteristics associated with younger workers, such as speed and innovation, while discounting those that are more commonly associated with older workers, such as knowledge, expertise, and loyalty (Van Dalen et al., 2010). Employers may also view older employees as less technologically proficient or less adaptable to new environments or practices and may invest less in training them. These forms of workplace discrimination affect workers' decisions to remain in their positions (Angrisani et al., 2016).

Individual characteristics also shape the opportunities for changing jobs or returning to work. Historically, employment opportunities have narrowed at older ages as the physical ability to perform work tasks deteriorates (Rutledge et al., 2017). However, technological change and economic shifts to jobs that are less dependent on manual and routine skills and favor those with cognitive and analytic skills (Autor et al., 2003) have allowed more older adults to remain in the labor force despite health limitations at older ages. The shift away from physically demanding occupations creates working environments in which health limitations are more easily accommodated by employers (Maestas and Zissimopoulos, 2010), but the higher-skill demands of these jobs prevent less educated workers from benefiting from these changes. This means that employment opportunities at older ages have increased for women—who are less likely to be employed in physically demanding occupations than men—and more educated workers but have remained narrow for less educated men (Rutledge et al., 2017), restricting the latter's ability to delay retirement.

Macroeconomic and local labor market conditions also play an important role in shaping opportunities for employment at older ages. Older workers who are near retirement age are more responsive to changes in the labor market, both positive and negative, than younger workers (Gorodnichenko et al., 2013; Maestas, Mullen, and Powell, 2013; Coile and Levine, 2011). Factors such as globalization and automation can change the demand for workers in specific industries and occupations (Lee and Angrisani, 2020; Maestas, 2010), and these changes can have much stronger effects on older workers. Moreover, older adults are less likely to relocate to areas with better employment prospects (U.S. Census Bureau, 2019), which leaves them more susceptible to changes in local economic conditions.

Negative labor market shocks, such as the onset of a recession, the ongoing COVID-19 pandemic, or the shuttering of a large employer, are more likely to affect the long-term employment behavior of older workers. As unemployment increases, full-time workers become more likely to transition into partial or full retirement, while those in partial retirement become more likely to enter full retirement (Papadopoulos et al., 2020; Gorodnichenko et al., 2013). Once unemployed, older workers face longer periods of unemployment than younger unemployed workers, are more likely to file unemployment claims than middle-aged workers (Neumark, 2018), and suffer larger losses in earnings than younger unemployed workers (Davis and von Wachter, 2011). Unemployment-induced earlier retirement is also associated with lower income in retirement and earlier mortality (Coile et al., 2014; Coile and Levine, 2011).

Public policies can play an important role in individual retirement decisions by setting the context for retirement and work decisions. The important roles of Social Security and Medicare in providing individual financial support and health insurance coverage are well established (for example, see Bee and Mitchell, 2017). But a host of other policies, addressing retirement savings, paid and unpaid leave to address caregiving responsibilities, subsidies to provide formal care, and retraining may also improve financial resources or opportunities to continue working at older ages. Beyond these individual effects, public policies can affect the incentives for organizations to implement workplace changes that enable or inhibit work at older ages. These policy environments are not set in stone, but are ever in flux.

Thus, to fully understand how individual characteristics affect the experience of work, their effects must be considered within the broader contexts through which they influence individual preferences, expectations, and constraints for work and retirement. This will provide a deeper understanding of the relationship between context and individual outcomes, providing a guide for future policymaking.

BOUNDARIES ON THE SCOPE OF THIS REPORT

The scope of the statement of task assigned to the committee was broad, which meant that producing a concise and useful summary of the research literature required the committee to identify clear boundaries to its review. Based on its statement of task and discussions with the study sponsor, the committee understood that its review should be centered on the behavioral and social factors associated with continuing work at older ages, with an eye toward the development of a clear research agenda identifying key topics that should be targeted in future research.

There were two topics that were relevant to the committee's task but so broad in scope that a thorough review of their content would not be feasible within the timeframe of the study. Moreover, because the committee's primary task was to identify and highlight new research questions and areas that have not received adequate attention within the field to date, the extensive extant literature on these two topics made them a less promising source for identifying new research questions. The two topics are the relationship between health and work and the role of public policy in shaping retirement decisions. Both of these factors play such important roles in transitions between work and retirement at older ages that they could not be ignored in their entirety. For this reason, the committee set boundaries regarding the coverage of these topics within this report.

One such boundary concerned the relationship between work and health. Health is one of the most important predictors of labor force participation at older ages, both because of the direct causal relationship between work and health and because of its relationship to other characteristics that shape opportunities for work, such as educational attainment (Jason et al., 2017; Zajacova et al., 2014; Cahill et al., 2006). The causal relationship between work and health can run in both directions. Health status can affect work and retirement decisions; poor health can lead an individual to discontinue working and leave the labor force (Zajacova et al., 2014; Warner and Brown, 2011), while improvements in health can enable individuals to continue working longer (Coile et al., 2017). At the same time, work can also affect health, both positively, by promoting physical, cognitive, and social engagement (Carr et al., 2021; Fitzpatrick and Moore, 2018; Berkman et al., 2014), and negatively, through physical demands and injuries and mental stress (Fisher, Chaffee et al., 2016). This complex relationship makes identifying the effect of health on work inherently difficult and has spawned an extensive literature that seeks to establish its causal nature.

The committee viewed health as one of the individual-level factors that predicts labor force participation at older ages, and therefore provides a brief review of the research establishing a causal effect of health on work. Beyond this, the committee considered the effects of health only insofar as they were related to other factors under consideration, such as caregiving or workplace accommodations. In particular, a review of the effect of work on health was considered outside the scope of the committee's statement of task.

The second boundary the committee established in its review focused on the relationship between public policy and work at older ages. As noted above, public policies play an important role in setting the contexts in which individuals' preferences, expectations, and constraints are defined. For example, the age-based eligibility requirements of older-age programs, such as Social Security and Medicare, can have strong effects on retirement decisions (Fadlon and Deshpande, 2020; Coile et al., 2019; Burtless and Moffitt, 1986). A wide variety of programs have been introduced to encourage saving behaviors at younger ages in order to financially prepare individuals and families for retirement (e.g., 401(k) plans and IRAs). In addition, many other age-neutral programs and policies, such as family leave and job retraining programs, can help older workers remain in the labor force. The wide-ranging variety and scope of such programs made a thorough review of the literature evaluating the effects of these programs infeasible. Such a review would constitute its own report. The committee compromised by including a chapter that provides a broad overview of both age-targeted and age-neutral public programs that may affect the work behaviors of older workers.

Although the statement of task explicitly charges the committee with a focus on what is known about the United States, population aging is occurring within many countries, and this has led to the creation of a rich and informative international literature on working longer that can help inform our understanding of working longer in the U.S. context. For this reason, the committee draws on this literature in places where similar research is lacking in the United States, when we wish to indicate that findings from the United States have shown broad applicability across countries, or when a comparative focus can reveal information about the specific U.S. context. However, the committee regarded research addressing how the U.S. context differs from that of other countries and how these differences explain international differences in work patterns at older ages as falling outside the scope of the report, and was mindful of these limits when discussing research conducted outside the United States.

UNDERSTANDING WORK AT OLDER AGES

The remainder of this introductory chapter briefly discusses what defines an older worker and introduces the theoretical concepts of expectations, constraints, and preferences for work and retirement, which the committee relies on as a frame for coverage of issues of an aging workforce.

Normative Expectations about Work at Older Ages

At what age do workers become "older workers?" There is no single, clear answer to this question to which the committee can point, because the relevant age range often depends on the topic of study. Federal laws targeting age discrimination in employment identify workers ages 40 and over as potential victims of age discrimination, while federal retirement policies are usually focused on adults in their 60s. The Health and Retirement Survey (HRS), a longitudinal panel study conducted biennially since 1992 by the University of Michigan, which is one of the most commonly used data sources for studying both retirement and preretirement behaviors of older adults in the United States, initially identified eligible households as those with at least one member who was between the ages of 51 and 61, in order to capture work behaviors prior to the initiation of retirement (Sonnega et al., 2014). As such, research on age discrimination in the workplace may consider "older workers" to include a younger age range than research focused on transitions to retirement or on re-entries into the labor force from retirement. Even when considering transitions to retirement, the employment experiences of and opportunities available to workers approaching retirement may differ substantially from those who are well past conventional retirement ages.

Thus, in many cases, the relevant definition of "older worker" is dependent on what is meant by "retirement age." Unlike some countries, the United States does not have an officially recognized mandatory retirement age; however, age-based eligibility requirements for older-age programs such as Social Security and Medicare have often served as benchmarks for establishing conventional retirement age (Coile et al., 2019; Gruber and Wise, 1999). This is in part because the benefits offered by these programs enable retirement (Song and Manchester, 2007), but also because normative expectations about what constitutes the appropriate age to retire underlie the establishment of their eligibility ages.

As a growing proportion of adults continues to work beyond conventional retirement ages, normative expectations about what constitutes retirement age could change. Such a change may be further incentivized by the need to bolster the solvency of social programs directed at older adults (U.S. Social Security Administration, 2020c), because policy changes such as raising the age at which enrollees receive partial or full benefits can reduce the overall costs of these programs (Olsen, 2012). In fact, fears that the dramatic increases in life expectancy that occurred in the mid-twentieth century (coupled with the effects of high inflation and unemployment rates in the late-1970s and early-1980s) would lead to the Social Security program's insolvency motivated the 1982 passage of legislation that gradually raised the age at which individuals became eligible for its full benefits, from age 65–67 (McSteen, 1985). However, due to concerns that not all workers benefited equally from these gains in longevity and that many adults faced difficulty remaining in the labor force at older ages, this legislation left the original age at which individuals became eligible for partial benefits at age 62. This latter decision did protect workers who were less able to continue working at older ages. Yet it also potentially widened economic inequality among older adults by constraining the qualification for full benefits for the most vulnerable older workers, that is, those with limited employment opportunities or with health conditions that restrict their activity. Some of these workers may retain eligibility under the Social Security Disability Insurance provisions, subject to establishing the presence of a qualifying disability.

Though many policies have aimed to improve the financial stability of older adults through the introduction of targeted retirement savings vehicles, research has consistently shown that working longer has a greater impact on financial outcomes than changing savings behaviors (Bronshtein et al., 2019). In addition, much of the research on work at older ages is focused on factors that enable these adults to remain in the labor force longer or on barriers that prevent them from doing so (e.g., Fast et al., 2020; Keating et al., 2019; Stoilko and Strough, 2019; Kalleberg, 2018; Gustafson, 2017; Fisher, Chaffee et al., 2016; Feldman and Beehr, 2011; Moen et al., 2006; Raymo and Sweeney, 2006; Dentiger and Clarkberg, 2002). One might plausibly conclude from this formulation of the research that there is an underlying normative expectation that these adults *should* be working longer. But this need not be the case; drawing this conclusion largely depends on how the research question is framed and presented. For example, research on factors that enable or prevent continued work at older ages could, where possible, more clearly identify and target older adults who express an interest in continuing to work.

Older adults who continue to work beyond traditional retirement ages are disproportionately those who are in good health, have more education, have better employment opportunities, and prefer to remain in the labor force (Moen, 2016b; Cahill et al., 2006)—precisely those who are most likely to experience work as a positive contribution to their well-being. This means that often research on older workers, particularly on those that remain in the labor force beyond traditional retirement ages, is based on population data, such as the HRS, in which the experiences of these well-off adults are well represented but, because less affluent adults are less likely to continue working, those of less affluent workers at these ages are not. This can obscure the work outcomes of less affluent older workers those of whose experiences in the labor force may be substantively different, creating a more positive representation of the effects of work on quality of life that could shift normative expectations about work and retirement at older ages. Thus, in presenting research on the older workforce, it is crucial to be clear about the characteristics of the study population to whom findings apply. Moreover, research that focuses on explicating the heterogeneity of work experiences at older ages would provide a more nuanced understanding of the role of work and reduce the likelihood of the ecological fallacy—in which the experiences of more economically advantaged adults will be seen as representative of the experiences of the older worker population as a whole—being applied to this population.

A Framework for Understanding Work at Older Ages

At the outset of our task, the committee members developed a framework for understanding the experience of work and transitions between work and nonwork at older ages. This framework relied on conceptual elements that were common across their respective research disciplines and provided a common language for presenting the research in this report. It is discussed in greater detail in Chapter 3, but at its core it conceptualizes work at older ages as being shaped by an individual's preferences for work and expectations about the future, as well as constraints on his or her ability to realize preferred work relationships. These three dimensions—preferences, expectations, and constraints—each shape the others and are mutually reinforcing.

Much of the research about work at older ages focuses on the role of constraints or barriers to labor force participation at older ages (Fisher, Chaffee et al., 2016). As noted, this focus can be accompanied by an often-unacknowledged assumption: that older adults should be working if they are able to do so. This, however, is a subjective value judgment rather than an empirically established fact. Incorporating the roles that preferences and expectations also play in shaping work outcomes acknowledges that work decisions are not based on work capacity or opportunities alone (James et al., 2016; Moen, 2016a). Individuals also weigh the relative value they place on engaging in other activities, such as leisure, travel, or volunteer work, when considering whether to continue working at older ages. These preferences shape and are shaped by expectations about how they will affect outcomes, such as financial stability, health, and quality of life (Boehm et al., 2014; Cahill et al., 2013; Wang and Shultz, 2010). Of course, constraints also play a significant role in whether individuals are able to fully realize their preferences for work at older ages, and these constraints also shape preferences for work and expectations for the future (Carr et al., 2016). Individuals face barriers to employment that can take many forms, such as health limitations on work capacity, caregiving demands, or lack of employment opportunities (Fast et al., 2020; Keating et al., 2019; Stoilko and Strough, 2019; Kalleberg, 2018; Gustafson, 2017; Feldman and Beehr, 2011; Moen et al., 2006; Raymo and Sweeney, 2006; Dentiger and Clarkberg, 2002).

Though the transition from work to retirement is often thought of as a single transition into an all-absorbing state, the reality is more complex and dynamic. Full retirement between ages 62 and 65 remains the most common pathway out of the labor force (Maestas, 2010), but a growing proportion of older Americans remain fully or partially employed in "bridge" employment (Ruhm, 1990) beyond these traditional retirement ages or return to work after a brief period out of the labor force (Fry, 2019; Quinn et al., 2019; Ameriks et al., 2018; Cahill et al., 2018; Maestas, 2010). Each of the three dimensions of preferences, expectations, and constraints can change over time, leading to multiple transitions between work and nonwork activities at older ages. Understanding how these forces affect the experience of work, as well as transitions into and out of retirement, can provide insight into the ways in which work contributes to well-being at older ages.

ORGANIZATION OF THE REPORT

The remainder of the report is organized into three parts. Part I provides background describing the aging workforce in the United States and further explicates the committee's conceptual framework for understanding pathways between work and retirement. It begins with a description of the aging workforce that includes the demographic and health characteristics of those who remain in the labor force at older ages and the types of work they perform (Chapter 2). It then discusses the potential pathways between work and nonwork and a number of commonly used conceptual models for understanding transitions within this framework (Chapter 3).

Part II of the report examines what is known about the experience of work at older ages, focusing on factors that affect older workers' preferences and their expectations for work and retirement, as well as the constraints that shape opportunities to realize these preferences and expectations. Chapters 4 through 8 are organized by the level of analysis at which the factors under consideration affect work at older ages. Chapter 4 begins with the most proximal factors, examining the individual and family-level characteristics associated with transitions between work and nonwork. Chapters 5 through 8 take a broader view, examining the ways in which context shapes and constrains the experience of work and pathways between work and nonwork at older ages. Chapter 5 focuses on the workplace and examines how workplace policies and practices can serve to enable or restrict the ability of older workers to remain in the labor force. Chapter 6 examines the role of age bias and discrimination in work-related experiences. Chapter 7 examines the role of labor markets in creating demand and opportunities for older workers to remain in the labor force. Chapter 8 focuses on the role of public policy in encouraging or enabling or, conversely, discouraging or operating as a barrier to labor force participation at older ages.

Part III of the report is a summary of the conclusions drawn from the preceding chapters and identifies key themes that cut across these chapters in order to outline a future research agenda on work at older ages. The final chapter (Chapter 9) draws from the findings of the earlier chapters. It identifies key conclusions that can be drawn from the extant research and proposes a detailed research agenda that, if enacted, would provide a comprehensive understanding of the social and economic role of work at older ages and the barriers older adults face in realizing their preferred work and retirement relationships.

Part I

2

The Emerging Older Workforce

During the two-decade period between 2000 and 2020, the share of employed workers ages 60 and over has doubled among both men and women (Figure 2-1). Specifically, the percent of all employed men who are in that age range rose from 7.4 to 14.8 percent, while among all employed women it rose from 6.3 to 14.0 percent. Although most of this increase, in absolute terms, was due to a growing share of the workforce entering their early 60s, the percentage of employed workers in each five-year age group over age 60 either doubled or nearly doubled during this period. The percentage ages 80 and over plateaued in the late-2010s (Figure 2-1, bottom panels).

This aging of the U.S. workforce is due in part to the overall aging of the U.S. population. Since 2006, when the sizable Baby Boom generation began to reach age 60, the proportion of the population that is ages 60 and over has grown dramatically, while younger age groups have remained steady or declined, with most of the decline occurring among those under age 40 (Figure 2-2, upper panels) as birth rates have continued to fall (Hamilton et al., 2021). The share of the population that falls in each of the over-60 age groups has increased substantially since 2010 (Figure 2-2, lower panels), particularly among those ages 60–74.

U.S. Census Bureau (2018) population projections predict that the U.S. population will continue to age with the median age of the population, which it projects to increase from 37.9 years in 2016 to 42.9 years by 2060. According to these projections, the percent of the population that is ages 60 and over will also continue to increase (Figure 2-2, upper panels). However, the largest increase is projected to occur among those ages 80 and over (Figure 2-2, lower panels), among whom employment rates are very low.

The percent of the population ages 60–69, those in the 60-and-over age group that are most likely to be employed, is expected to decline after 2020, before rising again after 2040 as the large Millennial cohort begins to reach age 60. If employment rates remained steady at their 2020 levels in subsequent decades among those ages 60 and over, the share of the workforce that is ages 60 and over would begin to decline after 2025, but would again increase after 2040, largely mirroring the share of the population in the 60–69 age group.

In fact, the aging of the U.S. population has not been as rapid as the aging of the workforce, suggesting that it is not only shifts in the age of the population that have led to the increasing number of older workers. If employment rates had remained steady throughout the 2000s and 2010s, the percentage of the workforce that was ages 60 and older would not have increased as dramatically. Thus, changes in labor force participation at all ages have also contributed to the increasing average age of the U.S. worker. The combination of decreasing labor

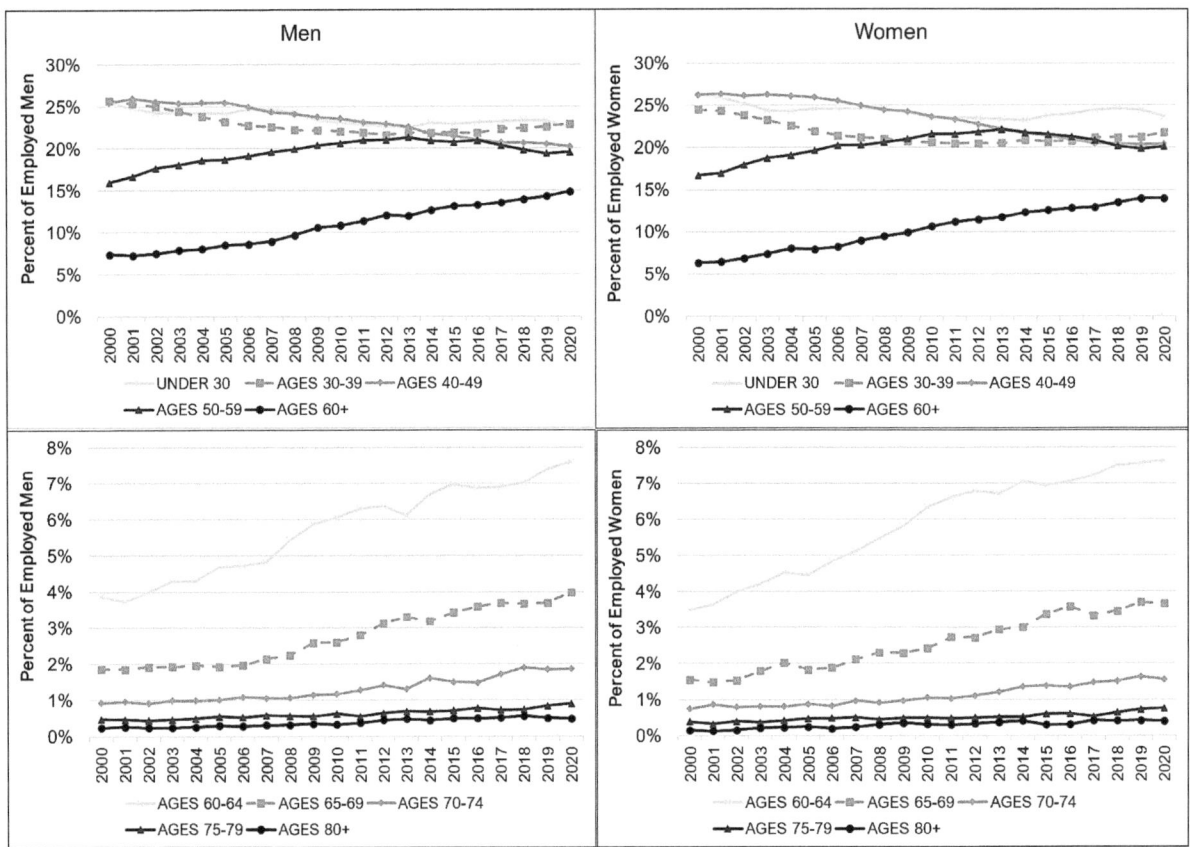

FIGURE 2-1 The age distribution of employed adults in the U.S. by gender, 2000–2020.
NOTE: Figure 2-1 shows the percent of employed adults that falls in each age group among men (left panels) and women (right panels).
SOURCE: Data from 2000–2020 March Current Population Survey Annual Social and Economic Supplement data files calculated by U.S. Census Bureau online data table tool (Beta version).

force participation rates among younger adults and increasing labor force participation rates at older ages has also contributed to the growing share of older workers (Figure 2-3). Over this same two-decade period, among both men and women participation fell among those under age 55 but increased among those ages 55 and over (Figure 2-3, middle and bottom panels).[1] This means that even if the age distribution of the population had not changed during this period, older workers would have constituted a larger share of the workforce in 2019 than they had in 2000.

HOW TRENDS IN LABOR FORCE PARTICIPATION ARE GENDERED

Although these overall trends have been present among both men and women, the magnitude of the changes at younger and older ages, as well as their relative importance, has differed by gender. The decline in labor force participation between 2000 and 2020 that occurred at younger ages has been larger among men than among women; however,

---

[1] To demonstrate the long-term trends and exclude any potential effects of the COVID-19 pandemic, the changes over time in labor force participation use 2019 as an endpoint.

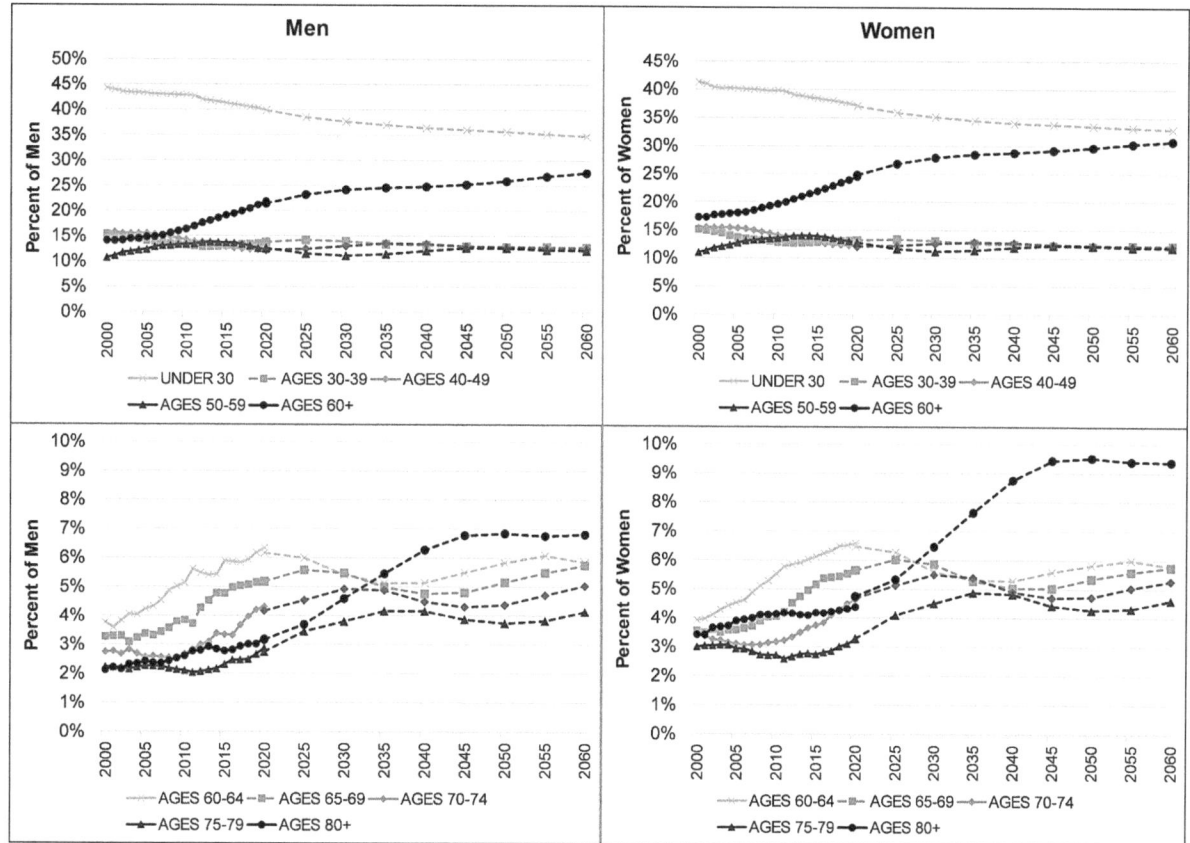

FIGURE 2-2 The age distribution of the U.S. population by gender, actual (2000–2020) and projected (2020–2060).
NOTE: Figure 2-2 shows the percent of the U.S. population that falls in each age group among men (left panels) and women (right panels). The age distribution for the 2000–2020 period is based on the actual age distribution of the U.S. population during this period. The distribution for the 2020–2060 period is based on U.S. Census Bureau 5-year population projections; this period is represented by dashed lines. Since the population projections are based on projecting from the base year of 2016, both the observed and projected distributions for 2020 (the first projected year) are included in the figure to show any discontinuities between the actual and projected numbers.
SOURCE: Data from 2000–2020 March Current Population Survey Annual Social and Economic Supplement data files calculated by U.S. Census Bureau online data table tool (Beta version) and 2020–2060 U.S. Census Bureau (2018) Population Projections.

the increase in labor force participation at older ages has been more pronounced among women, particularly among those in their sixties. These gender differences are the result of overall lower labor force participation among women. This lower participation holds true especially among younger women during the years in which they are raising children, but it carries forward into older ages as well.

The pattern of lower labor force participation among older women (relative to older men) is not unique to the United States; in fact, the United States enjoys higher labor force participation among older women than many other countries (Figure 2-4, right panel). Though both U.S. men and women were more likely to remain in the labor force after age 65 than similarly aged men in many other countries, this was particularly true among women. This is because many of the Latin American countries that have higher labor force participation among men than the United States also have lower participation among women. The countries with the smallest absolute difference in labor force participation rates between men and women (Figure 2-5) also tend to be those with low

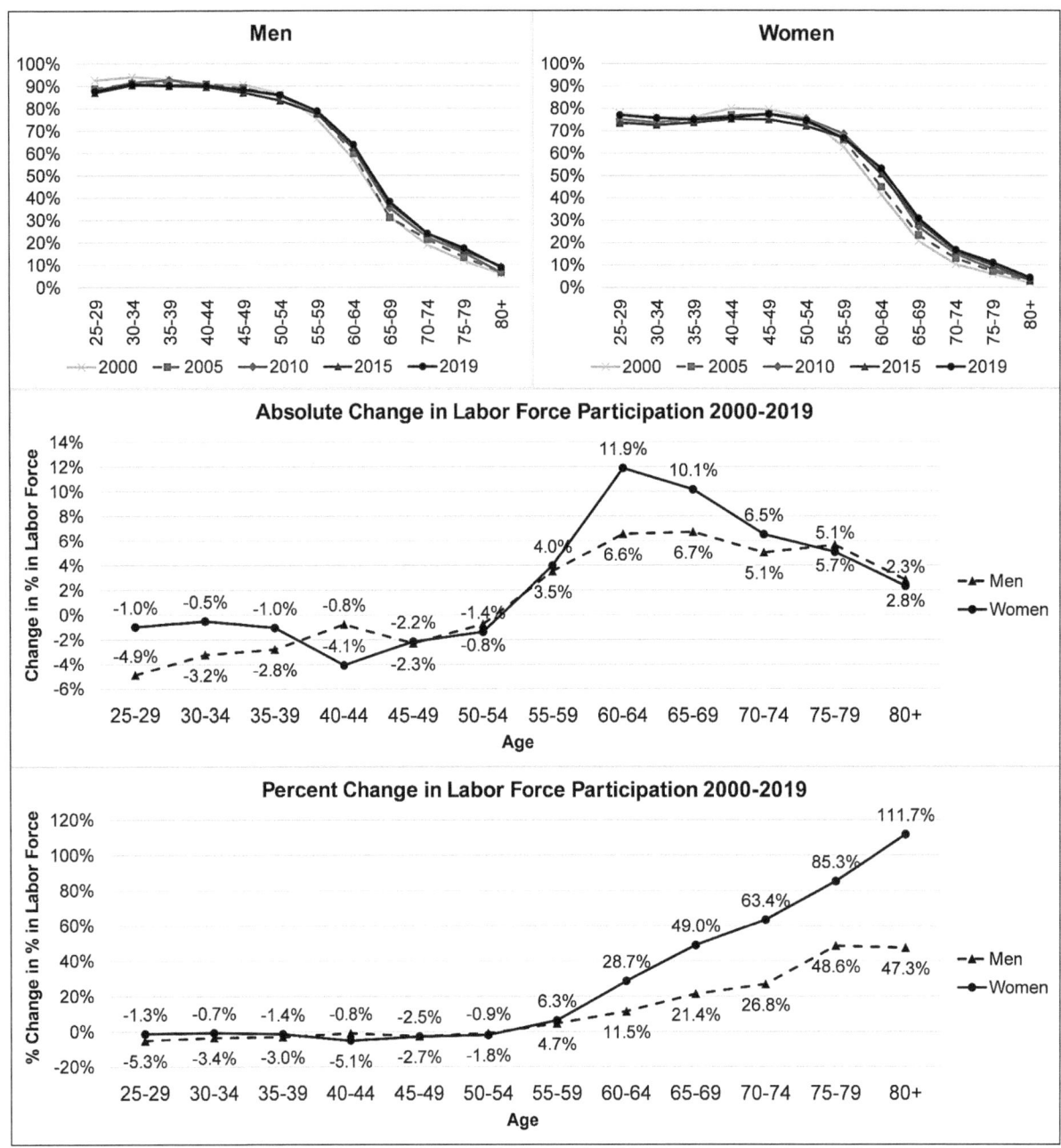

FIGURE 2-3 Labor force participation rates (and change in rates) by gender and age group, selected years, 2000–2019.
NOTE: Figure 2-3 shows the labor force participation rate by age group and gender in selected years between 2000 and 2019 (top panels), as well as the absolute change in the labor force participation rate (middle panel) and the percent change in the labor force participation rate (i.e., the absolute change in the labor force participation rate divided by the 2000 labor force participation rate; bottom panel). This figure is restricted to the 2000–2019 period to demonstrate the long-term trends without the influence of the COVID-19 pandemic.
SOURCE: Data from 2000–2019 March Current Population Survey Annual Social and Economic Supplement data files calculated by U.S. Census Bureau online data table tool (Beta version).

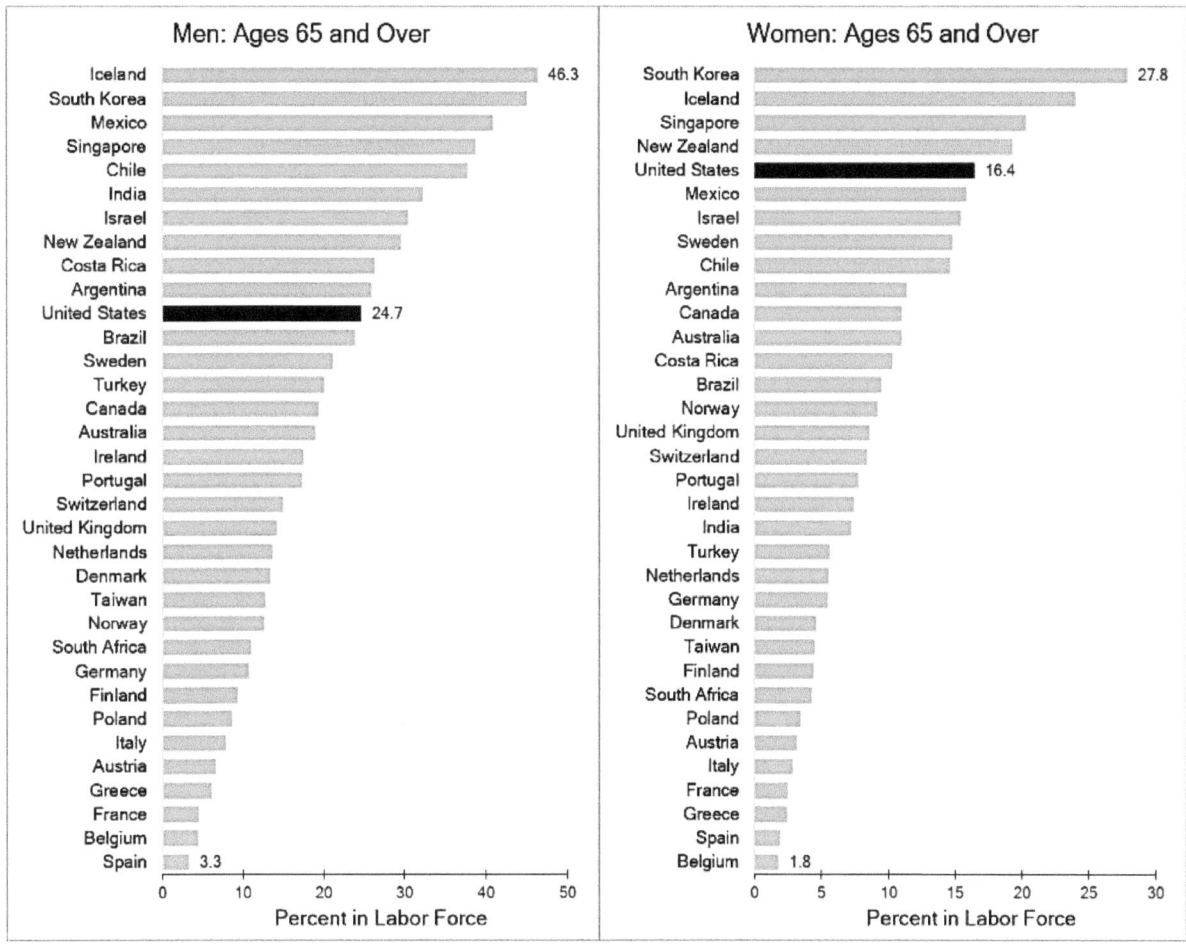

FIGURE 2-4 2019 labor force participation, adults ages 65 and over by country and gender.
SOURCE: Data from International Labour Organization (2021).

rates overall. For this reason, the gender gap in labor force participation among those ages 65 and over in the United States falls in the middle of the distribution of 34 countries shown in Figures 2-4 and 2-5. However, in the United States, labor force participation rates for men are only 33.5 percent higher than the rates for women. Of the 34 countries considered, only Norway (27.5% higher), Sweden (30.1%), and France (30.9%) have a smaller relative difference.

One of the most important demographic changes of the last half of the twentieth century in the United States was the dramatic increase in labor force participation among married women and women with children. This trend is reflected in the large increases in labor force participation at all ages across successive birth cohorts of women born between 1930 and 1954 (Figure 2-6, top right panel). Among cohorts born after 1955, these rates continued to increase when women were ages 25–34 but began to fall when they reached middle age. If these cohorts continue this pattern as they reach older ages, the growth in labor force participation at older ages may slow in the future among women. In contrast, the participation of younger men has declined modestly across cohorts, but remains near 100 percent (Figure 2-6, top left panel). It is not until after age 55, when men begin to leave the labor force in substantial numbers, that one begins to see larger changes in labor force participation among men.

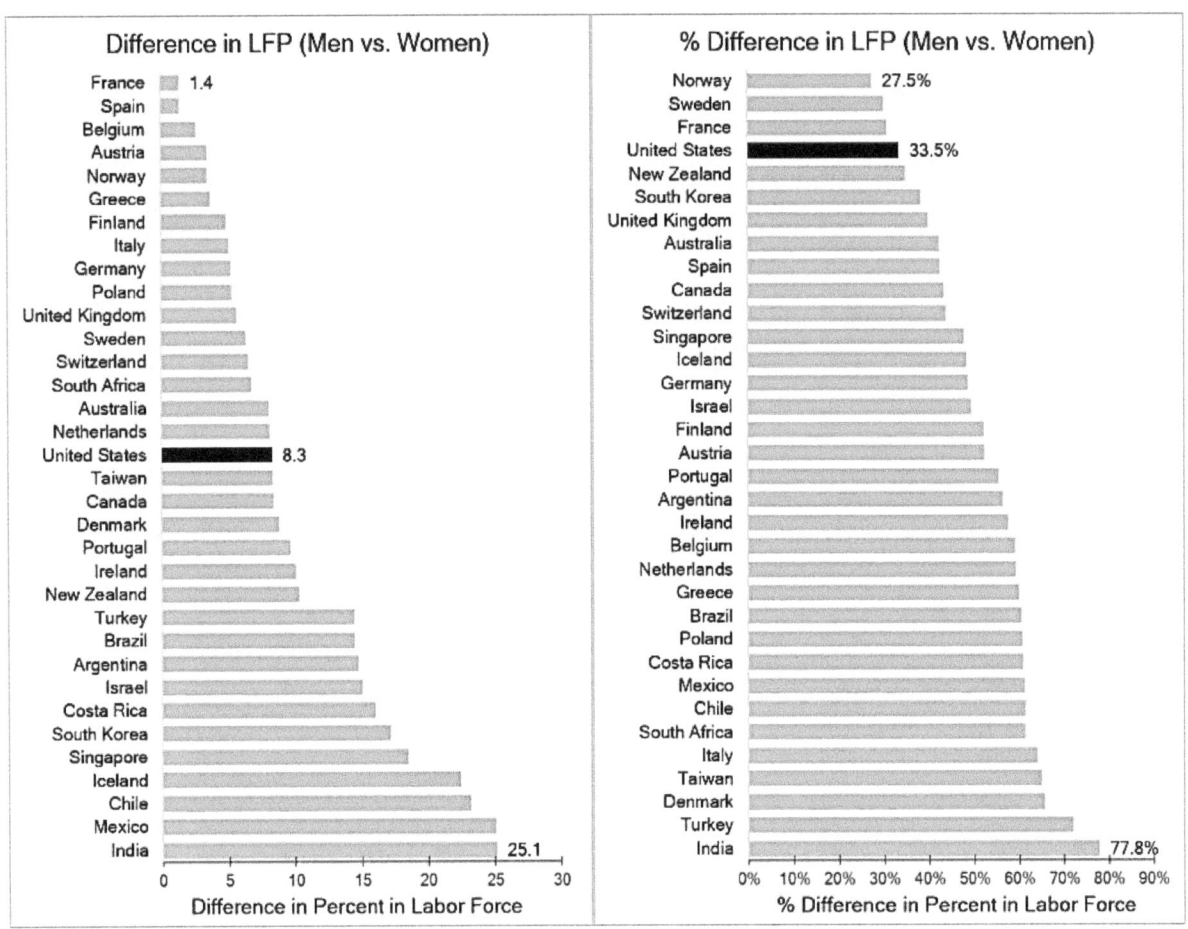

FIGURE 2-5 Gender difference in labor force participation (LFP) rates in 2019 by country.
NOTE: The left panel shows the absolute difference in rates. The right panel shows the difference as a percent of men's labor force participation.
SOURCE: Data from International Labour Organization (2021).

EMPLOYMENT CHARACTERISTICS OF OLDER WORKERS

What type of jobs are older workers most likely to be employed in? Table 2-1 shows the percent of workers within each age group who are employed within each of 25 broad occupation groups defined by their two-digit standard occupation code. The six occupation groups in which the highest percentages of workers ages 50 and over were employed in 2019 (Table 2-1, Panel A) were:

1. Management occupations;
2. Office and administrative support occupations;
3. Sales and related occupations;
4. Transportation and material moving occupations;
5. Education, training, and library occupations; and
6. Production occupations.

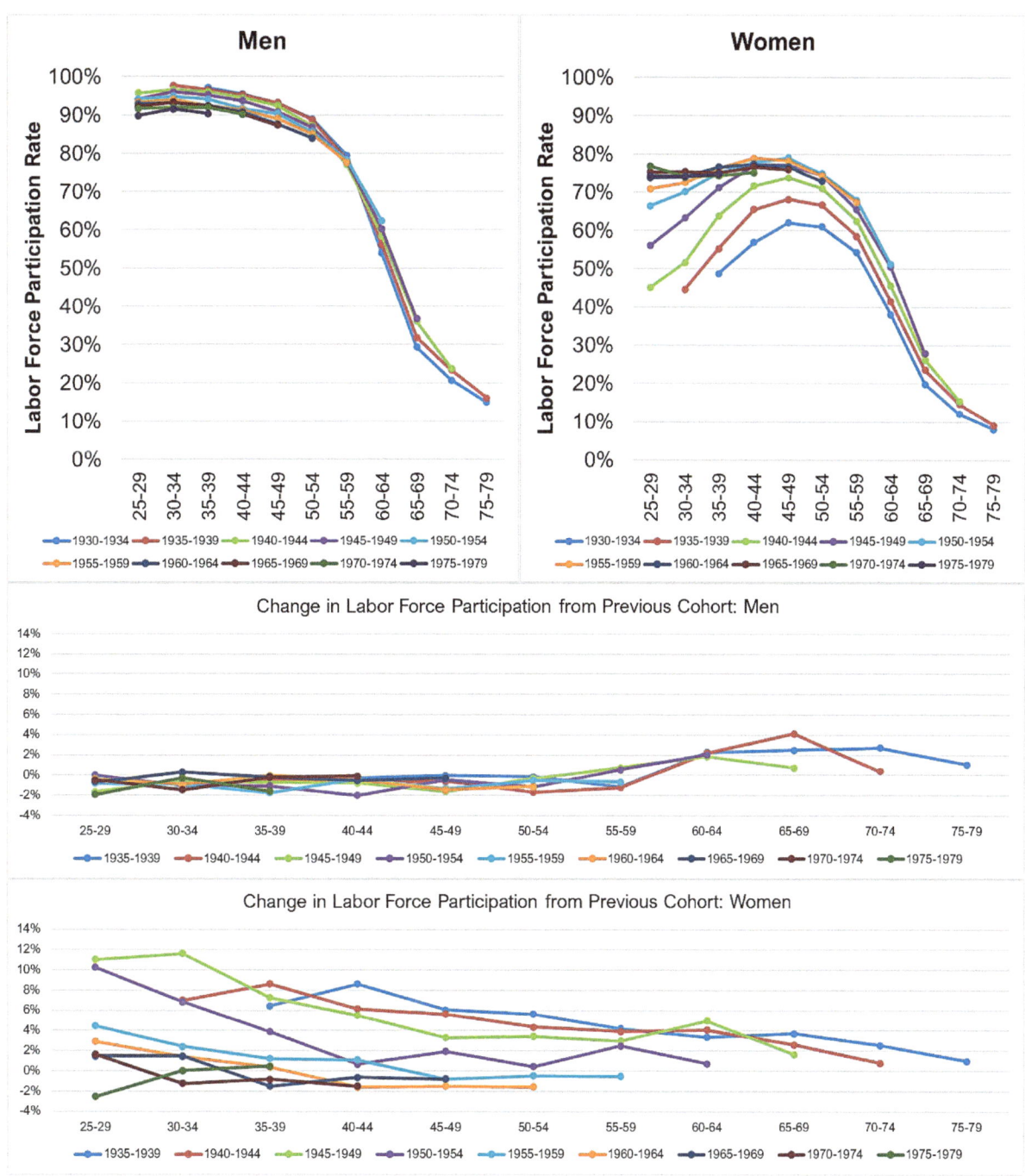

FIGURE 2-6 Labor force participation by age, gender, and birth cohort, ages 25–79.
NOTE: Figure 2-6 shows the average labor force participation rate within five-year age groups among men (top left panel) and women (top right panel) who are ages 25 and over for each five-year birth cohort born between 1930–1979, as well as the change in the labor force participation rate from the previous cohort among men (middle panel) and women (bottom panel). Following the method used by Goldin and Mitchell (2017), the average labor force participation rate is the average rate calculated from the five single-year ages for each of the five single-years of birth (25 values). More information on this calculation can be found in this chapter's Annex.
SOURCE: Data from 1965–2020 March Current Population Survey Annual Social and Economic Supplement data files.

TABLE 2-1 Distribution of Workers across Occupation Groups by Age Group, 2004 vs. 2019

PANEL A	Ages 50 and Over				Ages 40 and Under			
	2004		2019		2004		2019	
Occupation Group	Rank	%	Rank	%	Rank	%	Rank	%
Management Occupations	2	11.3	1	12.5	7	6.1	5	7.2
Office and Administrative Support	1	15.7	2	12.0	1	14.8	2	10.1
Sales and Related	3	11.3	3	9.4	2	12.9	1	11.2
Transportation and Material Moving	6	6.3	4	7.9	6	6.3	4	8.0
Education, Training, and Library	5	6.9	5	6.6	8	4.9	6	5.7
Production	4	7.5	6	6.0	5	6.4	8	5.2
Healthcare Practitioners and Technical	7	4.7	7	5.9	10	3.8	7	5.4
Construction	8	4.7	8	4.6	4	6.7	9	5.0
Building/Grounds Maintenance	9	4.4	9	4.4	9	3.9	12	3.5
Business Operations	14	2.1	10	3.2	18	1.6	14	2.9
Installation, Maintenance, and Repair	10	3.3	11	3.2	12	3.2	15	2.8
Healthcare Support	16	1.9	12	3.2	13	2.5	11	3.6
Food Preparation and Serving	12	2.9	13	3.1	3	8.6	3	9.4
Computer and Mathematical	20	1.4	14	2.5	14	2.3	13	3.3
Personal Care and Service	11	3.0	15	2.3	11	3.7	10	3.7
Financial Operations	13	2.2	16	2.3	17	1.9	19	1.7
Architecture and Engineering	15	2.0	17	2.1	19	1.5	18	1.8
Protective Service	17	1.9	18	2.0	15	2.3	17	2.3
Arts, Entertainment, Sports, Media	18	1.8	19	1.9	16	2.0	16	2.3
Community and Social Service	19	1.8	20	1.9	20	1.2	20	1.6
Legal	21	1.2	21	1.3	22	0.9	22	0.8
Life, Physical, and Social Sciences	22	0.9	22	0.9	23	0.9	21	1.1
Farming, Fishing, and Forestry	23	0.7	23	0.6	21	0.9	23	0.8
Extraction	24	0.1	24	0.1	25	0.1	25	0.2
Military	25	0.0	25	0.1	24	0.4	24	0.6

PANEL B	Ages 50–59				Ages 60–69				Ages 70 and Over			
	2004		2019		2004		2019		2004		2019	
Occupation Group	Rank	%	Rank	%	Rank	%	Rank	%	Rank	%	Rank	%
Management Occupations	2	11.7	1	13.0	3	10.6	2	12.0	3	10.8	3	11.6
Office and Administrative Support	1	15.4	2	11.4	1	16.2	1	12.7	1	15.9	1	12.9
Sales and Related	3	10.3	3	8.8	2	12.2	3	9.5	2	15.0	2	12.0
Transportation and Material Moving	6	6.0	4	8.1	5	6.7	4	7.7	4	6.7	5	7.8
Production	4	7.7	5	6.4	4	7.7	7	6.0	6	5.3	7	4.2
Education, Training, and Library	5	7.3	6	6.0	6	6.6	5	6.9	7	5.2	4	8.0
Healthcare Practitioners and Technical	7	5.1	7	5.6	9	4.1	6	6.4	9	3.8	6	5.5
Construction	8	5.0	8	5.3	8	4.2	9	4.3	10	3.8	12	2.8
Building/Grounds Maintenance	9	4.0	9	4.5	7	4.9	8	4.4	5	5.7	8	4.1
Installation, Maintenance, and Repair	10	3.6	10	3.4	11	3.1	11	3.2	15	2.0	17	2.4
Food Preparation and Serving	12	2.7	11	3.4	10	3.2	13	2.8	11	3.6	16	2.5

TABLE 2-1 Continued

PANEL B	Ages 50–59				Ages 60–69				Ages 70 and Over			
	2004		2019		2004		2019		2004		2019	
Occupation Group	Rank	%	Rank	%	Rank	%	Rank	%	Rank	%	Rank	%
Business Operations	14	2.2	12	3.3	14	2.0	10	3.2	17	1.9	11	2.8
Healthcare Support	16	2.0	13	3.2	16	1.9	12	3.2	19	1.7	10	2.9
Computer and Mathematical	20	1.7	14	2.9	20	1.0	16	2.3	23	0.4	21	1.3
Financial Operations	13	2.3	15	2.2	13	2.2	14	2.3	14	2.3	15	2.6
Personal Care and Service	11	2.7	16	2.2	12	3.1	17	2.2	8	4.3	9	3.3
Protective Service	18	1.8	17	2.1	15	2.0	20	1.7	13	2.4	18	2.1
Architecture and Engineering	15	2.0	18	2.1	17	1.9	15	2.3	18	1.7	19	2.0
Arts, Entertainment, Sports, Media	19	1.8	19	1.7	18	1.8	19	2.0	12	2.4	14	2.6
Community and Social Service	17	1.8	20	1.7	19	1.7	18	2.0	16	1.9	13	2.8
Legal	21	1.2	21	1.1	21	1.0	21	1.3	20	1.4	20	2.0
Life, Physical, and Social Sciences	22	0.9	22	0.8	22	0.8	22	1.0	22	0.8	22	1.2
Farming, Fishing, and Forestry	23	0.6	23	0.6	23	0.8	23	0.6	21	1.1	23	0.7
Extraction	24	0.1	24	0.1	24	0.1	24	0.1	24	0.0	24	0.1
Military	25	0.1	25	0.1	25	0.0	25	0.0	25	0.0	25	0.0

NOTE: In this table, the rank of each occupation is based on the percent of workers within each age group who are employed within that occupation. Occupation groups are assigned based on the two-digit Standard Occupational Classification (SOC) and are exhaustive of all paid occupations. Occupations are sorted in table based on 2019 rank for all older adults ages 50 and over in Panel A and the 2019 rank of adults ages 50–59 in Panel B. The 2019 data is classified using the 2018 version of SOC. The 2004 data is classified using the 2000 Census version of SOC. Differences in classification versions may affect comparisons over time.
SOURCE: Data from 2004 and 2019 American Community Survey Public-Use Microdata file calculated by U.S. Census Bureau online data table tool (Beta version).

In total, just over half of these older workers (54.4%) were employed within these six occupation groups in 2019. Though their rankings shifted slightly, workers ages 50 and over were also most likely to be employed in these six occupations in 2004, and these occupations groups then employed 59 percent of older workers. Within these six occupations there were declines in the percent employed in office and administrative support, sales and related, and production occupations and an increase in transportation and material moving occupations. With a few notable exceptions—business operations, healthcare support, computer and mathematical, and personal care and service occupations—rankings across all occupation groups changed little over the 2004–2019 period among older workers.

Since labor force participation drops significantly among those ages 60 and over, the rankings for those ages 50 and over largely reflect employment among those ages 50–59 (Table 2-1, Panel B). The three most common occupation groups for those ages 50 and over also employ the highest percentages of workers ages 60–69, and ages 70 and over, though their relative ranking shifts with age as higher proportions of older workers leave the labor force or shift their job arrangement to accommodate their changing preferences and needs. Office and administrative support occupations; sales and related occupations; and education, training, and library occupations each employed a higher percentage of those ages 70 and over than those ages 50–59. In contrast, the percentage of those ages 70 and over who were employed in management, production, and material moving occupations was lower than the percentage of those ages 50–59. This could suggest that these latter occupations have characteristics, such as long work hours or physical demands, that make them less preferable or accommodative to workers as they age (Ameriks et al., 2018; Angrisani et al., 2016). It could also be the result of broader changes in the occupational distribution of the workforce, in which younger workers are less likely to enter shrinking occupation groups while older workers who first entered these occupations in early periods (when the occupations were growing) remain.

Nevertheless, while these occupations employ much of the older workforce, this is not necessarily because they are more likely to accommodate the needs of these workers. Part of the reason such a high percentage of older workers is employed in these occupation groups is simply that these occupations employ many workers overall. In fact, five of the six most common occupation groups for older workers in 2019 were also among the top six occupation groups in which workers under age 40 were employed. Together, the top five occupations among those ages 50 and over also employed 42 percent of all workers under age 40, just slightly below the percentage of older workers employed in them. The sixth occupation, production occupations, declined across all age groups between 2004 and 2019 and was only the eighth most common occupation among those under age 40, suggesting that the labor market was shifting away from this type of employment over the period.

In contrast, younger workers were far more likely to be employed in food preparation and serving occupations than older workers; these occupations ranked third among those ages 40 and under in both 2004 and 2019, but 12th and 13th (respectively) among those ages 50 and over. This suggests that these occupations have characteristics that make them less attractive to older workers.

A more instructive method for looking at the occupations of older workers is to examine the age distributions within occupation groups to determine in which groups older workers constitute the highest share of workers. These are the occupations in which the workforce is aging more rapidly than the rest of the labor force, a pattern that could reflect a declining need for or availability of younger workers to enter these occupations and (or) might indicate that these occupations can more easily accommodate the physical and cognitive needs of older workers. Table 2-2 shows these occupations ranked by the percentage of workers that fall within each age group in 2004 and 2019, separately by gender.[2] The occupations with the highest percentage of older workers differ from those that employ the highest percentage of middle-aged and younger workers and these occupations differ by gender.

The five occupations with the highest percentages of workers who were ages 50 and over in 2019 were:

	Men	**Women**
1.	Legal	Office and administrative support
2.	Management occupations	Building/grounds maintenance
3.	Community and social service	Financial operations
4.	Architecture and engineering	Production
5.	Financial operations	Extraction

Comparing this list to the rankings in Table 2-1 shows that several of the occupations with the highest percentages of workers over age 50 are also those that employ fewer workers overall. Among men, only management occupations are also among the most common occupations in which older (or younger) men were employed, while among women, only office and administrative support occupations were. However, employment in management occupations increased among men (both older and younger) between 2004 and 2019, while employment in office and administrative support occupations decreased among women.

Among men, the three occupations that had the highest percentage of workers over age 70—legal, community and social service, and financial operations occupations—were among the five occupations that had the highest percentages of men ages 50 and over in 2019. However, among women, only office and administrative support occupations employed both the highest percentage of workers ages 50 and over as well as workers ages 70 and over in 2019. The occupations that had the second and third highest percentages of women ages 70 and over—arts, entertainment, sports, media, community, and social service occupations—had the 16th and ninth highest percentages of women ages 50 and over. This could be because these occupations have characteristics that allow workers to remain in them at older ages; however, community and social service occupations employed the third highest percentage of women in the 50–59 age group in 2004 and the 16th highest in 2019, suggesting that this could also reflect changes in the occupation distribution over time. In fact, the ranking of occupations among women changed substantially more than that among men between 2004 and 2019, perhaps reflecting the dramatic changes in the sex segregation of the labor market that occurred throughout these women's lives (Blau et al., 2013).[3]

---

[2]Results are presented separately by gender because sex segregation of occupations declined substantially during the lives of these older workers (Blau et al., 2013), but segregation patterns when entering the labor market may persist throughout the life course. The percentage of workers within each age group is provided in the Annex at the end of this chapter.

[3]They may also reflect changes in the overall distribution of occupations.

TABLE 2-2 Occupation Groups with the Highest Percentages of Oldest and Youngest Workers by Gender and Age Group, 2004 vs. 2019

PANEL A: MEN	Ages 50+		Ages 50–59		Ages 60–69		Ages 70+		Under Age 40	
Occupation	2004	2019	2004	2019	2004	2019	2004	2019	2004	2019
Legal	1	1	1	9	4	1	2	1	24	24
Management Occupations	3	2	2	1	5	3	7	8	25	25
Community and Social Service	2	3	3	12	2	2	1	2	23	23
Architecture and Engineering	8	4	7	4	10	4	16	12	20	22
Financial Operations	6	5	8	11	6	6	5	3	19	19
Business Operations	5	6	5	6	3	9	4	11	22	21
Healthcare Practitioners and Technical	7	7	6	13	13	7	8	5	21	20
Installation, Maintenance, and Repair	15	8	11	2	18	11	21	18	15	18
Building/Grounds Maintenance	11	9	14	7	7	10	9	14	13	15
Education, Training, and Library	4	10	4	16	1	8	12	4	18	17
Life, Physical, and Social Sciences	9	11	9	19	11	5	15	7	17	14
Production	12	12	10	3	16	12	19	20	16	16
Transportation and Material Moving	13	13	13	8	12	14	14	15	12	11
Sales and Related	10	14	12	14	8	13	10	9	14	10
Arts, Entertainment, Sports, Media	16	15	15	20	19	15	11	10	10	9
Protective Service	14	16	17	10	14	19	13	16	11	12
Construction	22	17	20	5	22	18	20	21	8	13
Farming, Fishing, and Forestry	19	18	22	18	15	17	6	13	5	7
Office and Administrative Support	17	19	18	17	17	16	17	17	7	6
Healthcare Support	21	20	19	21	21	20	18	19	4	4
Computer and Mathematical	23	21	21	15	23	23	24	22	6	8
Personal Care and Service	18	22	23	23	9	22	3	6	3	3
Extraction	20	23	16	22	20	21	23	23	9	5
Food Preparation and Serving	24	24	24	24	24	24	22	24	1	2
Military	25	25	25	25	25	25	25	25	2	1
PANEL B: WOMEN	Ages 50+		Ages 50–59		Ages 60–69		Ages 70+		Under Age 40	
Occupation	2004	2019	2004	2019	2004	2019	2004	2019	2004	2019
Office and Administrative Support	6	1	8	6	3	1	5	1	17	20
Building/Grounds Maintenance	4	2	9	3	1	3	1	8	23	24
Financial Operations	12	3	11	2	13	2	16	10	18	25
Production	3	4	5	5	2	4	7	12	24	21
Extraction	24	5	19	1	24	15	24	20	3	15
Management Occupations	2	6	2	4	7	8	9	11	25	23
Legal	16	7	10	7	20	7	19	6	12	22
Education, Training, and Library	1	8	1	13	4	6	8	4	22	19
Community and Social Service	5	9	3	16	6	9	12	3	20	18
Healthcare Practitioners and Technical	7	10	6	14	11	5	17	16	21	17
Transportation and Material Moving	9	11	12	8	5	14	13	14	15	14

continued

TABLE 2-2 Continued

PANEL B: WOMEN	Ages 50+		Ages 50–59		Ages 60–69		Ages 70+		Under Age 40	
Occupation	2004	2019	2004	2019	2004	2019	2004	2019	2004	2019
Business Operations	11	12	7	9	16	12	20	18	16	16
Healthcare Support	15	13	16	15	12	11	11	9	8	12
Installation, Maintenance, and Repair	8	14	4	12	15	10	21	19	19	11
Computer and Mathematical	19	15	13	10	23	17	23	24	13	13
Arts, Entertainment, Sports, Media	10	16	15	21	8	13	3	2	14	8
Sales and Related	17	17	20	20	9	16	4	5	4	4
Construction	21	18	18	11	22	22	18	22	10	9
Farming, Fishing, and Forestry	18	19	23	17	14	19	6	17	7	10
Protective Service	20	20	21	18	19	23	14	15	5	6
Personal Care and Service	13	21	17	22	10	21	2	7	9	3
Life, Physical, and Social Sciences	14	22	14	23	17	18	15	13	11	7
Architecture and Engineering	22	23	22	19	21	20	22	23	6	5
Food Preparation and Serving	23	24	24	24	18	24	10	21	2	2
Military	25	25	25	25	25	25	24	25	1	1

NOTE: Table 2-2 shows the 25 occupation groups ranked by the percentage of workers within that occupation who fall within each age in 2004 and 2019 by gender. Panel A shows the occupation rankings among men, while Panel B shows the occupation rankings among women. 2019 occupation groups are based on two-digit codes assigned using the 2018 version of the Standard Occupational Classification (SOC). The 2004 data is classified using the 2000 Census version of SOC. Differences in classification versions may affect comparisons over time. Each percentage is ranked from highest percentage to lowest percentage. Occupations are sorted in the table based on their ranking among all workers ages 50 and over.
SOURCE: Data from 2004 and 2019 American Community Survey Public-Use Microdata file calculated by U.S. Census Bureau online data table tool (Beta version).

WORK PREFERENCES OF OLDER WORKERS

Older workers are disproportionately more likely to value jobs that require moderate physical activity, sitting, and team-based evaluation and that offer schedule flexibility and work autonomy (Maestas et al., 2018). As noted above, several occupations ranked considerably higher among those ages 70 and over than they did among those ages 50–59. In 2019, these included: community and social service occupations; education, training, and library occupations; and arts, entertainment, sports, and media occupations. Among women, sales and related occupations and personal care and service occupations also ranked higher in their employment of workers ages 70 and over than of workers ages 50–59. Among men, financial operations occupations; education, training, and library occupations; healthcare practitioners and technical occupations; and life, physical, and social sciences occupations also ranked considerably higher in employing workers ages 70 and over than in employing those ages 50–59. Though these occupations cover a wide range, they likely possess characteristics that allow workers to continue working at older ages and make them more desirable occupations to older workers, such as autonomy and schedule flexibility.

The preference for greater work autonomy leads many workers to shift to self-employment, and this becomes increasingly common at older ages. Though the probability of being self-employed increases across the age range, it increases more dramatically after age 65 (Abraham, 2020). Figure 2-7 (top panel) shows the percentage of employed adults over age 50 who were self-employed in their current main job in 2004 and in 2019, by gender and age.[4] In 2019, only 8.6 percent of employed men ages 50–54 were self-employed, but this rose with age, reaching 15.4

---

[4]The committee also examined similar comparisons using self-employment measured by self-employment status of longest-held job and receipt of any self-employment income. Though the overall levels of self-employment differ somewhat—for example, using any self-employment income overall rates of self-employment across the age distribution are 10–20% higher than those in Figure 2-5—the trends by age, gender, and over time are similar.

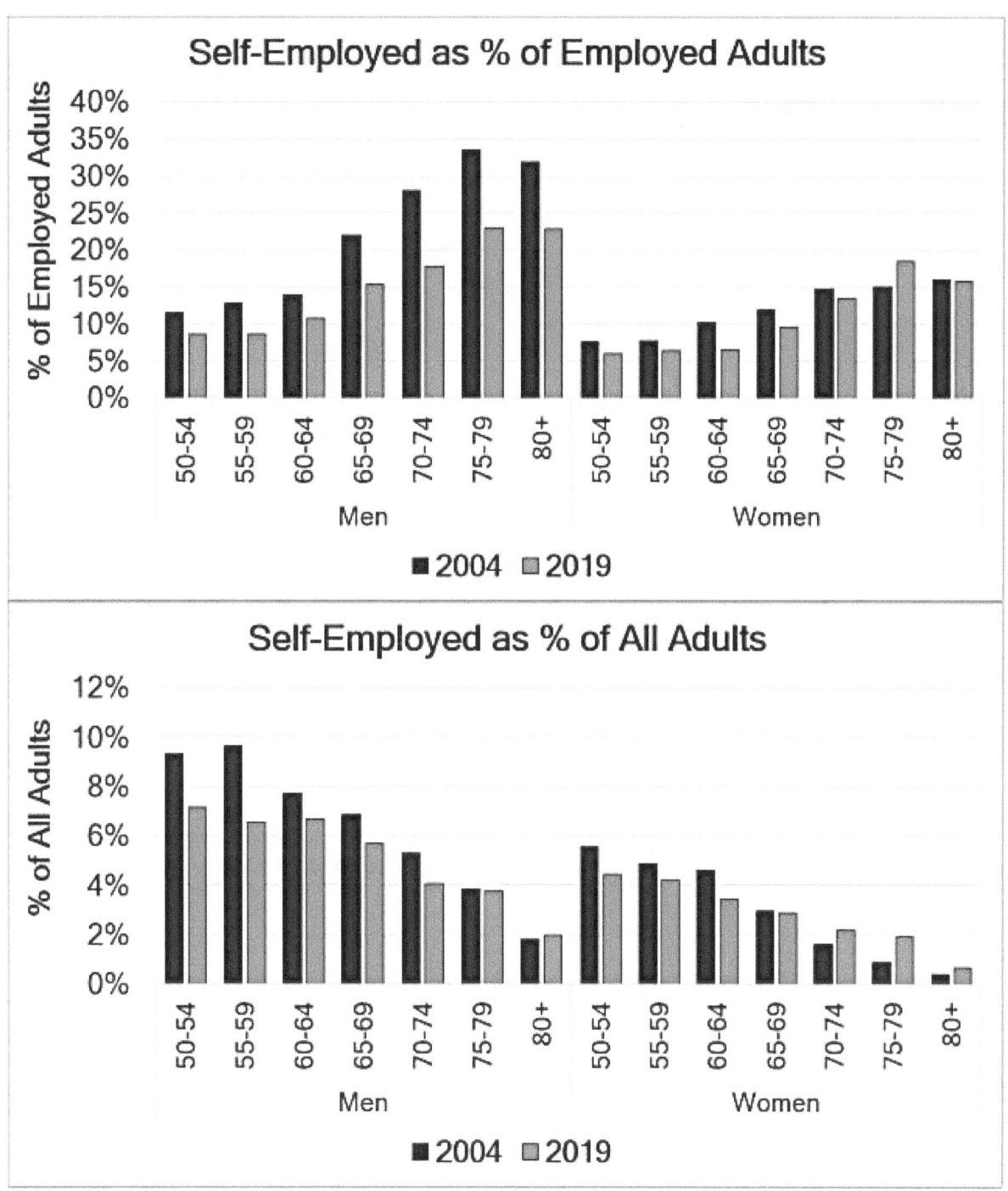

FIGURE 2-7 Self-employment in current main job, by age and gender, 2004 and 2019.
NOTE: Figure 2-7 shows the percentage of employed adults (top panel) and all adults (bottom panel) ages 50 and over who are self-employed in their current main job.
SOURCE: Data from 2004 and 2019 March Current Population Survey Annual Social and Economic Supplement data files calculated by U.S. Census Bureau online data table tool (Beta version).

percent of those ages 65–69 and 23.0 percent of those ages 75–79. These percentages marked a sizable decline in self-employment since 2004, when 11.5 percent of employed men ages 50–54 were self-employed, 22.0 percent of those ages 65–69, and 33.6 percent of those ages 75–79. Older employed women were less likely than men to be self-employed at every age; however, employed women over age 65 experienced smaller declines in self-employment between 2004 and 2019 than similarly aged men, and employed women who were ages 75–79 were *more* likely to be self-employed in 2019 than in 2004.

Though self-employment rates declined among all adults in their 50s—especially among men—between 2004 and 2019 (Figure 2-7, bottom panel), the decline in self-employment among workers ages 65 and over was in part due to the growth in employment among wage and salary workers during this period, which exceeded the growth among self-employed workers. Though the percentage of all men ages 65–74 who were self-employed also declined during this period (Figure 2-7, bottom panel)—indicating that self-employment rates within this age group did decline over the period—the declines are much smaller than those among employed men (Figure 2-7, top panel). In addition, self-employment *increased* within the oldest age groups. The percent of men ages 75 and over who were self-employed remained steady or increased even as the percentage of employed men who were self-employed declined. The percentage of women who were self-employed also increased among those ages 70 and over, while remaining stable among women ages 65–69.

Self-employment can take on a number of different forms. A small fraction of older self-employed adults engages in informal work, such as babysitting or elder care, maintenance work, or making and selling handcrafts (Abraham, 2020). Some older workers return to their prior employer as an independent contractor. These relationships allow employers to continue to benefit from their former employees without taking on the full cost and risk of employing them. Though these independent contractors often gain flexibility and greater autonomy over their schedules and work, they lose some of the benefits and protections of being an employee. About half of older self-employed workers work as independent contractors, independent consultants, or freelance workers, and about one-quarter of these workers are performing work for a prior employer (Abraham, 2020). It is not clear to what degree these workers choose this independent contractor relationship or are pushed into these arrangements by their prior employers as a condition of continuing their employment.

Accurate estimates of these employment relationships have proved elusive due to limitations in the most commonly used measures of employment characteristics (National Academies of Sciences, Engineering, and Medicine, 2020). These measures can lead to misclassification of some forms of self-employment, particularly informal, gig, mobile-platform-enabled, and contract work, as well as an underestimation of employment and labor force participation (see Box 2-1). The underestimation of labor force participation is particularly acute for the youngest and oldest workers in the labor market, who are more likely to work fewer than 15 hours per week and to engage in informal work arrangements (Abraham et al., 2021).

Older Workers Work Fewer Hours

The shift to self-employment among older workers is often driven by a desire for shorter or more flexible work hours. Few employers offer a phased retirement plan, which allows workers to reduce their work hours as they approach retirement (Society for Human Resource Management, 2018), and most workers do not believe their employer would allow them to reduce their hours (Abraham and Houseman, 2005). Nevertheless, many older workers who remain in the labor force reduce their work hours to part-time, and this is particularly true for those who are self-employed (Abraham et al., 2021). As was true for self-employment, part-time working arrangements become increasingly common with age (up until age 80), with steep increases occurring after age 65 (Figure 2-8).

Older women are more likely than similarly aged older men to work part-time. For example, at ages 50–54, employed women are twice as likely as employed men (22.8% vs. 10.6% in 2019) to work part-time, with part-time defined as working fewer than 35 hours per week. This gender disparity narrows among those in their 70s and older. In fact, in 2004 there was no difference by gender in the probability of working part-time among those ages 75 and over. Between 2004 and 2019, as labor force participation increased among older adults, the percentage working part-time declined, as those who remained in the labor force became more likely to work at least 35 hours

> **BOX 2-1**
> **Measuring Employment and Self-Employment among Older Workers**
>
> Most of the information presented in this chapter relies on data from the Current Population Survey (CPS), a monthly survey conducted by the U.S. Census Bureau that is the primary source for monthly labor statistics in the United States. This survey is one of the longest-running surveys conducted by the federal government, and many of the questions and measures included in it have been consistently measured for decades. That consistency allows users to examine trends in labor statistics over long periods of time; however, the measures used might not capture the full range of work activities in which U.S. workers are engaged.
>
> The limitations of the CPS measures were recently highlighted by a National Academies of Sciences, Engineering, and Medicine (2020) report on alternative work arrangements, which recommended the development of more detailed employment measures. The need for these changes has also been demonstrated in recent work by Katherine Abraham and her colleagues (2021). By adding an extensive set of employment questions that were designed to capture a wider range of work activities to four waves of the Gallup Education Consumer Pulse Survey conducted in 2018 and 2019, these researchers were able to demonstrate that the CPS underestimates rates of employment and self-employment among older workers and that this underestimation is larger among workers ages 70 and over. They found that their more extensive set of questions about work-related activities was able to capture more low-hour and informal work, leading to higher estimates of employment and part-time work in the Gallup data than in CPS data collected during the comparable period.
>
> As mentioned in the discussion of self-employment, many workers who are self-employed work as independent contractors under agreements to perform work they had previously done as employees, sometimes for their previous employers. This reclassification of a worker from employee to self-employed while performing similar duties for the same employer can lead to mismeasurement of his or her relationship to the employer—that is, as an employee rather than an independent contractor (Abraham, 2020). This measurement error can be substantial, with one estimate showing that 9–10 percent of all employed workers over age 65 are self-employed as independent contractors but would be misclassified as "employees" using CPS definitions of self-employment (Abraham, 2020).

per week. This change was very small among those in their 50s and primarily occurred among those ages 60 and over, with the largest changes among those ages 65 and over. Though both men and women were less likely to work part-time in 2019 than they were in 2004, the age-specific decreases in part-time work were larger among men. This meant that the gender gap in work hours either opened (ages 75 and over) or increased (ages 50–75) at each age throughout the age distribution.

THE CHANGING COMPOSITION OF THE OLDER WORKFORCE

The older workforce, like the U.S. population as a whole, has become more diverse and more educated over time. Immigrants, Hispanic Americans, and non-White populations alongside those who have a college degree each constitute a greater share of the older workforce in 2019 than they did in 2004 (Figure 2-9).[5] The gender distribution of the labor force changed little over the period (Figure 2-9, Panel A); 47.6 percent of adults ages 50 and over who were in the labor force in 2019 were women, compared with 47.3 percent in 2004. The gender gap in labor force participation is larger at ages 70 and over than at younger ages, though this older age group also

---

[5]The change in the demographic composition of the older workforce is presented for the period 2004–2019. Though data were available for 2020, they were not used for these analyses in order to exclude the effects of the COVID-19 pandemic. These comparisons could not be extended back to 2000 to match the figures in Tables 2-1 to 2-4, because beginning in 2003 Current Population Survey began to allow respondents to report more than one racial identity. It is not possible to generate comparable race-ethnicity measures for 2000.

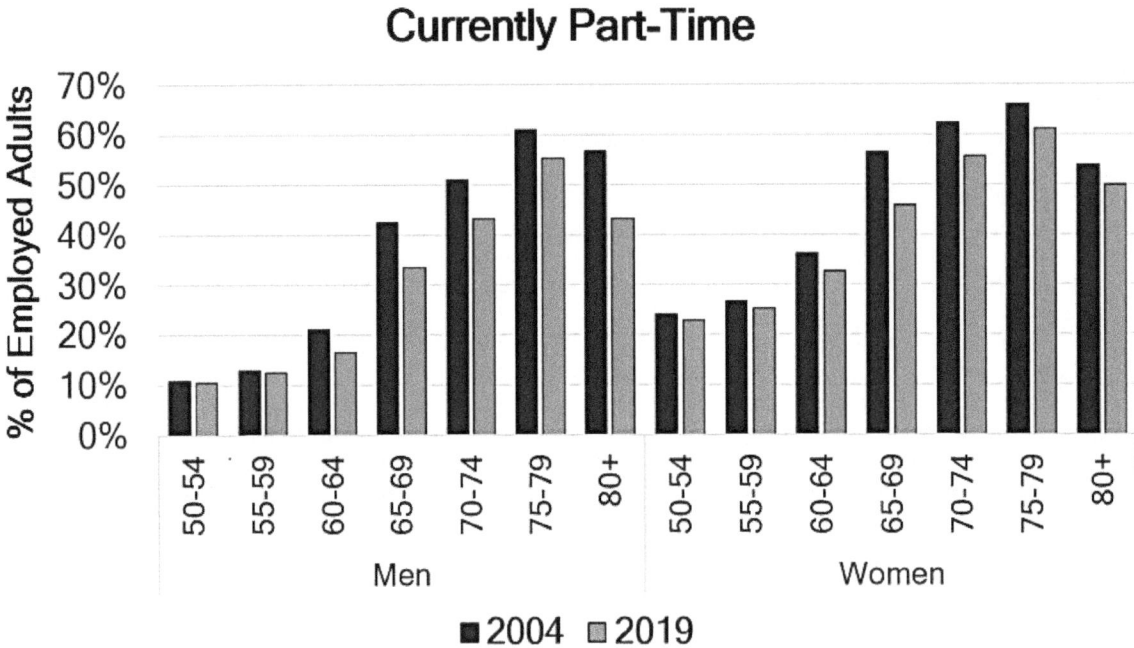

FIGURE 2-8 Percent of employed adults ages 50 and over currently working part-time, by age and gender, 2004 and 2019.
SOURCE: Data from 2004 and 2019 March Current Population Survey Annual Social and Economic Supplement data files calculated by U.S. Census Bureau online data table tool (Beta version).

saw the largest increase in the representation of women among labor force participants; the share in this age group who were women rose slightly between 2004 and 2019, from 42.5 to 43.6 percent.

Immigration status, in contrast, has changed a lot among older workers. The Immigration and Naturalization Act of 1965 abolished the immigration quota system that had been in place for decades and had restricted immigration to the United States based on nation of origin. This change in the law paved the way for dramatic changes in the nativity and racial-ethnic composition of the United States that occurred in subsequent decades and are ongoing as of the writing of this report. Though the effect of these compositional changes is lagged within the older population because individuals are more likely to immigrate at younger ages, the percent of the older workforce that is foreign-born has increased steadily over time (Figure 2-9, Panel B). In the period between 2004 and 2019, the foreign-born share of the labor force rose from 11.0 to 17.3 percent among those ages 50 and over, with the largest increase occurring among those ages 50–59 (from 11.0% to 19.1%). The accelerated increase at younger ages suggests that this trend is likely to continue in the near future.

As members of the foreign-born population and their native-born children aged, they began to constitute a larger share of the older labor force, changing and diversifying the racial-ethnic composition[6] of that population (Figure 2-9, Panel C). The fastest growth occurred in the number of Hispanic adults, though there

---

[6]The racial-ethnic composition of the older workforce is coded based on two measures included in the Current Population Survey (CPS) data files beginning in 2004: Hispanic/Latino origin and race. CPS race categories follow the Office of Management and Budget guidelines (first issued in 1997) that allow respondents to report more than one race and recommend that race categories be restricted to the following: White, Black, American Indian and Alaska Native, Asian, and Native Hawaiian and Pacific Islander. Respondents who report being of Hispanic or Latino origin are coded as Hispanic, regardless of race. Respondents who report themselves as multiracial are coded into a separate multiracial category. These racial-ethnic categories may not line up to individuals' self-identification. For example, many Hispanic respondents or those of Middle Eastern/Northern Africa descent report their race as "other" and are recoded into the existing Office of Management and Budget categories—often to White.

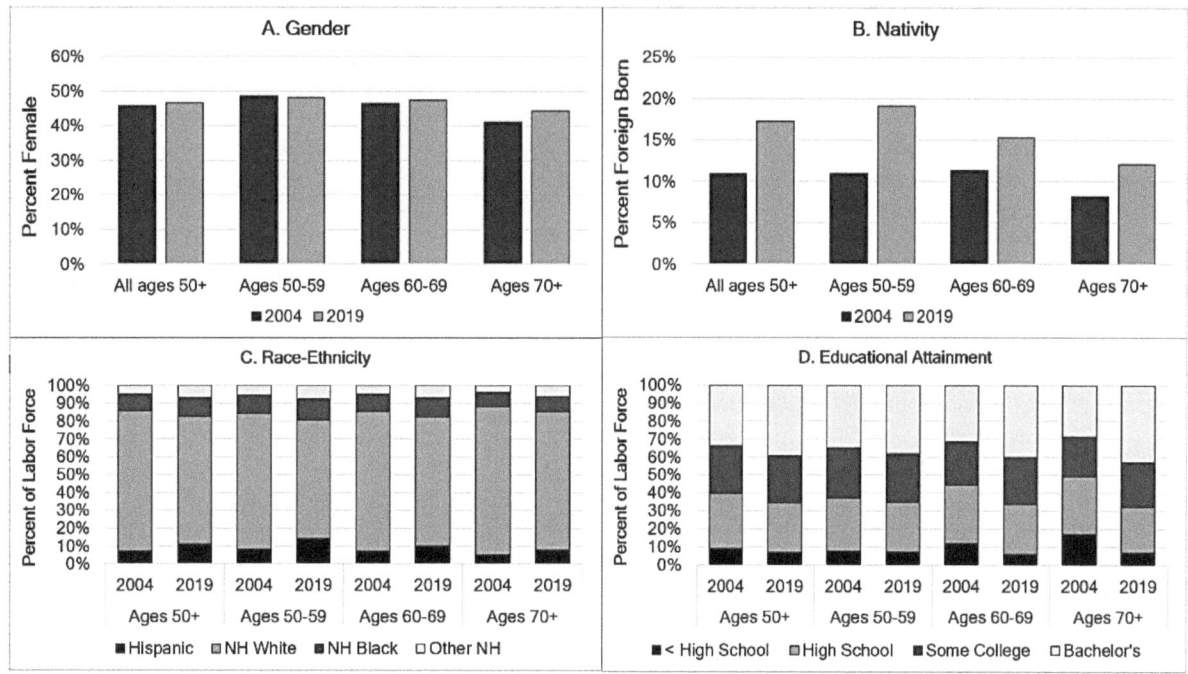

FIGURE 2-9 Demographic characteristics of the older labor force, ages 50 and over, 2004 vs. 2019.
SOURCE: Data from 2004 and 2019 March Current Population Survey Annual Social and Economic Supplement data files calculated by U.S. Census Bureau online data table tool (Beta version).

were also increases in the non-Hispanic Black and other non-White populations. Between 2004 and 2019, the Hispanic share of adults ages 50 and over in the labor force rose from 7.4 to 11.9 percent, while the share who were non-Hispanic Black rose from 8.8 to 10.0 percent, and the share who were of another non-White race (predominantly Asian)[7] increased from 5.0 to 7.0 percent. This movement toward greater racial-ethnic diversity occurred within each age group, though here too the largest shift occurred among those ages 50–59, suggesting that this population will continue the trend toward greater racial-ethnic diversity as these and younger cohorts age.

After World War II, the United States began to experience an expansion in educational attainment over time. This was driven by higher rates of college completion across birth cohorts born before the mid-1970s (Bauman, 2016). The share of workers ages 50 and over who had completed a four-year college degree increased from 33.6 percent to 39.1 percent between 2004 and 2019 (Figure 2-9, Panel D). The largest increase occurred among workers ages 70 and over, among whom it increased from 28.5 percent in 2004 to 42.8 percent in 2019, a 50 percent increase over the period. Though the share of workers in their 50s with a college degree increased slightly, from 34.8 to 38.0 percent, this change was small relative to the change among older age groups.

In part, this reflects a slowdown of the dramatic expansion of college education in the post-war period; however, it also reflects the increasingly important role that education plays in both health and changes in labor force participation at older ages. College completion rates did not increase significantly enough across birth cohorts to explain the large increase of college graduates among those ages 70 and over; much of this increase over time

---

[7] In addition to Asians, this category also includes non-Hispanic Native Hawaiians and Pacific Islanders, non-Hispanic American Indians and Alaska Natives, and non-Hispanic multiracial individuals. Due to the small number of Current Population Survey respondents within these other racial groups, these categories were collapsed with Asians who make up about three-quarters of those who fall in this category.

is due to both differential mortality and differences in labor force participation by education. (The latter trend is discussed in the next section.)

The United States has long experienced differential mortality rates by education, which have resulted in lower life expectancy for those with less education (first noted in Kitagawa and Hauser, 1973). However, these disparities have widened such that those with the highest levels of education can expect to live more than a decade longer than those with the lowest levels of education (the National Academies, 2021). As a result, those with a college degree are overrepresented among surviving adults in the oldest age groups.

DIVERSITY IN LABOR FORCE PARTICIPATION PATTERNS

In the previous section we noted that changes in the demographic composition of the labor force were sometimes larger than could be explained by concomitant changes in the composition of the U.S. population, but also reflected disparities in labor force participation. In this section, we examine differences in labor force participation by nativity, race-ethnicity, and educational attainment to assess how these factors shape labor force participation at older ages.[8]

Labor force participation varies significantly by nativity, race-ethnicity, and education. These differences reflect differential access both to employment and to alternative sources of support in retirement. Though many of those who immigrate to the United States become naturalized citizens and enjoy access to public programs that enable retirement, such as Social Security and Medicare, due to a combination of their immigration status and program eligibility requirements a sizable number remain ineligible for these programs and other retirement benefits and must rely on employment for financial support at older ages. Long-standing race-ethnic disparities in employment and work are often cumulative, leading to different trajectories at older ages. Finally, education shapes the opportunities available to individuals in the labor market, influencing their ability to continue to work, as well as their preferences regarding retirement.

At most ages, foreign-born men maintained higher labor force participation in 2019 (Figure 2-10, top panels) and experienced larger increases in participation between 2004 and 2019 than native-born men (Figure 2-10, middle and bottom panels). Between ages 30 and 54, the share of foreign-born men who were in the labor force in 2019 remained about four percentage points higher than that of native-born men, but this gap widened to 10 percentage points between ages 55 and 64 before narrowing at older ages. This higher labor force participation among foreign-born men may be the result of legal restrictions on immigration and public program eligibility. Immigration law requires immigrants and their families to maintain income support in order to remain in the United States. At the same time, many public programs have eligibility restrictions that prevent noncitizens from receiving benefits, increasing their reliance on employment at older ages. Among men ages 75 and over, there was no longer a difference in labor force participation by nativity. In 2004, foreign-born men ages 70 and over were less likely to be in the labor force than native-born men, but labor force participation at older ages increased more rapidly among foreign-born than native-born men between 2004 and 2019.

A different pattern was present among women. In 2019, foreign-born women had similar or lower labor force participation rates than native-born women at every age, except ages 65–69, when the rate of foreign-born women slightly exceeded that of native-born women. Foreign-born women were more likely than native-born women to be out of the labor force during their child-raising years but had similar labor force participation rates at older ages. Labor force participation among foreign-born women in their 30s was about 15 percentage points lower than that of native-born women, but this gap narrowed to two to three percentage points at ages 55–74.

Though foreign-born women were less likely than native-born women to be in the labor force in 2019, the gap was much smaller than it had been in previous decades—except among women ages 35–49. In 2004, labor force participation rates of foreign-born women were far below those of native-born women at every age. Between 2004

---

[8] Labor force participation is the sum of employment and unemployment rates, both of which are likely to differ by nativity, race-ethnicity, and educational attainment. Unemployment rates are difficult to measure and interpret for older workers. For those over age 65, unemployment rates are very low, which means estimates are less precise within this group and it is difficult to see trends. This is because they are based on whether an individual looked for work in the past week and older workers who have difficulty finding work are more likely to leave the labor force. For these reasons, trends in unemployment are not presented here.

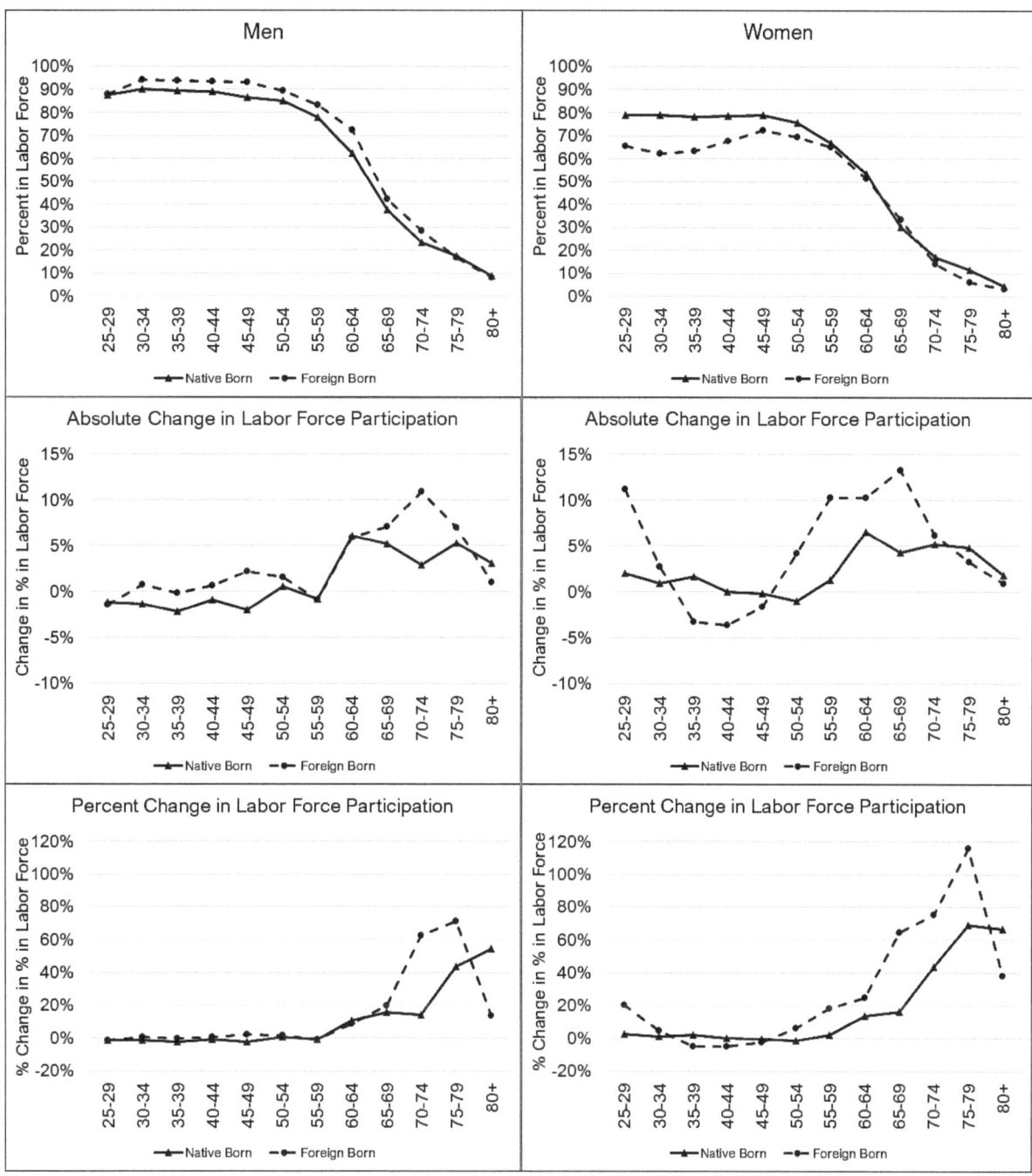

FIGURE 2-10 Labor force participation among adults ages 25 and over by gender and nativity, 2004–2019.
NOTE: Figure 2-10 shows the labor force participation rate in 2019 (top panels), the absolute change in the labor force participation rate between 2004 and 2019 (middle panels), and the percent change in the labor force participation rate over this period (i.e., the absolute change in the labor force participation rate divided by the 2004 labor force participation rate).
SOURCE: Data from 2004 and 2019 March Current Population Survey Annual Social and Economic Supplement data files calculated by U.S. Census Bureau online data table tool (Beta version).

and 2019, labor force participation increased more among foreign-born than native-born women. The only exception was in the 35–49 age range, within which foreign-born women experienced declining labor force participation, while native-born women experienced little change. Though native-born women ages 55 and older participated in the labor force at increasing rates, foreign-born women experienced much larger increases. These trends marked a convergence in the labor force participation rates of older foreign-born and native-born women over time.

Racial-ethnic disparities in the labor force are deeply entrenched and long-standing in the United States. Black men of all ages have long encountered reduced employment opportunities compared to other men due to structural racism, which has led them to leave the labor force in greater numbers. In 2019, non-Hispanic Black men had substantially lower labor force participation than other men (Figure 2-11, top left panel). At ages 34–44, the gaps between non-Hispanic Black men, on the one hand, and Hispanic, non-Hispanic White, and non-Hispanic Asian or Pacific Islander men, on the other, is greater than 10 percentage points. Beginning at age 50, non-Hispanic Black men leave the labor force at much higher rates than other men, so that by ages 60–64, labor force participation rates among these men are more than 16 percentage points lower than those of non-Hispanic White and Asian/Pacific Islander men and 20 points lower than Hispanic men.

The differences in labor force participation rates among Hispanic, non-Hispanic White, and non-Hispanic Asian/Pacific Islander workers were smaller. Hispanic men had the highest rates among men in their 30s and approaching retirement at ages 60–64. Between ages 40 and 59, non-Hispanic Asian/Pacific Islander men had the highest labor force participation rate, while non-Hispanic White men were most likely to be in the labor force at ages 65–74. Overall, non-Hispanic White and Asian/Pacific Islander men were more likely to remain in the labor force after age 65 than either Hispanic or non-Hispanic Black men. These two groups also experienced the largest and most consistent increases in labor force participation after age 65 between 2004 and 2019. The higher labor force participation among Hispanic and Asian men before age 65 might reflect the higher proportion of foreign-born men with higher overall rates of labor force participation within this population. The trends over time are more difficult to interpret for these two racial-ethnic groups because their composition has changed over time in response to shifts in migration from Latin American and Asian countries and, as well, labor force participation may differ by nativity (Budiman and Ruiz, 2021; Flores and Radford, 2017).

Among women, Hispanic women were consistently less likely than other women to be in the labor force at nearly every age. Younger non-Hispanic Asian/Pacific Islander women (ages 25–39) also had lower labor participation than non-Hispanic White and Black women; however, between ages 40 and 69, labor force participation among this group was comparable to that of non-Hispanic White women. Unlike non-Hispanic Black men, non-Hispanic Black women were as likely as non-Hispanic White women to be in the labor force between the ages of 25 and 49. However, as was true among non-Hispanic Black men, the labor force participation rates of non-Hispanic Black women ages 50–65 were lower than those of non-Hispanic White women, though this difference was much smaller than the one that occurred among men. After age 65, labor force participation was largely similar among non-Hispanic women, regardless of race; only Hispanic women experienced lower rates than other women. The changes in labor force participation between 2004 and 2019 among women were also largely similar across the four racial-ethnic groups.

The Role of Education in Defining Opportunity Increases at Older Ages

Educational attainment plays an important role in defining the labor market opportunities of older workers. Historically, employment opportunities have narrowed at older ages as physical ability to perform work tasks deteriorates (Rutledge et al., 2017). However, technological change and economic shifts to jobs that depend less on manual and routine skills and favor workers with cognitive and analytic skills (Autor et al., 2003) have allowed more Americans to remain in the labor force despite health limitations at older ages. The shift away from physically demanding occupations creates working environments in which health limitations are more easily accommodated by employers (Maestas and Zissimopoulos, 2010), but the higher-skill demands of these jobs prevent less educated workers from benefiting from these changes. This means that employment opportunities at older ages have increased for more educated workers but have remained narrow for those with less education (Rutledge et al., 2017).

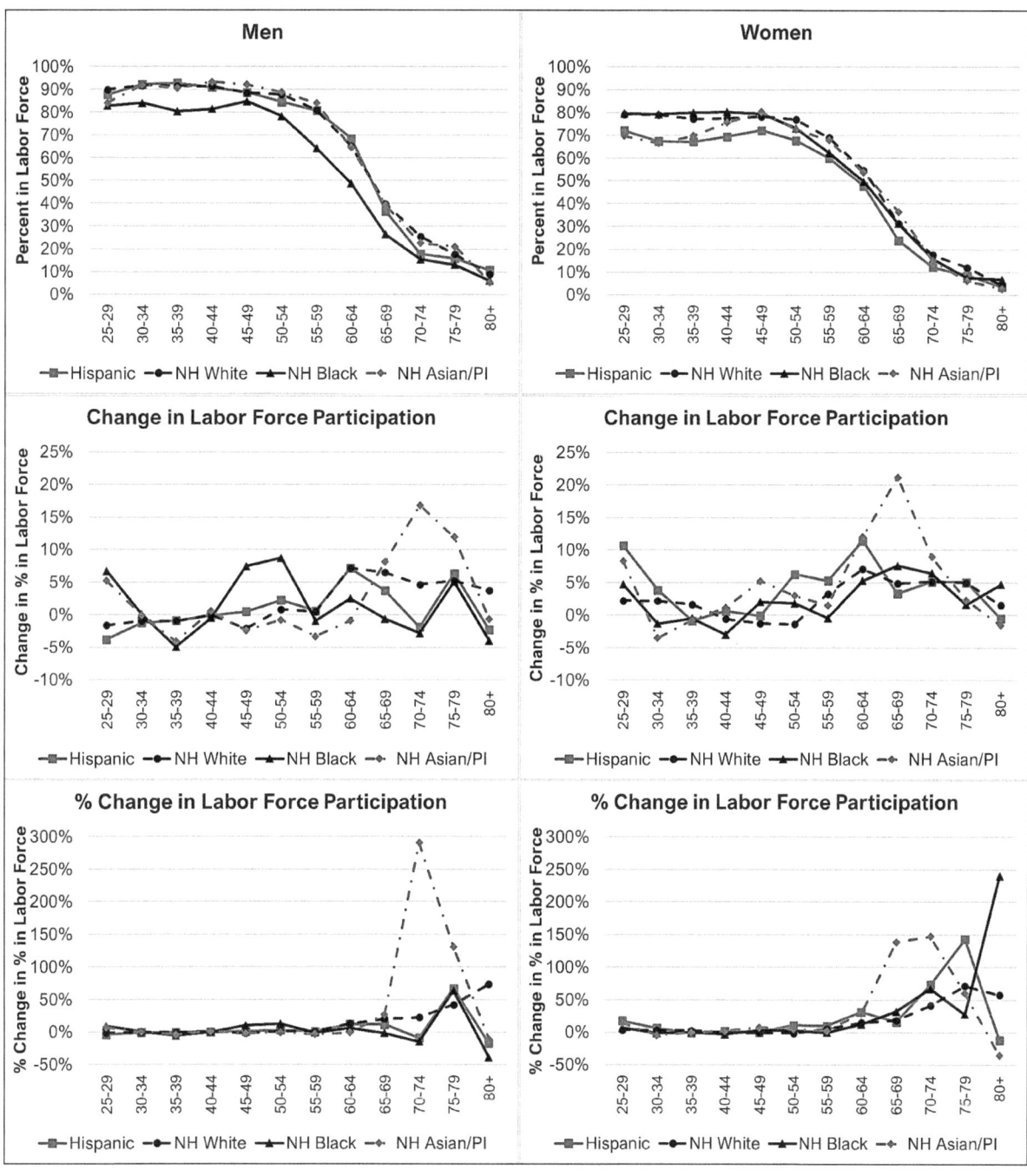

FIGURE 2-11 Labor force participation among adults ages 25 and over by age, gender, and race-ethnicity, 2004–2019.
NOTE: Figure 2-11 shows the labor force participation rate in 2019 (top panels), the change in the labor force participation rate between 2004 and 2019 (middle panels), and the percent change in the labor force participation rate over this period (bottom panels).
SOURCE: Data from 2004 and 2019 March Current Population Survey Annual Social and Economic Supplement data files calculated by U.S. Census Bureau online data table tool (Beta version).

In 2019, the largest differences in labor force participation rates the committee examined were those by educational attainment (Figure 2-12). At every age, labor force participation increased with education among men (Figure 2-12, top left panel), but the gap between the most and least educated group expanded with age, in part because those with less education began to leave the labor force at younger ages. The gap between college graduates and those with less than a high school degree was nearly 15 percentage points among those ages 25–29 (91.0% vs. 76.2%) and widened between ages 40 and 69, reaching 26 percentage points among those ages 65–69 (48.7% vs. 22.9%). Labor force participation rates began to decline at ages 40–44 among those who had not completed college, at ages 45–49 among those with a high school degree, at ages 50–54 among those who had attended college but not completed a degree, and at age 55–59 among those with a four-year college degree.

The changes in labor force participation between 2004 and 2019 (Figure 2-12, middle and bottom panels) did not differ substantively by education, with all four groups experiencing small declines in participation at younger ages and increases among those ages 60 and over. Men who had not completed college experienced somewhat larger decreases in labor force participation among those ages 25–29 and were also the only group to show declines in participation among those ages 65–69. Though the percent increase in labor force participation rates among men with a high school degree or less appears to be large for men ages 75 and over, this dramatic change should be interpreted with caution because it is the result of both low labor force participation rates in 2004 and a small sample size.

Among women in 2019 (Figure 2-12, top right panel), education-based disparities in labor force participation were significantly larger than those among men and followed a different age pattern. The gap in participation between those with the highest and lowest levels of education was largest at younger ages. Fewer than half (43.5%) of women ages 25–29 who did not complete high school were in the labor force, compared to 86.2 percent of those who had completed a college degree. Though labor force participation was higher among women ages 45–49 who did not have a high school degree (55.5%), it remained considerably below that of similarly aged women who had a college degree, among whom 85.4 percent were in the labor force. Among women in their 50s, labor force participation declined among all education groups but declined more among those with less than a high school degree than those with more education. The largest education-based gap occurred among women ages 55–59, reaching 37.3 percentage points (39.8% for women without a high school degree vs. 77.1% for women with a bachelor's degree). Beginning in their 60s, labor force participation began to drop off more rapidly among women with a bachelor's degree, narrowing the gap in labor force participation, though those with a college degree continued to be much more likely to remain in the labor force. After age 60, there was no difference in participation between those with a high school degree and those who had some college but had not completed a degree.

These disparities in labor force participation by educational attainment among women were much larger in 2019 than they had been in 2004 (Figure 2-12, middle and bottom panels), though there were already large gaps in that year. Between 2004 and 2019, participation rates fell among women under age 50 who had a high school degree or less,[9] but they increased among those who had a college degree. Among older women, labor force participation increased across all education groups; however, women with a college degree experienced the largest increase. Together, these changes led to a widening gap in labor force participation between college-educated women and women without a college degree. As is also the case for the changes observed among men, the large percent increases in female labor force participation at the oldest age groups should be interpreted with caution.

Although the committee did not examine racial-ethnic differences by education, previous research (Lahey, 2018) suggests that the education gap in labor force participation is particularly large for Black women. Among women with a high school degree or less, Black women who are under age 60 are less likely than White women of the same age to be in the labor force, but are more likely to be in the labor force at older ages—in part because earlier cohorts of these Black women had higher labor force participation rates at younger ages than did similarly educated White women. However, among women with a college degree, Black women are consistently more likely

---

[9] The one exception was among women ages 25–29 with a high school degree, who saw a small increase in labor force participation during the period.

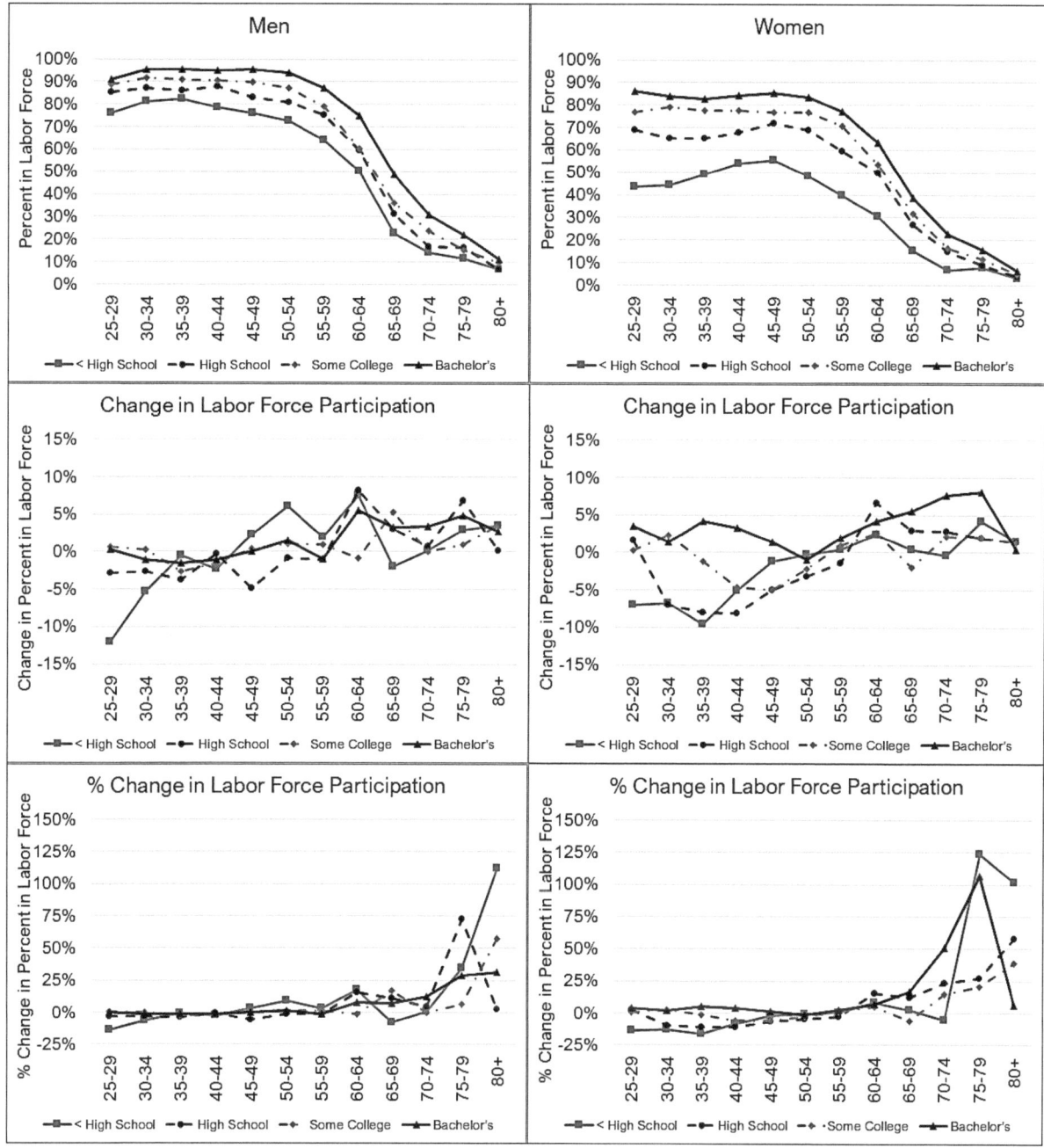

FIGURE 2-12 Labor force participation among adults ages 25 and over by age, gender, and educational attainment, 2004 and 2019.
NOTE: Figure 2-12 shows the labor force participation rate in 2019 (top panels), the change in the labor force participation rate between 2004 and 2019 (middle panels), and the percent change in the labor force participation rate over this period (bottom panels).
SOURCE: Data from 2004 and 2019 March Current Population Survey Annual Social and Economic Supplement data files calculated by U.S. Census Bureau online data table tool (Beta version).

than White women to be in the labor force, regardless of age, though this race-based disparity has declined over time as more White women with college degrees have remained in the labor force at older ages.

These large and growing education-based disparities, especially among women, explain the large shift in the proportion of the older workforce possessing a college degree between 2004 and 2019, particularly among those ages 70 and over. Though educational attainment has risen across birth cohorts, this shift alone could not explain the large increase in the proportion of the older workforce (ages 60 and older) with a college degree over this period. What can explain it is the combination of this shift with the large increase in labor force participation among older adults with a college degree and the education-based disparities in mortality discussed above.

THE INITIAL EFFECTS OF COVID-19 ON LABOR FORCE PARTICIPATION AND EMPLOYMENT

The committee had completed its first meeting as the effects of the COVID-19 pandemic began to be felt; however, it was clear from the outset that this disease could have severe and lasting repercussions for the work lives of older workers. Persons over the age of 65 who contract COVID-19 are more likely to experience severe symptoms than those who contract it at younger ages; this older age group represented the vast majority of COVID-related hospitalizations and about 80 percent of all mortality from the disease in 2020 (NCHS, 2020).

Thus, older workers, particularly those working in jobs that were deemed essential, were at a much higher risk of contracting the disease and experiencing more severe health effects. This could affect both the supply of and demand for older workers in the labor market. Fears about exposure to the virus may have made older workers wary of participating in jobs that required regular in-person interactions with the public or with coworkers. At the same time, employer concerns about the effects of disease severity on productivity and health care costs, as well as the possibility of being held legally liable for infection transmission in the workplace, could reduce the value of hiring and keeping older workers. In addition, any general decrease in labor demand could have a disproportionate effect on older workers if they are concentrated in hard-hit industries or experience more difficulty in finding new work after a job loss due to age discrimination or other issues.

The pandemic is ongoing at the time of this writing, and its long-term effects on the employment and labor force participation of older workers are yet to be experienced. However, monthly data from the Current Population Survey (CPS) can be used to assess its initial impact. Between January 2020, before the infection rate in the United States was measurable, and January 2021, a year later, the employment rate declined among adults 25 and over, regardless of age group (Figure 2-13). Among both men and women, the largest declines in the employment rate occurred at younger ages (Figure 2-13, middle panel); however, this was because employment was already higher at these ages. The percentage change in employment rates was similar for those under age 65 (Figure 2-13, bottom panel); employment rates were approximately five percent lower in January 2021 than they were a year earlier. Though the percentage point decline in the percent employed was smaller among those ages 65 and over (Figure 2-13, middle panel), it represented a larger share of older workers (Figure 2-13, bottom panel), particularly among women in their 70s. In January 2021, employment rates among men ages 70 and over were about 12 percent lower than they were in January 2020. The largest decrease occurred among women ages 70–74, whose employment rates were nearly 25 percent lower in 2021 than in 2020.

Older adults who lost employment could respond by either looking for a new job or leaving the labor force altogether. Most of those who lost their jobs during this period continued to look for work and were, therefore, unemployed, though the probability of looking for work depended on the age of the worker. The smaller difference between the change in the labor force participation rate and the employment rate at older ages suggests that older workers were more likely to respond to the loss of employment by leaving the labor force, and this was particularly true of older women.

The health and mortality effects of the COVID-19 pandemic did not affect the U.S. population equally. Racial and ethnic minorities have experienced much higher rates of infection, hospitalization, and mortality than non-Hispanic Whites persons (NCHS, 2020). Similarly, due to the broader socioecological effects of racial/ethnic inequality, the effects of the pandemic on employment and labor force participation have also been distributed unequally. For this reason, the committee also examined employment and labor force participation

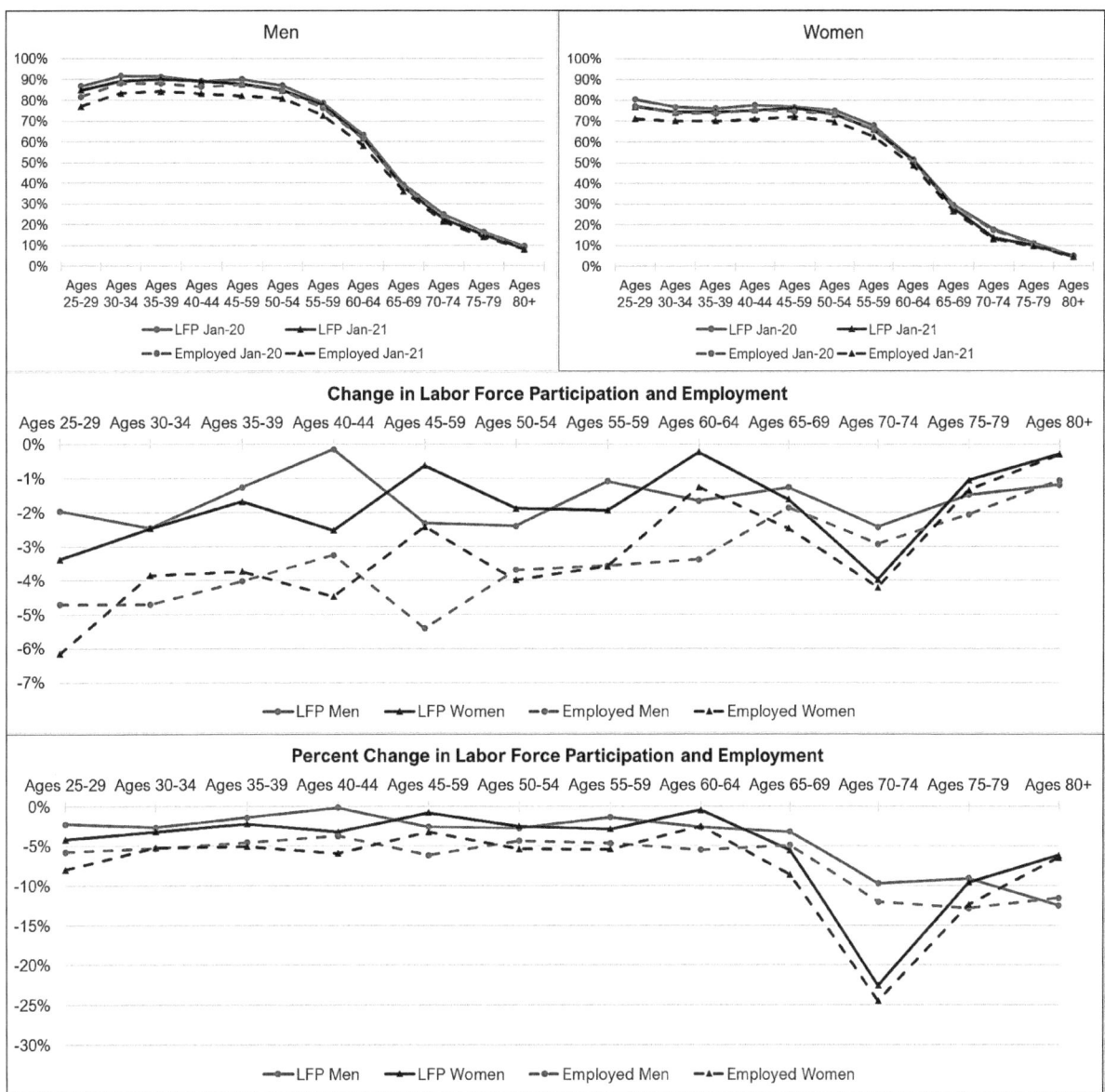

FIGURE 2-13 Labor force participation and employment status among adults by gender and age, January 2020–January 2021.
NOTE: The top panels of Figure 2-13 show the labor force participation (solid lines) and employment (dashed lines) rates for men (left panel) and women (right panel) in January 2020 and January 2021. The unemployment rate is represented as the gap between the labor force participation rate and the employment rate. The middle panel shows the change in each rate between January 2020 and January 2021, while the bottom panel shows the percent change in each rate over this period. A larger decrease in the employment rate than the labor force participation rate suggests that an increase in the unemployment rate occurred.
SOURCE: Data from 2020 and 2021 January Current Population Survey monthly data files calculated by U.S. Census Bureau online data table tool (Beta version).

(the sum of employment and unemployment) rates by gender, race-ethnicity, and age in January 2021 to that of January 2020 to determine the differential impact of COVID-19 on employment and labor force participation by race-ethnicity. The results for men can be found in Figure 2-14, and the results for women can be found in Figure 2-15.

Though men in all four racial-ethnic groups experienced declines in employment and labor force participation between January 2020 and January 2021, the largest decreases occurred among Hispanic and Asian men (Figure 2-14, middle panels). Across all age groups, Hispanic men most consistently saw larger decreases in employment than White or Black men. Asian men who were under age 50 experienced losses in employment that were comparable to those of White men; however, those age 50 and over experienced larger declines than men in any other racial-ethnic group. In general, changes in labor force participation largely mirrored those in employment, particularly at older ages. Younger men, in their late 20s, experienced the largest increase in their unemployment rates, while older men were more likely to leave the labor force altogether. The one exception was among Asian men approaching retirement: their unemployment rates increased most among those ages 50–64, even as labor force participation also declined. Only those ages 60–64 did not experience a contemporaneous decline in labor force participation.

The effect of the COVID-19 pandemic on racial-ethnic differences in employment and labor force participation followed different patterns among women, but these patterns also varied by age. The age-specific labor force participation profile changed most notably among younger Black and Hispanic women. In 2019 (Figure 2-11), labor force participation was flat between ages 25 and 49 among Black women, though it declined among other women in their 30s as they entered child-raising ages. However, in January 2021 (Figure 2-15, top panels), participation rates also declined among Black women in their 30s. In contrast, among Hispanic women though labor force participation rates were lower among Hispanic women in their 30s than those ages 25–29 in 2019, they held steady between ages 25 and 49 in January 2021 due to a decline in labor force participation among those ages 25–29 between 2020 and 2021 (Figure 2-15, middle panels). Asian women in their 50s experienced the largest declines in employment and increases in unemployment. However, in contrast to men, among older women there were no clear patterns in racial-ethnic differences in the changes in employment and labor force participation rates.

TRENDS IN HEALTH AND DISABILITY

Health is an important predictor of remaining in the labor market at older ages (Jason et al., 2017; Zajacova et al., 2014; Cahill et al., 2006). Poor health can limit work opportunities by reducing an individual's physical, cognitive, or mental capacity for engaging in work activities, and also by altering preferences for job characteristics, remaining in the labor force, and the type of work in which to engage. The latter half of the twentieth century saw dramatic improvements in health and longevity due to advances in medical care and public health, and these changes have contributed significantly to the increases in labor force participation among older adults in the United States (Goldin and Katz, 2018a; Coile et al., 2017).

However, more recently, these gains in health have begun to flatten and perhaps even reverse. In fact, within the United States, mortality rates have increased among working-age adults due to drug and alcohol use, suicide, and obesity, leading to a three-year decline in overall life expectancy, the most sustained decline in more than a century (the National Academies, 2021). Though these changes were initially concentrated among those younger than age 55, more recently they have begun to expand into older ages as these younger cohorts have aged (the National Academies 2021).

Though the percentage of adults ages 60 and over who report they are in "fair" or "poor" health steadily declined between 2000 and 2020 (Figure 2-16), signaling improving health over time, this was not the case for younger adults. Among those under age 60, the percentage in fair or poor health either remained stable or increased between 2000 and 2014. After 2014, overall health improved among men and women in their 50s and women in their 40s, but remained stable among younger adults. Though health improved among adults ages 60 and over between 2000 and 2020, these improvements were smaller among those in their 60s than among those in their 70s, leading to a convergence in the percentage in fair or poor health across these five-year age groups. These trends

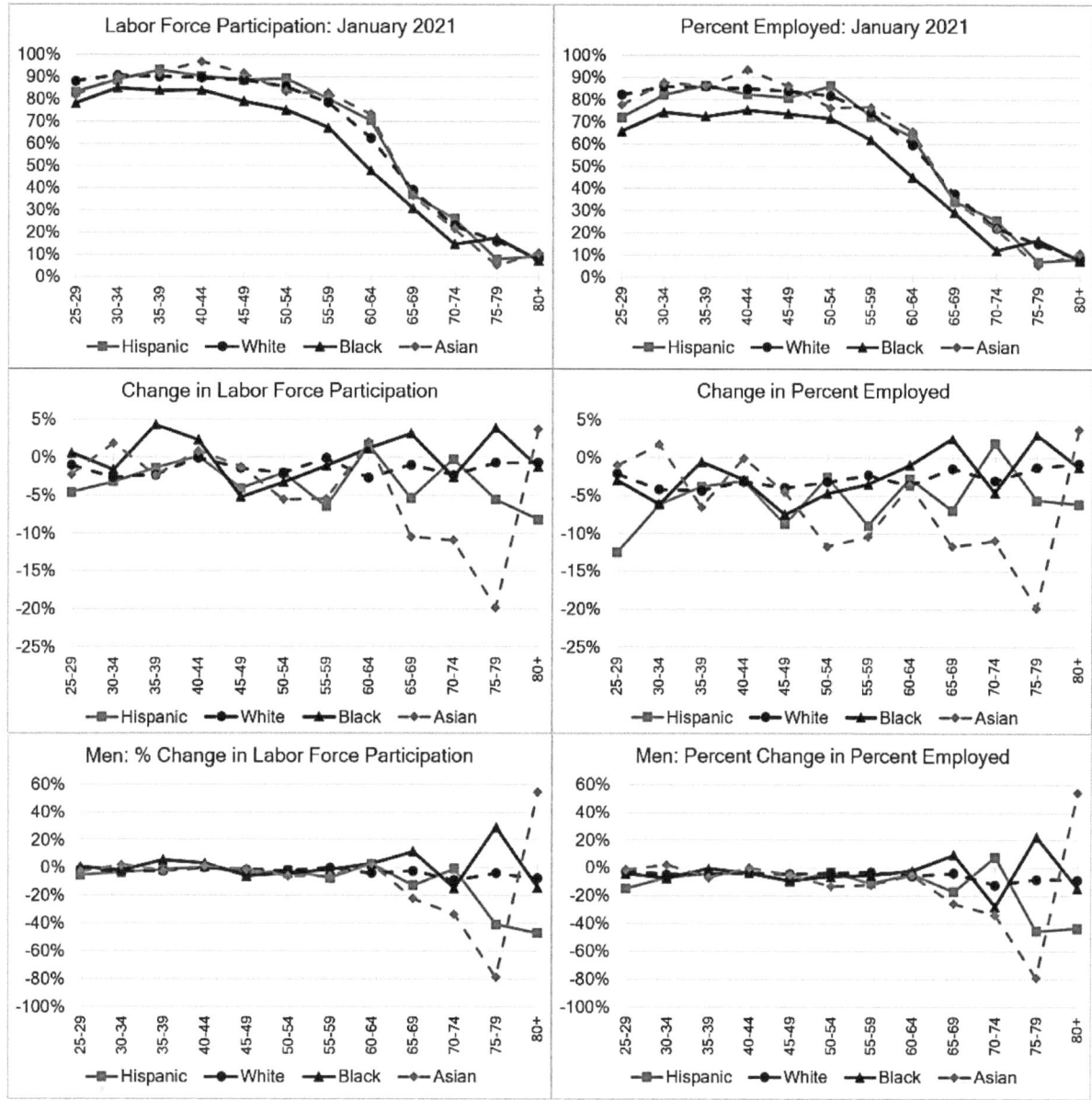

FIGURE 2-14 Labor force participation and employment status among men ages 25 and over by race-ethnicity and age, January 2020–January 2021.
NOTE: Figure 2-14 shows the percent of men who are employed (top right panel) and in the labor force (top left panel) in January 2021. The middle panels show the absolute change in the labor force participation rate (left panel) and employment rate (right panel) between January 2020 and January 2021. The bottom panels show the percent change in the labor force participation rate (left panel) and employment rate (right panel).
SOURCE: Data from 2020 and 2021 January Current Population Survey monthly data files calculated by U.S. Census Bureau online data table tool (Beta version).

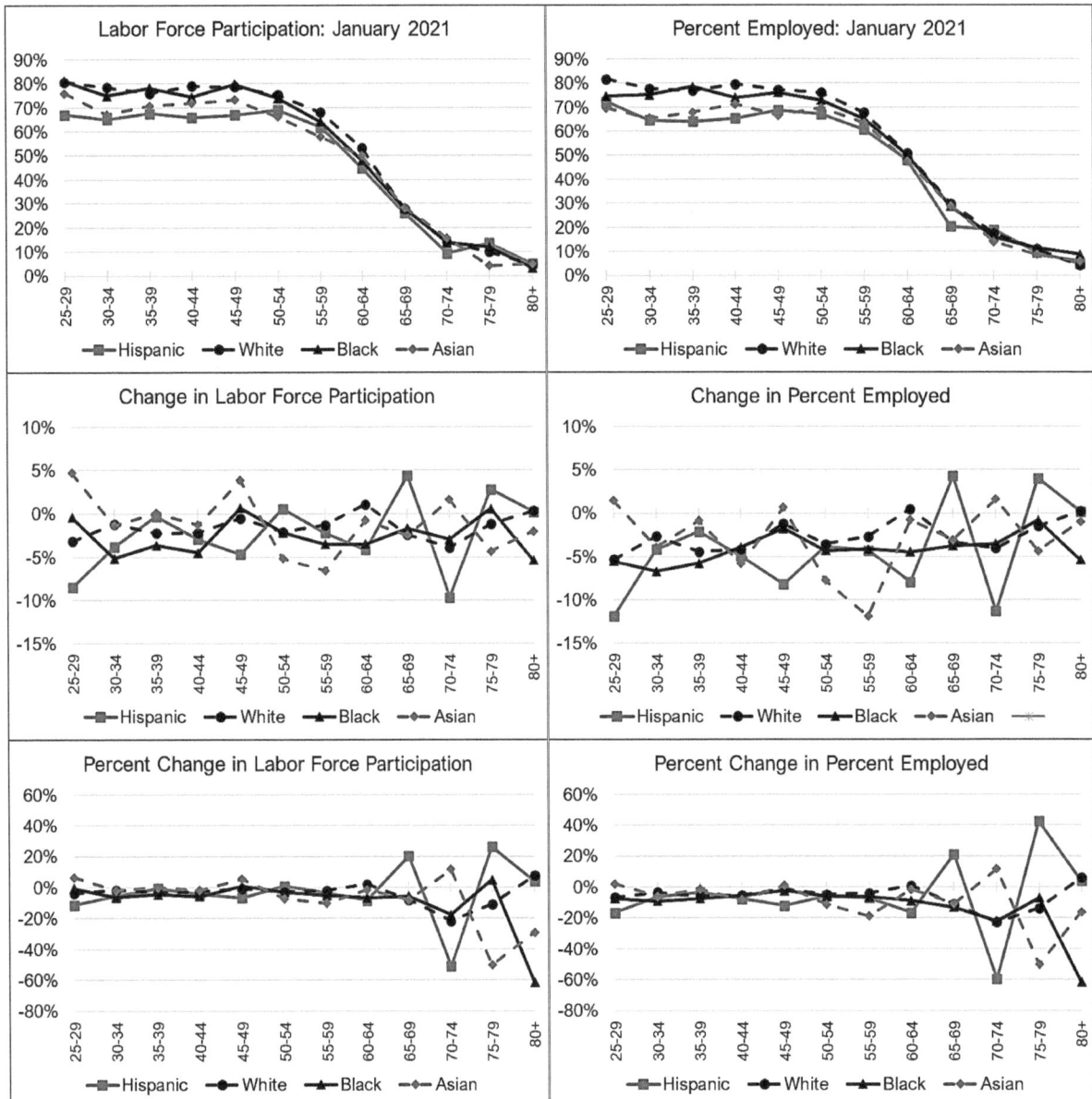

FIGURE 2-15 Labor force participation and employment status among women ages 25 and over by race-ethnicity and age, January 2020–January 2021.
NOTE: Figure 2-15 shows the percent of women who are employed (top right panel) and in the labor force (top left panel) in January 2021. The middle panels show the absolute change in the labor force participation rate (left panel) and employment rate (right panel) between January 2020 and January 2021. The bottom panels show the percent change in the labor force participation rate (left panel) and employment rate (right panel).
SOURCE: Data from 2020 and 2021 January Current Population Survey monthly data files calculated by U.S. Census Bureau online data table tool (Beta version).

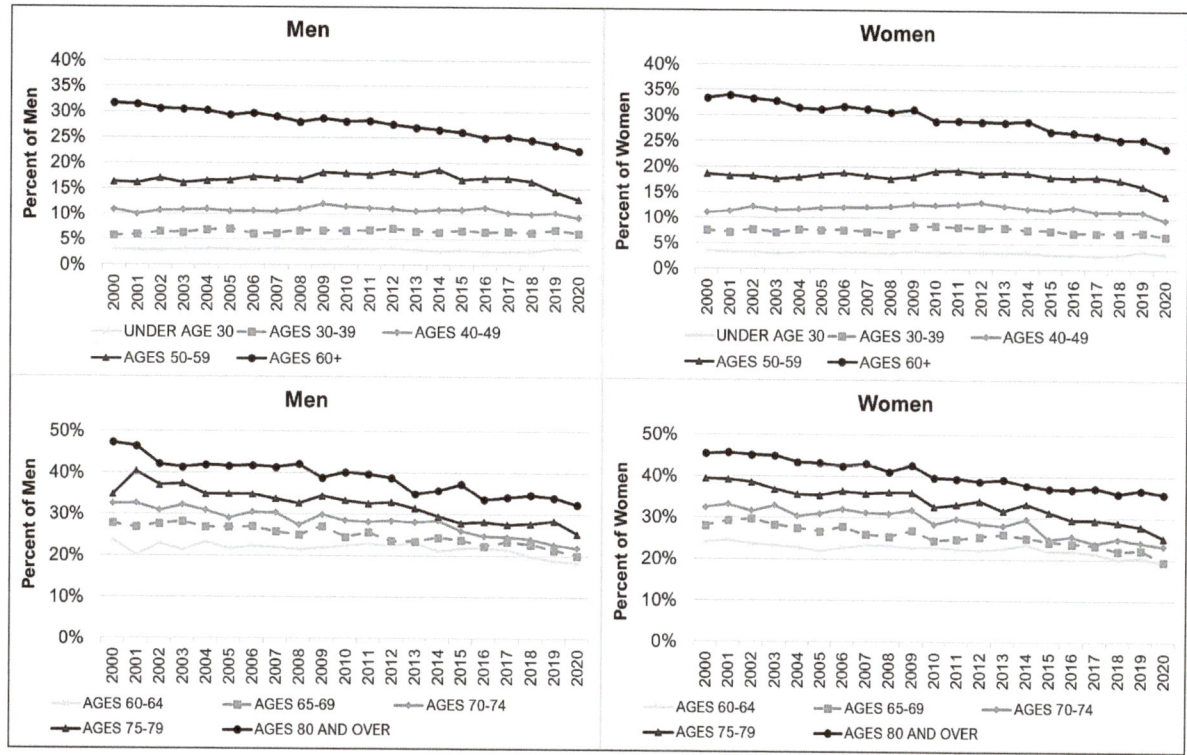

FIGURE 2-16 Percent of U.S. adults reporting their health as fair or poor, by gender and age, 2000–2020.
NOTE: Figure 2-16 shows the percentage of men (left panels) and women (right panels) who report their overall health as "fair" or "poor" (rather than "excellent," "very good," or "good").
SOURCE: Data from 2000–2020 March Current Population Survey monthly data files calculated by U.S. Census Bureau online data table tool (Beta version).

suggest that the gains in labor force participation among older adults that are due to improvements in health may be slowing. Moreover, the declining health among younger adults could presage future declines in labor force participation at older ages as these younger cohorts age and approach retirement.

As noted above, the United States has long experienced a large education-based gap in health and mortality that favors those with more education, particularly those with a college degree. The percentage of adults in fair or poor health decreases as levels of education increase, and the gap between those with the most and the least education widens with age (Figure 2-17, top panels). In 2019, among those ages 25 and over, adults with a four-year college degree were less likely to be in fair or poor health than those with less education, while those who did not complete a high school degree were the least healthy. This gap expanded with age, but more dramatically so after age 50. Among men with less than a high school degree, the percentage in fair or poor health was nearly twice as high among those ages 65–69 (at 42.2%) as it was among those ages 50–54 (at 22.1%). Among those with a bachelor's degree the percentage was only marginally higher (10.9% vs. 6.4%), though this also represented a large percentage increase. Among women, the decline in health among those with less than a high school degree began earlier, at ages 45–49, when 21.2 percent were fair or poor health, and increased by more to reach 46.0 percent among those ages 65–69. The percentage of women with a bachelor's degree who were in fair or poor health increased from 6.6 percent among those ages 45–49 to 12.9 percent among those ages 65–69.

This large education-based gap in overall health in 2019 represented an *improvement* from 2000 (Figure 2-17, bottom panels). Among both men and women who did not complete high school, the percentage in fair or

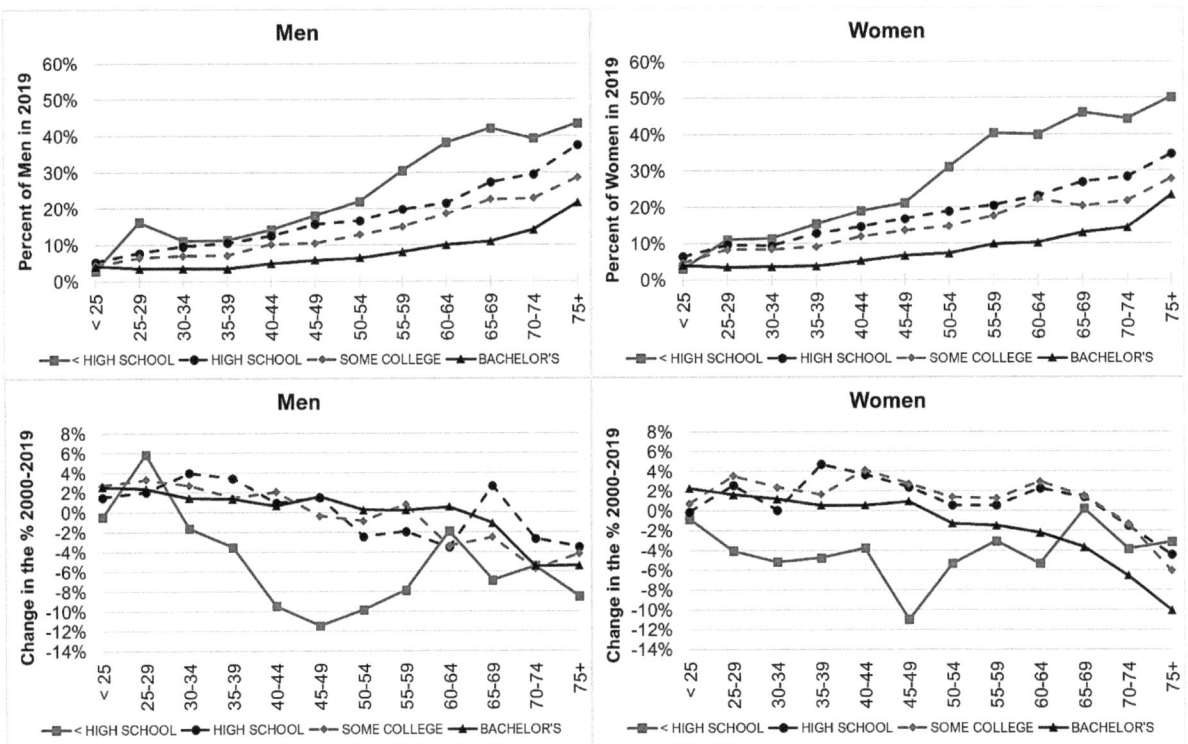

FIGURE 2-17 Percentage of U.S. adults reporting their health as fair or poor, 2019, and change in percentage, 2000 vs. 2019, by gender, age, and education.
NOTE: Figure 2-17 shows the percent of U.S. adults in 2019 whose overall health is "fair" or "poor" (rather than "excellent," "very good," or "good"; top panels) and the change in this percentage from 2000 (bottom panels). Men are shown in the left panels, women are shown in the right panels. The year 2019 is used instead of 2020 to eliminate the effect of the COVID-19 pandemic on health in the March 2020 Current Population Survey monthly data file.
SOURCE: Data from 2000–2019 March Current Population Survey monthly data files calculated by U.S. Census Bureau online data table tool (Beta version).

poor health declined substantially, particularly among those under age 60.[10] This was not the case for those who had a high school degree or more; among these more-educated adults, a higher percentage of those under age 50 were in fair or poor health in 2019 than in 2000. Though there was no clear relationship between the change in health and education among men, women who completed a bachelor's degree experienced larger improvements in health than did other women with a high school degree or more, increasing their advantage over the period.

Figure 2-18 restricts the population to those in the labor force. In general, though the overall percentage of workers in fair or poor health is lower than that of the general population, the trends across age groups and over time are largely similar. However, two key differences stand out. First, in 2019, among men ages 60–64 and women ages 55–64 who have a high school degree, the percent in fair or poor health is lower than among younger men and women, but rises again with age among those ages 65 and over. This suggests that many of these adults who are in fair or poor health are leaving the labor force early, perhaps when the men reach eligibility for partial Social Security benefits at age 62. The second difference is that the change in health

---

[10]This change could be the result of changes in the composition of those with less than a high school education. As high school attendance is compulsory within the United States, new immigrant populations are overrepresented within this less educated group.

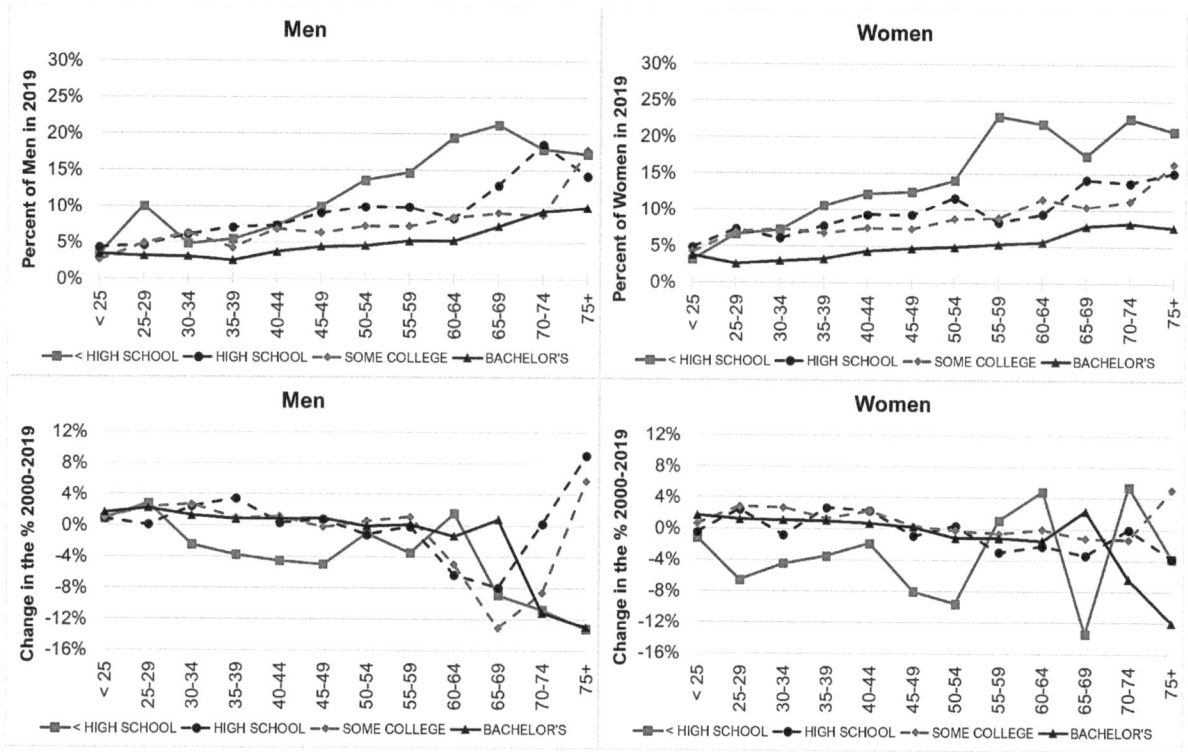

FIGURE 2-18 Percent of labor force reporting their health as fair or poor, by gender, age, and education, 2000 vs. 2019.
NOTES: Figure 2-18 shows the percent of U.S. adults in the labor force in 2019 who reported their overall health as "fair" or "poor" (rather than "excellent," "very good," or "good"; top panels) and the change in this percentage from 2000 (bottom panels).
SOURCE: Data from 2000–2019 March Current Population Survey monthly data files calculated by U.S. Census Bureau online data table tool (Beta version).

between 2000 and 2019 among women with a college degree is similar to that of other women with a high school degree or more.

These differences suggest that changes in health are made manifest, in part, through changes in labor force participation. The rising rates of younger workers in fair or poor health could portend lower labor force participation among these younger cohorts as they reach conventional retirement ages. However, these rising rates could also signal a growing need to expand workplace accommodations for health conditions if more individuals in fair or poor health remain the labor force.

Though the CPS is not designed to capture detailed health or disability information about the U.S. population or workforce, it contains several questions that the U.S. Census Bureau uses to generate a composite measure of whether respondents have a health limitation or disability that limits or restricts their ability to work, a more stringent criterion than an overall assessment of fair or poor health (see Figure 2-19). This measure may underestimate the size of the population with disabilities (Burkhauser et al., 2014) and is discussed in greater detail in the annex to this chapter. The results are substantively similar to those obtained using the broader overall health measure. They show that though labor force participation has been increasing among older adults, the percentage who have a work disability has declined over the past two decades, suggesting that the employed population has become increasingly selective of those in better health. They also demonstrate that the percentage of younger workers with a work-limiting disability increased over the period.

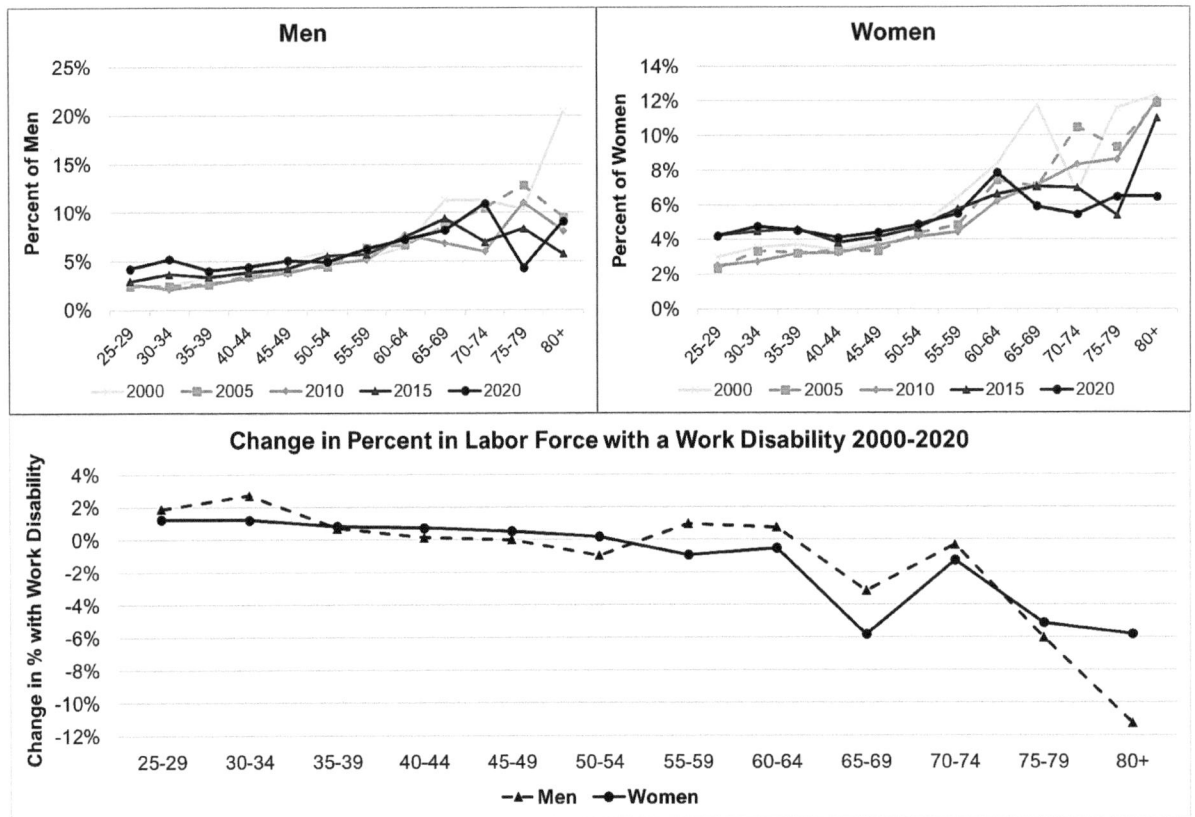

FIGURE 2-19 Presence (percent) of a work disability among labor force participants ages 25 and over, 2000–2020, and change in percent, 2000 vs. 2020.
NOTE: Figure 2-19 shows the percent of workers in the labor force who meet the Curret Population Survey criteria for having a work disability between 2000 and 2020 by gender and age group. These criteria are described in the annex at the end of this chapter.
SOURCE: Data from 2000–2020 March Current Population Survey Annual Social and Economic Supplement Data Files calculated by U.S. Census Bureau online data table tool (Beta version).

CONCLUSION

The U.S. workforce is aging, both because the population as a whole is aging and because more older adults are remaining in the labor force at older ages. Population projections suggest that the share of the U.S. population that is ages 65 and over will continue to grow, and current trends in labor force participation suggest the workforce will become increasingly diverse. The growing diversity of this labor force reflects changes in women's labor force participation as well as changes in the racial-ethnic composition and nativity of the U.S. population. At the same time, the older workforce has increasingly become selective based on education, with workers with a college degree disproportionately remaining in the labor force at older ages.

Older workers who remain in the labor force are more likely to be self-employed and working part-time, a likelihood that increases with age. Although those in their 50s are overrepresented within management occupations, as well as within blue-collar occupations such as production, maintenance, repair, and installation occupations, these occupations are less common among those who remain in the labor force in their 60s and older ages.

Though health has improved among older adults, declines in overall health and increases in work-limiting disabilities among younger workers are worrying and could presage comparative declines in labor force participation as these cohorts enter retirement ages or an increase in work-limiting disabilities that will require greater workplace accommodations.

This points to an important caveat regarding the use of current trends to predict the future. Chronological age is a measure of stages of life course development, but individuals experience age within the contexts of the birth cohorts and historical periods in which they live (Elder and George, 2015). Historical events (period-based changes) with broad societal impacts may change the context for current and future decision-making and outcomes. Moreover, the effects of these period-based changes may vary depending on an individual's life stage when the event happened. Thus, later life outcomes are shaped not only by an individual's chronological age but also by his or her birth cohort and the historical periods in which the person has lived.

For example, The Civil Rights Act of 1964, which banned discrimination based on race, color, sex, religion, and national origin, was passed when the youngest members of the Baby Boom cohort were just reaching adulthood. This meant that the Baby Boom cohort was the first cohort to begin their careers in a labor market in which racial-ethnic and sex-based discrimination were illegal. This dramatically expanded the education and employment opportunities available to women and racial-ethnic minorities born in this and later cohorts. In contrast, those born before 1946 generally entered adulthood with fewer opportunities available to them, and despite also benefiting from the passage of the Civil Rights Act, the effects of these early disadvantages are likely to have cumulated over the life course, affecting retirement outcomes many decades later.

The recent cohort-based increases in morbidity and mortality among younger adults may portend future declines in labor force participation among these cohorts as they age. If this is the case, the projected aging of the population may not lead to continued aging of the U.S. labor force in the future as these birth cohorts reach retirement age. Similarly, the period-based effects of the COVID-19 pandemic may vary across birth cohorts. The contemporary effect of the pandemic disproportionately affected labor force participation among older workers. It remains to be seen whether their participation rates will recover or remain depressed as the economy improves. Further, the long-term effects of COVID-19, or Long COVID, particularly among younger adults and children who experience lasting health effects remain unknown. They could further erode the health and well-being of these cohorts, affecting their economic outcomes and labor force participation as they age.

ANNEX

Distributions Within Occupation Groups by Gender 2004 vs. 2019

ANNEX TABLE 2-1 Age Distribution Within Occupation Group Among Men, 2004

MEN	2004									
	Ages 50+		Ages 50–59		Ages 60–69		Ages 70+		Under Age 40	
Occupation	Rank	Percent	Rank	Percent	Rank	Percent	Rank	Percent	Rank	Percent
Management Occupations	3	39.7	2	24.6	5	11.1	7	4.0	25	30.6
Business Operations	5	38.7	5	22.6	3	11.8	4	4.3	22	36.2
Financial Operations	6	35.5	8	20.9	6	10.4	5	4.3	19	40.5
Computer and Mathematical	23	19.0	21	14.0	23	4.3	24	0.6	6	55.0
Architecture and Engineering	8	33.1	7	21.1	10	9.1	16	2.9	20	38.4
Life, Physical, and Social Sciences	9	31.7	9	19.8	11	9.0	15	2.9	17	44.2
Community and Social Service	2	41.5	3	23.5	2	11.9	1	6.1	23	34.8
Legal	1	42.1	1	25.0	4	11.2	2	5.9	24	32.2
Education, Training, and Library	4	39.2	4	23.1	1	12.7	12	3.5	18	41.4
Arts, Entertainment, Sports, Media	16	27.1	15	16.5	19	7.0	11	3.6	10	50.9
Healthcare Practitioners and Technical	7	35.3	6	22.5	13	8.7	8	4.0	21	38.2
Healthcare Support	21	23.2	19	15.2	21	6.1	18	1.9	4	57.2
Protective Service	14	28.1	17	16.1	14	8.7	13	3.4	11	50.4
Food Preparation and Serving	24	10.1	24	6.1	24	2.9	22	1.1	1	78.3
Building/Grounds Maintenance	11	30.5	14	16.7	7	10.0	9	3.9	13	48.2
Personal Care and Service	18	25.7	23	11.7	9	9.1	3	4.8	3	58.4
Sales and Related	10	30.8	12	17.5	8	9.4	10	3.8	14	47.2
Office and Administrative Support	17	26.3	18	16.0	17	7.6	17	2.7	7	54.3
Farming, Fishing, and Forestry	19	25.5	22	12.8	15	8.5	6	4.2	5	55.4
Construction	22	22.5	20	15.0	22	5.9	20	1.7	8	52.8
Extraction	20	23.6	16	16.5	20	6.3	23	0.7	9	51.8
Installation, Maintenance, and Repair	15	27.9	11	18.7	18	7.6	21	1.5	15	44.9
Production	12	29.0	10	18.8	16	8.5	19	1.7	16	44.2
Transportation and Material Moving	13	28.9	13	17.0	12	8.9	14	3.0	12	48.3
Military	25	5.3	25	4.6	25	0.6	25	0.1	2	76.7

NOTES: Annex Table 2-1 shows the percent of male workers whose age falls within each age group in 2004 by occupation group and the rank of the occupation based on the percent of workers in that age group. The 2004 data is classified using the 2000 Census version of the Standard Occupation Classification. Differences in classification versions may affect comparisons over time. Each percentage is ranked from highest percentage to lowest percentage. Occupations are listed sorted based on their ranking among all workers ages 50 and over. Percentages for ages 50–59, 60–69, and 70 and over may not sum to Ages 50+ due to rounding. Table excludes percentage of employees who are ages 40–49.
SOURCE: Data from 2004 American Community Survey Public-Use Microdata file calculated by U.S. Census Bureau online data table tool (Beta version).

ANNEX TABLE 2-2 Age Distribution Within Occupation Group Among Men, 2019

MEN	2019									
	Ages 50+		Ages 50–59		Ages 60–69		Ages 70+		Under Age 40	
Occupation	Rank	Percent	Rank	Percent	Rank	Percent	Rank	Percent	Rank	Percent
Management Occupations	2	46.7	1	24.0	3	16.9	8	5.8	25	30.1
Business Operations	6	39.2	6	19.1	9	14.7	11	5.4	21	41.2
Financial Operations	5	40.7	11	17.3	6	15.8	3	7.6	19	41.8
Computer and Mathematical	21	27.7	15	16.5	23	9.5	22	1.8	8	50.0
Architecture and Engineering	4	41.2	4	19.9	4	16.4	12	4.9	22	39.9
Life, Physical, and Social Sciences	11	37.5	19	15.4	5	15.9	7	6.2	14	45.3
Community and Social Service	3	45.5	12	17.3	2	17.7	2	10.5	23	35.9
Legal	1	50.1	9	18.2	1	19.7	1	12.1	24	31.6
Education, Training, and Library	10	38.0	16	15.6	8	14.9	4	7.5	17	43.2
Arts, Entertainment, Sports, Media	15	33.2	20	15.1	15	12.5	10	5.6	9	49.3
Healthcare Practitioners and Technical	7	38.7	13	17.3	7	15.0	5	6.5	20	41.5
Healthcare Support	20	28.8	21	14.9	20	10.7	19	3.2	4	55.5
Protective Service	16	33.0	10	17.8	19	10.9	16	4.3	12	46.7
Food Preparation and Serving	24	14.0	24	8.4	24	4.5	24	1.1	2	74.2
Building/Grounds Maintenance	9	38.2	7	19.0	10	14.6	14	4.6	15	44.1
Personal Care and Service	22	26.8	23	10.9	22	9.6	6	6.3	3	60.6
Sales and Related	14	35.8	14	16.7	13	13.5	9	5.7	10	47.6
Office and Administrative Support	19	31.4	17	15.5	16	12.0	17	3.9	6	52.8
Farming, Fishing, and Forestry	18	32.1	18	15.4	17	12.0	13	4.7	7	51.0
Construction	17	33.0	5	19.3	18	11.3	21	2.4	13	45.3
Extraction	23	25.2	22	13.9	21	9.6	23	1.7	5	55.1
Installation, Maintenance, and Repair	8	38.2	2	20.6	11	14.2	18	3.4	18	42.7
Production	12	37.2	3	20.2	12	13.9	20	3.0	16	43.9
Transportation and Material Moving	13	36.1	8	18.3	14	13.3	15	4.5	11	46.8
Military	25	5.3	25	4.1	25	0.7	25	0.5	1	82.3

NOTES: Annex Table 2-1 shows the percent of male workers whose age falls within each age group in 2019 by occupation group and the rank of the occupation based on the percent of workers in that age group. Occupation groups are based on two-digit codes assigned using the 2018 version of the Standard Occupational Classification. Differences in classification versions may affect comparisons over time. Each percentage is ranked from highest percentage to lowest percentage. Occupations are listed sorted based on their ranking among all workers ages 50 and over. Percentages for ages 50–59, 60–69, and 70 and over may not sum to Ages 50+ due to rounding. Table excludes percentage of employees who are ages 40–49.
SOURCE: Data from 2019 American Community Survey Public-Use Microdata file calculated by U.S. Census Bureau online data table tool (Beta version).

ANNEX TABLE 2-3 Age Distribution Within Occupation Group Among Women, 2004

WOMEN	2004									
	Ages 50+		Ages 50–59		Ages 60–69		Ages 70+		Under Age 40	
Occupation	Rank	Percent	Rank	Percent	Rank	Percent	Rank	Percent	Rank	Percent
Management Occupations	2	33.3	2	23.2	7	8.1	9	2.1	25	37.0
Business Operations	11	27.8	7	20.2	16	6.3	20	1.2	16	44.9
Financial Operations	12	26.7	11	18.0	13	6.9	16	1.8	18	44.6
Computer and Mathematical	19	21.2	13	17.6	23	3.3	23	0.4	13	48.0
Architecture and Engineering	22	19.3	22	13.8	21	4.6	22	0.8	6	53.1
Life, Physical, and Social Sciences	14	25.4	14	17.3	17	6.3	15	1.8	11	51.1
Community and Social Service	5	32.2	3	22.2	6	8.1	12	1.9	20	43.5
Legal	16	24.8	10	18.3	20	5.2	19	1.3	12	48.3
Education, Training, and Library	1	34.2	1	23.4	4	8.7	8	2.1	22	41.1
Arts, Entertainment, Sports, Media	10	28.0	15	16.9	8	8.0	3	3.1	14	47.9
Healthcare Practitioners and Technical	7	29.4	6	20.3	11	7.4	17	1.7	21	42.0
Healthcare Support	15	25.0	16	15.9	12	7.1	11	2.0	8	52.6
Protective Service	20	21.2	21	13.9	19	5.4	14	1.8	5	55.6
Food Preparation and Serving	23	17.8	24	9.9	18	5.8	10	2.0	2	65.7
Building/Grounds Maintenance	4	32.3	9	19.0	1	9.8	1	3.5	23	41.0
Personal Care and Service	13	26.2	17	15.6	10	7.5	2	3.1	9	52.5
Sales and Related	17	24.7	20	14.0	9	7.7	4	3.0	4	56.1
Office and Administrative Support	6	31.7	8	19.5	3	9.4	5	2.9	17	44.6
Farming, Fishing, and Forestry	18	22.7	23	13.3	14	6.8	6	2.7	7	52.7
Construction	21	20.4	18	14.9	22	4.0	18	1.5	10	51.2
Extraction	24	16.9	19	14.2	24	2.8	24	0.0	3	60.0
Installation, Maintenance, and Repair	8	28.7	4	20.9	15	6.7	21	1.1	19	43.5
Production	3	32.8	5	20.6	2	9.7	7	2.5	24	39.8
Transportation and Material Moving	9	28.0	12	17.7	5	8.5	13	1.9	15	46.0
Military	25	4.6	25	3.5	25	1.1	24	0.0	1	81.0

NOTES: Annex Table 2-1 shows the percent of female workers whose age falls within each age group in 2004 by occupation group and the rank of the occupation based on the percent of workers in that age group. The 2004 data is classified using the 2000 Census version of the Standard Occupation Classification. Differences in classification versions may affect comparisons over time. Each percentage is ranked from highest percentage to lowest percentage. Occupations are listed sorted based on their ranking among all workers ages 50 and over. Percentages for ages 50–59, 60–69, and 70 and over may not sum to Ages 50+ due to rounding. Table excludes percentage of employees who are ages 40–49.
SOURCE: Data from 2004 American Community Survey Public-Use Microdata file calculated by U.S. Census Bureau online data table tool (Beta version).

ANNEX TABLE 2-4 Age Distribution Within Occupation Group Among Women, 2019

WOMEN	2019									
	Ages 50+		Ages 50–59		Ages 60–69		Ages 70+		Under Age 40	
Occupation	Rank	Percent	Rank	Percent	Rank	Percent	Rank	Percent	Rank	Percent
Management Occupations	6	40.2	4	22.7	8	13.9	11	3.6	23	36.2
Business Operations	12	34.8	9	19.5	12	12.7	18	2.6	16	44.2
Financial Operations	3	41.8	2	23.0	2	15.0	10	3.8	25	35.5
Computer and Mathematical	15	32.2	10	19.4	17	11.1	24	1.7	13	47.1
Architecture and Engineering	23	28.0	19	16.0	20	10.2	23	1.8	5	53.8
Life, Physical, and Social Sciences	22	28.3	23	14.0	18	10.8	13	3.5	7	53.1
Community and Social Service	9	35.9	16	17.2	9	13.8	3	4.8	18	43.3
Legal	7	38.7	7	20.2	7	14.3	6	4.3	22	39.3
Education, Training, and Library	8	37.4	13	18.1	6	14.6	4	4.7	19	41.6
Arts, Entertainment, Sports, Media	16	32.1	21	14.7	13	12.3	2	5.0	8	51.3
Healthcare Practitioners and Technical	10	35.7	14	17.9	5	14.6	16	3.3	17	43.8
Healthcare Support	13	34.4	15	17.8	11	12.8	9	3.8	12	47.5
Protective Service	20	29.5	18	16.7	23	9.5	15	3.3	6	53.6
Food Preparation and Serving	24	21.0	24	11.3	24	7.4	21	2.3	2	67.1
Building/Grounds Maintenance	2	42.0	3	22.9	3	14.9	8	4.2	24	35.6
Personal Care and Service	21	28.5	22	14.4	21	9.9	7	4.2	3	55.9
Sales and Related	17	31.4	20	15.1	16	11.7	5	4.6	4	53.9
Office and Administrative Support	1	42.9	6	20.5	1	16.9	1	5.5	20	40.1
Farming, Fishing, and Forestry	19	30.0	17	17.0	19	10.2	17	2.8	10	49.2
Construction	18	30.7	11	19.2	22	9.6	22	1.9	9	49.8
Extraction	5	40.3	1	25.8	15	12.1	20	2.3	15	45.8
Installation, Maintenance, and Repair	14	34.2	12	18.8	10	12.9	19	2.5	11	47.7
Production	4	40.5	5	22.3	4	14.7	12	3.5	21	39.9
Transportation and Material Moving	11	35.4	8	19.9	14	12.2	14	3.3	14	46.2
Military	25	5.1	25	4.3	25	0.7	25	0.0	1	85.9

NOTES: Annex Table 2-1 shows the percent of female workers whose age falls within each age group in 2019 by occupation group and the rank of the occupation based on the percent of workers in that age group. Occupation groups are based on two-digit codes assigned using the 2018 version of the Standard Occupational Classification. Differences in classification versions may affect comparisons over time. Each percentage is ranked from highest percentage to lowest percentage. Occupations are listed sorted based on their ranking among all workers ages 50 and over. Percentages for ages 50–59, 60–69, and 70 and over may not sum to Ages 50+ due to rounding. Table excludes percentage of employees who are ages 40–49.
SOURCE: Data from 2019 American Community Survey Public-Use Microdata file calculated by U.S. Census Bureau online data table tool (Beta version).

Data Sources

Except where noted, the data used in the analyses presented in this chapter are drawn from the 1965–2020 March CPS Annual Social and Economic Supplement Data Files. Results for 2019–2020 were generated from raw data files downloaded from the U.S. Census Bureau.[11] Results for 1988–2018 were generated from raw data files distributed by the National Bureau of Economic Research. Harmonized data on labor force participation for 1965–1987 were generated and distributed by the iPUMS project at the University of Minnesota.

Comparisons by race-ethnicity and educational attainment begin in 2004, because prior to 2003 respondents to the CPS could not report a multiracial background, which made the creation of similar race measures over time impossible.

Results from the 2004–2018 data were reproduced and verified using the U.S. Census Bureau's Current Population Survey Table Creator, while results from the 2019–2020 data were reproduced using the beta version of the U.S. Census Bureau's updated Table Creator, a publicly accessible online tool that allows users to produce weighted output tables based on Census Bureau data files. This tool was also used to generate the distributions of age within occupation and occupations within age in the 2019 American Community Survey, which are displayed in Tables 4-1 and 4-2.

Calculating Labor Force Participation Rate by Birth Cohort

The average labor force participation rate was generated using a similar method to that used in Goldin and Mitchell (2017) to calculate the labor force participation rate by birth cohort among women only. Though their results applied only to women and were displayed in figures that do not depict the exact values, their figure closely matches the one corresponding figure for women presented in this chapter.

To calculate the average labor force participation rate within each 5 × 5 (five-year age group by five-year birth cohort) combination, the single-year age-specific weighted population estimate for the number of adults in the labor force was divided by the adult civilian population for each year (wave) of the CPS. Each single-year age within each survey wave was allocated to a birth cohort using the method described below under *Identification of birth cohort*. Then, the 25 labor force participation rates for each five-year age group and five-year birth cohort group were averaged together with equal weight. All figures include averages only when all birth cohorts had reached the oldest age in the age range. For example, because the youngest member of the 1965–1969 birth cohort was age 50 in the 2020 March CPS data, the last labor force participation rate shown for this birth cohort is for ages 45–49.

Identification of Birth Cohort

The public use data files for the CPS include reported age in years but do not include information on date of birth. Birth cohort was determined by subtracting the reported age from the year in which the survey was conducted. However, because the reference week for the March CPS is the week in which the 12th day of the month falls, most individuals would not have had their birthday by the reference week. For this reason, the labor force participation rate for each single-year age was apportioned 20 percent to the current survey year birth cohort and 80 percent to the previous survey year birth cohort.

Definition of CPS Work Disability Indicator

The CPS measure used to indicate the presence of a work disability is constructed by the U.S. Census Bureau. It is based on responses to a series of questions about health limitations, disability, and enrollment in government

---

[11] See https://www.census.gov/data/datasets/time-series/demo/cps/cps-basic.html

programs associated with having a disability that affects an individual's ability to work. An individual is considered to have a work disability if she/he/they meets any of the following seven criteria:

1. The individual has a health problem or disability that prevents them from working or which limits the kind or amount of work they can do;
2. The individual ever retired or left a job for health reasons;
3. The individual is not in the labor force because of a disability;
4. The individual did not work at all in the previous year because of illness or disability;
5. The individual is under age 65 and is enrolled in Medicare;
6. The individual is under age 65 and received Supplemental Security Income in the previous year;
7. The individual received Veterans Administration disability income in the previous year.

It is important to note that the survey questions on which this indicator was based were not designed to measure disability, and therefore this indicator is not a comprehensive measure of the overall health of an individual or the impact of health conditions on work.

The measures included in the indicator capture different types of health limitations and disabilities. Though some of these criteria preclude an individual from remaining in the labor force, not all of them do, and many of those who report a work disability remain in the labor force. In addition, some of the criteria used to determine the presence of a work disability are age-based in ways that can affect the age-distribution of the presence of a work disability. For example, criterion five, enrollment in Medicare, is conditional on being under age 65 because only those who have a disability that affects their ability to work are eligible to enroll in Medicare before age 65. However, once such an individual turns age 65, she or he would be eligible for Medicare regardless of health status; therefore, this individual may no longer be counted as having a work disability unless she or he also met one of the other criteria, because enrollment in Medicare at ages 65 and over is no longer linked to health status. This leads to a discontinuity in the age distribution at age 65 in the work disability measure when applied to the adult population; however, because eligibility requirements for enrolling in Medicare disability coverage generally require exiting the labor force, this discontinuity is less evident when the population is restricted to those in the labor force as it is within this chapter.

3

Work and Retirement Pathways

In this chapter, we offer a conceptual framework to depict and understand the patterned work and retirement pathways of older adults. A key feature of this conceptual framework is its emphasis on the existence of multiple pathways for older adults to continue working, as well as to transition between working and nonwork states. This feature is aligned with the continuous trend for workers to move away from the traditional linear career progression over the past 30 years (e.g., see Figure 2-7 in this report for the increasing trend of self-employment from 2004 to 2019; also see Calvo et al., 2018; McDonough et al., 2017; Wang et al., 2013; Johnson et al., 2010). As such, instead of viewing full-time retirement as a one-time event and an inevitable end of one's workforce participation, we acknowledge that at least some individuals can remain active in various forms of workforce participation in later adult life and that such workforce participation can be flexible in nature until the very end of one's life (e.g., Moen, 2016a; Zhan et al., 2015; Wang et al., 2008).

On the basis of this conceptual framework, we then review the main theories that have been used to explain work and retirement pathways for older adults. Further, we consider the proximal forces that shape older adults' work and retirement pathways, which include the preferences, expectations, and experienced constraints regarding their workforce participation. We review research findings regarding these forces, especially on the effects of their various empirical referents and variables. Toward the end of this chapter, we review findings regarding disparities and heterogeneity in work and retirement pathways. Finally, we discuss challenges faced by this research area and make recommendations for future research.

A CONCEPTUAL FRAMEWORK OF WORK AND RETIREMENT PATHWAYS

In retirement research, *retirement pathways* typically refers to courses of action that people follow to exit the workforce (Szinovacz, 2003; Flippen and Tienda, 2000). Traditionally, and especially before mandatory retirement was abolished in the United States, the course of action was viewed as quite simple, containing a single transition from full-time employment to full-time retirement (Beehr, 1986). However, with changes in policies, work, and workforce, the courses of action for exiting the workforce have evolved to contain multiple possibilities.

Accordingly, retirement has been defined in various ways in the literature (Denton and Spencer, 2009), including:

- as nonparticipation in the labor force;
- as reduction in hours worked and/or earnings;

- as hours worked or earnings below some minimum cutoff;
- as the receipt of retirement/pension income;
- as the exit from one's main employer;
- as a change of career or employment later in life;
- based on a self-assessment of retirement; and
- as some combination of the previous seven definitions.

As a result of these multiple possibilities, the current literature generally agrees that retirement does not have to be a one-time permanent exit from the workforce but may be a process that occurs over a period of time, one that may involve moving in and out of work activities multiple times (Zhan and Wang, 2015a; Wang and Shi, 2014; Shultz and Wang, 2011; Cahill et al., 2006).

Indeed, many retirees now stay in the labor force and maintain certain levels of work engagement after starting to receive Social Security benefits and (or) retirement pension. Based on the data from the Health and Retirement Study (HRS), a large nationally representative longitudinal survey of Americans who were at least 51 years old (Fisher and Ryan, 2018), approximately 50–64 percent of retirees from full-time career jobs experienced employment in "bridge" jobs—jobs taken after leaving a full-time career job lasting 10 years or longer (Ruhm, 1990)—before they completely exit the workforce (Cahill et al., 2018, 2006; Pleau, 2010; Giandrea et al., 2009). A more recent investigation using HRS data (Quinn et al., 2019) showed that for Americans who were in the age range of 51–61 in 1992 (i.e., those born in 1931–1941) with full-time career jobs, three percent of men and one percent of women were still not retired in 2016, when they were ages 75–85, and 10 percent of men and 11 percent of women were still working in bridge jobs or had re-entered the workforce as of 2016. For adults in this 1931–1941 cohort who had fully exited the workforce by 2016, 53 percent of men and 53 percent of women took on bridge jobs or re-entered workforce after retiring from their career jobs. These labor force status patterns by year are plotted in Figure 3-1 (for private-sector men) and Figure 3-2 (for private-sector women), based on the data from Quinn and colleagues (2019).

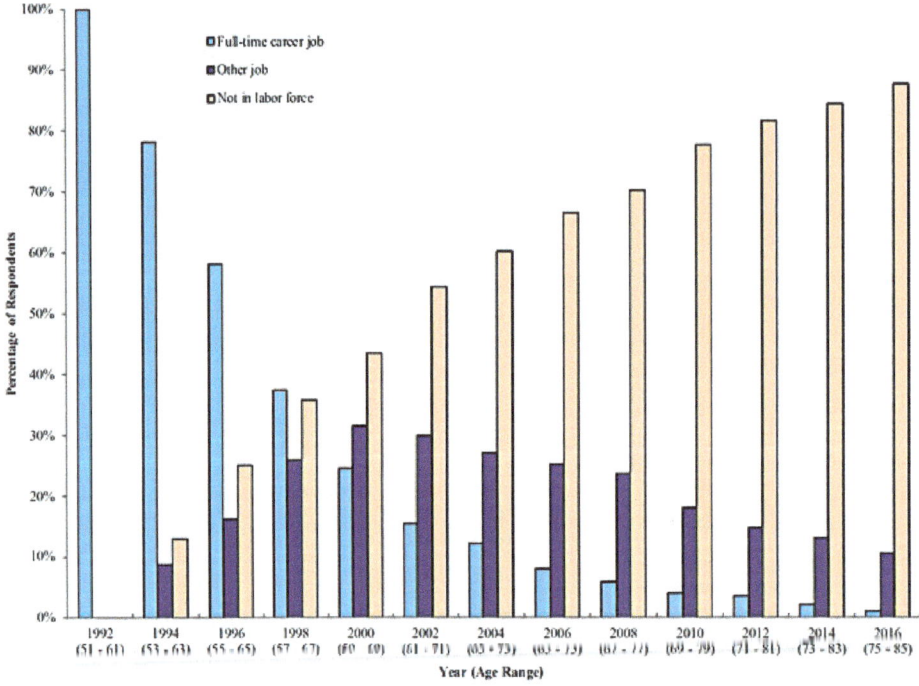

FIGURE 3-1 Labor force status among men in the private sector, by year, 1992–2016.
NOTE: Figure 3-1 depicts the percentage of respondents to wave 1 of the Health and Retirement Study with full-time career jobs.
SOURCE: Data from Quinn and colleagues (2019).

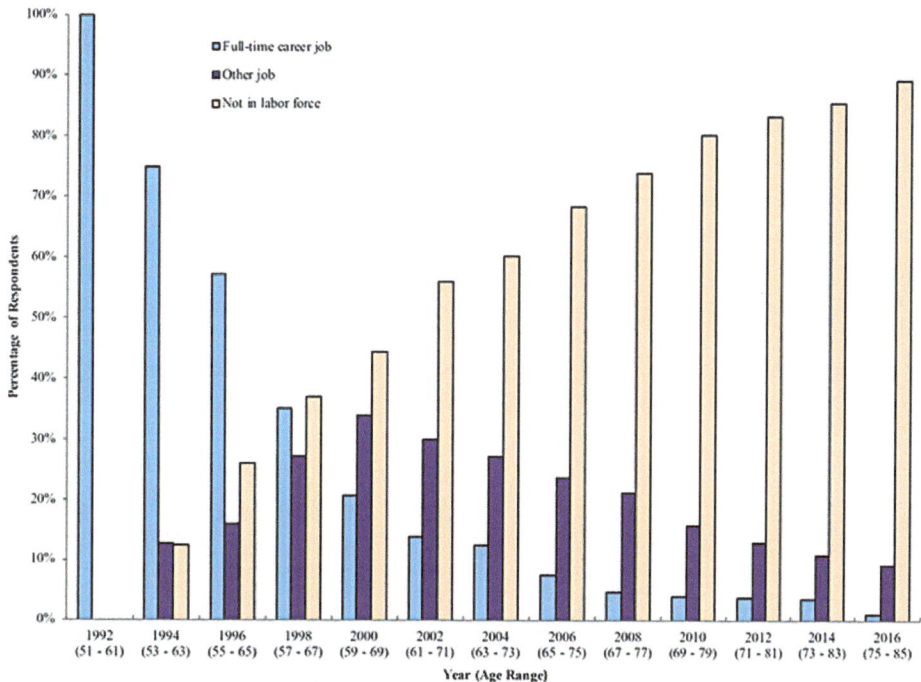

FIGURE 3-2 Labor force status among women in the private sector, by year, 1992–2016.
NOTE: Figure 3-2 depicts the percentage of respondents to wave 1 of the Health and Retirement Study with full-time career jobs.
SOURCE: Data from Quinn and colleagues (2019).

Research has also shown that the conventional, irreversible exit from full-time work to full-time retirement at around age 65 was not common among those born between 1931 and 1941, with only 18.43 percent following such a sequence (Cahill et al., 2016, 2015). The most common pathway for this older cohort is an early, but not necessarily permanent, exit, with over a third (36.6%) leaving the workforce by or before age 62 (Calvo et al., 2018). Others (15.5%) experience a partially retired sequence, scaling back to part-time hours before exiting completely, typically by age 66. Finally, about 11.67 percent follow a "late" path; these are workers invested in their "career" jobs as well as those who move to other full-time employment, continuing to work full-time into their late 60s and 70s.

Among older cohorts that presage the Baby Boom generation's entrance into retirement, unconventional retirement sequences are more commonly followed by women than men, by middle-educated individuals than lower- and higher-educated individuals, and by White and Black Americans than Hispanic Americans. The experiences of those now in the conventional retirement years (the large Baby Boom cohort—the 76 million men and women born between 1946 and 1964) also vary widely. A study of short-term (over 16 months) pathways of the Baby Boom cohort shows the wide variation in retirement timing (Moen et al., 2021). By age 62, when eligible for partial Social Security benefits, 35.9 percent of this cohort was retired; this share rises to 56.6 percent at age 65, the eligibility age for Medicare and full Social Security benefits, and increases to 80.8 percent for those age 72.

Given the blurring of the boundaries between work and retirement, we use the term "work and retirement pathways" to be more accurate in describing the work-related courses of actions in later adult life. Our conceptual framework is presented in Figure 3-3. At the far right side of the figure, the "time/aging" arrow provides a rough sense of life development and event sequencing for older adults. As the figure shows, at any given moment in later adult life, people can be in either a paid work state or an unpaid/nonwork state. Following Zhan and Wang (2015a), the work state can be described by considering features of paid work, such as the time commitment to work (full-time vs. part-time; Zhan et al., 2015), working field (same working field as the career job vs. a different

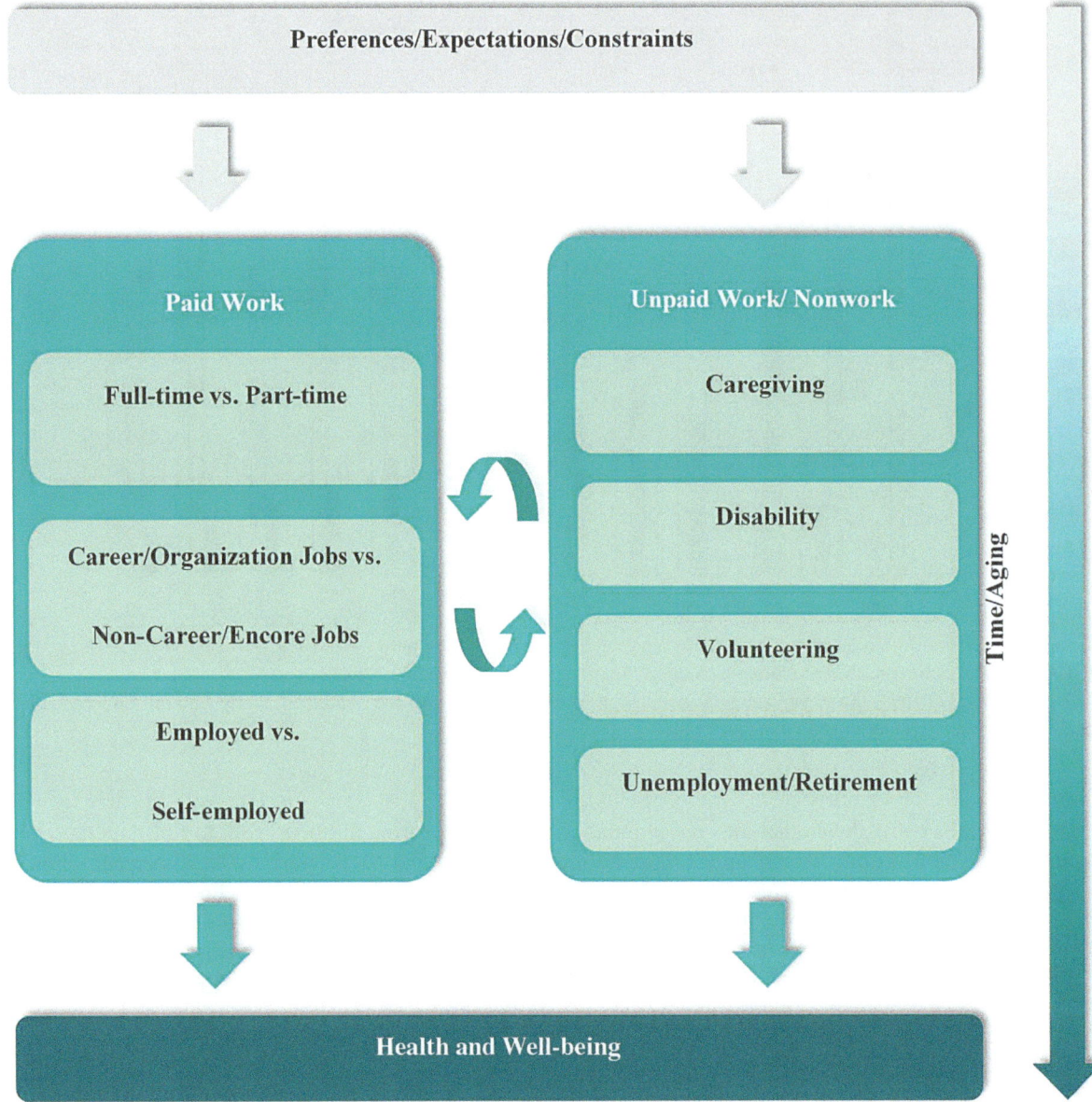

FIGURE 3-3 A conceptual framework of work and retirement pathways.

working field; Wang et al., 2008), organization (same organization as the long-term employment vs. a different organization; Zhan et al., 2013), and employment relationship (employed vs. self-employed; von Bonsdorff et al., 2017). The unpaid work/nonwork state can be described by considering the nature of the activities, such as caregiving (Keating et al., 2019), disability (Warner et al., 2010), volunteering (Matz-Costa et al., 2015, 2014), or full retirement (Wang and Shultz, 2010).

The reciprocal arrows between the paid work state and unpaid work/nonwork state illustrate that older adults can transition from one state to the other over time. As we will discuss in more detail later in this chapter, we consider older workers' preferences, expectations, and experienced constraints to be proximal forces that shape their workforce participation in later life.

Following our conceptual framework, an older adult's work and retirement pathway can be measured as their work/nonwork states sequenced over time. As such, this conceptual framework captures two important realities. First, in terms of tracing a person's workforce participation, it captures that an older adult can transition in and out of work over time. This matches the empirical findings from the first five waves of the HRS, which showed three workforce participation patterns after retirement from career jobs (Wang and Chan, 2011). The three patterns include two "stayer" classes, one containing retirees who were employed at each point in time after retirement and one containing retirees who were never employed at any point after retirement; and one "mover" class, which includes employees who transition between employment and retirement, back and forth. Other studies also found wide variability in the timing of "unretirement," that is, moving back into the workforce following an exit from one's career job (Moen et al., 2021; Calvo et al., 2018; McDonough et al., 2017; Cahill et al., 2016, 2015).

The second reality captured by the framework concerns individual differences in workforce participation over time: work and retirement pathways differ among older adults. Thus, this framework offers a way to conceptualize the heterogeneity in work and retirement pathways among older adults. This again matches the findings from Wang and Chan (2011) and others (Moen et al., 2021; Calvo et al., 2018; McDonough et al., 2017), which show that the years of education were a key predictor of retirees' workforce participation patterns. Specifically, retirees who had more years of education are less likely to be either "stayers who were never employed" or "stayers who were always employed" than to be "movers."

THEORETICAL MECHANISMS

In this section, we review the main theoretical approaches that have been used to explain work and retirement pathways for older adults. They are listed in Table 3-1.

Rational Choice Theory

Rational choice theory explains how older workers' financial resources and the external economic environment are related to their retirement decisions (Laitner and Sonnega, 2013). It considers the retirement decision to be the result of utility maximization. In particular, financial resources (both current and expected future) affect retirement decisions through their relationship to (current and expected future) consumption, and this relationship is affected by work decisions and saving and consumption decisions. Workers will retire when the utility they obtain from not working is higher than from continuing to work, which is more likely to occur when they place greater value on leisure time (nonwork) and when they have accumulated sufficient financial resources to finance their preferred consumption level in retirement. This depends on many things, including their actual and predicted health, expected returns on their assets, and more. They are more likely to continue to work when the utility of leisure time is lower, and when working longer will enable them to generate sufficiently higher utility from consumption after retirement to compensate for foregoing leisure (retirement) earlier.

TABLE 3-1 Theoretical Approaches

Theoretical Approaches	Key References
Rational choice theory	Lazear, 1986; Hanoch and Honig, 1983; Blinder and Weiss, 1976
Theory of planned behavior	Ajzen, 1991
Role theory	Barnes-Farrell, 2003; Ashforth, 2001
The life course perspective	Elder and Johnson, 2003; Elder, 1995
Meaningful life	King and Hicks, 2021
Socioemotional selectivity theory	Carstensen et al., 1999; Carstensen, 1991

Thus, when applying rational choice theory to consider retirement and workforce participation options, the concept of *subjective expected utility* is very useful. It guides researchers to consider older workers' subjective preferences and expectations regarding their workforce participation options. Accordingly, utility-maximizing models of labor supply, human capital investment, consumption, and retirement are useful in predicting and explaining people's workforce exit pathways (Lazear, 1986; Hanoch and Honig, 1983; Blinder and Weiss, 1976).

Theory of Planned Behavior

The theory of planned behavior (Ajzen, 1991; depicted in Figure 3-4) explains workers' workforce exit decisions by considering their attitudes toward their jobs, employers, careers, and retirement, as well as the norms in their workplace (e.g., Zhan et al., 2013; Shultz, 2003; Adams and Beehr, 1998) and perceived ability to control the behavior (that is, to make the choice consequential). This expectancy-value theory highlights the importance of workers' attitudes toward retirement, that is, whether they evaluate it favorably or unfavorably, and toward its alternative (continuing to work) in influencing their workforce exit decisions. It also emphasizes the role of perceived social influence, that is, the subjective norm—the belief about whether most people approve or disapprove of the behavior—regarding retiring in affecting an individual's workforce exit decision. Finally, perceived behavior control, that is, a person's perception of the ease or difficulty of performing the behavior of interest, is closely linked to constraints experienced by older workers when making workforce exit decisions. Together, these three dimensions—expected value, subjective norms, and perceived control about work and retirement—powerfully predict an individual's intentions, which in turn reliably predicts their planned behavior.

Role Theory

Role theory (Ashforth, 2001) focuses on how global identity derived from a social position with an expected behavioral repertoire shapes behavior. Once individuals adopt a specific role, such as a work role, their behaviors and decisions are influenced by the activated role identity. Role theory conceptualizes nonwork states as being free of work-role identity and considers the process of moving from employment to nonemployment as a role-based

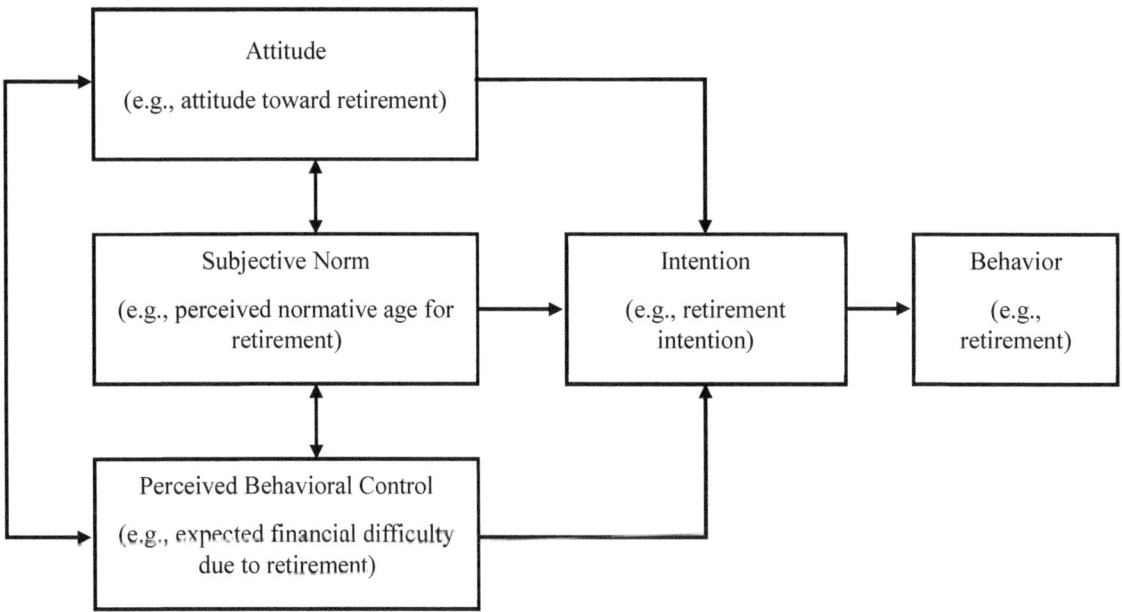

FIGURE 3-4 Theory of planned behavior.

transition (Wang et al., 2008). This transition can be eased by motivating retirees to replace their work-role activities with other forms of role involvement, or to create a new central identity in life. For example, retirees can continue working after retirement or they can fully exit work activities and become more involved in family or volunteer activities. Individuals may be pleased to lose their work roles, if they retire from unpleasant jobs. Many factors can make a job unpleasant, such as work stress, high workload, low salary, and unhealthy workplace relationships. Workers may view their retirement as an escape when they retire from unpleasant work roles (Barnes-Farrell, 2003).

The Life Course Perspective

The life course perspective is another theory often used to understand workforce exit decisions (Gee et al., 2019; Moen, 2016a, b; Shanahan et al., 2016; Elder and Johnson, 2003; Elder, 1995). This perspective, which is based on the dynamic ecological view of human development, articulates the importance of contextual embeddedness and the interdependence of life spheres. It emphasizes the influences of institutional constraints as well as individual attributes, job-related psychological variables, and family-related variables in workforce exit decision-making (Wang et al., 2008). Contextual embeddedness emphasizes that both life transitions and development occur under specific circumstances that are defined by historical, policy, and organizational and social contexts, previous job experience, family situational exigencies, and individual attributes with regard to work and retirement (Moen, 2016a, b; Wang, 2007). Individuals and couples make work and retirement decisions in light of the options available to them, including age-graded (and gender-graded) norms, social and organizational policies and practices, age, gender, and race/ethnic discrimination. All of this is embedded within shifting demographic, technological, social, economic, and labor market environments (Moen, 2016a).

According to the life course perspective, two major individual attributes are important in shaping the retirement processes. Poor financial status or severe health problems can significantly constrain retirement-related decisions (Wang et al., 2008; Shultz, 2003). Further, the notion of interdependent life spheres highlights that individuals' experience in one life sphere are affected by their experiences in other life spheres. Accordingly, nonwork life spheres, such as those of family and health, should also be studied to understand work and retirement pathways (Wang et al., 2008; Szinovacz, 2003). Overall, the life course perspective can be thought of as an expansion of the economic/rational choice model, one that includes a richer set of factors that can affect the subjective expected utility of work vs. retirement.

Meaningful Life

Life choices sometimes are not based on rational choice, specific attitudes, roles, or context, but rather on a search for meaning (King and Hicks, 2021), defined as the subjective experience of one's life as having significance, purpose, and coherence. A sense of meaning follows from factors that shape preferences—positive affect, social connections, religion or worldview, self-concept, forecasting, and mortality awareness. King and Hicks (2021) reviewed the literature and concluded that lack of meaning in life predicts disability, cardiovascular disease, dementia, job burnout, and other factors relevant to retirement decisions (as well as mortality). Those who draw meaning in life through paid work may continue to work in order to maintain this sense of meaning and purpose (Ward and King, 2017; Dik et al., 2013), while others may find meaning in other post-career activities.

Socioemotional Selectivity Theory

Socioemotional selectivity theory (Carstensen et al., 1999; Carstensen, 1991) posits that people in all cultures have a basic awareness of life passage, and this awareness influences people's emotions, cognitions, and motivations. Specifically, the theory argues that younger adults tend to view "time" as open-ended, because they are in the beginning of their life stages. Consequently, younger adults tend to have future-oriented goals. This means that when it comes to work, they will be more motivated to engage in knowledge acquisition, career planning, and developing ability and skills that will be useful in the future. Older adults, on the other hand, tend to view "time" as limited, because they are in the later stages of their lives. Thus, their goals are more present-oriented, such as maintaining positive emotions and pursuing positive relational experience with others. Overall, according to socioemotional selectivity theory, when it comes to work, older adults focus more on socioemotional experiences, whereas younger adults focus more on skill, knowledge, and opportunity development (Gielnik et al., 2018; Wang et al., 2015).

Summary

These five theoretical perspectives—rational choice theory, the theory of planned behavior, role theory, the life course perspective, meaningful life approach, and socioemotional selectivity theory—offer different framings of older adults' decision-making around paid and unpaid work and retirement paths. Despite their differences, all five perspectives are useful. All see older workers as active agents in shaping their own pathways, with clear preferences as to the types and timing of work-related transitions. However, some, including role theory, rational choice theory, and the life course perspective in particular, also emphasize the constraints limiting expectations and choices.

THE PROXIMAL FORCES THAT SHAPE THE WORK AND RETIREMENT PATHWAYS

Drawing from the theoretical mechanisms reviewed above, we consider older workers' preferences, expectations, and experienced constraints to be proximal forces that shape their workforce participation in later life. For example, the arrival of grandchildren may catalyze retirement through any of these. The notion of preferences is rooted in both the theory of planned behavior and rational choice theory, capturing older workers' subjective weighting of different workforce participation options. A grandparent may decide that cutting back to part-time work will allow active grandparenting and prefer that to continuing full-time work for the reasons that the theory of planned behavior and rational choice theory would explain: that spending daily time with a new grandchild would be rewarding (subjective utility), that the extended family would approve (social norms), and that the choice is the grandparent's to make (perceived behavioral control). Consequently, both the theory of planned behavior and rational choice theory could account for this preference. Grandparenthood also signals a new life course state, as well as a new role that could come to take precedence over ongoing intense occupational involvement.

The notion of expectation is rooted in both role theory and rational choice theory, capturing older workers' forecasts about their experiences with regard to choosing or not choosing certain workforce participation options. For example, these can include forecasts about whether continuing to work will be enjoyable, or forecasts about whether sufficient financial resources will remain if one takes full retirement. Again, if the grandparent role specifies daily time together, to benefit both parent and child, that expectation may govern a choice to work only part-time.

Finally, the notion of experienced constraints is rooted in each of the theory of planned behavior, rational choice theory, and a life course theoretical lens. Older workers in different social locations (such as gender, race/ethnicity, nativity, age) and with different resources (such as education, health, and savings) experience different constraints limiting their options for ongoing workforce participation. These constraints, in turn, can diminish their perceived behavior control (theory of planned behavior) and alter their subjective weighting of those options (theory of planned behavior, rational choice theory). In the following sections we review research findings related to each of these forces.

Preferences

Preferences result from two contrasting types of decision-making processes: both deliberation, implied by rational choice theory and the theory of planned behavior, and less systematic processes, implied by role theory and the theories of life course in context and meaning in life. Neither process produces preferences that reflect complete and unbiased information gathering, weighting, and inference (e.g., Fiske and Taylor, 2021). Instead, preferences for workforce exit pathways result from a combination of both thoughtful and unthinking considerations, including the weight of societal and organizational norms, policies, and practices.

Preferred Workforce Exit Pathways

In light of these factors, preferences as to when to exit the workforce differ across subgroups of the population, with women, those with less education, and those in physically demanding and low-status occupations more likely to prefer and take early exits, even as other psychosocial factors matter as well (Calvo et al., 2013; Zhan et al., 2013; Davies and Cartwright, 2011; Wang and Shultz, 2010; Wang et al., 2008; Barnes-Farrell, 2003). Preferences as to retirement timing do, in fact, predict actual timing of retirement and actual exits, although many find themselves "retired" before they expected as a result of poor health, caregiving obligations, buyouts, or layoffs (Moen, 2016a). One Swedish study finds that personal preferences for retirement timing have little effect on actual retirement timing net of other factors (e.g., health and other circumstances described in Chapter 4), suggesting that opportunities and constraints may outweigh subjective preferences in shaping pathways to retirement (Örestig et al., 2013). Further, preferences for working or retiring can be clouded by a sense of ambivalence for those who are not sure what retirement will bring, as well as for those who would like to work "some," but in less demanding, more meaningful, and more flexible ways but see no such options (Moen, 2007).

As women's labor market attachments have increased, decision-making and experiences around retirement timing have become more likely to be couple-based, not individual-based processes (Henkens and van Solinge, 2002). Older couples can confront disjunctures in both partners' work/nonwork preferences and behavior. Moreover, spouses may have preferences for their husbands' and wives' exits as well as their own. For example, a person's leisure may be more valuable if the spouse also retires, because the spouse's leisure time can augment the subjective utility of the person's leisure.

In the past, given their more variable attachments to the labor force, women have tended to tailor their work exits around those of their husbands, but this is changing as women begin to remain in the workforce throughout the life course, even when their children are young (Moen et al., 2006). A study using Swedish register data finds that for about one in four couples, both individuals retire within a year, and that women who synchronize retirement timing with their husbands tend to retire at earlier ages, even as men who synchronize with their wives are more likely to delay, thus retiring at later ages (Gustafson, 2017). A recent study of the oldest members of the Baby Boom cohort (using the HRS) shows that men influence their wives' retirement timing, even as women appear to have little influence on their husband's retirement timing (Stancanelli, 2017; Jackson, 2016), although these findings are not consistent with those of another study (also using the HRS) examining an earlier cohort (Coile, 2004), which found the opposite: men are responsive to their wife's retirement incentives, but not vice versa. Other factors such as maintaining access to employer health insurance may also affect spouses' retirement timing (Boyle and Lahey, 2016; Witman, 2015; see also Chapter 4).

Preferred Job and Workplace Characteristics

For some older adults, continued work in later life contributes to the fulfillment of psychological needs such as "the need to belong, to be a contributing member of society," and to stay engaged (James et al., 2016, p. 334; see James et al., 2020). In addition to greater financial security (and perhaps employee benefits), continued work in later life can confer a sense of belonging, self-esteem, identity continuity, and a way to structure time (Zhan et al., 2019; 2015; Smyer and Pitt-Catsouphes, 2007). The Special Committee on Aging report from the U.S. Senate (2017) concluded that work is also linked to improved mental and physical health and overall quality of life, although empirically this can be hard to distinguish from causality running in the other direction—with healthy and well people working longer. Chapter 5 includes a detailed discussion regarding elements of job and workplace characteristics that older workers prefer.

Expectations

People's expectations often determine their choices, but these processes are again a mix of thoughtful deliberation and less systematic beliefs. People's ability to forecast their future happiness is flawed; in a variety of life decisions, comparing expectations versus reality, affective forecasting is poor (Gilbert and Wilson, 2007). People's expectations about their work-exit pathway also include finances and work context.

Financial Considerations

One important expectation that accompanies remaining in the workforce is that work will provide better financial income. A person may expect to receive more income by working longer than the typical retirement age (Cahill et al., 2013), but this may not be the sole consideration. A job that meets such financial expectations may breach other expectations about engaging in meaningful work if there is a lack of person-job fit and the job is less intrinsically rewarding. Consistent with the distinction between push and pull factors of retirement (Wang et al., 2009; Shultz et al., 1998), retirees who are "pulled" into bridge employment due to positive expectations about work activities may have higher levels of retirement satisfaction than retirees who are "pushed" into bridge employment due to financial expectations.

Work Context Shaping Expectations

When making workforce exit decisions, older workers' expectations are likely shaped by factors in their work context. These include not only retirement-related organizational-level policies and norms, but also perceived biases and negative stereotypes that older workers encounter in their workplace or in society more broadly (Wang and Shultz, 2010). In particular, retirement age norms in the workplace and in society play important roles in shaping older workers' retirement expectations and plans (Settersten and Hagestad, 1996). Individuals who are behind normative career advancement schedules or have plateaued in their careers are less likely to expect investment and fair treatment from their organizations. Accordingly, they are more likely to feel pressure from the organization and society to retire.

Workplace policies and practices related to the treatment of older workers may also be critical in forming age-discrimination-related expectations that may influence older workers' attachment to organization and retirement intention (Boehm et al., 2014; Goldberg et al., 2013). For example, data from a sample of German companies showed that age-inclusive human resource practices (e.g., equal opportunities to training and promotion for all age groups) promoted the age diversity climate, leading older workers to expect fair treatment and positive social exchange with their supervisors, which enhanced their intentions to remain and work for the same organization (Boehm et al., 2014).

Finally, the workplace as a social community also provides important interpersonal context to expectations about the benefits of working longer. Research on employee retention has emphasized the role of interpersonal links in reducing employees' workforce turnover behaviors (Lee et al., 2004). The impact of interpersonal context might be stronger for older employees, as older adults value social goals such as maintaining and building satisfying social relationships to a greater extent than younger ones (Carstensen, 1995). For example, having a dense and strong friendship network in the workplace may enhance older workers' sense of social belonging and acceptance, likely to fulfill expectations of positive social experiences for continuing to work and thus serving as a key contextual factor in retaining older workers.

Constraints

Constraints for Work and Retirement Pathways

In addition to preferences and expectations, constraints also shape workforce exit pathways for older workers. Economic and health resources and shocks, such as changes in Social Security or Medicare policy, chronic strains, such as burnout and precarity, and family caregiving responsibilities and the circumstances of spousal work and income all influence both preferences for and the actual timing of exits (Fast et al., 2020; Keating et al., 2019; Stoilko and Strough, 2019; Kalleberg, 2018; Gustafson, 2017; Beehr and Feldman 2011; Raymo and Sweeney, 2006; Moen et al., 2006; Dentinger and Clarkberg, 2002). So too does a sense of perceived "workability," the subjective sense that one is able to do the job, which is related to health, a sense of control, and job demands (McGonagle et al., 2015). Related to the last, disability trends from 1997–2010 show increased disabilities for those ages 40–64 (Martin, Schoeni et al., 2010), leading to increased workforce exits (Warner et al., 2010).

Early evidence from CPS data (Flood et al., 2021; Moen et al., 2020) showed that COVID-19 caused significant increases in unemployment and being out of the workforce at all ages, but especially among women and those with less education. Looking specifically at older adults in their 50s and 60s (Flood et al., 2021) shows that those in historically disadvantaged locations, in terms of race and education as well as gender, were more apt to become unemployed or leave the labor force; there was no large upturn in retirement through December 2020. In contrast to the experiences of Black and Hispanic women and men, White men's employment was less disrupted and more apt to rebound during 2020 (see also Chapter 2). The COVID-19 pandemic significantly challenged marginalized older adults' prospects for working longer, especially among those with lower educational attainment.

There are other forces shaping work and retirement pathways as well: technological changes coupled with corresponding skill obsolescence, encouraged (forced) early retirement packages, societal as well as organizational norms and pressures, and limited phased or alternative work options, such as possibilities for bridge jobs or reduced or flexible hours, often come into play (Hess et al., 2018; Moen, 2016; Sweet and Moen, 2012). For example, studies using HRS data of the initial wave of the Baby Boom cohort show that they are apt to take alternative work options at later ages than earlier cohorts, that poor health leads to bridge jobs (Cahill et al., 2019), and that those reaching retirement ages during the Great Recession are more apt to experience layoffs (Cahill et al., 2015). A study in the Netherlands showed that some older workers are especially vulnerable to involuntary early exits (Visser et al., 2018).

Retirement and social welfare policies shape incentives and possibilities for early or late exits, as do educational and retraining options (Foster and Walker, 2015; Zhan and Wang, 2015b; Powers and Neumark, 2003). Taking various options also shapes older workers' relative propensity to return to work, with those taking the early Social Security option at age 62 having higher odds of subsequently doing part-time work (Kail and Warner, 2013). As discussed in Chapter 5, working conditions, such as greater control over the time and place of work, can also color expectations of older workers for the future, such as their expectations about working past certain ages (Moen et al., 2016; Pienta and Hayward, 2002).

As described in socioemotional selectivity theory, older adults selectively invest their time and energy resources as they recognize their time horizons are constrained (Carstensen, 2011). They also seek to exercise control over life transitions (Staudinger et al., 2016; Heckhausen and Schulz, 1995). Voluntary work and voluntary exits promote well-being (Rhee et al., 2015; Glavin, 2013; Calvo et al., 2009; Gallo et al., 2006; Kim and Moen, 2002). But institutionalized constraints around the clockworks of work (workdays, workweeks, work years, work lives) together with macroeconomic forces limit older adults' options for achieving their work and retirement preferences across the later life course (Moen et al., 2016; Moen, 2013).

In fact, as a life course approach underscores, paid work is organized in age-graded ways (Moen, 2016b; Settersten and Mayer, 1997). Young adults in their 20s and 30s are recruited for entry-level jobs, and occupational paths are designed for prime-age workers. Most organizational practices and pension policies are predicated on continuous full-time work throughout adulthood, followed by a one-time, one-way exit to full-time retirement, what Blau and Shvydko (2011) call labor market rigidities. This means that alternative paths—to unretire or, if working, to work less, more flexibly, and differently—are not institutionalized, rendering preferences for such options at odds with opportunities (Moen, 2016). The social organization of the work course can also foster situations like job lock, the problem that emerges when, because of Medicare health insurance eligibility, U.S. workers who would like to or need to scale back or exit the workforce are forced to continue working for the health insurance until they reach age 65 (Fisher, Ryan et al., 2016; Boyle and Lahey, 2010).

Taken together, constraints in the forms of personal, organizational, and societal circumstances and exigencies can create a mismatch between preferences and actual behavior around workforce exit-related transitions, leading to involuntary work and involuntary retirement, in contrast to similar but voluntary states (Sohier, 2019; Hershey and Henkens, 2014; Sweet and Moen, 2012; Kim and Moen, 2001). Research documents different types of mismatch, with older workers who would prefer to retire and others who would like to keep working beyond conventional retirement ages feeling unable to do so because of disability, caregiving demands, discrimination, automation, layoffs, workplace norms, or intense and rigid working conditions (Katz and Krueger, 2019; Ebbinghaus and Radl, 2015; van Solinge and Henkens, 2007).

There are those who are not working and would prefer to be working but find few if any opportunities for reemployment compatible with their skills and flexibility needs. There are also those who would like to retire but have little choice but to keep working (Sohier, 2019). These involuntary states can have harmful consequences for older workers' well-being (Sohier, 2019; Munnell and Sass, 2008; van Solinge and Henkens, 2007; Kim and Moen, 2002).

Involuntary Dislocation from Work

The evidence from both the United States and Europe shows that many later exits from the workforce occur despite adult workers' preference to continue working (Rhee et al., 2015; van Solinge and Henkens, 2007). These exits may take place because individuals are pushed out (Ebbinghaus and Radl, 2015; Reynolds and Wenger, 2010), experiencing health problems (Martin, Freedman et al., 2010), or serving as care providers for elderly parents, spouses, children, or grandchildren (Stoiko and Strough, 2019; van der Horst et al., 2017). Assumptions about a customary and voluntary work-to-retirement experience are clearly obsolete.

Indeed, although older workers in large numbers have reported an interest in continuing work past conventional retirement ages, there is a question about the extent to which jobs will be available to them. In the 2017 Retirement Confidence Survey[1] of American workers, only 27 percent of individuals ages 65 and older report that they have actually been able to continue working as long as planned (Greenwald et al., 2017). Chronic illnesses (self or family) often force people to work into retirement age, in order to maintain health insurance, but for this same reason, people may not be able to work as long as they need to (Homaie Rad et al., 2017).

Further, as Heidkamp and Van Horn (2020, p. 337) note,

> Many aspiring older workers [especially those seeking full-time jobs with benefits] face tremendous challenges in the labor market—including age discrimination and outdated job search, technology and workplace skills—contributing to significantly higher rates of long-term unemployment for workers (55+) compared to prime age (16–54) workers.

Using data from the U.S. Bureau of Labor Statistics, for the Employment Data Digest of AARP, Schramm (2018) reports that in February 2018 the long-term unemployment rate for these older job seekers was 27.2 percent, compared to 19.0 percent for prime-age workers. Audit studies examining the effect of age on employer callbacks for unemployed workers have found employers are less likely to contact those ages 50 and over (Farber et al., 2019; Farber et al., 2016).

Thus, older job seekers must make difficult adjustments. The longer one is in a job search, the greater the stigma of unemployment, both in the United States (Liu et al., 2014; Kroft et al., 2013) and in Germany (Nüß, 2018). Older workers are typically unfamiliar with current job search techniques using social media, technology, and networking, and they often lack the training or skills for the jobs that exist (Heidkamp and Van Horn, 2020). Additionally, the growing gig economy is often less appealing to workers who are seeking stable jobs (Heidkamp and Van Horn, 2020). Together, this means that many older adults who become unemployed end up underemployed, if they find work at all, and without access to retirement benefits, paid leave, or health care (if they are under 65).

Involuntary dislocation from work is associated with an increased risk of negative health outcomes for older workers in the United States, including increased risk of cardiac disease and stroke (Gallo et al., 2006). Similarly, a study conducted in Sweden using linked employer-employees data reveals that involuntary job loss increases the risk of hospitalization, not due to strokes but to alcohol-related conditions, among both men and women, and to traffic accidents and self-harm, among men only (Eliason and Storrie, 2009). These authors report that the overall mortality risk among men increased by 44 percent during the first four years after job loss, but did not increase for women. For both sexes there was an increase in suicides and alcohol-related mortality.

It is important to note that methodologically, studying involuntary dislocations and involuntary early retirement helps researchers overcome problems of reverse causality (e.g., in measuring the influence of unemployment or

---

[1] The Retirement Confidence Survey is an annual online survey of American workers and retirees ages 25 and over conducted by the Employee Benefits Research Institute.

early retirement on health). Since involuntary job changes are often due to exogenous changes in the economic environment, instrumental variable techniques can be used to estimate the causal impact of job changes on health and mortality. A number of studies have used these and similar techniques to examine the effects of plant closures and layoffs on subsequent mortality rates, finding that these events are associated with significant increases in suicide (Classen and Dunn, 2011), opioid overdose deaths (Venkataramani et al., 2020), and overall mortality rates (Sullivan and von Wachter, 2009).

These findings are not unique to the United States; similar findings have been noted in other countries with different policy environments. For example, Kuhn and colleagues (2020) studied involuntary early retirement in Austria in the late 1980s in response to the international steel crisis. They estimated the causal effect of an early retirement policy on mortality for blue-collar workers. The policy allowed workers in eligible regions to withdraw from the labor market up to 3.5 years earlier than workers in noneligible regions. For males, they found that a reduction in the effective retirement age caused a significant and quantitatively important increase in the risk of premature death. Advancing the date of permanent exit from the work force by one year led to an increase in the risk of premature death of 2.4 percentage points, resulting in a large relative increase of about 13.4 percent.

In summary, constraints in the form of public and organizational policies and practices, but also in terms of older workers' health, spousal circumstances, and family care obligations, shape retirement pathways, including whether retirement timing is voluntary or involuntary, as well as opportunities to unretire. The role of external forces is underscored by COVID-19; the ensuing lockdown pushed many older (as well as younger) workers into unemployment or else out of the workforce. But constraints are not evenly distributed across the population of older workers, as described in the next section and more fully in Chapters 4 and 6.

DISPARITIES AND HETEROGENEITY IN WORK AND RETIREMENT PATHWAYS

Demographic-based Disparities in Work and Retirement Pathways

Research shows disparities in pathways to retirement by gender and race (Moen et al., 2021; Calvo et al., 2018; McDonough et al., 2017; Fasang, 2010; Warner et al., 2010). Black and Hispanic Americans, as well as women, in their 50s and 60s are more likely to experience involuntary job separation and less likely to be reemployed, resulting in labor force withdrawal (Flippen and Tienda, 2000). These racial differences are related to differences in education, health, and employment characteristics. Married women are more likely to leave the labor force earlier because they often retire at the same time as their husbands. Women are also more likely to leave the labor force due to family caregiving (Dentiger and Clarkberg, 2002). Women's labor histories are more intermittent than men's and typically feature low-skill jobs without private pensions.

As a result, retirement may have a different meaning for women and minorities. One study found that women's (but not men's) odds of being retired (both in terms of pension retirement and self-attributed retirement) increase dramatically if they have more dependents living with them (Talaga and Beehr, 1995). The same data showed that women whose spouses are in poor health are more likely to retire than those whose spouses are not in poor health, while the opposite is true for men (see also Dentinger and Clarkberg, 2002).

A review on pathways to retirement for minority workers suggests that discontinuous work histories and poor health increase minority workers' chances of involuntary job loss in the years prior to retirement (Flippen, 2005). This, in turn, affects their financial security in old age. Analyzing retirement pathways for women, Brown and Warner (2008) find large racial and ethnic disparities in pathways to retirement that emerge in midlife. Black and Hispanic women are more than twice as likely as White women to experience disability as a retirement pathway (Lahey, 2018). This finding is attributed to differences in health and socioeconomic inequality, which are often the result of larger structural disadvantages that shape life course trajectories (Rothstein, 2017). This is discussed in greater detail in Chapter 4. Minority women close to retirement face barriers to employment because of their poor health and economic capital, which reduces their chance to exit the labor force voluntarily (Lahey, 2018).

Given the higher risks for minority workers to enter retirement involuntarily, it is also concerning that minority workers tend to be less prepared for retirement. In a qualitative study in the United States, Blanco and colleagues (2017) find a lack of preparedness for retirement for poor older Hispanic people. Older adults, in that study, report wanting to continue working until they are unable to do so; and respondents report a lack of tradition in terms of preparedness for retirement, saying their parents never spoke to them about a plan for retirement.

Life Course Disparities in Work and Retirement Pathways

Looked at in light of the life course cumulative advantage/disadvantage thesis (Dannefer, 2020; DiPrete and Eirich, 2006; O'Rand, 1996), opportunities and constraints accumulate across the life course to generate disadvantage or advantage in later adulthood. This means that historically disadvantaged subgroups are further disadvantaged, because they are less able to accrue the necessary resources to make the options that allow them to enact their preferences available. Life course scholars describe cycles of control (Moen, 2013; Elder, 1985) as shifts in constraints and opportunities occur across the life course, further advantaging some, disadvantaging others. For example, standardized retirement protections are unraveling, and retirement feels riskier for those without pensions or considerable savings.

As a consequence, there are likely widening disparities between subgroups regarding their sense of control over their lives, with disadvantaged older subgroups experiencing a limited sense of control over whether they are working or not. Thus, preference/behavior mismatches around work and nonwork are not evenly distributed across subpopulations. Those with greater educational and health resources and those in professional occupations are most able to achieve their preferences to work more flexibly, to tailor their jobs, or else to retire early, on-time, late, or not at all (Calvo et al., 2018; Ebbinghaus and Radl, 2015; Munnell and Sass, 2008; Ebbinghaus, 2006). Flippen and Tienda (2002) also find that individuals who had limited opportunities (in low-skill occupations or in work for small firms) in their prime working years also faced large disadvantages close to retirement age, which led to involuntary labor force withdrawal.

Recent research shows gender, educational, and race/ethnic divergences in full-time and long-hour work pathways, as well as in disability-related and other exit pathways (Moen et al., 2021; Calvo et al., 2018; McDonough et al., 2017; Fasang, 2010; Warner et al., 2010). The disability/work relationship is complicated because paid work promotes health (Zulkarnain and Rutledge, 2021; Carr et al., 2020), and yet disability paths can become a safety net for older workers with health conditions unable to find employment who are not yet eligible to receive Social Security benefits (see Freedman, 2018; Pfeffer, 2018). Disability pathways disproportionately characterize the experiences of those with less education as well as Black and Hispanic women and men. Black men and women with a high school degree or less are most likely to experience this disability pathway, especially when in their 50s, though probabilities decline and converge across race, gender, and education as individuals move into their late 60s and early 70s. In contrast, Hispanic and Asian women often leave the workforce to provide family caregiving (Moen et al., 2021).

Some older adults in their 50s are not in the workforce and, therefore, are excluded from studies of retirement that begin with samples of workers employed at least full-time. Older Black and Hispanic adults, in particular, are more likely to experience labor market constraints that limit their work options (Moen, 2016; Munnell and Sass, 2008; Flippen and Tienda, 2000). This disparity has been highlighted once again by their disproportionate exits from employment as a result of the COVID-19 pandemic (Flood et al., 2021).

Heterogeneity in Working Longer and Part-time Work

In terms of working longer, findings regarding patterned pathways (Moen et al., 2021) show that Black men are the most disadvantaged in being less likely to follow either the long-hour (50 hours or more) or full-time pathway in their 50s, 60s, and early 70s, especially those with at most a high school degree. Among women, there is less of a clearly patterned differentiation in long-hour and full-time pathways by race, with fewer older women than men working long hours, and a steeper decline in full-time hours with age. Socioeconomic status in combination with gender clearly matters; older women with a high school degree or less consistently have the lowest probabilities of following full-time or long-hour pathways, even lower than White men with some college education.

Most obvious is the cumulation of advantage with education for older White men; those who had attended college are far more likely to continue working long hours (50 or more per week) as they move to and through the conventional retirement years. Comparing women to men, women in their 50s and 60s with at least some college follow long-hour and full-time pathways at similar levels as less-educated men (those with only a high school degree or less).

Employment in the form of part-time work appears to be a pathway for well-educated women and men in their 60s (Moen et al., 2021). The probabilities of participation in this pathway are slightly higher for White women than for other women and for White men in their 60s compared to same-age men of color. There is divergence in the probability of participation in the part-time work pathway in the 60s and 70s, with the highest educated White men having higher odds of pursuing it. Older women of Hispanic or Asian/Pacific Islander background are most likely to follow the unemployed/other pathway, most typically leaving the workforce because of family-care reasons.

Gender-based Heterogeneity in Bridge Employment Decision Making

According to social gender role theory, gender roles are formed as a result of people's social beliefs about gender differences in psychological and behavioral characteristics (Eagly et al., 2000). Gender roles in turn cultivate real gender differences in behaviors (Konrad et al., 2000). In other words, though such beliefs do not have actual roots in biological differences, they can be learned and internalized by people through socialization and impact people's cognitions and behaviors (Eddleston et al., 2006). Given that social gender roles are associated with various work attributes, men and women may react differently to specific aspects of work (Konrad et al., 2000).

For example, people tend to expect men to pay more attention to status, prestige, and recognition that are ascribed by others. This is because striving to elicit the immediate attention of others is an important masculine role characteristic (Williams and Best, 1990). Accordingly, both meta-analytical review (Konrad et al., 2000) and empirical studies (e.g., Eddleston et al., 2006) show that men value the status aspect of a job more than women do. On the other hand, people tend to expect women to be more active in seeking positive personal relationships (i.e., "affiliation"; Williams and Best, 1990). Based on this gender characteristic, women are expected to prefer working with people rather than working alone. As such, the desire for social communion is expected to be more salient for women than men in making bridge employment decisions (Zhan et al., 2015). However, longitudinal data from a representative sample from China, controlling for age, health, education, finance, family context, preretirement job conditions, and retirement attitudes, showed that communion striving and generativity striving were positively related to bridge employment participation for both male and female retirees. However, status striving was positively related to bridge employment participation for male retirees but not for female retirees. Taken together, these findings suggest that retirees' actual decisions to work after retirement were at least partly shaped by different needs associated with their social gender roles.

Summary

In summary, the demography of and processes leading to later adult work and retirement pathways paint a picture of enduring inequalities by historically disadvantaged subgroups who are less apt to have either resources or opportunities to work longer. The evidence to date points to the need for an intersectional approach (Lahey and Oxley 2021; Collins and Bilge 2020; Romero, 2018) to examine the effects of overlapping social statuses (such as gender, race/ethnicity, nativity as well as age), in order to promote understanding of disparities in work pathways, including the inability to exit work because of the absence of savings or a pension (see also Chapter 4) or the inability to keep working because of poor health (see also Chapter 4), working conditions (see also Chapter 5) or discrimination (see also Chapter 6). Intersectional analysis could also provide a window into the distinctive retirement preferences and experiences, as well as the gaps between them, among different subgroups of older individuals and couples. For example, this would permit a focus on the ways racism and sexism experienced early in the life course play out in the later life course, even as reports of agism increase (Gee et al., 2019).

CHALLENGES AND FUTURE RESEARCH DIRECTIONS

One challenge to understanding the dynamics and disparities in later adult work and retirement patterns is that scholars use different definitions of retirement and, accordingly, different measures (Ekerdt and DeViney, 1990). For example, "work" is often defined as full-time, long-tenure (career) employment, more typical of white-collar and unionized blue-collar White men than of those in other subgroups. However, because older adults follow multiple pathways to working in later life, it is necessary to capture specific features of work activities, such as work hours, the nature of employment, and the employment relationship.

A second challenge is that research often considers single transitions, such as from full-time work to retirement (with nonemployment equated with retirement; Radl, 2013), or from retirement to reemployment (Kail and Warner, 2013). But considering transitions this way cannot quantify the patterning or range of routes to eventual retirement, ignoring the variety of pathways (see Figure 3-3 above) followed from work to complete retirement. Recent innovations in sequence analysis, as well as panel data, are resulting in scholarship that captures the varied and unequal later life course paths older individuals experience in the United States and Europe (Moen et al., 2021; Calvo et al., 2018; McDonough et al., 2017; Fasang, 2010). Longitudinal analytic techniques can also help better depict and predict qualitative changes over time (Wang and Chan, 2011).

A third challenge involves the samples of individuals studied. Social research typically looks in the rearview mirror, drawing on available data, often decades old, from earlier populations of older adults. This is a key issue in times of rapid social change, when the nature of both work and retirement are in flux, even as traditional safety nets are eroding (Moen, 2016). It also points to the complexity of the relationship between age, period, and cohort (Elder and George, 2016; Alwin and McCammon, 2003). Age reflects career and life course stages, but also locates people in particular socio-historical contexts. Past studies on the work and retirement pathways of earlier populations of older workers who faced very different organizational and economic environments may not apply to the experiences of contemporary older workers. Moreover, the timing of external events in the later life course matter. Consider, for example, the different experiences of Americans in the face of the COVID-19 lockdown. Older Americans in their 70s were mostly already out of the workforce, whereas those in their 50s were more vulnerable to job loss (Flood et al., 2021). This points to the need for more rapid collection and dissemination of data on contemporary older workers, as well as attention to the timing of social changes in people's lives. It also suggests that extrapolating future trends from the experiences of recent cohorts should only be done with caution.

Relatedly, many work- and retirement-related phenomena are fundamentally intertwined with their specific socioeconomic and policy contexts (Costa, 1998). Changes have often occurred in these contexts over time, such as economic booms due to technology innovation, Social Security reform, health care reforms, and early retirement incentive practices (Wang, 2015). These changes can alter the research questions investigators ask. For example, at the end of the 1990s and in the early 2000s, much effort was invested in studying early retirement, because there was a clear trend of workers retiring earlier and earlier. However, the population aging trend, in combination with the 2008–2010 economic recession, seems to have reversed this phenomenon, and more and more older workers are choosing to postpone their retirement and stay in the workforce. As such, bridge employment becomes a focal research topic for investigation. This type of shift in research phenomena is challenging and rewarding at the same time, as new issues surface constantly.

In addition, given the context changes, the same phenomena are likely to be influenced by different factors at different points in time, which often facilitates theoretical and methodological innovations in tackling those issues. Given the disruption caused by the COVID-19 pandemic to public health, social interaction, and employment attachments, it is crucial to understand the effects of COVID-19 on subsequent work and retirement pathways.

Finally, research is still lacking regarding independent contracting and self-employment as workforce participation activities for older adults. The growth of the gig economy raises the question of the extent to which older workers are *attracted* to independent contractor work or are being *pushed* toward it. In addition, given the difficulties of measuring these populations (discussed in Chapter 2), what is the prevalence of older workers among the self-employed, and how has it changed over time? Understanding these questions could be helpful in providing a fuller picture of the employment experience of older workers. HRS data provide some insights into the prevalence of older workers among the self-employed over time, showing that Americans ages 50 and older who identify as self-employed have consistently made up about 10 percent of the population and 20 percent of the working population since 2004 (Halvorsen and James, 2020). In addition, the rate of self-employment among older workers also increases with age, particularly in the late 60s and early 70s (Chapter 2).

Abraham (2020) finds working as an independent contractor[2] is the primary form of self-employment for older workers. Of those working as an independent contractor, 23–25 percent work for a prior employer. Among those who work as an independent contractor, their primary reason for doing so is to earn income, followed by a desire to stay active and connect with others. In addition, the highly educated make up the greatest proportion of independent contractors. These results leave several unanswered questions, including, as mentioned above, whether older workers enter independent contractor relationships by choice or because they have been pushed into the arrangement by their former employer. Also, why are less-educated older people less likely to be working as independent contractors? What barriers do they face?

CONCLUSION

A large body of research in the United States and Europe shows that later adult work and retirement patterns are in flux. There are also wide disparities and heterogeneities in work and retirement pathways for older adults. In this chapter, we offered a conceptual framework to depict and understand these work and retirement pathways, highlighting the flexibility and constraints that older adults experience in their workforce participation in their later life stage. We also summarized the main theories and empirical findings that explain the various work and retirement pathways for older adults. These offer a foundation for us to dive further, in subsequent chapters, into more detailed individual and household factors, workplace and job factors, and labor market factors that can shape work and retirement pathways.

It is important to emphasize that much of what we know about the later work course comes from studies of earlier birth cohorts who were confronting very different demographic, technological, social, and economic forces, as well as very different private sector and public policy regimes. For this reason, the experiences of more recent cohorts of older adults may differ in substantive ways.

Moving forward, it is important to examine whether age discrimination in hiring and retention has been made more severe by the COVID-19 pandemic, as older job applicants and workers may be seen to have greater health risks than their younger counterparts (van Dalen and Henkens, 2020). Consequently, it is also important to examine whether the economic and health effects of the pandemic have discouraged older adults who were laid off from continuing the job search, eventually pushing them out of the workforce permanently. Finally, the impact of government policies (e.g., Gelfand et al., 2021) and organizational practices (e.g., Chang et al., 2021) introduced to counter the ripple effects of the COVID-19 pandemic on older adults' workforce participation warrants careful investigation. It is essential for future research to produce insights on the contemporary and dynamic experiences of work and retirement as they are transforming before our eyes.

---

[2]Identification of independent contracting relationships among older workers is complex and prone to measurement error. See Box 2-1 in Chapter 2 for more information about the measures used by Abraham (2020) and her colleagues.

Part II

4

Individual and Social Factors That Influence Employment and Retirement Transitions

Individual and social resources associated with work and retirement in later life are dynamic, complex, and multidimensional (Moen, 2020; Zhan et al., 2019; Munnell and Sass, 2008; Morrow-Howell et al. 2001). Research on labor force transitions at the individual and household levels has grown significantly over the past decades due to the availability of longitudinal population-based studies in the United States and abroad. This research has resulted in greater insights and understanding of individual and social factors that contribute to the diversity of work and retirement pathways.

The theoretical framework of person-environment fit provides a way to conceptualize the reciprocal relationship between individuals and the environments within which they are situated (Hansson et al., 2018; Zhan et al., 2015; Tang et al., 2013; Burr and Mutchler, 2007; Ostroff and Schulte, 2007; Morrow-Howell et al., 2001; Caplan, 1987). To help understand the "person" in the "person-environment fit" perspective, this chapter highlights research on individual factors, such as health, education, financial resources, the many meanings of work and work satisfaction, as well as economic factors. It also highlights the social resources that enable or constrain the pathways to work and retirement at older ages, such as family and household structure and social capital. Later chapters (5, 6, and 7) will elaborate on the "environmental" aspects of that fit, examining the work environment, the supply and demand of the labor market, and social policy.

The individual factors reviewed within this chapter shape the timing of retirement exits, and their effects can be viewed through the lens of our framework of preferences, expectations, and constraints. For example, health, education, and financial resources can be enablers of preferences and expectations of working longer, even as their absence constrains opportunities to do so. Similarly, a number of individual-level resources and family and household structures enable or constrain individuals' ability to achieve their anticipated or preferred path from work to retirement.

This chapter also advances our understanding of life course processes, recognizing that later-life course resources enabling both working and retiring reflect cumulative advantages and disadvantages shaped by early life experiences as well as institutionalized systems of inequality (Dannefer, 2020; Ferraro and Shippee, 2009). Accordingly, we consider evidence of the disparate distribution of health and other resources by people's social locations in terms of their gender, race, ethnicity, and education. We also consider the evidence of the disparate distribution of health and other resources by age/cohort, nativity, and sexual and gender minority status, recognizing the value of an intersectional approach by considering these categories where possible as jointly configured (Collins and Bilge, 2020). Doing so points to divergent labor force participation and retirement pathways among what is a very heterogeneous U.S. population (Moen et al., 2021; Calvo et al., 2018; Cahill et al., 2015; Warner and Brown, 2011; Warner et al., 2010).

The chapter begins by reviewing the literature on individual resources that affect work at older ages, beginning with the relationship between health and retirement. As noted in Chapter 1, the committee limited its consideration of the relationship between health and work at older ages to the role of health in determining retirement timing and does not provide a review the effects of work and retirement on health. This is followed by a review of the relationship between education and work at older ages.

Since financial security plays an important role in shaping preferences and expectations for work and constraints on work opportunities at older ages, the next sections focus on contributors to financial security at older ages: financial literacy, employer pensions, Social Security, wealth and income, and debt. The discussion then turns to family and household characteristics, including the roles of caregiving, joint retirement, and family structure. It also covers the role of social capital in finding employment at older ages.

We conclude this chapter by identifying cross-cutting themes, underscoring new scientific findings, and pinpointing gaps in knowledge to shape a research agenda on work and retirement for the 21st century.

INDIVIDUAL LEVEL RESOURCES

Health

Studies using large-scale national surveys of older workers find that healthy older people are more apt to keep working (Cahill et al., 2006; Kim and DeVaney 2005; Henretta et al., 1992), even as doing so appears to have protective health effects (Fitzpatrick and Moore, 2018; Berkman et al., 2014). This makes it difficult to tease out the causal linkage between the two. Still, the evidence shows that the onset of a health condition can trigger labor market exits of older workers (Zajacova et al., 2014; Warner and Brown, 2011), suggesting that health is causally linked to working at older ages.

Many older workers experience health issues that constrain opportunities for working longer. Among individuals ages 55 to 64, seven in 10 have been diagnosed with at least one of six common chronic conditions: diabetes, cardiovascular disease, chronic obstructive pulmonary disease, asthma, cancer, or arthritis—and nearly four in 10 have at least two of these conditions (National Center for Health Statistics, 2009). More than 40 percent of people ages 50 to 64 report difficulty with at least one of nine physical functions because of a health problem, while four percent report difficulty performing activities of daily living (e.g., bathing, dressing, eating, moving from bed to chair, going to the toilet) or instrumental acts of daily living (e.g., preparing meals, shopping for groceries, making telephone calls, assisting with medications; Martin, Freedman et al., 2010).

Large health disparities by race, ethnicity, and socioeconomic status (SES) (National Center for Health Statistics, 2015) result in an unequal incidence of health problems across groups of older workers. These disparities are likely to be compounded by the effects of COVID-19 (see Box 4-1). Black and Hispanic individuals near retirement age have lower baseline health status and experience larger declines in health as they age, when compared to their White counterparts (Sudano and Baker, 2006). Although much has been made of the Hispanic health "paradox"—the lower mortality rates of Hispanic people despite their generally lower SES—it is not clear that this advantage extends to other dimensions of health (Hayward et al., 2014). A life course perspective is invaluable for understanding health disparities by race and ethnicity at older ages, which reflect the cumulative effect of early-life health, social, and economic disadvantages (Brown, 2009).

Health disparities among older Americans by education are also large—the share of college graduates reporting fair or poor health at age 70 is reached by high school graduates by ages 40 to 55 and exceeded by high school dropouts before age 40 (Zajacova et al., 2014). While there are differences in educational attainment by race, research indicates that race and education are both key determinants of health and work (Farmer and Ferraro, 2005). Health deteriorates more rapidly with age for workers engaged in manual work, suggesting that some of the effect of education on later adult health likely occurs through selection into occupation (Case and Deaton, 2005). There are also well-documented disparities in health by gender, with women having longer life expectancies but higher morbidity (Bird and Rieker, 2008). These disparities reflect gender differences in health behaviors and life course paths, although they may also be partially attributable to biological differences between men and women (Adler and Rehkopf, 2008).

Evidence suggests that health at midlife has been declining in recent years, while mortality has been rising (National Academies of Sciences, Engineering, and Medicine, 2021). The share of men and women ages 55 to 64 reporting themselves to be in fair or poor health rose between the mid-1990s and the mid-2010s, as did the share reporting chronic pain (Hudomiet et al., 2022). There was also an increase in diabetes and overweight status over this period, although smoking decreased. Similarly, there are increases in self-reports of functional limitation, depression, and work limitations over the past two decades (Waidmann et al., 2020). Among non-White Hispanic people, differences in health status across education groups have become more pronounced over time (Case and Deaton, 2017).

These racial-ethnic, gender, and education-based disparities in overall health are manifest in disparities in labor force participation at older ages. While many studies document an association between poor health and retirement (Jason et al., 2017; O'Donnell et al., 2015), the work-nonwork-health interface in later adulthood unfolds over time in complex and unequal ways. Though some types of occupations can reduce activity limitations and improve health—for example, working, as opposed to retirement, delays the onset of cognitive impairment (Carr et al., 2021)—poor health can also constrain opportunities to remain in the labor force. Race and educational disparities in disability pathways, captured in large-scale national surveys that follow older Americans over a period of time (the National Academies, 2018), reveal gender, race, and educational disparities in the timing of exits because of functional limitations (disability), with less-educated Black men in their 50s and early 60s particularly at risk (Moen et al., 2021, 2020; Warner and Brown 2011).

Determining the causal effect of health on retirement is challenging. The first issue is how to measure health. Self-reported health status and work-limiting disability are useful summary measures that are frequently available in survey data. However, these more subjective measures may be subject to justification bias, that is, where people who are out of the labor force characterize their health as poor in order to explain why they are not working (Black et al., 2017). Objective health measures may be subject to reporting error and only imperfectly correlated with work capacity (Baker et al., 2004), and this may vary by occupation or education; using these measures in conjunction with subjective measures may yield clearer results (Bound, 1991). Another major concern is the potential for retirement to affect health (Neuman, 2008). This could create an association between health and retirement that does not reflect the true causal impact of health. Further complicating the relationship between health and retirement timing is the job lock phenomenon, which occurs when an individual continues to work in order to maintain access to health insurance benefits until they reach the age of eligibility for Medicare, regardless of the presence of health conditions (Fisher, Ryan et al., 2016). Individuals in poor health may also retire earlier as a response to their shorter life expectancy.

Using health shocks (unexpected changes in health) to measure the effect of health on retirement may overcome some of these issues by exploiting the arrival of new health information unrelated to the worker's preferences prior to retirement. Concerns about this approach include the potential for error in measuring changes in health (French and Jones, 2017) and the possibility that workers may respond differently to a temporary vs. a permanent change in health (Blundell et al., 2016). Health shocks are associated with an increase in the probability of retiring, retiring earlier than planned, and revising retirement expectations to anticipate an earlier retirement (Munnell, Webb et al., 2018; McGarry, 2004; McClellan, 1998).

Yet while health is a critical determinant of retirement for some individuals, others exit the labor force for reasons unrelated to health and have substantial work capacity at older ages (Coile et al., 2017; Cutler et al., 2013). The role that health disparities play in explaining the large disparities in work at older ages by race, ethnicity, and education has yet to be fully explored. The fact that there are large disparities in health at older ages across groups, and the fact that health is a critical factor in retirement decisions, together suggest that health inequities may be an important reason why some groups tend to retire earlier than others (Brown, 2009), but further work is needed to determine this definitively.

More work is also needed to explore how the opioid crisis is affecting work at older ages. In theory, if used properly, opioids could enable workers to manage pain and remain in the work force, but they could also interfere with the ability to hold down a job if abused. Employment rates have dropped more in counties with higher numbers of opioid prescriptions, though this fact does not establish the direction of causality (Krueger, 2017). Currie and colleagues (2019) find that prescriptions for working-age people—as predicted based on the level of prescriptions to elderly people in the same area—have a small positive effect on employment for women and no effect for men.

Although earlier literature largely focused on physical health, mental health may also affect retirement. Nearly one in five adults in the United States lives with a mental illness, and nearly one in 20 has a serious mental illness (National Institute of Mental Health, 2019). At all ages, adults with mental illness are less likely than others to be in the labor force, and this participation gap increases dramatically with the severity of psychological distress (Frank et al., 2019). In the United States, among those working in late middle age, depression increases the probability of retirement (Doshi et al., 2008); there are similar results in Australia, Denmark, and Finland (Sewdas et al., 2020; Oleson et al., 2012; Harkonmäki et al., 2006). However, the small literature on mental health and retirement has largely left the issue of causality unaddressed (Fisher, Chaffee et al., 2016). The vast majority of studies on mental health and retirement examine how retirement affects mental health, rather than the reverse (Rohwedder and Willis, 2010).

Cognitive health may also affect retirement. Most of the empirical work in this area focuses on estimating how cognition changes with age and how these changes may affect job performance and be mitigated by work arrangements, questions that we take up in Chapter 5. There is a literature examining how retirement affects cognition, which has not yet reached a clear consensus (Mazzonna and Peracchi, 2017; Coe et al., 2012). Fewer studies examine how cognition affects retirement, though one finds that cognitive decline is associated with workers moving to a less demanding job or retiring earlier than expected (Belbase et al., 2015).

In sum, the evidence suggests a strong relationship between poor health and retirement that appears to be causal; however, mental and cognitive health have received less research attention than physical health. Despite portrayals of later adulthood as increasingly a time of vitality and engagement, poor health and disability are key contingencies pushing people out of paid work and even limiting volunteering (Zajacova et al., 2014; McNamara and Gonzales, 2011; Warner and Brown 2011; Brown and Warner, 2008; Choi et al., 2007).

Education

Research using national surveys shows that older college-educated adults are less likely to retire from full-time employment or from the workforce altogether than are those with less education (Moen et al., 2021; Cahill et al., 2006; Reitzes and Mutran, 2004; Han and Moen, 1999). They are also more likely to participate in other ways, such as volunteering for an organization (McNamara and Gonzales, 2011; Choi et al., 2007).

The differences in labor force participation at older ages by education are striking. As noted in Chapter 2, differences by education are larger than those by gender, race-ethnicity, or nativity. These gaps exist at all ages but increase at older ages—for men, the gap between the participation rate of college graduates and that of individuals who have not completed high school reaches 26 percentage points at ages 65–69, while for women the gap peaks at 37 percentage points at ages 55–59. Male college graduates retire on average 3 years later than male high school graduates, at about age 66 vs. age 63 (Rutledge, 2018). This gap has widened over time, though interpreting this trend is complicated by changes over time in the share of the population in each education group (Bound et al., 2014).

Several hypotheses have been suggested to explain this pattern. The first is the wage premium for college graduates, which is substantial and has grown over time (Binder and Bound, 2019). Economic theory suggests that a higher wage could lead workers to choose less leisure time because of its higher cost (substitution effect) or more leisure time due to their increased resources (income effect). Later retirement among those with higher education could arise if the former effect is dominant. A second hypothesis relates to health. Given the strong association between education and health (Cutler and Lleras-Muney, 2008) and the effect of health on retirement, earlier retirement among the less educated could be due to their poorer health. A third theory concerns occupation. Occupations requiring a high school degree or less have higher physical demands and lower cognitive demands than do occupations requiring a bachelor's degree, and physical abilities decline more rapidly with age than do cognitive abilities (Lopez et al., 2019). Workers with lower levels of education might be less able to remain in their career job as they age or have fewer potential occupations for which their skills meet the job demands. Moreover, changes in technology and economic shifts to jobs that are less dependent on manual and routine skills and favor those with cognitive and analytic skills (Autor et al., 2003) have allowed more older adults to remain in the labor force despite health, but the higher-skill demands of these jobs prevent less educated workers from benefiting from these changes.

Levels of education in the older population have risen in recent decades. As discussed in Chapter 2, the share of the population ages 50 and above with a college degree rose from 34 to 39 percent between 2004 and 2019; however, the rate of increase is now slowing, as the cohorts that experienced the most rapid gains in educational attainment have already reached age 50. While trends for men and women are similar (Coile, 2019), recent increases in education have been larger for Black men, leading to a substantial narrowing of the Black-White gap in the share of men ages 45 to 54 with a college degree (Coile and Duggan, 2019). Yet the share of Black and Hispanic adults age 25 and above with a college degree remains far lower than the equivalent share of White adults, despite large increases in college attendance in recent decades for Black and Hispanic youth (U.S. Department of Education, 2019).

Combining the known differences in labor force participation by age with the increase in education levels over the past several decades suggests that rising education could help to explain the trend of higher labor force participation at older ages (Burtless, 2013). An important caveat, however, is that the level of education was also increasing during the earlier period when labor force participation rates were declining. This points to the difficulty of definitively establishing the role of education in labor force trends from this type of analysis (Coile, 2019).

Indeed, ascertaining the causal effect of education on retirement and the mechanisms responsible for this effect is inherently difficult. An individual's level of education may be influenced by any number of factors—family background, race and ethnicity, willingness to trade between present costs and future benefits, and so on—that may continue to have a direct effect on labor force participation throughout the life course and at older ages, making it difficult to draw conclusions from an observational study. Future work in this area might fruitfully make use of exogenous variation in education, for example variation due to changes in compulsory schooling laws, which previously had been used to study the effect of education on health (Lleras-Muney, 2005). Research is also needed into the mechanisms underlying the strong relationship between education and work at older ages, which might include the cumulative effects of education on health, occupation, earnings, and wealth throughout the life course.

Financial Literacy

Financial literacy is another individual resource that is potentially important for retirement decision-making. Financial literacy refers to "peoples' ability to process economic information and make informed decisions about financial planning, wealth accumulation, debt, and pensions" (Lusardi and Mitchell, 2014, p. 6).

Financial literacy is increasingly important for retirement security, given the ongoing shift in employer-sponsored pensions from defined-benefit (DB) to defined-contribution (DC) plans. Among the roughly two-thirds of households ages 51 to 56 with a retirement plan, the share with a DC plan (only) more than doubled from 1992 to 2010, from 20 to 43 percent (Munnell et al., 2017). In such a plan, the employee typically must decide whether to participate, how much to contribute, how to allocate the portfolio across investment options, whether to annuitize, and how quickly to spend down any non-annuitized assets during retirement. The responsibility of managing investment, inflation, and longevity risks and of ensuring an adequate replacement rate is shifted from employer to employee (Broadbent et al., 2006).

The standard measure of financial literacy, developed by Lusardi and Mitchell (2008), consists of three questions designed to assess numeracy and ability to make interest rate calculations, understanding of inflation, and understanding of risk diversification. Financial literacy peaks in midlife and declines at older ages (Finke et al., 2017), an effect that may primarily reflect the effect of declining cognitive abilities (Lusardi et al., 2014). Only one-third of older individuals answer all three questions correctly (Lusardi and Mitchell, 2011).

Within the population age 50 and above, rates of financial literacy vary systematically across groups. Older women have lower levels of financial literacy than do older men (Lusardi and Mitchell, 2008). Black and Hispanic individuals provide fewer correct answers to literacy questions than do their White counterparts (Clark et al., 2021). Individuals with less education also score lower than those with more education. The magnitude of the gaps across gender, race, and education groups is fairly similar, ranging from one-quarter to one-half of a standard deviation in an index of questions answered correctly (Lusardi et al., 2014).

Financial literacy at younger ages is also important for retirement security, because financial well-being in retirement depends on financial decisions made throughout one's lifetime (Morrow-Howell and Sherraden, 2015). As with the older population, financial literacy among the young is low, with only about one-quarter of young adults answering all three standard questions correctly (Lusardi et al., 2010). Literacy in this age group is strongly related to sociodemographic characteristics, with lower rates of literacy among women, Black and Hispanic individuals, and those with less education or lower cognitive ability. Family background also plays a key role, as those whose parents have had more education or own stocks or retirement savings accounts have higher rates of financial literacy.

Financial literacy may play a role in retirement decisions by enabling planning and thus allowing workers to retire earlier (and/or with higher retirement resources) relative to those who do not plan. Individuals with higher levels of financial literacy are more likely to plan for retirement and to stick with the plan (Lusardi and Mitchell, 2011), though it is not clear if this association is causal. Recent evidence from a number of randomized controlled trials suggests that financial education can improve financial literacy and affect financial behaviors (Kaiser et al., 2020); however, as of yet, this literature does not examine its effects on retirement. The design of financial education may be important for reaching vulnerable subgroups (Olsen and Whitman, 2007). In an interesting counterpoint, some analysts suggest that the savings behaviors that could be affected by financial literacy—saving more, from an earlier age, and in lower-fee investments—have modest effects on retirement resources as compared to the gains available from working longer (Bronshtein et al., 2019).

Financial literacy is important to save for retirement but likely insufficient (Birkenmaier et al., 2016; Sherraden et al., 2015; Morrow-Howell and Sherraden, 2014; Johnson and Sherraden, 2007). Individuals also need access to financial institutions, such as banks and credit unions, financial products and services, such as savings and checking accounts, and policies that protect the consumer (Birkenmaier et al., 2016). Women, racial and ethnic minorities, and individuals with low levels of education are at greater risk of financial fragility and lack access to products to save (see discussion below on pensions, wealth and income and Chapter 7).

Successful interventions, in particular Individual Development Accounts (IDAs), suggest that low-income adults can and do save with financial literacy trainings and access to saving products (Sherraden, 1991). An IDA is a type of savings account designed to help low-income individuals build assets and achieve financial stability and long-term self-sufficiency (Kagan, 2021). They have helped low-income adults reduce debt, purchase homes, and attend college, although the effects are small to moderate and are uneven across race, ethnicity, and gender (Huang et al., 2017; Grinstein-Weiss et al., 2013, 2008; Mills et al., 2006). There is limited evidence of its effects on saving for retirement (Grinstein-Weiss et al., 2015), suggesting a need for additional research in this area.

Employer-Sponsored Pensions

Employer-sponsored pensions before the 1990s were mainly DB systems. Under such systems, employers bear the investment risks, and the pension benefits are based on a defined formula that accounts for age, earnings history, and length of service. In recent decades, DC systems have become more common than DB systems. In DC plans, employees bear the investment risks and decide how much to contribute and how to invest the contributions. Examples of DC schemes include 401(k) and 403(b) plans, to which employers may also make contributions (Gustman et al., 2010). Defined contribution plans are increasingly common for both public and private sector workers, though many public sector workers still have defined benefit plans. From 1980 to 2007, the share of private sector workers covered by defined benefit plans decreased from 39 percent to 20 percent, while the share covered by DC plans increased from seven percent to 31 percent (Cushing-Daniels and Johnson, 2008). Among private sector workers, 51 percent participate in employer-sponsored pension plans; among public sector workers, nearly 100 percent do so (Cushing-Daniels and Johnson, 2008).

A higher proportion of older workers are enrolled in employer-sponsored pensions, which is explained by the different types of work that older and younger workers do and the changes over time in the willingness of employers to offer pension plans to new employees. Similar proportions of men and women participate in employer-sponsored pensions, though the earnings gap between men and women means women have lower pensions in retirement (Butrica and Johnson, 2010).

There are large differences by race in the proportions of workers covered by employer-sponsored pensions. Employer-sponsored plans cover 64.6 percent of non-Hispanic White workers, 55.7 percent of Black workers, and 38.4 percent of Hispanic workers. These differences are explained by differences in firm size, proportion of employees in full-time and part-time jobs, and occupational segregation. Non-Hispanic White people are more likely than Black and Hispanic people to be employed in firms with more than 1,000 employees, which in turn are more likely to offer these pensions. Black people are more likely to be employed in the public sector, where participation in pension plans is nearly universal. Hispanic people are more likely than non-Hispanic White people and Black people to be employed in firms with less than 100 employees and to work part-time, which are both settings that are less likely to offer employer benefits such as pension plans. Hispanic people are also more likely to work in occupations, such as service, farming, fishing, forestry, and construction jobs, in which employers are less likely to provide pensions. Both Black and Hispanic people are more likely to work in low-paying jobs that do not offer employer-sponsored pensions (Butrica and Johnson, 2010). Wage gaps between non-Hispanic White workers and Black and Hispanic workers translate to lower pension benefits for Black and Hispanic people in retirement. Smith et al., (2004) also found that Black and Hispanic workers enrolled in employer-sponsored pension plans contribute a lower proportion of their income than non-Hispanic White workers, which may lead to lower pension benefits for them in previously defined DC schemes.

DC plans require participants (rather than financial experts) to decide how much to contribute and how to invest the contributions in stocks, bonds, or other financial instruments. Butrica and Johnson (2010) found that 59 percent of Hispanic people, 43 percent of Black people, and 26 percent of non-Hispanic White people did not take financial risks. This may be a result of minorities having lower levels of financial literacy or individual preferences to maintain limited wealth, as the willingness to invest in riskier assets may increase with wealth (Bajtelsmit and Bernasek, 2001). Being averse to investments may make Black and Hispanic people less likely to enroll in employer-sponsored pensions, particularly DC programs, when they have the opportunity to do so (Butrica and Johnson, 2010).

There are differences in risk-taking by gender as well. Women are less willing to take financial risks and tend to hold less risky assets than men (Butrica and Johnson, 2010), which leads to lower asset accumulation on average but also reduces the risk of a very poor outcome (Barber and Odean, 2001). A higher proportion of men than women are overconfident investors in the financial market, with higher levels of stock trading, while women are more likely to "buy and hold," which can be a better long-term strategy for investing in the financial market (Barber and Odean, 2001). These differences in behavior could also be due to differences in financial literacy (discussed above).

Social Security

Earnings history is one of the primary determinants of Social Security[1] benefits (U.S. Social Security Administration, 2019b). Social Security has a moderate redistributional effect, because its benefits are distributed more equally than preretirement income (Crystal et al., 2017). Nevertheless, Social Security benefits for workers in the top income quintile have been more than twice as great as those for workers in the lowest quintile (Crystal et al., 2017), due in part to large education-based inequality in preretirement income and in work opportunities available to those approaching retirement age. This is troublesome because lower-income older adults are more reliant on Social Security for their income. Among older adults in the highest income quintile, Social Security benefits comprise less than one-fifth of their income, while among those in the lowest quintile these benefits provide most of their income (Crystal et al., 2017).

Recent cohorts of older adults have faced greater inequality in preretirement income as a result of declining job opportunities and work benefits for the least-educated, as well as the shift from DB to DC pensions (Crystal et al., 2017). Increasing income inequality has particularly affected low- and mid-skilled workers, who find decreasing demand for their labor (e.g., Autor et al., 2008; Blau and Kahn, 1994). Both low-skilled and mid-skilled workers

---

[1]This section focuses on research on the U.S. Social Security program. Social Security programs in other countries often have different eligibility requirements and therefore likely have different effects on retirement and work.

TABLE 4-1 Average Social Security Wealth at Age 51–56 by Quintile of Wealth Within Race/Ethnicity, 2016 Dollars

	White	Black	Hispanic
Bottom quintile	88,800	30,900	44,400
2nd quintile	165,000	92,000	104,700
Middle quintile	200,900	148,400	151,000
4th quintile	222,700	169,900	179,000
Top quintile	262,800	191,100	196,800

SOURCE: Data from Hou and Sanzenbacher, 2020.

may perform tasks that can be easily automated, which forces their early involuntary withdrawal from the labor force (Acemoglu, 1999; Katz and Murphy, 1992). Displacement by automation of mid-skilled jobs has particularly affected Hispanic and Black workers (Lund et al., 2019). The decline of mid-skilled occupations has reduced options for workers with no more than a high school education. This, in turn, has led to lower life-time earnings and, therefore, lower Social Security benefits for such workers.

Due to large disparities in mortality by SES, lower-income individuals also experience shorter life expectancy than higher-income ones (e.g., Deaton and Paxson, 2001; Attanasio and Hoynes, 2000). As a result, such individuals receive Social Security benefits for a shorter period of time than higher-income individuals (Smith et al., 2003). With the growing gap in life expectancy by lifetime income (Chetty et al., 2016), higher-income individuals are increasingly receiving more in Social Security benefits over their lifetimes (the National Academies, 2015).

Social Security income and wealth[2] have differed by race and ethnicity. Black and Hispanic people historically have had lower average earnings than non-Hispanic White people, and hence they have received lower Social Security benefits. The redistributive component of Social Security has meant that, in 2016, the average Social Security replacement rate (that is, the portion of previous annual wages that Social Security replaced) was 45 percent for Black and Hispanic people and 36 percent for non-Hispanic White people (Munnell, Hou et al., 2018). Still, in 2016 among persons 51 to 56 years of age, average Social Security wealth of non-Hispanic White households was higher at all levels of wealth (Table 4-1) (Hou and Sanzenbacher, 2020).

Black, Hispanic, and women workers close to retirement age have had higher odds of experiencing involuntary job separation and subsequent withdrawal from the labor force and are more likely to have discontinuous work histories, as well as to be in poor health, leading to involuntary job loss in the years prior to retirement (Flippen, 2005; Flippen and Tienda, 2000). This history of job loss, in turn, can lead to lower lifetime earnings and fewer qualifying years of employment, resulting in lower levels of Social Security benefits, and in some cases, a failure to qualify for benefits. Time spent out of the labor force or with low earnings directly reduces the value of and eligibility for Social Security benefits, because these benefits are based on an individual's highest 35 years of earnings and require individuals to contribute to the program for a minimum of about 10 years to qualify (Hendley and Bilimoria, 1999).

Among Hispanic workers, the foreign-born have lower levels of Social Security benefits, often because they have more truncated labor histories (Johnson et al., 2013). Some immigrants return to their country of origin before achieving Social Security eligibility, or even acquiring an authorized Social Security number, and hence do not collect Social Security benefits (Aguila and Vega, 2017). Most immigrants returning to their country of origin who qualify for Social Security benefits in the United States cannot expect to receive these benefits unless their country of origin has a totalization agreement with the United States that makes Social Security contributions portable between countries (Aguila and Zissimopoulos, 2013). Among male Mexican workers who migrated to the United States and later returned to Mexico, 32.0 percent reported making U.S. Social Security contributions; however, only 5.1 percent received or expected to receive U.S. Social Security benefits in the future (Aguila and Vega, 2017).

---

[2] Social Security wealth is defined as the present-day value of the stream of future benefits the household can expect to receive over time.

Changes in family structure in recent decades have also affected Social Security eligibility. There have been large gaps in retirement wealth between single older adults and older married couples, with single females having particularly low levels of retirement wealth (Wolff, 2003). Since eligibility for spousal or widowhood Social Security benefits requires the spouse or widow to have been married to their qualifying partner for a minimum of 10 years, the proportion of women eligible to claim spouse or widowhood Social Security benefits has declined as the proportion of middle-aged and older women who are never married, divorced, or married for less than 10 years has decreased (Tamborini et al., 2009).

Wealth and Income

Income inequality has increased for several decades, leading to a "hollowing out" of the income distribution within the United States. Between the early 1970s and the late 2010s, the proportion of households considered to be "middle-income" has decreased while the proportions considered to be "lower" and "higher" income both increased (Table 4-2). Here, middle-income households are defined as those having annual household incomes that are between two-thirds of and double that (about 67 to 200 percent) of the national median. Lower-income households have household incomes below the lower-bound of the middle-income household income range, while higher-income households have incomes above the upper bound of that range. Additionally, average household income grew more among higher-income households than among others in this time (Horowitz et al., 2020).

The income gap between men and women has decreased since the 1970s, but income inequality by education and work experience has increased (Blau and Kahn, 1994). For non-Hispanic White, Black, and Hispanic people the median income increased for those at the 10th, 50th, and 90th percentiles between 1970 and 2016 (Table 4-3). At the same time, income differences between White workers, on the one hand, as well as Black and Hispanic workers, on the other, have persisted (Kochhnar and Cilluffo, 2018).

Much of the income gap among racial and ethnic groups and between men and women is due to the higher proportions of Black, Hispanic, and women workers who work in low-paying jobs that offer few benefits, in part because they are also more likely to have lower levels of educational attainment (Tali et al., 2018). These differences cumulate over the life course and contribute to considerable differences in wealth across race and ethnic groups. In 2016, the median net wealth of non-Hispanic White households was 7.2 times higher than that of Black households and 5.4 times that of Hispanic households (Munnell, Hou et al., 2018).

Inequality in wealth—the value of housing, savings, and other assets minus debt and an indicator of household financial security—has grown even faster than income inequality in recent decades. Though wealth grew for households at all income levels between 1983 and 2001, it decreased for low- and middle-income households between 2001 and 2016 (Table 4-2), despite continuing to increase for high-income ones. This decline occurred because wealth for low- and middle-income households is concentrated in housing value, which decreased as a result of the "Great Recession." In contrast, higher-income households possess a more diversified portfolio of wealth that is less concentrated on real estate value and, therefore, were able to recover faster (Horowitz et al., 2020). Moreover, many social safety net programs in which low-income individuals or families are enrolled provide

TABLE 4-2 Income and Wealth Changes by Income Level

		Lower-income	Middle-income	Higher-income
Percent of all households	1971	25	61	14
	2019	29	51	20
Percent growth in average income	1970–2018	43	49	64
Percent change in median wealth	1983–2001	67	42	85
	2001–2016	−45	−20	33

SOURCE: Data from Horowitz et al., 2020.

TABLE 4-3 Changes in Median Income by Race and Ethnic Origin and Income Percentile, 1970 to 2016

Percent growth in income	White	Black	Hispanic
10th percentile	45	67	37
50th percentile	52	66	36
90th percentile	80	79	58

Income as a percent of that for Whites at comparable percentile*			
1970	White	Black	Hispanic
10th percentile	100	47	69
50th percentile	100	59	71
90th percentile	100	68	74
2016	White	Black	Hispanic
10th percentile	100	54	66
50th percentile	100	65	63
90th percentile	100	68	65

*Table indicates, for example, that, in 2016, Blacks at the 90th income percentile for all Blacks received 68 percent of the income that Whites at the 90th percentile for all Whites received.
SOURCE: Data from Kochhar and Cilluffo, 2018.

a disincentive for retirement savings or wealth accumulation: the main safety net programs make ineligible individuals with assets above a given threshold, reducing incentives for low-income earners to save or accumulate above that level (Yoong et al., 2019).

Within the United States there are large disparities in wealth accumulation by race, ethnicity, and gender. Longitudinal analyses from the Health and Retirement Study (1992–2010; Brown, 2016) revealed wealth accumulation patterns among non-Hispanic White people that were consistent with the life cycle hypothesis of Modigliani (1975), which proposes that individuals smooth their consumption over the life course, borrowing during periods in which income is lower and saving when income is higher. Non-Hispanic White people increased their savings at a higher rate during the period approaching retirement, when lifetime income trajectories peak, and then began to spend down their wealth in retirement; however, this theoretical perspective was not empirically supported by the wealth accumulation behaviors of racial and ethnic minorities. Among Mexican Americans, wealth accumulation peaked earlier, around age 60—several years before retirement—before beginning to decline, while non-Hispanic Black people experienced little change in wealth throughout the life course.

These racial-ethnic disparities in wealth may be better explained by the cumulative impact of economic (dis) advantages experienced throughout the life course by racial-ethnic minorities due to the effects of systemic discrimination and resource hoarding by racial-ethnic majorities (Rothstein, 2017). Non-Hispanic White women and women of color have had similar disparities in wealth accumulation compared to men (Brown, 2012).

These disparities in income and wealth are important for understanding financial security in old age, because financial security is highly correlated to income and wealth during working life. It is more tenuous for workers without access to employer-sponsored pensions, savings in the financial sector, or other sources of retirement income. Munnell, Hou, and colleagues (2018) found that, among U.S. households headed by persons 30–59 years of age, the proportion "at risk" for financial insecurity in old age increased from 44 percent in 2007 to 50 percent in 2016.

Hispanic and Black workers in 2016 were more at risk for financial insecurity in old age than non-Hispanic White workers (Table 4-4); in part, because Hispanic and Black people are less likely to participate in an employer's retirement plan (Butrica and Johnson, 2010) and more likely to lack bank accounts (Blanco et al., 2018). Most of the difference in unbanked rates between non-Hispanic White, non-Hispanic Black, and Hispanic workers are accounted for by lower individual and neighborhood SES (non-Hispanic Black workers) and language barriers (Hispanic workers; Blanco et al., 2018). The effect of these differences on financial security at older ages is compounded by the other disparities noted above, namely, Black and Hispanic people receiving lower

TABLE 4-4 Indicators of Possible Financial Insecurity in Old Age

	Whites	Blacks	Hispanics
Percent of households with head 30–59 "at risk" for financial insecurity in old age	48	54	61
Percent of workers participating in employer retirement plan	54	46	34
Percent of households "unbanked" (lacking bank accounts)	4	21	20

SOURCES: Data from Munnell, Hou et al., 2018; Federal Deposit Insurance Corporation, 2016.

lifetime Social Security benefits (Yoong et al., 2019), being less likely to invest in high-risk and high yield assets (e.g., stocks), and being more likely to invest in real estate than non-Hispanic White people, who have more diversified investment portfolios (Yoong et al., 2019).

Yoong et al. (2019) found that non-Hispanic White workers have Social Security wealth 40 percent higher than that of Black and Hispanic workers. They also found that Black and Hispanic people were less likely to invest in high-risk and high-yield assets (e.g., stocks) and more likely to invest in housing or other real estate than non-Hispanic White people who have more diversified investment portfolios.

Rising Debt

Debt is rising among older adults and some evidence suggests it is an important contributor to working longer (Butrica and Karamcheva, 2018, 2013; Mann, 2011; Belkar et al., 2007; Lahey et al., 2006). In 1989, approximately 38 percent of adults ages 65+ had debt, and this figure increased to 61 percent in 2016 (Congressional Research Service, 2019). At the same time, the real average debt increased from $29,916 to $86,767 among this age group. Pre-retirees (those ages 55+) similarly experienced an increase in the percentage of adults with debt, though more recently, their average debt load has declined. The percentage of adults ages 55+ who had debt increased from approximately half (54%) to 68 percent between 1992 and 2016 (Copeland, 2018). However, between 2010 and 2016, the average size of their debt decreased from $82,968 to $76,679. This debt is largely from mortgage-related debt and an increase in student loan debt (Congressional Research Service, 2019; Zinshteyn, 2019; Copeland, 2018).

Longitudinal analyses from the Survey of Consumer Finances[3] (1989–2016) reveal that indebted older adults are more likely to work, less likely to be retired, and, on average, expect to work longer than those with less debt (Butrica and Karamcheva, 2019). These findings are similar to analyses of the Health and Retirement Study (1992–2008),[4] which found that those with higher debt in later life were more likely to remain attached to the labor force (Mann, 2011). Among older women, mortgage debt was positively associated with a higher propensity to be currently working and they also had a higher expectation that they would be working at age 65 (Lusardi and Mitchell, 2016). Debt appears to be a more important predictor of remaining in the labor force for women and women with young children, than it is for men (Belkar et al., 2007). While Black and Hispanic workers ages 75+ had higher levels of debt overall compared to White workers, there is little evidence that this disparity leads to racial-ethnic differences in the association between labor force attachment and debt (Mann, 2011). The relatively small literature on debt and labor force participation generally uses race and ethnicity as a covariate rather than a predictor of interest. Research that examines cohort differences, race and ethnicity, gender, education, and type of debt is warranted.

---

[3]The Survey of Consumer Finances is a triennial cross-sectional survey of U.S. families sponsored by the Federal Reserve Board in cooperation with the Department of the Treasury. It includes information about families' balance sheets, pensions, income, and demographic characteristics. Though the survey is cross-sectional, there were two periods during which longitudinal data were collected. The 1983 panel of respondents were reinterviewed in 1986 and 1989, while the 2007 panel was reinterviewed in 2009.

[4]The Health and Retirement Survey is a longitudinal survey of older adults (ages 51 and over) conducted biennially since 1992 by the University of Michigan.

Health Insurance

Health insurance plays a uniquely important role in retirement decisions in the United States, because there is a strong link between health insurance coverage and employment. About six in 10 adults ages 19[5] through 64 receive health insurance through their own or a family member's employer (Kaiser Family Foundation, 2020). Medicare provides near-universal health insurance coverage starting at age 65. Individuals who retire prior to age 65 may be eligible for retiree health insurance through their former employer, although such coverage has become less common over time (Fronstin and Adams, 2012). Workers retiring before age 65 who lack retiree health insurance or access to insurance through an employed spouse may purchase private insurance on the individual (or nongroup) market. However, this market was subject to high premiums due to adverse selection—the tendency of high-risk (less healthy) buyers to be overrepresented in the market—prior to the passage of the Affordable Care Act (ACA) (Hackmann et al., 2015). Medicare and the ACA are discussed in more detail in Chapter 8.

The existing literature consistently finds that access to health insurance is a key driver of retirement decisions. Numerous studies indicate that having retiree health insurance through an employer raises the probability of retirement by 30 to 80 percent, reducing the average age of retirement by six to 24 months (Gruber and Madrian, 2004). These findings have been confirmed in more recent studies on both private and public sector workers (Shoven and Slavov, 2014; Fitzpatrick, 2013; Nyce et al., 2013; Boyle and Lahey, 2010). Some may work in order to provide health insurance for a spouse, as men are more likely to retire when their wives turn 65 and gain access to Medicare (Madrian and Beaulieu, 1998); however, younger spouses are also more likely to become uninsured when an older spouse turns 65 (Witman, 2015) and wives of male veterans increase their labor supply—potentially to qualify for employer-sponsored insurance—after an expansion of eligibility for veterans' health insurance because they are ineligible for veterans' coverage (Boyle and Lahey, 2016). A number of studies explore the effect of health insurance on retirement as part of a broader model in which consumers make retirement and savings decisions based on their future medical expenditure risk; their estimates of the role of health insurance are largely consistent with the rest of the literature (French and Jones, 2017).

MEANING OF WORK, SATISFACTION OF WORK, AND SENSE OF PURPOSE

Up to this point, this chapter has focused on economic reasons for engaging in work at older ages. However, adults engage in work for a wide range of noneconomic reasons as well (Maestas, 2010; Walajtys, 2007; Singh and Verma, 2003; Choi, 2000; Hayward et al., 1994). The meaning of work subtly shifts as one ages (Smyer and Pitt-Catsouphes, 2007). Some argue that there is a national movement toward finding a sense of purpose and contribution to society through paid or volunteer work in later life (Freedman, 2007). Older adults are motivated to work for a number of different psychological and social factors, such as to remain productive ("to feel useful," "to give myself something to do," "to be with other people;" Rosentiel, 2009; Walajtys, 2007), to contribute to society through their work (Montenegro et al., 2002), and dissatisfaction with retirement (Walajtys, 2007). Forced retirement (either due to downsizing or a "golden handshake") is positively associated with reentering the workforce in later life (Walajtys, 2007). For some older women, returning to work is a way to gain independence from men or to achieve lost dreams and resolve regrets generated by their inability to participate in the workforce during their years of family child-rearing responsibility (Altschuler, 2004).

This points to the importance of investigating how life course processes of accumulating advantage and disadvantage (Dannefer, 2020; O'Rand, 1996) shape and constrain the universe of choices for both work and retirement that are available to individuals in later adulthood. This includes factors that shape retirement timing and the availability of possible alternatives to retirement, such as reduced work hours or greater schedule flexibility. People coming to the conventional retirement ages with higher levels of education, those in professional jobs, and those following "orderly" career paths (Wilensky, 1961) are better positioned to follow their goals and motivations. Unfortunately, those who are unable or choose not to remain continuously in the workforce or in full-time employment in relatively secure jobs confront more limited options. Those facing enduring disadvantages throughout the

---

[5]Health insurance coverage rates for adults generally exclude 18-year-olds because eligibility for children's coverage through Medicaid and state health insurance programs extends to those under age 19.

life course—women, minorities, immigrants, those with less education—have less control or choice over transitions into or out of the workforce or between jobs (Choi et al., 2016; Zajacova et al., 2014; Warner and Brown, 2011; Brown and Warner, 2008; Willson, 2003; Choi, 2000). Thus, pathways to work that provide meaning and purpose are also constrained for less advantaged workers at older ages.

FAMILY AND HOUSEHOLD STRUCTURE

Family roles and responsibilities, as well as evolving household structures, shape work and retirement trajectories at older ages. This section reviews how unpaid work in the form of informal caregiving constrains opportunities for, and choices to, engage in paid work in later adulthood, particularly for women, racial and ethnic minorities, and individuals with limited education. We then describe and analyze complex processes of joint retirement decisions. We end this section by reviewing how family and household structures have evolved significantly over time, shifting from marriage as a normative and universal practice in the 20th century to the current diversity of family types in the 21st century, and discussing the implications of these changes for work and retirement research.

Informal Caregiving

According to a recent survey of caregivers in the United States conducted by AARP (2020), approximately 53 million adults in the United States provide unpaid care for others, and six out of 10 of these caregivers are also employed. Over a third (35%) of caregivers are ages 50–64 AARP (2020); however, this study did not separately examine the experiences of these older caregivers. Informal caregivers assist others with activities of daily living and are not paid for providing their assistance. Informal caregiving is highly gendered; the majority of informal caregivers, regardless of age, are women. These caregivers are most likely to assist one recipient (often a relative), though approximately 18 percent provide care to multiple recipients.

Informal caregivers who also are employed are engaged in a variety of employment contexts (AARP, 2020). Slightly over half (54%) are paid hourly in their main job, while nearly four out of 10 report being salaried. A smaller percentage report that they are self-employed or own their own business. Men who provide care are more likely than women to be salaried. White, Black, and Hispanic informal caregivers are more often employed in hourly paid jobs, while Asian American informal care providers are more likely to be salaried. Long-distance caregivers, caregivers to a spouse, and high or medium-intensity care providers are more likely to indicate that their supervisor is aware of their caregiving responsibilities. Among individuals who are not self-employed, approximately half of informal caregivers reported their employer offers paid sick days (58%), flexible work hours (56%), and unpaid family leave (53%), while only a quarter reported programs to help with caregiving responsibilities (26%; information, referral, employee assistance programs) or telecommuting (25%). In 2020, White caregivers report more paid family leave, while Black caregivers are more likely to have paid sick days. Since 2015, more employers have provided paid sick days and paid family leave, possibly in response to the growing attention to caregiving in the United States (AARP, 2020).

Although there is great diversity of informal care work and paid work arrangements, longitudinal studies in both the United States and abroad suggest that informal older caregivers are more likely to reduce their hours at work, be forced into retirement, retire earlier, and they are less likely to return to work after retirement (Fahle and McGarry, 2018; Gonzales et al., 2017; Szinovacz and Davey, 2005; Dentinger and Clarkberg, 2002; Pavalko and Artis, 1997). When compared to older men, older women were more likely to permanently leave the labor market, more likely to be working part-time due to informal care, and more likely to take time off of work each week due to the demands of care, while controlling for occupations and industries that are gendered, job tenure, and union membership (Smith et al., 2020). As the intensity of providing care increases, the odds of returning to work decrease (Gonzales et al., 2017). Taken together, these findings suggest that the roles of "worker" and "caregiver" are not complementary, but compete with each, forcing many caregivers to leave the labor force (Fabius et al., 2020; Smith et al., 2020; Kamakura, 2009; Southerton and Tomlinson, 2005; Moen et al., 1995).

Contrary to the studies above, there is a small body of research suggesting that informal care is associated with delaying retirement or going back to work after retirement. Caregiving is costly. Informal caregivers spend approximately $7,000 per year on out-of-pocket expenses related to care (Rainville et al., 2016). These out-of-pocket expenses are felt more acutely among low-income families, Hispanic people, long-distance caregivers, those caring for an adult who is age 50 or over, and when the care recipient has dementia. Because older Black caregivers are more likely than older White caregivers to provide care in excess of 40 hours per week, care for an older adult with dementia, and live below the federal poverty limit (Fabius et al., 2020), these costs would have a disproportionate impact on them. A cross-sectional study found that among caregivers considered to have "high financial strain," 24 percent had put off retirement or decided to never retire, compared to only 12 percent and four percent with moderate or low financial strain, respectively (AARP, 2020). Similarly, qualitative research on grandparents who gain full custody of their grandchildren finds that these grandparents often report that they returned to work and/or delayed retirement as a result of these custody arrangements (Gonzales et al., 2019; Hayslip, et al., 2009).

Nearly one in 10 caregivers (of all ages) identifies as lesbian, gay, bisexual, or transgender (AARP, 2017); sexual and gender minorities are more likely to become caregivers than the general population, are more likely to be caring for another individual who identifies as a sexual or gender minority, are less likely to have support from their biological family members, report higher levels of workplace discrimination due to caregiving, and also encounter fewer culturally competent support services (AARP, 2020, 2017; Meyer et al., 2018; Knauer, 2016).

In sum, informal caregiving is associated with earlier retirement and a lower probability of returning to the labor force after retirement. However, a small body of literature suggests that the costs of providing such care may also lead some caregivers to extend employment at older ages. More research is needed to fully understand the heterogeneity of caregiving experiences among older informal caregivers, the ways in which caregiving contexts shape and constrain work opportunities and the quality of work available to caregivers, and work characteristics that enable or constrain caregivers' ability to engage in both informal caregiving and paid employment. Intervention studies examining the effects of flexible work arrangements as well as state and federal policies and practices on paid employment among caregivers are also warranted.

Joint Retirement

Among two-earner couples, the retirement behavior of each partner may influence that of the other. Nearly one-third of couples retire jointly, or within 12 months of each other (Ho and Raymo, 2009). There are several reasons why this could occur. First, a couple may face a shared financial situation, so the need to work longer (or ability to retire early) will be common to both members. Second, assortative mating may occur. The tendency of people with similar levels of education to marry each other is well documented (Domingue et al., 2014), and the similarities between partners could extend to characteristics like retirement preferences. Finally, complementarity of leisure—the notion that leisure time is more valuable when spent with one's spouse—may be important.

Two types of studies have examined couples' retirement behavior. The first estimates structural models of retirement in which each partner is an independent decision maker facing shared finances (see Casanova, 2010, for a review). Several of these studies conclude that complementarity of leisure is critically important in explaining joint retirement (Gustman and Steinmeier, 2004; Maestas, 2001). A second set of studies examines whether public and private pension provisions affecting one spouse have spillover effects onto the retirement decision of the other spouse, indicating that one partner's retirement behavior influences the other's. Studies in both the United States and the United Kingdom find evidence of such spillover effects and attribute them primarily to complementarity of leisure (Banks et al., 2007; Coile, 2004).

In sum, there is some tendency for both members of married/partnered couples to retire together. This could arise for several reasons in an economic model: (1) assortative mating; (2) shared household budget constraints; (3) complementarity of leisure. Previous work has established the importance of the last factor. Changing marriage/divorce patterns can affect work at older ages.

Household Structure

Marriage was a normative and nearly universal experience of U.S. adults in the 20th century (Carr, 2020). Household structure has become far more diverse in the 21st century due to a combination of extended longevity;

disparities in longevity along the lines of gender, race, and ethnicity; and changes in personal and structural constraints. Older women, Black workers, Hispanic workers, and individuals of lower SES are less likely engage in marriage or remained married in later life. Older women are more likely to be single than older men, partly because wives tend to outlive their husbands and are less likely to remarry in later life (U.S. Census Bureau, 2015; England and McClintock, 2009). White people are more likely to be married than Black people, partly due to the destabilizing effects of systemic racism such as the War on Drugs, mass incarceration, and reverberating effects of the Great Recession (Carr, 2020; Hayslip et al., 2019). Women of color are more likely to live alone. Being single, whether through divorce, never marrying, or becoming widowed, means an individual cannot pool resources to cover costs with a spouse or partner, and may not benefit from social insurance programs that privilege marriage (such as Social Security). Living alone in mid- and later-life increases the likelihood of experiencing acute financial strain to cover basic costs of living such as rent/mortgage, student loans, credit card debt, food, medicine, and transportation.

Household structures thus may influence the timing of retirement. In the United States, single women (never married, widowed, divorced) reported lower levels of retirement confidence when compared to married women (Copeland, 2020). In addition to working longer for financial reasons, single workers may lack meaningful relationships at home and derive greater benefit from the social connections with work colleagues (Smeaton and McKay, 2003). A cross-sectional study from the Netherlands examined retirement preferences between single and married workers (Eismann et al., 2019). They classified spouses into three categories: "pulling" (spouses who prefer the worker to retire), "neutral" (spouses who did not have a preference for the worker's retirement age) or "pushing" (spouses who wanted the worker to remain in the labor force). Results indicate that single workers preferred to work longer when compared to workers with a "pulling" spouse but preferred earlier retirement when compared to workers with "pushing" spouses. There was no statistical difference between single workers and workers with a neutral spouse. Research is needed to understand the push and pull factors to work and retirement by household structure given this emerging diversity by gender, race, ethnicity, and SES in the 21st century.

SOCIAL CAPITAL

Acquiring, maintaining, and advancing one's career is a social process (Smith, 2017; Granovetter, 1995, 1973). Yet research establishing the mechanisms through which social networks, and social capital embedded within them, play a significant role for acquiring employment is mixed (Gayen et al., 2019; Smith, 2017). Scant research has focused on the social processes of older job seekers (Gayen et al., 2019) and even less on older racial and ethnic minorities and low-income older adults. There is evidence that suggests that without social networks, the odds of acquiring employment are reduced, particularly among low-income job seekers (Fernandez and Fernandez-Mateo, 2006; Newman, 1999; Newman and Lennon, 1995) although there are ongoing debates about the causal nature of this relationship (Smith, 2017, 2010; Mouw, 2003).

There are many definitions and dimensions to social networks and social capital (Son et al., 2008; van Deth, 2003; Portes, 1998; Coleman, 1988). Social *support*, for example, is a type of social capital that helps one "get by or cope" (Briggs, 1998, p. 178) while social *leverage* is a form of social capital that enables individuals "to get ahead or change one's opportunity set through access to job information . . . or a recommendation for a scholarship or loan" (Briggs, 1998, p. 178). Social support and leverage may offer different types of support among low-income populations. Free or cheap childcare by friends and relatives to assist a job seeker may be just as important as job information and personal referrals (Dominguez and Watkins, 2003). Thus, Smith (2017) argues both of these social relations may be equally important to formal labor force participation.

Weak versus *strong* social ties may also play an important role when searching for employment (Granovetter, 1995, 1981; Marsden and Campbell, 1984). From the perspective of social stratification, individuals within homogenous social networks tend to have strong social ties but redundant information about economic opportunities, thereby limiting new information concerning job opportunities; whereas weak social ties are a product of heterogeneous social networks that promote nonredundant information that may foster new information concerning jobs (Granovetter, 1981). There is some evidence to support Granovetter's (1983, 1973) argument that weak social ties—friend's friends or acquaintances—are more important than strong social ties (Hällsten et al., 2017; Snijders et al., 2010; Yakubovich, 2005; Calvo-Armengol and Jackson, 2004).

Yet, Gayen and colleagues (2019) found that older adults transitioning out of unemployment did so by accessing strong social ties, as opposed to weak ones. Granovetter (1995) later suggested that individuals from low SES may not benefit from weak social ties when compared to those from high SES because friends of friends within poor social networks may not have information and access to job opportunities. Others argue that there is a *ceiling effect* among high-status job seekers (Lin and Dumin, 1986; Lin et al., 1981) and that low-status job seekers may benefit more from weak social ties. The evidence supporting these perspectives is mixed (Smith, 2017).

Stemming from ecological systems theory, social theorists have expanded the lens of studying social networks to the role and function of neighborhood organizations and government. Neighborhood organizations, it is argued, are important to social networking and social capital (Smith, 2017; Small, 2010; Putnam, 2000). Membership to civic and noncivic organizations within neighborhoods foster social ties, and over time, trust, reciprocity, and norms help to build social capital. Policies from the state, federal, and supraorganizational bodies of authority, shape networks and social capital (Small, 2010). This perspective underscores the importance of building the capacity of institutions to facilitate meaningful productive roles for older adults, an important concept within the productive aging literature (Morrow-Howell et al., 2001).

Civic organizations at the national, state, and local levels can help build social capital within neighborhoods and within groups, while also promoting the health of older adults (Morrow-Howell et al., 2001). These social and health resources could then be used to acquire employment in later life for older adults who need and/or want to work. Carr and Kail (2013) found that older adults who engaged in paid work and formal volunteering prior to full retirement were more likely to continue to volunteer during retirement and subsequently return to work compared to those who did not volunteer. They speculated that social resources associated with volunteering had facilitated the transition out of retirement to paid work. Gonzales and Nowell (2017) expanded this literature by examining social bonding (close social ties among family members), social bridging (looser social ties among friends and neighbors that "bridge" people horizontally within a social stratum, p. 1102) and social linking (social ties that connect individuals to others in higher and lower social stratum) within the context of retirees returning to work. They found that retirees who helped friends, neighbors, or relatives, as well as those engaged as formal volunteers with religious, educational, health-related, or other charitable organizations, significantly increased their odds of returning to work, after controlling for factors associated with un-retirement (e.g., health, education, lifetime occupational status, wealth). They also found a dose response, where high-intensity volunteering, either formal or informal, significantly increased the odds of returning to work when compared to individuals who did not volunteer or only engaged in low-intensity volunteering. These findings offer some support that social bridging, such as informal volunteering, and social linking, such as formal volunteering, are important resources to obtaining employment in later life.

Smith (2017) argues social compositions and social structures vary by race, ethnicity, gender, and nativity, and may contribute to longstanding labor force participation inequities. Age is another important dimension, as older adults are more likely to access their social capital to find employment, whereas younger people are more likely to rely on their human capital (Gayen et al., 2010). Ajrouch et al., (2016) also argue social capital might be more important than human capital for older adults seeking employment, particularly for low socioeconomic populations. Additional research that clarifies the social mechanisms predictive of formal labor market participation in later life is warranted given scant and mixed evidence among working individuals generally, and the limited research on older adults more specifically.

CROSS-CUTTING THEMES OF INEQUITY: A LIFE COURSE PERSPECTIVE

Life Course Disparities

The move away from a standardized normative life course, standardized career paths, and conventional retirements (Carr et al., 2021; Calvo et al., 2018; Warner et al., 2010; Kohli, 2007) in tandem with a transforming global economy and shifting policies in both Europe and the United States (including the demise—

in the United States at least—of mandatory retirement ages) means that older individuals and couples find they must customize their own employment and retirement decisions (Hofäcker et al., 2016; Ebbinghaus and Hofäcker, 2013; Cahill et al., 2015, 2006). Decision-making involves more than simply deciding on the timing of exits, and can involve decisions around whether to move to more limited engagements, take on bridge jobs, or, if retired, to seek reemployment (Kail and Warner, 2013; Tang et al., 2013; Warner et al., 2010; Moen, 2007). Such choices are made in the face of current and perceived future demands, resources and risks, as well as motivations and goals (Kojola and Moen, 2016; Wang et al., 2011). But demands, resources, and risks are factors in motion. Unexpected exigencies, such as an acute health condition, job loss, the sudden need to provide family care, enhanced job demands, layoffs, an economic downturn, or a health pandemic—all can shift the calculus around continued work engagement, retirement, disability or family-care exits or reemployment.

Decision-making is often couched in terms of weighing various options and making optimal choices. But choice around labor market continuities and exits are often constrained, with freedom of choice differentially distributed across older adult populations (Moen, 2016; Sohier, 2019). Control over deciding when, where, and how much to work or retire is limited for those in historically disadvantaged social positions (women, minorities, immigrants, the less educated—see Brown and Warner, 2008; Choi et al., 2016; Warner and Brown, 2011; Zajacova et al., 2014). Moreover, decisions about work and retirement in later adulthood are made without knowledge of the consequences of doing so, as well as possible future circumstances, particularly with regard to individual and family members' future health and income, but also possibilities in terms of, for example, future employer buyouts or reemployment.

These decisions can be viewed from a model of decision-making behavior called *prospect theory*, which applies particularly to risky or uncertain choices. "Risky" choices are defined as decisions made "without advance knowledge of their consequences" (Kahneman and Tversky, 1984, p. 341). Kahneman and Tversky find that people typically conceptualize outcomes in terms of *gains* or *losses* relative to a given reference point, rather than as final assets. Losses usually loom larger than gains; an individual is more distressed at the prospect of a loss than pleased by a potential gain ("loss aversion"). Given declines in social protections like secure DB pensions and increased longevity, retirement can be seen as a risky choice for some older adults who fear they may outlive their savings. People tend to be risk-*averse*, but if staying in their current jobs might mean a possible loss, risk *seeking* is observed (Kahneman and Tversky, 1979). Given rising intensity and precarity of work (Kelly and Moen, 2020; Kalleberg, 2018), others might see exiting in the form of retirement, disability, or because of caregiving demands, as a potential gain over remaining in a state of chronic pain or stress, especially coupled with some, even minimal, guaranteed income in the form of Social Security benefits. Those in poor health may view remaining in their current jobs as a potential further loss of health and well-being, compared to the relief of full-time retirement leisure.

Race and ethnicity may also shape the timing of exits, with White people both better positioned in the labor market and having more resources (health, education) than Black people, Hispanic people, or other minority groups (Moen et al., 2021; Lahey, 2018; Stainback et al., 2018; Zajacova et al., 2014; Warner and Brown, 2011; Willson, 2003), favoring greater time in paid work.

Certain working conditions can also be beneficial or harmful for health (Kelly and Moen, 2020; Staudinger et al., 2016). Noxious environments and physically demanding jobs obviously take their toll, leading to early retirements when financially possible. But psychosocial conditions also matter; jobs with high demands, low control, and little support lead to poor health outcomes for workers of all ages and life stages (Karasek and Theorell, 1990). Alternatively, those who feel satisfied with their jobs, coworkers, and bosses are apt to avoid risks around the uncertainties of leaving, while those who feel they cannot sustain the level of work required and who cannot scale back or move to a more supportive manager will take on the risks associated with exiting. Greater flexibility and control, together with supportive supervisors, can be conducive to deciding to remain with one's employer longer (Moen et al., 2016a).

Recall losses usually loom larger than gains; for healthy college-educated workers, retirement can be seen as the loss of interesting, meaningful activity as well as a paycheck. For those older workers remaining in the workforce past age 65, the health and personal development aspects of work ran parallel to that of the financial motivations (Reynolds and Wenger, 2012). By contrast, for workers in poor health and with little education, exits concomitant with Social Security eligibility may render retirement a welcome risk and even gain in the face of the difficulties of working and the uncertainties around both jobs and earnings.

It is worth highlighting that the population 65 years old or older is becoming more racially diverse. Older Hispanic adults in the United States are one of the fastest-growing population groups in the United States (U.S. Census Bureau, 2018; Flores and Radford, 2017). Hispanics were 6.9 percent of the U.S. population ages 65 and older in 2010, and they are projected to comprise 18.6 percent of the U.S population that is ages 65 and older in 2050 (U.S. Census Bureau, 2018). Among Hispanics 65 years old or older, 56 percent are foreign-born (Johnson et al., 2013). Poverty rates among minority older adults 65 years old or older in the United States is higher among Blacks and Hispanics than among non-Hispanic Whites. Poverty rates among older adults are 16.2 percent for Blacks, 17.7 percent for Hispanics, and 6.6 percent for non-Hispanic Whites. Foreign-born older Hispanics poverty rate is 20.1 percent, compared to 14.7 percent for Hispanic U.S.-born (Flores and Radford, 2017).

According to the life course theory, early SES and social interactions affect adulthood social conditions that in turn affect health at older ages (e.g., Berkman, 2009). According to Flippen and Tienda (2002), race, ethnicity, and gender are ascribed characteristics associated with education, occupation, and marital status. All of these factors are associated with employment stability, income and wealth trajectories, saving for retirement, and health status, which in turn affect retirement behavior and income security in old age. Adults that face limited work opportunities during their prime working years continue to face a considerable disadvantage when reaching retirement (Flippen and Tienda, 2002).

Racial-ethnic disparities in economic outcomes begin to appear at young ages and expand throughout the life course. Although differences in education can only partially explain these disparities in economic outcomes at older ages, older Black and Hispanic people have completed less education than have older White people. Black and Hispanic people are less likely to have completed a bachelor's degree; in 2014, only 11 percent of Hispanic older adults 65 years old or older had completed college, compared to 15 percent of Black older adults and 26 percent of non-Hispanic White older adults.

The economic effects of these differences in education on employment and income cumulate over the life course, affecting access to public and private retirement benefits and wealth accumulation, resulting in large racial-ethnic disparities in financial resources and security at older ages. Although almost 90 percent of older non-Hispanic White workers receive Social Security benefits, only 81 percent of older Black workers, and 75 percent of older Hispanic workers do so. Non-Hispanic White workers are also more likely (39%) to receive employer provided pensions than Hispanic workers (22%). An important component of wealth for older adults is housing, and here too, non-Hispanic White people enjoy a large advantage in homeownership, even as they also enjoy the benefits of possessing a more diverse asset portfolio that is less reliant on housing value (Johnson et al., 2013). As a result, only four percent of non-Hispanic White workers had zero or negative net wealth, compared to 19 percent of Black workers and 23 percent of Hispanic workers. These racial-ethnic disparities in financial security differentially constrain retirement and work options at older ages, leaving racial-ethnic minorities less able to realize their preferences for work and retirement.

Life course research, in conjunction with cumulative (dis)advantages and inequality, has expanded our conceptual understanding of work and retirement trajectories among diverse older adults. Given the challenges of adopting an intersectional approach, critical race theory (which holds that legal and social institutions are designed in ways to enforce and perpetuate social, economic, and political inequalities between White people and non-White people) and perspectives on scarcity may yield important insights on how individuals and households make complicated decisions in a context of resource scarcity (Collins, 2019; Calasanti and King, 2015; Collins and Bilge, 2015; Mani et al., 2013; Mullainathan and Shafir, 2013; Shah et al., 2012; Delgado and Stefancic, 2000; Crenshaw, 1991). Further, much of our longitudinal and/or population data have limited sample sizes on race and ethnicity or gender and sexual minorities. There is great heterogeneity within these subgroups, and exploring this heterogeneity across time within life course, critical race, and scarcity perspectives, may prove useful to developing sensitive policies and practices at the national, state, and employer levels.

> **BOX 4-1**
> **COVID-19**
>
> The COVID-19 pandemic is likely to upend retirement plans for many older workers. Although the ultimate effect of the pandemic on retirement cannot yet be discerned, through May 2021 the labor force participation rate of those ages 55 and above was 1.5 percentage points lower for women and 2.3 percentage points lower for men, relative to pre-pandemic levels (Congressional Research Service, 2021). As a share of pre-pandemic employment, the decline in participation has been far greater among those 65 and up than among those ages 55 to 64 (Johnson, 2021).
>
> The most direct pathway for an effect of the pandemic on retirement is through unemployment, as is discussed in Chapter 6. However, the pandemic is also likely to alter some retirement plans through its effect on some of the individual and household factors discussed in this chapter. One such factor is health. While medical research on the long-term effects of COVID-19 will be carried out for years to come, early evidence suggests that a minority of those infected experience post-acute COVID-19 (Long COVID), with symptoms lasting months if not longer (Sudre et al., 2021). These health effects may lead some to retire earlier than planned.
>
> On the other hand, the pandemic may cause some people to work longer due to reduced retirement resources. Some individuals may need to use their retirement savings to pay for ongoing living expenses if they experience unemployment or another COVID-related work disruption. The CARES Act of 2020 increased the ability to borrow and take distributions from retirement accounts, and some employers temporarily froze retirement plan contributions during the pandemic (Plan Council Sponsor of America, 2020a, b). The pandemic may have also affected retirement through caregiving responsibilities, as some family caregivers may have been precluded from providing care for fear of infecting the care recipient or needed to take over for paid caregivers no longer able to perform their duties.
>
> Longstanding inequities by race and ethnicity, education, gender, and health may become exacerbated during shocks, such as recessions as well as pandemics (Gonzales, Gordon et al., 2021; Garcia et al., 2020). Emerging research suggests COVID-19 has had particularly acute impacts on the labor force participation of Black, Indigenous, and People of Color, as well as older adults (Miller, 2020; Moen et al., 2020). Low-income older workers had heightened concerns about work-related health risks as well as a greater financial imperative to work (Agovino, 2020; Halvorsen and Yulikova, 2020b). These workers face health risks in getting to work, as they tend to rely heavily on public transportation. Paid sick leave and work flexibility as well as expanded unemployment insurance benefits and stimulus payments may have helped older workers sustain income during the pandemic. Women and racial minorities have a heavier burden caring and working for pay, and it is unknown how the pandemic has exacerbated work-family strain. Shocks disrupt assumptions about work and retirement patterns, and research is needed to help shape effective policies and practices to promote health and choice for work and retirement before, during, and after national shocks.

RESEARCH IMPLICATIONS

The science on work and retirement trajectories at the individual and social levels is complex. Social research has clarified longstanding research questions, yet there is much that we do not know. Below are the most promising areas for future research.

- Health is a key determinant of retirement for some workers, while others retire for nonhealth-related reasons and retain substantial work capacity during the early years of retirement. Health disparities by race-ethnicity and education are a leading candidate to explain group-level differences in work at older ages, but more research is needed to establish this connection. Similarly, more research into the work capacity of different types of older workers would be of great value, given that policy discussions frequently include proposed reforms aimed at encouraging longer work lives. In addition, more research on the causal effects of mental and cognitive health on retirement is needed, as much of the existing literature focuses on physical health or on the health effects of retirement.

- The differences in labor force participation at older ages by education group are strikingly large. However, the existing literature has not established the extent to which this reflects a causal effect of education on retirement, the underlying mechanisms for this association, or the role that rising education has played in the recent increase in labor force participation at older ages. More work on all of these questions is urgently needed, because differences in work at older ages translate into meaningful differences in retiree well-being. Importantly, this work needs to take account of the fact that education-based differences in labor force participation rates begin long before traditional retirement ages.
- Research is needed to understand barriers to saving for retirement, particularly for low-income, women, and minorities including the role of (1) financial literacy, (2) access to employer-sponsored pensions, (3) other mechanisms to save for retirement, and (4) social insurance programs that may reduce incentives to save and accumulate wealth. In addition, we need to develop and test culturally competent incentive mechanisms and financial literacy programs to diverse populations.
- Changes in the retirement landscape—notably the shift from DB to DC pension plans—have put much more responsibility on workers to make financial decisions that affect their retirement security. Research suggests that financial literacy can affect financial decision-making, and also that pension plan provisions such as default contribution rates or investment allocations strongly influence decisions. In a sense, these represent two options for changing retirement savings behavior, and additional research may help to clarify their relative efficacy.
- The association of informal caregiving and labor force attachment is dynamic and complex due to workplace policies and job characteristics that can support caregiving, resources and characteristics of the care provider, the type of dyadic relationship between care provider and receiver, as well as the demands of the caregiving role (Clancy et al., 2020). Research is needed to understand how informal caregiving interacts with household and employment characteristics over time by gender, race, ethnicity, education, and SES. Longitudinal population studies that explicitly ask about employment policies and practices among informal caregivers would enable research on employment and retirement trajectories among a diverse U.S. population.
- Household structures have become far more varied than in the past. Research that provides greater insight into the health, economic, social, and psychological factors to work and retire by household structure, and quality of household ties, is warranted.
- What social processes are most effective for older adults to work and retire? How might social support and leverage enable low-income older adults, caregivers, or individuals with health limitations to obtain and maintain work should they want and/or need to work? Are weak or strong social ties most effective for low-income older job seekers? How might the social composition of an older worker evolve as they transition between work and retirement, and possibly back to work? What federal, state, and community policies and practices enhance social capital among older adults to achieve their preferences for work and retirement?
- A common theme that emerged in the extant research on individual and social resources is the lack of data and knowledge on Black, Indigenous, and People of Color as it relates to work and retirement. Further research is needed to explore heterogeneity and disparities across race and ethnicity, as well as within racial and ethnic groups. Emerging theories from the fields of critical gerontology, sociology, law, public health, and social work are critical race theory, standpoint theory, intersectionality, health equity, and systemic racism, which have helped to guide some empirical knowledge base on health, education, financial assets, and financial capacity. These theoretical perspectives will likely help to center the lives of racial and ethnic minorities in work and retirement inequities research, which can then inform policies and practices to promote choices and opportunities for work and retirement in later life for a growing diverse and aging population.
- Research using a life course perspective has expanded our conceptual understanding of work and retirement trajectories among diverse older adults and provided a lens through which the processes that generate cumulative (dis)advantages and inequality among older adults can be observed and elaborated. Further elaboration of the processes through which early life experiences shape late-life outcomes is needed.

5

Workplace and Job Factors

In this chapter, we examine the influence of workplace and job-related factors on the employment decisions of older workers. We recognize that organizations continue to define the work experience through the implementation of practices and the structuring of job tasks. These work practices define the employment relationship by establishing a set of conditions, such as pay, work schedule, benefits, the degree of job flexibility, training opportunities, and health and safety conditions. In addition, these conditions link to the work process and the resulting job characteristics experienced by workers.

Organizations and the conditions they establish affect the career decisions workers make over their life course. So much of the retirement literature focuses on individual decisions and the role public policy plays in them; however, organizations and workplace practices also play a critical role in shaping retirement pathways. These practices influence whether older workers continue to develop their skills as they age (McNamara and Pitt-Catsouphes, 2020), stay engaged at the workplace, remain healthy (Chang et al., 2021), and are able to balance work and nonwork roles over the life course (Pitt-Catsouphes et al., 2015). Workplace practices thus establish workers' constraints, shape expectations, and guide preferences.

Workplace practices may be either age-related or age-neutral. Age-related practices are those focused on the needs of a specific age group workers. For example, training may be designed around the learning styles of older employees (Kubeck et al., 1996), or partial retirement initiatives may be created to help extend working lives (Berg and Piszczek, 2021). Age-related practices can be problematic to the extent that they reinforce stereotypes or raise legal concerns over promoting differential treatment based on age (discrimination). In contrast, age-neutral practices are designed without consideration of age-based differences and thus can impact people positively and negatively across the age distribution (Piszczek and Pimputkar, 2020; Korff et al., 2017; Kooij and van de Voorde, 2015).

Currently workplaces are undergoing tremendous change. New technologies are impacting work processes, in some cases intensifying work while in other cases simplifying it, as well as demanding that employees continually update their skills. At the time of this writing, the nation is in the midst of the COVID-19 pandemic. Remote working has increased dramatically (Brynjolfsson et al., 2020; Parker et al., 2020) and concerns about workforce safety have become more of a priority for organizations.[1] Today's workplace is also characterized by great inequality in working conditions and access to employee benefits (Kristal et al., 2020). It is in this

---

[1] We discuss the effects of COVID-19 in the workplace in a box at the end of this chapter.

context that we write about the workplace and job-related factors that influence the employment decisions of older workers.

We begin with a discussion of various theoretical approaches that provide insight into the purpose and effects of workplace practices on working conditions and workers. These theoretical approaches include a job-quality perspective, a total-worker-health approach, and an interest-based perspective. Based on the literature, we then classify age-related workplace practices into various categories and discuss their implications for older workers. Next, we focus on a set of key workplace practices and factors that influence the employment of older workers. We conclude by identifying areas for future research, highlighting the need for a national longitudinal organization-level survey to provide the necessary data to address key research questions about workplace practices.

THEORETICAL APPROACHES

Some theoretical approaches emphasize universal working conditions, focusing on the conditions that characterize good workplaces for employees. The job quality and total-worker-health approaches have implications for older workers, but they typically emphasize practices that affect all workers regardless of age. In contrast, the interest-based perspective can be used to show how employer and employee interests shape workplace practices for older workers; whose interests are being met depends in large part on the types and structure of practices implemented. Table 5-1 summarizes the key insights from these various approaches.

Job Quality

Kalleberg and colleagues have written extensively about the changing composition of jobs and job quality over the last 40 years, which has given rise to more "bad jobs" than "good jobs" (Appelbaum et al., 2019; Kalleberg and Dunn, 2016; Kalleberg, 2011). Although all jobs can have both good and bad features, classifying them as "good jobs" or "bad jobs" is a dichotomous way to discuss the overall characteristics of job quality, and is a useful heuristic for contrasting a set of dimensions in the labor market. Bad jobs are those with low wages,

TABLE 5-1 Theoretical Approaches

Theoretical Approach	Key Features	Key References
Universal Conditions		
Job Quality	Eight dimensions of the work experience create a comprehensive definition of job quality.	McNamara and Pitt-Catsouphes, 2020; Appelbaum et al., 2019; Kalleberg and Dunn, 2016; Pitt-Catsouphes et al., 2015; Kalleberg, 2011.
Total Worker Health	Three areas of concern: workplace safety and health; employment security; and worker well-being.	Punnett et al. 2020; National Institute for Occupational Safety and Health, 2018; Schill and Chosewood, 2013.
Interest-based Perspectives		
Institutional Logics	Socially constructed, historical patterns of practices that reinforce a binary retirement choice for workers.	Moen et al., 2017; Thornton and Ocasio, 2008.
Human Capital Approach	Organizations view workers as bundles of human capital in ways that can downplay other older workers' contributions and preferences.	Berg and Piszczek, 2021; Nyberg and Ployhart, 2013; Becker, 1964.
Categorization of Practices	Accommodation, developmental, retention and exit, and age-inclusive practices. The structure and content of these practices reflect the tensions between employer and employee interests.	Jungmann et al. 2020; van Dalen et al., 2015; Kooij et al., 2014; Wang and Shultz, 2010.

few (if any) benefits, little opportunity for advancement, and little autonomy or control; importantly, these jobs are highly precarious, providing no job security. Good jobs are, of course, the opposite: they offer good wages, benefits, development and growth opportunities, schedule control, and greater job security.

Similarly, Clark (2015), among many others, points to the multiple-dimensionality of job quality. That is, job quality includes not only pay and compensation but satisfaction with the number of hours, the promise of promotion opportunities and job security, satisfaction with the type of work (whether hard physical labor and whether exhausting or dangerous), the content of the work (whether it is interesting, involves contributing to society, is meaningful), and satisfaction with interpersonal relationships (with both peers and managers).

The Sloan Center on Aging & Work at Boston College has tested a model of eight elements of job quality that employers can strengthen in ways that improve the fit between employee needs and preferences and those of the organization, all of which have been shown to be very important to older workers (McNamara and Pitt-Catsouphes, 2020; Pitt-Catsouphes et al., 2015). Following is a list of these elements of job quality with examples of research on the relevance each one has for older workers:

1. *Constructive relationships*: A supportive supervisor, for example, and good friends at work are associated with job satisfaction for workers over the age of 50 (Maestas et al., 2017; see Eppler-Hattab et al., 2020; and James et al., 2010).
2. *Fair compensation and benefits*: Workers over the age of 50 are more likely than younger workers to say that pension and retirement benefits are important to them (Maestas et al., 2017). This factor has become more important to older workers who have been caught in the transition from defined-benefit (DB) to defined-contribution (DC) retirement policies (Quin, 2010; Munnell and Sass, 2008).
3. *Culture of respect, inclusion, and empathy*: While this element is related to job satisfaction for workers of all ages (Pitts, 2009), more women over the age of 50 cite this element as "moderately" or "very important" to them (Pitt-Catsouphes et al., 2015; see also Mor Barak, 2015).
4. *Opportunities for training, learning, development, and advancement*: While findings on this element are mixed, the 2015 American Working Conditions Survey (Maestas et al., 2017) shows that among workers over the age of 50, the ability to acquire skills was related to job satisfaction, even though these older workers were less likely than younger workers to report that they had jobs that allowed them to learn "new things" (McNamara and Pitt-Catsouphes, 2020, p. 381). Similarly, opportunities for training and development are a significant factor in levels of employee engagement for workers up to the age of 65 (James et al., 2010).
5. *Workplace flexibility, autonomy, and control*: Older workers' reports of work engagement are related to their satisfaction with these elements of job quality (James et al., 2010; Swanberg et al., 2011; Pitt-Catsouphes et al., 2015). The importance of workplace flexibility (when, where, and how much to work) is probably one of the most robust areas of research, as workplace flexibility has been shown to be important to workers of all ages, including older workers.
6. *Provisions for employment security and predictability*: These provisions are linked to psychological and economic concerns related to job insecurity and unemployment (Punnett et al., 2020) and precarious employment conditions., e.g., contingent work or underemployment (Benach et al., 2014). For older workers, these provisions are related to decisions about working longer and to work engagement (Pitt-Catsouphes et al., 2015; see also Taylor et al., 2010.)
7. *Opportunities for meaningful work:* Although approximately one-fourth of all workers felt that it was "very important" that their work be "morally, socially, personally, or spiritually significant" (Maestas et al., 2017; p. 50), workers over the age of 50 report the importance of these qualities of the job in greater numbers than younger workers. This element of job quality has also been found to be related to work engagement (Pitt-Catsouphes et al., 2015).
8. *Wellness, health, and safety at the workplace*: More workers over the age of 50 than younger workers say that it is important that their jobs be less physically demanding (Maestas et al., 2017). In a study at the Center on Aging & Work, more women than men said that wellness and health and safety protections were important to them (Pitt-Catsouphes et al., 2015).

A study using data from the Time and Place Management Study[2] found that, among older workers (ages 50 and older), those who were less satisfied with compensation, opportunities to engage in meaningful work, and clear and effective information with respect to employment security were less likely to say that they planned to stay with the organization more than five years than stay with the organization until they retired (McNamara and Pitt-Catsouphes, 2020). The authors of the study conclude ". . . quality jobs can reduce the number of older adults who slip into retirement even though they may have wanted to work longer . . . results indicate that this factor is particularly important for older adults who are vulnerable in terms of physical and mental well-being" (p. 392). In summary, the extent to which jobs confer positive or negative outcomes, especially in terms of health and well-being, depends greatly on the nature of the work (or the quality as noted above), the amount of the work, and the level of engagement or affective attachment to the work (Matz-Costa et al., 2014).

Total Worker Health

Total Worker Health is a holistic approach designed to improve the safety, physical health, and psychological well-being of workers, thereby achieving the goal of enhancing workforce well-being and productivity (National Institute for Occupational Safety and Health, 2018). Total Worker Health is based on a recognition that employment conditions are a critical social determinant of health that can affect workers' long-term health and well-being through their effect on the distribution of money and resources (Benach et al., 2007). The approach emphasizes the importance of protecting worker safety, health, and well-being by reducing occupation-related injuries, preventing occupational diseases, alleviating occupational stress, and encouraging work-life balance in order for workers and their employers to reach their potential productivity goal (Chang et al., 2021).

More specifically, the Total Worker Health approach highlights three major areas of concern: workplace issues, employment issues, and workers' issues (Schill and Chosewood, 2013). *Workplace issues* refers to the physical and psychosocial environmental risk factors that can threaten workers' safety, health, and well-being. For example, hazard exposure risks and a poor safety climate can be viewed as potential physical and psychosocial threats to worker safety (Chang et al., 2021). *Employment issues* refers to policies and practices designed to preserve and cultivate human resources in the workplace. These issues include job insecurity and unemployment (Punnett et al., 2020), precarious employment conditions such as contingent work or underemployment (Benach et al., 2014) as well as costs and availability of health care and other benefits. All of which are human resource policy issues that affect decisions about working longer. Third and finally, *workers' issues* refers to factors that impact workers' well-being. Examples of these factors include pay, paid leave, work hours, opportunities to facilitate optimal functioning of workers (e.g., promoting work-family balance and employee health), and accommodations for workers with disabilities who may be at-risk for occupational injuries and illness (Schill and Chosewood, 2013).

Importantly, the Total Worker Health approach is intended to bring benefits not only to individual workers, but also to their employing organizations by enhancing innovation, productivity, and efficiency and by reducing the costs associated with injuries and illnesses (National Institute for Occupational Safety and Health, 2018). The dimensions of job quality and the total worker health approach primarily reveal a set of characteristics that reflect the interests of employees and what they would like from the work experience. This is also consistent with an economic framework where employees are constantly weighing the relative utility of work and leisure in decisions about whether to keep working.

Interest-Based Perspective

The work practices associated with an aging workforce that are actually implemented in organizations reflect both employer and employee interests. This *interest-based perspective* is a key aspect of employment relations

---

[2]The Time and Place Management Study is a large-scale random assignment study of more than 9,000 employees in more than 600 units of a regional healthcare provider in the United States. Workplace policy changes were assigned at the unit level and employees were surveyed longitudinally.

theory, which states that conflict is an inherent aspect of the employment relationship because the interests of employers and employees differ (Kochan, 1980). These differing interests can create tension at the workplace that can result in various practices that satisfy the interests of one party over the other, but this tension is not insurmountable because interests can also align around particular issues.

One can understand employer interests through different theoretical lenses. Moen and colleagues (2017) use institutional logic to show the disconnect between age-related work practices offered by firms and the preferences of older workers. Institutional logics are socially constructed, historical patterns of practice by which individuals and organizations provide meaning (Thornton and Ocasio, 2008, p. 2). Institutional logics emphasize that organizations are embedded in an institutional structure that makes organizations resistant to changing existing practices. Moen and colleagues (2017) argue that organizations have established retirement practices based on a one-way, full-time work model that culminates in a one-time exit to retirement. Although—as demonstrated in Chapter 3—this model no longer fits the preferences and experiences of older workers, practices that do fit these preferences, such as phased retirement or continuous training for older workers, are rarely implemented because they do not fit the prevailing logic.

In addition, the flow of human capital in organizations is another lens through which to view the implementation of age-related work practices from the interest of employers (Berg and Piszczek, 2021; Nyberg and Ployhart, 2013; Becker, 1964). Organizations will institute age-related work practices either to retain human capital in their organizations or to facilitate the exit of human capital based on the needs of their business. This theoretical framework emphasizes that organizations view older workers as bundles of human capital and that work practices will reflect the value the organizations put on particular skills and abilities workers possess. Thus, organizations may in fact pursue work practices that encourage the exit of older workers as much as they may put in place practices to encourage working longer.

Considering employer and employee interests draws attention to how age-related workplace practices are the result of tensions between employers and employees. In some cases, interests align. For example, practices attentive to safety and ergonomics generally meet the interests of both employers and employees regardless of age. Moreover, alignment of employer and employee interests may vary by the skills of older workers. High-skilled workers typically have more power to obtain practices from employers that match their preferences than do lower-skilled workers because they face a more favorable labor market that offers them wider employment opportunities (see Chapter 7 for more discussion of the role of labor markets). This power difference can lead to disparities in workplace practices across skilled work groups. In other cases, interests will differ. For example, older workers' interests in more flexible retirement pathways or flexible work arrangements may conflict with employers' interests in facilitating the exit of older workers.

Categorization of Practices

Much of the literature classifies age-related work practices primarily from the perspective of individual interests, but employer interests can also shape these practices. We discuss four bundles of practices classified in the literature, demonstrating where employer and employee interests align and differ: accommodation practices, developmental practices, retention and exit practices, age-inclusive practices.

Accommodation Practices

Age-related *accommodation practices* refers to workplace practices that recognize the possible declines in older workers' physical and cognitive capacities due to aging and are designed to compensate for such declines (van Dalen et al., 2015; Kooij et al., 2014). Accommodation practices can affect older workers directly by improving or sustaining their physical and cognitive health, as well as indirectly by facilitating an organizational climate that cares for older workers (Froidevaux et al., 2020; Wang and Fang, 2020; Kooij et al., 2014).

For example, making ergonomic changes in the workplace can accommodate physical decline for those working in physically demanding jobs. Some of these changes may include adopting better equipment (e.g., larger computer screens) or altering the job design to minimize physical strain (e.g., rearranging the physical space to reduce repetitive movements; Froidevaux et al., 2020; Wang and Fang, 2020). Another accommodation practice for older workers is telecommuting, that is, allowing individuals to work from home with the help of information and communication technologies. Allowing older workers to work where and when it is most convenient for them provides them with flexibility and autonomy and signals that the organization values and supports them (Cleveland and Maneotis, 2013). However, sometimes "allowing" flexibility is an option available not to all workers but limited to favored workers (Kelly and Moen, 2020).

Employers can also accommodate older workers' needs by reassigning older workers to less-demanding jobs if these reassignments are preferred or needed (Armstrong-Stassen and Schlosser, 2011). One example of job reassignment is to switch older workers from night shifts to day shifts. Similarly, another form of accommodation is job crafting, that is, allowing workers to modify their tasks at work in order to improve their person-job fit (Kooij et al., 2020).

From their multinational investigation of the predictors of accommodation practices, van Dalen and colleagues (2015) conclude that organizational characteristics (e.g., proportion of older workers, seniority-based compensation), characteristics of the economy (e.g., recruitment problems), and labor unions' involvement predicted whether employers used accommodation practices for their older workers. Of the four accommodation practices examined in 3,780 European organizations, ergonomic practices were the most widely implemented by organizations (34%), followed by the reduction of working time before retirement (24%), decreasing the workload of older workers (24%), and setting age limits for irregular work/shift work (11%). However, few empirical studies have directly examined the expected beneficial effects of accommodation practices for older workers.

Developmental Practices

Age-related *development practices* refers to workplace practices that help older workers acquire new knowledge, skills, and abilities (van Dalen et al., 2015; Kooij et al., 2014). Given the continuously increased use of technology in most workplaces and the shift from production work to information and service work, employees need to constantly learn new skills. This is particularly important for older workers who typically have not had recent training (Beier and Ackerman, 2005). Engaging in development and training at work provides general benefits, such as ensuring that employees have basic skills to work and helping them understand how to work effectively in teams. In addition to those benefits, older workers' participation in skill development may help combat age-related declines in cognitive and physical abilities, providing not only a private benefit but a social one as well (Kooij et al., 2014; Oude Mulders and Henkens, 2019). Moreover, development practices are important because skill obsolescence and lack of updated training are prevalent threats to older workers' careers (Charness and Czaja, 2006).

The aim of development practices can vary, as they can focus on maintenance or job mobility or, in differing degrees, on both (Oude Mulders and Henkens, 2019). Development practices that are maintenance-focused can help older workers perform their current jobs better. In this case, the goal of development is to improve older workers' ability and skills to better fit the demands and responsibilities entailed in their jobs. Development opportunities may also be focused on job mobility, offered to older workers as part of an organization's workforce planning. In the latter case, development is focused on updating older workers' skills, replacing those that are no longer pertinent to their jobs with new skills to ensure they have the appropriate resources to continue working. When organizations offer such developmental initiatives to promote internal job mobility, they can better utilize older workers' human capital resources by transferring them to positions that will maximize the combination of their individual capabilities.

Of the three development practices studied by van Dalen and colleagues (2015), European organizations provided continuous career development the most (32%), followed by promoting internal job mobility (28%) and offering training programs for older workers (20%). The predictors of development practices are comparable to those of accommodation practices. These included the proportion of older workers in the organization, the recruitment problems, the training requirements, and knowledge intensity of the work. Despite evidence showing that organizations are beginning to implement development practices, their impact on older workers remains unclear.

Retention and Exit Practices

Age-related exit and retention practices can serve different purposes (Wang and Shultz, 2010). For organizations that experience labor force shortages or potential talent loss, the goal is to retain the human capital provided by older workers. The typical practices include offering phased retirement, contingent work arrangements, and comprehensive benefit packages. Phased retirement means allowing older workers to continue working at a reduced workload and gradually moving into retirement. Contingent work arrangements mean rehiring retired workers as independent contractors or temporary workers. Comprehensive benefit packages include retention bonuses, pension supplements, and health care benefits.

For organizations that aim at restructuring human resources and altering skill and knowledge combinations, practices that facilitate retirement and exit, such as by offering early retirement incentives, are often adopted. Serving both purposes, another common age-related practice is succession planning, which allows organizations to actively forecast the positions that will be vacant and consider potential employees whom they can develop to fill the vacancies (Froidevaux et al., 2020; Rau and Adams, 2013). This practice enables organizations to minimize knowledge loss due to retirement by encouraging older workers' mentorship and knowledge transition to younger workers before exit. It also maximizes the time for organizations to prepare for older workers' exit. Indeed, retention and exit practices are more effective when organizations are tracking and measuring employee skills in order to understand where potential skill gaps may occur. Although these last practices are valuable, Berg and Piszczek (2021) find that few U.S. employers actually track employee skills systematically.

Of the two exit practices studied by van Dalen and colleagues (2015), European organizations provided early retirement schemes (31%) more often than part-time retirement (26%). The predictors of these exit practices included the proportion of older workers in the organization, the job's training requirements, and labor union's involvement. The literature has consistently shown that offering early retirement incentives can increase the likelihood that older workers will retire, whereas offering contingent work arrangements can extend older workers' workforce participation (Peiró et al., 2013). Further, phased retirement has been shown to be associated with better retirement adjustment (Wang and Shultz, 2010). Nevertheless, it is important to note that the majority of firm- and workplace-level research documenting age-related exit practices is Europe-based, where work and policy contexts are quite different from those in the United States.

Age-inclusive Practices

Age-inclusive practices focus on making all employees in an organization, regardless of their age, feel welcomed, accepted, and fairly treated, thus protecting workers from age-related stereotypes, prejudice, or discrimination (Parker and Andrei, 2020). To prevent age-based exclusion, organizations need to ensure compliance with antidiscrimination laws, such as actively avoiding the prohibited practices stipulated in the Age Discrimination in Employment Act, which include using age preferences, limitations, or specifications in job advertisements (Wang and Fang, 2020).

To counter age-related stereotypes and discrimination, organizations also implement training programs for their employees and supervisors. These training programs typically include:

> (1) introduction to age-related changes in performance and work motivation; (2) discussion and explanation regarding the development and consequences of age stereotypes, as well as the appreciation of age differences in the workplace; and (3) encouragement of trainees (supervisors of age diverse groups) to discuss strategies and come up with practical implications for their everyday work life. (Wang and Fang, 2020, p. 121).

Such training programs were effective in reducing age-related team conflicts and increasing appreciation of age diversity in the workplace (Jungmann et al., 2020). Practices that promote inclusion often involve explicitly appreciating the differences that diverse workforces bring to an organization (Parker and Andrei, 2020).

Age-inclusive practices can mobilize knowledge exchange among workers and their social connections in age-diverse workforces (Li et al., 2021). This is because age-inclusive practices promote fairness and eliminate discrimination, which provide employees from all age groups with equal opportunities to contribute and succeed

(Dwertmann et al., 2016). Thus, they generate a welcoming and accepting environment whereby employees of all ages are valued by and integrated into the organization. For example, a study of 93 German small and medium-sized companies with 14,260 employees (Boehm et al., 2014) found that age-inclusive practices facilitated strong and mutually caring, supportive, and loyal relationships between workers of all ages and their employers, which subsequently led to higher company performance and lower employee turnover intention. Further, a large-scale study of U.S. companies (Li et al., 2021) used data from 3,888 organizations based on the Annual Workplace Survey implemented by the Society for Human Resource Management and showed that when age-inclusive practices were implemented, age diversity at workplaces had stronger positive effects on human capital and social capital, which eventually facilitated organizational performance.

KEY PRACTICES

In this section, we focus on particular practices associated with job quality: flexible work arrangements, training practices, a supportive climate for age diversity and inclusion, and compensation and benefits. We examine how these practices are shaped by employer and employee interests and where research gaps exist.

Flexible Work Arrangements

Flexible work arrangements are important practices that can meet the interests of employees, employers, or both. These practices are important components of job quality for workers of all ages. Work arrangements can affect employee retention, conflict between work and care obligations, and psychological well-being both positively and negatively; inflexible ways of working can have deleterious effects on retention (Moen et al., 2017) and on health (Berkman et al., 2010). Studying the impacts of flexible ways of working for the older workforce is increasingly salient in the wake of the COVID-19-driven push of office workers into working remotely, which may well drive greater flexibility in the future of work.

Simply contrasting flexible from inflexible practices is not ideal for capturing the costs and benefits of each, because workers may be in different occupations, have different supervisors, and engage in different types of work. The best way to capture the effects of flexible work arrangements is to introduce them into an organization and then compare current to previous outcomes for the same employees. Where possible, the gold standard is a randomized trial, contrasting changes in the "flexibility innovation" group with a control group of workers who did not gain access to flexibility.

Two studies have examined the effects of this innovation. One was a natural experiment in the headquarters of a Fortune 500 firm, which observed an employer-generated change that would have happened whether or not it was studied. The other was a five-year randomized field trial of 1,000 professionals, technicians, and managers undertaken by the Work, Family, and Health Network (Kossek et al., 2014) in another Fortune 500 firm that introduced greater employee control over the time and place of work (flexibility) to workers across the age spectrum. Results from the latter study showed this innovation in job quality reduced expectations of exiting, lowered employees' actual turnover rates, and produced later ages of anticipated retirement (Moen et al, 2017, 2016a, b; Moen, Kelly et al., 2011). These changes in job quality reduced work-family conflict (Kelly et al, 2014; Kelly et al., 2011) and time strain (Moen et al., 2013), enhancing psychological well-being (Fan et al., 2019; Moen et al., 2016b). Moreover, there were no differences in the beneficial effects of the flexibility innovation based on the ages of workers. However, except for the analysis of retirement ages, there was little specific focus on older workers.

This set of studies describes outcomes for professionals, not the larger workforce, and yet there are real distinctions in policies and practices for health, retail, and service workers compared to professionals (Henly and Lambert, 2014; Lambert et al., 2012). A study of healthcare workers in extended care settings finds that those whose managers are supportive of employees' work–family needs, including offering flexibility regarding work schedules, report lower cardiovascular disease risk and longer sleep than those with less supportive supervisors (Berkman et al., 2010). This was not the case for those working with less supportive, less flexible supervisors. Another study, this time of European older workers ages 50 and above, found real inequalities regarding which workers had flexible work arrangements (Andersen et al., 2019). Older women and those with less education as well as other subgroups were particularly disadvantaged.

This is a fertile area for future research in the United States. Additional investigations of possible distinctions and disparities by workers' ages and life course stages, as well as by their social class, race, and ethnicity, could identify specific flexibility preferences and experiences of older workers in different types of occupational and life circumstances.

The randomized field trial study described above (Kossek et al., 2014) finds that the effectiveness of flexible work arrangements, such as remote work or alternative schedules, is essentially determined by whether they are voluntary, chosen and desired by workers, or involuntary, implemented by managers or employers for business reasons. For example, it demonstrates that working remotely involuntarily has negative impacts on worker health and well-being (Kaduk et al., 2019). However, additional studies are needed to examine whether involuntary remote work and other mandated flexibilities for business needs (such as expectations of instant responsiveness or being forced to work at the office or remotely) tend to push older workers out of the workforce. As precarity increases in the U.S. economy, heightened instability is evident in work schedules that are more often designed to benefit employers than employees (Schneider and Harknett, 2019; Kalleberg, 2018). And flexibility policies can be "on the books"—stated in organizational handbooks—but rarely granted, typically granted only as a special accommodation to highly valued employees (Kelly and Moen, 2020).

Studies chronicling the availability and use of various flexibility arrangements among older workers would be especially valuable in light of the increase in remote work concomitant with the COVID-19 dislocation. Having large numbers of employees working from home during the pandemic may jumpstart a nationwide trend toward partial (hybrid) or full remote work practices for jobs that make it practical to do so. We need to know more about the conditions under which older workers appreciate remote ways of working, even as others may see it as fostering longer hours and expectations of instant accessibility.

Another form of flexibility involves work and retirement pathways. As discussed in Chapters 3 and 4, older workers often have a preference for options to scale back on job obligations, including reducing their work hours, whether as part-time work, through phased retirement paths, or by being rehired for contract work (Timmons et al., 2011; Moen, 2007). But there is insufficient evidence on the retirement timing effects of the ability to customize exit pathways in the United States. One study using European data[3] finds that older workers who decrease their hours actually exit the workforce *earlier* than those continuing in full-time schedules (Hess et al., 2018), but it is not clear whether decreased hours were voluntary. A 10-year follow-up study of older English workers showed that high job demands predicted preferences for early exits, even as some control (decision latitude) predicted both preferences for and actual later exits (Carr et al., 2016). A large survey of older workers in Europe found that older workers in non-physically-demanding jobs would consider working longer if they had greater flexibility (Andersen et al., 2020). In addition, the impact on workers of changing work hours or a work schedule depends on whether this is done voluntarily or involuntarily. Older workers who are involuntarily "demoted" are more likely to reduce their organizational commitment and leave their jobs (Hennekam and Ananthram, 2020).

There is a clear need in the United States for scholarship on whether and what kinds of flexible arrangements affect the timing of retirement exits. Studies on specific types of voluntary alternative work-hour arrangements and late career pathways, as well as how they meet the interests of older employees in different occupations and industries, would be especially valuable for promoting understanding of working longer.

Another key area for future research is the role of intersecting social locations (overlapping positions related to gender, class, race/ethnicity, nativity, age—see Collins and Bilge, 2020; Romero, 2018) in shaping who has access to flexible work arrangements, alternative work paths, and other aspects of the opportunity structure. Corporate as well as public labor market and retirement policies and practices were developed in the middle of the last century

---

[3]Data are from The Survey of Health, Ageing, and Retirement in Europe (SHARE) and the English Longitudinal Study of Ageing (ELSA). The SHARE study is a pan-European social science panel study providing internationally comparable longitudinal data on adults ages 50 and older from 28 European countries and Israel. ELSA is a nationally representative panel study of adults ages 50 and older living in households in England.

with a mindset characterizing workers as White men following standardized paths, namely, continuous, full-time work until continuous, full-time retirement (Moen and Roehling, 2005).

But today's—and tomorrow's—older workforce increasingly consists of women as well as men, and is increasingly diverse in age, race, and ethnicity as well as preferences for and options regarding how and how long they work. Research shows that social class, gender, and race (as well as country) affect retirement pathways and possibilities (Moen, 2016a, b; Radl, 2013; Blossfeld et al., 2011; Raymo et al., 2011). For example, it is important to consider alternative pathways from work to retirement experienced by older adults with few job options, by people who are disproportionately Black and Hispanic, by women, and by men without a college degree (Moen et al., 2020).

Existing organizational arrangements and expectations of standardized full-time employment and standardized one-way, one-time retirement typically constrain older workers' employment and retirement options, impeding flexible pathways and flexible ways of working (Kojola and Moen, 2016; Johnson, 2011; Johnson, Butrica, and Mommaerts, 2010; Peterson and Murphy, 2010; Armstrong-Stassen, 2008; Pitt-Catsouphes and Matz-Costa, 2008; Hedge et al., 2006b; Siegenthaler and Brenner, 2001). This constraint can be demonstrated in how public polices influence organizational practices. For example, federal retirement policies intent on clarifying the distinction between "worker" and "retiree" impede some organizations from hiring their own recent retirees for a year after their retirement. Disability policies that classify workers as "disabled" (and unable to work) or "not disabled" often prevent the option of possible part-time work. In addition, the Fair Labor Standards Act regulations constrain possible flexibility policies around the time and timing of work. A fruitful area for future research is to assess the unintended as well as intended consequences of both existing and changing labor market and retirement policies in the ways they affect organizational practices and constrain or open up options for continued participation in paid work by older workers.

Despite possible limiting factors, organizational changes in how, when, and where work is accomplished *can* and *do* happen (Kelly and Moen, 2020; Cahill et al., 2015; Oude Mulders, Henkens, and Schippers, 2015; Conen et al., 2014; Kossek et al., 2014). Indeed, the COVID-19 pandemic demonstrates how quickly working conditions can change. Even prior to the pandemic, some organizations were proactively addressing the needs and desires of their aging workforces by offering schedule flexibility, late career development, and ways to scale back (Dychtwald et al., 2013), as well as rehiring their retirees (Oude Mulders, Henkens, and Schippers, 2015). Most tend to adopt age-neutral policies, rather than focus specifically on older workers, which can be a limitation to options like phased retirement. The evidence suggests that many workers of all ages and life stages need or want to scale back on work or to have greater flexibility in terms of where, when, and how they do so (Moen et al., 2016a; Johnson, 2011; Timmons et al., 2011; Moen, 2007). Table 5-2 summarizes differences in flexible work arrangements that are structured to meet employee interests (voluntary) and those structured to meet employer interests (involuntary).

In summary, work arrangements with flexible work times and places are increasingly common. Moreover, it appears that some forms of remote or hybrid work are likely here to stay. These could be a boon to older workers who want greater flexibility, but research evidence points to the importance of employee control over where and when they work, not whether their organizations have flexibility policies and practices, underscoring the costs of inflexible arrangements to workers of all ages. Additionally, some flexibility polices are voluntary, designed to benefit employees, even as others are involuntary, designed to meet business needs. There is insufficient knowledge about whether and under what conditions older workers find working from home, hybrid work, and other flexibility practices or, conversely, stringent inflexibilities, to be salutary or stressful, much less the degree to which these arrangements promote working longer. This constitutes an important agenda for future scholarship.

Training Practices

Employer-provided training programs are examples of other practices that can bring important benefits to older workers, increasing their engagement and job quality. Human capital theory predicts that firm-specific training increases productivity and wages relative to alternative employment opportunities, allowing the firm that offers training to pay higher wages and providing incentives for both employers and employees to maintain the employment relationship (Becker, 1962). Yet research on training and retaining older workers has yielded

TABLE 5-2 Age-Related Flexibility Practices Shaping Later Adult Work

	Voluntary (Employee Interests)	Involuntary (Employer/Managerial Interests)
Temporal/Spatial Flexibilities		
Schedule	Ability of workers to customize schedules.	Just-in-time scheduling; supervisor changes in schedule.
Place	Ability of workers to do remote/hybrid work.	Remote/hybrid work arrangements; 24/7 accessibility.
Work Path Flexibilities		
Scaling Back	Part-time options; job/task shift options.	Employer-mandated hours; reductions or job/task shifts.
Alternative Paths	Phased retirement; bridge jobs; rehiring of retirees.	Incentivized or pressured early exits; layoffs; rehiring of retirees.

conflicting results. One study using data from Europe finds that training led to greater worker retention in the Netherlands for workers ages 50–64 (Picchio and van Ours, 2013). Other studies also find a positive relationship between training and retention (Armstrong-Stassen and Ursel, 2009; Herrbach et al., 2009), whereas Boockmann and colleagues (2012) find no relationship between training and exit rates of employees ages 40–65. They speculate that this result may be due to the limited resources provided for training and the redesign of workplaces or other difficulties related to implementation.

The way training is conducted can influence the effectiveness of the training itself and its relationship with retention. Organizations can offer programs that include older workers in a standard training program designed for their entire workforce, offer targeted training programs, or use some combination of these two delivery methods. Older workers have different traits and skills and process information differently than younger workers, so they may benefit more from some training methodologies than from others (Callahan et al., 2003). Studies in the organizational psychology training literature suggest that training that is targeted toward older workers is more effective at providing extensive human capital development and a stronger positive relationship with wages (Hedge et al., 2006b; Charness et al., 2001; Sterns and Doverspike, 1988; Sterns, 1986). Based on this literature, we expect establishments that offer targeted training programs to have higher retention rates among older workers.

Employers often introduce training programs for workers when processes change or new technologies are introduced. Yet older workers may be less motivated to pursue training opportunities (Bertolini et al., 2011), and organizations may be less likely to offer training to them, given that older employees have fewer remaining years of work during which employers could reap the returns on their training investment (van Dalen et al., 2015). Thus, even if training increases productivity and wages, the effort required to participate in it may outweigh the benefits because the individual is close to retirement age. Whether older workers participate in training may depend on their income level as well.

Whereas training may seem like a straightforward practice to encourage older workers to remain in employment, more research is needed to determine specific factors, such as training methods and wage levels, that influence this relationship.

Supportive Climate for Age Diversity and Inclusion

The climate within organizations relating to perceptions of age, diversity, and generational differences impacts the employment decisions of older workers. In a recent Transamerica survey (Collinson, 2017), employers report increasing awareness that their older employees may plan to work past conventional retirement ages. Seventy-seven percent of employers agree with the statement, "Many employees at my company plan to continue working either full-time or part-time after they retire," including 24 percent who "strongly agree" and 53 percent who "somewhat agree." Still greater numbers of employers (81%) agree that they are supportive of employees who plan to work longer. Yet fewer than half of employers surveyed offer the kinds of flexible work options and transition strategies that older workers indicate are needed to make working longer possible. Neither have employers included age in their diversity and inclusion strategies (only 8% according to the PricewaterhouseCoopers (2015) 18th annual CEO survey). Such oversights represent a disconnect between employers' beliefs and workers' perceptions.

When diversity efforts do exist, they are typically organized around overcoming stereotypes or bridging generational differences and tensions. The literature has largely rejected the idea that generations have distinct attitudes and values (Rudolph et al., 2020). Nevertheless, when employees identify with the idea that generations are associated with shared characteristics and values, this can add tension to workplace interactions and exchanges across age groups (North, 2019). North and Fiske (2015a) note that interventions to mitigate such tensions and conflicts across ages make use of either educational or contact approaches that are limited in scope and, as such, show mixed results. Educational approaches, for example, may affect knowledge about older adults, but seldom change attitudes toward them. Similarly, increasing contact between and among generations has shown mixed results. These authors recommend intervention strategies that (1) help employers recognize both the positives and the everyday realities of aging workers; (2) help older workers to resist "self-handicapping" with their own internalized ageist beliefs; and (3) decrease competition between and among the four generations currently in the workforce. More scholarship is needed for testing the effectiveness of any of these strategies.

Although chronological age continues to be a useful indicator of changes across the lifespan, it is an imprecise measure. Pitt-Catsouphes and colleagues (2012) note that certain thresholds and passages based on age have changed in ways that make chronological age less meaningful than it might have been in earlier times. Today, for example, a 40-something can be a first-time parent or a grandparent. A 50-year-old can be starting a new career or enjoying 30 years of tenure in an organization. A college student can be a retired veteran returning for an advanced degree. Thus, age might be better thought of as a prism with many different facets (Pitt-Catsouphes et al., 2012). According to North (2019) these other facets interact in ways that affect attitudes and capabilities having to do with later life work.

Much has been made in recent years about generational age or the extent to which individual employees are shaped during their coming of age during important social and political events, such as the Great Depression, the Vietnam War, Civil Rights activism, or today's pandemic. But tenure with an organization, not to mention lifetime experience, for example, might be more relevant to assessments of performance than age *per se*; similarly, whether one is in early career or late career can vary by age. Indeed, as North (2019) points out, such intersections within age may explain many of the null findings and/or conflicting findings within the still small literature on aging and work. Trawinski (2016a) sums this up succinctly: "Age is a number, not a credential" (p. 3).

Ideally, supervisors would make a clear and evidence-based assessment of an individual's ability, skills, experience, motivations, and knowledge and how that particular employee adds value to teams and the overall performance of the organization, rather than rely on generic assumptions based on age or other sociodemographic characteristics. A report by AARP on leveraging the value of an age-diverse workforce suggests diversity and inclusion efforts must be part of the organization's overall strategy, holding managers accountable for implementing diversity and inclusion initiatives throughout all levels of the organization, and suggests that the workforce should mirror the diversity of the organization's customer or client base (Trawinski, 2016a, b).

North advocates for more scholarly work to examine generation, age, tenure, and experience simultaneously, in order to deconstruct the prism of age and better understand the relationships between these facets and important organizational outcomes, especially productivity and performance. Rigor is lacking in many studies throughout the diversity and inclusion literature. Most of the research is based on cross-sectional quantitative data or else is qualitative but with small sample sizes. Additional research is needed to overcome these significant methodological limitations.

Compensation and Benefits

Compensation and benefits are key elements that define a job as "good" and are another set of practices that affect retirement decisions. It is well established that compensation (earnings as well as pension wealth) increases over much of the life course. The human capital model and the long-term incentive-contract model are the two main models that describe the relationship between productivity, compensation, and age.

General human capital refers to skills and abilities that typically increase with experience and are equally useful at jobs within and outside of one's current employer. Specific human capital refers to skills and abilities that typically increase with tenure at a person's current job and are productive only within the firm where the skills are acquired. These forms of human capital increase earnings over much of the life course (Becker, 1964).[4] This occurs because investments in human capital increase employee productivity; thus, both productivity and wages rise over much of the life course. General human capital investment causes wages to rise in lock-step with productivity. In contrast, workers and employers share in both the costs of and the returns (higher productivity) to specific human capital investment. Since the value of specific human capital isn't realized outside of the current employment relationship, productivity and wages still rise over the life course, but wages grow more slowly—starting out higher than productivity but ending up lower as productivity rises faster.[5]

A long-term incentive contract provides a different model of the age-earnings profile, in which a rising earnings profile is generated even when productivity is flat over the life course (Lazear, 1979). Under such a contract, if the worker is paid less than his contribution to productivity when young, with the promise of earning more than his or her contribution later, then the worker effectively commits to providing high effort in the early years in exchange for higher compensation later during his job tenure. This Lazear contract encourages the worker to exert effort and benefits the worker as long as the present value of compensation is greater than the minimum acceptable wage the worker believes she can earn elsewhere in the labor market. In contrast to the human capital model, in the Lazear model earnings rise faster than productivity over the life course.[6]

These alternative models of rising earnings profiles provide different explanations as to why firms offer pensions to employees in an effort to shape retirement behavior.[7] As Becker (1964) points out, investments in specific human capital give employers an incentive to offer pensions that reward workers for long tenure until their investments are recouped. DB pension plans do this quite naturally by tying benefits to years of service and the high wages earned late in the career.

Part of the delayed payments in Lazear contracts may come in the form of a pension upon retirement. The backloading of DB pension plans provides a way to delay compensation and encourage retirement on a specific date. A DB pension plan could be structured in a way that induces retirement by setting the maximum present value of the pension to peak on a certain date (Lazear, 1995). For example, Kotlikoff and Wise (1989) study a 1979 survey of pension plans, focusing on DB plans that based benefits on past earnings. Pension plans typically specify certain retirement ages, including, for example, early and normal retirement ages. The earlier a worker takes retirement, the longer the benefits will be received, but in return the benefit amounts are lowered. However, if the benefit reductions are actuarially unfair, so that pensions taken at these early retirement ages are not adjusted downward by as much as they should be to compensate for the greater number of years for which they will be received, then after each of these ages pension accrual rates (the rate of growth of pension wealth from period to period) can fall sharply and typically become negative. Kotlikoff and Wise show that such accrual patterns characterize DB pension plans in the United States and argue that these kinds of patterns in pension wealth suggest explicit attempts to induce retirement at specific ages, as we would expect to arise under Lazear contracts.[8]

DC retirement plans, on the other hand, do not have either of these features. They do not particularly bind workers to firms, because they are portable; moreover, because they continually grow (as long as the assets in which they are invested grow), they do not serve explicitly to induce retirement. Nonetheless, DC pensions

---

[4]There is little dispute that labor market experience contributes to rising wages, but some dispute about how much tenure increases wages, because better worker-employer matches result in higher wages and also last longer (e.g., Topel, 1991).

[5]Nevertheless, versions of models with specific human capital investment can be constructed in which wages rise faster than productivity (Carmichael, 1983).

[6]The Lazear model pertains more to earnings growth with tenure than to growth with experience, because subsequent employers would have no reason to compensate a worker for the below-productivity wage earned on a previous job. However, most workers in the U.S. economy settle into long-term jobs (Hall, 1982), a finding that has changed little despite some changes in job attachment in U.S. labor markets (Neumark, 2000). Thus, the evolution of earnings during workers' tenure with their employers plays an important role in the life-cycle pattern of earnings.

[7]There are other theories about why employers provide pensions, including: tax incentives because earnings of pension assets are not taxed until benefits are paid; insurance against the risk of living a long time after retirement (for DB plans, a role also played by public pensions); and shifting the risk on retirement-related benefits to employers (in the case of DB plans). See Dorsey et al., (1998).

[8]Employers' ability to use changes in pension wealth to induce retirement is not unrestricted. The 1990 Older Workers Benefits Protection Act regulated financial inducements to retire.

create other inducements to retire. One inducement is the ability to begin making withdrawals from DC plans at age 59.5, which in the presence of liquidity constraints should result in increased acceptable wages to stay in the labor market.

There has been a sea change in pension provision since the early 1980s, with the shift from DB to DC retirement plans (including 401(k) plans). For example, Papke (1996) reports that for single-employer pension plans with 100 or more participants, the number of DB plans fell from over 22,000 in 1980 to 17,000 in 1992, and the number of active participants fell from 21.9 million to 19.8 million. During the same period, the number of DC plans rose from 13,000 to 38,000, and the number of participants from 15 million to 29 million, while the number of 401(k) plans and participants rose even more strongly. And Friedberg and Webb (2003) report that the percentage of pensioned full-time employees with a DC plan rose from 40 to 79 percent between 1983 and 1998, while the percentage covered by a DB plan fell from 87 to 44 percent over the same period.

The shift from DB to DC plans would appear to undermine what may be one of the principal roles of pensions in the interplay between productivity and compensation. In both the specific human capital model and the Lazear contract model, backloading of pensions plays an important role. DC plans, however, typically do not have backloading, but instead generally result in contributions of a given share of wages, and workers are fully vested relatively quickly (a maximum of six years under 401(k) plans). And in a world of Lazear contracts, DB plans, but not DC plans, can create strong incentives for workers to separate at the right retirement age, from the perspective of the implicit long-term incentive contract.[9]

Thus, the shift in pensions in the U.S. economy could possibly threaten or limit the ability of workers and employers to enter into long-term relationships whose productivity is enhanced by either greater specific human capital investment, or greater incentives to exert effort. If the underlying importance of long-term employment relationships—stemming from either specific human capital investment or Lazear-type contracts—has not changed, then the shift in pensions may be alarming. In this view, whatever has spurred the shift to DC plans and away from DB plans ultimately threatens the ability of employers and workers to form these productive long-term relationships. Moreover, with the aging of the Baby Boom generation, employers may be likely to be hit with rapidly aging, highly paid workforces, with little leverage with which to encourage retirement, especially given the threat of age discrimination claims. This "perfect storm" of an increasing burden of highly paid older workers and an inability to "lock in" younger workers may be viewed as presenting severe challenges to companies in the next couple of decades.

On the other hand, a concern that the shift from DB to DC plans makes it difficult to induce older workers to retire may be misplaced in some important respects, which instead point to the challenge of trying to keep older individuals employed. Moreover, with an aging workforce, employers may face some difficulties in meeting labor demand needs if they cannot induce enough older individuals to remain in the labor market. Thus, the reduced incentives to retire generated by the shift from DB to DC plans may, over the next few decades, offer some advantages because of the need to try to keep older individuals working, even if, in the steady state, the shift in pensions might otherwise pose challenges to employers.

KEY FACTORS OF INFLUENCE

Job Control

Employers are often locked into thinking that work can only be organized in a specific way, although research demonstrates that the organization of where and when work is done can vary. Moreover, who controls the timing of work can differ across industries, as well as across jobs and workers within organizations. However, these disparities within organizations and occupations are not inevitable. For example, teams of workers in hourly service jobs could self-organize to enhance the flexibility of all team members. Professional, administrative, and clerical jobs could be designed more flexibly, especially given rapidly evolving technologies (Kelly and Moen, 2020; Fan et al., 2019). Though shifts in organizational policies and practices often occur at a glacial pace, the COVID-19 pandemic has shown that many jobs can be quickly redesigned and reimagined so that people can work more flexibly and remotely.

---

[9]Friedberg and Webb (2003) present evidence that the shift to DC plans leads to later retirement ages.

Prior to COVID-19, a five-year randomized field trial (described above in the section on Flexible Work Arrangements; Kelly and Moen, 2020) demonstrated that providing employees with more control over when and where they worked, together with supervisors who are supportive of employees' family and personal lives, not only increased health and well-being, it also promoted greater job satisfaction and lowered turnover rates for workers of all ages. Older workers participating in the flexibility redesign planned on remaining with their firms for a longer period of time than those in the comparison group following usual practices (Moen et al., 2016a; see also Cahill et al., 2015). This was not a form of special accommodation for a few employees; rather, flexibility became part of team practice and culture, "the way we work here," so long as deadlines and goals were met. In other words, it became the default for everyone, including those who chose to continue to work conventional hours at the workplace; they too had the latitude to change when and where they accomplished their tasks.

Job control involves both decision authority or latitude over key decisions regarding how work is done and the sense that one's skills are utilized (Bakker and Demerouti, 2017, 2007; Karasek and Theorell, 1990). *Schedule control* is distinct from job control, but baseline evidence from the randomized trial found that those who have more control over how they work (job control) also tend to have more control over when and where they work (schedule control). This is not surprising since, in many organizations, higher-status employees tend to have more autonomy and flexibility, while those in the lower ranks have less freedom to decide how they approach their tasks and whose schedules are monitored more closely. A similar randomized controlled trial revealed that employees of all types in a large hospital system who were given more control over their schedules were able to better meet budget guidelines (James et al., 2015), improve their workability[10] (Morelock et al., 2017), and reverse early retirement expectations (Cahill et al., 2015) than their peers in the control group.

As we have seen in connection with work-at-home mandates during the COVID-19 pandemic, new communication technologies facilitate possibilities for working anywhere, anytime. But this also means that coworkers and managers often feel free to reach out for work matters at any time and everywhere, 24/7. These managerial practices, coupled with instant-availability communication technologies, can make remote work more stressful than working at a workplace. Employees' sense of control over both their jobs and their schedules can make the difference between positive and negative outcomes of these changes. Despite ratcheting job demands and "always on" expectations, both job control and schedule control appear to reduce burnout and turnover and to promote job satisfaction, health, and well-being (Fan et al., 2015; Moen et al., 2017, 2011; Moen, Fan et al., 2013). Additional research is needed to follow older workers over time as both demands and control options shift within organizations, or as they move to different jobs.

Employee Voice and Participation

Mechanisms of *employee voice* are means by which older workers can influence their employment conditions. Employee voice has many different aspects and meanings. For example, voice typically refers to how workers communicate with management, the say workers have about their work tasks, and the participation workers have in organizational decision-making (Wilkinson et al., 2014). As a key form of collective employee voice, unions are an important element of the workplace that provides additional benefits to older workers, increasing their power and connection to the organization. In the United States, labor unions typically negotiate seniority provisions across economic and noneconomic bargaining issues. Time served in a job or with an organization defines seniority, which provides benefits to older workers with greater tenure than younger workers. Pay systems in unionized organizations are often structured to increase wages as employee seniority increases. Overtime premiums, preferences on vacation periods and length of vacation, eligibility for promotions and transfers, and protection from layoffs are other benefits that also come with seniority.

Seniority provisions fall into two categories: benefit-status and competitive-status seniority (Fossum, 2012). *Benefit-status seniority* refers to benefits employees receive due to organizational tenure. For example, the length of vacation allowed depends on seniority benefit status. *Competitive-status seniority* refers to preferences employees receive in competition for a new position or in determining the order of layoffs. In union contracts, seniority is

---

[10]"Workability" refers to the competence, health, and other mental and physical characteristics that workers need to meet the demands of their jobs.

often a deciding factor for promotions if the qualifications of competing employees are otherwise equal. In addition, layoffs are typically determined in a way that protects employees with the highest seniority. These seniority provisions are most typical in manufacturing and emerged as a form of protection against arbitrary treatment by supervisors.

For older workers, labor unions provide a form of protection and voice at the workplace. They provide representation when older workers have grievances and advocate for them in discussions with management as they would advocate for any worker. In the United States, labor unions have typically not negotiated specific benefits for workers based on age; although seniority provisions are highly correlated with age, they are based on longevity. In contrast, labor unions in other countries have been more proactive in negotiating provisions that benefit older workers directly, such as partial retirement schemes or demography funds for older worker training (Flynn et al., 2013). Additional research on the role played by labor unions and other forms of employee voice at the workplace in affecting older worker retention or retirement would be helpful in better understanding the impact of older worker empowerment on employment outcomes.

The Impact of Technology

There is very limited research on how the implementation of technology in the workplace is impacting older workers in particular. By contrast, there is extensive research on the general effects of various forms of technology—including artificial intelligence, robotics, the internet, and data driven management—on jobs, job tasks, and the workplace (Neufeind et al., 2018; Brynjolfsson and McAfee, 2014). The effects of such technologies on jobs are mixed. Some argue that new technologies will have positive effects leading to improved productivity, upskilling of jobs, and growing employment in certain occupations (McGuinness et al., 2019; Autor, 2015; Mokyr et al., 2015). Others suggest new technology will have more negative effects by eliminating jobs with routine tasks or jobs that lack social intelligence, further exacerbating inequality (Fonseca et al., 2018; Adermon and Gustavsson, 2015; Goos et al., 2014).

It is unclear which perspective will best describe the future. When it comes to technology such as machine learning, the effects on the workforce can be varied and depend on many factors (Brynjolfsson and Mitchell, 2017). More than just replacing jobs with routinized tasks, machine learning is likely to affect particular tasks within jobs that have specific strategic goals and from which data can be generated to help automate decision-making. The extent to which machine learning impacts particular jobs and occupations will depend on the demand and supply of specific skills, the extent to which tasks act as substitutes or complements, and price, income, and supply elasticities.

Coughlin (2020) suggests four areas for which the technologies adopted by employers affect a multigenerational workforce: for safety and well-being, for onsite assistance, for workforce transitions, and for knowledge management. *Safety and well-being* involves using technology to design workplaces so they reflect the physical needs of older workers, such as ergonomic elements or using wearable technology (wrist bands) that monitor physical depletion or mental engagement. *Onsite assistance* is the use of technology to monitor repetitive tasks, such as lift and positioning technology on assembly lines, and through "cobots" to aid workers in expanding worker strength. These technologies are designed for all workers but would typically benefit older workers to a greater degree and help extend working life.

Workforce transitions involves the use of technology to expand online learning as a form of lifelong learning. Technology is also used to develop app-based work that can serve to keep people employed, despite the increased risks workers bear as independent contractors. *Knowledge management* refers to the use of technology to help older workers learn on the job, for example through virtual reality wearables or by using data-driven technology to conduct reverse mentoring.

The extent to which technology extends the employment of older workers depends on several factors, including organizational culture, employee skill level, and technology design. An inclusive organizational culture that welcomes age-diversity is more likely to implement technology in a way that increases the ability of older workers to be productive. Higher-skilled workers, regardless of age, are more likely to receive training in new technology and benefit from technological innovation. In contrast, lower skilled workers may find their jobs replaced by automation and technology that can perform repetitive tasks (Mercer and Wyman, 2019). Technology design also plays a big role in the usability of technology by older workers and its effectiveness in raising older worker productivity (Thompson and Mayhorn, 2012). Yet we should be cautious about designing technology too specifically to meet older worker needs because of the risk of stigmatizing older workers and encouraging firms to replace them. More research is needed to sort out the differential effects of various forms of technology and technology design on older workers.

IMPLICATIONS FOR FUTURE RESEARCH

The literature regarding age-related organizational practices reveals areas in need of more research. First, most existing studies focus on *age-specific practices*, but not *age-neutral practices*. These two types of practices reflect two different approaches for managing workers and their aging processes (Yeatts et al., 1999). On the one hand, age-specific practices are developed to counter potential age-related declines among older workers. They may be well intended, but the specialized attention on age at work risks putting a "stamp" on older workers and highlighting their identity as "a devalued social group" (Froidevaux et al., 2020), contributing to stigmatization. In addition, age-specific practices can expand retirement pathways, address age stereotyping, more effectively develop human capital, and increase retirement security. But again, such targeted practices can draw organizational resources to a specific group and contribute to discord and resentment within the workforce. On the other hand, age-neutral practices consider all workers, regardless of age, as important human resources to their organization. Investment and development in human resources through age-neutral practices would conceivably reduce stigmatization and discord. There is currently a lack of research comparing the effectiveness of age-specific and age-neutral practices and the theoretical assumptions behind them.

Second, most existing studies focus on measuring the availability of age-related organizational practices, but not the actual utilization of these practices by workers. It is well known that merely offering organizational practices as policies does not necessarily lead to the policies' utilization (e.g., Wright and Nishii, 2013; Nishii et al., 2008). The differences between access to practices and the use of practices have been well documented in the work-family literature (Berg et al., 2014; Kossek et al., 2006; Eaton, 2003). Many older workers have limited access to flexible work options, with college-educated white men the most apt to have choices as to when, where, how, and how long to work (Moen, 2016a, b; Moen, 2013). Yet, more research is needed to fully understand the barriers for older workers to actually take advantage of the beneficial practices offered by their organizations. For example, more comparative studies that consider the effects of the institutions within which organizations are embedded would be particularly helpful in determining what drives older workers to access and use specific age-related practices.

Third, the organizational context is often lacking in studies of aging and workplace practices (Lee et al., 2017). Suggestions of age-related practices are often made without regard to potential organizational factors that may drive the response. Studies that seek to determine why some firms implement age-related practices and others do not are difficult to conduct due to the lack of longitudinal data in the United States to deal with issues of endogeneity. Thus, the classification and analysis of practices is most often focused on how practices affect individual outcomes and well-being. We recommend that government agencies establish or expand an existing longitudinal, representative sample of organizations with questions focused on older workers and practices so more research could be conducted on the determinants of offering age-related practices within organizations.

Fourth, we would encourage more research using the interest-based perspective to determine what age-related and age-neutral practices are offered by organizations, what types of older workers have access to these practices, and who actually uses them. Such studies could examine the role of managerial strategy as a reflection of employer interests or the role of institutions in distributing power across employers and employees. For example, research has shown that employers who analyze business needs have positive attitudes toward their older workers, and those who have large numbers of older workers are more apt to have policies that better fit with the needs of older workers (van Dalen et al., 2015; Lee et al., 2012; Loretto and White, 2006).

We can see this tension between employer and employee interests play out in employee access to and use of flexibility work arrangements. Older workers express preferences for greater "flexibility," but do not always have access to the flexible work arrangements that would keep them in their jobs. There are real equity concerns when flexibility is allocated in ways to meet the needs of some workers but not others. Better educated workers, high-income workers, and those who could easily find another job tend to be able to have their needs "accommodated" (Glauber, 2011; Swanberg et al., 2005; Golden, 2001). Workers lower in the occupational hierarchy are more likely to be in place-bound jobs or have rigid shifts (such as jobs in retail, restaurants, or hospitality). More research would be welcome that examined the implications of these practices for those in later adulthood who wish to scale back or work more flexibly in terms of time and place.

CONCLUSION

This chapter examines a variety of theoretical approaches and work practices impacting older worker employment. We recognize that there is no universal set of workplace characteristics desired by all workers, especially older workers. Dimensions of job quality and the total worker health approach emphasize the importance of constructive relationships, a culture of respect, opportunities for training and meaningful work, good pay, flexibility and control, safety, and stability—all important features of workplaces valued by workers. Whether these practices are implemented at the workplace, however, depends very much on the interests of both employers and employees, which we emphasize throughout our discussion of workplace practices.

We highlight various practices, including flexible work arrangements, training practices, a supportive climate for age diversity and inclusion, and compensation and benefits. Our discussion of these practices shows how different interests of employers and employees can shape practices and their influence on older worker employment decisions. Throughout this chapter we call for more research in key areas that relate to whether and what kinds of flexible arrangements affect the timing of retirement exits, the effect of compensation systems on retirement decisions, and implications of the intersectionality of a variety of age-related practices that affect older workers.

We also discuss various factors that influence how older workers experience workplace practices. The extent of job control and schedule control is critical for helping older workers manage their work and nonwork commitments, though more research is needed to fully understand how control affects the path toward retirement. Employee voice and participation is another factor that can empower older workers to better shape work practices in their interest. Technology is also impacting job tasks and shaping how older workers experience work. Much more research is needed about how new forms of technology are either fostering older workers' employment or leading to more early exits.

BOX 5-1
The Effects of COVID-19 on Workplace Practices and Older Workers

The COVID-19 pandemic presents both challenges and opportunities with regard to older workers' employment. The pandemic has forced employers to restructure workplaces with health and safety standards in mind. COVID-19 testing, social distancing where possible, and remote working have increased dramatically. Communication software such as Zoom and Microsoft Teams has increased in use and replaced face-to-face meetings. Two aspects of pandemic-affected work are salient for older workers:

- *Employees over the age of 60 are more vulnerable to infection than are younger workers.*
  - Employer COVID-testing programs and vaccine mandates, especially for essential workers, have been important in lowering the level of risk.
  - Concerns about the vulnerability of older workers to infection have increased the risk of age discrimination at the workplace (Morrow-Howell and Gonzales, 2020).
- *Remote working has gained acceptance in organizations as managers have seen that workers can be productive working from home.* This could lead to a more flexible work environment after the pandemic subsides.
  - Remote working has created opportunities for older workers by providing a way for them to remain socially distanced while keeping their jobs and income, especially for those in jobs with higher-level skills and those in professional jobs.
  - On the other hand, workers who are not able to work remotely face greater risk of infection. These different experiences exacerbate inequalities in how the virus affects income and occupational groups.

6

Age Discrimination, One Source of Inequality

INTRODUCTION

Ageism contributes to disparities for older workers. This chapter describes the measurement and impact of ageist treatment in the workplace and the labor market. It moves from the micro (interpersonal-level) view to the macro (society-level) view, beginning with face-to-face workplace issues. It then examines aggregated experiences within the workplace. Finally, it looks at the labor market.

Interpersonal or *face-to-face workplace issues* are those in which societal images and expectations about older workers (both explicit and implicit assumptions about their performance or behavior) are reflected in what these workers report regarding their experiences of workplace discrimination. These experiences of discrimination are associated with their mental and physical well-being. Universally beneficial remedies to such discrimination—the type of remedies most likely to be widely acceptable—aim to develop inclusive workplace climates, adopt realistic assessments of workers' cognitive capacity, and focus on measuring their actual job performance. Although age-based analyses find no consistent performance differences across workers, older workers consistently report experiencing discrimination. However, beyond well-documented ageism in hiring processes, proof of discrimination within workplace settings is elusive. Even less is known about how these age-related work experiences and their personal correlates vary as age intersects with other marginalized categories, such as those based on gender or race-ethnicity.

When individuals are aggregated at the *workplace level,* analyses of plant and office age-related productivity also find no clear performance differences, suggesting that assumptions about age-related performance differences are not supported by evidence. Finally, anticipating the next chapter, the current chapter also examines the *labor market*—older workers' aggregate productivity and employers' aggregate age discrimination. Analyses of direct and indirect evidence, and especially audit studies of job applications, show that stereotypes about older workers affect labor-market demand for their work, constraining their work opportunities as they age. This discussion paves the way to the next chapter, which examines age-related labor market supply and demand.

All three levels of analysis—interpersonal, workplace, and labor market—reveal sources of inequality based on age.

DISTINCT FEATURES OF AGEISM

Most workforce variables apply in some form to all workers. For example, individuals' career paths always depend on their training, on having other breadwinners or caregivers in the household, on organizational climate, and on job characteristics and the labor market. As the prior chapters show, personal (individual and household) factors, as well as organizational (workplace and job) characteristics, shape the pathways of older workers as well.

In addition, older workers, as a group, have the distinct potential to experience age discrimination, which overlaps somewhat but also differs from other forms of discrimination (see Fiske and Taylor, 2021). For example, the old-age category is permeable, and people generally hope to join it someday (but just not yet, as the boundary always recedes). Compared with other characteristics, age more often appears as a continuous variable, sometimes categorized into life stages ("old"), relative standing ("older than me"), cut-offs ("eligible for discount"), or changing roles ("grandparent").

Another distinctive feature of age as an identity group membership is that, as with gender, people have older and younger people within their own families, something that is less often true for some other categories (e.g., race, religion). This means that older and younger people are often interdependent in the home. Nevertheless, families can treat older members (interpersonally; North and Fiske, 2012) based on age-related preferences, expectations, and constraints. Older individuals can internalize ageism; they may prefer, expect, and constrain themselves to act stereotypically (*intra*-personally; Levy, 2009). Ageism and age discrimination demonstrably operate at these intrapersonal, interpersonal, and structural levels (Chang et al., 2020); the workforce review here emphasizes the latter two levels, moving from workplace encounters to aggregated workplace profiles to labor-market outcomes.

Each of these distinctive features of age—a continuous variable often treated categorically, with permeable and moving boundaries; self-relevant; involving family relations—altogether complicates measurement. The meaning of "older" age depends on perspective, context, and purpose: who is asking about it, where, and why. As Chapter 5 noted, even within a single organization, a person's chronological age is associated with other factors that are related to their treatment, such as birth generation, employee tenure, and work experience, each of which may have different effects. Where possible, this review aims to be clear about what a given study means by "older."

FACE-TO-FACE AGEISM: HOW PEOPLE VIEW OLDER WORKERS

Ageism theoretically has a variety of plausible origins, each of which implies a different workplace intervention (though this is not our focus here; see Box 6-1). In describing the work-related manifestations of ageism, this chapter relies on some theories already introduced, including rational choice and human capital, but also introduces new ones: *implicit bias, stereotype content,* and *prescriptive ageism* (see Table 6-1).

The evidence presented throughout this chapter shows that, as with race and gender, people treat older workers as a category. Responses range from explicit and overt bias (regular, reportable attitudes) to implicit, latent bias (subtle, modern, covert incivilities; Cortina, 2008). Social psychology distinguishes among key indicators of both explicit and implicit bias: simple evaluative attitudes (preferences), cognitive stereotypes (beliefs, expectations), emotional prejudices (specific affect, such as pity or resentment), and discriminatory behavior (constraining action) (Fiske, 1998). The evidence for ageism, reviewed here, includes *perceivers'* explicit and implicit attitudes, cognitive beliefs and stereotypes, and emotional prejudices about older workers, as well as *older workers' own reports* of behavioral discrimination. Hence, the review begins with the individual perceiver's explicit attitudes and then moves to define and discuss implicit ones.

Explicit Attitudes and Preferences

Simple evaluative-preference judgments stigmatize older adults more than they stigmatize some societal groups and less than others. The Project Implicit website collects data from visitors who take implicit and explicit attitude measures on a variety of demographic targets (https://implicit.Harvard.edu). After nearly 15 years of data collection, the results show that Americans who volunteered their explicit attitudes toward older people (online respondents, N = 588,230) display moderate negativity (Figure 6-1; Charlesworth and Banaji, 2019). But this masks a gradual change in attitudes over time. Overall, 4.4 million online volunteers expressed their explicit attitudes toward at least some of six social groups: age, race, sexuality, disability, skin tone, and body weight (Charlesworth and Banaji, 2019). In just over a decade, all these self-reported attitudes moved toward neutral on seven-point scales, away from expressing preferences for or against specific groups (e.g., young over old versus old over young). Anti-old, pro-young bias changed less than did sexuality and racial biases, but more than disability, skin-tone, and weight biases (see bottom

**BOX 6-1
Theories of Ageism's Origins, with Implications for Interventions***

Theory of Ageism and Its Origins	Main Premise	If Ageism Is Modifiable, by What Mechanisms?
Individual Threats		
Terror Management	Older people make mortality salient, so others avoid them	Salience varies
Social Identity	People seek belonging with valued, similar others, e.g., youth	Identity varies
Ego-Protective Function	People avoid death thoughts and thus elders	Function varies
Interpersonal Stigma		
Negative halo	Older appearance (unattractive) cues overall negativity	Difficult to change
Overgeneralization	Aged appearance implies traits (older face cues poor health)	Difficult to change
Social affordances	Older people do not provide preferred activities	Elders' other offers
Evolutionary Value		
Fitness cues	Older people look sick, contagious	Hard-wired, fixed, but education could modify
Socio-evolutionary	Older people lack useful resources	Reframing is possible
Sociocultural Roles		
Socio-historical	Older people's functions replaced by technology (collective memory) and social change (nuclear families)	Change roles from traditional to modern
Social Role	Older people fill cooperative but low-status roles	Highlight other roles

*For references and more context, see North and Fiske, 2012.

TABLE 6-1 Theories Applied to Ageism in the Workforce*

Ageist Preferences, Evaluations, Attitudes	
Explicit bias	Not a theory, but a measurement method assuming the veracity of self-reported answers to attitude questions.
Implicit bias	Immediate associations favoring ingroups and devaluing outgroups.
Ageist Expectations, Beliefs, Stereotypes and Emotional Prejudices	
Stereotype Content Model	Stereotypes focus on warmth (trustworthy, friendly) and competence (capability, confidence). Warmth x competence interaction predicts distinct prejudices (contempt, envy, pity, pride).
Ageism as a Prescriptive Constraint	
Succession, Consumption, Identity	Elders should cede power, forfeit resources, defer.
Perceived Age Discrimination	
Selective Incivility	People perceive unusual, ambiguous, exclusionary behavior as potential discrimination.
Links to Well-Being and Exit Decisions	
Stereotype Embodiment	Targets internalize others' stereotypes, tending to confirm.
Intersectionality	
Double Jeopardy	Two marginalized identities multiply the risks of each.
Invisibility	Two marginalized identities exclude the target from both.

*See text for references.

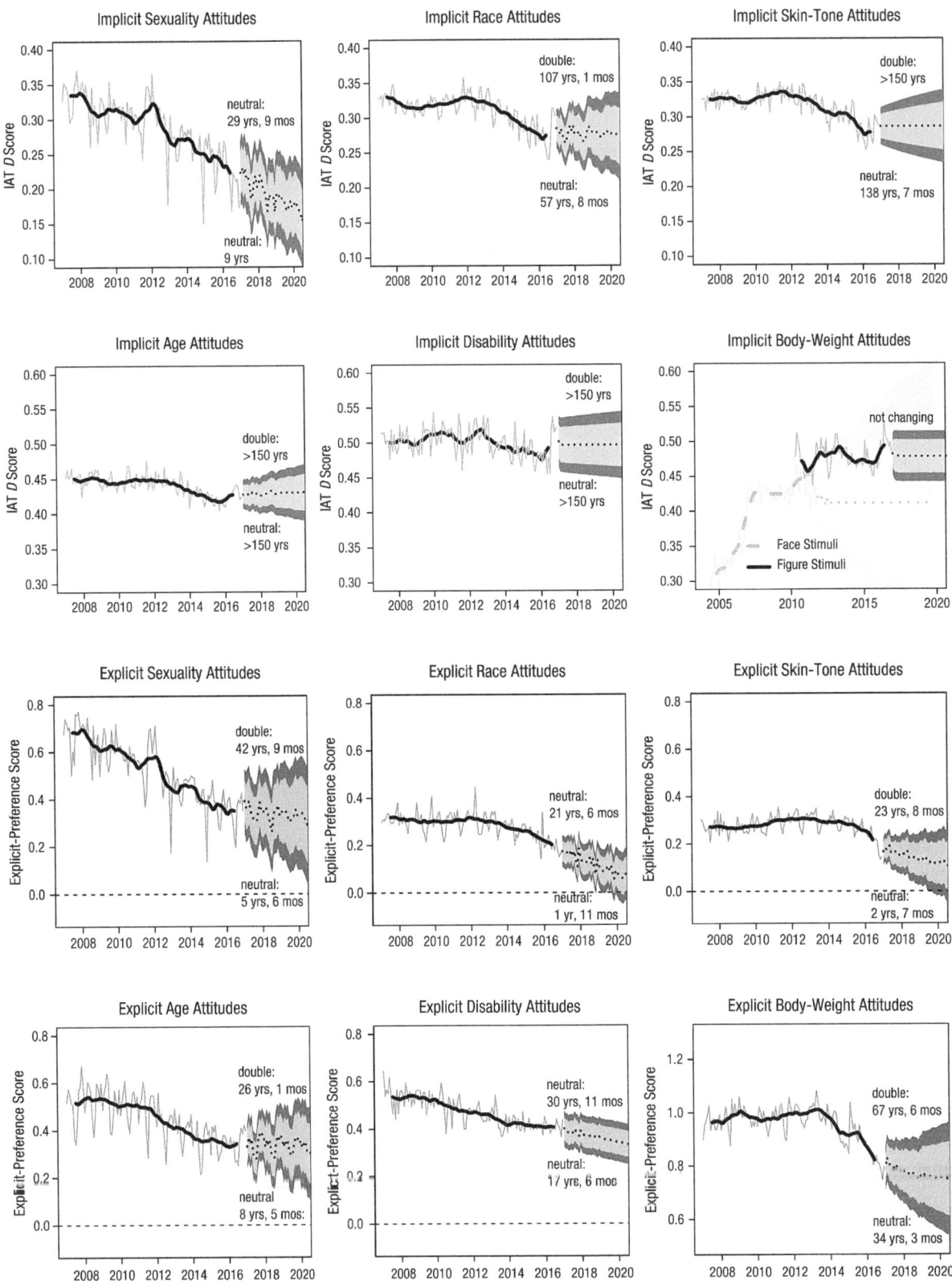

FIGURE 6-1 Change and predicted change in implicit and explicit attitudes from 2007 to 2020.

half of Figure 6-1). Overt ageism, like all self-reported intergroup prejudices, is becoming less acceptable, at least in some public arenas.

A note of caution, because this online sample of respondents is not representative but tilts younger, female, liberal, and educated, compared to the general population, the responders might have adjusted their responses to reflect civility norms, downplaying their own biases. Their socially desirable responses promote equity but also create challenges for accurate measurement. Among researchers, debates center on defining the "true" attitude, as previous biases may co-exist with reconsidered updates (Wilson et al., 2000); if this is true, then rejected attitude habits can leak out in unguarded moments.

One conclusion for research follows: Whether and when the original, unfiltered attitude or the newer, socially desirable, revised attitude guides age-related workplace behavior, including discrimination, remains an empirical question. But measurement is not straightforward and requires development.

Furthermore, contrary to popular intuition, reported ageism is worse in modern East Asia than in the West (across 23 countries, N = 21,090; North and Fiske [2015b] meta-analysis).[1] Ageism appears to be a function of intergenerational resource tensions. That is, when younger people are expected to provide greater support for their elders, they are more biased against them. These cross-cultural findings merit greater elaboration in workplace data.

Implicit Attitudes and Preferences

Less direct measures focus on people's *implicit* evaluative associations (latent preferences) about societal groups. *Implicit* biases are unconscious attitudes and associations that individuals hold about specific groups. Indirect measures of these attitudes about older adults assess the degree to which when the concept of older person comes to mind, negative associations also come to mind. The most common measure assesses speed of pairing in-group or outgroup (e.g., *young, old*) with other positive or negative concepts (e.g., *good* or *bad; sunny* or *cloudy*). On some trials, participants sort words or images of old people on the same side of the screen as negative concepts not relevant to age; simultaneously, they sort young people and positive concepts together. Then, on other trials, by instruction, they sort together *old* and *good*, *young* and *bad*. The logic is that if negative associations have faster response times (*old* and *bad* go together) than do positive associations, this reflects some evaluative tendency stored in the mind. Implicit associations are detectable, but relatively automatic and unexamined, in this view. (For examples, see the Project Implicit website, below; for theory, see Greenwald and Lai, 2020.) The Implicit Association Test (IAT) has its critics (e.g., Fiedler et al., 2006), but recent comprehensive meta-analyses provide convincing evidence of its validity, as follows.

Compared with explicit reports of in-group favoritism and out-group derogation, implicit preferences reduce the biases in measurement that stem from social desirability, that is, from people protecting their reputation when surveyed. For controversial attitudes such as prejudice, implicit and explicit evaluations may not correlate because people report no bias but show faster negative associations with outgroups than ingroups. The correlation of the IAT with explicit self-reports was .24 in one meta-analysis of 126 studies (Hofmann et al., 2005), .36 in another (57 object pairs; Nosek, 2005), and .36 in another (184 samples; Greenwald et al., 2009). A meta-analysis of the IAT with behavior (217 research reports) found that the correlations vary depending on study focus, methods, and attitude polarity; higher-quality studies report bigger effects, but most studies are statistically underpowered (Kurdi et al., 2019; see also Greenwald et al., 2009).

The widespread use of these measures attests to their intuitive appeal. The theory holds that most people have positive associations concerning themselves and associate themselves with certain in-groups (e.g., their age cohort), so they also have positive associations attached to their in-groups—and less positive associations with out-groups (Greenwald and Lai, 2020). Overall, implicit in-group positivity (and relative outgroup negativity) predicts a range of behavior toward a range of out-groups. Applying these measures to ageism therefore seems useful.

Implicit associations with the concept "old" are, along with obesity and disability, the most negative associations among six out-groups (Figure 6-1). These negative age implicit-association results were also stable over the preceding 15 years, even as other implicit attitudes were becoming more neutral (see top half of Figure 6-1;

---

[1] In the United States, the exceptions—samples where young people do reportedly admire their elders—include African Americans (Fiske et al., 2009) and Native Americans (Burkley et al., 2017).

Charlesworth and Banaji, 2019). The correlation between implicit and explicit ageism is only r = 0.12, meaning the two forms of ageism are effectively independent. To the extent respondents might want to conceal their ageist bias—an understudied assumption—measuring both implicit and explicit responses would be useful.

In conclusion: to supplement existing research on explicit attitudes, the impact of implicit ageism on workplace behavior specifically could use rigorous, high-powered investigation. From a practical perspective, if the attitudes are implicit, people cannot individually track their effects on, for example, their own hiring or promotion decisions. Workplace research should therefore monitor patterns that might show unexamined bias.

Stereotypes: Mixed Expectations

Stereotypes, which are generalized beliefs based on group membership, underlie evaluative attitudes. Some stereotypes describe default expectations of a group and are openly reportable cognitions; these are explicit, descriptive stereotypes. As organizational psychology shows, stereotypes about older workers are mostly negative (Ng and Feldman, 2012), though not entirely; they are often ambivalent or mixed (Burn et al., 2020; North and Fiske, 2015b). Starting with the general content of older-adult stereotypes provides context to the older-worker stereotypes.

Historically, stereotypes of elders were probably more positive, according to a text analysis of five million books published between 1880 and 2020 (Mason et al., 2015). However, these older stereotypes were based predominantly on those for men, because younger and older women appeared less frequently in the database of texts. This is consistent with other research that finds that male members of a category often serve as the default (e.g., that a generic "American" refers to a male citizen; Eagly and Kite, 1987). Adjectives associated with (male) older people began to shift in the early 1900s, a change that researchers have speculated was due to society devaluing older people as their roles changed: (1) widespread literacy and mass media replaced a reliance on elders' wisdom; (2) industrialization required nimble adaptation to changeable modern skill sets, rather than traditional practices; (3) families became more nuclear and had less need for multigenerational contributions (Butler, 2009; Nelson, 2005).

Currently, ambivalence toward older people is the most common stereotype, not just within the United States, but globally (Table 6-2). Across a variety of countries, older people are universally viewed as well-intentioned

TABLE 6-2 Mixed Stereotypes about Older Adults and Older Workers

Source	(Not) Competent	Warm-Trustworthy	Other
Fiske et al., 2002			
	less competent	warm	
	less skilled	friendly	
	less intelligent	trustworthy	
	less confident	sincere	
Ng and Feldman, 2012			
	less motivated	less trusting	less healthy
	less willing to train and develop		
	more resistant and less willing to change		
	more vulnerable to work-family imbalance		
Marcus et al., 2016			
	incompetent	warm	not adaptable
Burn et al., 2020			
	lower ability to learn	dependable	less attractive
	less adaptable	careful	hard of hearing
	worse communication skills	better communication skills	less physically able
	less (more) productive	warm personality	
	worse with technology	negative personality	
	less creative		
	worse memory		
	more experienced		

but incompetent, "doddering but dear."[2] Older people are supposedly warm and friendly, but less ambitious, less responsible, and less intelligent (Andreoletti et al., 2001; Rubin and Brown, 1975). Ambivalent stereotypes are often unexamined and harder to detect, because they mix both positive and negative attributes (Fiske et al., 2002), but a reliable and valid scale has proven able to establish ambivalent ageism (Fiske and North, 2014). This ambivalence is reflected in mixed behavior. For example, during the COVID-19 pandemic, because elders are especially vulnerable to severe infections, protective measures such as senior shopping hours and early vaccine access were provided to offer support to this population; however, at the same time, public discourse reflected a resentment of older people's priority for health care (Monahan et al., 2020).

The Work-related Age-based Stereotypes Scale (WAS; Marcus et al., 2016) builds on these concepts to show that stereotypes of older workers are multidimensional, incorporating both negative (incompetent, not adaptable) and positive (warm) aspects. WAS has demonstrated validity in measuring stereotypes about older workers across lab and field settings (N = 1,245; see Table 6-2). The older-worker stereotypes considered suggest similar ambivalence: incompetent but trustworthy, if also unhealthy.

A meta-analysis (Ng and Feldman, 2012) of 418 nonlaboratory empirical studies (representing a total sample size of 208,204 participants) examined whether empirical evidence supports six common stereotypes of older workers, namely, that they are less motivated, less willing to participate in training and career development, more resistant and less willing to change, less trusting, less healthy, and more vulnerable to work-family imbalance. All these alleged attributes relate to workplace competence, except perhaps being less trusting, which reflects the interpersonal dimension of warmth and communion, though it is not equivalent to one's own trustworthiness. The meta-analysis finds support for the incompetence stereotype, but only for the belief that older workers are less willing to participate in training or development (see Table 6-2); it is uninformative about the warmth dimension.

In a more recent study that used language processing techniques to examine the use of age-related stereotypes in job applications, Burn and colleagues (2020) reviewed literature in industrial psychology and related disciplines to identify 17 stereotypes related to health, personality, and skills that are commonly associated with workers in their 50s and 60s. Although more of these stereotypes were negative than positive,[3] when they are sorted according to their relationship to the two validated dimensions of age stereotypes discussed above (warmth and competence), they yield a more coherent picture that is consistent with previous findings across countries: one of ambivalence.

It is notable that these 17 stereotypes include several contradictory pairs (both worse and better communication skills, both less and more productive, and both negative and warm personality) and "less attractive" (as low warmth), which may reflect individual heterogeneity of beliefs, with different individuals subscribing to each. Alternatively, the contradictions may reflect construal by subtypes of older targets, as occurs in subtypes for gender (Eckes, 2002), race (Fiske et al., 2009), and sexuality (Clausell and Fiske, 2005). For example, subtypes of older people have included *grandmother* (all warmth), *elder statesman* (all competence), and *senior citizen* (neither warm nor competent; Brewer, Dull, and Lui, 1981), though these are not exhaustive.

In addition, this most recent meta-analysis of older-worker stereotypes included the dimension of being unhealthy (see Table 6-3). The mixture of positive (warmth) and negative (incompetent, unhealthy) stereotype dimensions regarding the older worker—and older adults generally—has costs to both individuals and society, as later sections indicate.

Conclusion: The measurement of older-worker stereotypes could benefit from more systematic investigation of the warmth dimension (being trustworthy as well as friendly). Also, closer description of elder subtypes might increase the accuracy of predicting their effects.

Prescriptive Stereotypes: Beliefs as Constraints

In addition to descriptive stereotypes, which affect expectations about older workers' characteristics (e.g., doddering, health issues), some stereotypes are prescriptive constraints, seeking to control older adults so they will "cooperate" (e.g., "be a dear"). People of different ages depend on each other's resource allocations, whether

---

[2] Based on data from six countries in Cuddy et al., (2005) and Fiske (2017); see also North and Fiske (2015b) for a meta-analysis of 23 countries.

[3] 11 are negative (lower ability to learn, less adaptable, less attractive, worse communication skills, less physically able, less productive, worse with technology, less creative, worse memory, hard of hearing, and negative personality), and six are positive (more productive, dependable, careful, more experienced, better communication skills, and warm personality).

TABLE 6-3 Stereotypes about Older Workers' Health

Aggregate Stereotype	Phrasing	Source
Less Attractive	"wrinkled," "unattractive," "not neat"	Kite et al. (1991)
	"less attractive"	Levin (1988)
	"worse-looking when older"	Zepelin et al. (1987)
Hard of Hearing	"hard of hearing"	Kite et al. (1991)
	"worse hearing," "think people speak too softly," "frustrated when not hearing," "think other people speak too fast," "often ask others to repeat"	Ryan et al. (1992)
	"worse hearing"	Hummert et al. (1995)
Worse Memory	"worse memory"	Hendrick et al. (1988)
	"worse memory"	Ryan et al. (1992)
	"worse memory"	Ryan and See (1993)
	"worse memory"	Hummert et al. (1995)
Less Physically Able	"lower physical capacity"	Kroon et al. (2016) (p. 16)
	"[worse] physical capability and health"	van Dalen et al. (2009) (p. 21)
	"sedentary," "physically handicapped," "slow moving," "sick," "shaky hands," "fragile," "poor posture"	Schmidt and Boland (1986)
	"less qualified for a physically demanding job"	Finkelstein et al. (1995)
	"tired," "scared of becoming sick or incompetent"	Hummert et al. (1994)
	"[lower] activity," "[less] energy," "[worse] health," "[less] speed"	Levin (1988) (p. 142)
	"less physically active," "unhealthy," "moves slowly"	Kite et al. (1991)
	"worse psychomotor speed"	Hendrick et al. (1988)

this concerns sharing money, handling tasks, or sharing information or time. Ageism's roots in intergenerational tensions lead younger and middle-aged people to endorse constraints for elders (North and Fiske, 2012, 2015a). These stereotypes highlight competition over (1) resources controlled by elders (e.g., orderly succession of power), (2) resources shared by everyone (e.g., unequal consumption of healthcare), and (3) resources identified with youth (e.g., social media savvy). In six studies (N = 1,022) using vignettes and simulated interactions, younger people (compared with middle-aged and older) liked older adults who stepped aside—who ceded power, passed up shared resources, and avoided youth culture—but did not respect them. Older adults who refused to comply with these behaviors were respected but disliked (North and Fiske, 2013). These prescriptive prejudices differentiate stereotypic warmth and competence, but go farther; for example, the most common result of an online search for "old people shouldn't" comes out with the top choice as "drive": literally constraining them to get out of the way.

Prescriptive stereotypes' constraints operate in the workforce as well. For example, succession plans may pressure older workers to retire promptly, ceding power and resource control (a later section returns to this point).

ASSESSING THE ACCURACY OF AGEIST STEREOTYPES: COGNITIVE CAPABILITIES IN LATER LIFE

Despite stability in ageist attitudes and stereotypes (and, as discussed in a later section, stability in older worker reports of discrimination), a critic might ask whether these stereotypes about older workers' ability are grounded in evidence. This section explores current evidence of age-related cognitive capacity. Longstanding stereotypes of older workers as ineffective (Avolio and Barrett, 1987; Singer, 1986; Rosen and Jerdee, 1976a, b) have confronted equally longstanding and contradictory evidence of their validity (for a review, see McCann and Giles, 2002). The newer evidence is even more comprehensive.

To be sure, individuals do experience physical and psychological changes as they age. This is a natural part of everyone's development process, as a result of transitions and experiences that impact what they learn and how they develop. As the field of cognitive aging agrees, declines in healthy aging are exaggerated; rather, variability in these processes is the rule (Tucker-Drob, 2019). For an aging workforce, the central questions about cognitive decline over time are, for any given occupation: when and whether declines start to occur, with perhaps few if any effects on performance; when such declines might affect performance, but can diminish with training or by changing the work context; and when such declines become irreparably detrimental to performance (see, for example, Rizzuto et al., 2012).

Answers to these questions are complicated by methods used to investigate them, including whether the research is lab-based or field-based, whether data is longitudinal or cross-sectional, and which types of cognition it assesses (whether memory, processing speed, executive functioning, verbal skills, spatial skills, or reasoning). In longitudinal studies of cognitive performance, two categories of intelligence are relevant: *fluid* intelligence (identifying patterns and relationships, working memory, information processing speed) tends to decline, but *crystallized* intelligence (knowledge acquired over time, vocabulary, experience) remains stable, perhaps even increasing over time (Salthouse, 2019). Thus, the data support *two lifespan trends*: steady growth in wise intelligence (accumulated knowledge) until older old age, along with declining speed over time starting in early adulthood (Salthouse, 2018; cf. Wang et al., 2013). For the most part, these latter fluid abilities are largely preserved through the typical working years (Schaie, 2013). If and when they occur, declines are not precipitous and might even be imperceptible to colleagues up until the 70s. Moreover, these changes may not have a negative (or positive) impact on actual job performance in older adults (Peng et al., 2018; Wang et al., 2013; Charness and Czaja, 2006). Most of the cognitive tests used to assess older adults were in fact designed for children and adolescents, not intended to test real-world behavioral outcomes such as job performance.

Various moderators further complicate cognitive performance. Individual differences affect whether and how cognitive decline manifests, especially among educated older adults (Bosma et al., 2003), and how older adults adapt to such changes, such as by optimizing their strengths and minimizing their weaknesses (e.g., Niessen et al., 2010; Baltes and Lindenberger, 1997). The organizational context can also be noteworthy by offering policies and practices that can minimize the impact of declines, such as providing supervisor support, flexible work arrangements, and other inclusive efforts (Veth et al., 2019).

In addition, the effect of age-related declines can vary depending on the type of decline, the type of job, and the age juncture; for example, declines may affect performance earlier in life for baseball players, later for air traffic controllers, and still later for professors and judges (Ackerman and Kanfer, 2020). Finally, current tests do not assess many job-dependent cognitive skills, such as employees' domain knowledge of job requirements, critical thinking, reading and writing skills, and individual motivation for engaging the work.

Overall, the elder stereotypes seem mostly inaccurate and certainly lack nuance. Nevertheless, they likely trigger prejudices and discrimination, as the next sections review.

Emotional Prejudices: Missing Link between Stereotypes and Discrimination?

If stereotypes are cognitive beliefs and expectations, prejudices are affective responses, as noted earlier. Affect includes both good-bad evaluation (attitudes, preferences) and more complex emotions (pity, disgust, pride). Targeted emotions (differentiated prejudices) matter because they reliably predict differentiated discriminatory behavior. The default old-age stereotype of doddering-but-dear evokes pity and active helping in response to older people's warmth, but neglect and disrespect in response to perceived incompetence (Cuddy et al., 2005; Fiske et al., 2002). The opposite stereotype of "greedy geezer"—not warm but competent and assertive—violates ageist prescriptions to step aside, so the key emotion is resentful envy. Envy predicts both associating (because they have resources) and harming (because they violate prescriptions to yield the resources). The stereotype combinations of warmth and competence predict distinct emotional prejudices, which are more specific than simple valenced preferences; these in turn predict differentiated discrimination.

The default older-adult stereotype—well-intentioned but inept—predicts pity, along with ambivalent protection and neglect. The ambivalent stereotype is well supported in many countries, as noted above. U.S. participants report the same stereotypes, associated emotions, and behaviors, as well as supporting that causal sequence (Cuddy et al., 2007; a correlational study from a representative U.S. sample and three experiments with undergraduates).

Research to date has not pursued measurement of these emotions in workplaces; such research would be useful to predict specific patterns of discrimination.

Another neglected source of emotional prejudices against elders is mortality salience. Ageism includes aversion to reminders of death (Martens et al., 2005). Evidence is scant so far: ageism correlates with death anxiety and risk-seeking behavior in one study of undergraduates (Popham et al., 2011). Aversion predicts avoidance (Cuddy et al., 2007). This pattern is plausible in the workplace, but it remains to be studied.

In conclusion, because emotional prejudices predict discrimination even better than stereotypes do (Fiske and Taylor, 2021), the neglected role of emotional prejudices in discrimination needs to be examined through evidence from the workplace. The interpersonal-level phenomena continue at the labor-market level, which is discussed later.

Conclusions about Ageist Attitudes, Stereotypes, and Prejudices at Work

Attitudes toward older people are generally and stably negative, but only moderately so. Whether and when the original, unfiltered attitude (moderate negativity) or the socially desirable, revised attitude guides age-related workplace behavior, including discrimination, remains an empirical question. But measurement is not straightforward and requires development.

Implicit attitudes also need clearer links to workplace behavior. A favorite of diversity, equity, and inclusion training, they may create a teachable moment, but the workplace dynamics of implicit, unexamined biases await more thorough investigation.

Ageist attitudes' slight overall negativity masks a mixed stereotype: the default attitude expects an older person to be incompetent but well-meaning. Assuming an attitude-behavior or stereotype-behavior linkage in the workplace, one implication is that monitoring ageist biases does not translate directly into monitoring a single attitude, such as purely negative reactions. Biases are not uniform, one-size-fits-all phenomena. Older workers are not typically hated or feared—they may even be liked—but they are often disrespected. Interventions, too, would differ, based on the ageist configuration of stereotype components. Workplace research needs to verify these robust basic research results: Ambivalent ageist stereotypes likely predict ambivalent discriminatory behavior (e.g., protect but also exclude).

Even the simple ageism-discrimination link (the unambivalent default that a negative attitude toward older people predicts discriminatory behavior) remains understudied as an individual dynamic. Meta-analysis identifies few estimates of the link between ageism and discrimination (10 effect sizes, as of Jones et al., 2017), compared with links between sexism (43) or racism and discrimination (30). And in that overall prejudice-discrimination literature, most targets are hypothetical (46), not real people (10), and the raters are students (56), not other adults (27). Ageism's link to discriminatory hiring selection (five studies) averages ~$r = .21$, small but higher than ageism's link to biased performance evaluation ~$r = .09$ (three studies). Ageism's effects are rarely tested.

The ageism literature contains an odd anomaly in testing the prejudice-discrimination link: different people report different parts of the causal chain, with targets reporting perceived discrimination, but the possible discriminators reporting only their prejudices and stereotypes. Research thus needs to link these *other people's* (supervisors' and coworkers') self-reported age-related preferences (attitudes, prejudices) and expectations (stereotypes) with the constraints (discriminatory behavior) that *older workers* report. Perhaps those other people's (coworkers' and managers') self-reported behavior toward older people is missing because such reports of discrimination could not be trusted, for social and legal reasons. Instead, usually in "the lab," student respondents encounter hypothetical scenarios that explore attitudes or stereotypes regarding older workers, rarely tying them to discriminatory, possibly adverse decisions about older workers (Kite et al., 2005; Gordon and Arvey, 2004). This leaves the causal chain that produces discrimination incomplete, because while these observers report their beliefs and stereotypes, their emotions, and their prejudices, only the targets report discrimination.

Altogether, more complete mapping of the psychology would yield insight into leverage points for intervention. The measurable causal chain can go from the potential discriminators' predispositions to their behavior and then to the target perceiving that behavior as discrimination. The science of social perception informs measurement of potential biases and their mechanisms (process mediators and situational or personal moderators), all candidates for intervention.

WORKPLACE AGE DISCRIMINATION AND EXCLUSION: OLDER WORKERS' REPORTED EXPERIENCE

Having summed up how observers view older workers, we turn to look at how these workers themselves report experiencing ageism, including links to health and well-being, and we look at experiences of inclusion. Older workers do report perceived discriminatory behavior toward themselves—as well as describing their response and well-being—but rarely report their view of the putative causes (others' attitudes, stereotypes, and prejudices about themselves). Admittedly, all these perceptions are subjective, but people's perceptions drive their behavior and well-being, so measuring both causal and outcome variables would be useful. As a later section indicates, the most reliable indicators of age-related discrimination are audit studies (e.g., examining correspondence and resumés) and hiring studies (as in other types of discrimination; National Research Council, 2004).

Older Adults' Experiences of Work-Related Stereotypes of Aging

Aging stereotypes are culturally shared and absorbed; as just reviewed, they prominently include cognitive incompetence. Many older people eventually apply age stereotypes to self (Levy, 2009). As people age, they worry that they actually might be, or might be seen as, losing their memory and general cognitive ability (Barber, 2017). Older people also worry too much about other people's stereotypes, which are more positive than they think (Finkelstein et al., 2015). Worrying not only about their individual performance, other people's stereotypes about their performance, but also about fulfilling the stereotype is termed *stereotype threat*. When the situation makes their age salient, stereotype threat does undermine older people's performance on cognitive tests, relative to their individual potential (Lamont et al., 2015). When self-stereotyping and stereotype threat combine with perceived discrimination, all this could affect mental health and well-being, topics considered next.

Scales of Perceived Age Discrimination in the Workplace

Only recently have social scientists validated instruments to measure targets' reported experiences of age discrimination. Four examples of psychometrically sound instruments are:

1. The Nordic Age Discrimination Scale (NADS; Furunes and Mykletun, 2010);
2. The Workplace Age Discrimination Scale (WADS; Marchiondo et al., 2016);
3. The Work-related Age-based Stereotypes Scale (WAS; Marcus et al., 2016); and
4. Workplace Intergenerational Climate Scale (WICS; King and Bryant, 2016).

These few examples of sound instruments aim to measure modern forms of age discrimination in the workplace, as reported by older workers themselves (Lagacé et al., 2020). Among the less obvious forms is incivility—"low-intensity deviant behavior with ambiguous intent to harm the target" (Cortina, 2008; p. 56).

Whether age discrimination is routine or "deviant" is an empirical question answerable by several methods. One approach compares the average perceived discrimination to the scale endpoints (no discrimination, much discrimination) or to the presumably neutral-scale midpoint. This allows comparing different subgroups on the same scale. Even the within-scale comparisons are not absolute in any sense, but they do show degrees of perceived discrimination. Unfortunately, only rarely does research address perceived age discrimination at work from large and population-representative samples.

For example, WADS, validated in the United States, assesses perceived age-based discrimination among individuals ages 18 and up. Respondents indicate the frequency of experiencing nine incidents of discrimination (on a scale from 1 = *never* to 5 = *very often*; see Table 6-4; Marchiondo et al., 2016). Average perceptions of workplace age discrimination from three online samples revealed perceived discrimination overall between 1 and 2, well below the scale neutral point of 3, closer to "never" than at least sometimes. But within this range, perceived discrimination was higher at *both* ends of the age distribution. For two online samples of older workers (ages 50 or older, N = 338 and 390) mean scores were 1.68 and 1.69. For two online samples of younger workers

TABLE 6-4 Workplace Age Discrimination Scale (WADS)

Respondents report how often they have experienced nine items (1 = never, 5 = very often):
• *I have been treated as though I am less capable.*
• *I've been given fewer opportunities to express my ideas due to my age.*
• *I have unfairly been evaluated less favorably due to my age.*
• *I have been passed over for a work role/task due to my age.*
• *I receive less social support due to my age.*
• *My contributions are not valued as much due to my age.*
• *I have been treated with less respect due to my age.*
• *Someone has delayed or ignored my requests due to my age.*
• *Someone has blamed me for failures or problems due to my age.*

SOURCE: Adapted from Marchiondo et al., 2016.

(ages 18–30, N = 294 and 403), the mean scores were close: 1.75 and 1.92. For middle-aged workers (ages 31–49, N = 407), the mean score was lower, 1.42. Combining the samples suggests a curvilinear relationship between age groups and perceived age discrimination at work. Across these separate samples, a U-shaped distribution of perceived discrimination across the working lifespan was evident, in which young and older workers reported experiences of age discrimination to be more frequent than did middle-aged workers (see Table 6-4; Marchiondo et al., 2016). All of the age groups averaged well below the scale midpoint, at least in this online sample (which is likely slightly more liberal and more educated than the average worker).

Another mean estimate comes from nationally representative data (N = 3,957) on Americans ages 51 years and older, collected in the 2010, 2012, and 2014 waves of the Health and Retirement Study (HRS). On a 4-point Likert scale (higher scores representing greater perceived age discrimination at work), the estimated mean score for perceived age discrimination at work was 2.02 in 2010 (Marchiondo et al., 2019), below the scale's neutral point (i.e., 2.5). The estimated change coefficient over time is quite small (estimate = 0.01), indicating that perceived age discrimination at work is relatively stable.

In conclusion, the consistent reporting of low-grade but enduring discrimination is consistent with the stable, moderately negative expression of implicit and explicit attitudes reported earlier. But current data are limited. More research could address perceived age discrimination at work from large and population-representative samples.

Links among Perceived Discrimination, Health, and Work

Both overt and covert forms of age-based discrimination are correlated with health as well as with labor force attachment. Perceived age discrimination has been associated with mental health, stress, job satisfaction, turnover intentions, and retirement intentions in the expected directions (Marchiondo et al., 2016). Such correlational evidence makes a plausible argument that ageism is bad for the heath of older people. Showing these linkages is a first step, necessary but not yet sufficient for inferring causality.

Adding time to the correlation strengthens the argument for causality. Another investigation utilized latent growth modeling based on Health and Retirement Study 2010–2014 data to establish this relationship between age discrimination and health (Marchiondo et al., 2019). In this study, workplace age discrimination measures were direct (e.g., "In decisions about promotion, my employer gives younger people preference over older people," and "My co-workers make older workers feel they ought to retire before age 65") and associated over the long term with mental health, self-rated health, and occupational health, but not with retirement intentions. Health might mediate the relationship between perceived discrimination and retirement age.

Subsequently, analysis of a representative sample of older adults in the United States from the Health and Retirement Study (2006–2014) revealed that (1) mental health only partially mediated the relationships between major lifetime, *work-related* discrimination and retirement, whereas (2) mental health fully mediated the relationship between *everyday* discrimination (outside of work) and retirement age. Individuals who reported high levels of daily-life discrimination retired earlier than individuals who did not experience discrimination (controlling for demographics, marital status, household income and assets, and health insurance; Gonzales, Lee et al., 2019).

A meta-analysis of studies conducted throughout the world found 27 that addressed workplace ageism (e.g., perceived hiring and training discrimination) and its association with worse mental health, such as depressive symptomology, and physical health, such as long-term illness (Chang et al., 2020). People reporting ageism were also more likely to retire early. These findings from 17 countries support selective incivility and stereotype embodiment theories (Levy, 2009; Cortina, 2008), which suggests ageism could impact health through three separate but interrelated components: "age discrimination (i.e., detrimental treatment of older persons); negative age stereotypes (i.e., beliefs about older persons in general); and negative self-perceptions of aging (e.g., beliefs held by older persons about their own aging)" (Chang et al., 2020, p. 2). These external and internal experiences relate to decreased self-efficacy, perceived control, and purpose in life, which may moderate the relationship between ageism and health.

A small but growing body of research suggests that discrimination within the workplace may also cause distress at home (Ferguson, 2012; Cortina et al., 2001). Analyses of 299 couples in the Health and Retirement Study revealed that workplace incivility was associated with targets' well-being, which was subsequently associated with life dissatisfaction, interference with work, and lower overall health (Marchiondo et al., 2020), confirming previous findings. In a novel finding, workplace incivility perceived by the target was associated with declines in their partners' well-being.[4]

Discrimination and incivility at work are stressful. This stress likely permeates the targets' social network, affecting the health of partners at home. More research is needed to discern how retirement decisions made by couples are influenced by these spillover effects. Future research could also clarify whether these experiences are tied to ageism, racism, sexism, or a combination of marginalized identities; this evidence could inform workplace interventions.

Overall, perceived workplace discrimination is associated with various aspects of health, such as hypertension, depression, anxiety, self-esteem, and global health (Marchiondo et al., 2019; Pascoe and Smart Richman, 2009; Lim et al., 2008; Garstka et al., 2004), as well as lower levels of job satisfaction (Taylor at al., 2013) and turnover intentions (Lim et al., 2008). Granted, the direction of causality is not established because these findings are based on necessarily correlational designs.

The relationship between workplace discrimination and health also depends on employees' inner resources and how they can cope with discrimination (Charles, 2010; Holland, 1997). Perceived control, Big Five personality traits, optimism, and coworker/supervisor support may all moderate the relationship (Tett et al., 2013; Tett and Burnett, 2003). For example, employees with high neuroticism, high extraversion, and high agreeableness have more negative responses to perceived workplace discrimination (Xu and Chopik, 2020). Perceived control was a protective factor for health within the context of workplace discrimination. Similarly, employees high in negative affect (e.g., chronically resentful) were more likely to perceive age discrimination, especially when they reflected on their experiences over five years, as opposed to the past year (Marchiondo et al., 2017). Irritable people might (mis) perceive more discrimination; without disrespecting individual experience, research should probe this possibility.

In conclusion, reported experiences of discrimination occur along with a constellation of signs of lower health and well-being and along with a higher likelihood of work exit. Studies deploying longitudinal designs could help unpack the causal directions of these relationships. Also, assessing the role of additional covariates (e.g., optimism, personality, and support) may clarify and isolate the relationships among perceived workplace discrimination, health, and labor force participation.

---

[4]This crossover effect of stress at work to health outcomes at home varied by gender. After men experienced incivility, their affective well-being was associated with their female partners' overall life satisfaction. Women's experiences of workplace incivility were directly associated with the affective well-being of their male partners.

A Note Regarding the COVID-19 Pandemic

With the data arriving as we write, the COVID-19 pandemic's effects on older workers appear mixed. As other chapters indicate, COVID-19 evidently disrupted many older workers' pathways to retirement, accelerating the transition in many cases. Workers' age, ethnicity, gender, and education interact to predict COVID-19's economic hit to at least some older workers, but other evidence indicates that younger workers—in various combinations with the same factors—may have been at least as vulnerable (Moen et al., 2020). The COVID-19-related unemployment pattern could be curvilinear by age, but it might not represent discrimination in any case.

Intersection with Other Forms of Discrimination

Depending on their race and ethnicity, older adults report experiencing varying levels of lifetime discrimination at work and in their everyday lives. Recent analyses of the Health and Retirement Study (Gonzales, Lee et al., 2021) suggest that 20 percent of older Black workers report being unfairly dismissed from a job, a rate similar to that reported by older White workers (19%), and slightly higher than Hispanic workers (15%). Approximately 13 percent of older Black people reported unfairly not being hired for a job, a rate significantly higher than those reported by White people (7%) and Hispanic people (5%). Older Black workers were nearly twice as likely to not be promoted at work (15%) as White workers and Hispanic workers (9% in each case) were. Respondents also reported everyday incivilities, such as being unfairly treated with less courtesy or respect, being threatened, or being harassed. Older Black people again reported the highest rates (21%) of experiencing two or more of these everyday incivilities, followed by older Hispanic people (13%), and White people (12%).

Respondents also reported *why* they believed they were the targets of everyday discrimination. Age discrimination is a common experience among older adults—White, Black, and Hispanic workers—yet their meaning-making attributions to these experiences differ somewhat. Racial and ethnic minorities tie these experiences to their race, nativity, age, and gender, whereas older White people mostly attribute these experiences to age and gender. Ageism and age discrimination are a shared experience across racial and ethnic membership groups, yet various attributions underscore the need for an intersectional lens to understand discrimination in later life.

Multiple marginalized characteristics—including older age, racial/ethnic minority status, and less education—increase the risk for discrimination (Chang et al., 2020). For example, older applicants were sorted into lower-paid employment vacancies, when compared to their younger counterparts, yet older racial/ethnic minority applicants were less likely to be interviewed than White older applicants (Drydakis et al., 2018). Also, older targets with less education faced higher risks of age discrimination, compared to the more educated group (Chang et al., 2020). These findings inform double- and triple-jeopardy hypotheses (Sidanius and Veniegas, 2000), as well as intersectionality theory (Purdie-Vaughns and Eibach, 2008), which posit that those at the intersection of multiple disadvantages (e.g., older Black women) have compounded experiences of disadvantage and seek to understand the complexity of identities and vulnerability within workplace settings. More systematic work is needed.

Experiences of Organizational Inclusion

Organizational climate can offset tendencies toward age discrimination and its likely effects. The U.S. Office of Personnel Management (2011, p. 5) describes organizational inclusion as a collective commitment to connection, collaboration, flexibility, fairness, diversity, and opportunity. Similarly, "in inclusive organizations and societies, people of all identities and many styles can be fully themselves while also contributing to the larger collective, as valued and full members" (Ferdman, 2017, p. 235). With an inclusive climate, organizational practices aim to welcome, accept, and treat all workers fairly, rather than excluding as a result of stereotypes, prejudice, or discrimination (Parker and Andrei, 2020).

Two general practices are critical components of a climate of organizational inclusion aiming to prevent discrimination and bias at work (Janssens and Zanoni, 2008). Specifically, organizations need to ensure the same treatment across employees, while simultaneously acknowledging employees' individual differences. The effective organizational practices often include recruitment of diverse workers based on both their individual capabilities and their demographic group membership, building diverse teams with equal-status jobs, and designing task-interdependent teams, allowing for frequent interaction and communication among diverse team members (Janssens and Zanoni, 2008).

A climate of organizational inclusion demonstrably promotes employees' psychological safety, offering a place where diverse workers can behave authentically (Shore et al., 2018). Such safety can allow employees in different identity groups to comfortably express views that differ from others at work. An inclusion climate moderates the relationship between workplace diversity and relationship conflict (Nishii, 2013). In particular, workplace diversity correlates with employee conflict in low-inclusion work units, but diversity negatively associates with conflict in high-inclusion work units.

More specific to workplace age discrimination, an organization's age diversity could enable an age-discrimination climate, which collectively undermines affective commitment (attachment, belonging) and damages the organization's performance (N = 8,651 in 128 organizations; Kunze et al., 2011). In contrast, older workers experienced less age discrimination when they worked in an inclusive climate and when they were included in the manager's in-group (Nishii and Langevin, 2009). Although a culture of respect, inclusion, and empathy relates to job satisfaction for workers of all ages (Pitt-Catsouphes et al., 2015), older women especially are likely to say that such a culture is important to them (Pitts, 2009).

Conclusions about Self-reported Experiences of Workplace Age Discrimination

Psychometrically validated scales document older workers' reports of discrimination, which covary with job dissatisfaction and poor health, though the evidence establishing causality awaits better designs. Other forms of discrimination intersect with ageism, but more work is needed to understand these relationships. Some intersections may amplify stigma (e.g., an older person who uses a wheelchair); others may eliminate it (e.g., an "elder statesman;" a Black grandmother); still others may make the person invisible (older White women). An inclusive climate benefits all workers, offsetting the risks of friction that may occur with age diversity.

Having addressed face-to-face ageism (attitudes, stereotypes, prejudice, discrimination, and inclusion), the review moves up a level to age-related performance in the aggregate.

AGE AND JOB PERFORMANCE

On the job, older people's actual performance matters. What some older workers report as age discrimination, employers might justify, hypothetically, based on older workers' stereotypically expected inadequate job performance on average. However, not much evidence shows a consistent relationship between age and performance.

The first meta-analysis (based on 13 studies) shows age to be *positively* correlated with job performance and productivity: Older workers were objectively more productive than their younger counterparts (Waldman and Avolio, 1986). Peer ratings also favored older workers. However, supervisor ratings of job performance declined with employee age. Taken together, these results suggest *supervisor biases against older workers*. This bias appeared to be stronger for nonprofessional positions than for professional positions—perhaps related to the physical demands of nonprofessional jobs. Still, ratings of older professional (knowledge-based) workers were still lower than ratings of their younger counterparts, indicating supervisors' potential age bias. Supporting this finding of rater bias, some individuals are indeed predisposed to rely on negative stereotypes of older workers and evaluate their performance more negatively (Perry et al., 1996).

Yet another meta-analysis (based on 65 studies) shows no relationship between age and job performance (McEvoy and Cascio, 1989). A subsequent narrative review of 117 publications focused on age stereotypes (Posthuma and Campion, 2009) also found little evidence that performance declines with age. Consistent with the earlier meta-analysis results for peer and objective measures, this last review demonstrated job performance improving with age; any declines in performance were quite small. In fact, health status and individual skill levels were more predictive of performance than age was.

On the other hand, in a set of three meta-analyses by Sturman (2003), the heterogeneity of the results depended on performance measures (objective vs. supervisor) and job complexity. Sturman investigated job experience and

TABLE 6-5 Age and Job Performance Factors

Unrelated to Age (Competence)	Positively Related to Age (Warmth)
core task performance	organizational citizenship behaviors
creativity	safety performance
performance in training programs	(avoid) general counterproductive work behavior
	(avoid) self-rated workplace aggression
	(avoid) self-rated on-the-job substance use
	(avoid) tardiness
	(avoid) absenteeism

NOTE: An earlier meta-analysis did find age-related decline in training performance (Kubeck et al., 1996), but the more recent Ng and Feldman (2008) does not.
SOURCE: Data from Ng and Feldman, 2008.

performance (on 58 studies, N = 87,189), organizational tenure and performance (on 74 studies, N = 59,444), and age and performance (115 studies, N = 96,866). All three indicators of worker "age"—experience, tenure, and actual age—showed inverted U-shaped relationships with performance in low-complexity jobs. High-complexity jobs also showed nonlinear (but not curvilinear) patterns. Measures of worker "age" need to be compared, as do features of the job itself.

Given such widely disparate and inconsistent results, the range of performance measures could matter (Ng and Feldman, 2008). Prior meta-analyses had measured performance by core tasks, that is, by job accountabilities and activities. The expanded definition of job performance used by Ng and Feldman includes 10 factors related to employee actions and behaviors, all of which impact the work context and, therefore, performance measurement (see Table 6-5). Using this approach, age is found to be unrelated to performance on core task performance, creativity, and training-program performance. However, a positive relationship emerged between age and *organizational citizenship behaviors*: actively upholding organizational norms, helping coworkers who needed assistance, and avoiding negative behaviors such as gossiping and complaining. This split between performance and being a good person fits the universal elder stereotype split between disputed competence and presumed warmth, described earlier.

Throughout, the literature fails to agree on what to measure, how to measure it, and whom to ask. In psychological research, lack of agreement on how to measure the concept of age is a final reason for the different outcomes among studies designed to measure the relationship between age and job performance. Specifically, multiple ways of defining age go beyond simple chronological age (Cleveland and Lim, 2007; see Sturman, 2003, just noted). These include person-based measures of age, such as subjective, personal, or perceived age (i.e., how old or young individuals perceive themselves to be), as well as functional or biological age. In addition, within organizations, context-based age measures include psychosocial measures (e.g., self-perceived or other perceived age) and organizational measures (e.g., self-perceived or other perceived age in relation to other work group members).

How one defines the concept of age can impact how age relates to performance, management, training, and leadership. One attempt to systematize the age variable, as noted, defines age in different ways based on the purpose of the measure—as generation, chronological age, tenure in the job, and experience (North, 2019)—and some seemingly inconsistent results become clearer when they distinguished by these measures of age. As noted earlier, the predominant age stereotype concerns incompetence, but the simple conclusion regarding its accuracy is a lack of consistent evidence, and some contrary evidence, especially regarding older people's advantage in knowledge and experience. Although cognitive speed may decline with chronological age, experienced older workers create work-arounds to compensate for this. But only older workers with more job-specific experience would have the knowledge to develop these compensation techniques. In this way, job experience would moderate the negative effects of chronological age on productivity.

The other likely dimension of age stereotypes, benign intentions, suggests some basis for accuracy, when measured in organizational citizenship behaviors. Measures of worker "age," worker character, job factors, and performance measures all matter to the analysis of stereotype accuracy, performance, and discrimination. New research needs to acknowledge these complexities.

Aggregating Age-Productivity Profiles: Workplace-Level Analyses

The widely presumed age-productivity profiles are also hard to evaluate because performance itself is hard to measure, hard to isolate, and may depend on the level of aggregation. Even so, moving from individual to the workplace (factory or firm) level of analyses still fails to find productivity declining with age.

Assessment Issues

The impression that human productivity rises quickly until it reaches a peak at a relatively young age and then declines is widespread and implicit in many discussions about aging. Macroeconomics usually assumes an increasing and then decreasing profile, with a peak somewhere between ages 30 and 45 (e.g., Altig et al., 2001). Often regarded as an established fact, the hypothetical age-productivity profile matters to countries' retirement policy (Lahey, 2008), employers' expectations, and employees' choices. From a macroeconomic point of view, if the impression were true, as the population's share of older workers rises aggregate productivity should fall, a result that has some support (Maestas et al., 2016). This more or less implicit assumption creates the pessimistic undertone in the debate about stagnation due to aging populations (Gordon, 2016; Lee, 2014; Summers, 2014; Lee and Mason, 2010; Feyrer, 2007) despite some contradicting micro- and macroeconomic evidence (Acemoglu and Restrepo, 2017; Kluge et al., 2014; Mokyr, 2014; Kwon et al., 2010).

Labor economists have long estimated age-productivity profiles in numerous empirical studies (early reviews are Kutscher and Walker, 1960; Mark, 1957; more recent reviews are Gelderblom, 2006; Skirbekk, 2004). However, they face a host of methodological challenges (Börsch-Supan and Weiss, 2016; Göbel and Zwick, 2012), including measurement, selectivity/endogeneity, and aggregation that make results difficult to interpret.

First Challenge: Measuring Productivity

Productivity resists direct measurement, as noted earlier. Although biophysical markers deteriorate with age, social experience increases; that is, people learn to work well with others, on average. But wisdom is more difficult to measure than speed, for example. Since the easily measured abilities peak early, the focus of research on these abilities may contribute to the age-productivity myth (Börsch-Supan, 2013). A similar argument holds for cognition. While fluid intelligence, often associated with the speed with which new tasks are learned, is relatively easy to measure, crystalized intelligence, associated with knowledge and experience, is much harder to measure (Salthouse, 2012).

On-the-job measures might seem reasonable, and early studies used wages as a measure of productivity (e.g., Kotlikoff and Gokhale, 1992; Kotlikoff and Wise, 1989). But independent of productivity, age and seniority tend to increase wages, and wages rarely decrease, which limits their usefulness as a measure (e.g., Laitner and Stolyarov, 2005; Salthouse and Maurer, 1996; McEvoy and Cascio, 1989; Medoff and Abraham, 1980). Finally, as the previous sections suggest, managers, whose evaluations determine wages, may themselves be biased about the age-productivity profile.

Second Challenge: Causal Ambiguity

Age composition of the labor force has a potential endogeneity problem, making it causally ambiguous as an indicator, due to selection processes (Börch-Supan, 2013). Working is both a predictor variable and an outcome variable, because productive workers are more likely than unproductive workers to keep their jobs. When plants close or firms reduce positions, and some employees must retire early, employers prefer to keep productive workers, creating positive selection. Age structure at the company level has a related endogeneity problem. Productive firms are profitable firms, and they tend to hire more people. Expanding their workforce leads them to favor younger hires (Ouimet and Zarutskie, 2013). When this occurs, company productivity would show a spurious negative correlation linking youth and productivity.

Third Challenge: Finding the Right Level of Aggregation

Aggregation takes account of productivity associated with teamwork, allowing workers' productivity to be interdependent. Teammates influence the work climate. Older workers are more likely to spend time helping others, so an individual-level analysis would underestimate their contribution and overestimate the contribution of the younger workers they helped. The aggregate productivity measure would better capture this dynamic.

However, a company view also falls short because it collapses over heterogenous jobs, motivations, and productivity. That is, some jobs offer continuing advancements, keeping motivation at older ages (e.g., management), whereas other jobs top earlier (e.g., shop floor). Age-productivity profiles would differ accordingly, and averaging over them, as in company-level aggregation, could be misleading.

Most age-productivity studies correlate workplace productivity with the age composition of its employees (e.g., Daveri and Maliranta, 2007; Haltiwanger et al., 1999; Hellerstein et al., 1999; Hellerstein and Neumark, 1995). Workplace productivity is easy to measure reliably, and it offers a compromise between individual productivity and the productivity of the entire company. Nevertheless, workplace age structure is probably not exogenous (a straightforward predictor), as noted above. New econometric methods have solved many problems but sacrificed precision. The best estimates show that productivity increases until a worker is 50–55 years old, and then it levels out (Göbel and Zwick, 2012; Malmberg et al., 2008; Aubert and Crépon, 2007; Aubert, 2003). The more sophisticated the methods, the more productivity increases with age (although confidence intervals, and thus the precision of these estimates, also widen).

Finally, many studies measure individual productivity directly (Börsch-Supan et al., 2021): by the number of peer-reviewed publications (Oster and Hamermesh, 1998) or Nobel Prizes (Jones, 2010), by the prices obtained for paintings (Galenson and Weinberg, 2001), by sports records (Fair, 1994), or by completed court cases (Backes-Gellner et al., 2011). Although precise, these measures apply only to some occupations and then only to top performers, whose work is often achieved earlier and recognized later. Ordinarily, workflow is set up for average performance (Börsch-Supan, 2013), which does not decline with age, despite the common expectation.

Aggregating Productivity as a Function of Age

Workplace-level analyses of productivity offer the use of big data sets and econometric methods, thereby avoiding labor-market selection effects (Börsch-Supan et al., 2021; Börsch-Supan and Weiss, 2016). Two cases illustrate the principles in quite different industries: a truck factory and an insurance office.

In a truck factory, assembling a standardized product, the ability to simply avoid errors is a precise measure of productivity: here, the inverse of the number mistakes made in a given time (Börsch-Supan and Weiss, 2016). Given the sheer physical demands of these jobs, productivity in such a plant might best detect age-related decline. Nevertheless, an evaluation of more than 1.2 million observations in this plant find no decline in productivity within the relevant age range. Instead, individual worker productivity increases monotonically until age 65, when everyone retires. Any age-related declines in strength are offset by harder-to-measure outcomes, including experience, teamwork, and coping with emergencies, all of which apparently improve with age.

Analysis of a large international company in the service industry (insurance, Börsch-Supan et al., 2021) shows the importance of job type. Routine, undemanding jobs show age-related productivity decline for ages 30–55. More complex professional jobs (most employees) show no age-performance relationship. However, the most challenging jobs, those of advanced specialists, show a reliable, steady increase in productivity across all ages.

Conclusions about Age Profiles and Workplace Productivity

The current literature on workplace productivity finds no solid evidence that productivity generally declines with age. Hence, any claim that stagnation over time is due to population aging rests on weak evidence. Some traction results from distinguishing between the productivity of top performers and productivity in ordinary jobs. More specific differences between jobs may determine the age-productivity profile: Performance of purely physical work may decline with age, and performance of boring jobs may decline with age (or tenure). More challenging jobs that profit from experience, teamwork, and insights into human nature—as well as sustained interest—may increase performance with age (or experience).

Many of the studies in this area are flawed, due to the difficulties in measuring productivity and in avoiding selection and aggregation biases. New research is needed to provide unbiased data and to filter the age effect out of many other determinants of day-to-day productivity. There are no up-to-date company studies in the United States.

AGE DISCRIMINATION IN THE LABOR MARKET FOR OLDER WORKERS

As a nation, Americans apparently believe that if older people, specifically those past the traditional retirement age of 65, want to work, discrimination (on any basis) should not prevent them from doing so. This is evident in the passage of the Equal Pay Act (1964), Title VII the Civil Rights Act (1964), the Age Discrimination in Employment Act (ADEA, 1967), and the Americans with Disabilities Act (1991). Moreover, labor market participation at older ages could reduce the budgetary impact of an aging population on public programs such as Social Security. Ageist discrimination therefore deserves attention as a constraint that limits individual preferences and societal expectations.

In individual and interpersonal settings seen earlier, ageism manifested in attitudes, implicit and explicit bias, stereotypic beliefs, and emotional prejudices—all psychological antecedents to the discrimination sometimes reported by older workers.

Nature of Evidence for Employer Discrimination

These considerations raise a central question: is age discrimination a significant problem for older workers? (Chapter 8 discusses policy responses.) Research that attempts to provide an aggregate, quantitative answer to this question focuses on the market-level outcomes that can be measured in the available data sources, for example, in household surveys, employer surveys, or hiring data collected by researchers. The kinds of interpersonal experiences related to age discrimination discussed earlier in this chapter have typically been quantified with psychometrically valid measures of individuals' interpretations of their lived experiences.

Economists and other social scientists typically are cautious about interpreting differences between groups as evidence of discrimination. Observing differential outcomes by age (e.g., longer times to find a job) does not necessarily imply age discrimination, though it is consistent with it. Instead, other explanations, such as chronic illness, must be eliminated. Rarely does blatant, direct evidence of intentional discrimination appear in the current era, partly because age discrimination is no longer legal. (Before the ADEA, job ads explicitly set age restrictions, but this is no longer the case; U.S. Department of Labor, 1965.) More often, evidence is indirect and by itself inconclusive, because alternative explanations for the findings cannot be excluded. As a result, researchers have turned to experimental and other methods to produce more rigorous evidence on age discrimination.

Indirect Evidence of Employer Discrimination

Evidence of discrimination is considered indirect if it is based on differences in the observed behavior of older worker relative to that of younger workers or on the differential treatment of older workers by other agents. A prominent example is the consistently longer unemployment durations experienced by older job seekers in their 50s and early 60s compared with younger ones. This difference suggests that employers exhibit age bias in hiring, although it does not show it conclusively (Neumark and Button, 2014). For example, older workers could be more selective when pursuing new opportunities because they reject some types of work or expect higher pay based on their experience at their previous job.

Indirect evidence includes identifiable patterns of worker behavior. When workers report age discrimination, these reports are often associated with other subsequent adverse work experiences, including separating from jobs, longer periods of unemployment, slow wage growth, and earlier expectations for retirement (Adams, 2002; Johnson and Neumark, 1997). This constellation of adverse experiences is consistent with age discrimination, but it could also be due to contemporaneous changes in health, such as an increase in chronic pain, high standards, or depression. Or, when asked, older workers may just attribute many negative outcomes to age discrimination.

Changes in labor market outcomes of older workers that occur after new laws that protect them from employment discrimination are passed can also provide indirect evidence of age discrimination. Indeed, passage of both state and federal legislation protecting older workers has preceded their higher employment rates (Adams, 2004) and increased longer-term attachments of older workers to firms, benefiting firms and older workers alike (Neumark and Stock, 1999). Of course, alternative explanations remain possible: places becoming more hospitable to older workers for other reasons (e.g., due to population shifts) might change both their laws and their employer-employee norms.

More recently (2003–2008), changes in Social Security decreased benefits for early retirees (age 62) and gradually increased the retirement age from 65–67. Older workers responded by working longer and claiming benefits later in states with better age-discrimination laws (increased damages in age-discrimination suits; expanded coverage to include smaller firms; Neumark and Song, 2013). (See Chapter 8 for more discussion of Social Security.)

Although evidence of the effectiveness of age-discrimination laws can suggest that age discrimination had been present, this evidence is considered indirect, because age discrimination laws are not perfect. In theory, for example, workers could use the laws simply to contest a disliked outcome, such as being fired, paid less, or passed over. That, in turn, might lead employers to terminate fewer older workers, or increase their pay, even in the absence of actual discrimination. Though this is unlikely (especially given the evidence discussed below), this possibility cannot be dismissed. Additionally, antidiscrimination laws could, in theory, reduce hiring of older workers by making employers more cautious about hiring these workers; these effects would depend on the laws' content and enforcement.

Direct Evidence of Discrimination: Audit and Correspondence Studies

Audit and correspondence studies are the gold standard for inferring discrimination in the labor market (e.g., National Research Council, 2004; Fix and Struyk, 1993). In contrast to observational studies from which evidence of discrimination can only be inferred, audit and correspondence studies allow researchers to manipulate age (or race, gender, etc.) in ways that are unrelated to other worker characteristics, and thus directly measure discrimination. *Audit studies* use actual job applicants coached to act alike and measure discrimination as differences in job-offer rates. *Correspondence studies* create fake applicants (on paper or electronically) and capture callbacks for job interviews. Both kinds of studies' artificial applicants have resumés indicating equal qualifications, except for their belonging to a demographic group protected by law (e.g., being older or younger, often indicated by graduation year). Absent any average differences between groups, employers should treat them identically, unless they prefer one group over the other, which is known as having a "taste for discrimination." (Taste discrimination occurs because of having animus against, or a distaste for, the group in question.) Alternatively, employers might be making inferences based on group membership (see the earlier discussion of stereotypes), unjustified by individuating information. (Statistical discrimination uses actual or perceived group differences—such as stereotypes—to make inferences about an individual from the group and hence treat that individual differently.) Either way, group disparities generate a strong inference of discrimination.

Audit studies take more time because they entail interviews, so they have samples of a few hundred observations at most. Also, they risk experimenter expectancy effects because the actors can easily infer the hypotheses and inadvertently behave accordingly (Heckman and Siegelman, 1993). Correspondence studies, because they entail "paper people," can collect far larger samples of job-application outcomes. Though correspondence studies capture only callbacks and not actual job offers, callbacks seem to capture most of the relevant discrimination. For example, 90 percent of the discrimination detected in International Labour Organization studies occurs at the selection-for-interview stage (Riach and Rich, 2002; see also Neumark, 1996).

This type of experimental research provides stronger demonstration that age can drive the labor market decisions of employers. Although these types of studies are focused on hiring choices and, therefore, might not seem relevant to extending the work lives of older adults, these audit or correspondence studies are directly related to older adults' ability to transition to new jobs. Age discrimination in hiring can prevent them from moving to a new employer, acquiring a part-time or less-demanding job that provides them with a bridge to retirement, or unretiring and returning to the labor force. Many older workers extend their work lives in these ways (Johnson, 2014; Maestas, 2010; Cahill et al., 2006). Additionally, employers who engage in discriminatory hiring practices may be more likely to also engage in other forms of workplace age discrimination. Thus, understanding these easier-to-measure forms of discrimination could provide insights into how those same employers treat older adults in their employ.

As an illustration of what can and should be done with appropriate resources: A recent large-scale study of age discrimination in hiring (Neumark et al., 2019) focused on ages near retirement, precisely when policy incentives aim to encourage people to work longer. The authors identified advertisements for jobs in occupations that hire low-skilled workers from all adult age groups, such as administrative assistants and secretaries (female applicants' resumés), janitors and security guards (male applicants), and retail sales (both genders). They designed realistic resumés for fictitious applicants for these positions that differed only by age of the applicant. Each resumé was assigned to one of three age groups: young (ages 29–31), middle-aged (ages 49–51), and older (ages 64–66). Three otherwise identical resumés (one from each age group) were sent to apply for each of more than 13,000 open positions they had identified, which were located in 12 cities within 11 states.

Across the board, callbacks were higher for younger applicants than for older applicants, consistent with age discrimination in hiring, in every job category. And discrimination was worse just before retirement age. Moreover, women experienced more age discrimination than men: female applicants to administrative and sales jobs showed a large and steadily decreasing decline in callbacks with age. For men, the young-old difference was substantial but smaller, and middle-aged men in sales and janitorial services got a break, getting called back as often as younger men.

Two additional points are key. First, although methods have improved over time, findings are consistent (Farber et al., 2017; Lahey, 2008; Riach and Rich, 2010, 2006; Bendick et al., 1999; Bendick et al., 1997); a sizable body of work indicates age discrimination.

Second, age discrimination against older women is consistently higher than that for older men (Farber et al., 2017; Lahey, 2008). Several factors might contribute. Judgments based on appearance favor the young, for both genders, but women pay a higher price for an aging appearance (e.g., Deutsch et al., 1986), and gender roles emphasize appearance more for women (Jackson, 1992) than for men. In job descriptions posted on Internet job boards in China and Mexico, employers often expressed preferences for workers based on age and sex (Hellester et al., 2020; Kuhn and Shen, 2013). This research found a twist: greater preference toward women in job descriptions seeking young workers, and for men in job descriptions seeking older workers.

Generally, older women are in a bind regarding employment discrimination, because age discrimination is worse for them (Lahey and Oxley, 2021; Burn et al., 2020), but they cannot generally have straightforward recourse to both age and sex discrimination laws at once. Age discrimination laws do less to protect older women than older men (McLaughlin, 2020).

A parallel dilemma faces older Black Americans, who have worse economic outcomes than older White Americans; part of this gap reflects current job prospects. To the extent that racial and age discrimination combine, the ADEA limits enforcement where age is one of multiple factors (Delaney and Lahey, 2019). Clearly, more work needs to examine the intersections of gender and race with age, given the stronger age discrimination experienced by older women and by older minorities.

Stereotypes about Older Workers Affect Demand

Older workers may be targets of stereotypes about their skills or abilities on average (reviewed earlier), or what labor economists might refer to instead as statistical discrimination, which in this case refers to assumptions about the average abilities of older workers that are applied to all older workers.

What we do not know from this literature, however, is how these stereotypes affect demand for older workers in the actual labor market. A large-scale correspondence study of age discrimination, which provided experimental measures of discrimination across thousands of employers, was combined with a computational linguistics analysis of the text of the job ads from this study (Burn et al., 2020). The aim was to ask whether employers who use more age-related stereotypes in their job ads—especially negative stereotypes about older workers—are more likely to discriminate against older workers in hiring.

This could happen for two reasons, both consistent with lower demand for older workers. Employers who are predisposed to discriminate could signal their preference for younger workers by using job-description language that conveys positive young-person stereotypes. This might then discourage older workers from applying in the first place, concealing any age bias in the hiring process. This process could reflect taste-for-discrimination (employer animosity) or statistical discrimination (stereotypical belief about the group average). Another possibility is that employers could assume, based on their belief in stereotypes about older workers, that older workers will be less able to meet the advertised job requirements. In that case, these beliefs would clearly reflect statistical discrimination and could shape not only the job-description language and pool of applicants, but also the probability that older workers would receive a callback when they apply.

Job ads' age stereotypic language (see section above on Stereotype Content) is related to fewer callbacks for older applicants—across both jobs and genders (Burn et al., 2020). The ageist language about both men and women describes the required (youthful) personality for the job. For men, the ageist descriptions also refer to robust health and cutting-edge skills. Research needs to extend these findings across race and cultures to better understand how cultural understandings of age may affect these outcomes.

Conclusions about Labor Market Demand

Stereotypes about older workers do affect employment decisions and the demand for older workers. Not only do these results need replication, but more detail is needed about the processes involved in order to document mediators, moderators, and possible points of intervention.

CONCLUSION

Summary

This chapter reviewed evidence of discrimination against older workers on three levels, going from the micro to macro: age-related interpersonal interactions at work, workplace aggregated age profiles of performance, and labor markets manifestations of age-related productivity and discrimination.

Starting with interpersonal *face-to-face workplace issues*: societal images of older workers (explicit and implicit) align with their reported experiences of workplace discrimination; these experiences have associations with their mental and physical well-being. Universally beneficial—and therefore more likely to be widely acceptable—remedies aim for inclusive climates, realistic assessment of workers' cognitive capacity, and measuring their actual job performance. Age-based analyses find no generalized performance differences but consistent reports of discrimination. However, beyond well-documented ageism in hiring processes, proof of discrimination is elusive. Even less is known about how these age-related work experiences, and their personal correlates, vary as age intersects with other marginalized categories.

Aggregating over individuals, at the *workplace,* analyses of age-related productivity also find no performance differences. Finally, anticipating the following chapter, the current review examined the *labor market*—older workers' aggregate productivity and employers' aggregate age discrimination. Analyses of direct and indirect evidence, and especially audit studies of job applications, show that stereotypes about older workers affect labor market demand—paving the way to the next chapter on age-related labor market supply and demand.

Research Implications

Research agendas need to address how societal expectations about aging workers (e.g., stereotypes) affect employers and managers' preferences (e.g., attitudes) and how these in turn constrain older workers' options (e.g., discrimination), despite scant evidence of age-related performance issues. Research implications go from workplace interactions to firm-level productivity to labor market outcomes.

Ageist Attitudes and Stereotypes at Work

The science of social perception informs measurement of potential age-related biases, their mechanisms (process mediators and situational or personal moderators), and points of leverage for intervention. This raises several issues for understanding how ageism occurs.

Research needs to address the relationship between implicit and more explicit workplace attitudes and behavior, although measurement is not straightforward and requires additional development. For example, as ageism becomes less acceptable, research could address whether and when the original, old-fashioned, unfiltered attitudes or newer, more socially desirable, revised attitude guides age-related workplace behavior, including discrimination. Implicit attitudes also need clearer links to workplace behavior. Knowledge about the workplace dynamics of implicit, unexamined biases await more thorough investigation regarding on-the-ground behavior.

Another form of unexamined bias is mixed beliefs that include both positive and negative valence. Workplace research needs to verify basic research results: many ageist stereotypes are mixed (e.g., "doddering but dear") and likely predict ambivalent and ambiguous behavior (e.g., liking but disrespecting). Since this is harder to detect, but identifies a form of ambivalent discrimination that is distinctive to older people, good measurement is essential.

Finally, other forms of discrimination intersect with ageism, but more work is needed to measure and understand this phenomenon.

The Broken Causal Chain: From Observer Expectations and Preferences to Older Workers' Reports of Discriminatory Constraints

The link between employers', supervisors', and co-workers' self-reported age-related preferences (attitudes, prejudices) and expectations (stereotypes) and their behaviors (discrimination) that constrain outcomes for older workers. The causal chain that produces discrimination is incomplete because these observers report their thoughts and feelings (their beliefs, stereotypes, emotions, and prejudices), but only the targets report behavior (discrimination). All of the links in the chain need to be documented: from reports of the evaluators to those of the evaluated, as well as differences in the treatment or evaluation of older workers that are not viewable to the target of discrimination.

Self-reported Experiences of Workplace Age Discrimination and Well-Being

Psychometrically validated scales have documented older workers' reports of discrimination, showing that they covary with job dissatisfaction and poor health; however, the evidence of causality awaits better research designs. Longitudinal studies would help; converging reports and data collected in the same workplace would help.

Stereotype Accuracy

Measures of worker "age," worker character, job factors, and performance measures all matter to the analysis of the accuracy of stereotypes regarding older worker performance. New research needs to acknowledge these complex relationships.

Age Profiles and Firm-level Productivity

Measuring productivity is complicated and new work needs to create unbiased data and to filter the age effect out of many other determinants of day-to-day productivity. Most of the existing research has occurred within other countries; there are no up-to-date company studies conducted within the United States.

Stereotypes about Older Workers Affect Demand

The best evidence establishing age discrimination comes from the rarely conducted audit study, which shows discrimination against older workers. Not only do these results need replication, but more detail is needed to outline the processes that are involved in generating these discriminatory practices, in order to document mediators, moderators, and possible points of intervention.

7

The Labor Market for Older Workers

As discussed in earlier chapters, the population of the United States is aging. When combined with the lower labor force participation of older adults, this aging of the population suggests that the size of the labor force will grow more slowly than that of the population. As a result, the U.S. dependency ratio—the ratio of nonworkers to workers in the economy—will rise. One policy response has been to try to boost the employment rates of older adults, which could lower the dependency ratio, increase tax revenues, and decrease public expenditures on health insurance, retirement benefits, and income support.[1]

This has led to a number of policy reforms that have the goal of encouraging employment (or increasing the number of work hours) of older adults who would otherwise retire, such as reducing Social Security benefits received upon early retirement at age 62; gradually increasing the age at which adults become eligible for full benefits from age 65 to 67 (Munnell et al., 2004; American Academy of Actuaries, 2002); and changing the taxation of benefits among Social Security enrollees in several ways that include reducing the marginal tax rate on earnings in excess of the earnings cap, increasing the amount of earnings that are exempt from taxation, and broadening the age range that is exempt from the earnings test (Friedberg, 2000). As the possibility of insolvency of the Social Security program approaches, additional changes or reforms to the system may be considered. However, these policy reforms may be less effective than hoped if other factors or changes in the economy reduce labor demand for older workers or reduce the labor supply of older workers.

Thus, this chapter considers the evidence on a large number of influences on the demand and the supply of older workers—mainly on demand-side influences. On the supply side, the chapter considers the impact of the age structure of the workforce, that is, the larger relative cohort size of the older population owing to population aging. On the demand side, the following influences on the labor market for older workers are considered: automation; other technological change; globalization; immigration; and age discrimination against and stereotyping of older workers (considered in more detail in Chapter 6). The chapter also considers hypothesized influences on the balance between supply and demand for older workers, including: the "lump of labor" fallacy; labor mobility and the geography of labor demand; supply-demand mismatch; changes in the demand for and supply of skills; and the business cycle and economic shocks and crises. Figure 7-1 lists the factors this chapter discusses, and identifies them as primarily supply factors, primarily demand factors, or a reflection of both supply and demand (and hence the balance between them).

---

[1] The dependency ratio is sometimes defined with respect to working ages (15–64) vs. nonworking ages (0–14 and 65+). But, of course, work at older ages is changing, so defining this for fixed ages seems inappropriate, and we think of the dependency ratio as a measure that can decline if the employment of older workers is increased.

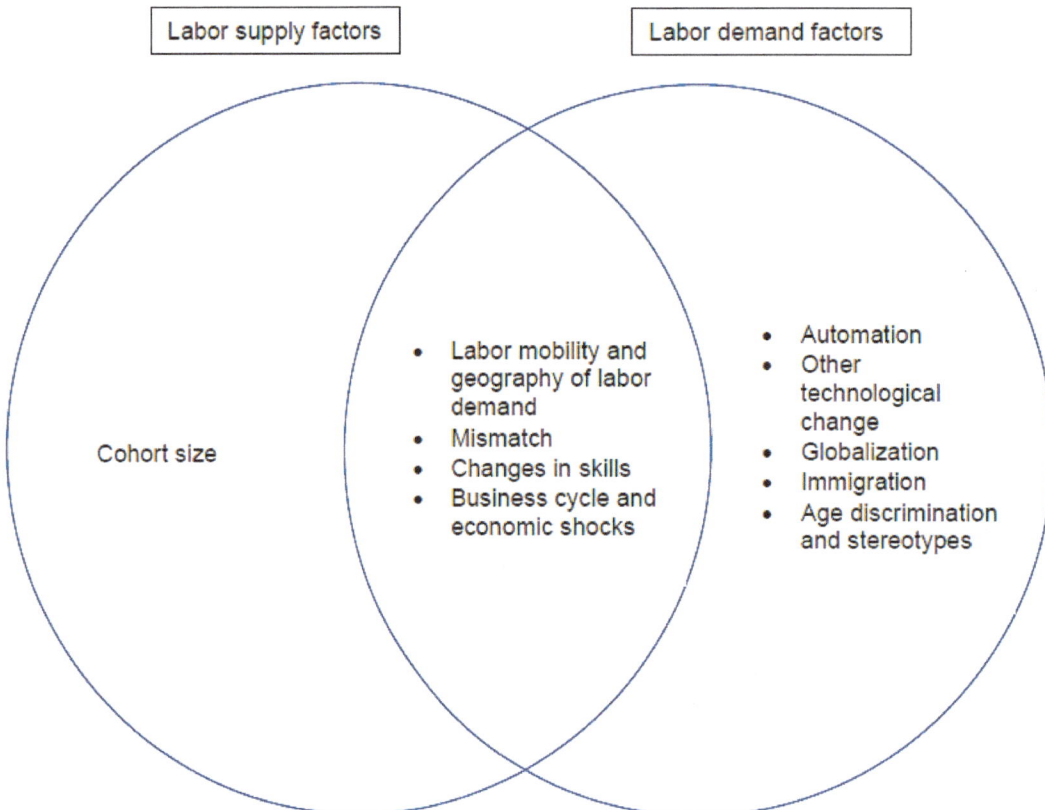

FIGURE 7-1 Factors affecting labor demand for and labor supply of older workers.

Not all the influences on labor supply or labor demand for older workers necessarily lower labor demand for or the labor supply of older workers, although many might. From a policy perspective (see Chapter 8), there may be a good rationale for trying to mitigate the influence of behaviors or economic changes that inhibit labor demand for or labor supply of older workers.[2] This may be particularly important because, if current reforms fail to increase employment at older ages, the resulting fiscal strains may compel policy makers to enact even stronger or harsher policies to encourage older adults to delay retirement, including reducing Social Security benefits overall or further increasing the age of eligibility for full benefits. Changes such as these could negatively affect some older workers, specifically those with disabilities or in declining health who are more likely to have difficulty extending their work life into older ages. In other words, supply-side incentives to work, such as reducing Social Security benefits prior to full retirement, may be undermined by demand-side barriers to work due to age discrimination.

More generally, this chapter is about labor supply and labor demand. The standard economist's view of supply and demand is that they equilibrate to clear markets. There are many reasons why this perspective may be too simple when applied to labor markets, including rising interest in imperfect competition in labor markets (e.g., Boeri and van Ours, 2013) and other sources of friction like the costs of mobility or retraining (Becker, 1964). This chapter focuses on factors that may influence labor supply or labor demand for older workers, often in ways that may lead to lower employment of older individuals. The factors considered range broadly, covering some that may have shorter-term effects, like the impact of the business cycle or other economic crises on older workers, and

---

[2]Population aging and the fiscal challenges it poses are not the only rationale for policies to reduce demand-side or supply-side barriers to the employment of older workers. Removing these barriers may also simply help older individuals remain employed and productive, with benefits for both the economy and for themselves, including their physical and mental health (see Chapters 3 and 4).

some that may have longer-term effects, like age discrimination, the shifting age structure, and the weak incentives for older workers to retrain or move to stronger labor markets.

We first discuss the supply of older workers, before turning to factors that primarily affect the demand for older workers, although in quite a few cases there can be effects on both sides of the market. We then turn to considerations regarding labor market equilibrium and what they might imply for older workers.

THE LABOR SUPPLY OF OLDER WORKERS

Population aging affects the age structure of the workforce (or the potential workforce, when we consider the decision of whether to work or not). How does a rising share of those at older ages, a relatively larger cohort of older workers, affect older workers' employment?

Most of the research on this question comes from the perspective of labor supply, studying the effects of the Baby Boom and less-notable variations in the sizes of birth cohorts that generated sizable shifts in the age distribution of the population. Much of this work conducted in the United States has examined the effects of *own* cohort size on wages (e.g., Macunovich, 1999; Easterlin, 1980; Welch, 1979), and sometimes on employment or unemployment (e.g., Korenman and Neumark, 2000) among youths born into large cohorts first entering the labor market. In general, these studies, as well as those in other countries (such as Morin [2015], for Canada), find that these youths fare worse than those from smaller birth cohorts, at least initially; they earn lower wages and, as a result, have lower employment rates. These effects of a cohort's relative size are interpreted as "relative supply" or "cohort crowding" effects, in which a large cohort shifts out labor supply, leading to lower wages, and hence reductions in employment or labor force participation (due to the reservation wage effect). This implies that workers in different age cohorts are only imperfectly substitutable for each other, and some of this research (e.g., Morin, 2015) suggests that as the age difference between cohorts increases, the degree of substitutability between them declines.

Despite the generally consistent finding that young workers from large cohorts experience lower wages and employment rates when entering the labor market than those from smaller cohorts, there is reason to expect that relative cohort size will not have similar effects on older workers.[3] Several studies have found evidence that these negative effects weaken (Welch, 1979) or dissipate (Wright, 1991) with age. However, these studies are quite dated, and neither focused explicitly on older individuals. Moreover, because earnings-experience profiles flatten by middle age (Heckman et al., 2006), this could lead to a higher degree of substitution between older cohorts and other more-experienced workers, which would reduce the effect of being born into a large birth cohort on wages or labor force participation among older workers.

On the other hand, there are other reasons to expect that relative cohort size may have a sizable impact on labor market outcomes for older workers. Employment rates among individuals in their 50s or 60s are lower than those of adults in their 30s or 40s, and among older workers retirement is quite fluid, as described in Chapter 3. Together, this suggests that, in contrast to workers (especially men) of other ages, older workers may have an elastic labor supply on the extensive margin. If true, the effects of large cohort size on wages—and through wages, on labor force participation or employment—could be sizable for older workers (French and Jones, 2012; Evers et al., 2008). Moreover, if the type of work older workers enter in partial retirement differs substantially from that of their career jobs (i.e., lower-skilled or less-demanding), this could reduce their substitutability with prime-age workers, leading to effects of cohort size on wages among older adults similar to those for young labor market entrants.

Although the relative supply hypothesis about cohort size predicts that there will be negative effects of large relative cohorts on labor force participation and wages, there are two factors that could push in the opposite direction, toward a positive effect. Both of these stem from possible effects relative cohort size could have on labor demand. In particular, we might expect the age structure of the population to affect the composition of consumption and hence labor demand. For example, Reinhardt (2003, Exhibit 1) reports that per-capita health spending for 55–64 year-olds is double that for 25–34 year-olds, and Cohen (2006) documents that the nursing workforce in the United States—which will be in greater demand as the population ages—is itself aging.

---

[3]Much of this discussion draws from Neumark and Yen (2020), discussed in more detail below.

TABLE 7-1 Percent Retired within Age Group, 2012-2017

Age Group	Percentage Retired
16–24	0.26%
25–49	0.81%
50–59	6.14%
60–69	40.94%

NOTE: The percentage retired is computed from the employment status question, which captures respondents saying that they are not in the labor force due to retirement.
SOURCE: Data from 2012-2017 March Current Population Survey Annual Social and Economic Supplement Data.

Second, as the proportion of the population that is ages 60–69 increases, the proportion(s) within some other age cohorts must necessarily decrease. If the skills of two age cohorts are substitutable, then when the relative size of one of them declines, the demand for the other may increase. For example, as a large cohort of older workers shifts to partial or bridge retirement, these "post-retirement" workers may move into lower-skilled jobs that were often held by younger workers. In this case, older workers and younger workers would be substitutable, which could increase demand for a large cohort of 60–69 year-olds. Alternatively, if the skills of older workers make them more substitutable for those in the prime/middle-aged cohort, then when the cohort of 60–69 year-olds is large relative to that of this middle cohort, demand for the large 60–69 cohort to remain in peak career positions may increase.

In recent work, Neumark and Yen (2020) explore the effects of age cohort size on the labor force participation and wages of older individuals. They focus on the age group in which labor force participation begins to decline (ages 50–59) and the age range when most people retire (ages 60–69) (see Table 7.1). The latter age group is the age range most likely to be targeted by policy makers interested in incentivizing delayed retirement and working longer, often by introducing reforms to public pension systems (e.g., Gruber and Wise, 2007). Moreover, because labor force participation rates are low at these ages, policy targeted at this age group can have a greater impact on labor force retention (see Chapter 2).[4] When estimating the effects of a large older cohort relative to the working-age population as a whole, Neumark and Yen find that when older cohorts are large relative to the younger cohort (ages 16–24), the larger relative older cohort experiences lower labor force participation and wages, consistent with the relative-supply hypothesis. But when the older cohorts are large relative to the middle-range cohort of 25–49 year-olds, older workers experience higher labor force participation, although there is little evidence of a change in wages; results that are more consistent with a relative demand shift.[5] As discussed in Chapter 2, over the first half of the twenty-first century, the age distribution of the United States is projected to see rising shares of 50–69 year-olds relative to the adjacent prime/middle-age group, rather than to the particularly small cohort of the youngest workers. As such, the results suggest that this population aging will likely lead to rising labor force participation and employment of older individuals.

FACTORS PRIMARILY AFFECTING THE DEMAND FOR OLDER WORKERS

Automation

On the labor demand size, machines are replacing not only workers performing manual jobs but workers performing jobs that involve cognitive tasks (Autor, Levy, and Murnane, 2003). Recent research has found that humans have a comparative advantage over machines for jobs requiring both hard *and* soft skills, such as creativity, nonroutineness, and social intelligence (e.g., Frey and Osborne, 2017; Autor et al., 2003).

---

[4] Neumark and Yen did not include the 50–59 year-olds with 25–49 year-olds, because they found that the behavior of 50–59 year-olds was similar to that of 60–69 year-olds, rather than that of 25–49 year-olds.

[5] The demand shift may occur because when prime-age workers are scarce relative to older workers, firms may try to retain or hire older workers. Also, older workers' extensive-margin labor supply elasticity may be quite high, and older workers often enter into different jobs or employment relationships with more flexible, lower-paying work, which can explain the absence of wage increases.

Other research has documented how automation is replacing mid-skilled workers but not low- or high-skilled ones, resulting in job polarization (Acemoglu, 1999; Katz and Murphy, 1992). Mid-skilled workers—such as those in sales, office, and administrative support, or in craft and repair occupations—perform routine codifiable tasks. Automation has had little impact on low-skilled and service jobs because such jobs require physical dexterity, face-to-face communication, adaptability, and visual recognition. The decline of mid-skilled occupations has reduced options for workers with no more than a high school education, who are concentrated in such jobs.

Lund et al., (2019) found that such displacement may have particularly strong effects on Hispanic and African American workers, whose rates of potential displacement are about 25 percent. Jobs with higher technology displacement include food preparation, retail sales, office clerks, stock clerks and order fillers, bookkeeping, accounting, auditing clerks, cashiers, secretaries and administrative assistants, and food servers. These jobs have large concentrations of Hispanic workers, Black workers, and women. They also have large concentrations of older adults with lower levels of education. Specifically, adults 51–65 are concentrated in bookkeeping, accounting, auditing clerk, secretaries, and administrative assistant occupations with high technology displacement. As such, the effects of automation on labor demand may vary by race, gender, and skill level of middle-aged and older adults.

Displaced older workers are less likely than other displaced workers to be reemployed (Farber, 2015). Training that could improve displaced workers' hard and soft skills could promote labor market reentry. However, the success of such training programs may depend on whether those in need have access to them, as well as on the feasibility for older adults to make changes in their lines of work. Some older adults may be precluded from taking advantage of training programs due to poor health or having to provide caregiving to other family members that impose additional barriers to change their line of work.

Research documenting the effects of automation on labor demand is still at a very preliminary stage (see, e.g., Acemoglu and Restrepo, 2018, for theory and evidence). Moreover, there appears to be even less research on the dimensions of automation that might replace some cognitive tasks, for example through machine learning and artificial intelligence.

Effects on Retirement

While automation has its direct effects on labor demand, labor supply responses can influence the impact of automation on the labor market for workers in general and older workers in particular. Likely the most important factor is the possibility of workers retraining for the new jobs that automation offers; conversely, automation may have adverse effects on older workers who are unable to modify their skills or do not find the necessary retraining profitable because of their relatively short time horizon in the labor market. This, in turn, can affect retirement plans and the length of older workers' effective working life.

Some research has been done to assess the effects of automation on retirement decisions. Angrisani and colleagues (2016) find that using computers is associated with a lower likelihood of retirement for middle-aged and older adults. Angrisani and colleagues (2016) additionally find that workers who are open to new experience (personality trait) and who use computers are more likely to remain in the labor force than others. Lee and Angrisani (2020) find that technology *complements* individuals who have skills at which human workers hold a comparative advantage over machines. At the same time, technology replaces workers with automatable skills. In this last study, Lee and Angrisani created an index of worker skills, focusing not on educational attainment but on worker creativity, ability to handle nonroutine tasks, and social intelligence (i.e., the skills that render individuals more automation-resistant). They find that workers who score well in these three areas are more likely to postpone retirement.

Maestas (2010) documents "unretirement" decisions, that is, decisions to reenter the workforce after retirement. Altogether, more than one in four retirees studied over the 1990s unretire. Automation may affect unretirement decisions, though there is scarce research on this. Lee (2020) measures the level of protection from automation retirees had for their work skills. She explores how this level of protection from automation—determined by skills such as creativity, ability to handle nonroutine tasks, and social intelligence—influenced unretirement decisions. She finds that workers with higher automation-protection are more likely to unretire, and that those who unretire choose jobs whose task-specific automation-protection matches their skills. Aging individuals are highly likely to make unretirement decisions based on their "soft skills."

Other Technological Change

The technological change that has been most studied by labor economists is the growth of computer technology and its use in the workplace. Much of their research has focused simply on whether this technological change was responsible for the large growth in economic returns to education, in the context of a broader phenomenon referred to as "skill-biased technical change." (For a review of the evidence, see Katz, 2000.) As discussed in Burstein et al., (2019), the rise in the skill premium was much larger among middle-aged and younger workers than among older workers. Card and Lemieux (2001) attributed this to changes in labor composition, specifically in the relative supply of more-educated workers among different age cohorts. But Burstein, Morales, and Vogel find this has more to do with changes in equipment productivity, in particular because the computer-use differential between college and non-college-educated workers was higher for young and middle-aged workers.

Globalization

The globalization of economic activity, including trade in goods and services as well as outsourcing, can potentially impact older workers in the United States, just as it can impact workers anywhere else in the world. For example, if the industries in which they are concentrated suffer from globalization, their own employment prospects may worsen, in particular when switching industries is costly, as we might expect it to be for older workers. Ashournia (2018) formalizes this in a model of the effects of international trade shocks when mobility is costly; in the model, mobility is costlier for older workers than others because they have fewer years left to acquire the experience that is valuable in the new industry. If outsourcing is skill-biased—with somewhat lower-skilled jobs being outsourced but the highest-skilled jobs remaining domestic—older workers could be disadvantaged if they do not have the requisite skills, or do not (because of their shorter projected work life) have as much incentive to acquire these skills. Ebenstein and colleagues (2014) present evidence that offshoring (or outsourcing, measured as employment of U.S. multinationals at affiliate locations in low-income countries) disproportionately hurt the wages of workers ages 40 and over.

The impact of aging can also run in the opposite direction. For example, Gu and Stoyanov (2019) present evidence that population aging reduces the comparative advantage of countries in industries intensive in the skill-adaptability of workers. They attribute this to lower ability (or perhaps incentive?) to update skills among older workers. They argue that variation in demographic composition across countries is as important for international trade flows as the variation in standard factors of production, such as physical capital and skilled labor. If true, this could provide a strong incentive for governments (or specific industries) to incentivize the upgrading of older workers' skills.

Immigration

Immigration leads to increases in the supply of labor, which can in turn impact the demand for native workers. The effects of immigrants on wages and on the employment prospects of native workers (or more broadly, workers already here) depends on a number of factors:

- the effects of the product market demands of immigrants;
- the effects on the productivity of native workers who might be either substitutable or complementary with immigrant labor (e.g., Peri, 2016);
- internal migration in response to immigration to particular areas (Borjas, 2006); and
- other effects that change the input mix of native labor or other factors, such as the evidence in Foged and Peri (2016) that low-skilled natives move out of manual occupations in response to low-skilled immigrant inflows, or the evidence in Lewis (2011) that capital investment responds to low-skilled immigration.

While immigration is often viewed, in the public debate, as largely an inflow of unskilled workers, in fact U.S. immigration consists of both less-educated and more-educated labor, from different countries. Peri (2016) argues that a balanced composition of immigrants, coupled with these other responses, has led to relatively small effects of immigration on relative and absolute wages.

However, that is not a settled view, and Borjas (2016) argues that at least some of the research concluding that effects of immigration are modest is flawed by ignoring the internal migration that mitigates the local effects of immigration.

In an earlier paper, Borjas (2003) uses a strategy that does not focus on effects in local labor markets, and concludes that when we look at workers with similar education and experience, immigration inflows do result in lower wages.

These two different conclusions likely reflect, in part, heterogeneous effects among workers, as reflected in the conclusions of a National Academies of Sciences, Engineering, and Medicine (2017) report, which notes that when adverse wage and employment effects are found, they are found for the closest substitutes. This means the effects include lower wages for prior immigrants and native-born high school dropouts, lower employment for prior immigrants, and lower hours for teens (National Academies of Sciences, Engineering, and Medicine, 2017, pp. 5–6). Still, as the National Academies of Sciences, Engineering, and Medicine report notes, researchers continue to disagree about the effects for narrow subgroups.

Given this unsettled debate, it is hard to draw any firm conclusions about the effects of immigration on particular groups of workers. Moreover, there is very little focus on workers differentiated by age. Borjas (2003) is an exception, as he studies the effects of immigration on (male) native workers broken out by education and by labor market experience. He finds that the effects are strongly correlated with age, especially because he uses a "potential experience" measure that estimates the number of years since a person completed school, a measure which is more reliable for men than for women, especially in older cohorts when women worked more intermittently. Borjas similarly classified immigrants based on their education and estimated experience, although this overstated their experience in the U.S. labor market. Using the data this way, Borjas can measure the labor supply shocks of immigrants, differentiated by education and experience. One conclusion of interest is that, for a given level of education, immigrants are more substitutable with natives with similar experience, based on occupational similarities. Using the variation within education and experience cells, Borjas finds a negative relationship between immigrant supply and both earnings and employment (fraction of time worked). And he concludes that it is generally not only the low-educated who drive these results.

If we consider the implications of this work for older workers, the conclusions might be relatively sanguine, because, overall, recent immigration has skewed young (see Borjas, 2003, Figure I); his most recent data are for 2000. At the same time, this pattern varies by education, and in the 2000 data the low-skilled immigration shock is more experienced, suggesting—if we accept Borjas' conclusions—that this immigration may have adversely affected the earnings and employment of older, less-skilled workers. Overall, though, immigrants remain relatively young, although the share ages 50 and over has increased from about 11–17 percent in recent decades, largely because of family-sponsored migration (Carr and Tienda, 2013).

Age Discrimination

Is age discrimination a significant demand-side barrier to the employment of older workers? As discussed in greater detail in Chapter 6, many types of evidence suggest there is labor market discrimination against older workers, lengthening the durations of their unemployment spells. Moreover, this discrimination leads to more separations of older workers from their current employers, lower employment rates, slower wage growth, and reduced expectations of working past their mid-60s (Adams, 2002; Johnson and Neumark, 1997). Indirect evidence of age discrimination also comes from research showing that stronger age discrimination laws (at the federal and state level) have boosted the employment of older workers (Adams, 2004) and strengthened the employment relationship between older workers and firms (Neumark and Stock, 1999). Moreover, stronger state laws have increased the responsiveness of older workers to increases in the Social Security Full Retirement Age—working longer and claiming Social Security benefits later—pointing to important complementarities between supply-side incentives (Social Security reforms) and reducing demand-side barriers (Neumark and Song, 2013).

The most compelling evidence comes from field experiments, "audit" or "correspondence" studies in which researchers send out applications for fictitious job applicants, experimentally manipulating the ages listed on the applications to isolate the effect of age on hiring (see Chapter 6). Although hiring discrimination may seem less relevant to whether or not older people lengthen their work lives, it may be a critical determinant of whether many older adults are able to transition to part-time or shorter-term "partial retirement" or "bridge jobs" toward the end of their careers (Johnson, 2014; Cahill et al., 2006), or return to work after a period of retirement (Maestas, 2010).

These studies generally find strong evidence of discrimination against older workers in hiring, with more and stronger evidence of age discrimination against older women (Neumark et al., 2019; Farber et al., 2017; Lahey, 2008). However, it is more difficult to determine the source of discrimination against older workers. One source may be aversion to hiring older workers—much as labor economists model discrimination against, say, minorities. Another source of discrimination against older workers may be stereotypes employers hold about their skills or abilities, or what labor economists might refer to instead as "statistical discrimination," which in this case means employers' assumptions about the average skills or abilities of older workers that are applied in part to all older workers.[6]

While economists are interested in the nature of discriminatory behavior, both forms (statistical and taste) of discrimination are illegal under U.S. law. Equal Employment Opportunity Commission regulations state: "An employer may not base hiring decisions on stereotypes and assumptions about a person's race, color, religion, sex (including pregnancy), national origin, age (40+), disability or genetic information."[7] From a legal perspective, it is not relevant whether the stereotypes are correct (i.e., on average); however, economists would more likely view these actions from an efficiency perspective and be more concerned about whether these stereotypes are supported by evidence (see Chapter 6 for evidence on stereotypes).

THE BALANCE BETWEEN LABOR SUPPLY AND LABOR DEMAND

The "Lump of Labor" Fallacy

In considering what public policies might encourage or discourage the continued employment of older workers—such as mandatory retirement, retirement policy generally, or policies to reduce age discrimination—it is important to dispel the fallacy that there is a given "lump sum" amount of paid work to be done in the country at any given time. Such an assumption would imply that enabling older people to work longer would damage employment prospects for younger workers. Economists call this the "lump of labor" fallacy. This fallacy has been used to argue against immigration, to argue that automation necessarily reduces jobs, to argue that restricting work hours will lower unemployment, and, most importantly in our context, to argue that we should compel older workers to retire in order to create jobs for younger workers (Kemmerling, 2016). The flaw in this fallacy is ignoring the fact that when more people work, the economy expands, more jobs are created, and so on.[8]

Gruber and colleagues (2010) list many examples of policy makers in different countries trying to ease older workers out of the labor market to create more jobs for younger workers.[9] For example, Kemmerling (2016) shows that in European countries where voters think there is a trade-off between the employment of older and younger workers, voters are more hostile to reforms that lead to longer working lives. Gruber and colleagues (2010) describe results from a set of papers in a volume they edited that addresses this question. They first show that employment rates of older and younger worker covary *positively*, because they both reflect underlying macroeconomic conditions. These positive relationships weaken but remain with controls for the economic conditions. They then ask the question more specifically in the context of retirement policy, focusing on within-country policy changes that changed retirement ages. The answer is clear. To quote the authors:

> There is no evidence that reducing the employment of older persons provides more job opportunities for younger persons. And, there is no evidence that increasing the labor force participation of older persons reduces the job opportunities of younger persons (Gruber et al., 2010, pp. 13–14).[10]

---

[6] Neumark and colleagues (2019) present a good deal of evidence against their results being driven by statistical discrimination.

[7] See http://www1.eeoc.gov//laws/practices/index.cfm?renderforprint=1

[8] As Autor (2015) points out, for example: "While intuitively appealing, this idea is demonstrably false. In 1900, for example, 41 percent of the United States workforce was in agriculture. By 2000, that share had fallen to 2 percent, after the Green Revolution revolutionized crop yields. But the employment-to-population ratio rose over the twentieth century as women moved from home to market, and the unemployment rate fluctuated cyclically, with no long-term increase" (pp. 237–238).

[9] For example, they quote the French Prime Minister, in 1981: "when it is time to retire, leave the labor force in order to provide jobs for your sons and daughters" (p. 2).

[10] Some recent work (Bianchi et al., 2019) finds that an unanticipated pension reform in Italy led to sudden retirement delays, which blocked *internal* upward progression of other workers in the same firm in which the retirement delay occurred. This work does not address the lump of labor fallacy, because it does not account for any increased demand for goods and services from older workers working longer. Indeed, the paper is presented as providing evidence on how internal labor markets work.

Similarly, Munnell and Wu (2012) review existing evidence and present new evidence for the United States. They conclude that there is no evidence for the "lump of labor" theory.

Labor Mobility and the Geography of Labor Demand

Economic outcomes have always varied across U.S. regions, owing to numerous factors including differences in transportation, natural resources, locations of universities and other sources of concentration of highly-educated workers, and agglomeration economies from early growth, as well as public policy. At the same time, there was evidence of long-term forces moving toward an economic convergence of regions (Barro and Sala-i-Martin, 1991), owing to the migration of labor toward high-income regions and of capital to lower-wage areas.

However, as documented by Couillard and colleagues (2021) and Austin and colleagues (2018), which also draw on earlier work, this convergence has slowed or even reversed, as a result of two forces. First, it appears that with changes in economic structure, the forces that led to job growth and increased labor demand in underperforming areas have weakened. Most notably, they have been weakened by the continuing decline in manufacturing, coupled with strong economic performance in particular regions—especially so-called "superstar cities" (Gyourko et al., 2013)—with concentrations of high-skilled labor, perhaps owing in part to the growth of the knowledge economy (Davis and Dingell, 2019). Second, there has been a decline in migration to high-income regions and less migration generally, perhaps owing in part to rising house price differentials associated with inelastic housing supply in some of the growing regions (Gyourko et al., 2013). As evidence, Foote and colleagues (2019) document that whereas in the past, in response to large negative shocks to local labor markets (mass layoffs), the largest contributor to reductions in the labor force was through out-migration, but during and after the Great Recession growth in nonparticipation in the labor market became the primary source of adjustment.[11] The combination of these forces has led to large and now persistent differences in rates of employment and nonemployment across regions.

This literature has tied emerging employment differences across regions to the rising nonemployment (combined unemployment and not in the labor force) of men ages 25–54, the upper bound of which includes older adults. As an example of the variation across regions, Austin, Glaeser, and Summers (2018) note that in 2016 the nonemployment rate of 25–54 year-old men was higher than 35 percent in Flint, Michigan, but was only five percent in Alexandria, Virginia. Austin, Glaeser, and Summers note that major social problems, including high levels of nonemployment, disability, opioid deaths, and increases in mortality, are concentrated together in the states that are east of the Mississippi River and extend south to north from Mississippi to Michigan, excluding the Atlantic coastal states. They argue that these regional disadvantages have calcified over time, which presents policy makers with a choice: either let these differences continue to fester or adopt place-based policies to stimulate economic activity in these depressed areas.[12] Their argument marks a break with that of some urban and regional economists (and, in some cases, with their own earlier views) in which migration between these and better-performing areas could address these differences (e.g., Glaeser, 2009).

To the best of our knowledge, this literature has not focused on older workers per se. But to the extent that mobility declines with age after ages 25–29 (see Figure 7-2), it seems likely that these geographic disparities in economic opportunity could particularly harm the employment prospects of older workers. Since older adults are less geographically mobile, this suggests that place-based policies along the lines suggested by Austin, Glaeser, and Summers (2018) might be most successfully targeted at creating jobs for older workers, and this in turn raises the question of what place-based policies would do this. Here a strong cautionary note is in order: Many, if not most, place-based policies have shown limited if any effectiveness at creating jobs (for a review, see Neumark and Simpson (2015). However, in the United States, these efforts have typically been narrowly targeted (especially enterprise zones) and there is continuing debate about whether alternative place-based policies at a broader geographic level may be more effective (Bartik, 2020). At the same time, to the extent that these policies focus on training or retraining workers for new jobs, their effectiveness for older workers may be limited (as discussed more below).

---

[11] Moreover, touching on a topic this chapter returns to later, among workers ages 55+, mass layoffs lead to increases in county-level disability insurance applications.

[12] Place-based policies target incentives or benefits to areas based on the socioeconomic characteristics of those residing in or near the areas, as opposed to "people-based" policies that target them based on individual or family characteristics.

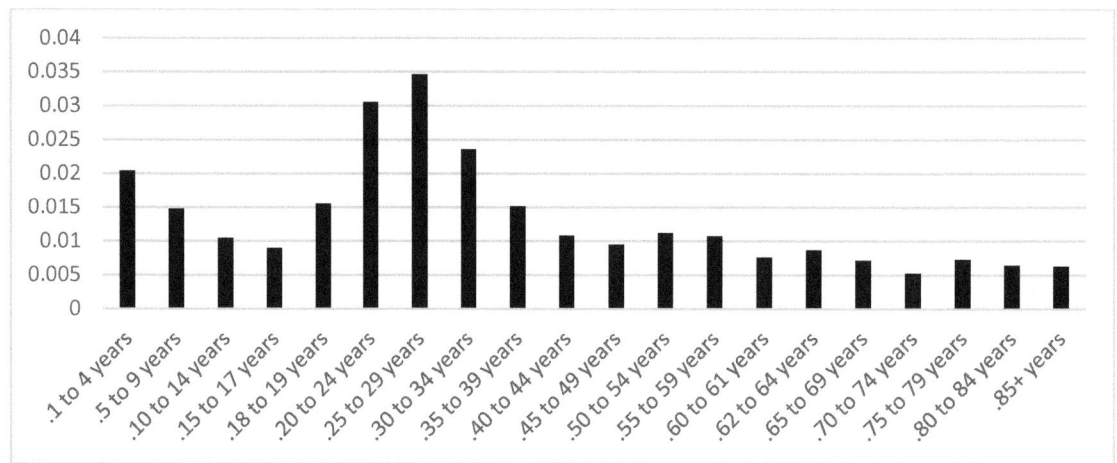

FIGURE 7-2 Mobility rates by age, CPS ASEC (2019).
NOTE: These are one-year mobility rates.
SOURCE: Data from U.S. Census Bureau (https://www.census.gov/data/tables/2019/demo/geographic-mobility/cps-2019.html) Table 1.

Mismatch

When there is reallocation of labor demand, either across geographic areas or by skills required by employers, the possibility of "mismatch" arises. Such a mismatch can be between the skills people have and the ones employers want, or between the areas where labor demand is strong and those where workers tend to reside.[13] The mismatch that results is referred to as "structural unemployment," as opposed to the purely cyclical form of unemployment that stems from fluctuations in labor demand and labor supply (depending on one's perspective on macroeconomic models). This issue has typically become a concern after large economic changes, for example due to the deindustrialization of jobs that became prominent in the 1970s and with the continuing decline in manufacturing (Kollmeyer and Pichler, 2013; Lilien, 1982). Another example is the sharp changes in employment and unemployment, accompanied by the possibility of restricted mobility because of housing price declines, after the Great Recession. Concerning the Great Recession, Pissarides (2013) suggests that structural unemployment emerged in the United States, based on evidence of rising vacancies at a given level of unemployment (or an outward shift in the Beveridge curve). However, Valletta (2013) presents evidence suggesting that "housing lock" did not contribute to long unemployment durations during this period, and Neumark and Valletta (2012) summarize research suggesting that the Great Recession did not create skill mismatch.

As with other areas of research and evidence, research on mismatch to date has not focused on older workers. However, there are indications that problems associated with job loss and reemployment can be more severe for older workers, likely because of the lower geographic mobility documented and discussed earlier and the weaker incentives older workers have to invest in retraining. In fact, these same weak incentives, owing to a shorter period to recoup the gains, may also account for the lower mobility of older workers. For example, Neumark and Button (2014) show that unemployment durations after the Great Recession increased substantially more for older workers, men and women ages 55+. Looking over a longer period (1981–2001), Farber (2004) shows that the reemployment rates of displaced workers (those who lose jobs involuntarily for economic reasons) are substantially lower for workers ages 55 and over, and correspondingly, long-term earnings losses are higher for older workers (ages 51–60, in Davis and von Wachter, 2011), although job displacement rates are lower for older workers.

---

[13]There is also a large body of work on "spatial mismatch" within urban areas, but this usually refers to mismatch between supply and demand between urban and suburban areas (e.g., Kain, 1968).

A different type of mismatch, which has received less attention from economists, pertains to the preferences of older workers for particular job characteristics, in contrast to the characteristics of the jobs employers offer (see the discussion in Chapter 5). This mismatch may stem in part from the health problems of older workers, for whom flexible work-time and workplace flexibility may be more desirable and may contribute to better health as well (Vanajan et al., 2020). Similarly, allowing for phased rather than complete retirement might attract a continuing labor supply from older workers (Siegenthaler and Brenner, 2001). In this case, employers may be constrained by laws that prevent the offering of fringe benefits only to older part-time workers rather than to all part-time workers, and by laws that limit paying out partial retirement benefits to employees working some hours (Johnson, 2011).

One question is whether government employment services can help match older workers with jobs requiring their skills. For example, the United States has American Job Centers that offer services to job seekers, including training referrals, career counseling, job listings, and similar employment-related services. To the best of our knowledge, there is no research on the effectiveness of these centers nor any material on efforts devoted to older workers, although the CareerOneStop website associated with the program that runs these centers does provide specific advice to older workers,[14] and some centers appear to have a focus on older workers.[15] The U.S. Department of Labor also has a Senior Community Service Employment Program (SCSEP), which is described as "a community service and work-based job training program for older Americans."[16] This program is authorized by the Older Americans Act and provides training for low-income, unemployed seniors ages 55 and over. SCSEP is discussed in greater detail in Chapter 8. As discussed there, the Department of Labor recently characterized the program as ineffective, but there appears to be limited evaluation of this program, without comparing participants to a control group of nonparticipants (Kogan et al., 2012).[17] Moreover, to the best of our knowledge, research on SCSEP has not focused explicitly on the role of reducing mismatch between older workers' skills and job preferences, on the one hand, and employer demands on the other.

An interesting model is Japan's Silver Human Resource Centers, which help place retirees in jobs that are part-time and temporary in nature, and typically provide community-based services (Flynn, 2014; Bass and Oka, 1995). We are unaware of evaluations of this program or the existence of evaluations of similar programs in other countries. Developing an inventory of such programs and evaluations of them (if any exist) would be useful, as would an evaluation of the U.S. SCSEP.

Changes in Skill Demands and the Supply of Skills

Technological and market changes often require workers to learn new skills. Lately these have included computerization in white-collar work, computer-aided design/computer-aided manufacturing, robotics, green technologies, and more. As discussed earlier, however, worker retraining is an investment on the part of the worker, entailing both direct training costs (whether paid by workers or employers) and the opportunity cost of lost earnings. Older workers may have less incentive to invest in this retraining, and employers may have less incentive to invest in those workers if their likely remaining work life is relatively short.

However, to some extent lower rates of retraining may be driven by other factors, such as stereotypes about the ability of older workers to learn new skills (Posthuma and Campion, 2009). Both conjectures are consistent with evidence of lower participation in training with increasing age in the European Union and many individual countries (Picchio, 2015). Picchio suggests that some evidence is consistent with older adults taking longer to acquire new skills and having worse training performance (Charness and Czaja, 2006; Kubek et al., 1996). Piccho (2015) further suggests that some types of training programs (self-paced, job-related, and integrated with work; Zwick, 2012) can offset these difficulties, and also that subsidies may be needed to incentivize training for older workers.

---

[14] See https://www.careeronestop.org/ResourcesFor/OlderWorker/older-worker.aspx

[15] See, e.g., https://www.careeronestop.org/LocalHelp/EmploymentAndTraining/find-older-worker-programs.aspx?location=80401&radius=25&persist=true

[16] See https://www.dol.gov/agencies/eta/seniors

[17] The Workforce Investment Act (now Workforce Innovation and Opportunity Act) offers career counseling, training, etc. However, an earlier report (U.S. Government Accountability Office, 2003) suggested that performance measures for the Workforce Investment Act may have discouraged a focus on older workers (mainly because older workers tended, in part from taking part-time jobs, to be less likely to show earnings gains, leaving SCSEP as, functionally, the main such program for older workers.

There is other evidence on the effects of retraining for older workers who need to retrain. Jacobson and colleagues (2005a) studied the impact of community college on displaced workers in Washington State. Although their definition of "older" is quite broad—age 35 and up[18]—they estimate similar effects on long-run earnings regardless of age. For older men, a year of community college schooling boosts earnings by about 7 percent, and 10 percent for older women. These estimates are similar for younger men and women, leading the authors to conclude that "at least among those who participate in retraining, older workers acquire new skills about as effectively as do younger workers" (Jacobson et al., 2005a, p. 406). However, underscoring the effects of the opportunity cost of foregone earnings, and the shorter prospective work life,[19] Jacobson and colleagues estimate that the internal rate of return to the investment for older displaced workers is about half of what it is for comparable younger displaced workers. This calculation raises legitimate questions about the net social benefit from retraining older displaced workers, although the authors point out that the internal rate of return calculation is more favorable for courses teaching more quantitatively oriented material, or courses in health occupations or the trades.[20]

There is also evidence on training older workers in the European context, in this case training currently employed workers. Picchio and van Ours (2013) estimate the effects of retraining provided by current employers on the future employment of workers, possibly via retention at the current job, although the authors could not measure that. They find positive effects for prime-aged as well as older workers (aged 26–34, 35–49, and 50–64). Similarly, Dauth and Toomet (2016) study a German program that subsidizes training for workers at least 45 years old employed in small- and medium-sized firms, and find positive impacts on remaining in paid employment in the two-year post-treatment period, with larger impacts for those ages 56 and older. Presumably, the idea of this program is to subsidize employers to train older workers to keep them employable, and the subsidy may be needed because employers might not otherwise see the training of older workers as profitable because of limited future tenure with the firm. In contrast, Schwerdt and colleagues (2012) find no gains from an adult education voucher program in Switzerland, although this program did not target older workers per se. Instead, it was available to those ages 20–60, and take-up (compliance, since it was a randomized controlled trial) was similar for those above age 30. The authors also find that there was crowding-out of firm-financed training.

Impacts of the Business Cycle and Economic Shocks and Crises

Earlier, we discussed the potential for mismatch between older workers' skills and the skills employers demand, or for mismatch between where jobs are growing and where older workers live. This kind of mismatch can also be generated from adverse business cycle shocks that are followed by reallocation of jobs to other regions, or to other industries with different skill needs. At the same time, recent empirical evidence from the Great Recession suggests that, for that episode at least, the recession did not contribute to skill mismatch (Abraham, 2015); this evidence does not, however, address older workers specifically.

Retirement plans may be disrupted by a late-career job loss. The risk of job loss facing American workers is considerable: from 1990 to 2011, an average of seven percent of all jobs ended each quarter due to employer-initiated separations, representing about nine million layoffs per quarter (Davis and von Wachter, 2011).[21] Older workers have historically experienced lower rates of layoff than younger workers, due partly to the protective effect of job tenure, but this advantage has largely evaporated in recent years (Farber, 2015). Compared to younger displaced workers, older workers who experience a job loss take longer to find a new job, experience larger declines in earnings, and are more likely to exit the labor force (Farber, 2015). Older workers who experience a late-career

---

[18] The older men and women average about age 44 vs. about 29 for the younger men and women, in the Jacobson and colleagues (2005a) study.
[19] This argument is laid out formally in Jacobson et al. (2005b).
[20] Cummins (2015) discusses community college outreach to displaced older workers, emphasizing (based on observations of key informants and other literature) that it is important to reach these workers quickly, to provide them with a realistic assessment of the labor market and how well their skills do or do not match current employer needs (career counseling), and to help with job search. However, this study does not assess effectiveness. Catalfamo (2018) describes a qualitative study of a "Second Career" program at a Canadian college, highlighting both the challenges in balancing school-life demands, but also positive outcomes in terms of skills, confidence, and more.
[21] Farber (2015) presents measures of job loss based on the Current Population Survey's Displaced Workers Survey, whereas this estimate is based on the Job Openings and Labor Turnover Survey. The two sources do not provide strictly comparable measures.

job loss are substantially less likely to be employed years after the loss and have lower earnings as compared to similar nondisplaced workers (Couch, 1998; Chan and Stevens, 2001, 1999).

During a labor market downturn, the risk of layoff increases and the probability of finding new work decreases. As a result, retirement transitions rise with the unemployment rate, although this effect is primarily evident among workers who have reached (or nearly reached) the age of eligibility for Social Security benefits (Marmora and Ritter, 2015; Coile and Levine, 2007). Higher unemployment is similarly associated with earlier retirement in Sweden and the United Kingdom (Disney et al., 2015; Hallberg, 2011). U.S. workers who experience a weak labor market in their late 50s and early 60s claim Social Security benefits earlier and have lower retirement income (Coile and Levine, 2011). They also experience higher mortality, which is plausibly due to the reductions in employment, health insurance coverage, and health care utilization in the years following a job loss (Coile et al., 2014).

These factors are likely magnified during the COVID-19 crisis, which led to an economic downturn that was to some extent government-engineered. In the early part of the pandemic, employment rates fell fastest and unemployment rates rose fastest for those ages 65 and older, in contrast to past (more typical) recessions (Bui et al., 2020). This was the result not only of layoffs and retirements from career jobs that occurred during the downturn, but also of the targeted economic shutdowns, which may have made it harder for older workers to find "bridge" or "partial retirement" jobs on the path to permanent retirement, particularly if these jobs were more likely to involve face-to-face contact (Montenovo et al., 2020). Moreover, the higher morbidity and mortality risk that older workers exhibited during the on-going pandemic might give employers pause when they consider hiring or re-hiring older workers, particularly if they may be liable for healthcare costs or work-related infections. As of the time this report was being completed, the end of the COVID-19 pandemic remained elusive, so the full effects of this event on retirement and work among older adults remain to be documented and examined by future researchers.

SUMMARY

We have surveyed an extensive list of factors that can influence the labor supply of older workers, labor demand for older workers, and the balance between them. Many of the findings of existing research on these factors suggest concerns about older workers' employment as the population ages, but there is also some evidence pointing to more sanguine perspectives. In some cases, the research base needs to be strengthened considerably.

Summary Findings

We summarize the findings from each subsection of this chapter, as follows.

- While a rising share of the population at older ages has typically been viewed as a source of lower employment rates for older workers, the evidence is more nuanced, with some evidence that population aging can increase labor demand for older workers, especially when the older cohort is large relative to the cohort just below it in age.
- We do not know much about the effects of automation on labor demand for older workers. There is some evidence that some types of automation, at least, increase demand for older workers, especially for those who adapt to the new technologies. But other types may have the opposite effect. Most work on the effects of automation is speculative at this stage, with only limited empirical evidence on recent changes.
- While computerization has increased demand for more-skilled workers, this change was less in evidence for older workers.
- Globalization leads to changes in the industrial and occupational structure of employment. The lower mobility of older workers can leave them at a disadvantage when labor demand for the jobs they have occupied declines. In addition, in the United States (and other advanced economies), globalization may increase the premium for learning new skills. Evidence suggests that countries with older workforces tend to lose out, perhaps because of less skill adaptability. On the other hand, globalization could perhaps spur governments to invest more in retraining older workers.

- There is compelling evidence that older workers suffer from age discrimination in hiring, which constrains labor demand for older workers.
- There is rather strong evidence against the "lump of labor" fallacy. Countries that have reformed retirement systems to encourage people to work to later ages have not seen concomitant declines in the employment of younger workers.
- Growing regional disparities in economic outcomes in the United States have left behind rising numbers of people in areas with low employment rates, high unemployment rates, and related social ills, and the role of geographic mobility in reducing these disparities has weakened. These issues are likely quite salient for older individuals, given their low mobility, although research has not focused on older individuals per se.
- Mismatch between workers' skills and the skills employers demand can arise from economic dislocations, and there is evidence that this mismatch can be worse for older workers, in part because of weaker incentives to invest in training or in moving. There are some government programs in the United States that try to help displaced older workers find new jobs, but their effectiveness has not been evaluated. More work on such programs in other countries, such as Japan, would be useful. Governments may also be able to do more to allow more flexibility in the work arrangements of older workers, to better enable employers to offer working conditions more amenable to older employees.
- Changing the supply of skills among older workers to respond to changes in the composition of jobs is a challenge, because incentives for workers or firms to invest in retraining may be weak. There is evidence that some kinds of retraining—like community college education in the United States and firm training subsidies in Germany—boost earnings and employment, although the social returns may be relatively low if workers are relatively close to retirement.
- Adverse economic shocks tend to result in less job loss for older workers but larger and more persistent earnings declines and more exit from the labor force when these job losses occur, which can spur early retirement. Early evidence from the COVID-19 crisis points to particularly strong adverse outcomes for older workers in contrast to more "normal" recessions, and there are factors unique to the pandemic that may imply adverse longer-run effects as well.

Implications for Research

The above findings, and the gaps in knowledge that this chapter has identified, prompt the following implications (needs) for future research.

- We need more research on the effects of automation on workers generally, and a deeper understanding of the implications for older workers and how policy might respond to mitigate adverse impacts.
- We need more research to understand the effects of globalization on older workers and how globalization might require governments to adapt to encourage employment at older ages.
- Researchers thus far have not figured out how to generate rigorous evidence on age discrimination along dimensions other than hiring; this is a critical challenge for research.
- Research on the labor market effects of immigration on older workers would be useful, although we might be doubtful whether this research will be any more decisive than similar, existing evidence that does not focus on older workers.
- Policies to stimulate labor demand in distressed regions may help all workers in these regions, and particularly less-mobile older workers. But we need to know more about what effect even successful place-based policies (and many have been unsuccessful) have had on older workers.
- More research would be useful to measure the effectiveness of programs in other countries, such as Japan, that help displaced older workers find new jobs.
- We need evaluations of initiatives to encourage the retraining of older workers, including cost/benefit analyses.
- It is important to obtain early evidence on the effects of the COVID-19 crisis on the employment and retirement of older workers.

8

Public Policy

INTRODUCTION

A wide range of government policies affect the ability of individuals to remain in the work force at older ages as well as their need to do so. To begin to understand how these policies affect older workers in the United States, it may be useful to characterize them along several dimensions, as shown in Table 8-1.

Policies fall into two categories: those that aim to support work and those that aim to support financial security. Within the set of policies that aim to support work, a further distinction may be made between policies that apply to workers of all ages and policies that are specific to older workers. The former group includes legal protections for disabled workers, family and medical leave policies, and workers' compensation. Broadly speaking, all of these policies are designed to aid workers who are dealing with a disability or other health issue to remain employed. While these policies are not age-specific, they may have greater relevance for older workers due to the higher risk of disability and health issues at older ages. Next, there are a number of policies that apply only to older workers, including age-based legal protections, mandatory retirement (or the elimination thereof), gradual retirement policies, and job training authorized under Title V of the Older Americans Act. Unlike the first set, this set of policies is designed to boost the employment prospects of older workers specifically.

The second category of policies relevant for older workers are those policies that aim to enhance the financial security of disabled or retired individuals. This category includes several of the largest federal government programs: Disability Insurance, Social Security, and Medicare. In 2019, these three programs paid cash benefits or provided health insurance coverage to 9.9, 54.1, and 61.2 million people, respectively, at a combined cost of $1.8 trillion (OASDI Trustees, 2020). These social insurance programs are designed to protect workers against a variety of risks, including the risk of career-ending disability, of outliving one's retirement resources, and of incurring medical expenses while disabled or in old age. While the focus of these programs is on risk protection, their existence can make retirement possible when it might not otherwise have been possible. These programs can also affect the financial incentive to continue working at older ages, potentially affecting the timing of retirement.

This category of policies that support the financial security of disabled and retired workers includes other programs, notably retirement savings policies. In addition, several policies in this category are designed to boost retirement security among low-income individuals specifically. These include Supplemental Security Income (SSI), Medicaid, and retirement savings policies that target low-wage workers.

TABLE 8-1 Public Policies Relevant to Older Workers

	Non-Age-Specific	Age-Specific
Policies to support work	• Legal protections for disabled workers (the Americans with Disabilities Act) • Family and medical leave • Worker's compensation	• Legal protections for older workers (the Age Discrimination in Employment Act) • (End of) Mandatory retirement • Gradual retirement policies • Senior Community Employment Program
Policies to support financial security	• Disability Insurance • Social Security • Supplemental Security Income (SSI)* • Retirement saving policies* • Health insurance policies*	

*Includes policies designed to support low-income individuals.

Throughout this report, we frame work at older ages as being shaped by preferences, expectations, and constraints. Some of the policies discussed in this chapter may be viewed as loosening constraints and enabling workers to achieve a work-to-retirement path more in line with their preferences. For example, legal protections for disabled and older workers may open up a wider range of employment opportunities. Access to family and medical leave may allow workers dealing with a personal or family crisis to step away from work temporarily and then return to their jobs. Policies that boost access to health insurance outside of employment may enable retirement for those who were working primarily to obtain insurance. In other cases, policies may create constraints, such as when workers who prefer to take an earlier retirement are unable to access their Social Security benefits until they reach the early eligibility age.

Another important theme is disparities in retirement experiences. Among the policies that we review are benefit programs that essentially cover all workers, notably Social Security and Medicare, and legal protections that similarly apply to most or all workers. Other programs we review are in theory available to all yet end up being used more by some groups than others. For example, higher-income individuals are more likely to use retirement savings programs that are regulated and subsidized by the government, while less-educated individuals are more likely to receive Social Security Disability Insurance (SSDI) benefits. Our review includes a handful of programs, like SSI, that are explicitly targeted at lower-income individuals. Where there are large differences in the use or importance of these programs to different groups, we include this in our discussion.

In this chapter, we provide a comprehensive discussion of the full range of policies that may affect work at older ages. We organize this discussion to follow the categories above, first discussing non-age-specific policies that support work, then age-specific policies that encourage employment, and finally policies that support the financial security of disabled and retired workers. For each policy, we provide an introduction to relevant institutional details as well as the literature exploring the effect of the policies on older workers. We conclude with a summary of key lessons from this review of policies, emphasizing areas where future research is needed.

NON-AGE-SPECIFIC POLICIES THAT SUPPORT WORK

We begin with a discussion of non-age-specific policies. The concept of universal design may provide a useful lens through which to view these policies. First introduced in the context of the built environment, universal design refers to design that focuses on ensuring accessibility for all. Applying this principle leads to the incorporation of elements that may be crucial for some groups to access the environment on an equal basis and are neutral or helpful for other groups—for example, in the built environment context, having a ramp in addition to stairs at a building entrance. In the context of social policies to promote employment, universal design means designing policies that may be of value to individuals at all stages of the life course, with special attention to the needs of disabled or older workers, who may face additional challenges in maintaining employment.

Americans with Disabilities Act (ADA)

One policy that seeks to promote equal access to employment is the ADA. The ADA, enacted in 1990, is meant to protect the disabled from discrimination. The employment portion of this act protects persons with disabilities who are qualified for a specific employment position "with or without reasonable accommodation" (Americans with Disabilities Act of 1990). The definition of disabled in the ADA includes those who have a "physical or mental impairment that substantially limits one or more major life activities," have a record of such an impairment, or are regarded as disabled (Americans with Disabilities Act of 1990). This definition is more generous than that for SSDI or SSI, both of which require that the disability be work-limiting (Burkhauser and Daly, 2002). In 2008, an amendment to the act broadened the definition of "disability" further in order to offset U.S. Supreme Court rulings that limited those protected by the ADA (ADA Amendment Act of 2008).

Although the ADA does not target older workers, the likelihood of being disabled increases with age, especially after age 50 (e.g., Rowe and Kahn, 1997; U.S. Department of Commerce, 1997), and almost 60 percent of charges of ADA violations between 1993 and 2007 were filed by individuals over age 40 (Bjelland et al., 2010). From this we can infer two things. First, employers might reasonably project that hiring older workers could result in additional costs in the future, based on the combination of age-related increases in the probability that the worker will develop a disability during their tenure and the ADA legal requirement that employers make reasonable accommodations for workers who have disabilities. Second, disability protections may become increasingly important for protecting older workers from age discrimination as work lives extend into older ages. Indeed, disability discrimination laws may be more effective for protecting older workers than age discrimination laws. Some health ailments that commonly develop as part of the aging process have been legally classified as disabilities (Sterns and Miklos, 1995), and the presence of these ailments can give older workers the option of filing their discrimination claims under either the ADEA or the ADA (or corresponding state laws). In addition, because the ADA includes the requirement that employers make reasonable accommodations for their workers' disabilities and does not include a bona fide occupational qualification exception (see ADEA discussion below), the ADA is better able to limit employer defenses against discrimination claims.

As they have done regarding age discrimination laws, researchers have studied the effects of disability discrimination laws, both in the United States and in other countries. Some of these studies find that these laws have negative effects on employment (Acemoglu and Angrist, 2001; Bell and Heitmueller, 2009; DeLeire, 2000; Jolls and Prescott, 2004), while some find no effects (Houtenville and Burkhauser, 2004; Hotchkiss, 2004; Stock and Beegle, 2004). More recent studies point to positive effects (Ameri et al., 2018; Armour et al., 2018; Button, 2018; Kruse and Schur, 2003a). However, with the exception of the work by Ameri and colleagues (2018), none of these studies uses direct measures of discrimination to ask whether these laws reduce discrimination. Further, it appears that those studies that define disability as *having a work-limiting disability* find negative effects of the ADA on employment for the disabled (Acemoglu and Angrist, 2001; DeLeire, 2000, 2003), whereas studies that further restrict the definition to people who said that they were "able to work at all" (excluding those with a work-limiting disability who were unable to work) find positive effects (Hotchkiss and Rovba, 2003; Kruse and Schur, 2003a, b). Blanck and colleagues (2003) argue that neither of these definitions of disabled covers the population targeted by the ADA, and thus the true impact of the ADA on the population targeted is still an open research question.

Summary

Although the definitions of disability are different for the ADA than for transfer programs targeting those with disabilities, it was hoped that the ADA would decrease the need for SSI and SSDI by enabling the disabled to work. However, that does not seem to be the case. Burkhauser and Daly (2002) find that people with disabilities were much more sensitive to government transfer program rules than they were to the ADA, which suggests that proposals targeting such transfer programs may provide maximal impact on the labor force participation of older disabled people.

Family and Medical Leave Policies

Policies that allow workers to take time away from work (on a paid or unpaid basis) in order to deal with a health or family crisis and then return to their jobs may enhance workers' ability to remain in the work force. Older workers face a significant risk of experiencing such crises. One in five male workers and one in six female workers between the ages of 50 and 69 experience an acute health event—including a heart attack, stroke, new cancer diagnosis, new chronic illness diagnosis, or accident—over a two-year period (Coile, 2004). One in five individuals ages 51 to 61 has a frail parent or parent-in-law, and one in four will experience new frailty in a parent or parent-in-law over a 10-year period (Johnson et al., 2005). As discussed in Chapter 4, many older workers serve as informal caregivers, and such service is associated with an increased probability of labor force exit.

The Family and Medical Leave Act (FMLA) allows employees to take up to 12 weeks of unpaid, job-protected leave to address their own serious health condition or the serious health condition of a family member, including the care of a newborn child. The 1993 law applies to employees who have been at their job for at least one year, are working at least 1,250 hours per year, and are employed by a firm with at least 50 workers. Due to these restrictions, only 55 percent of the private-sector workforce is covered by the FMLA (Jorgensen and Applebaum, 2014).

There is currently no federal *paid leave* policy in the United States. There are ongoing legislative efforts to enact such a policy—most recently, the Family and Medical Insurance Leave (FAMILY) Act, which was introduced in the House and the Senate in 2019 and would provide up to 12 weeks of partial income to address a worker's own serious health problem or that of a family member (including the birth or adoption of a child). The Family First Coronavirus Response Act, passed in 2020, provides for paid leave for certain COVID-19 related leaves on a temporary basis.

In the absence of a federal policy, a growing number of states have passed paid family leave policies. California adopted the first such policy in 2004, and currently seven additional states and the District of Columbia offer paid leave or will do so within the next few years (Congressional Research Service, 2019b). These policies generally provide benefits in the event of a serious health condition of a close family member or the arrival of a child; some policies also offer benefits for a worker's own serious medical condition, while other states provide this coverage through a separate state disability insurance program. The maximum duration of family leave varies by state, from four to 12 weeks, and maximum weekly benefits range from $667 in New Jersey to $1,300 in California. Finally, many employers choose to offer at least some amount of paid sick leave to their workers. In 2017, 87 percent of full-time workers and half of part-time workers worked in firms that offered this benefit (Kaiser Family Foundation, 2020a).

Most of the research to date on family leave policies focuses on their use for childbirth-related leaves. Therefore, it is not well understood if the FMLA or paid leave policies affect employment rates at older ages by helping older workers weather their own health problems or those of a spouse or parent while maintaining employment. However, a few pieces of evidence suggest that these policies could play an important role. Among workers age 50 and above, about one in seven took an FMLA leave over an 18-month period, a rate similar to that among younger workers (Mayer, 2013). The introduction of paid family leave in California led to an 11 percent decrease in elderly nursing home utilization, raising the possibility that the policy may have allowed some workers to take time off to care for a parent or older spouse without leaving their jobs (Arora and Wolf, 2018).

Summary

Access to paid or unpaid family leave could help older workers stay in their present job while managing a health or family crisis. However, most of the research to date on family leave policies does not elucidate whether the FMLA or other paid-leave policies affect the employment rates of older workers.

Workers' Compensation

An unfortunate but, to some extent, inevitable consequence of work is the occurrence of workplace injuries. In the United States, workers injured at work are covered by workers' compensation, a system that provides medical care for treatment of the injury, as well as indemnity benefits for time away from work. Indemnity benefits are often short term, until workers recover fully and return to work. In this sense, workers' compensation can be considered to be among the set of policies that support work. In cases where injuries result in permanent disabilities, which can range from partial to full disability (defined in terms lost earnings capacity), indemnity benefits can be indefinite, although often lump-sum settlements are used. Workers' compensation laws in the United States are set at the state level, and while the core structure of the program is similar across states, there are very important differences in the generosity of benefits and many other aspects of state programs (see, e.g., Rothkin, 2019). Separate federal workers' compensation programs cover federal employees and workers in specific high-risk occupations, such as coal miners and longshoremen (Sengupta et al., 2012).

One key piece of evidence to keep in mind in thinking about older workers and workplace injuries is that, overall, workplace injuries are declining across all age groups (Coate, 2019), with the sharpest declines among younger workers—a change that is not attributable to changes in the composition of occupations but rather to occupations becoming safer (Restrepo and Shuford, 2011). Still, potentially important age differences remain.

Data from the Bureau of Labor Statistics (BLS) indicate that, in recent years, overall rates of lost work time due to injuries and illnesses do not differ much by age (whereas younger workers used to have higher rates [Restrepo and Shuford, 2011]). However, the evidence sometimes differs. For example, in a large sample of workers' compensation claims in Australia, Berecki-Gisolf and colleagues (2012) found increased injury rates through age 60, after which they declined a bit. The most recent evidence for the United States (Savych and Ruser, 2019), from a database of workers' compensation claims covering a large share of the United States, indicates that injury rates and the rates of injuries with lost work time are not very different for older workers (and are highest for younger workers). But the nature of injuries differs, with older workers more likely to be injured in falls and to have fractures. And BLS data point to a much higher fatality rate for older workers, for example, the rate is five times as high for workers ages 65+ than for those ages 20–24.

The evidence generally indicates that when older workers are injured on the job, their injuries tend to be more severe (Pransky et al., 2005b; Rogers and Wiatrowski, 2005). In BLS data covering all reported injuries, days away from work rise monotonically with age, from a median of about five days for ages 20–24 to 18 days for ages 65 and over (Rogers and Wiatrowski, 2005). Restrepo and Shuford (2011) show that measuring severity by indemnity payments indicates uniformly higher severity with age (with severity highest in the oldest group included, ages 55–64). These age differences have been persistent over time, and the same is true when severity is measured by medical payments. About half of these differences are due to the more severe injuries older workers experience. For example, older workers are more likely to have rotator cuff and knee injuries and lower-back nerve pain, and younger workers are more likely to have sprains and lower-back pain. In a related study using BLS data and focusing on workers ages 65 and over, Wolf (2010) finds that falls, slips, and trips were the largest cause of injury among older workers in this age group.

On the other hand, the frequency of workers' compensation claims for this 65+ age group is generally lower, owing to lower employment in the more hazardous and injury-prone occupations. Algarni and colleagues (2015) discuss evidence of a higher prevalence of musculoskeletal injuries and slower recovery among older workers, likely associated in part with age-related physical changes. In data from Australia, Smith and Berecki-Gisolf (2014) document that both age and physical demands at work are associated with more musculoskeletal injuries, and the relationship with age was stronger in more physically demanding jobs, although this tends to attenuate after age 45.[1] In data from 2003, the types of injuries that occur also change with age, with a higher share of fractures among those ages 55–64 and especially 65 and older, and a corresponding lower share of sprains, strains, and tears. Biddle and colleagues (2003) report a higher rate of permanent disabilities for older workers injured on the job than for younger workers.

The fatality rate jumps substantially for those ages 65 and older, to nearly three times the rate at other ages (and the rate at other ages varies little); see Rogers and Wiatrowski (2005). Berecki-Gisolf and colleagues (2012) also report that days until return to work rise with age, largely plateauing after age 45, while recurrences of injuries

---

[1] One factor the authors emphasize as potentially mitigating evidence of greater likelihood of injury among older workers is the "healthy worker effect," in which, especially with age, only the healthiest workers tend to select (or get selected into) physically-demanding jobs. It remains on open question whether increases in employment among older workers are likely to reinforce this effect, with healthier workers choosing to continue working, or to undercut it—if more older workers choose to continue working of necessity.

increase into the 50s and then decline somewhat. Looking at Colorado workers' compensation claims, Schwatka and colleagues (2012) find rising medical and indemnity costs, owing in part to more severe injuries, among construction workers. Some evidence indicates, not surprisingly, that age differences in preexisting health conditions contribute to the greater severity of workplace injuries among older workers, looking at musculoskeletal injuries (Smith et al., 2014).[2]

The most recent data (from Savych and Ruser, 2019) point to higher indemnity payments with age (although with declines for those aged 65 and older), due to longer duration of temporary disability, greater likelihood of permanent disability payments (and higher amounts), and higher pre-injury wages (which influence indemnity payments via the replacement rate). Medical payments generally increase with age. It's also true that recovery tends to decline with age, but only slightly, and the percentage of workers without "substantial" return to work increases with age.

There is less research about age differences in treatment for injuries covered by workers' compensation. This may be relevant, because some types of common treatments, or treatments for common injuries, are controversial. For example, there has been rapid growth in opioids prescribing for workers' compensation injuries, and opioid prescriptions, including for longer-term use, are frequent.[3] But longer-term opioids prescribing is associated with slower return to work (Savych et al., 2019), and opioids prescribing increases with age (Thumula and Liu, 2018). Back injuries are very common for workers and are a major cost of workers' compensation. Treatment for back injuries—in particular, whether to use surgery—is highly controversial (e.g., Maghout-Juratli et al., 2006). We are not aware of evidence on differences in treatment and efficacy by age.

Workplace injuries among older workers—especially given their greater severity—may lead to retirement and participation in other public disability programs. With regard to retirement, Pransky and colleagues (2005a) studied workers who filed workers' compensation claims with lost work time, and found that among those ages 55 and over, 11 percent planned to retire earlier due to a workplace injury; this was more likely among those with prior health problems. Scott and colleagues (2018) report similar evidence for Canada, for a subsample of those with permanent impairments (for whom this response seems particularly likely).

Burton and Spieler (2001) identified the problem of increased participation in public disability programs early, in light of what they saw as declining availability of permanent disability benefits. They also pointed out a potential externality problem: state policy to reduce the generosity of these kinds of workers' compensation benefits could simply shift costs to other, primarily federal, programs. Burton and Spieler also noted that some evidence suggested that workers do turn to SSDI for income support when workers' compensation benefits are unavailable, based simply on opposite trends in these two programs.[4] Evidence of injured workers covered by workers' compensation ending up on SSDI is reported by O'Leary and colleagues (2012), Parent and colleagues (2012), and Sengupta and Baldwin (2015). Aside from the externality problem, this shift could be problematic because workers' compensation is an experience-rated system, which is intended to create incentives to keep workplaces safe, whereas SSDI is not. The implications for worker well-being are potentially ambiguous. SSDI benefits tend to be lower, although the benefits may be more secure and medical care is provided, as SSDI recipients receive Medicare after 24 months (Burton and Spieler, 2001).

Summary

Older workers do not have higher injury rates or more frequent workers' compensation claims than younger workers. However, their injuries are more severe, resulting in higher payments, longer periods of benefit receipt, and higher fatality rates. Older workers who are injured on the job and receive workers' compensation benefits, particularly those with preexisting health problems, are more likely to report that they plan to retire earlier than

---

[2]One conflicting study is Pransky and colleagues (2005b), who study a sample of workers with workplace injuries that entailed lost work time, comparing those ages 55 and over to those younger than 55, matching on gender, injury code, and injury date. Older workers report more severe injuries, and (not surprisingly) had more preexisting comorbidities. But they did not have worse outcomes (looking at time until return to work, change in ability to perform job, post-injury pain, and many other outcomes).

[3]Some recent reforms appear to be reducing the prescribing of opioids (e.g., Thumula et al., 2017).

[4]See Mont and colleagues (2000) and recent work on this question by McInerney and Simon (2012) and Buffie and Baker (2015).

they previously intended. There is some tendency of injured workers receiving workers' compensation benefits to transition to SSDI.

AGE-SPECIFIC POLICIES THAT SUPPORT WORK

The policies discussed so far may be of particular importance for older workers, but they cover all workers. We now turn to a set of policies that apply exclusively to older workers. Older workers are a group of special concern due to their potential to be negatively impacted by age discrimination in the work force, as discussed in Chapter 6; age-discrimination legislation may mitigate this risk. Similarly, the elimination of mandatory retirement has made it easier for U.S. workers to work in old age, even as such policies remain in force in many other countries. If many workers prefer gradual retirement, as suggested in Chapter 3, it is worth considering whether public policies can support that option. Finally, job training for older workers merits discussion, as the need to help workers retool for available jobs will need to be balanced against the generally lower number of remaining work years when considering the value of training for this group.

Age Discrimination in Employment Act (ADEA)

The federal Age Discrimination in Employment Act (1967) protects people over the age of 40 from discrimination in hiring (including prohibiting age-related advertisements), firing, promotion, layoff compensation, benefits, job assignments, and training. In addition, most states have their own age discrimination laws, which may differ from the federal law, for example by allowing for larger damages or applying to workers at smaller firms.

The ADEA affects organizations that regularly employ 20 or more employees. The current law also protects against mandatory retirement for most occupations (Lahey, 2008). Exemptions to the ADEA include a "bona fide occupational qualification," or BFOQ, that is directly related to age, for example, in an acting position. In practice, the courts have also allowed age to be considered a BFOQ in cases where public safety may be affected, including occupations such as pilots, air traffic controllers, and bus drivers. The federal law also exempts high-salaried policy-making positions from age discrimination law.

Unlike the Civil Rights Act, the ADEA does not allow damages for emotional pain and suffering or for punitive damages. Damages are limited to "make whole" damages and lawyer fees. Although these awards can include requirements to hire, reinstate, promote, provide back pay, and restore benefits, in practice most of what is awarded under the ADEA goes to paying lawyer fees. Additional damages are awarded only in rare cases in which the defendant has willfully violated the law, and these damages are limited to twice the amount of actual damages (Lindemann and Kadue, 2003; O'Meara, 1989). Initial examinations of cases brought under the ADEA showed that, because of these limits on the awards under the ADEA, most plaintiffs were White male middle managers in their 50s who had lost sizable salaries and benefits (O'Meara, 1989). The average amount awarded per ADEA suit has only recently increased and become closer in size to awards for Title VII suits (Causey and Lahey, 2013).

A strict interpretation of the ADEA allows only for cases of disparate treatment, requiring proof of intentional discrimination. However, another interpretation of ADEA allows for disparate-impact cases, in which a policy indirectly impacts a protected group differently than the unprotected group. In ADEA cases, workplace decisions that are based on seniority or wages—for example, firing those with the highest salaries or who have the longest tenure at the firm—are considered to have a disparate impact on older workers. Initially, the Equal Employment Opportunity Commission (EEOC) held the position that an employment practice that had a disparate impact on individuals within the protected age group could not be considered to be due to a "reasonable factor other than age" unless it was justified as a business necessity. However, in *Smith v. City of Jackson*,[5] the United States Supreme Court held that the ADEA authorizes recovery for disparate-impact claims of discrimination and that the "reasonable factors other than age" test, rather than a "business necessity" test, is the appropriate standard for determining the legality of practices that disproportionately affect older individuals.

---

[5]*Smith v. City of Jackson*, 544 U.S. 228, 241 (2005).

Since the 1970s, rulings in ADEA cases have shifted the burden of proof from defendant to plaintiff and back. Currently, the 2005 *Smith v. City of Jackson* ruling is that

> it is not enough to simply allege that there is a disparate impact on workers, or point to a generalized policy that leads to such an impact. Rather, the employee is 'responsible for isolating and identifying the specific employment practices that are allegedly responsible for any observed statistical disparities' (*Smith v. City of Jackson*, 2005, citing *Wards Cove Packing Co. v. Atonio*, 1989).

In its 2009 *Gross v. FBL Financial Services* ruling, the High Court found that unlike Title VII legislation, the burden of proof would not shift from the plaintiff to the defendant in a "mixed-motive" case in which age is one of many factors resulting in an adverse decision. Instead, the plaintiff must show "but-for" causation, in which age was the factor resulting in that decision.[6] Currently proposed legislation, the Protecting Older Workers Against Discrimination Act (POWADA, H.R. 1230, S. 485)[7] signals a motivation by some members of Congress to reinstate the legal standards of ADEA to their pre-2009 evidentiary threshold, where age can be a factor but need not be the determining factor in finding age discrimination. Legislators and others believe this would expand protection from age discrimination and would likely lead to an increase in successful age discrimination claims and settlements (Miller, n.d.).

Evidence on the Impact of ADEA

The ADEA has been widely used since it was passed by the Congress. Although, as noted, initially most plaintiffs were White male middle managers in their 50s (O'Meara, 1989), over time there has been an increase in the share of claims filed by female, non-White, and older (55 and above) workers (U.S. Equal Employment Opportunity Commission, 2021). In the last two decades alone, there have been more than 30,000 settlements for ADEA claims filed with the EEOC. Moreover, the EEOC's press releases constantly reveal age discrimination lawsuit settlements against organizations in different industries (e.g., in medicine; see *Equal Employment Opportunity Commission v. Professional Endodontics*[8]). This highlights the prevalent use of this legislation by older workers to protect their legal rights when they encounter age discrimination in the workplace.

The abolition of mandatory retirement under the ADEA has increased labor force participation rates among older workers. Von Wachter (2002) examined the shift of mandatory retirement to age 70 in 1978 and its end in 1986 using the imputed probability of being covered by mandated retirement, finding that the labor force participation of workers age 65 and older increased by 10 to 20 percent in 1986 in specific industries. Similarly, when mandatory retirement was phased out for industries with tenure in 1994, retirement rates declined among college professors who were ages 70 and 71 (Ashenfelter and Card, 2002).

There is also evidence that the ADEA was partly responsible for the rise of human resource practices in the 1970s and that these practices continue to govern organizations' resource allocation decisions in order to help them ensure compliance with labor laws and regulations (Dobbin and Sutton, 1998). Specifically, Ollier-Malaterre and colleagues (2013) find that organizations attaching higher levels of importance to compliance with labor laws and regulations (the ADEA and ADA among them) were more likely to adopt age assessment practices (e.g., analyzing projected retirement rates) and older-worker-related practices in their management.

Economic research evaluating the effectiveness of age discrimination laws suggests that they have improved labor market outcomes for older workers. For example, the arrival of (first) state and (then) federal age discrimination laws raised the employment of older workers (Adams, 2004), and strengthened the employment relationship between older workers and firms (Neumark and Stock, 1999), suggesting that age discrimination laws made it more difficult for employers to fire older workers with long tenure at the firms.

However, these findings do not provide insight into the effects of age discrimination laws on age discrimination in hiring. Age discrimination in hiring may be the most important form of discrimination to consider in light of population aging. First, as discussed in Chapter 3, the transition to retirement is often gradual, with many

---

[6] *Gross v. FBL Financial Services Inc.*, 557 U.S. (2009).
[7] See https://www.congress.gov/bill/116th-congress/house-bill/1230/text
[8] *Equal Employment Opportunity Commission v. Professional Endodontics*, P.C., 4:17-cv-13466 District Court, E. D. Michigan (2018).

people taking bridge jobs or moving to partial retirement, possibly as a result of declining health (Cahill et al., 2006; Johnson, 2014; Johnson et al., 2009; Maestas, 2010). As more workers continue working into older ages, the demand for less physically demanding jobs will likely result in an increase in partial retirement. Second, the most rigorous evidence establishing age discrimination—from correspondence studies such as those discussed in Chapter 6—is focused on discrimination in hiring.

Third, both empirical evidence (Adams, 2004; Neumark and Stock, 1999) and the workings of age discrimination enforcement suggest that, at present, the ADEA is more effective at reducing age discrimination in terminations than in hiring (Neumark, 2009), because in hiring cases it is difficult to identify a class of affected workers, and economic damages are smaller than in termination cases.[9] Fourth and finally, as a result of their effectiveness in making the termination of older employees more difficult, stronger age discrimination protections can have the unintended consequence of *increasing* hiring discrimination. In particular, if age discrimination laws less effectively reduce discrimination in hiring than in terminations, they could deter employers from hiring older workers by raising the expected cost of hiring them (Adams, 2004; Bloch, 1994; Posner, 1995). Thus, determining the effects of age discrimination laws on the hiring older workers is of great importance.

Earlier studies that use state-level variation in age-discrimination laws to examine the effect of these laws on the hiring of older adults find no evidence that these laws are effective in improving the hiring of older workers (Adams, 2004; Lahey, 2008). Instead, they find that such laws might have had the opposite effect and reduced hiring, particularly among those ages 65 and over (Adams, 2004; Lahey, 2008). However, these earlier studies either rely on data that measure employment overall and are not well suited to directly measuring changes in hiring (Adams, 2004) or their findings are also consistent with alternative interpretations that could suggest that these laws led to increases in hiring (Lahey, 2008; Neumark, 2009).

More recently, Neumark and Song (2013) used variations across states in older workers' responses to the changes in Social Security that were phased in between 2003 and 2008 for cohorts born after 1938—a reduction in benefits for those retiring early at age 62 and a gradual increase in the age of full retirement from 65 to 66—to estimate the impact of age discrimination laws. They found that in states that had stronger age discrimination laws (those that allowed for larger damages and/or extended coverage to small firms exempt from federal age discrimination law), older workers were more likely to work longer and claim Social Security benefits later, and that these increases in employment were due to increases in the hiring of older workers. In particular, employment increased for those between the original age of full retirement (age 65) and the new, higher age (by 2008, it reached age 66), the specific age range targeted by these reforms to Social Security. This study points more directly to the ways in which policy can jointly create supply-side incentives to encourage older workers to extend their work lives and demand-side reductions in age discrimination.

Subsequent research using correspondence studies (discussed in Chapter 6) has confirmed and extended the finding that state age discrimination laws that allow plaintiffs to seek increased damages (compared to the federal ADEA) reduce age discrimination in hiring (Neumark et al., 2019; Neumark et al., 2019). In one such study covering retail hiring in all U.S. states, the authors find evidence of lower levels of discrimination against older men and women when state age-discrimination laws allow plaintiffs to file for larger damages (Neumark et al., 2019). Because employers in these states could expect higher costs associated with dismissing older workers, this evidence more strongly rebuts the hypothesis that stronger age discrimination laws may lead employers to reduce their hiring of older workers.

However, research has not consistently found that stronger age discrimination laws *increase* the hiring of older workers. There is some contrary evidence examining these effects during the economic downturn of the Great Recession (Neumark and Button, 2014). During this period, there is very little evidence that stronger-age discrimination protections improved employment rates or reduced unemployment rates or durations among older workers relative to younger workers, and in some cases the evidence suggests that stronger age discrimination protections were associated with more-adverse effects on older workers (Neumark and Button, 2014). It is possible that severe labor market disruptions that involve significant layoffs, such as the Great Recession, make it harder to discern discrimination in hiring and terminations, which weakens the benefits of stronger state protections for age-discrimination. It is also possible

---

[9]That said, the studies of the effectiveness of the ADEA examine somewhat different environments (e.g., the Great Recession in Neumark and Button, 2014; recessions vs. other periods in Dahl and Knepper, 2020; and earlier state laws and the federal laws in Lahey, 2008).

that the potentially higher costs of terminating older workers loom larger for employers in periods of economic uncertainty, reducing their willingness to hire older workers. However, these results are less a contradiction of other findings suggesting positive effects of age discrimination laws than specific to a highly unusual labor market period.

One interesting observation is that the few studies that have examined differences in the effectiveness of age discrimination laws by gender and race/ethnicity have not found similar effects for either women or racial-ethnic minorities. Specifically, neither Lahey (2008) nor McLaughlin (2020) found effects of ADEA laws for women. Lahey (2008) also did not find effects of ADEA laws for minorities. This could in part be due to the limits on damages that can be sought by plaintiffs under the ADEA. As noted earlier, most early ADEA claims were filed by older White male middle-managers with substantial salary and benefit losses; because older women and minorities are historically less likely achieve these high-paying jobs with extensive benefits, the high cost of litigation relative to the potential award may discourage these groups from filing cases. As another potential explanation of these null findings, Delaney and Lahey (2019) argue that although older women and minorities experience discrimination—the source of which is not always obvious to the target—the ADEA and Title VII employment laws were separate laws and thus limited intersectional claims between age, race, and gender. Nevertheless, this explanation has not received rigorous empirical testing yet.

Summary

In general, the balance of the evidence suggests that stronger state age-discrimination laws improve the hiring and retention of older workers, particularly older White men. Beyond this, there is even clearer evidence that stronger age-discrimination laws do not produce the unintended consequence of creating incentives for employers to reduce their hiring of older workers—with the possible exception of during unusual periods of economic disruption. Thus, one might argue that, at a minimum, these laws do no harm.

Affirmative Action

A potential policy change that would go beyond age discrimination protection would be to extend affirmative action mandates for federal contractors to include older workers. This would require federal contractors to demonstrate that they have developed and enacted measures to ensure that they employ older workers throughout their organization. One rationale for such a policy is that evidence suggests that age discrimination in hiring is a particularly serious problem, and reducing discrimination is an important way to help society adapt to population aging. One might also argue that age discrimination protections should be on par with protections based on race, sex, ethnicity, and religion. This extension of affirmative action could be done by expanding on previously issued executive orders that require federal contractors to take affirmative action to improve representation of other protected groups to cover age as well.[10] There is evidence that affirmative action policies have been successful in boosting employment for other covered groups (for reviews, see Holzer and Neumark, 2000; and Kurtulus, 2012) and, therefore, would likely improve employment prospects for older workers.

(Elimination of) Mandatory Retirement

In a sense, *mandatory retirement* is the ultimate form of age discrimination—a policy allowing (if not requiring) the employer to set an age at which an employee must retire, regardless of the employee's wishes or job performance. A popular theory for the existence of mandatory retirement is that it is a mutually beneficial arrangement for workers and firms (Lazear, 1979). According to this theory, workers are paid less than the value of their marginal product when young and more than this amount when old in order to induce workers whose performance cannot be perfectly monitored to perform at a higher level of effort when young. Mandatory retirement ensures that workers leave the

---

[10]The key prior executive orders with regard to hiring and employment include no. 10925 (1961), instructing federal contractors to "take affirmative action to ensure that applicants are treated equally without regard to race, color, religion, sex, or national origin"; no. 11246 (1965), requiring all government contractors to take affirmative action to expand employment opportunities for minorities, establishing the Office of Federal Contract Compliance; and no. 13672 (2014), amending no. 11246 to cover sexual orientation or gender identity.

firm at the previously agreed-upon date. Jolls (1996) posited that the elimination of mandatory retirement would indeed encourage the use of Lazear contracts, a theory tested empirically and affirmed by Neumark and Stock (1999).

Mandatory retirement at age 65 was common in the 1960s and 1970s in the United States, affecting an estimated 40 percent of the male workforce (von Wachter, 2002). While the 1967 ADEA originally protected workers only through age 65, amendments in 1978 and 1986 first outlawed mandatory retirement before age 70 and then abolished the practice. Currently, mandatory retirement exists only in occupations deemed too physically or cognitively challenging for workers to continue beyond a certain age. These occupations include federal law enforcement officers, national park rangers, and firefighters, who generally must retire at age 57 (Costello, 2019); pilots, who must retire by age 65 (previously age 60) and air traffic controllers, who must retire by age 56 (with exceptions up to age 61; Federal Aviation Administration, 2019); employees who enter into contractual agreements at the time of appointment or partnership (for example, lawyers); and certain state officials, particularly judges (Sciocchetti, 1991).

During the period when mandatory retirement at age 65 was in effect, workers covered by this policy had a very high incidence of retirement at age 65. The elimination of mandatory retirement at age 65 is estimated to have increased the labor force participation of workers ages 65 to 69 by five to 20 percent relative to then current levels (Morrison, 1988; von Wachter, 2002).

Despite its virtual elimination in the United States, mandatory retirement is still in place in many high-income countries (Organisation for Economic Co-operation and Development [OECD], 2017a). While Australia, Canada, and New Zealand abolished mandatory retirement along with the United States, the only OECD countries within Europe to have done so are the United Kingdom, Denmark, and Poland.[11] This is in spite of a recommendation by the European Parliament that European Union (EU) member states "put a ban on mandatory retirement when reaching the statutory retirement age, so as to enable people who can and wish to do so to choose to continue to work beyond the statutory retirement age or to gradually phase in their retirement" (European Parliament, 2013).

Mandatory retirement still exists in other EU countries, set at age 67 in Sweden, age 68 in Finland, age 70 in France, Iceland, and Portugal, and age 72 in Norway, for example. In these countries, when an employee reaches mandatory retirement age the employer must either create a new employment contract or renew the existing one if the employee is to continue their employment relationship. Since there is limited data on this process, it is unclear how often mandatory retirement ages actually prevent older workers from continuing to work.

Although mandatory retirement policies have largely ended in the United States and several other countries, ending these policies in other countries has remained controversial (Organisation for Economic Co-operation and Development, 2017b). Employers in these countries often argue that mandatory retirement improves the efficiency of their businesses. Therefore it can be difficult to provide objective measures of the performance of workers that can justify dismissing those with poor performance, mandatory retirement offers employers a convenient mechanism for terminating these workers, particularly in countries in which employment protection rules are rigid. Mandatory retirement policies are also sometimes urged based on the (unsubstantiated) belief that they benefit younger workers (but see the discussion of this "lump of labor" fallacy in Chapter 7).

An interesting counterpoint to mandatory retirement is Japan's Elderly Employment Stabilization Law, which requires employers to provide continuous employment until the pension eligibility age.[12] The law increased employment at older ages for employees of larger firms, for whom the law was binding (Kondo and Shigeoka, 2017).

Partial Retirement

Partial retirement refers to a policy that allows workers to select partial pension receipt in combination with part-time work in order to make a gradual exit from the labor force. It is easy to imagine that many workers might elect this option if available; indeed, the popularity of part-time work and bridge jobs in the United States, discussed in Chapters 2 and 3, points to a preference among many for gradual retirement, even in the absence of a natural

---

[11] A 2007 European Court of Justice ruling (*Palacios de la Villa v. Cortefiel Service SA*) affirmed that the EU's Equal Treatment Framework Directive does not preclude a national law allowing compulsory retirement clauses to be contained in collective agreements under certain conditions.

[12] Prior to the law's passage, many firms had a long-standing policy of mandatory retirement at age 60, leaving workers to retire, seek new employment, or continue working for the same employer under a new contract, if offered by the firm. Once the pension eligibility age was raised beyond 60, individuals could be left without means of support. The law required firms to offer a new contract for employment until the pension age.

way to combine this with partial pension receipt. Some have suggested that the ADEA could be amended to establish a legal right to phased retirement at one's current job where feasible (Gotbaum and Wolfe, 2018). The federal government has offered partial (or "phased") retirement since 2014 (U.S. Office of Personnel Management, 2019).

In the United States, there is no formal partial retirement option. An informal option does exist for certain workers to work while receiving only a portion of their full Social Security benefit. Workers who claim benefits prior to the full retirement age are subject to the Retirement Earnings Test, in which earnings beyond an exempt amount trigger a reduction in benefits. Workers are later compensated for the lost benefits in the form of an increased actuarial adjustment, with their benefit amount increased as though they had originally claimed at a later date. A worker younger than the full retirement age who claims benefits and has earnings between the exempt amount and the level at which benefits are reduced to zero will thus receive a partial benefit. In practice, the option to receive a partial pension does not appear to be well understood, given the ample evidence that workers misperceive the Retirement Earnings Test as a pure tax. For example, workers tend to "bunch" at a level of earnings just below the exempt amount (Gelber et al., 2020).

In the absence of any experience with a partial retirement policy in the United States, its effect can be simulated using a model of retirement behavior (Gustman and Steinmeier, 1983). Results of this exercise suggest that workers will retire earlier if they face a minimum hours constraint—for example, if they are required to either work full-time or retire—than if they are given the option to freely set their preferred number of hours.

Partial retirement policies exist in many European countries. An international comparison of nine OECD countries that have introduced such policies suggests that the policies increase labor force participation (extensive margin) but also decrease the average hours worked (intensive margin; Börsch-Supan et al., 2018). Overall, these policies have either had no significant effect on total labor supply or have decreased it.[13]

Summary

While partial retirement policies may have intuitive appeal, it is unclear whether their introduction would lead to an increase or decrease in work at older ages. Although some workers who would have retired early in the absence of a partial retirement option might choose to extend their working lives on a part-time basis if this option were available, some workers who would have otherwise worked full-time might also elect this option, leading to a reduction in their hours worked (Börsch-Supan et al., 2017, 2018). Whether this policy option ultimately leads to more work at older ages is thus an empirical question.

The Senior Community Employment Program

A final type of policy that may support work at older ages is job training. The Senior Community Employment Program (SCSEP) is a training program for older workers based on community service and work, authorized by Congress under Title V of the Older Americans Act (OAA) of 1965. The OAA promotes a range of services that support economic opportunity and health among older adults, including adult day care, senior centers and activities, legal support, health promotion, disease prevention, and transportation. SCSEP is focused on employment and civic engagement for older adults.

SCSEP provides subsidized, part-time, community service work-based training for low-income older individuals that have poor employment prospects (U.S. Department of Labor, 2020a). The program helps to meet urgent needs in the community that "might otherwise go unmet while empowering participants to become self-sufficient, thus avoiding public assistance as they provide essential community services and gain the necessary confidence and job skills for obtaining unsubsidized employment" (National Council on the Aging, 2001, p. iv). Program participants must be at least age 55, be unemployed, and have a family income of no more than 125 percent of the

---

[13]For evidence from a specific country, see Graf et al., (2011) for evidence on Austria; Huber et al., (2013) and Berg et al. (2020) for evidence on Germany; Ilmakunnas and Ilmakunnas (2006) for evidence on Finland; and Brinch et al., (2015) for evidence on Norway. For European studies demonstrating older workers' preference for reducing their working hours in a gradual shift toward their retirement over full retirement, see Gielen (2009), Büsch and colleagues (2010), and Cihlar et al. (2014).

federal poverty level. Priority is given to persons who are over age 65, have a disability, have low literacy skills or limited English proficiency, reside in a rural area, or have failed to find employment after using services through the American Job Center System. A variety of organizations are involved in administering SCSEP programs.[14]

SCSEP enrollees work with a social worker or case manager on an individual employment plan to assess their skills, interests, capabilities, and needs. They are then placed in community service jobs, such as schools, libraries, social service organizations, or senior-service organizations (Collins, 2019). SCSEP participants receive a stipend based on the typical wage for the job in which they are employed or minimum wage, whichever is higher. The average duration of participation should not exceed 27 months, although this may increase to 36 months in circumstances such as high unemployment or for individuals with severe disability or advanced age (Collins, 2019; Halvorsen and Yulikova, 2020a). The program enrolls only a small fraction of the eligible population (Halvorsen and Yulikova, 2020a).

Since 2016, SCSEP's performance measures have shifted from a person-centered program (Gonyea and Hudson, 2011; National Council on the Aging, 2001) to emphasize unsubsidized employment and earnings after the program (Collins, 2019). Given these performance measures, the U.S. Department of Labor recently evaluated SCSEP as ineffective (U.S. Department of Labor, 2020b), with some discussion of eliminating the program:

> . . . while the program provides some income support to about 60,000 individuals each year, it fails to meet its other major statutory goals of fostering economic self-sufficiency and moving low-income seniors into unsubsidized employment. (p. 12)

Widening the lens provides a more complex picture. SCSEP participants face many barriers to work, including but not limited to health, social, and economic shocks; age discrimination; caregiving; homelessness or being at-risk of homelessness; limited education; limited English proficiency; chronic health conditions; and/or physically demanding lifetime jobs that are a mismatch with their health (Carolan et al., 2020; Gonzales et al., 2019). In spite of these challenges, participants contribute approximately 40 million hours to communities (U.S. Department of Labor, 2020a) and some find unsubsidized employment.

Other program benefits include improvements in social well-being and health. SCSEP participants report improved self-esteem, larger social networks, improved work skills, and a stronger belief that they can find and keep jobs (Aday and Kehoe, 2008; Carolan et al., 2020; Gonzales et al., 2019). Nearly seven out of ten participants report their health has improved because of the program (Gonzales et al., 2019; U.S. Department of Labor, 2020c).[15] These findings underscore the positive relationship between work and health when the person/environmental fit is optimal (Armstrong-Stassen and Ursel, 2009; James et al., 2011; Pak et al., 2018; Slack and Jensen, 2008; Smyer and Pitt-Catsouphes, 2007; Staudinger et al., 2016; Steenstra et al., 2017).

One analysis suggests that the benefits of SCSEP outweigh the costs, with a gain of nearly $3,000 per participant per job obtained (Mikelson, 2017). Further, the demand for workforce programs serving older workers is on the rise with population aging and increases in the desire or need to work longer. This demand will likely grow due to the economic crisis associated with COVID-19 and the need to retool and reskill low-income older adults for emerging jobs post-COVID-19.

Summary

The SCSEP is the only federally funded program to assist low-income older adults with multiple barriers in finding employment. The program provides income support for this vulnerable population and is associated

---

[14]Key stakeholders include SCSEP grantees, One-Stop Career Centers, and private-sector adult education and literacy agencies. State agencies and 19 national nonprofit organizations (e.g., AARP, Experience Works, Goodwill Industries International, National Council on the Aging, Center for Workforce Inclusion—formerly Senior Service America, Inc.) make up SCSEP grantees. In most states, the governor selects the State Office on Aging to administer the program.

[15]As Gonzales, Lee, and Harootyan (2019) report, one participant said: "I was depressed. Actually, working over there [SCSEP] helped get me out of my depression. I was happy [laughs], I had a social life and working and I lost weight too . . . physically, mentally, everything. I felt better . . ." (p. 218).

with improvements in social well-being and health but is not currently meeting its statutory goals of fostering economic self-sufficiency and moving low-income seniors into unsubsidized employment.

POLICIES TO SUPPORT THE FINANCIAL SECURITY OF DISABLED AND RETIRED WORKERS

From the perspective of older workers, there are many policies that may affect employment decisions at older ages, only some of which are designed to support work at older ages. The next set of policies we discuss are generally designed to enhance the financial security of disabled and retired workers and protect them against a variety of risks. By providing cash or health insurance benefits upon becoming disabled or reaching a certain age, or by encouraging workers to save for retirement, these policies may enable retirement. Moreover, specific program elements, such as the age of benefit eligibility, may influence the timing of retirement. A number of these programs are focused on low-income individuals, and we pay special attention to them in the discussion below.

Disability Insurance

Disability insurance provides protection against the earnings loss associated with a long-term work-limiting disability. An estimated one-quarter of 20-year-olds are projected to become disabled before reaching retirement age (U.S. Social Security Administration, 2020a). In the United States, workers are covered by SSDI, which has been part of the Social Security program since 1956.

SSDI benefits are available to workers who meet medical eligibility and work requirements. The worker must have sufficient recent and lifetime contributions: five of the prior 10 quarters and at least 40 quarters over the work life, or less if disabled at a young age. An applicant must be determined to have a disability, defined as "the inability to engage in substantial gainful activity by reason of any medically determinable physical or mental impairment(s) which can be expected to result in death or which has lasted or can be expected to last for a continuous period of not less than 12 months."[16] Applicants must have earnings below the substantial gainful activity level ($1,260 per month in 2020), and beneficiaries whose earnings exceed this level will have their benefits suspended after a trial work period.

The review of an SSDI application can be a lengthy, multistep process. A state Disability Determination office makes the initial decision, but denied applicants have up to four levels of appeals available to them. Although only one-third of applicants have been allowed in the initial determination, nearly two-thirds of original applicants are ultimately awarded benefits (Maestas, Mullen, and Strand, 2013). Once an award is made, benefits are paid (retroactively, if need be) starting five months after disability onset. The benefit calculation is essentially the same as for Social Security retired worker benefits, except that benefits are not reduced for claiming before the full retirement age.[17] Benefits are financed through the Social Security payroll tax. SSDI beneficiaries are also eligible for Medicare after a two-year waiting period. The vast majority of SSDI beneficiaries receive benefits until death or reaching the Social Security full retirement age, when they move to the rolls of that program. Fewer than 10 percent of beneficiaries ever exit SSDI to return to the labor force (Raut, 2017), though a larger share are employed with earnings below the substantial gainful activity level at some point while receiving benefits (Liu and Stapleton, 2011).

The share of nonelderly adults receiving SSDI has risen over time, from 2.2 percent in the late 1970s to 4.6 percent in 2013 (Liebman, 2015). There are a number of possible explanations for the rise in SSDI receipt, including demographic, program, and economic factors.

Population aging is one such factor, since SSDI rates rise with age and the Baby Boom generation has recently aged into the peak ages for SSDI receipt. The rising participation of women in the labor force has increased the fraction of women who are insured for SSDI. There have also been changes in the stringency of medical screening over time, notably a 1984 federal law that instructed examiners to place more weight on applicants' reported pain and discomfort, relax screening of mental illness, consider multiple nonsevere impairments as constituting a disability even if no single impairment is by itself disabling, and put more weight on medical evidence provided

---

[16]Code of Federal Regulations § 404.1505. Basic definition of disability. See https://www.ssa.gov/OP_Home/cfr20/404/404-1505.htm

[17]In the case of younger applicants, fewer years of earnings are used to calculate average earnings.

by the applicants' own health care providers (Autor and Duggan, 2006). Liebman (2015) assesses the relative importance of these factors in the growth of SSDI from 1985 to 2007, attributing half to the increased award rate (likely related to the 1984 law), one-fifth to population aging, and one-eighth to rising rates of SSDI coverage, primarily among women. The rapid growth over time in awards for mental and musculoskeletal disorders also supports the importance of the 1984 changes in medical screening procedures, as these kinds of awards might be expected to be particularly sensitive to these changes (Autor and Duggan, 2006).[18]

In addition to these demographic and legal factors, economic factors may have contributed to the increase. The SSDI replacement rate has risen over time for low-wage workers due the interaction between the benefit formula and rising income inequality (Autor and Duggan, 2006). Autor and Duggan (2003) estimate that the combination of rising replacement rates, reduced medical stringency, and declining demand for less-skilled workers made high school dropouts two to three times more likely to apply for SSDI and nearly twice as likely to exit the labor force in response to demand shocks after 1984. SSDI payments respond counter-cyclically to boom and bust cycles in the coal and oil and gas industries (Charles et al., 2018; Black et al., 2002). Similarly, SSDI applications rise with the unemployment rate (Cutler et al., 2012; Stapleton et al., 1998). While recession-related changes in awards are more muted than changes in applications (Center on Budget and Policy Priorities, 2019), recent evidence suggests that the Great Recession induced nearly one million SSDI applications and 400,000 new awards that would not otherwise have occurred, representing nine percent of all new beneficiaries between 2008 and 2012 (Maestas, Mullen et al., 2018). These studies linking economic conditions to SSDI receipt indicate that the program serves as a safety net for some individuals who meet medical eligibility criteria but would work if jobs were available. Finally, the increase in the Social Security full retirement age from age 65 to age 67 has increased the relative value of SSDI.[19] Duggan et al. (2007) estimate that the rise in the Social Security full retirement age led an additional 0.6 percent of men and 0.9 percent of women ages 45 to 64 to be receiving SSDI.

Somewhat surprisingly, the number of SSDI beneficiaries has been falling since 2014, due not only to a rise in people moving off the program due to death or attainment of the full retirement age, but also to a decline in new awards (Congressional Research Service, 2018). Among the hypotheses for this decline are the availability of jobs during the economic expansion between the Great Recession and COVID-19 pandemic, the Baby Boom generation's beginning to age out of SSDI, the reduced attraction of SSDI's Medicare benefit following the passage of the Affordable Care Act (ACA), and a decline in the SSDI allowance rate. While determining the relative importance of these factors is difficult, the last one seems important. The total allowance rate at all adjudicative levels fell from 62 percent in 2001 to 48 percent in 2016 (Congressional Research Service, 2018), potentially as a result of changes in the SSDI adjudication process as well as an improving economy (Social Security Technical Panel, 2015, 2019). Negative trends in health at midlife, discussed in Chapter 4, raise the concern that the demand for SSDI benefits may increase in the future (Waidmann et al., 2020).

SSDI receipt varies systematically with a number of individual characteristics, including age. The ratio of beneficiaries to insured workers is 1 percent at ages 30 to 34 vs. 12 percent at ages 55 to 59 and 17 percent at ages 60 to 66 (Center on Budget and Policy Priorities, 2019). There is a strong education gradient in SSDI receipt, with high school dropouts being five to six times as likely to receive benefits at ages 55 to 64 than college graduates (Coile, 2016). While differences in health explain part of this gradient, conditional on health, those with lower education are still about 50 percent more likely to receive SSDI. One factor that could contribute to age and educational differences in SSDI receipt is the medical-vocational grid, which is used in the final step of the SSDI review.[20] The

---

[18]Some indirect evidence on the role of medical screening comes from international comparisons (Wise, 2012). Among a dozen developed countries, the share of individuals on disability insurance varies a lot across countries and over time, with this variation depending much more on stringency of medical screening than on differences in health.

[19]With a Full Retirement Age (FRA) of 65, a worker claiming Social Security retired-worker benefits at age 62 receives a monthly benefit equal to 80 percent of their Primary Insurance Amount (PIA). Once the FRA rises to age 67, the same age-62 claimant receives 70 percent of PIA. A successful SSDI applicant receives 100 percent of PIA. Thus the relative benefit of being an SSDI recipient vs. retired worker beneficiary is rising with the FRA.

[20]If an applicant has met the work requirements and is found to have a condition that is sufficiently severe that is not included in the Listing of Impairments (or deemed to be of equal severity) and who is found to be unable to engage in his or her previous employment but able to undertake some form of work is evaluated using this grid. Age, education, language, and previous work skills are used in the evaluation, making it easier for older or less skilled workers to be awarded benefits than for younger or more skilled workers with the same medical condition.

worker's age, education, English language proficiency, and work skills factor into the award decision for disabled applicants who do not have a qualifying condition and retain some residual functional capacity (Warshawsky and Marchand, 2015). The probability of an award among applicants reaching the final step jumps by an estimated 9 percentage points at age 50 and by 25 percentage points at age 55 (Chen and van der Klaauw, 2008).

Rates of SSDI receipt are substantially higher for Black people than for White people (Autor and Duggan, 2006), potentially reflecting the effect of racial disparities in health and education. There is also striking geographic variation in rates of SSDI receipt. The sources of this variance are not yet well understood, but demographic and labor market factors appear to play a role (Gettens et al., 2016; Michaud et al., 2019).

Disability insurance benefits may affect labor supply decisions. In an ideal world with perfect medical screening, benefits would be strictly targeted to those who are unable to work, negating the possibility of work disincentives. In reality, this kind of targeting is impossible, both because disability occurs on a spectrum and because determining the work capacity of applicants is quite difficult. In the face of imperfect medical screening, the availability of SSDI benefits may induce some individuals who have work capacity above the substantial gainful activity level to apply for benefits. Some analysts have argued that the SSDI screening process is broken (Autor and Duggan, 2006), although the recent decline in award rates might call for new work on this question.

Estimating the effect of SSDI benefits on labor supply is inherently challenging, because the analyst does not observe the counterfactual—how much the SSDI recipient would have worked in the absence of the program. Comparing outcomes of SSDI recipients to the population as a whole is clearly unworkable due to the poorer health of beneficiaries. An early solution to this quandary was to assume that the earnings of unsuccessful applicants after rejection serves as an upper-bound estimate of the potential work capacity of those with successful SSDI applications, because the former group is likely in better health (Bound, 1989). Subsequent studies raised and debated potential problems with this approach (Bound, 1991; Lahir et al., 2008; Parsons, 1991).

More compelling recent evidence identifies plausibly exogenous sources of SSDI receipt. Maestas, Mullen, and Strand (2013) exploit variation in the allowance rates of disability insurance examiners at the first step of the determination process. They find that among those applicants on the margin of program entry, employment would have been nearly 30 percentage points higher in the absence of SSDI. French and Song (2012) similarly make use of variation in the assignment of SSDI cases to administrative law judges, while Chen and van der Klaauw (2008) use the variation in receipt arising from the medical-vocational grid; the latter two studies obtain estimates in the range of the former's results.

The long-term rise in the SSDI rolls has generated interest in existing or prospective policies that might increase labor force participation and reduce SSDI receipt among disabled individuals who retain some work capacity. One such policy is state vocational rehabilitation programs, which provide employment-related services to individuals with disabling conditions. These services are associated with higher labor force participation and reduced take-up of SSDI (Dean et al., 2014; Loprest, 2007; O'Neill et al., 2015). Individuals who face a longer wait time for these services are more likely to end up on SSDI, suggesting that they play a causal role in SSDI deterrence (Hyde et al., 2014).

Some analysts have called for firms to be required to provide short-term disability insurance for a period of time before individuals could apply for SSDI (Autor and Duggan, 2010). Firms may be in the best position to offer accommodation and rehabilitation to a newly disabled worker, and requiring them to bear some share of the cost of disability benefits may induce them to do so. A reform of this type in the Netherlands led to higher labor force participation and reduced use of long-term disability benefits (van Sonsbeek and Gradus, 2013). Others have suggested that contributions to the SSDI program could be experience-rated, where firms whose workers have been more likely to use SSDI face a higher payroll rate (Burkhauser and Daly, 2011).

Finally, the Social Security Administration and other federal agencies have conducted a number of large-scale demonstration projects to test various interventions that aim to support employment and reduce SSDI receipt among people with disabilities. The best-known of these is the Ticket to Work program, which provided SSDI beneficiaries with greater access to job placement, job training, and other services. The Ticket to Work program increased use of these services but had no consistent effect on SSDI use (Stapleton et al., 2014). A pilot program allowing SSDI recipients to keep part of their benefits if they earned more than the substantial gainful activity level did not have significant effects on employment (Weathers and Hemmeter, 2011). In general, these demonstration projects have had fairly small effects on employment and earnings, relative to what might be needed to replace SSDI, with somewhat bigger impacts for programs targeted at younger disabled persons (Wittenburg et al., 2013).

Summary

In sum, the SSDI program provides important protection against the risk of earnings loss due to a work-limiting disability. The long period of growth and very recent decline in the SSDI rolls is likely due to many factors. Changes in the program, including a 1984 law to liberalize medical screening, seem quite important, but demographic factors also play a role. There is ample evidence that economic factors matter also. Long-term structural decline in the demand for low-skilled workers appears to increase SSDI applications, and recessions or industry-specific busts lead to an increase in both applications and awards.

There is a strong relationship between age and SSDI receipt, and there is a steep education gradient that is not fully explained by differences in health. Recent evidence suggests that employment rates of marginal SSDI applicants would be about 30 percentage points higher in the absence of SSDI. Interventions designed to support employment and reduce SSDI use among disabled individuals have a mixed record of success, although there is some evidence that providing access to vocational rehabilitation services and employer-provided short-term disability benefits may support work.

Social Security

Established by the Social Security Act of 1935, the Social Security program provides benefits to retired workers and their dependents and survivors. Workers and their employers make payroll tax contributions on earnings (up to a taxable maximum) and those with 40 quarters of contributions receive retired worker benefits. Benefits are calculated based on the worker's highest 35 years of wage-indexed earnings. The benefit formula is progressive, such that the replacement rate (benefit as a share of average earnings) is higher for lower-wage workers, although the benefit amount is lower. The mean replacement rate is 44 percent among all workers, 69 percent for workers in the lowest quintile of lifetime earnings, and 31 percent for workers in the highest quintile (Khan et al., 2017). The average replacement rate in the United States is lower than that in most advanced economies (Ruffing, 2013). The average monthly benefit for workers claiming benefits in 2018 was $1,481 (U.S. Social Security Administration, 2019a).

Retired worker benefits are first available at age 62 but may be claimed as late as age 70. The benefit calculation is centered on the Full Retirement Age (FRA), historically age 65 but rising to age 67 for those born in 1960 or later. Claiming benefits before the FRA results in a lower benefit due to an actuarial adjustment, while claiming after the FRA results in a higher benefit due to the Delayed Retirement Credit. A worker whose FRA is 66 receives 75 percent of the FRA-level benefit by claiming at age 62 and 132 percent of this benefit by claiming at age 70. Workers may claim benefits and continue working, but a Retirement Earnings Test applies for workers below the FRA; this test reduces benefits by $1 for each $2 in earnings beyond an exempt amount ($18,240 in 2020). While the benefit amount is later adjusted to compensate for lost months of benefit receipt, there is ample evidence that workers perceive the Retirement Earnings Test to be a tax (Gelber, Jones, and Sacks, 2020).

Dependent spouses can receive a benefit of 50 percent of the retired worker benefit, although spouses entitled to a retired worker benefit receive their own benefit plus a "top-up" to the spousal benefit (if larger), but not both. Women's rising labor force participation has diminished the importance of dependent benefits over time, a trend that is projected to continue. More than 80 percent of married women in the late Baby Boom (born 1956–1965) and Generation X (1966–1975) cohorts will receive benefits based solely on their own earnings (Iams, 2016). Surviving spouses receive 100 percent of the retired worker benefit; dependent children of retired or deceased workers receive benefits also.

Social Security protects workers against a number of risks. First, since benefits last until death, the program protects workers against the risk of outliving their retirement resources. Second, benefits are indexed to the Consumer Price Index, providing protection against inflation risk. Third, survivor benefits protect the worker's family in the event of the worker's death. Finally, to the extent that some workers may fail to save optimally for retirement due to heuristics and biases in savings decisions (Benartzi and Thaler, 2007), Social Security ensures a base level of consumption during retirement. Notably, Social Security benefits are themselves at some risk due to the program's long-term financial deficit. The combined Social Security and Disability Insurance Trust Fund is currently projected to be depleted in 2035, and at that point, tax revenue would be sufficient to pay 79 percent of scheduled benefits (U.S Social Security Administration, 2020c).

Social Security plays a central role in the retirement income of older Americans. Among persons age 65 and above, 86 percent live in a family that receives Social Security income (Waid, 2016). These values are slightly higher for White people (89%) and lower for Black (82%), Hispanic (75%), and Asian people (69%). Social Security is distributed far more equally across the income distribution than are other sources of retirement income. The probability of having Social Security income is quite similar across income quintiles. By contrast, families in the highest quintile of income are at least four times as likely to have income from pensions and retirement savings and twice as likely to have income from other assets than are families in the lowest quintile (Waid, 2016). Overall, Social Security represents about half of income for households ages 65 and above, though the share is higher in low-income households (Bee and Mitchell, 2017).

Including the value of Social Security benefits in calculations of retirement wealth dramatically reduces inequality across race and ethnic groups. Excluding Social Security, wealth at ages 51 to 56 for middle-wealth households born between 1960 and 1964 is $25,000 for Black people, $35,000 for Hispanic people, and $177,000 for White people. This results in Black:White and Hispanic:White wealth ratios of 14 percent and 20 percent, respectively. Including the value of Social Security in retirement wealth raises these values to 46 percent and 49 percent, respectively (Hou and Sanzenbacher, 2020). While Social Security wealth is distributed far more equally than other sources of wealth, average Social Security wealth is higher for White people than for Hispanic people and Black people due to differences in earnings histories, as discussed in Chapter 4.

Effects of Social Security on Retirement

With respect to the older workforce, Social Security is important in two respects. First, Social Security provides resources that make retirement possible, at least for those workers lacking other resources with which to finance retirement. Second, Social Security may affect the timing of retirement, as the availability of benefits at age 62 as well as the way in which benefits change if workers claim later may affect retirement decisions.

To use the language of economic theory, these two mechanisms correspond roughly to wealth effects and accrual effects. Social Security wealth can be calculated as the present-day value of the stream of Social Security benefits that the worker can expect to receive over their lifetime, where future years of benefits are discounted (worth somewhat less from today's perspective) to account for mortality risk and the preference for money today over money in the future. A recent estimate put Social Security wealth (as measured at ages 51 to 56) for individuals born between 1960 and 1964 at about $200,000 for White people in the middle of the Social Security wealth distribution and at about $150,000 for Black people and Hispanic people (Hou and Sanzenbacher, 2020). A higher value of Social Security wealth is expected to lead to earlier retirement, as more wealth enables households to consume more of the things they value, including leisure time.

The effects of working longer on Social Security wealth are complex. The worker (if age 62 or older) foregoes one year of benefits by delaying retirement and claiming but receives a higher future benefit due to the actuarial adjustment. The additional year of earnings may factor into the benefit computation, replacing a lower earnings year. The worker and employer pay additional payroll taxes.[21] The net of all of the effects of working longer can be to increase or decrease Social Security wealth. Two useful measures of the financial incentive to work longer are the accrual, or change in Social Security wealth associated with working one year longer, and the tax rate, which is the (negative of the) accrual scaled by earnings—the latter can be interpreted like a standard tax rate, reflecting the share of earnings lost by working one year longer. A third measure, peak value, is similar to the accrual but measures the change in Social Security wealth arising from working to the age when wealth is maximized (Coile and Gruber, 2007).

---

[21] Economic theory suggests that contributions by employers are fully "passed through" to workers in the form of lower wages, indicating that they are also paid by workers. Recent evidence indicates that this is the case when there is a clear link between a higher contribution and a future higher benefit, but less true when there is no such link (Bozio et al., 2019).

There is substantial evidence that workers' retirement decisions are responsive to these financial incentive measures. International comparisons offer one fruitful way to explore this issue, as different countries have adopted different program provisions, creating different incentives. This evidence consistently indicates that retirement decisions are responsive to financial incentive measures like the tax rate, as detailed in Box 8-1. Studies of U.S. workers also find that they are responsive to financial incentives. A one-standard-deviation increase in peak value reduces the probability of retirement by 1.1 percentage points, or 16 percent of the average retirement rate, while a one-standard-deviation increase in Social Security wealth increases the probability of retirement by one point (Coile and Gruber, 2007).

BOX 8-1
International Social Security (ISS)

As a federal program, Social Security is more difficult to study than programs that have state-level diffferences in eligibility or benefits. Social Security benefits vary across individuals due to differences in earnings or family circumstances, factors that may have an independent effect on work at older ages. There have been few changes to the program over time for analysts to study.

International comparisons offer a potentially appealing way to learn more about how social security program provisions affect behavior. Differences in provisions across countries create a natural laboratory that can be used to explore their effect on employment. The ISS project is a collaboration among researchers in Canada, Japan, the United States, and nine European countries. The project was launched in the late 1990s, motivated by a long-term decline in men's labor force participation as well as large cross-country differences in work at older ages. For each project phase, research teams use a harmonized approach to conduct country-specific studies, whose results are combined to draw meaningful cross-country comparisons.

The project's first phase established that there is an extremely strong cross-sectional relationship between the financial incentive to work at older ages for a typical worker, as determined by the country's social security provisions, and the country's unused capacity, or share of older men not in the labor force (Gruber and Wise, 1999); this finding was subsequently confirmed for more countries (Blöndal and Scarpetta, 1999). Studies of individual countries indicate that program provisions, at least in some instances, were adopted to encourage older workers to leave the labor force, potentially because it was thought that this would increase opportunities for younger workers.

A subsequent phase of the project conducted country-specific analyses of retirement behavior, relying on within-country variation across individuals in the financial incentive to work longer. The models produce "strikingly common findings" in virtually all the countries, showing that workers with a stronger incentive for continued work retire later than other workers (Gruber and Wise, 2004).

The project's most recent phases exploit the social security reforms that occurred throughout the industrialized world in recent decades. Interestingly, employment at older ages has risen rapidly for both men and women over the same period, offering the opportunity to explore whether reform-driven variation in incentives within and across countries over time can explain these increases in work. Coile and colleagues (2019) find no evidence that changes in health and education are key drivers for the rise in work, while Börsch-Supan and Coile (2020) document that pension reforms strengthened the incentive to work at older ages starting at the same time that employment began to rise. In order to establish a causal interpretation for this finding, the most recent phase of the project estimates regression models using several decades of microdata, spanning the recent period of reform (Coile et al., 2022).

The central finding of the ISS project is that retirement incentives affect behavior. But another enduring lesson of the ISS project is the power of its approach. There are many useful studies of single countries, which often yield compelling evidence of the effects of specific social security provisions on retirement in their own contexts, but comparisons of findings across studies and countries is complicated by differences in the institutional context and in the choices made by researchers. These studies are also less well-positioned to examine broader questions, such as how much of the increase in employment at older ages over the past two decades can be attributed to reforms. Studies based on international comparisons that exploit differences in program provisions and the timing of reforms can provide evidence needed by policy makers facing difficult choices.

Studies that have focused on changes in the individual program elements that factor into the overall incentive to work have also shown that workers respond to Social Security. When the FRA was increased from age 65 to age 66, each two-month increase in the FRA led to a one-month increase in the average age of retirement (Mastrobuoni, 2009). Benefit claiming is even more responsive to changes in the FRA than employment, moving essentially in lockstep (Duggan et al., 2021; Song and Manchester, 2007). The increase in the Delayed Retirement Credit from 3 percent to 8 percent credit per year of delay (phased in for the 1925–1943 cohorts) has strengthened the incentive to work at older ages, resulting in an increase in employment after age 65 (Coile, 2020; Pingle, 2006).

Workers are also quite responsive to the age of first benefit eligibility (Early Eligibility Age). In the United States, the spike in retirement at age 62 (i.e., the increased tendency to retire at this age) only emerged once the Early Eligibility Age was lowered from age 65 to age 62 (Burtless and Moffitt, 1986). Interestingly, claiming Social Security benefits at age 62 has become much less popular in recent decades, with 52 percent of men and 64 percent of women born in 1923 claiming benefits at age 62, versus 36 percent of men and 40 percent of women born in 1951 (Munnell and Chen, 2015). In other countries, the tendency to retire at either the Early Eligibility Age or the FRA has historically been very high, with some 60 to 80 percent of workers who remain in the labor force retiring when they reach one of these ages, as compared to roughly 20 percent in the United States (Gruber and Wise, 1999). As other countries have raised the Early Eligibility Age or FRA, there have been sharp increases in participation at the affected ages (Coile et al., 2019).

Social Security policy changes implemented in the last several decades—the increase in the FRA, the increase in the Delayed Retirement Credit, and the elimination of the Retirement Earnings Test after the FRA in 2000—have strengthened the incentive for American workers to continue working after age 65. These changes have generally not affected the incentive to work before age 65, nor to work after age 70, yet the labor force participation rate has risen in all of these age groups. Future research may provide a more complete accounting of the share of increased labor force participation at older ages that can be attributed to changes in Social Security vs. other factors.

Research has begun to explore policy options that could further strengthen the incentive to work at older ages. These include increasing the number of years in the benefit averaging formula from 35 to 40 (potentially in combination with other changes so that average benefits are not reduced), eliminating payroll taxes after a certain number of years of contributions or a certain age (Goda et al., 2009; Reznik et al., 2009), or changing the benefit formula to directly incorporate each year's earnings and not only average lifetime earnings (Bipartisan Policy Center, 2016). Research has also examined various proposals to strengthen benefit adequacy. Social Security has a special minimum benefit, but in recent years this benefit has applied to almost no new beneficiaries (Johnson, 2020). There have been numerous proposals for a higher minimum Social Security benefit that could reduce elderly poverty (Favreault et al., 2006; Herd et al., 2018; Rupp et al., 2007).

Other possible changes, such as raising the FRA further or increasing the cap on wages subject to taxation, are usually discussed in the context of reforms intended to improve the program's long-term solvency, yet any such changes would also affect the incentive to work at older ages and the adequacy of benefits. Research has also begun to highlight how rising socioeconomic disparities in health and longevity are affecting the progressivity of Social Security under current rules and to suggest that this context may be important in analyzing the effects of Social Security reforms (Biggs et al., 2021; the National Academies, 2015; Zajacova et al., 2014).

Supplemental Security Income Program

Supplemental Security Income (SSI) seeks to provide a minimum income or safety net for basic needs. The program, administered by the Social Security Administration, began in 1974, replacing state programs that had different benefits and eligibility rules. SSI was incorporated into Title XVI of the Social Security Act and is funded by federal tax revenues. The program provides means-tested benefits for citizens living in the United States who are blind, disabled, or at least 65 years of age. Recipients cannot have assets exceeding $2,000 for individuals or $3,000 for couples.

In 2020, SSI provides federal monthly cash transfers of up to $783 for an individual and $1,175 for a couple. The benefit is reduced dollar-for-dollar (after a small offset) against income, including SSDI or Social Security benefits; the program thus serves as a "top-up" for some low-income beneficiaries. Benefits for couples are lower than the sum of two individual benefits because of assumed reductions in expenses for individuals living together. The benefit amount also varies by living arrangements and income. Some states provide additional income to account for differences in living expenses. Individuals who receive SSI are eligible for other welfare programs including Medicaid and the Supplemental Nutrition Assistance Program (commonly known as food stamps; U.S. Social Security Administration, 2020b; Daly and Burkhauser, 2003).

Among adults age 65 and older, SSI coverage decreased from more than nine percent of these adults in 1973 to less than five percent in 2019. This reduced coverage was a result of means-testing rules on income and assets that have not changed much over time and have not been adjusted for inflation. In 2019, 11 percent of older adults with SSI also received Social Security benefits. SSI has increased its coverage of nonelderly individuals with disabilities. Among adult SSI recipients age 65 and older, 42 percent have income (including SSI benefits) below the poverty line (Center on Budget and Policy Priorities, 2020), and 71 percent are women (Sweeney and Fremstad, 2005).

There is some research exploring the effects of SSI on health and preretirement labor. SSI improved the health of older recipients within three years of program introduction (Taubman and Sickles, 1983), while higher SSI benefits are associated with lower disability rates (Herd et al., 2008). Perhaps surprisingly, only 56 percent of eligible individuals claim SSI, and claiming is associated with being in poverty and lacking any other sources of income (McGarry, 1996). Low-income older adults close to the eligibility threshold are less likely to apply. SSI recipients who are enrolled in multiple safety net programs have fewer incentives to work, given cumulative marginal tax rates and the complexity of satisfying multiple program requirements (Daly and Burkhauser, 2003). More generous SSI benefits reduce employment and the work hours of likely SSI participants among low-income adults 62 to 64 years old (Neumark and Powers, 2005). Some low-income individuals claim SSI as an early retirement option before claiming Social Security benefits (Neumark and Powers, 2000).

Supplemental income programs such as SSI have been introduced around the world to alleviate poverty among older adults. Most programs are universal or have few means-testing rules and cover a large proportion of older adults with generous benefits (Willmore, 2007). Research on South Africa, Brazil, Mexico, and other Latin American countries has found that supplemental income programs reduced household poverty and inequality (Ali et al., 2010; Barrientos et al., 2003).

Summary

In the United States, the increasingly strict rules for SSI have made it a welfare program for those in severe poverty. Over time, it has had less influence on reducing poverty or affecting the labor supply of low-income older adults because of reduced benefits and lack of program participation. To our knowledge, no studies have shown how SSI has functioned as a safety net during economic recessions. One study suggests that for low-income older adults who are able to work, the rules of SSI and other safety net programs function more as a poverty trap than as a means to improve recipient well-being (Daly and Burkhauser, 2003). Nonetheless, SSI is a relevant safety net program for nonelderly individuals with disabilities, both children and adults, as well as for low-income elderly.

Retirement Savings Policies

Government policies that support saving for retirement may increase the likelihood that workers nearing traditional retirement ages have adequate resources to retire.

Adequacy of Retirement Saving

There is an active debate in the literature over whether people are saving enough for retirement. Using a life-cycle model to estimate the optimal level of saving for households, Scholz, Seshadri, and Khitatrakun (2006) conclude that less than 20 percent of retirement-age households are saving too little. Following a similar approach, Scott and colleagues (2020) find that it may be optimal for very low earners to save little or not at all, due to the high replacement rate of Social Security for such workers. A different approach to determining savings adequacy is proposed by Munnell and colleagues (2006). They project households' retirement income based on assets and entitlements to Social Security and pensions, and then calculate whether income is sufficient for households to maintain their preretirement standard of living; they assume that 65 to 85 percent of preretirement income is needed, depending on family type and income level, as older households do not save for retirement and pay less in taxes. In the most recent update, they estimate that 50 percent of households are at risk of falling at least 10 percent below this benchmark and that this figure could rise to 55 percent due to COVID-19–related unemployment (Munnell et al., 2020).

Analysts have scrutinized changes in consumption at retirement as another possible indicator of retirement saving adequacy. A simple life-cycle model suggests that people will prefer constant consumption over time. If households experience an unexpected drop in consumption at retirement, this may indicate that they are surprised to find that they have inadequate savings. The literature on this question is generally reassuring when it comes to the population as a whole. Consumption drops are largely anticipated (Hurd and Rohwedder, 2003) and concentrated in food and work-related expenditures, while food intake remains constant (Hurst, 2008). While up to one-quarter of households experience a drop at consumption in retirement, this is concentrated among households experiencing involuntary retirement due to health shocks (Hurst, 2008); low-income older adults are also more likely to have such a drop (Bernheim et al., 2001). Hurst (2004) finds that 20 percent of individuals did not plan adequately for retirement. Aguila and colleagues (2011) find that the lowest income quartile dropped their nondurable consumption by 36 percent when the head of household retired.

Another issue that may shed light on retirement savings adequacy is the inability of low-income households to smooth their consumption between Social Security payments. Stephens (2003, 2006) finds that recipients' expenditures increased during the first weeks after check receipt and then decreased until the arrival of the next payment. Shapiro (2005) and Mastrobuoni and Weinberg (2009) document a similar pattern for caloric intake. Studies of other countries have found that more frequent benefit payments increase food availability, health care use, and health.[22] Similar U.S.-based studies could reveal whether varying the frequency of Social Security, SSI, or other benefit payments would affect the well-being of resource-constrained households.

Older adults may spend larger payments quickly because of their lack of options, such as a bank account, for storing money safely (Blanco et al., 2018). Older unbanked adults are more likely to have lower income, to be non-White, to have fewer savings, and to face higher monetary costs for everyday transactions (Carbó et al., 2005; Thaler 1999). Gaining access to bank accounts resulted in mental health benefits for older low-income Hispanics who lacked access to the financial sector (Aguila et al., 2016).

Employer-sponsored Pension Plans

We turn now to the role of the government in promoting and regulating retirement saving. Retirement saving may occur in employer-sponsored pension plans or in other designated accounts. The government's role includes setting pension plan regulations, which may affect an employer's willingness to offer a plan, the type of plan offered, and other plan provisions, as well as providing tax incentives for saving.

One type of employer-sponsored pension is the defined benefit plan. Defined benefit plans were first regulated under the 1974 Employee Retirement Income Security Act, which established minimum funding requirements and set up the Pension Benefit Guarantee Corporation to insure benefits against plan insolvency.[23] In a defined benefit plan, the employee receives a regular benefit payment from retirement until death. While details vary across plans, the benefit is generally calculated using a formula based on the worker's years of service and average earnings near the end of a career. A certain tenure at the firm is usually required to be vested in the plan. Most plans have both early and normal retirement ages, and the benefit amount is often adjusted for claiming age in a way that creates strong financial incentives to work to these ages and retire and claim thereafter—for example, increasing for each year the worker delays between the early and normal retirement ages (Stock and Wise, 1990).

---

[22]Evidence from Mexico and Kenya suggests that one-time or less frequent payments are more likely to be used for durable goods while more frequent payments increase food availability and health care use (Haushofer and Shapiro, 2016; Aguila, Kapteyn et al., 2017). More frequent payments to low-income older adults in Mexico also improved health and well-being more than less frequent, larger payments did (Aguila and Smith, 2020), potentially because of the difficulty of smoothing consumption between payments.

[23]Multiemployer plans are a type of plan protected by the PBCG. Some of these plans are significantly underfunded—currently one million employees (10% of those in multiemployer plans) are in plans that could run out of money within 15–20 years. The PBCG estimates that its multiemployer insurance program will run out of money within 10 years (Munnell et al., 2017).

The other main retirement plan type is the defined contribution plan. These plans are often referred to as 401(k) plans, after the section of the Internal Revenue Code that governs them (Employee Benefit Research Institute, 2018). In a defined contribution plan, the employer and/or employee make contributions to a retirement account. The employee determines where contributions are invested, choosing from a set of investment options selected by the firm. Employee contributions are exempt from income taxation, and investment earnings accrue tax-free. Withdrawals are subject to income tax, as well as a 10 percent penalty before age 59.5. Defined contribution balances are portable—employees who change jobs can roll their account balances into a defined contribution plan at a new job (if applicable) or another retirement account or withdraw them. Some defined contribution plans allow employees to annuitize account balances. Some plans offer workers the opportunity to contribute to a Roth individual retirement account (IRA) rather than a traditional 401(k) (Ebeling, 2014).

Individual Retirement Accounts (IRAs)

IRAs were first introduced in 1974 to provide a retirement savings plan for workers not covered by an employer-sponsored plan. The tax treatment of IRAs mirrors that of 401(k)s, but contribution limits are lower: a maximum of $6,000 in 2020 for IRAs, versus $19,500 in 401(k)s (limits are somewhat higher for those 50 and above). Those who are covered by a pension plan at work may contribute to an IRA, but the contribution is not tax-deductible (except for lower-income households). For both IRAs and 401(k)s, individuals are required to begin making withdrawals no later than age 72.

Depending on income, workers may be eligible to contribute to a Roth IRA. Contributions to a Roth IRA are not tax-deductible, but investment earnings receive the same favorable tax treatment as in traditional IRAs and 401(k)s. Distributions from Roth IRAs are not subject to tax and there are no requirements to take distributions. For an individual who is eligible to contribute to either a traditional or Roth IRA, expectations of current vs. future tax rate are important in determining the relative merit of the two options.

There are currently seven states that have enacted auto-IRA programs. These programs require employers who do not offer a pension plan to automatically enroll employees in a state-sponsored IRA program. Oregon was the first state to implement such a program, beginning in 2017. Other states that have adopted them include California, Colorado, Connecticut, Illinois, Maryland, and New Jersey (Center for Retirement Initiatives, 2020). Six states have adopted other policies that aim to boost retirement saving by reducing the administrative burden of offering a pension plan, including voluntary payroll deduction, Roth IRAs, multiple employer plans, and retirement marketplaces (Gale and John, 2018).

Effects on Retirement

Among the employer-sponsored plans, defined benefit and defined contribution plans offer very different incentives for retirement. As discussed above, defined benefit plans include strong incentives for work and retirement at particular ages, since the value of the pension increases with additional work in a highly nonlinear way. Many studies indicate that workers are quite responsive to these incentives (Stock and Wise, 1990; Asch et al., 2005). In a defined contribution plan, pension wealth evolves smoothly with additional work. Friedberg and Webb (2005) estimate that the lack of age-based incentives in defined contribution plans leads workers to retire two years later. The large shift from defined benefit to defined contribution pension plans in the United States (discussed in Chapter 4) might be expected to contribute to the trend of working longer. Mermin et al., (2007) attribute one-fifth of the increase in the expected probability of working past age 62 over a 25-year period to the decline in defined benefit coverage.

All of the retirement savings policies discussed thus far could potentially affect retirement behavior by boosting retirement resources. Putting aside for a moment the question of whether these policies do increase savings, estimating the effect of retirement savings on retirement is difficult. Economic theory indicates that a forward-looking individual will make labor supply and savings decisions jointly (French, 2005), suggesting that any correlation between retirement wealth and retirement behavior might not reflect a causal effect of wealth on retirement. Researchers seeking to estimate this relationship have made use of unanticipated changes in wealth arising from higher (or lower) than usual stock market returns or unexpected inheritances. There is only weak evidence of an effect of wealth on retirement in the former case (Hurd et al., 2009) but stronger evidence in the latter case (Brown et al., 2010).

Effects on Saving

The U.S. federal government provides $250 billion per year in tax incentives for retirement saving through defined contribution plans and IRAs (Tax Policy Center, 2020). Using the model of a rational, forward-looking consumer, these tax incentives may affect saving through several pathways. First, defined contribution plans and IRAs increase the rate of return to saving. They do so by enabling individuals to invest funds on a pre-tax basis (to invest a full dollar of earned income, rather than the fraction remaining after income tax) and by allowing investment earnings to compound tax-free before being taxed at withdrawal. In theory, the impact of an increased rate of return on saving behavior is ambiguous. Consumers may choose to save more since a dollar of foregone spending today yields more spending in the future when the rate of return is higher (substitution effect), but they also may choose to spend more today and save less because the higher return has made them better off (income effect). Saving will increase if the former effect dominates. A second pathway, also consistent with this model, is that exposure to a retirement savings plan may increase financial literacy, through financial education offered by the firm or peer effects (Duflo and Saez, 2004; Lusardi, 2009), which could lead to higher retirement saving.

Running counter to the standard model is the insight that saving for retirement is "both a difficult cognitive problem and a difficult self-control problem" (Mullainathan and Thaler, 2001). It is now well understood that there are many biases present in human decision-making that can affect saving and other decisions. For instance, individuals approach tradeoffs between present and future in a way that is dynamically inconsistent, reflecting a bias toward the present (Laibson, 1997). Procrastination leads to a tendency to stick with the status quo (Samuelson and Zeckhauser, 1988). Exponential growth bias refers to the tendency of individuals to underestimate the gains from compound interest (Stango and Zinman, 2009). Under mental accounting, labeling funds as being for current vs. future spending can impact their use (Shefrin and Thaler, 2004). The effect of retirement plans on saving may be quite different from what the standard model predicts if behavioral biases are important. For example, auto-enrollment in a pension plan or auto-escalation of contributions, either of which is easily undone by a rational consumer, will have a greater impact if status quo bias is important (Thaler and Bernartzi, 2004). Introducing tax-advantaged retirement accounts may lead to new saving, rather than the diversion of existing assets into the new accounts, if mental accounting is present.

Turning to the evidence, the early literature on 401(k)s and IRAs and saving focused on whether retirement account balances constitute new savings or a reallocation of savings that would have occurred elsewhere. This question has been intensely debated (Poterba et al., 1996; Engen et al., 1996). An arbiter examining evidence on both sides conservatively estimates that at least 26 cents of every dollar of IRA contributions represents new saving while 401(k) contributions "largely" represent new saving (Hubbard and Skinner, 1996).

More recently, the literature has focused on the role of defaults in defined contribution plans. Employers with such plans decide whether employees are automatically enrolled in the plan and often set a default for the contribution rate, asset allocation, and post-retirement distribution. An employee who is automatically enrolled may opt out of the plan or change other defaults, but this requires an action on their part. A large literature has established that such defaults have a very substantial effect on savings decisions (U.S. Government Accountability Office, 2009; Beshears et al., 2007). For example, in a firm adopting auto-enrollment, the plan participation rate at 3 to 15 months after hire was 86 percent in the group hired after auto-enrollment, as compared to 37 percent at a similar point post-hire among those hired under an opt-in regime (Madrian and Shea, 2001). Effects were larger among employees from groups that were historically less likely to participate, including younger, lower-income, Black, and Hispanic employees.

The literature has also begun to explore whether auto-enrollment promotes new saving or a reallocation of other resources into retirement accounts. In the Danish context, a one percentage point increase in mandatory savings contributions is associated with a 0.8 percentage point increase in total savings (Chetty et al., 2014). Interestingly, 85 percent of Danish individuals are passive savers who are influenced by defaults but not by financial incentives to save, while those who do respond to financial incentives were saving already, implying that financial incentives are not particularly effective in increasing savings among those who are unprepared for retirement. Recent evidence from the United States as to whether there is any crowd-out of default-induced savings is more mixed. Workers who are automatically enrolled in their current job's pension plan contribute less to a following job's opt-in pension (Choukhmane, 2019), but auto-enrollment is not associated with an increase in debt (Beshears et al., 2019).

In the wake of this influential research, there is now an understanding that defaults are not neutral but, in fact, are likely to either encourage or inhibit retirement saving. The 2006 Pension Protection Act encouraged firms to adopt auto-enrollment by providing a safe harbor from antidiscrimination tests (which require firms to certify that the plan does not discriminate in favor of highly-compensated employees), so long as the plan has adequate default contribution levels, a qualified default investment fund such as a "target-date" retirement fund, and an adequate employer match. The Pension Protection Act also protected firms selecting a qualified default investment fund from fiduciary liability in the event of investment loss. Between 2005 and 2008, the share of firms using a money market fund as a default investment dropped from 25 to two percent, while the share selecting a target-date fund rose from 42 to 87 percent (U.S. Government Accountability Office, 2009). Given the difference in the expected rate of return by fund type, such changes can meaningfully impact account balances at retirement.

Evidence on state-established auto-IRA programs thus far primarily comes from Oregon. Among eligible employees in firms with at least 50 workers, 62 percent are participating in the plan (Belbase and Sanzenbacher, 2018). Of those not participating, the most commonly reported reasons are not being able to afford to save (30%) or having another retirement saving plan (19%). Over 90 percent of participants keep the default contribution rate of five percent. In the program's second year, 20 percent of those with account balances made a withdrawal from their account. While these "leakages" inhibit the accumulation of retirement assets, they also suggest that auto-IRA balances may serve as a valuable source of precautionary saving (Quinby et al., 2019). In the first year after California adopted an auto-IRA program, new employer-sponsored plans were nine percent of the total plans in the state, well above the national average; Illinois also experienced an increase in new plans in the year after implementation (Scott, 2021).

Models from outside the United States may also prove informative. In the United Kingdom, a 2008 law required all private-sector employers to auto-enroll their employees in a plan. Several years after implementation, enrollment rates for employees in medium and large firms were nearly 90 percent, similar to rates in large U.S. firms with auto-enrollment, and nearly 70 percent in small firms (Cribb and Emmerson, 2019). Exploiting variation in the timing of the roll-out, the auto-enrollment mandate is found to raise participation in the smallest firms (under 30 employees) by 44 percentage points. In other countries, such as Australia, a mandatory retirement savings program is one of the pillars of the retirement system. In the Australian case, employers contribute 12 percent of earnings, which are invested in Superannuation Funds at the employee's direction (Agnew, 2013).

Policies for Low-income Savers

As discussed in Chapter 4, there are substantial differences in wealth by race and socioeconomic status. One key factor driving these differences is the disparity in the probability of being offered a pension. The share of wage and salary workers offered a pension by their employer is 65 percent for White workers, as compared with 56 percent for Black workers and 38 percent for Hispanic workers; conditional on offer, White workers are about 5 percentage points more likely to participate than non-White workers (Butrica and Johnson, 2010). Similarly, in a comparison of higher and lower wage workers, differences in the probability of offer are much larger than differences in conditional participation (Wu and Rutledge, 2014). Differences in financial literacy may contribute to the wealth gap. Finally, providing financial incentives for retirement savings in the form of a tax deduction favors high-income workers, who face higher marginal tax rates; an alternative would be to offer tax credits, which do not depend on tax rate.

A few programs have aimed to promote retirement savings for low-income workers who lack access to employer-provided pensions. MyRA, which started in 2014 and ended in 2018, targeted employees in firms without employer-provided pensions. This program failed because of low participation and high management costs (Powell and Ferraro, 2018); low participation is unsurprising given that enrollment was voluntary (Munnell, 2015). The Saver's Credit program provides a nonrefundable federal income tax credit of up to 50 percent of contributions to a 401(k) or IRA by low-income filers. The nonrefundability of the credit limits eligibility, because many low-income filers have no tax liability (Koenig and Harvey, 2005). Duflo and colleagues (2006) find that the saving response to the Saver's Credit is smaller than what is obtained in a randomized controlled trial offering a match to IRA contributions, potentially due to the opacity of the credit and framing.

More general evidence on IRAs suggests that these programs have not been particularly successful in closing the racial wealth gap. Among older adults (age 65 or older) in 2012, 46 percent of non-Hispanic White people but only 12 percent of Black people and 14 percent of Hispanic people held an IRA. For older adults between the 10th and 50th percentiles of wealth, IRAs represented six percent of total wealth for non-Hispanic White people and one percent for Black and Hispanic people. For older adults between the 50th and 90th percentiles of wealth, IRAs represented 20 percent of total wealth for non-Hispanic White people, four percent for Black people, and five percent for Hispanic people (Johnson et al., 2013).

Health Insurance Policies

Government policies that facilitate access to health insurance at older ages are potentially important in the employment decisions of older workers. The United States has the distinction of being the only large, wealthy country without universal health coverage. As discussed in Chapter 4, a majority of nonelderly Americans receive health insurance through their own or a family member's employer. The share of workers who have retiree health insurance—coverage from their employer after leaving the job—has declined over time. Workers with access to retiree health insurance retire substantially earlier than other workers. Government policies that provide access to health insurance to older individuals may facilitate retirement by addressing one possible motivation for continued work at older ages.

Medicare

Medicare is central in any discussion of health insurance and older Americans. Established in 1965 through Title XVIII of the Social Security Act, Medicare provides health insurance to people age 65 or older and to SSDI beneficiaries (after a two-year waiting period).[24] The Medicare program has several components: Part A, which covers inpatient hospital services; Part B, which provides physician and outpatient services; Part D, which offers prescription drug coverage; and Part C, or Medicare Advantage, which allows beneficiaries to enroll in a private insurance plan for their Part A, B, and D benefits.[25] Most Medicare beneficiaries pay no premiums for Part A benefits but have premiums for Parts B and D as well as deductibles and co-insurance payments (Kaiser Family Foundation, 2015). The cost-sharing in Medicare leaves beneficiaries with a substantial risk of out-of-pocket medical expenditures (Goldman and Zissimopoulos, 2003). Nearly nine in ten beneficiaries have some protection against these expenses, through enrollment in a Medicare Advantage plan or a secondary insurance plan such as an employer-sponsored plan, Medicaid, or a "Medigap" policy (Kaiser Family Foundation, 2015). Nearly 11 million of Medicare's 61 million beneficiaries are dually eligible for Medicare and Medicaid, based on having low income and assets (Grabowski et al., 2017). Medicare expenditures on this group are twice as high as for Medicare beneficiaries as a whole, due in large part to their poorer health.

The probability of retirement has historically been higher at age 65 than at surrounding ages (Coile, 2004). This phenomenon could reflect the role of Medicare eligibility in retirement decisions, but there are several other possible explanations. The Social Security FRA was age 65 for people born before 1938, potentially creating a social norm of retirement at this age (Behaghel and Blau, 2012). Earlier cohorts faced financial disincentives to work past age 65 due to a less-than-fair actuarial adjustment for delayed claiming (Coile, 2020). Defined benefit pension plans typically feature strong disincentives for work beyond the plan's early or normal retirement age, often ages like 55, 60, and 65 (Stock and Wise, 1990).

---

[24]Medicare also covers people with end-stage renal disease and Amyotrophic Lateral Schlerosis or Lou Gehrig's disease.

[25]For more details about the benefits provided under each part of Medicare, as well as other background information on the program, see Kaiser Family Foundation (2015).

Turning to the evidence, similar exit rates at age 65 among those with and without retiree health insurance casts doubt on the role of Medicare in the spike (Lumsdaine et al., 1996). Early evidence indicating that the rise in the FRA from age 65 to 66 led the age-65 spike in retirement to largely vanish also argued against a role for Medicare (Behaghel and Blau, 2012). However, a more recent analysis concludes that the age-65 spike persists among cohorts with an age-66 FRA (Fadlon and Deshpande, 2020). Support for a role of Medicare in retirement decisions comes from the introduction of Part D (prescription drug coverage) in 2006. Workers who had been dependent on employment for drug coverage decreased their rate of full-time employment at age 65 by 8.4 percentage points (or 24%) more after 2006 than they did before, while a control group that had drug coverage both before and after 2006 exhibited no change in behavior (Wettstein, 2020).

Medicare could also affect employment decisions before age 65. The provision of Medicare benefits to SSDI beneficiaries raises the value of SSDI receipt, potentially encouraging some people to leave the labor force and apply for benefits. Several studies estimate structural models in which individuals facing medical-expenditure risk make decisions about work, consumption, and SSDI application. Kitao (2014) estimates that SSDI receipt would be 30 percent lower and Kim (2012) estimates that the labor force participation rate of men ages 23 to 62 would be 0.7 percentage points higher if Medicare benefits were not available to SSDI beneficiaries.

In recent years, there have been calls to raise the Medicare eligibility age to 67, matching the rise in the Social Security FRA. Others have suggested lowering the Medicare eligibility age or allowing some individuals to buy in to Medicare as a means of moving toward universal health care coverage in the United States. Based on existing empirical evidence, it is difficult to predict how such policy changes might affect employment at older ages.

The Affordable Care Act (ACA)

The 2010 ACA brought major changes to the health insurance landscape, including several provisions designed to increase insurance coverage. First, the ACA expanded Medicaid—a program that had primarily covered pregnant women, children, and long-term care expenses for low-income seniors—to cover low-income adults (up to 138% of the poverty line). A 2012 U.S. Supreme Court ruling made Medicaid expansion optional for states; to date, 38 states and the District of Columbia have chosen to do so. Second, the ACA provided income-based subsidies for moderate-income households (up to 400% of the federal poverty line) to help them buy insurance on new health insurance exchanges. Insurers participating in the exchanges are required to accept all consumers, regardless of health status, and charge premiums that differ only by geography, family size, and age, with a maximum 3-to-1 ratio across age groups.[26] Third, the ACA included an individual mandate to have health insurance, although a 2017 tax law eliminated the tax penalty that served as an enforcement mechanism.

By increasing access to health insurance outside of employment, the ACA may allow older workers to retire, reduce hours below the threshold required for benefits at their job, or move to a new job without benefits. Thus far, however, there is little evidence that the ACA is having these kinds of effects. Levy and colleagues (2018) find that the implementation of the ACA starting in January 2014 did not lead to a change in the probability of retirement or full-time work among older workers, either overall or in Medicaid expansion states. Gustman and colleagues (2019) compare retirement behavior before and after the ACA for the group most likely to be affected—those with employer-sponsored health insurance but not retiree health insurance—to the behavior of workers with both or neither of these benefits. They find no evidence that the ACA changed retirement or retirement expectations.

Analyses of the earlier Massachusetts health reform, which served as the model for the ACA, are also informative. These studies generally estimate differences-in-differences models, comparing the change in Massachusetts after vs. before the reform to the change in a control group of states. Heim and Lin (2017) find that the Massachusetts reform led to an increase in retirement and in part-time work among older women but not among older men. Sanzenbacher (2014) reports a decline in labor force participation among older men. Niu (2014) finds that the reform led to an increase in self-employment among older workers. However, Coe and colleagues (2016) find no effect on retirement or job changes.

Especially prior to the ACA, continuation-of-coverage mandates—often referred to as COBRA, after the law that established the federal mandate—were a means of obtaining health insurance after a job departure. These laws

---

[26]Premiums may also differ based on tobacco usage, at a maximum 1.5-to-1 ratio (Centers for Medicare and Medicaid Services, 2020).

allow individuals to buy in to a former employer's plan for 18 months (in case of the federal mandate; state laws may vary). They have been shown to raise the retirement rate of men by 30 percent (Gruber and Madrian, 1995), which is at the low end of the estimated effect of retiree health insurance on retirement (Gruber and Madrian, 2004). This is a large effect, given that retirees are fully responsible for COBRA premiums and that coverage is available for a limited time only. The size of the effect could reflect the value retirees place on maintaining coverage for preexisting health conditions, as prior to the ACA these could be excluded from coverage under a new health insurance plan (Currie and Madrian, 1999).

Summary

In sum, the evidence that government policies affect retirement behavior at older ages is surprisingly mixed, given the strong and consistent effect of employer-provided retiree health insurance on retirement. It is unclear if the spike in retirement at age 65 can be attributed to Medicare, though a recent study suggests that the availability of prescription drug coverage through Part D increases retirement at that age. There is little evidence so far that the ACA has altered the employment decisions of older workers, but some evidence that the earlier Massachusetts health reform did so. Continuity-of-coverage mandates have also been shown to have a large effect on retirement in the pre-ACA era, though their role could be supplanted by the ACA.

CONCLUSIONS

In this chapter, we have surveyed a broad range of public policies that may support work at older ages, encompassing both non-age-specific and age-specific policies, as well as an extensive set of policies that may enhance the financial security of workers in retirement. The existing literature suggests that many of these policies affect retirement decisions. In other cases, the literature has yet to reach a conclusion as to the employment effects of these policies. We first review the key findings from each section of this chapter, before presenting our recommendations for future research.

Findings: Non-age-specific Policies

- The ADA protects workers of all ages from disability-based discrimination but is of potentially greater relevance for older workers due to their increased risk of being disabled. Research on the employment effects of the ADA has yielded inconclusive results.
- The FMLA provides access to 12 weeks of unpaid leave for workers dealing with their own or a family member's health issues, while a growing number of states offer paid family leave for use in similar circumstances. Existing research on these programs has largely focused on their use following the birth of a child.
- Workers' compensation provides access to medical care and compensation for lost wages following a workplace injury. While there is no clear relationship between age and the probability of a workplace injury, older workers tend to experience more severe injuries and are less likely to return to work.

Findings: Age-specific Policies

- The ADEA protects workers age 40 and over from discrimination in the workplace on the basis of age. Some states provide stronger age-based protections. The ADEA led to changes in human resources practices and stronger relationships between older workers and their employers. Stronger state-based age discrimination laws do not reduce the hiring of older workers.
- Mandatory retirement has been abolished in the United States since 1986 (except in a few occupations), though it is still in effect in many high-income countries. The elimination of mandatory retirement after the ADEA's passage led to an increase in work after age 65.
- Partial retirement programs allow older workers to combine partial benefit receipt with part-time work; these programs exist in some European countries, but not in the United States. Research indicates that these

policies either reduce labor supply at older ages (as some individuals shift from full- to part-time work) or have no effect on labor supply.
- The Senior Community Employment Program is a community service and work-based training program for low-income older workers with poor employment prospects. While the program has had limited success in helping participants achieve economic self-sufficiency, it increases health and well-being while providing income for recipients and service hours to their communities.

Findings: Policies to Support Financial Security

- SSDI provides income support to individuals experiencing a long-term work-limiting disability. Growth in SSDI over time has been driven by changes in medical stringency, population aging, rising female labor force participation, and economic factors. Use of SSDI is higher among the less educated. There is non-trivial residual work capacity among SSDI recipients on the margin of program entry. Interventions that aim to boost employment and reduce SSDI use among disabled individuals have had only modest effects.
- Social Security is a critical source of income for older Americans that is distributed far more equally than other sources of retirement income (or wealth). Program provisions shape the financial incentive to work at older ages, and workers are highly responsive to these incentives. Changes to the program over the past several decades have strengthened the incentive to work at ages 65–69.
- SSI is a cash benefit program for very low-income elderly adults as well as disabled adults and children. The share of older individuals receiving SSI has declined over time as means-tested income and asset limits have not been updated for inflation. SSI improves health and reduces the labor supply of older recipients.
- Workers face increasing responsibility to plan for their own retirement, due to the ongoing shift from defined benefit to defined contribution pension plans. Defined contribution plan defaults for participation, contribution, and asset allocation tend to be "sticky," exerting a powerful impact on retirement saving. Evidence suggests that a substantial share of retirement account balances represent new saving, rather than assets shifted from nonretirement accounts. Whether most households have adequate retirement savings remains a hotly debated question. While most households are able to maintain their previous level of consumption at retirement, lower-income households experience consumption declines as well as difficulty smoothing consumption between benefit checks. Low-income workers are less likely to have IRAs and defined contribution pensions, and special programs targeting this group have only a mixed record in promoting saving.
- Most Americans obtain health insurance through their own or a spouse's employer. As discussed in Chapter 4, having access to employer-provided retiree health insurance is strongly associated with earlier retirement. While access to coverage through Medicare at age 65 and through the ACA would be expected to increase the probability of retirement, the evidence on this point is surprisingly mixed.

Implications for Research

Impact of Age-specific Policies

More research is needed on how non-age-specific policies that support work are affecting older workers. While all of these policies have been extensively studied, research on how they affect older workers is quite limited. Researchers could make use of differences in state disability laws to explore whether disability protections affect hiring or other employment outcomes for older workers, as has been done for state age discrimination laws. For the FMLA and state family leave policies, research could exploit the introduction of these policies or their applicability by firm size to explore whether these policies help older workers manage their own or a family member's health crisis. For the Workers' Compensation program, more research is needed into how to deter injuries and their impact on return to work, how to hold down Workers' Compensation costs for older workers, and whether the risk of more serious injury deters employment of older workers.

Effects of Age Discrimination Protections on Outcomes Other Than Hiring

More research is needed into the effect of age discrimination protections on outcomes other than hiring, such as on job training for older workers, and on the intersectionality of race and gender in the realm of age discrimination protections. While the ADEA has been extensively studied, the most compelling work explores its effects on hiring. As discussed in Chapter 6, new approaches are needed to identify the effect of age discrimination protections on other aspects of employment for older workers. There is some mixed evidence on the effects of the ADEA for women and minorities, indicating a need for more research on these groups and at the intersection of race and gender. There is also scant research on evidence-based job training interventions for older workers, beyond analyses of the Senior Community Service Employment Program, which targets a narrow segment of the older workforce. Such research would help policy makers understand which types of job training are efficacious, efficient, and cost-saving.

Implications of Decline in SSDI Enrollment

More research is needed to better understand the recent decline in the SSDI program rolls and to understand whether there are policies that can assist individuals with health problems to maintain employment. While lower SSDI enrollment is beneficial from a fiscal standpoint, it is important to ascertain whether the program is providing adequate support to those who lack the capacity for substantial gainful employment. Although past demonstration projects of interventions aiming to boost employment and reduce SSDI use for disabled individuals have had mixed results, providing more vocational rehabilitation services and shifting more responsibility to employers in the period after disability onset appear to merit additional study.

Adequacy of the Safety Net for Very-Low-Income Elderly

More research is needed to understand whether Social Security and SSI are providing an adequate safety net for very low-income elderly and disabled households. The share of older adults on SSI has been declining and there is very little recent work exploring the effects of the program on older beneficiaries. The Social Security minimum benefit has applied to almost no new beneficiaries in recent years. More analysis of how these programs serve vulnerable groups could guide policy discussions around a possible change to the Social Security minimum benefit.

Retirement Saving Behavior and Racial Wealth Gaps

More research exploring the racial wealth gap and other differences in retirement saving behavior across demographic groups and saver types is needed to ensure that all households are adequately prepared for retirement. Certain groups continue to have very low levels of retirement savings, decades after the introduction of IRAs and the start of the shift from defined benefit to defined contribution pensions. Several programs designed to benefit low-income savers have had mixed results. Further research on auto-IRA programs as they mature and other interventions targeting low-wage workers is needed to determine how policy can enhance retirement security for vulnerable groups.

Impact of Medicare and the ACA on Employment at Older Ages

More research is needed to reconcile the results of recent studies on the impact of Medicare and the ACA on employment at older ages with the earlier literature on these policies and employer-sponsored retiree health insurance. Such research is critically needed to understand the current impact of these important policies and to assess how policy changes, such as raising or lowering the age of Medicare eligibility, might affect the older workforce.

Weathering the COVID-19 Crisis

Research will be needed to understand how older workers have relied on government programs and employment protections to help them weather the COVID-19 crisis (see Box 8-2). Such research can help policy makers assess whether programs are adequate to help older workers cope with future shocks.

> **BOX 8-2**
> **The COVID-19 Crisis and Public Policy**
>
> While the full effects of the COVID-19 crisis will not be known for years, it is probable that the crisis will lead older workers to rely on government programs and employment protections to a greater degree than usual. The pandemic led to a sharp initial increase in unemployment among older workers (Bui et al., 2020), and it is likely to lead to sustained reductions in older employment and an increase in retirements, as occurred during the Great Recession (Coile and Levine, 2011). During the first year of the pandemic, employment fell by 5.7 percentage points for 50–61 year-olds and by 3.9 percentage points for 62–70 year-olds relative to what would have been predicted based on seasonal and other patterns (Goda et al., 2021).
>
> Displaced older workers seeking new jobs may hope to benefit from the ADEA's employment protections. However, there is evidence that stronger age discrimination protections did not benefit older workers during the Great Recession (Neumark and Button, 2014). The pandemic raises urgent questions about how the Workers' Compensation system can help employers navigate and mitigate the costs of COVID-19 related illness among workers and about whether the ADA will assist workers struggling with long-term effects of the illness. Workers may rely on the Family and Medical Leave Act (FMLA) or state paid family leave (where available) to help them get through their own or a family member's COVID-19 illness.
>
> The pandemic-related recession may lead to an increase in SSDI applications, as occurred after the Great Recession. Long-term health impacts of COVID-19 could also lead to an increase in applications. Whether SSI serves as a buffer against recessions and other shocks is not well understood. Some displaced older workers are likely to retire and claim Social Security retired worker benefits earlier than planned and to have lower retirement income as a result, as has happened in other times of high unemployment (Coile and Levine, 2011). Others may draw on their retirement savings to finance consumption during a period of unemployment. Displaced workers who have lost employer-provided health insurance may turn to the ACA's health insurance exchanges and Medicaid for coverage. Early evidence indicates a decrease in SSI and SSDI applications since the beginning of the pandemic, which might be due to the temporary availability of extended unemployment benefits and stimulus payments or to access problems due to the closure of Social Security Administration field offices and of public internet access sites like libraries (Goda et al., 2021). Applications for Social Security retired worker benefits are thus far at normal levels. Future research will be needed to better understand the extent to which all of these programs serve to protect older households from the shock of the COVID-19 crisis.

Part III

9

A Research Agenda to Promote Understanding of Employment among Older Workers

Older adults in the United States are working longer than they have in the past, with more extending their work lives into increasingly older ages (Chapter 2).[1] The chapters of this report document a growing body of scholarship that chronicles remarkable changes and growing diversity in late-life adult work paths and retirement timing. Taken together, an aging workforce, extended healthy life expectancy, mounting inequality, new technologies, heightened economic and job precarity, and changes to social support policies mean that work arrangements among older adults are in flux. Instead of viewing full-time retirement as a one-time event and an inevitable end of one's work engagement, growing numbers of older adults are sustaining various forms of workforce participation even though they are retired from their main or career jobs (Chapter 3). These patterned shifts challenge the definitions of what it means to "work" and to "retire" in the United States. Scientific understanding of older workers' pathways into and exits from the workforce has not always kept pace with social, economic, technological, and demographic transformations. These transformations are reshaping the possibilities and precarities that characterize the later life course among an increasingly diverse and heterogeneous older population.

This report focuses on identifying the factors that shape older workers' preferences and expectations for work at older ages, as well as factors that constrain the opportunities of older workers and prevent them from realizing their preferred work and retirement arrangements. When the literature on work at older ages is viewed through this conceptual lens, two overarching conclusions emerge.

CONCLUSION I: Older workers' preferences for work and specific work arrangements, their expectations about available work opportunities and financial stability, and the constraints on their work opportunities and behaviors reflect the impact of both age bias and social and economic inequalities. This bias and these inequalities structure economic opportunity throughout the life course and lead to wide disparities in employment and retirement pathways at older ages.

CONCLUSION II: The experiences of vulnerable older populations remain understudied within the current literature. These populations include women, racial and ethnic minorities, immigrants, those with less education, those who have low income or limited savings and wealth, those living in rural or

---

[1]This chapter provides a summary and integration of the findings from the preceding chapters. Where relevant, we reference the report chapter that contains a more detailed discussion of the evidence underlying the findings and conclusions presented. Where the findings of specific studies are discussed, the original references are provided.

economically disadvantaged areas, and those with multiple intersecting vulnerabilities. The fact that they are understudied limits our understanding of the ways in which inequality in retirement and work opportunities and outcomes contribute to broader social and economic inequality that affects the well-being of older adults.

The first conclusion points to the need for future research to recognize the ways in which age bias and social and economic inequality, as well as changes in them over time, set the contexts in which individual preferences, expectations, and constraints on work and retirement behaviors at older ages are shaped. Individuals' preferences and expectations for work as well as their ability to realize these preferences are constrained by the opportunity structures in which they live. These structures do not suddenly emerge at older ages but are the result of social and economic inequalities that shape economic and health outcomes throughout the life course and as individuals move through changing historical contexts. As a result, adults with higher levels of education and wealth experience fewer constraints that prevent them from extending their working life beyond traditional retirement age, and education-based gaps in employment rates increase with age among older adults (Chapters 2 and 4).

These differences in employment rates have implications for what we know about work at older ages. Because older workers who remain in the labor force are on average more affluent than older adults in the population, data and research that focuses on older workers will reflect the relative affluence of this population. However, these findings may not represent the experiences of less affluent populations that face a more restrictive opportunity structure. The second conclusion draws attention to the need to better understand the heterogeneity within the older worker population to ensure that the experiences of vulnerable populations are well-represented in research and policy discussions. Considering the diversity of experiences and outcomes within the older worker population, as well as the ways opportunities are shaped by inequality throughout the life course, can provide important research insights—even when research is not explicitly focused on social and economic inequality.

As an example, consider the efficacy of the Age Discrimination in Employment Act (ADEA) and other state age discrimination policies reviewed in Chapter 8. Though on balance the evidence suggests that—outside of periods of significant economic recession and disruption, such as the Great Recession—strong age discrimination laws are effective in improving employment among older workers, the limited number of studies that have examined whether their effects differ by gender or race suggest that they have little or no effect on reducing discrimination among older women or racial minorities. Moreover, when age discrimination laws are weak (i.e., place more restrictions on the damages plaintiffs can seek), most plaintiffs under the ADEA are highly paid White male middle-managers. These differences are especially concerning given the higher rates of hiring discrimination experienced by older women and Black adults (Chapter 6). They suggest that more affluent White male workers may experience greater protections from age discrimination than other older workers, compounding the effects of labor market advantages they experience throughout their working lives. However, the reasons underlying these differences are not yet well understood.

Taken together, these two overarching conclusions provide a framework though which the research agenda laid out in this chapter can be viewed. They can serve as a call to ensure that future research considers the heterogeneity of experiences within the older worker population, including the diverse ways in which work and retirement outcomes are shaped by broader contexts of age bias and social and economic inequality throughout the life course. Considering this heterogeneity will provide a more comprehensive and robust understanding of the benefits and disadvantages of extending work lives, which in turn can inform the development of policies that enable work at older ages in ways that account for the specific challenges vulnerable populations face and, therefore, improve their well-being.

DEFINING A RESEARCH AGENDA

These overarching conclusions provide the context for a future research and data collection agenda. Work and retirement preferences, expectations, and behaviors are shaped by many factors that operate at different levels of analysis, including continuity and change in individual and family characteristics and resources, workplace policies and practices, age discrimination, labor market opportunities, and social policies. When considered as a whole, the findings within the preceding chapters reveal a research agenda that, if enacted, would provide a deeper and more comprehensive understanding of the employment experiences of older workers and the constraints that shape their opportunities for work at older ages. They identify three lacunae in existing scholarship that cut across multiple levels of analysis and are the most promising areas for future research:

1. the employer–older employee relationship;
2. work and resource inequalities in later adulthood; and
3. the work-health-caregiving interface.

In the remainder of this chapter, each of these topics is considered in turn, drawing on the findings of the previous chapters to identify key gaps in the literature and research questions that remain unaddressed. It is important to note that many of these research gaps remain not because of a failure of imagination on the part of researchers in this area, but because their efforts are constrained by the limitations of the tools available to them. Thus, this chapter highlights research areas where the development of methodological innovations and improvements to current data infrastructure may be required.

The Relationship Between Employers and Older Employees

The role workplaces play in affecting older adults' work and retirement pathways has received relatively less research attention than the role individuals play (Chapter 5). Organizations are the crucial link between macro-level public policies and individual-level outcomes among workers. The employer-employee relationship translates national policies into organizational practices that set the stage for individual decisions to continue in their current job, accept a similar position at another firm, transition to bridge employment or part-time work, or leave the labor force. To ignore this relationship in understanding late-career behavior and outcomes has major repercussions for getting a clearer picture of the way older adults approach workforce participation and retirement.

CONCLUSION 1: Retirement is too often viewed as an overly individualized process of workers stimulated or constrained by macro-level forces. However, other forces shape work and retirement pathways by constraining or increasing older workers' agency in making decisions. These forces include workplace norms, policies, and practices, within the context of the employer-employee relationship.

Employer discretion is particularly important in determining what types of workers are hired, trained, and retained, as well as the types of workplace policies and programs that are put in place to recruit and retain workers within labor markets. Employer decisions directly affect the extent to which workers experience longer, healthier, and more engaged working lives. Moreover, the preretirement performance and well-being of older workers cannot be understood without sufficient knowledge of workplace practices and policies. Understanding the role of employers and employees in facilitating longer working lives is paramount today, in light of the unprecedented aging of the population and the resulting pension reforms that are being implemented to deal with this demographic reality. Important areas for future research include the implementation of workplace policies; policies and practices that affect work and retirement; and the role of age discrimination.

Implementation of Workplace Policies and Practices

The employer-employee relationship in the workplace is shaped by the interests of both the employer and the employee. These interests can differ or align depending on the workplace issue, for example whether it is safety procedures or compensation. The institutional environment also affects the interests of employers and employees. Laws that distribute rights and power to employers or employees influence the ability of either party to enact practices that reflect their interests, as does the quality of labor markets, which can enable or inhibit workers from finding new positions and employers from hiring new workers. Crucial to understanding the purpose of various workplace policies and practices affecting older workers is the employer-employee relationship and its institutional environment. Therefore, we encourage researchers to explicitly account for employer and employee interests and the institutional context when analyzing workplace policies and practices affecting older workers.

Employee voice is one key aspect of the employer-employee relationship that can shape workplace policies and practices (Chapter 5). The extent to which employees have a say in their work can influence the type of age-related or age-neutral practices employers implement. For example, employees may prefer particular flexible scheduling arrangements or certain ergonomic practices. Employee voice can be part of independent collective representation that engages in negotiations with employers, or it can occur when individual employees are able to express their concerns and opinions directly to employers. Greater employee voice at the workplace can be instrumental in expanding work options for older employees, such as part-time work, remote work, or partial retirement. Moreover, greater employee voice can help reduce inequalities by fostering greater access to practices across ages and historically disadvantaged subgroups.

Forms of employee voice often vary by country, reflecting different laws, norms, and levels of union activity. Thus, international comparative studies can be particularly useful in demonstrating the influence of employee voice on the types of practices implemented within organizations. We encourage researchers to examine the role that employee voice can play in reducing inequality in access to and use of various workplace practices that affect older workers.

CONCLUSION 1.1: Both employer and employee interests shape the employer-employee relationship at the workplace. Though this relationship is crucial to understanding the purpose of various workplace policies and practices affecting older workers, few researchers account for employer and employee interests and the institutional context when analyzing workplace policies and practices affecting older workers. Moreover, little research examines the potential role of employee voice in shaping the organizational practices and context that affect older workers.

When employers introduce new workplace practices that benefit older workers, they can do so in either age-specific or age-neutral ways. Unfortunately, only limited research compares the effectiveness of age-specific and age-neutral practices on the employment decisions of older workers (Chapter 5). Age-specific practices are tailored to older workers and can be useful in meeting their specific needs, but these practices run the risk of stigmatizing older workers as a "special group" and encouraging discrimination against older employees (Chapters 5 and 6). Moreover, these policies can be problematic to the extent that they reinforce stereotypes or raise legal concerns of promoting differential treatment based on age, making the employer vulnerable to claims of age discrimination (Chapter 8). Age-neutral practices are designed for all workers and therefore avoid age-based stigmatization; however, when the needs of older workers differ from those of younger workers, such practices risk losing the effectiveness they would have had had they been specifically designed for older workers. More research and organizational data sources are needed to better understand the implications of these tradeoffs.

CONCLUSION 1.2: The relative effectiveness of age-specific and age-neutral practices in improving outcomes for older workers has not been adequately examined. Additional research is needed to assess the tradeoffs between the costs and benefits of both age-specific and age-neutral practices.

Policies and Practices That Affect Work and Retirement

Older employees are more likely to report a desire for flexible work arrangements than younger workers (Maestas et al., 2018), and that greater flexibility would increase their ability to remain in the labor force at older ages (Anderson et al., 2020). Flexibility can also help organizations adapt their operations, but differences in how, why, and for whom these arrangements are available can lead to very different employee experiences (Chapter 5). Methods of introducing flexibility into work practices, such as through remote work, flexible hours, or alternative schedules, can be voluntary, chosen by workers; involuntary, implemented by managers or employers for business reasons; or mandated by the government due, for example, to a pandemic or natural disaster. These differences can affect whether the introduction of flexible arrangements improves the retention of older workers and the working conditions of workers more generally. Some forms of flexibility can lead to increases in work hours or reduced employee control over work schedules, which in turn can lead to reduced retention of older workers. More research is needed on the effects that voluntary and involuntary flexibility in hours, in the ability to take time off, and in work location have on older workers' decisions to exit or remain employed.

Clearly identifying both the type of flexibility and whether it is voluntary will be crucial for ascertaining the effects of flexible work arrangements on the retention of older workers. Only limited research examines the effects of different forms of flexible arrangements on the timing of retirement. Europe offers some comparative models for allowing reduced hours of work as a form of partial retirement, a practice more commonly encountered there than in the United States (Chapters 5 and 8). Moreover, little is known about how experiences of remote working during the COVID-19 pandemic serve to increase older workers' preferences for continued work participation, including their demands for partial retirement schemes. Research linking flexible work practices to later-life work could investigate not only exits from the workforce, but also the effects of these arrangements on older workers' health and well-being, work-life balance, and ability to provide caregiving (Chapter 4). These outcomes are important in their own right, but they are also important as possible mechanisms through which flexible work arrangements influence individual pathways into and out of the workforce.

CONCLUSION 1.3: Though older employees express a desire for flexible working arrangements, these arrangements can involve flexible work hours, time off, or remote work and be voluntarily chosen by workers or involuntarily imposed by employers for business reasons. There is insufficient research on whether and what kinds of flexible arrangements affect the timing of retirement and older workers' decisions to exit or remain employed.

Employers also influence the ways in which technological innovations are introduced in the workplace. Innovations in technology and automation are rapidly changing the way work is carried out in organizations today (Chapter 5). There is evidence that such innovations can support older workers in their efforts to continue working in a variety of ways. For example, technology can make jobs safer by monitoring repetitive tasks or providing lift and positioning technology on assembly lines or using "cobots" to aid workers' strength (Coughlin, 2020). On the other hand, there is evidence that technological innovations are eliminating the need for some jobs, especially those involving repetitive tasks that do not require higher education (Chapter 7). The elimination of these occupations, in turn, reduces the number of employment opportunities for workers without a college degree and increases economic inequalities. Although it is difficult to study an ever-moving target (the technologies themselves are changing rapidly), it is imperative to better understand which technologies are beneficial and which are destructive to making continued work in later life a reality for those who need it or would prefer to continue working. Research examining the implementation of technology in the workplace, including the reasons for its introduction and the impact it has on the health, well-being, and employment opportunities of older workers, is important for understanding both its benefits and its role in limiting older workers' job opportunities.

CONCLUSION 1.4: Little research has focused on the implementation of enabling technologies in the workplace and, although the effects of technological innovation on job elimination have been examined, their impact on older workers specifically has not. More research that assesses both the positive and negative impacts of technological change and innovation on the employment of older workers is needed.

Worker training and skill plays an important role in employee retention at older ages. Keeping skills up to date is critical for older workers who are interested in working longer (Chapters 5, 7, and 8). These human capital endowments are important factors that employers use to make decisions regarding practices that can increase the retention of older workers or expand their roles within an organization. Yet employee access to training programs depends on many factors, including occupation, manager discretion, and individual incentives to participate (Chapter 5). Older workers are often excluded from training and development programs due to employer assumptions that older workers are uninterested in these programs and will not provide a sufficient return on their investment in training (Chapters 5 and 7). We do not yet fully understand the distribution of training and development access across employees within organizations or the consequences of access to these programs in shaping the timing of retirement.

Although the data are mixed concerning the extent to which older workers are interested in training and development, some studies show that older employees who have access to programs that enhance their ability to perform their jobs have higher levels of job satisfaction and employee engagement (James et al., 2010; McNamara and Pitt-Catsouphes, 2020). There is also evidence that training programs that are tailored to their age and career stage improve the training performance of older workers (Piccho, 2015). Thus, future research needs to address whether the reason older workers are less likely to receive training is because they have fewer incentives to pursue training opportunities due to their shorter remaining work lives or because organizations are less likely to offer them those opportunities (Chapters 5 and 7). This research should take a multilevel approach to examine the joint implications of individual and workplace factors for older workers' training and development participation.

We also know little about whether older worker-focused training is effective in retaining older workers. Such investigation is crucial, because recharging older workers not only enhances their productive capacity and removes potential barriers for them to continue working, but also enriches organizations' reservoir of knowledge. Identifying training programs that are efficient, cost-effective, and adaptable to the needs of older workers, as well as programs that improve the retention of older workers with different wage and skill levels, could provide greater incentives for employers to offer these programs to a wider range of their employees.

CONCLUSION 1.5: Worker training programs are critical for helping older workers keep their skills up to date; however, older workers are less likely to have access to these programs. It is not clear whether the reason older workers are less likely to receive training is because they are less motivated to pursue training opportunities or because organizations are less likely to offer them such opportunities. Moreover, more research is needed to determine whether older-worker-focused training is effective in retaining older workers.

The Role of Age Discrimination

Workplace age discrimination can occur in many forms, some of which are subtle or complex, presenting significant measurement and methodological challenges (Chapter 6). The gold standard for measuring discrimination is the audit study (i.e., resumé experiment). Audit studies provide direct evidence of age discrimination in hiring, especially for those near the age of normal retirement, with women facing greater odds of experiencing age-based discrimination in later life than men. Such experiences can be the result of implicit or explicit biases. Most on-the-job measures of discriminatory treatment rely on perceived discrimination reported by the target, capturing only one aspect of this phenomenon. More subtle forms of bias, as well as discrimination that is unseen by the target, are not captured by these measures. Although they are less rigorous than the evidence from audit studies, these self-reports of perceived discrimination have provided extensive evidence of disparate treatment of older workers within organizations. This disparate treatment includes exclusionary or demeaning interpersonal treatment of older workers; biased employee evaluations and promotions; less access to workplace training; few education programs tailored to older workers' needs; and inadequate health and retirement policies. There is a great need for the development of rigorous research methods to measure these other forms of bias.

CONCLUSION 1.6: Current research suggests that older workers experience age discrimination in hiring, promotions, performance evaluations, and workplace opportunities and climate; however, the quality of evidence varies, with the strongest evidence presented from audit studies demonstrating clear discrimination in hiring. High-quality studies addressing whether, when, and how discrimination occurs on the job, carried out with a rigor equal to that of audit studies, are needed.

Not only do the results on perceived discrimination need replication, but the processes need elaboration, to document mediators, moderators, and possible points of intervention. Both implicit and explicit biases about older workers are widespread among workers of all ages (Chapter 6). The science of social perception informs measurement of potential biases, their mechanisms (process mediators and situational or personal moderators), and leverage points for intervention. To be sure, ageism sometimes operates in blatant, easily measured ways, but increasingly it functions in various less-examined ways. If the biases are ambivalent, implicit, ambiguous, and latent, then people cannot individually track their own biases in hiring, managing, or promotion decisions; instead, a firm should watch for patterns that might result from many instances of unexamined bias. Unexamined ageism needs to be explored with more direct evidence, especially at work. Because undertaking such measurements is not straightforward, it requires development.

Implicit attitudes toward older people are, on average, negative, but only moderately so, and they have remained stable over time (Chapter 6). At the same time, the social acceptability of expressing explicit ageism appears to have declined over time. Ageist attitudes' slight negativity masks a mixed stereotype: expecting an older person to be incompetent but well-meaning. However, age can interact with other individual characteristics (e.g., gender, race, or sexuality) to produce stereotypes of elder subtypes that differ from the "incompetent but well-meaning" stereotype. Documenting unexamined workplace biases might include identifying whether, when, and how:

1. an original, unfiltered attitude or a newer, socially desirable, revised attitude guides age-related workplace behavior, including discrimination;
2. implicit ageism results in unmonitored behavior that unintentionally leaks a negative attitude;
3. mixed ageist stereotypes ("doddering but dear") predict ambivalent (e.g., patronizing) behavior; and
4. elder subtypes (e.g., "grandmother," "recluse," "statesman") might increase the accuracy of predicting biases and their effects.

Additional research is needed to assess whether each subtle form of bias might require different forms of detection and mitigation.

Despite evidence of biased attitudes about older workers (Chapter 6) and age-based discrimination in the workplace (Chapters 6 and 8), the causal chain that produces age discrimination is incomplete, because while observers can report their stereotypes and prejudices, only the targets report discrimination (Chapter 6). The current evidence base is missing the link between supervisors' and co-workers' reported age-related preferences (attitudes, prejudices) and older workers' reports of discrimination: coworkers' and managers' reported and observed discriminatory behavior toward older people. There is compelling evidence from field experiments that older workers suffer from age discrimination in hiring, demonstrating that stereotypes about older workers do affect employment decisions, which constrains labor demand for older workers. Discrimination against older workers seems to be reinforced by negative stereotypes about them. However, there is not the same kind of rigorous evidence on age discrimination along dimensions such as promotion, selection for training, and terminations (Chapters 6 and 8). Researchers thus far have not developed methods that generate rigorous evidence on age discrimination along dimensions other than hiring; this is a critical challenge. Funding agencies and foundations could encourage researchers to think outside the box about how to bring rigorous—likely experimental—evidence to bear on these other dimensions, including, for example, running experiments inside organizations.

CONCLUSION 1.7: Though older workers report being the target of discriminatory behavior and employers and workers often subscribe to negative stereotypical beliefs about older workers, the causal chain is incomplete, because it lacks evidence of coworkers' and managers' reported and observed discriminatory behavior toward older people. These processes require further elaboration through innovative studies that produce rigorous evidence.

Within workplaces, age-related biases operate not only within interactions at the interpersonal level but can infuse the broader organizational climate (Chapters 5 and 6). Consistent with the evidence and conclusions regarding ageism, research is needed to understand inclusive organizational policies that mitigate against age-related biases entering into decisions at all levels—hiring, supervising, and promoting. Moreover, organizational climate determines whether older workers feel valued. An inclusive culture makes older workers (and everyone else) feel that they belong. If latent prejudice cannot be eliminated entirely, organizations can still develop policies that help to keep it from creating an unfair and unwelcoming work environment.

Organizations often describe themselves as having a culture of inclusion, but investigations of organizational culture necessitate better conceptual and operational definitions of inclusive organizational policies, as well as multi-level models of their antecedents, indicators, and consequences (Chapters 6). These factors link to other efforts for workplace flexibility, voice, and retention (see discussion above). In addition to developing methods of measuring organizational culture, research should assess whether interventions implementing policies to improve the inclusivity of workplace cultures actually create a more inclusive culture for older workers. Findings to date are mixed, and they neglect the question of whether age-discrimination regulations affect the existence and experience of age-based discrimination in the workplace; a later section returns to this point.

CONCLUSION 1.8: Investigations of organizational culture necessitate better conceptual and operational definition of inclusive organizational policies, as well as multi-level models of their antecedents, indicators, and consequences. Research is needed to understand inclusive organizational policies that mitigate against age-related biases entering into decisions at all stages and levels of analysis and whether these policies actually create a more inclusive culture.

Organizational decisions affect the assessment, formal or informal, of the productivity of older workers, and there is also concern that age bias in evaluations of performance and productivity negatively affect older workers. Productivity is hard to measure, causally ambiguous, sensitive to level of aggregation, and distinct by job type, but on balance research does not show clear age-related productivity declines (Chapter 6). Older workers generally underperform relative to younger workers on speed (fluid intelligence) but outperform their younger counterparts on certain other performance-related measures, such as experience (crystalized intelligence) and workplace citizenship (social intelligence), yet researcher and employer evaluations of employee performance often omit these latter factors because they are more difficult to measure. As a result, assessments of older workers' contributions may be biased, because these performance strengths are seldom examined and often discounted by both employers and researchers. Research that evaluates the impact of the exclusion of such older-worker strengths on researcher, supervisor, and peer estimates of worker productivity and performance would add precision to studies of older workers' productivity and workplace performance as well as the value of retaining older workers.

Just as complex are the interrelationships between measures of worker "age," worker character, job factors, and performance, which all contribute to analyzing expectation accuracy regarding performance. For example, as discussed in Chapters 5 and 6, in practice chronological age confounds the effects of the number of years lived, the generation into which an individual is born, job tenure, and work experience. There is a real need for scholarship using data that can filter out age effects from the many other determinants of day-to-day productivity. Determining the independent effects of each of these conceptually distinct factors is difficult, and more research is needed to clarify these complex concepts. Similarly, the way age intersects with other identities also contributes to underestimating the contributions of older workers. For example, there is insufficient understanding of the potentially stronger age discrimination experienced by older women compared to older men (Chapters 6 and 8). Workers who face disadvantage due to their race, ethnicity, sexuality, or immigrant status might experience multiplier effects as they age—or conversely, become invisible and immune to age effects (Chapter 6). Research needs to consider age-related intersectionality in the workplace, seeking both patterns and distinctive effects on older-worker pathways.

CONCLUSION 1.9: Negative stereotypes about declining productivity may motivate discriminatory treatment of older workers. Productivity is hard to measure, causally ambiguous, sensitive to level of aggregation, and distinct by job type, and the most common measures omit dimensions on which older workers outperform younger workers, possibly resulting in biased assessments of older worker performance. More research is needed to evaluate how this exclusion affects researcher, supervisor, and peer estimates of worker productivity, workplace performance, and the value of retaining older workers.

Older workers' reports of discrimination covary with job dissatisfaction and poor health (Chapter 6), though the evidence of causality awaits better designs because third variables, such as depression, might explain both. Research that includes such covariates (e.g., optimism, personality, support, intersectional identities) will likely clarify and isolate the relationships among perceived workplace discrimination, health, and labor force participation. Research needs to establish the presence of a causal relationships between these factors.

CONCLUSION 1.10: Though reports of discrimination have been linked to job dissatisfaction and negative health outcomes, the causal link has yet to be established.

Given the wide perception of age bias, mitigation efforts are needed at all levels of decision-making in organizations today (Chapter 6). To some extent, Equal Employment Opportunity Commission requirements capture biased patterns but not the variables that might explain them or show how to mitigate them. Organization-level research needs to address how and when organizations can monitor the emergence of bias most effectively. There is a need for research that examines inclusive organizational polices designed to mitigate against biases entering into decisions at all levels—hiring, supervising, promoting—and that addresses the extent to which such policies do in fact increase employees' perception of the workplace as being fair and inclusive.

New Data Collection Strategies

Addressing these research gaps regarding workplace practices requires gathering data on actors in the employment relationship, as well as understanding the organizational context and the perspectives of managers and older workers within that relationship. The importance of the organizational context on employee responses to and outcomes of any policy and/or practice underscores the necessity of having matched employer and employee data over time. Most of the existing panel surveys sponsored by the U.S. federal government focus on sampling individuals or households; such surveys might inquire about participants' work, but they examine little about the context of their work or even, in some cases, their industry sector.

To date, research on workplace policies and practices in the United States has typically relied on access granted by individual companies or establishments within industries. While this approach has resulted in insightful research, such findings may not be generalizable beyond the organizations studied. More importantly, such access is very difficult to obtain in the United States and even more difficult to sustain over time. Negotiating individually with companies for access to survey managers and workers is time-consuming and requires demonstrating the benefits of the research to a specific company rather than the more general contribution to the advancement of knowledge. In addition, certain topics, such as discrimination, are legally sensitive, making it difficult to gain company consent to the participation of employees and managers.

Government surveys have a much greater chance of obtaining consistent data from establishments and workers over time. However, federal surveys by the U.S. Census Bureau, such as the Longitudinal Employer-Household Dynamics survey and the Management and Organizational Practices Survey, are designed with very limited organizational questions. Neither survey asks about human resource practices or age-related workplace practices, so neither addresses the fundamental question of access to and use of various practices at the workplace. Understanding the ability of individuals to access and use practices is critical to analyzing practice impact on older workers.

The National Compensation Survey by the Bureau of Labor Statistics suffers from the same problem. Although it includes a question about flexible schedules, it does not go beyond this practice, nor does it address access to or use of the practice. A more recent data set, called the Census-Enhanced Health and Retirement Study, links a range of establishment characteristics to the Health and Retirement Survey, focusing on older workers. This approach has some promise, but the establishment questions do not address key age-related workplace practices, focusing more on the economic characteristics of establishments.

In sum, no nationally representative longitudinal panel exists that samples U.S. workplaces and also contains multilevel matched data between employers and workers. To study the multi-layered and dynamic impact of workplace practices on work and retirement pathways, it would be invaluable to establish a panel survey or modifying an existing federal survey with sufficient variation at both the workplace and individual levels. Such a panel survey should collect data from a random selection of workplaces from the population of employers, covering all sectors and all sizes of workplaces. Within each workplace, data should also be collected from a random sample of older workers to directly gauge how older workers react to various workplace practices over time.

Having such survey data would allow researchers to better understand the roles of employer practices and workplace context when studying older adults' work and retirement pathways. We recognize the costs of developing a new panel survey could be substantial. As an alternative, adding questions about age-related and age-neutral practices to existing surveys would be a step in the right direction. Questions about age-related practices would be most welcome, such as questions about partial retirement, mixed age/experience teams, training that targets older workers, and workforce age assessments. Questions about age-neutral practices would also be welcome, such as questions on the use of flexible schedules, the use of ergonomic technology, employee participation, and skills training.

It is critical that we become able to more consistently and comprehensively address research questions about the effects of workplace policies and practices. Employers are the crucial link between macro-level public policies and individual level outcomes of workers. They are also the main actors in society translating national policies into organizational practices that, in turn, set the stage for individual decision making, including workforce participation and retirement. Workplace practices shape the incentives and opportunities for older workers to remain productive and engaged. Understanding the role of these practices in facilitating longer working lives is crucial during this period of unprecedented population aging.

CONCLUSION 1.11: Research on workplace policies and practices in the United States has typically relied on access granted by individual companies or establishments within industries. This access is difficult to negotiate and sustain over time and results in findings that are usually not generalizable beyond the organizations studied. A nationally representative longitudinal panel that focuses on sampling U.S. workplaces and also contains multilevel matched data between employers and workers does not currently exist but would be an invaluable resource for advancing research on the role of employers and workplaces on older workers' employment experiences.

Work and Resource Inequalities in Later Adulthood

Another gap in research reflects the unknowns about divergences and disparities in the work experiences of different subgroups of older people and how these contribute to social and economic inequality in later life. The older working population, like the U.S. population more broadly, is becoming remarkably diverse in race/ethnicity, nativity, family circumstance, education, occupational background, gender, and the intersections of these social identities. Labor force participation differs substantially across education groups and between Black men and other men (Chapter 2). These gaps exist at younger ages but are even wider at older ages, indicating that these groups have distinct experiences throughout the life course as well as different propensities for early retirement.

Race, ethnicity, and gender are social-locational characteristics that are associated with later-life outcomes, such as education, occupation, and marital status. As such, they are also associated with employment stability, income and wealth trajectories, saving for retirement, and health status (Chapter 4). These, in turn, affect retirement behavior and income security in old age. Adults who face limited work opportunities during their prime working years will face a considerable disadvantage when reaching retirement. Historically disadvantaged subgroups are more likely to face involuntary retirement due to disability and job loss and are less likely to have control over when, where, and how much to work (Chapters 4 and 5). They are less apt to have the resources and options to enact their preferences, and this likely shapes their expectations for work and retirement (Chapter 3). Those who have already left the labor force by their early- to mid-50s are likewise a vulnerable group that is often overlooked in studying later-life employment transitions. Much future research is still needed to understand how preferences, expectations, and constraints reflect these differences and translate into different employment patterns at older ages.

These differences in employment patterns at older ages are important not only in their own right but also because of their effects on economic inequality at older ages. Wealth disparities by education and race/ethnicity are substantially larger than income disparities, even after factoring in Social Security wealth (Chapter 4). Older adults with higher socioeconomic status, who already enjoy greater wealth accumulation throughout their life course, are also more likely to work at older ages (Chapter 2), providing an additional source of income that increases their economic advantage relative to those with lower socioeconomic status. However, there is currently little research examining the ways in which disparities in employment patterns contribute to social and economic inequality between older adults.

CONCLUSION 2: Much of the research on older workers focuses on the experiences of socially and economically advantaged workers, because they are more likely to work longer. Historically disadvantaged subgroups are less likely to have control over when, where, and how much to work or the resources and opportunities to enact their preferences for work at older ages. But less is known about how preferences, expectations, and constraints reflect these differences, intersect with age biases, and translate into different employment patterns at older ages and how this contributes to social and economic inequality in later life.

Answers are not likely to be simple. Multiple identities, defined by characteristics beyond age, intersect to create distinct opportunities and constraints, shaped by forms of discrimination that play out at all life stages and accumulate in later-adult-workforce advantages and disadvantages. Disparities across demographic groups in work-related resources and options in later adulthood are found in health, caregiving responsibilities, household structure, financial literacy, job experience and skills, job insecurity, employment opportunities, lifetime earnings, wealth, and access to employer-provided pensions and health insurance (Chapter 4). The next sections, respectively, suggest research needed to address disparities from three perspectives: life-course dynamics that produce inequality throughout the lifespan, inequality in access to employment opportunities and experiences, and inequality in financial stability.

A Life Course Perspective of Inequality

Though research on older workers often focuses on workers ages 50 and over, the processes that structure unequal work and retirement pathways at older ages do not begin at age 50. Applying a life-course lens to work and retirement pathways means recognizing that the resources and work/retirement options available in mid- and later-life accumulate and are shaped through prior life-course experiences of advantages and disadvantages; the relationships in which individuals are embedded; and the historical, policy, organizational, and social contexts in which they occur (Chapters 3 and 4). A fundamental life-course theme is that transitions, such as the nature and timing of later adult exits from or reentries into paid work, occur within trajectories of experience that give them shape and meaning.

Adopting a life-course conceptual lens can promote a better understanding of disparities in later adulthood by improving our understanding of the processes that lead to inequality in retirement (Chapters 3 and 4). Individuals from different backgrounds come to later adulthood with divergent histories. People reaching conventional retirement ages with higher amounts of education, those in professional jobs, and those following orderly career paths are better positioned to follow their goals and motivations. Unfortunately, those unable to remain continuously in the workforce or in full-time, relatively secure jobs confront limited options. By shifting the research focus to how early experiences and contexts influence the current preferences, expectations, and constraints on opportunities for work of older workers, a life course perspective can identify how historical structural inequalities continue to affect inequality in work outcomes at older ages.

A second life-course theme concerns the interdependence of lives—not only across different life spheres but also across social ties. Couples often make decisions around retirement timing together, or in light of each partner's preferences (Chapters 3 and 4). And family situational exigencies, such as the need to care for a grandchild or an aging family member, may well alter work and retirement preferences and expectations. A better understanding of these interdependent relationships would provide a more complete understanding of the contexts and constraints under which work transitions occur.

Yet a third life-course theme locates individual transitions and trajectories within historical time as well as within existing policy and institutional arrangements. Contextual embeddedness implies that life transition and developmental trajectories occur under specific circumstances, including historical, policy, organizational, and social contexts. Individuals are embedded within multiple contexts (e.g., households/families, neighborhoods, states, nations), and individuals shape and are shaped by these contexts (Chapters 5, 6, 7, and 8). Failure to consider these contexts may lead scientists to put too much emphasis on the effects of individual characteristics and to fail to recognize the ways in which the effects of individual characteristics are constrained by the contexts in which they are embedded and the changes in these contexts over time.

CONCLUSION 2.1: The processes that structure unequal work and retirement pathways at older ages do not begin at age 50. Research adopting a life-course conceptual lens can promote understanding of disparities in later adulthood by underscoring the cumulative impact of the multilayered embeddedness of lives in ongoing biographies and in historical and institutional environments.

Inequality in Work Opportunities

Though work at older ages can substantially improve the economic security of older adults, work opportunities are not always available. Opportunities to remain in the labor force often reflect the underlying economic inequality in opportunities by socioeconomic status and geography (Chapters 4 and 7). Labor market factors such as globalization and automation target specific occupations and locations, affecting work opportunities within some geographic areas or for some classes of workers, often defined by skill level or type, but also defined by gender and race-ethnicity due to labor market segregation (Chapter 7). These changes often reinforce existing economic inequalities, because displaced older workers are less likely to be reemployed.

Though there has been extensive research on the labor market effects of globalization and automation, this research has not specifically examined the impact of these changes on older workers (Chapter 7). Globalization leads to changes in the industrial and occupational structure of employment. The lower geographic and occupational mobility of older workers can leave them at a disadvantage when labor demand for the jobs they have occupied declines. In addition, in the United States (and other advanced economies), globalization may increase the premium for learning new skills. Broadly, countries with older workforces tend to be more likely to lose out, perhaps because of less skill adaptability within their labor force, but there is little research that has examined the direct impact this has on older workers. Similarly, the effects of automation on labor demand for older workers specifically, as well as the long-term implications of automation-related job loss at younger ages, are not known (Chapter 7). Some evidence indicates that certain types of automation, at least, increase demand for older workers, especially for those who adapt to the new technologies, but other types may have the opposite effect. Most research on the effects of automation is speculative at this stage, with only limited empirical evidence on recent changes and little research that goes beyond more "traditional" forms of automation to look at the automation of cognitive tasks by machine learning and artificial intelligence.

Globalization and automation have contributed to and expanded on the effects of growing regional disparities in economic outcomes in the United States, which have left rising numbers of people in areas with low employment rates, high unemployment rates, high rates of Social Security Disability Insurance receipt, and related social ills, which might have broader repercussions for their well-being (Chapters 7 and 8). The role of geographic mobility in reducing these disparities has weakened over time (Chapter 7). There are reasons to suspect that older workers, who are less mobile than their younger counterparts, are more likely to be affected by geographic disparities in these labor market changes. However, research has not focused on older individuals per se, leaving knowledge about these age-related disparities as purely speculative.

In general, more research is needed to understand the impact of globalization, automation, and geographic disparities on the work opportunities available to older workers, and how public policy might respond to mitigate adverse impacts. Moreover, little is known about the long-term impact of job loss at younger ages from these forces and how that could affect work at older ages by altering employment prospects, health, or take-up of Disability Insurance benefits (Chapters 4, 7, and 8). Research is needed on regional place-based policies that might boost employment in poorly performing areas and how such policies might begin to reverse the decline in employment, particularly among lower-skilled older men (Chapter 7).

CONCLUSION 2.2: Historically disadvantaged subgroups are more likely to face constraints in employment opportunities at older ages. Though research has documented the differential effects on employment opportunities by educational attainment of automation, globalization, and geographic disparities, less is known about the specific impact of these factors on older workers or about public policies that reduce their adverse impact.

Mismatch between workers' skills and the skills employers demand can arise from economic dislocations and changes in the demand for skills. The effects of this mismatch can be worse for older workers, in part because of weaker incentives to invest in training or in moving (Chapter 7). Opportunities for retraining are often available through employers, but older workers are less likely to participate in these programs (Chapters 5 and 7). Organizational policies and practices occur in the context of larger public policies that may also have broader effects (Chapter 8), including for those who are not currently employed. The long-term effects of automation- and globalization-related dislocation could perhaps spur governments to invest more in the retraining of older workers, but the effectiveness of programs (using methods such as cost/benefit analyses) that help or encourage older workers to invest in skills that match employer needs is not known (Chapters 7 and 8). Some government programs in the United States try to help displaced older workers find new jobs, but their effectiveness has not been evaluated. Some kinds of retraining—like community college education in the United States and firm training subsidies in Germany—boost earnings and employment, although the social returns may be relatively low if workers are relatively close to retirement (Chapter 7). Additionally, programs in other countries—such as Japan—merit evaluation.

CONCLUSION 2.3: Though social policies have been introduced to improve the economic opportunities of displaced workers, such as through local or regional economic revitalization or worker retraining or reskilling, little is known about the effectiveness of these policies in engaging older workers and improving the work opportunities available to them, nor the comparative impact of integrative policies from other countries.

To better understand work and resource inequalities in later adulthood, we need rich information about the most vulnerable populations in the labor market. These include less-educated, minority, women, self-employed, and "gig" and informal workers, as well as workers with disabilities, those in poor health, those who are noncitizen immigrants, and those living in rural areas. In particular, we need to understand their labor transitions in and out of work and in and out of the formal and informal sectors, because these are likely to be more complex than those of more advantaged workers and are not always captured using common measures of employment (Chapter 2). We also need to understand any simultaneous participation in formal and informal sector jobs, involuntary job separations that lead to labor force withdrawal before normal retirement age, barriers to work at older ages, sources of income, multiple occupations, sporadic jobs, access to health care and other labor benefits, and eligibility and take-up rates of supplemental income support programs for these low-income older adults (Chapters 4 and 8).

Vulnerable older adults may face unique labor market entry barriers. These barriers may relate to their education level, age, race/ethnicity, gender, health status, and access to urbanized areas (Chapters 2 and 4). Because there is significant heterogeneity within these populations and in their experiences, a full understanding of their diverse work pathways requires comparatively large samples for analysis. It also requires more detailed survey questionnaires that can capture the complexity of their work experiences, including multiple occupations, sporadic or gig jobs, and frequent transitions into and out of work (Chapter 2). Previous qualitative and quantitative work may be extended to develop further understanding of these populations.

Social networks and social capital may play an especially important role in identifying employment opportunities for older adults with more tenuous and less formal contact with the labor market (Chapter 4). These social connections inform and enable varied paths through work and retirement. Only limited research has addressed the role of key social mechanisms in obtaining employment in mid- and later life; even less empirical research focuses on older racial and ethnic minorities across socioeconomic status. Much of existing research is focused on youths and adults whose social networks (both strong and weak social ties, social support and social leverage, and homogenous/heterogeneous networks) play significant roles in labor force participation and job-seeking (Chapter 4). These factors all help to understand the process of finding meaningful and satisfying work, yet we know little about how these social mechanisms function with advancing age, as social networks retract, especially when individuals are pressed to retire or if they live in communities with few employment opportunities. These social resources may benefit older job seekers up to only a certain point; their efficacy may depend on the socioeconomic characteristics of the social network and the levels of trust and reciprocity among members of the group.

National, state, and local organizations are institutions that can help build social capital among older adults (Chapters 4 and 8). For example, formal volunteering could expand and strengthen social ties, while also bolstering various dimensions of health (Morrow-Howell et al., 2001; Gonzales and Nowell, 2017). These social and health resources generated and maintained by volunteering might then help older adults who need or want to work to acquire employment in later life. The pathways between paid work, retirement, civic engagement, and returning to the labor market are not fully understood. For example, some large companies provide volunteer opportunities to pre-retirees to help smooth the transition between paid work and retirement. Volunteering offers pre-retirees a purposeful role as a potential substitute for their work identity. Another pathway is probably more common: individuals transitioning from employment to retirement, engaging in some leisure, and then starting to volunteer. In either pathway, some volunteers transition out of retirement and go back to work (Carr and Kail, 2013; Gonzales and Nowell, 2017). The many pathways between work, civic engagement, and retirement have not been empirically identified, nor do we know which path optimizes health and retirement security. Knowing and tracing these pathways, especially across a diversity of populations, could help clarify the role of employment and civic engagement policies and practices in later life.

CONCLUSION 2.4: Social networks play an important role in labor force participation and employment opportunities among younger workers; however, less is known about how these social mechanisms function with advancing age, as social networks retract, especially when individuals are pressed to retire or if they live in communities with few employment opportunities.

Inequality in Financial Security

Financial security is one of the most important considerations workers face in decisions to retire or continue working longer. Inadequate retirement savings may constrain older individuals in deciding when to retire (Chapter 4). There is considerable debate regarding whether Americans have adequate savings for retirement (Chapter 8). Studies that use an "optimal saving model" to estimate whether individuals are saving optimally for retirement find that the vast majority of households reach this goal, while studies that use the "target replacement rate model" report widespread inadequacy.[2] No matter which point of view is taken, however, experts agree that workers today face growing challenges in saving adequately for retirement due to the increased life expectancy, decreases in Social Security benefits as the full retirement age rises, changes in employer-sponsored pensions, declining real interest rates, and other changes that have increased the need for higher ratios of wealth to income (Chapters 4 and 8).

While there is no clear consensus on whether the population as a whole is saving adequately for retirement, there is growing concern about the large wealth gaps by race, ethnicity, and education (Chapter 4). Financial security in old age is more tenuous for members of historically disadvantaged groups due to their lower wealth. Lower lifetime earnings and less access to employer-sponsored pensions impede retirement savings. Safety net programs make ineligible those individuals with assets above a certain level, reducing incentives for low-income earners to save or accumulate above that level. A lack of financial literacy and access to financial institutions, financial products and services, and opportunities for building savings and other assets across the life course can be additional barriers.

---

[2]Optimal savings approaches model consumption over the life course to develop household-specific optimum wealth targets and compare these to savings behaviors to determine savings adequacy (Scholz et al., 2006). Target replacement rate models compare projected household retirement income from assets, Social Security, and pensions to pre-retirement standard of living (Munnell et al., 2006). A more detailed discussion appears in Chapter 8.

The Great Recession of 2008 had a significant effect on the retirement security of older Americans (Chapters 4 and 8), and the COVID-19 pandemic is expected to have a lasting impact on older workers' quality of life and their ability to retire with adequate income for years to come. Historically disadvantaged groups have been more negatively impacted by these shocks. Households may turn to the informal sector or use risk management strategies to mitigate the effects of economic shocks. These strategies can include reducing savings and assets, adjusting labor supply, and changing consumption patterns even in the presence of previously arranged insurance mechanisms. Public programs, social networks (religious and community organizations), and family transfers may also help reduce the effects of an economic shock (Chapter 8). The impact of an economic shock may be more severe for low-income older adults, given that they have fewer labor opportunities at advanced ages (Flippen and Tienda, 2000).

It is critical to conduct research that analyzes the lifetime earnings, saving, and wealth accumulation of historically disadvantaged groups, including lower-skilled vulnerable workers with discontinuous work histories and multiple or sporadic jobs, to better understand their pathways to retirement and income security in old age. It is important to understand barriers to saving for retirement particularly for low-income people, women, and minorities, including the roles of (1) financial literacy, (2) access to employer-sponsored pensions, (3) other mechanisms to save for retirement, and (4) social insurance programs that may reduce incentives to save and accumulate wealth.

New retirement savings policies, such as "auto-IRAs," as well as culturally competent incentive mechanisms and financial literacy programs may have the potential to boost saving among diverse populations, but their impact remains understudied (Chapters 4 and 8). Further development of this research area may require finding innovative ways to collect longitudinal data for gig and temporary workers, the self-employed, and those who work in the informal sector, to better understand trajectories of wages and benefit access in these populations (Chapter 2).

Social policy supports play an important role in income security and employment decisions at older ages, particularly for vulnerable populations (Chapter 8), but more research is needed to understand how these programs affect decisions to remain in the labor force at older ages. Previous studies have found that older workers close to retirement age who are minorities, women, or in low-skill occupations are more likely to suffer involuntary job separation and have lower chances to be reemployed (Chapters 4, 7, and 8). Transitions from unemployment to retirement increase once individuals attain eligibility for Social Security, suggesting that this near-universal retirement income program also serves as a safety net for laid-off older workers (Chapter 8).

Older workers with less education are more likely than those with more education to experience both poor health and less access to alternative work arrangements and opportunities that can accommodate their health limitations (Chapters 4 and 5). As a result, they are more likely to receive Social Security Disability Insurance (SSDI) benefits prior to reaching eligibility for Social Security benefits (Chapter 8). Disabled and elderly beneficiaries who have very low incomes receive additional benefits through the Supplemental Security Income (SSI) program. SSDI program rolls have declined in recent years for reasons that are not well understood, because this decline runs counter to the trend of declining health and increasing mortality in middle age among those with less education (Chapter 8). In the United States, public policy is focused on income maintenance for those who are unable to work; however, other countries have taken alternative approaches. International comparative research examining the effectiveness of these alternatives and how they interact with organizational policies within countries could provide insights in identifying other policies that can help individuals maintain employment following the onset of a disability or health issue. Further studies could also help to assess whether Social Security and SSI are providing an adequate safety net for very-low-income elderly and disabled households.

CONCLUSION 2.5: Inadequate retirement savings constrains older individuals' retirement decisions. Although there remains considerable debate regarding whether older adults have adequate savings for retirement, there is a consensus that workers today face growing challenges in saving adequately for retirement. Financial security in old age is more tenuous for members of historically disadvantaged groups due to their lower wealth. It is critical to conduct research that analyzes the lifetime earnings, saving, and wealth accumulation of historically disadvantaged groups, including lower-skilled vulnerable workers with discontinuous work histories and multiple or sporadic jobs, to better understand their pathways to retirement and income security in old age, including the effectiveness of public policy supports.

New Data Collection Strategies

Addressing these key issues will require improvements to the current data infrastructure and data analyses. To date, most existing data collection and analysis focus on individuals' experiences at particular points in time, absent the rich insights that multilayered processual and contextual data could provide. Collecting life histories of individuals' previous pathways would advance our understanding of life course development. These longitudinal data would particularly address inequalities, social capital, and the nexus between work, health, and caregiving, yielding rich but admittedly expensive data. Life-history data would illuminate the differential biographical experiences of those disadvantaged by class, race, ethnicity, gender, and nativity throughout the life course, thereby opening up or limiting opportunities and capacities to remain working in their 50s, 60s, and 70s.

In addition to improving access to life-history data, collecting data on partners' work and retirement preferences and actions, as well as on other family circumstances (and changes in them), would offer insights as to how preferences, expectations, and actual behaviors evolve over time. Contextual data are often available from other data sources that can be linked to existing survey data. Systemic efforts and supports need to link different data sets and merge contextual data with the individual experiences captured in population-based surveys. Expanding the accessibility and use of contextual data—for example, through the use of geographic identifiers—would improve our understanding of the ways these contexts shape the environments where work and retirement occur.

Combining information on individual work and retirement pathways with their past life histories, their household and family circumstances, and relevant administrative, regional, and state data illuminating the particular institutional and geographic contexts in which lives play out is key to understanding these pathways in later adulthood. Surveys that rely on respondents' recollection are insufficient and are fraught with biases and scientific limitations. Data need to disentangle the sequence of life events, not just their summary recollections. Older workers make work and retirement decisions in light of the options available to them, including age-graded (and gender-graded) norms, social and organizational policies and practices, age, gender, and race/ethnic discrimination, all embedded within shifting demographic, technological, social, economic, and labor market environments. Those facing enduring disadvantages throughout the life course—women, minorities, immigrants, the less-educated—have little control or choice as to whether they are in or out of the workforce or when they transition from one employment status to another or whether they have access to meaningful and satisfying work (Chapters 3 and 4). But it is not clear how public and workplace policies, discriminatory practices, and the social organization of work and retirement perpetuate or, conversely, ameliorate these disadvantages.

CONCLUSION 2.6: Understanding the ways in which earlier life experiences shape the resources and options available to older workers will require expanding data collection strategies to incorporate life-history, relational, and contextual data.

An inequalities agenda could document how existing institutional and organizational arrangements serve to structure inequalities in later-life work—and nonwork—outcomes, particularly within the current context in which the nature of work is in flux. Future research could prioritize the necessary data and analytic methods to document both disparate pathways and their antecedents, keying in on the distinctive work and retirement preferences and experiences of subgroups of older individuals, as well as the heterogeneity and disparities within as well as across subgroups. Such scholarship is necessary to understand inequalities in the opportunity to work longer and to understand the need for recasting policies and practices at the national, state, and employer levels in ways that facilitate longer working lives.

To better understand work and resource inequalities in later adulthood, researchers need rich information about the most vulnerable populations in the labor market. These include less-educated, minority, women, self-employed, and gig and informal workers, as well as workers with poor health, those with disabilities, those who are noncitizen immigrants, and those living in rural areas. In particular, it is necessary to understand their labor transitions in and out of work, and in and out of the formal and informal sectors. There is also a need to better understand any simultaneous participation in formal and informal sector jobs, involuntary job separations that lead to labor force withdrawal before normal retirement age, barriers to work at older ages, sources of income, multiple occupations, sporadic jobs, access to healthcare and other labor benefits, and eligibility and take-up rates of supplemental income support programs for low-income older adults because these likely differ in important ways from those of more affluent older adults.

Vulnerable older adults may face unique labor market entry barriers. These barriers may relate to their education level, age, race/ethnicity, gender, health status, and access to urbanized areas. The heterogeneity of these populations and their experiences requires large samples for analysis. It also requires more detailed survey questionnaires that can capture multiple occupations, sporadic or gig jobs, and frequent transitions in and out of work. Previous qualitative and quantitative work may be extended to develop further understanding of these populations.

Limited sample sizes on racial, ethnic, gender, and sexual minorities in existing longitudinal and population data may present a challenge for this type of work. Larger sample sizes, where feasible, could help address issues of inequality in particular, as well as distinctive workplace experiences (e.g., training, voice, climate) and issues related to health, disability, and caregiving. Longitudinal data could oversample low-income neighborhoods and rural areas to understand vulnerable populations there.

There is little existing research on Native American and other minority older adults, such as Native Hawaiians and Pacific Islanders, and little research on noncitizen immigrant older adults as well. More extensive collection of data among these populations could yield new insights into them, including the dynamics within them. For example, some research has focused on Hispanics generally, but it has not differentiated among Hispanic populations, even though those from Mexico, Cuba, Puerto Rico and other Hispanic populations differ from one another in their socioeconomic status, health status, and levels of cultural assimilation (U.S. Department of Health and Human Services Office of Minority Health, 2021; Noe-Bustamante, 2019). Better understanding of these differences, and the challenges they pose, would require larger samples of different Hispanic ethnic subgroups. Similarly, research differentiating between Asian ethnic subgroups would provide similar insights, but it would require oversamples within these populations.

Promoting innovative methods to collect data on vulnerable populations will help develop a better understanding of retirement pathways. Increasing the size of survey samples of minorities and other vulnerable populations will be necessary to produce rigorous analyses. The focus on underrepresented populations is particularly relevant given the increasing diversity of the older U.S. population and the widening income and wealth gap. New data and research will help policymakers identify what changes are needed, by existing policies and programs related to older adults, and to design new policies and programs as well.

Combining survey data, administrative records, and other contextual data would be a first step in using current data sources to understand these vulnerable populations. A second step would be extending nationally representative surveys to gather more detail about labor and income among vulnerable workers. In particular, such surveys should gather more data on workers with frequent labor transitions, on jobs in both the formal and informal sectors, on work schedules and benefits, on workers with and without labor contracts, on methods of payment for workers, and on other variables that could provide a better understanding of the labor history for vulnerable individuals. Previous qualitative and quantitative research in the United States on self-employed gig workers, the informal sector, and low-income populations, as well as surveys developed for other countries with large proportions of individuals in poverty, could provide insights on how to better collect data for workers with complex work arrangements, multiple jobs, frequent transitions in and out of the labor force, or jobs in the informal sector or in the gig economy (Chapter 2).

Quantitative, qualitative, and ethnographic work are needed to uncover gender, racial and ethnic, cultural, time, and space differences in formal and informal work. Such data can yield timely and relevant information for policymakers seeking to improve the labor conditions of the current generation of working adults as well as the income security of future generations. Current safety net policies for older adults are not aimed at improving the income security of a large proportion of low-income older adults. More data on the experiences of low- and mid-income adults could facilitate research on culturally competent interventions that would improve labor market outcomes and retirement savings for such adults. Research that combines qualitative and quantitative approaches would likely yield greater insights and knowledge. For example, quantitative data could help clarify the structure of social networks, whereas qualitative and ethnographic studies could help deepen our knowledge about key concepts, such as trust and reciprocity.

CONCLUSION 2.7: The ability to document the experiences and challenges of vulnerable populations has been constrained by both a lack of measures to capture the full range of diversity of their work experiences, such as participation in the informal labor sector or in precarious, sporadic, or "gig" work, and a lack of sufficient samples of respondents from these populations in most data sets. Innovative data collection and research strategies are needed to better understand and address the needs of these populations.

The Interface Between Work, Health, and Caregiving

While many studies document an association between poor health and retirement, determining the causal effect of health on retirement or other late exits is challenging due the difficulty of determining the appropriate way to measure health; the interrelationship between health and other factors associated with retirement; and the subsequent effect of retirement on health. Despite these challenges, a causal relationship between poorer health and retirement has been well established across a wide number of studies (Chapter 4). However, filling several gaps in the existing research would improve understanding of the mechanisms that guide this relationship and suggest evidence-based interventions that could reduce the role of health problems as a barrier to work among older adults. These research gaps concern improving measures of health to identify specific health conditions and limitations that constrain work at older ages and gain a better understanding of the role of mental health and cognitive health; understanding the recent erosion in health status in midlife and at older ages and its consequences for work at older ages; identifying jobs and job characteristics that are associated with working longer with health conditions; and evaluating workplace health accommodation practices.

The most commonly used measures of health in research on the relationship between health and work are self-reported health status and presence of a work-limiting disability (Chapter 2). These are useful summary measures that are frequently available in survey data, but they are largely focused on physical health. Mental and cognitive health may also be important for continued employment at older ages (Chapter 4). In general, less is known about the relationship between mental and cognitive health and retirement, because fewer studies have examined it, and even these studies have not addressed the issue of causality.

The long-term trend of improving health over time and across cohorts has stalled or even reversed (Chapters 2 and 4). In recent years, a growing number of adults at midlife and at younger ages have reported poorer health and chronic health conditions, while mortality has increased (National Academy of Sciences, 2021). Importantly, these trends are more pronounced among less educated individuals, resulting in growing disparities in health by educational attainment. This negative trend exists for a wide array of health measures, such as self-reported health and activities or instrumental activities of daily living as well as for diabetes, cancer, and BMI, though not for strokes or heart disease (Chapter 4). Moreover, this reversal in health improvement appears to be especially salient for mental health.

This decline in health will have important implications for trends in the employment of older workers. The presence of chronic health conditions may affect the labor force participation and productivity of older workers in current and future cohorts. Poor health can be a constraint on labor supply, forcing some workers into early retirement (Chapter 4). Workers in poor health may be less productive, may require disability accommodations, or may generate higher health care costs for employers—or employers may perceive this to be the case, whether true or not (Chapters 4, 5, and 6). These factors could have a negative effect on the demand for older workers (Chapter 7). Moreover, racial and socioeconomic disparities in health outcomes will exacerbate disparities in access to employment opportunities at older ages, leading to greater economic inequality in retirement (Chapter 4). Understanding the reasons for this underlying trend may provide insights into future trends in work at older ages and the potential need for workplace accommodations.

The Americans with Disabilities Act requires employers to make reasonable accommodations for workers with health-related limitations that affect their ability to work (Chapter 8). Accommodation practices are expected to affect older workers directly, by improving their physical and cognitive well-being, as well as indirectly by demonstrating an organizational climate that cares for the safety and health of its workers. However, too few empirical studies have directly examined the expected beneficial effects of accommodation practices for older workers and their effects on enabling employment at older ages (Chapter 5). The alarming downward shift in the health of workers after a decades-long positive trend underscores the importance of identifying accommodative practices that may help enable old-age employment for the post-baby-boom generation.

Though much of the current research on health has focused on the effects of workers' own health on their employment, the health and caregiving needs of family members also affect work and retirement decisions (Chapter 4). Informal unpaid caregiving also follows identifiable, patterned pathways, meaning the intensity and duration of providing care to family members often conflicts with employment and often leads to part-time work and forced retirement (Chapters 3 and 4). The interrelationship between caregiving and labor force participation is dynamic and complex as they jointly play out in later life. Differences in the type and intensity of the caregiving needs of the recipient as well as the likely interaction effects between the health, social, and economic status of the informal caregiver and that of the care receiver add to the complexity of this relationship. It is likely that there are interaction effects as well between working conditions, employment policies, and practices shaping resources for caregiving (Chapters 4, 5, and 8). The fluctuation of caregiving demands affects the timing of retirement and other exits from the labor force (Chapter 4). These individual, dyadic, and employment dynamics are further shaped by state and federal policies, such as paid family and medical leave (Chapter 8). Research has not yet modeled these conjoint later-life-course dynamics, nor examined how they differ across diverse groups of caregivers and care receivers.

Informal caregiving responsibilities influence both preferences for and the actual timing of labor force exits (Chapter 4). Older workers may prefer working beyond conventional retirement ages, but they face constraints because of caregiving and family demands. Amid great diversity of caregiving and work arrangements, longitudinal studies in the United States and abroad suggest that older informal caregivers often reduce hours at work, feel forced into retirement, retire earlier, and do not return to work after retirement (Chapter 4). Women are more likely to leave the labor market permanently, more likely to work part-time due to informal care, and more likely to take time off work due to the demands of care, even controlling for gendered occupations and industries, job tenure, and union membership (Chapter 4). As the intensity of providing care increases, the likelihood of returning to work decreases.

However, in contrast to this consistent finding, a small body of research associates informal care with delaying retirement or going back to work after retirement (Chapter 4). The costs of caregiving can push older workers to remain in or reenter the workforce to provide financial support. Research can examine the tradeoffs between the demands of informal caregiving and those of employment and how these dynamics influence retirement pathways.

Caregiving demands may also create barriers for public policies that aim at facilitating employment for older adults, such as the Senior Community Employment Program (Chapter 8). Such community service and work-based training programs for older adults usually require that participants invest a significant amount of time, so caregiving demands can manifest as a barrier for participants. More future research on evidence-based interventions could create robust benefits for older workers with caregiving demands. Intervention studies of flexible work arrangements as well as state and federal policies and practices are warranted.

We know too little about the health and well-being of older workers, as well as of those who are not working but may wish to do so under certain conditions and those who are working unwillingly. For example, too little is known about the micro-level impacts on older adults' work and retirement of large-scale social changes—in technology, the economy, the labor market, and society writ large. Much of what we know about the later work course in relation to health and well-being comes from studies of earlier cohorts confronting very different demographic, technological, social, and economic forces, as well as different private sector and public policy regimes. Beneficial future research could explore the contemporary—and changing—experiences of work and retirement and the conditions shaping health and well-being. Long-term trends may affect work at older ages: rising inequality in income, wealth, and health; changes in the nature of work and employer-provided benefits; changes in family structure, caregiving needs, and women's roles; and the rising share of Hispanics in the U.S. population. Across socioeconomic status and demographic groups, the heterogeneous effects of these trends, as well as of the current COVID-19 pandemic and economic recession, demand investigation.

CONCLUSION 3: Although the relationship between physical health and work at older ages has been well established, less is known about other aspects of the relationship between health and work at older ages, such as the role of one's own mental health; the health and caregiving needs of family members; and how accommodative practices can enable working longer. Moreover, little is known about how recent declines in health at midlife and younger ages, particularly among those with less education, will affect labor force participation and worker needs for accommodative practices in the future.

BOX 9-1
The COVID-19 Pandemic and Work at Older Ages

As this report was being finalized, the nation (and the world) was still in the midst of the COVID-19 pandemic. The wider social and economic ramifications of the pandemic for older workers are only beginning to be studied. This pandemic has in many ways led to a remarkable confluence of events that has illustrated and underscored the importance of the issues addressed within this report. The health and mortality effects of COVID-19 disproportionately fell upon older adults, with nearly 80 percent of mortality occurring among those ages 65 and over (National Center for Health Statistics, 2021). Fear of workplace-acquired infection and reductions in access to health and caregiving support led greater numbers of older workers to leave the labor force and retire in the early months of the pandemic (Bui et al., 2020; Coibion et al., 2020).

Though the long-term effects of these exits are not yet known, like those who retired during the Great Recession these older adults may be less likely to return to work after the pandemic has ended, arresting the trend toward working longer. However, it is also possible that the financial effects of this unexpected job loss could lead some older adults to enter the informal work sector or seek to extend their work lives into older ages after the threat of infection has passed.

COVID-19 has had a dramatic impact on workplace conditions and the ways in which work is conducted. The economic impact of the pandemic across sectors has been unusual in comparison with previous downturns, because it is concentrated in jobs with face-to-face contact. This has likely affected the pathways between work and retirement for older workers, because many forms of bridge employment, particularly those adopted by women, involve face-to-face contact (Montenovo et al., 2020). Concerns about in-person transmission of infection have forced employers to restructure workplaces with health and safety standards in mind. COVID-19 testing and vaccination mandates, social distancing where possible, and remote working have increased dramatically, underscoring the importance of employers in establishing workplace policies and practices that increase employee safety and enable continued work. Depending on how they are implemented, these changes could have long-term benefits for older workers by increasing flexibility in work hours and schedules, or they could create new barriers to work by creating the expectation that remote workers are available "on demand." Moreover, the shift to remote work may have reduced the impact or visibility of older workers' social- and knowledge-based contributions to productivity, reducing their value to employers.

The disparate health and economic impacts of the pandemic have occurred along familiar lines, reinforcing and exacerbating race/ethnic and socioeconomic inequality. Hospitalization and mortality rates among many non-White populations, including Black, Hispanic, American Indian, and Alaska Native people have been substantially higher than those among White people within every age group (National Center for Health Statistics, 2021). Moreover, there is evidence that discrimination against Black and Asian Americans has increased during the pandemic (Ruiz et al., 2020). Increases in unemployment have been largest among those with less education and the smallest among those with a college degree or more (Moen et al., 2020). Health and mortality disparities are likely driven, in part, by the overrepresentation of non-White and less educated adults within occupations considered "essential," which often involve in-person contact with either co-workers or the public (Dubay et al., 2020). Nearly two-thirds of those with a college degree were able to shift to teleworking during the pandemic, compared to less than one-quarter of those with a high school degree or less (Dey et al., 2020). The health and economic impacts of these disparities will likely continue to be felt in the future.

The pandemic has demonstrated both the importance and limitations of existing social safety net policies within the United States. The dramatic rise in unemployment rates and subsequent increase in filings of unemployment claims have highlighted weaknesses in many state unemployment programs. The lingering effects of pandemic-related job loss will probably lead older workers to rely on government programs and employment protections to a greater degree than usual. However, programs such as Social Security and Medicare provided many older workers with a safety net that cushioned the effects of the economic downturn, though the decision to enroll in Social Security at younger ages could have long-term effects for financial security. Social Security Disability Insurance may also serve as a safety net for displaced workers with health issues, although there is no evidence applications have increased to date. Family leave policies allowed many older workers the flexibility to care for loved ones affected by the pandemic. It is clear that the wide-ranging impacts of the COVID-19 pandemic will provide fruitful areas of study in the future. Only time will tell whether its effects will interrupt the long-term trend toward working longer or, alternatively, enable that trend to continue through changes within workplaces and in social policies.

CONCLUSION

Work and retirement decisions are the result of the combined effects of individual preferences for work, expectations about the future, and constraints on work behaviors. To fully understand the ways individual-level characteristics affect the experience of work at older ages, their effects must be considered within the broader contexts through which they influence individual preferences, expectations, and constraints. But these individual preferences, expectations, and constraints operate within complex systems of social and economic inequality that develop throughout the life course, and thus may be specific to the historical circumstances in which individuals enter adulthood and, later, retirement ages.

Despite substantial research on older workers over the past several decades, we know too little about the well-being of older workers, that of older individuals who are not working but may wish to do so under certain conditions, and that of older individuals working despite their preference to retire. For example, too little is known about the micro-level impacts on older adults' work and retirement of large-scale social changes—in technology, the economy, the labor market, and society writ large. Much of what we know about the later work course comes from studies of earlier cohorts confronting very different demographic, technological, social, and economic forces, as well as different private sector and public policy regimes. Beneficial future research could explore contemporary—and changing—experiences of work and retirement and the conditions shaping health and well-being.

References

AARP. (2017). *Finding LGBT-Friendly Care*. Report by AARP, Washington, DC. https://www.aarp.org/caregiving/local/info-2017/lgbt-resources.html

AARP. (2020). *Caregiving in the U.S.* Research Report by AARP and the National Alliance for Caregiving, Washington, DC. https://www.aarp.org/content/dam/aarp/ppi/2020/05/full-report-caregiving-in-the-united-states. https://doi.org/10.26419-2Fppi.00103.001.pdf

Abraham, K.G. (2015). Is skill mismatch impeding U.S. economic recovery? *Industrial and Labor Relations Review, 68*(2), 291–313.

Abraham, K. (2020). *Contract Work at Older Ages*. Presentation for the Committee on Understanding the Aging Workforce and Employment at Older Ages at the National Academies of Sciences, Engineering, and Medicine, June 9–10, Washington, DC.

Abraham, K.G., Hershbein, B.J., and Houseman, S.N. (2021). Contract work at older ages. *Journal of Pension Economics & Finance, 20*(3), 426–447.

Abraham, K.G., and Houseman, S.N. (2005). Work and retirement plans among older Americans. *Reinventing the Retirement Paradigm*, 70–91. New York: Oxford University Press.

Acemoglu, D. (1999). Changes in unemployment and wage inequality: An alternative theory and some evidence. *American Economic Review, 89*(5), 1259–1278.

Acemoglu, D., and Angrist, J.D. (2001). Consequences of employment protection? The case of the Americans with Disabilities Act. *Journal of Political Economy, 109*(5), 915–957.

Acemoglu, D., and Restrepo, P. (2017). Secular stagnation? The effect of aging on economic growth in the age of automation. *American Economic Review: Papers & Proceedings, 107*(5), 174–179.

Acemoglu, D., and Restrepo, P. (2018). Low-skill and high-skill automation. *Journal of Human Capital, 12*(2), 204–232.

Ackerman, P.L., and Kanfer, R. (2020). Work in the 21st century: New directions for aging and adult development. *American Psychologist, 75*(4), 486–498. https://doi.org/10.1037/amp0000615

Adams, G.A., and Beehr, T.A. (1998). Turnover and retirement: A comparison of their similarities and differences. *Personnel Psychology, 51*(3), 643–665.

Adams, S.J. (2002). Passed over for promotion because of age: An empirical analysis of the consequences. *Journal of Labor Research, 23*(3), 447–461.

Adams, S.J. (2004). Age discrimination legislation and the employment of older workers. *Labour Economics, 11*(2), 219–241.

Aday, R.H., and Kehoe, G. (2008). Working in old age: Benefits of participation in the Senior Community Service Employment Program. *Journal of Workplace Behavioral Health, 23*(1–2), 125–145.

Adermon, A., and Gustavsson, M. (2015). Job polarization and task-biased technological change: Evidence from Sweden, 1975–2005. *The Scandinavian Journal of Economics, 117*(3), 878–917.

Adler, N.E., and Rehkopf, D.H. (2008). U.S. disparities in health: Descriptions, causes, and mechanisms. *Annual Review of Public Health, 29*, 235–252.

Age Discrimination in Employment Act (ADEA). (1967). Statute of the United States Government. https://www.eeoc.gov/statutes/age-discrimination-employment-act-1967

Agnew, J. (2013). *Australia's Retirement System: Strengths, Weaknesses, and Reforms,* Issue Brief No. 13-5, Center for Retirement Research at Boston College, Chestnut Hill, MA. https://crr.bc.edu/briefs/australia%E2%80%99s-retirement-system-strengths-weaknesses-and-reforms-2

Agovino, T. (2020). *COVID-19 Deals a Dual Threat to Older Workers: The Pandemic Poses the Grim Potential of Job Loss and Health Risks, Which Makes for a Complex Landscape of Employment Issues.* https://www.shrm.org/hr-today/news/all-things-work/pages/covid-19-deals-a-dual-threat-to-older-workers.aspx

Aguila, E., and Smith, J.P. (2020). Supplemental Income program design: A cluster-randomized controlled trial to examine the health and wellbeing effects on older adults by gender, duration, and payment. *Social Science & Medicine, 259*, 113–139.

Aguila, E., and Vega, A. (2017). Social Security contributions and return migration among older male Mexican immigrants. *The Gerontologist, 57*(3), 563–574. https://doi.org/10.1093/geront/gnw140

Aguila, E., and Zissimopoulos, J. (2013). Retirement and health benefits for Mexican migrant workers returning from the United States. *International Social Security Review, 66*(2), 101–125. https://doi.org/10.1111/issr.12014

Aguila, E., Angrisani, M., and Blanco, L.R. (2016). Ownership of a bank account and health of older Hispanics. *Economics Letters, 144*(C), 41–44. https://econpapers.repec.org/article/eeeecolet/v_3a144_3ay_3a2016_3ai_3ac_3ap_3a41-44.htm

Aguila, E., Attanasio, O., and Meghir, C. (2011). Changes in consumption at retirement: Evidence from panel data. *Review of Economics and Statistics, 93*(3), 1094–1099.

Aguila, E., Kapteyn, A., and Perez-Arce, F. (2017). Consumption smoothing and frequency of benefit payments of cash transfer programs. *American Economic Review Papers and Proceedings, 107*(5), 430–435.

Ajrouch, K.J., Antonucci, T.C., and Webster, N.J. (2016). Volunteerism: Social network dynamics and education. *The Journals of Gerontology, Series B, Psychological Sciences and Social Sciences, 71*(2), 309–319.

Ajzen, I. (1991). The theory of planned behavior. *Organizational Behavior and Human Decision Processes 50*(2), 179–211.

Algarni, F.S., Gross, D.P., Senthilselvan, A., and Battié, M.C. (2015). Ageing workers with work-related musculoskeletal injuries. *Occupational Medicine 65*(3), 229–237.

Ali, R., Dethier, J.-J., and Pestieau, P. (2010). *Universal Minimum Old Age Pensions: Impact on Poverty and Fiscal Cost in 18 Latin American Countries.* Working Paper No. WPS5292, Washington, DC: The World Bank. http://documents.worldbank.org/curated/en/397501468299147949/Universal-minimum-old-age-pensions-impact-on-poverty-and-fiscal-cost-in-18-Latin-American-countries

Altig, D., Auerbach, A.J., Koltikoff, L.J., Smetters, K.A., and Walliser, J. (2001). Simulating fundamental tax reform in the United States. *American Economic Review, 91*(3), 574–595.

Altschuler, J. (2004). Beyond money and survival: The meaning of paid work among older women. *International Journal of Aging and Human Development 58*(3), 233–239.

Alwin, D.F., and McCammon, R.J. (2003). Generations, cohorts, and social change. *Handbook of the Life Course*, 23–49. New York: Kluwer Academic/Plenum.

Ameri, M., Schur, L., Adya, M., Bentley, F.S., McKay, P., and Kruse, D. (2018). The disability employment puzzle: A field experiment on employer hiring behavior. *Industrial and Labor Relations Review, 71*(2), 329–364. https://journals.sagepub.com/doi/pdf/10.1177/0019793917717474

American Academy of Actuaries. (2002). Raising the Retirement Age for Social Security. Issue Briefs of the American Academy of Actuaries, October, Washington, DC. https://www.actuary.org/sites/default/files/pdf/socialsecurity/age_oct02.pdf

Ameriks, J., Briggs, J., Caplin, A., Lee, M., Shapiro, M.D., and Tonetti, C. (2018). *Shocks and Transitions from Career Jobs to Bridge Jobs and Retirement: A New Approach.* Michigan Retirement Research Center Working Paper Series No. 2018-380. Institute for Social Research, University of Michigan, Ann Arbor. https://mrdrc.isr.umich.edu/publications/papers/pdf/wp380.pdf

Andersen, L.L., Jensen, P.H., and Sundstrup, E. (2020). Barriers and opportunities for prolonging working life across different occupational groups: The senior working life study. *European Journal of Public Health, 30*(2), 241–246. https://doi.org/10.1093/eurpub/ckz146

Andersen, L.L., Jensen, P.H., Meng, A., and Sundstrup, E. (2019). Strong labour market inequality of opportunities at the workplace for supporting a long and healthy work-life: The senior working life study. *International Journal of Environmental Research and Public Health, 16*(18), 3264. https://doi.org/10.3390/ijerph16183264

REFERENCES

Andreoletti, C., Maurice, J. K., and Whalen, H. (2001). *Gender, race, and age: Compound stereotypes across the lifespan.* Paper presented at the Second Annual Meeting of the Society for Personality and Social Psychology, San Antonio, TX.

Angrisani, M., Hurd, M.D., Meijer, E., Parker, A.M., and Rohwedder, S. (2017). Personality and employment transitions at older ages: Direct and indirect effects through non-monetary job characteristics. *Labour (Rome), 31*(2), 127–152.

Angrisani, M., Kapteyn, A., and Meijer, E. (2016). *Non-Monetary Job Characteristics and Employment Transitions at Older Ages.* SSRN. https://ssrn.com/abstract=3238248

Appelbaum, E., Kalleberg, A., and Rho, H.J. (2019). Nonstandard work and older Americans, 2005–2017. *Challenge, 62*(4), 219–241.

Armour, P., Button, P., and Hollands, S. (2018). Disability saliency and discrimination in hiring. *American Economic Association Papers and Proceedings, 108*, 262–266. https://econpapers.repec.org/article/aeaapandp/v_3a108_3ay_3a2018_3ap_3a262-66.htm

Armstrong-Stassen, M. (2008). Organisational practices and the post-retirement employment experience of older workers. *Human Resource Management Journal, 18*(1), 36–53.

Armstrong-Stassen, M., and Schlosser, F. (2011). Perceived organizational membership and the retention of older workers. *Journal of Organizational Behavior, 32*(2), 319–344. https://onlinelibrary.wiley.com/doi/10.1002/job.647

Armstrong-Stassen, M., and Ursel, N.D. (2009). Perceived organizational support, career satisfaction, and the retention of older workers. *Journal of Occupational and Organizational Psychology, 82*(1), 201–220. https://bpspsychub.onlinelibrary.wiley.com/doi/full/10.1348/096317908X288838

Arora, K., and Wolf, D.A. (2018). Does paid family leave reduce nursing home use? The California experience. *Journal of Policy Analysis and Management, 37*(1), 38–62.

Asch, B., Haider, S.J., and Zissimopoulos, J. (2005). Financial incentives and retirement: Evidence from federal civil service workers. *Journal of Public Economics, 89*(2–3), 427–440.

Ashenfelter, O., and Card, D. (2002). Did the elimination of mandatory retirement affect faculty retirement? *American Economic Review, 92*(4), 957–980.

Ashforth, B. (2001). *Role Transitions in Organizational Life: An Identity-Based Perspective.* Mahwah, NJ: Erlbaum.

Ashournia, D. (2018). Labour market effects of international trade when mobility is costly. *Economic Journal, 128*(616), 3008–3038.

Attanasio, O., and Hoynes, H. (2000). Differential mortality and wealth accumulation. *The Journal of Human Resources, 35*(1), 1–29. https://doi.org/10.2307/146354

Aubert, P. (2003). *Productivity, Wage, and Demand for Elder Workers: An Examination on French Matched Employer-Employee Data.* National Institute of Statistics and Economic Studies Technical Report, Paris, France.

Aubert, P., and Crépon, B. (2007). Are Older Workers Less Productive? Firm-Level Evidence on Age-Productivity and Age-Wage Profiles. Mimeo. *Economie et Statistique, 368*, 95–119.

Austin, B., Glaeser, E., and Summers, L. (2018). Jobs for the heartland: Place-based policies in 21st-century America. *Brookings Papers on Economic Activity,* Spring, 151–232. https://www.brookings.edu/wp-content/uploads/2018/03/AustinEtAl_Text.pdf

Autor, D.H. (2015). Why are there still so many jobs? The history and future of workplace automation. *Journal of Economic Perspectives, 29*(3), 3–30.

Autor, D.H., and Duggan, M.G. (2003). The rise in the disability rolls and the decline in unemployment. *The Quarterly Journal of Economics 118*(1), 157–206.

Autor, D.H., and Duggan, M.G. (2006). The growth in the Social Security disability rolls: A fiscal crisis unfolding. *Journal of Economic Perspectives 20*(3), 71–96.

Autor, D.H., and Duggan, M.G. (2010). *Supporting Work: A Proposal for Modernizing the U.S. Disability Insurance System.* Washington, DC: Center for American Perspective and the Hamilton Project.

Autor, D.H., Katz, L.F., and Kearney, M.S. (2008). Trends in U.S. wage inequality: Revising the revisionists. *The Review of Economics and Statistics, 90*(2), 300–323.

Autor, D.H., Levy, F., and Murnane, R.J. (2003). The skill content of recent technological change: An empirical exploration. *Quarterly Journal of Economics 118*(4), 1279–1334.

Avolio, B.J., and Barrett, G.J. (1987). Effects of age stereotyping in a simulated interview. *Psychology and Aging, 2*, 56–63.

Backes-Gellner, U., Schneider, M.R., and Veen, S. (2011). Effect of workforce age on quantitative and qualitative organizational performance: Conceptual framework and case study evidence. *Organization Studies, 32*(8), 1103–1121.

Bajtelsmit, V.L., and Bernasek, A. (2001). *Risk Preferences and the Investment Decisions of Older Americans.* Washington, DC: AARP.

Baker, M., Stabile, M., and Deri, C. (2004). What do self-reported, objective, measures of health measure? *Journal of Human Resources, 39*(4), 1067–1093.

Bakker, A.B., and Demerouti, E. (2007). The job demands-resources model: State of the art. *Journal of Managerial Psychology*, 22(3), 309–328. https://doi.org/10.1108/02683940710733115

Bakker, A.B., and Demerouti, E. (2017). Job demands-resources theory: Taking stock and looking forward. *Journal of Occupational Health Psychology*, 22(3), 273–285.

Baltes, P.B., and Lindenberger, U. (1997). Emergence of a powerful connection between sensory and cognitive functions across the adult life span: A new window to the study of cognitive aging? *Psychology and Aging*, 12(1), 12–21. https://doi.org/10.1037/0882-7974.12.1.12

Banks, J., Blundell, R., and Rivas, M.C. (2007). *The Dynamics of Retirement Behavior in Couples: Reduced-Form Evidence from England and the U.S.* University College London, Mimeo. https://www.researchgate.net/publication/260403390_The_dynamics_of_retirement_behavior_in_couples_Reduced-form_evidence_from_England_and_the_US

Barber, B.M., and Odean, T. (2001). Boys will be boys: Gender, overconfidence, and common stock investment. *The Quarterly Journal of Economics*, 116(1), 261–292.

Barber, S.J. (2017). An examination of age-based stereotype threat about cognitive decline: Implications for stereotype-threat research and theory development. *Perspectives on Psychological Science*, 12(1), 62–90.

Barnes-Farrell, J.L. (2003). Beyond health and wealth: Attitudinal and other influences on retirement decision-making. *Retirement: Reasons, Processes and Results*, 159–187. New York, NY: Spring Publishing Company, Inc.

Barrientos, A., Ferreira, M., Gorman, M., Heslop, A., Legido-Quigley, H., Lloyd-Sherlock, P., Vianna W., and M.L.T. (2003). *Non-Contributory Pensions and Poverty Prevention: A Comparative Study of Brazil and South Africa*. The Institute of Development and Policy Management and Help Age International. https://www.helpage.org/silo/files/noncontributory-pensions-and-poverty-prevention-a-comparative-study-of-brazil-and-south-africa-.pdf

Barro, R.J., and Sala-i-Martin, X. (1991). Convergence across states and regions. *Brookings Papers on Economic Activity*, 1, 107–182.

Bartik, T.J. (2020). Smart place-based policies can improve local labor markets. *Journal of Policy Analysis and Management*, 39, 845–851.

Bass, S.A., and Oka, M. (1995). An older-worker employment model: Japan's Silver Human Resource Centers. *The Gerontologist*, 35(5), 679–682.

Bauman, K. (2016). *College Completion by Cohort, Age, and Gender: 1967–2015*. Paper presented at the 2016 Population Association of America Annual Meeting. Washington, DC.

Becker, G.S. (1962). Investment in human capital: A theoretical analysis. *Journal of Political Economy*, 70(5), 9–49.

Becker, G.S. (1964). *Human Capital*. University of Chicago Press.

Bee, A., and Mitchell, J. (2017). *Do Older Americans Have More Income Than We Think?* Proceedings, 110, 1–85. Annual Conference on Taxation and Minutes of the Annual Meeting of the National Tax Association. National Tax Association.

Beehr, T.A. (1986). The process of retirement: A review and recommendations for future investigation. *Personnel Psychology*, 39(1), 31–56.

Behaghel, L., and Blau, D.M. (2012). Framing Social Security reform: Behavioral responses to changes in the full retirement age. *American Economic Journal: Economic Policy*, 4(4), 41–67.

Beier, M.E., and Ackerman, P.L. (2005). Age, ability, and the role of prior knowledge on the acquisition of new domain knowledge: Promising results in a real-world learning environment. *Psychology and Aging*, 20(2), 341–355.

Belbase, A., and Sanzenbacher, G. (2018). *How Have Workers Responded to Oregon's Auto-IRA?* Issue Brief No. 18-22, Center for Retirement Research at Boston College, Chestnut Hill, MA.

Belbase, A., Khan, M., Munnell, A., and Webb, A. (2015). *Slowed or Sidelined? The Effect of 'Normal' Cognitive Decline on Job Performance Among the Elderly*. Working Paper No. 2015-12, Center for Retirement Research at Boston College: Chestnut Hill.

Belkar, R., Cockerell, L., and Edwards, R. (2007). *Labour Force Participation and Household Debt*. Research Discussion Paper No. 2007-05. Sydney: Reserve Bank of Australia. https://www.rba.gov.au/publications/rdp/2007/pdf/rdp2007-05.pdf

Bell, D., and Heitmueller, A. (2009). The disability discrimination act in the UK: Helping or hindering employment among the disabled? *Journal of Health Economics*, 28(2), 465–480.

Benach, J., Muntaner, C., and Santana, V. (2007). *Employment Conditions and Health Inequalities*. Final Report to the WHO Commission on Social Determinants of Health. Employment Conditions Knowledge Network. https://www.researchgate.net/publication/242774540_Employment_Conditions_and_Health_Inequalities

Benach, J., Vives, A., Amable, M., Vanroelen, C., Tarafa, G., and Muntaner, C. (2014). Precarious employment: Understanding an emerging social determinant of health. *Annual Review of Public Health*, 35, 229–253. https://doi.org/10.1146/annurev-pubhealth-032013-182500

Benartzi, S., and Thaler, R. (2007). Heuristics and biases in retirement savings behavior. *Journal of Economic Perspectives*, 21(3), 81–104.

Bendick, M., Brown, L.E., and Wall, K. (1999). No foot in the door: An experimental study of employment discrimination against older workers. *Journal of Aging & Social Policy*, *10*(4), 5–23.

Bendick, M., Jackson, C.W., and Romero, J.H. (1997). Employment discrimination against older workers: An experimental study of hiring practices. *Journal of Aging & Social Policy*, *8*(4), 25–46.

Berecki-Gisolf, J., Clay, F.J., Collie, A., and McClure, R.J. (2012). The impact of aging on work disability and return to work. *Journal of Occupational and Environmental Medicine*, *54*(3), 318–327.

Berg, P., and Piszczek, M.M. (2021). Organizational response to workforce aging: Tensions in human capital perspectives. *Work, Aging, and Retirement, WAAB026*. Oxford University Press.

Berg, P., Hamman, M.K., Piszczek, M., Ruhm, C.J. (2020). Can policy facilitate partial retirement? Evidence from a natural experiment in Germany. *ILR Review*, *73*(5), 1226–1251.

Berg, P., Kossek, E.E., Misra, K., and Belman D. (2014). Work-life flexibility policies: Do unions affect employee access and use? *Industrial and Labor Relations Review*, *67*(1), 111–137.

Berkman, L.F. (2009). Social epidemiology: Social determinants of health in the United States: Are we losing ground? *Annual Review of Public Health*, *30*, 27–41. https://doi.org/10.1146/annurev.publhealth.031308.100310

Berkman, L.F., Kawachi, I., and Glymour, M. (2014). *Social Epidemiology* (2nd ed.). New York: Oxford University Press.

Berkman, L.F., Buxton, O., Ertel, K., and Okechukwu, C. (2010). Managers' practices related to work-family balance predict employee cardiovascular risk and sleep duration in extended care settings. *Journal of Occupational Health Psychology*, *15*(3), 316–329. https://doi.org/10.1037/a0019721

Bernheim, B.D., Skinner, J., and Weinberg, S. (2001). What accounts for the variation in retirement wealth among U.S. households? *American Economic Review*, *91*(4), 832–857. https://www.aeaweb.org/articles?id=10.1257/aer.91.4.832

Bertolino, M., Truxillo, D.M., and Fraccaroli, F. (2011). Age as moderator of the relationship of proactive personality with training motivation, perceived career development from training, and training behavioral intentions. *Journal of Organizational Behavior*, *32*(2), 248–263. https://onlinelibrary.wiley.com/doi/full/10.1002/job.670

Beshears, J., Choi, J.J., Laibson D., and Madrian, B.C. (2007). *The Importance of Default Options for Retirement Saving Outcomes: Evidence from the United States*, NBER Working Paper No. 12009, National Bureau of Economic Research. https://www.nber.org/system/files/working_papers/w12009/w12009.pdf

Beshears, J., Choi, J.J., Laibson, D., Madrian, B.C., and Skimmyhorn, W.L. (2019). *Borrowing to Save? The Impact of Automatic Enrollment on Debt*, NBER Working Paper No. 25876, National Bureau of Economic Research. https://www.nber.org/system/files/working_papers/w25876/w25876.pdf

Bianchi, N., Bovini, G., Li, J., and Paradisi, M. (2019). *Career Spillovers in Internal Labor Markets*. SSRM Electronic Journal. https://www.researchgate.net/publication/336832798_Career_Spillovers_in_Internal_Labor_Markets

Biddle, J., Boden, L.I., and Reville, R.T. (2003). *Older Workers Face More Serious Consequences from Workplace Injuries*. Health and Security for an Aging Workforce (5). Washington, DC: National Academy of Social Insurance.

Biggs, A.G., Chen, A., and Munnell, A.H. (2021). *The Consequences of Current Benefit Adjustments for Early and Delayed Claiming*, Working Paper No. WP2021-3, Chestnut Hill, MA: Center for Retirement Research at Boston College.

Binder, A.J., and Bound, J. (2019). The declining labor market prospects of less-educated men. *Journal of Economic Perspectives*, *33*(2), 163–190.

Bipartisan Policy Center. (2016). *Securing Our Financial Future*. Report of the Commission on Retirement Security and Personal Savings. Washington, DC. https://bipartisanpolicy.org/report/retirement-security

Bird, C.E., and Rieker, P.P. (2008). *Gender and Health. The Effects of Constrained Choices and Social Policies*. Cambridge University Press. https://psycnet.apa.org/record/2009-01087-000

Birkenmaier, J., Sherraden, M.S., Frey, J.J., Callahan, C., and Santiago, A.M. (2016). Financial capability and asset building: Building evidence for community practice. *Journal of Community Practice*, *24*(4), 357–367. https://doi.org/10.1080/10705422.2016.1233519

Bjelland, M., Bruyère, S., von Schrader, S., Houtenville, A., Ruiz-Quintanilla, A., and Webber, D. (2010). Age and disability employment discrimination: Occupational rehabilitation implications. *Journal of Occupational Rehabilitation*, *20*(4), 456–471.

Black, D.A., Daniel, K., and Sanders, S.G. (2002). The impact of economic conditions on participation in disability programs: Evidence from the coal boom and bust. *American Economic Review*, *92*(1), 27–50.

Black, N., Johnston, D.W., and Suziedelyte, A. (2017). Justification bias in self-reported disability: New evidence from panel data. *Journal of Health Economics, Elsevier*, *54*(C), 124–134.

Blanck, P.D., Schur, L., Kruse, D., Schwochau, S., and Song, C. (2003). Calibrating the impact of the ADA's employment provisions. *Stanford Law & Policy Review*, *14*(2), 267–290. https://bbi.syr.edu/wp-content/uploads/application/pdf/bio/2003-blanck-calibrating-impact-ada-accessible-DK.pdf

Blanco, L.R., Aguila, E., Gongora, A., and Duru, K. (2017). Retirement planning among Hispanics: In God's hands? *Journal of Aging and Social Policy*, *29*(4), 311–331. https://doi.org/10.1080/08959420.2016.1272161

Blanco, L.R., Marco, A., Emma, A., and Mei, L. (2018). Understanding the racial/ethnic gap in bank account ownership among older adults. *Journal of Consumer Affairs, 53*(2), 324–354. https://onlinelibrary.wiley.com/doi/abs/10.1111/joca.12188

Blau, D., and Shvydko, T. (2011). Labor market rigidities and the employment behavior of older workers. *Industrial and Labor Relations Review, 64*(3), 464–484.

Blau, F., and Kahn, L. (1994). Rising wage inequality and the U.S. gender gap. *The American Economic Review, 84*(2), 23–28. www.jstor.org/stable/2117795

Blau, F., Brummard, D., and Liu, A.Y.-H. (2013). Trends in occupational segregation by gender 1970-2009: Adjusting for the impact of changes in the occupational coding system. *Demography, 50*(2), 471–492. https://doi.org/10.1007/s13524-012-0151-7

Blinder, A.S., and Weiss, Y. (1976). Human capital and labor supply: A synthesis. *Journal of Political Economy, 84*(3), 449–472.

Bloch, F. (1994). *Antidiscrimination Law and Minority Employment.* University of Chicago Press.

Blöndal, S., and Scarpetta, S. (1999). *The Retirement Decision in OECD Countries. OECD Economics Department Working Papers, 98*(15). Paris, France: Organisation for Economic Co-operation and Development. https://www.oecd-ilibrary.org/economics/the-retirement-decision-in-oecd-countries_565174210530

Blossfeld, H., Buchholz, S., and Kurz, K. (2011). *Aging Populations, Globalization and the Labor Market: Comparing Late Working Life and Retirement in Modern Societies.* Edward Elgar Publishing.

Blundell, R., French, E., and Tetlow, G. (2016). Retirement incentives and labor supply. *Handbook of the Economics of Population Aging, 1*, 457–566. Elsevier.

Boehm, S.A., Kunze, F., and Bruch, H. (2014). Spotlight on age-diversity climate: The impact of age-inclusive HR practices on firm-level outcomes. *Personnel Psychology, 67*(3), 667–704.

Boeri, T., and van Ours, J. (2013). *The Economics of Imperfect Labor Markets* (2nd ed.). Princeton: Princeton University Press.

Boockmann, B., Fries, J., and Göbel, C. (2012). *Specific Measures for Older Employees and Late Career Employment*, IAW Discussion Papers No. 89, Institut für Angewandte Wirtschaftsforschung (IAW), Tübingen, Germany. https://econpapers.repec.org/paper/iawiawdip/89.htm

Borjas, G.J. (2003). The labor demand curve *is* downward sloping: Reexamining the impact of immigration on the labor market. *The Quarterly Journal of Economics, 118*(4), 1335–1374.

Borjas, G.J. (2006). Native internal migration and the labor market impact of immigration. *Journal of Human Resources, 41*(2), 221–258.

Borjas, G.J. (2016). Low-Skill Immigration. *The US Labor Market: Questions and Challenges for Public Policy.* Washington, DC: American Enterprise Institute.

Börsch-Supan, A. (2013). Myths, scientific evidence, and economic policy in an aging world. *The Journal of the Economics of Ageing, 1–2*, 3–15.

Börsch-Supan, A., and Coile, C.C., (Eds.). (2020). *Social Security Programs and Retirement Around the World: Reforms and Retirement Incentives.* University of Chicago Press.

Börsch-Supan, A., and Weiss, M. (2016). Productivity and age: Evidence from work teams at the assembly line. *Journal of the Economics of Ageing, 7*(C), 30–42. https://econpapers.repec.org/article/eeejoecag/v_3a7_3ay_3a2016_3ai_3ac_3ap_3a30-42.htm

Börsch-Supan, A., Bucher-Koenen, T., Kutlu-Koc, V., and Goll, N. (2018). Dangerous flexibility—retirement reforms reconsidered. *Economic Policy 33*(94), 315–355.

Börsch-Supan, A., Härtl, K., and Nuno Leite, D. (2017). *Earnings Test, Non-Actuarial Adjustments and Flexible Retirement*, MEA Discussion Paper No. 06-2017. Munich: Munich Center for the Economics of Ageing, Max Planck Institute for Social Law and Social Policy.

Börsch-Supan, A., Hunkler, C., and Weiss, M. (2021). Big data at work: Age and labor productivity in the service sector. *Journal of the Economics of Ageing, 19*(5), 100319.

Bosma, H., van Boxtel, M.P.J., Ponds, R.W.H.M., Houx, P.J.H., Jolles, J. (2003). Education and age-related cognitive decline: The contribution of mental workload. *Educational Gerontology, 29*(2), 165–173.

Bound, J. (1989). The health and earnings of rejected disability insurance applicants. *American Economic Review, 79*(3), 482–503.

Bound, J. (1991). Self-reported versus objective measures of health in retirement models. *Journal of Human Resources, 26*(1), 106–138.

Bound, J., Geronimus, A.T., Rodriguez, J., and Waidmann, T. (2014). *The Implications of Differential Trends in Mortality for Social Security Policy.* Michigan Retirement Research Center Research Paper No. 2014-314. Ann Arbor: University of Michigan.

Boyle, M.A., and Lahey, J.N. (2010). Health insurance and the labor supply decisions of older workers: Evidence from U.S. Department of Veterans Affairs Expansion. *Journal of Public Economics, 94*(7–8), 467–478.

Boyle, M.A., and Lahey, J.N. (2016). Spousal labor market effects from government health insurance: Evidence from a Veterans Affairs Expansion. *Journal of Health Economics, Elsevier, 45*(C), 63–76.

Bozio, A., Breda, T., and Grenet, J. (2019). *Does Tax-Benefit Linkage Matter for the Incidence of Social Security Contributions?* IZA Institute of Labor Economics Discussion Paper No. 12502, Bonn, Germany. https://docs.iza.org/dp12502.pdf

Brewer, M. B., Dull, V., and Lui, L. (1981). Perceptions of the elderly: Stereotypes as prototypes. *Journal of Personality and Social Psychology, 41*(4), 656–670. https://doi.org/10.1037/0022-3514.41.4.656

Briggs, X.S. (1998). Brown kids in White suburbs: Housing mobility and the many faces of social capital. *Housing Policy Debate, 9*(1), 177–221.

Brinch, C.N., Vestad, O.L., and Zweimüller, J. (2015). *Excess Early Retirement? Evidence from the Norwegian 2011 Pension Reform.* Working Paper. University of Zurich.

Broadbent, J., Palumbo, M., and Woodman, E. (2006). *The Shift from Defined Benefit to Defined Contribution Pension Plans—Implications for Asset Allocation and Risk Management.* Reserve Bank of Australia, Board of Governors of the Federal Reserve System and Bank of Canada, 1–54.

Bronshtein, G., Scott, J., Shoven, J.B., and Slavov, S.N. (2019). The power of working longer. *Journal of Pension Economics and Finance, 18*(4), 623–644.

Brown, E. (2009). Work, retirement, race, and health disparities. *Annual Review of Gerontology and Geriatrics, 29*(1), 233–249.

Brown, J.R., Coile, C.C., and Weisbenner, S.J. (2010). The effect of inheritance receipt on retirement. *The Review of Economics and Statistics, 92*(2), 425–434.

Brown, T.H. (2012). The intersection and accumulation of racial and gender inequality: Black women's wealth trajectories. *Review of Black Political Economy, 39*(2), 239–258. https://doi.org/10.1007/s12114-011-9100-8

Brown, T.H. (2016). Diverging fortunes: Racial/ethnic inequality in wealth trajectories in middle and late life. *Race and Social Problems, 8*(1), 29–41.

Brown, T.H., and Warner, D.F. (2008). Divergent pathways? Racial/ethnic differences in older women's labor force withdrawal. *Journals of Gerontology, Series B: Psychological Sciences and Social Sciences, 63*(3), S122–S134.

Brynjolfsson, E., and McAfee, A. (2014). *The Second Machine Age: Work, Progress, and Prosperity in a Time of Brilliant Technologies.* W.W. Norton and Company, Inc.

Brynjolfsson, E., and Mitchell, T. (2017). What can machine learning do? Workforce implications. *Science, 358*(6370), 1530–1534.

Brynjolfsson, E., Horton, J.J., Ozimek, A., Rock, D., Sharma, G, and TuYe, H.-Y. (2020). *COVID-19 and Remote Work: An Early Look at US Data.* NBER Working Paper No. 27344. htttps://doi.org/10.3386/w27344

Budiman, A., and Ruiz, N.G. (2021). *Key Facts About Asian Origin Groups in the U.S.* Pew Research Foundation, Washington: DC. https://www.pewresearch.org/fact-tank/2021/04/29/key-facts-about-asian-origin-groups-in-the-u-s

Buffie, N., and Baker, D. (2015). *Rising Disability Payments: Are Cuts to Workers' Compensation Part of the Story?* CEPR Reports and Issue Briefs No. 2015-21, Washington, DC: Center for Economic and Policy Research.

Bui, T.T.M., Button, P., and Picciotti, E.G. (2020). *Early Evidence on the Impact of COVID-19 and the Recession on Older Workers.* NBER Working Paper No. 27448, Cambridge, MA. https://www.nber.org/system/files/working_papers/w27448/w27448.pdf

Burkhauser, R.V., and Daly, M.C. (2002). U.S. disability policy in a changing environment. *Journal of Economic Perspectives, 16*(1), 213–224.

Burkhauser, R.V., and Daly, M.C. (2011). *The Declining Work and Welfare of People with Disabilities: What Went Wrong and a Strategy for Change.* Washington, DC: AEI Press. https://www.rand.org/content/dam/rand/www/external/labor/aging/rsi/rsi_papers/2011/Burkhauser1.pdf

Burkhauser, R.V., Houtenville, A.J., and Tennant, J.R. 2014. Capturing the elusive working-age population with disabilities: Reconciling conflicting social success estimates from the Current Population Survey and American Community Survey. *Journal of Disability Policy Studies, 24*(4), 195–205.

Burkley, E., Durante, F., Fiske, S.T., Burkley, M., and Andrade, A. (2017). Structure and content of Native American stereotypic subgroups: Not just (ig)noble. *Cultural Diversity and Ethnic Minority Psychology, 23*(2), 209–219.

Burn, I., Button, P., Figinski, T.F., and McLaughlin, J.S. (2020). Why retirement, Social Security, and age discrimination policies need to consider the intersectional experiences of older women. *Public Policy and Aging Report, 30*(3), 101–106.

Burr, J., and Mutchler, J. (2007). Employment in later life: A focus on race/ethnicity and gender. *Generations, 1*(8), 37–44.

Burstein, A., Morales, E., and Vogel, J. (2019). Changes in between-group inequality: Computers, occupations, and international trade. *American Economic Journal: Macroeconomics, 11*(2), 348–400.

Burtless, G. (2013). *Can Educational Attainment Explain the Rise in Labor Force Participation at Older Ages?* Issue Brief No. 13-13, Center for Retirement Research at Boston College, Chestnut Hill, MA.

Burtless, G., and Moffitt, R.A. (1986). Social Security, earnings tests, and age at retirement. *Public Finance Quarterly, 14*(1), 3–27.

Burton, J.F., and Spieler, E.A. (2001). Workers' compensation and older workers. *Ensuring Health and Income Security for an Aging Workforce*, 41–82. W.E. Upjohn Institute for Employment Research.

Butler, R.N. (2009). Combating ageism. *International Psychogeriatrics, 21*(2), 211. https://doi.org/10.1017/S104161020800731X

Butrica, B.A., and Johnson, R.W. (2010). *Racial, Ethnic, and Gender Differentials in Employer-Sponsored Pensions*. Statement to the ERISA Advisory Council, U.S. Department of Labor, Washington, DC. https://www.urban.org/research/publication/racial-ethnic-and-gender-differentials-employer-sponsored-pensions

Butrica, B.A., and Karamcheva, N.S. (2013). *Does Household Debt Influence the Labor Supply and Benefit Claiming Decisions of Older Americans?* Working Paper No. 2013-22, Center for Retirement Research at Boston College, Chestnut Hill, MA.

Butrica, B.A., and Karamcheva, N.S. (2018). In debt and approaching retirement: Claim Social Security or work longer. *AEA Papers and Proceedings, 108*, 401–406.

Butrica, B.A., and Karamcheva, N.S. (2019). *Is Rising Household Debt Affecting Retirement Decisions?* Wharton Pension Research Council, Working Paper No. 2019-14. University of Pennsylvania. https://ssrn.com/abstract=3540387

Button, P. (2018). Expanding employment discrimination protections for individuals with disabilities: Evidence from California. *Industrial and Labor Relations Review, 71*(2), 365–393.

Cahill, K.E., Giandrea, M.D., and Quinn, J.F. (2006). Retirement patterns from career employment. *The Gerontologist, 46*(4), 514–523.

Cahill, K.E., Giandrea, M.D., and Quinn, J.F. (2013). Bridge employment. *The Oxford Handbook of Retirement*, 293–310. Oxford University Press.

Cahill, K.E., Giandrea, M.D., and Quinn, J.F. (2015). Retirement patterns and the macroeconomy, 1992–2010: The prevalence and determinants of bridge jobs, phased retirement, and reentry among three recent cohorts of older Americans. *The Gerontologist, 55*(3), 384–403.

Cahill, K.E., Giandrea, M.D., and Quinn, J.F. (2016). Evolving patterns of work and retirement. *Handbook of Aging and the Social Sciences*, 271–291. Elsevier/Academic Press.

Cahill, K.E., Giandrea, M.D., and Quinn, J.F. (2018). Is bridge job activity overstated? *Work, Aging, and Retirement, 4*(4), 330–351.

Cahill, K.E., Giandrea, M.D., and Quinn, J.F. (2019). Retirement Patterns of the Early and Middle Baby Boomers. *U.S. Bureau of Labor Statistics Working Paper, 512*(April).

Cahill, K.E., James, J.B., and Pitt-Catsouphes, M. (2015). The impact of a randomly assigned time and place management initiative on employee retirement decisions. *Work, Aging, and Retirement, 1*(4), 350–368.

Calasanti, T., and King, N. (2015). Intersectionality and age. *Routledge Handbook of Cultural Gerontology*. Routledge.

Callahan, J.S., Kiker, D.S., and Cross, T. (2003). Does method matter? A meta-analysis of the effects of training method on older learner training performance. *Journal of Management, 29*(5), 663–680.

Calvo, E., Haverstick, K., and Sass, S.A. (2009). Gradual retirement, sense of control, and retirees' happiness. *Research on Aging, 31(1)*, 112–135.

Calvo, E., Madero-Cabib, I., and Staudinger, U.M. (2018). Retirement sequences of older Americans: Moderately destandardized and highly stratified across gender, class, and race. *The Gerontologist, 58*(6), 1166–1176. https://doi.org/10.1093/geront/gnx052

Calvo, E., Sarkisian, N., and Tamborini, C.R. (2013). Causal effects of retirement timing on subjective physical and emotional health. *Journals of Gerontology, Series B: Psychological Sciences and Social Sciences, 68*(1), 73–84

Calvo-Armengol, A., and Jackson, M.O. (2004). The effects of social networks on employment and inequality. *American Economic Review, 94*(3), 426–454.

Caplan, R.D. (1987). Person-environment fit theory: Commensurate dimensions, time perspectives, and mechanisms. *Journal of Vocational Behavior, 31*(3), 248–267.

Carbó, S., Gardener, E.P.M., and Molyneux, P. (2005). *Financial Exclusion*. Palgrave Macmillan.

Card, D., and Lemieux, T. (2001). Can falling supply explain the rising return to college for younger men? A cohort-based analysis *Quarterly Journal of Economics, 116*(2), 705–746.

Card, D.C., Maestas, N., and Purcell, P. (2014). *Labor Market Shocks and Early Social Security Benefit Claiming*. Michigan Retirement Research Center Working Paper Series No. UM11-14. Institute for Social Research, University of Michigan, Ann Arbor.

Carmichael, L. (1983). Firm-specific human capital and promotion ladders. *The Bell Journal of Economics, 14*(1), 251–258.

Carolan, K., Gonzales, E., Lee, K., and Harootyan, R.A. (2020). Institutional and individual factors affecting health and employment among low-income women with chronic health conditions. *The Journals of Gerontology: Social Sciences 75*(5), 1062–1071. https://academic.oup.com/psychsocgerontology/article/75/5/1062/5253675

Carr, D.C. (2020). Families in later life: A consequence and engine of social inequalities. *Annual Review of Gerontology and Geriatrics, 40*, 43–68.

Carr, D.C., and Kail, B.L. (2013). The influence of unpaid work on the transition out of full-time paid work. *The Gerontologist, 53*(1), 92–101.

Carr, D.C., Matz, C., Taylor, M., and Gonzalez, E. (2021). Retirement transitions in the US: Patterns and pathways from full-time work. *Public Policy and Aging Research, 31*(3), 71–77. https://doi.org/10.1093/ppar/prab013

Carr, D.C., Willis, R., Kail, B.L., and Carstensen, L.L. (2020). Alternative retirement paths and cognitive performance: Exploring the role of preretirement job complexity. *The Gerontologist, 60*(3), 460–471. https://doi.org/10.1093/geront/gnz079

Carr, E., Hagger-Johnson, G., Head, J., Shelton, N., Stafford, M., Stansfeld, S., and Zaninotto, P. (2016). Working conditions as predictors of retirement intentions and exit from paid employment: A 10-year follow-up of the English Longitudinal Study of Ageing. *European Journal of Ageing, 13*(1), 39–48. https://doi.org/10.1007/s10433-015-0357-9

Carr, S., and Tienda, M. (2013). Family sponsorship and late-age immigration in aging America: Revised and expanded estimates of chained migration. *Population Research and Policy Review, 32*(6), 825–849.

Carstensen, L.L. (1991). Selectivity theory: Social activity in life-span context. *Annual Review of Gerontology and Geriatrics, 11*, 195–217.

Carstensen, L.L. (1995). Evidence for a life-span theory of socioemotional selectivity. *Current Directions in Psychological Science, 4*, 151–156.

Carstensen, L.L. (2011). *A Long Bright Future: Happiness, Health and Financial Security in an Age of Increased Longevity.* Public Affairs.

Carstensen, L.L., Isaacowitz, D.M., and Charles, S.T. (1999). Taking time seriously: A theory of socioemotional selectivity. *American Psychologist, 54*(3), 165–181.

Casanova, M. (2010). *Happy Together: A Structural Model of Couples' Joint Retirement Choices.* Working Paper, Department of Economics, UCLA. http://www.econ.ucla.edu/casanova/Files/Casanova_joint_ret.pdf

Case, A., and Deaton, A.S. (2005). Broken Down by Work and Sex: How our Health Declines. *Analyses in the Economics of Aging*, 185–212. National Bureau of Economic Research, Inc., Cambridge, MA. https://ideas.repec.org/h/nbr/nberch/10361.html

Case, A., and Deaton, A.S. (2017). Mortality and morbidity in the 21st century. *Brookings Papers on Economic Activity, 48*(1), 397–476.

Catalfamo, H. (2018). An analysis of a government-sponsored retraining program: Implications to educational planning. *Educational Planning, 25*(2), 55–72.

Causey, C.L., and Lahey, J.N. (2013). Employment law and retirement. *The Oxford Handbook of Retirement*, 388–401. Oxford University Press.

Center for Retirement Initiatives. (2020). *State Initiatives 2020: New Programs Begin Implementation While Others Consider Action.* Georgetown University, McCourt School of Public Policy, Washington, DC.

Center on Budget and Policy Priorities. (2019). *Chart Book: Social Security Disability Insurance.* Washington, DC.

Center on Budget and Policy Priorities. (2020). *Policy Basics: Supplemental Security Income.* Washington, DC. https://www.cbpp.org/research/social-security/policy-basics-supplemental-security-income

Centers for Medicare and Medicaid Services. (2020). *Market Rating Reforms.* Baltimore: MD. https://www.cms.gov/CCIIO/Programs-and-Initiatives/Health-Insurance-Market-Reforms/Market-Rating-Reforms

Chan, S., and Stevens, A.H. (1999). Employment and retirement following a late-career job loss. *American Economic Review, 89*(2), 211–216.

Chan, S., and Stevens, A.H. (2001). Job loss and employment patterns of older workers. *Journal of Labor Economics, 19*(2), 484–521.

Chang, C., Shao, R., Wang, M., and Baker, N. (2021). Workplace interventions in response to COVID-19: An occupational health psychology perspective. *Occupational Health Science, 5*(5), 1–23.

Chang, E.-S., Kannoth, S., Levy, S., Wang, S.-Y., Lee, J.E., and Levy, B.R. (2020). Global reach of ageism on older persons' health: A systematic review. *PLoS ONE 15*(1), e0220857. https://www.ncbi.nlm.nih.gov/pmc/articles/PMC6961830

Charles, K.K., Li, Y., and Stephens, Jr., M. (2018). Disability benefit take-up and local labor market conditions. *Review of Economics and Statistics, 100*(3), 416–423.

Charles, S.T. (2010). Strength and vulnerability integration (SAVI), A model of emotional well-being across adulthood. *Psychological Bulletin, 136*(6), 1068–1091.

Charlesworth, T.E.S., and Banaji, M.R. (2019). Patterns of implicit and explicit attitudes: I. long-term change and stability from 2007 to 2016. *Psychological Science, 30*(2), 174–192.

Charness, N., and Czaja, S.J. (2006). *Older Worker Training: What We Know and Don't Know*. AARP Public Policy Institute Report No. 2006-22, Washington, DC.

Charness, N., Kelley, C.L., Bosman, E.A., and Mottram, M. (2001). Word-processing training and retraining: Effects of adult age, experience, and interface. *Psychology and Aging, 16*(1), 110–127.

Chen, S., and van der Klaauw, W. (2008). The work disincentive effects of the disability insurance program in the 1990s. *Journal of Econometrics, 142*(2), 757–784. https://econpapers.repec.org/article/eeeeconom/v_3a142_3ay_3a2008_3ai_3a2_3ap_3a757-784.htm

Chetty, R., Friedman, J.N., Leth-Petersen, S., Nielsen, T.H., and Olsen, T. (2014). Active vs. passive decisions and crowd-out in retirement savings accounts: Evidence from Denmark. *The Quarterly Journal of Economics, 129*(3), 1141–1219.

Chetty, R., Stepner, M., Abraham, S., Lin, S., Scuderi, B., Turner, N., Bergeron, A., and Cutler, D. (2016). The association between income and life expectancy in the United States, 2001–2014. *Journal of the American Medical Association, 315*(16), 1750–1766. https//:doi.org/10.1001/jama.2016.4226

Choi, N.G. (2000). Determinants of engagement in paid work following Social Security benefit receipt among older women. *Journal of Women & Aging, 12*(3/4), 133–154.

Choi, N.G., Burr, J.A., Mutchler, J.E., and Caro, F.G. (2007). Formal and informal volunteer activity and spousal caregiving among older adults. *Research on Aging, 29*(2), 99–124.

Choi, E., Tang, F., and Copeland, V.C. (2016). Racial/ethnic inequality among older workers: Focusing on Whites, Blacks, and Latinos within the cumulative advantage/disadvantage framework. *Journal of Social Service Research, 43*(1), 18–36. https://doi.org/10.1080/01488376.2016.1235068

Cihlar, V., Mergenthaler, A., and Micheel, F. (2014). Erwerbsarbeit & informelle Tätigkeiten der 55- bis 70-Jährigen in Deutschland. Wiesbaden.

Choukhmane, T. (2019). *Default Options and Retirement Savings Dynamics*. Yale University, Mimeo. https://tahachoukhmane.com/wp-content/uploads/2019/01/Choukhmane_JMP.pdf

Clancy, R.L., Fisher, G.G., Daigle, K., Henle, C.A., McCarthy, J., and Fruhauf, C.A. (2020). Eldercare and work among informal caregivers: A multidisciplinary review and recommendations for future research. *Journal of Business and Psychology, 35*, 9–27. https//:doi.org/10.1007/s10869-018-9612-3

Clark, A. (2015). What makes a good job? Job quality and job satisfaction. *IZA World of Labor, 215*. https://econpapers.repec.org/article/izaizawol/journl_3ay_3a2015_3an_3a215.htm

Clark, R., Davis, H., Lusardi, A., and Mitchel, S. (2021). *Financial Well-being Among Black and Hispanic Women*. TIAA Institute. https://www.tiaainstitute.org/publication/financial-well-being-among-black-and-hispanic-women

Classen, T., and Dunn, R. (2011). The effect of job loss and unemployment duration on suicide risk in the United States: A new look using mass-layoffs and unemployment duration. *Health Economics, 21*(3), 338–350. https://onlinelibrary.wiley.com/doi/abs/10.1002/hec.1719

Clausell, E., and Fiske, S.T. (2005). When do the parts add up to the whole? Ambivalent stereotype content for gay male subgroups. *Social Cognition, 23*, 157–176.

Cleveland, J.N., and Lim, A.S. (2007). Employee age and performance in organizations. *Aging and Work in the 21st Century*, 109–138. Psychology Press.

Cleveland, J.N., and Maneotis, S.M. (2013). Recruitment and retention strategies for mature workers. *The Oxford Handbook of Retirement*, 431–448. Oxford University Press.

Coate, P. (2019). *Changing Workforce Demographics and Workplace Injury Frequency*. National Council on Compensation Insurance, Inc. Report, Boca Raton, FL. https://www.ncci.com/Articles/Documents/Insights-WorkforceDemographics.pdf

Coe, N.B., von Gaudecker, H.M., Lindeboom, M., and Maurer, J. (2012). The effect of retirement on cognitive functioning. *Health Economics, 21*(8), 913–927.

Coe, N.B., Hou, W., Munnell, A.H., Purcell, P.J., and Rutledge, M.S. (2016). *The Impact of Massachusetts Health Insurance Reform on Labor Mobility*. Working Paper No. 16, Center for Retirement Research at Boston College, Chestnut Hill, MA. https://crr.bc.edu/working-papers/the-impact-of-massachusetts-health-insurance-reform-on-labor-mobility

Cohen, J.D. (2006). The aging nurse workforce: How to retain experienced nurses. *Journal of Healthcare Management, 51*(4), 233–245.

Coibion, O., Gorodnichenko, Y., and Weber, M. (2020). *Labor Markets During the COVID-19 Crisis: A Preliminary View*. Working Paper No. 2020-41, Becker Friedman Institute for Economics at the University of Chicago, Chicago, IL. https://bfi.uchicago.edu/wp-content/uploads/BFI_WP_202041.pdf

Coile, C.C. (2004). Retirement incentives and couples' retirement decisions. *The B.E. Journal of Economic Analysis & Policy, 4*(1), 1–30.

Coile, C.C. (2015). Economic determinants of workers' retirement decisions. *Journal of Economic Surveys, 29*(4), 830–853.

Coile, C.C. (2016). Disability insurance incentives and the retirement decision: Evidence from the United States. *Social Security Programs and Retirement around the World: Disability Insurance Programs and Retirement*, 1–44. University of Chicago Press.

Coile, C.C. (2019). Working longer in the United States: Trends and explanations. *Social Security Programs and Retirement around the World: Working Longer*, 299–324. University of Chicago Press.

Coile, C.C. (2020). The evolution of retirement incentives in the US. *Social Security Programs and Retirement around the World: Reforms and Retirement Incentives*, 435–459. University of Chicago Press.

Coile, C.C., and Duggan, M.G. (2019). When labor's lost: Health, family life, incarceration, and education in a time of declining economic opportunity for low-skilled men. *Journal of Economic Perspectives, 33*(2), 191–210.

Coile, C.C., and Gruber, J. (2007). Future Social Security entitlements and the retirement decision. *Review of Economics and Statistics, 89*(2), 234–246.

Coile, C.C., and Levine, P.B. (2007). Labor market shocks and retirement: Do government programs matter? *Journal of Public Economics, 91*(10), 1902–1919.

Coile, C.C., and Levine, P.B. (2011). Recessions, retirement, and Social Security. *American Economic Review, 101*(3), 23–28.

Coile, C.C., Levine, P.B., and McKnight, R. (2014). Recessions, older workers, and longevity: How long are recessions good for your health? *American Economic Journal: Economic Policy, 6*(3), 92–119.

Coile, C.C., Milligan, K., and Wise, D.A. (2017). Health capacity to work at older ages: Evidence from the United States. *Social Security Programs and Retirement around the World*, 359–394. University of Chicago Press. https://doi.org/10.7208/9780226442907-01

Coile, C.C., Milligan, K., and Wise, D.A. (2019). *Social Security and Retirement around the World: Working Longer*. University of Chicago Press.

Coile, C.C., Wise, D.A., Börsch-Supan, A., Gruber, J., Milligan, K., Woodbury, R., Baker, M., Banks, J., Behaghel, L., Bingley, P., et al. (2022). Social Security and Retirement Around the World: Lessons from a Long-Term Collaboration. NETSPAR Working Paper. https://documentos.fedea.net/pubs/dt/2022/dt2022-02.pdf

Coleman, J.S. (1988). Social capital in the creation of human capital. *The American Journal of Sociology, 94*(Supplement), S95–S120.

Collins, B. (2019). *Older Americans Act: Senior Community Service Employment Program*. Washington, DC: Congressional Research Service.

Collins, P.H., and Bilge, S. (2015). *Intersectionality*. Policy Press.

Collins, P.H., and Bilge, S. (2020). *Intersectionality* (2nd Ed.). Policy Press.

Collinson, C. (2017). *All About Retirement: An Employer Survey*. Los Angeles, CA: The Transamerica Center for Research Studies. https://www.transamericacenter.org/docs/default-source/employer-research/tcrs2017_sr_employer_research.pdf

Conen, W., Henkens, K., and Schippers, J. (2014). Ageing organisations and the extension of working lives: A case study approach. *Journal of Social Policy, 43*(4), 773–792.

Congressional Research Service. (2018). *Trends in Social Security Disability Insurance Enrollment*. CRS Report No. R45419, Washington, DC.

Congressional Research Service. (2019a). *Household Debt Among Older Americans, 1989–2016*. Congressional Research Service, Washington: DC. https://sgp.fas.org/crs/misc/R45911.pdf

Congressional Research Service. (2019b). Paid Family and Medical Leave in the United States. Congressional Research Service. https://sgp.fas.org/crs/misc/R44835.pdf

Congressional Research Service. (2021). *Unemployment Rates During the COVID-19 Pandemic*. CRS Report Prepared for Members and Committees of Congress, Washington, DC. https://fas.org/sgp/crs/misc/R46554.pdf

Copeland, C. (2018). Debt of the elderly and near elderly, 1992–2016. *Employee Benefit Research Report Issue Brief, 443*. https://www.ebri.org/docs/default-source/ebri-issue-brief/ebri_ib_443_debt-5mar18.pdf?sfvrsn=3a35342f_2

Copeland, C. (2020). *Retirement Confidence Survey: Attitudes Toward Retirement by Women of Different Marital Statuses*. Issue Brief No. 507, Employee Benefit Research Institute, Washington, DC.

Cortina, L.M. (2008). Unseen injustice: Incivility as modern discrimination in organizations. *The Academy of Management Review, 33*(1), 55–75.

Cortina, L.M., Magley, V.J., Williams, J.H., and Langhout, R.D. (2001). Incivility in the workplace: Incidence and impact. *Journal of Occupational Health Psychology, 6*(1), 64–80. https://doi.org/10.1037/1076-8998.6.1.64

Costa, D. (1998). *The Evolution of Retirement: An American Economic History 1880–1990*. University of Chicago Press.

Costello, M. (2019). *Special Retirement Coverage for Law Enforcement Officers and Firefighters*. Department of Defense: Defense Civilian Personnel Advisory Service. https://www.dcpas.osd.mil/Content/documents/Events/DBS/WBW04_SpecialRetirementWorkshopR.pdf

Couch, K.A. (1998). Late life job displacement. *The Gerontologist, 38*(1), 7–17.

Coughlin, J. (2020). *Technology in the Workplace*. Public Session for the Committee on Understanding Aging in the Workforce and Employment at Older Ages at the National Academies of Sciences, Engineering, and Medicine, Washington, DC.

Couillard, B.K., Foote, C.L., Gandhi, K., Meara, E., and Skinner, J. (2021). Rising geographic disparities in U.S. mortality. *Journal of Economic Perspectives, 35*(4), 123–146.

Crenshaw, K. (1991). Mapping the margins: Intersectionality, identity politics, and violence against women of color. *Stanford Law Review, 43*(6), 1241–1299.

Cribb, J., and Emmerson, C. (2019). *Requiring Auto-enrollment: Lessons from UK Retirement Plans*. Issue Brief No. 19-6, Center for Retirement Research at Boston College, Chestnut Hill, MA.

Crystal, S., Shea, D.G., and Reyes, A.M. (2017). Cumulative advantage, cumulative disadvantage, and evolving patterns of late-life inequality. *The Gerontologist, 57*(5), 910–920. https://doi.org/10.1093/geront/gnw056

Cubanski, J., Swoope, C., Boccuti, C., Jacobson, G., Casillas, G., Griffin, S., and Neuman, T. (2015). *A Primer on Medicare: Key Facts About the Medicare Program and the People it Covers*. Kaiser Family Foundation, San Francisco: CA. https://www.kff.org/report-section/a-primer-on-medicare-what-is-medicare

Cuddy, A.J.C., Fiske, S.T., and Glick, P. (2007). The BIAS map: Behaviors from intergroup affect and stereotypes. *Journal of Personality and Social Psychology, 92*(4), 631–648.

Cuddy, A.J.C., Norton, M.I., and Fiske, S.T. (2005). This old stereotype: The pervasiveness and persistence of the elderly stereotype. *Journal of Social Issues, 61*(2), 267–285.

Cummins, P.A. (2015). The role of community colleges in career transitions for older workers. *Community College Journal of Research and Practice, 39*(3), 265–279.

Currie, J., and Madrian, B.C. (1999). Health insurance and the labour market. *Handbook of Labor Economics, 3*(C), 3309–3416. Elsevier. https://econpapers.repec.org/bookchap/eeelabchp/3-50.htm

Currie, J., Jin, J., and Schnell, M. (2019). *U.S. Employment and Opioids: Is There a Connection?* NBER Working Paper No. 24440. National Bureau of Economic Research, Cambridge, MA. https://www.nber.org/system/files/working_papers/w24440/w24440.pdf

Cushing-Daniels, B., and Johnson R.W. (2008). *Employer-Sponsored Pensions: A Primer*. The Retirement Policy Project, Urban Institute's Income and Benefits Policy Center, Washington, DC.

Cutler, D., Ghosh, K., and Landrum, M.B. (2013). Evidence for significant compression of morbidity in the elderly U.S. population. *National Bureau of Economic Research Working Papers*, 19268. Cambridge, MA.

Cutler, D.M., and Lleras-Muney, A. (2008). Education and health: Evaluating theories and evidence. *Making Americans Healthier: Social and Economic Policy as Health Policy*, 29–60. Russell Sage Foundation.

Cutler, D.M., Meara, E., and Richards-Shubik, S. (2012). *Unemployment and Disability: Evidence from the Great Recession*. National Bureau of Economic Research, Retirement Research Center, Working Paper No. NB12-12. https://www.nber.org/sites/default/files/2020-08/orrc12-12.executive_summary.pdf

Dahl, G.B., and Knepper, M.M. (2020). *Age Discrimination Across the Business Cycle*. NBER Working Paper No. 27581, National Bureau of Economic Research, Cambridge, MA. https://www.nber.org/system/files/working_papers/w27581/w27581.pdf

Daly, M., and Burkhauser, R.V. (2003). The Supplemental Security Income Program. In R.A. Moffitt (Ed.), *Means-Tested Transfer Programs in the United States* 4, 79–140. National Bureau of Economic Research, Cambridge, MA. https://www.nber.org/books-and-chapters/means-tested-transfer-programs-united-states/supplemental-security-income-program

Dannefer, D. (2020). Systemic and reflexive: Foundations of cumulative dis/advantage and life-course process. *Journals of Gerontology, Series B: Psychological Sciences and Social Sciences, 75*(6), 1249–1263.

Dauth, C., and Toomet, O. (2016). On government-subsidized training programs for older workers. *Labour, 30*(4), 371–392.

Daveri, F., and Maliranta, M. (2007). Age, seniority, and labour costs: Lessons from the Finnish IT Revolution. *Economic Policy, 22*(49), 117–175.

Davies, E., and Cartwright, S. (2011). Psychological and psychosocial predictors of attitudes to working past normal retirement age. *Employee Relations, 33*(3), 249–268.

Davis, D.R., and Dingell, J.I. (2019). A spatial knowledge economy. *American Economic Review, 109*(1), 153–170.

Davis, S.J., and von Wachter, T. (2011). *Recessions and the Costs of Job Loss*. Brookings Papers on Economic Activity. The Brookings Institution, Washington, DC. https://www.brookings.edu/bpea-articles/recessions-and-the-costs-of-job-loss

Dean, D., Pepper, J.V., Schmidt, R.M., and Stern, S. (2014). State vocational rehabilitation programs and federal disability insurance: An analysis of Virginia's vocational rehabilitation program. *IZA Journal of Labor Policy, 3*(7). https://link.springer.com/article/10.1186%2F2193-9004-3-7

Deaton, A.S., and Paxson, C. (2001). Mortality, education, income, and inequality among American cohorts. *Themes in the Economics of Aging*, 129–170. University of Chicago Press. http://www.nber.org/chapters/c10324

Delaney, N., and Lahey, J.N. (2019). The ADEA at the intersection of age and race. *Berkeley Journal of Employment and Labor Law, 40*(1), 61–90.

DeLeire, T. (2000). The wage and employment effects of the Americans with Disabilities Act. *Journal of Human Resources, 35*(4), 693–715.

DeLeire, T. (2003). The Americans with Disabilities Act and the employment of people with disabilities. *The Decline in Employment of People with Disabilities: A Policy Puzzle*, 259–278. Kalamazoo, MI.

Delgado, R., and Stefancic, J. (2000). *Critical Race Theory: The Cutting Edge* (3rd ed.). Temple University Press.

Dentinger, E., and Clarkberg. M. (2002). Informal caregiving and retirement timing among men and women: Gender and caregiving relationships in late midlife. *Journal of Family Issues, 23*(7), 857–879.

Denton, F.T., and Spencer, B.G. (2009). What is retirement? A review and assessment of alternative concepts and measures. *Canadian Journal on Aging/La revue Canadienne du Vieillissement, 28*(1), 63–76.

Deutsch, F.M., Zalenski, C.M., and Clark, M.E. (1986). Is there a double standard of aging? *Journal of Applied Social Psychology, 16*(9), 771–785.

Dey, M., Frazis, H., Loewenstein, M.A., and Sun, H. (2020). Ability to work from home: Evidence from two surveys and implications for the labor market in the COVID-19 pandemic. *Monthly Labor Review*. 1–19.

Dik, B.J., Byrne, Z.S., and Steger, M.F. (2013). *Purpose and Meaning in the Workplace*. American Psychological Association.

DiPrete, T.A., and Eirich, G.M. (2006). Cumulative advantage as a mechanism for inequality: A review of theoretical and empirical developments. *Annual Review of Sociology, 32*, 271–297.

Disney, R., Ratcliffe, A., and Smith, S. (2015). Booms, busts, and retirement timing. *Economica, 82*(327), 399–419.

Dobbin, F., and Sutton, J.R. (1998) The strength of a weak state: The rights revolution and the rise of human resources management divisions. *American Journal of Sociology, 104*(2), 441–476.

Doshi, J.A., Cen, L., and Polsky, D. (2008). Depression and retirement in late middle-aged U.S. workers. *Health Services Research, 43*(2), 693–713.

Domingue, B.W., Fletcher, J., Conley, D., and Boardman, J.D. (2014). Genetic and educational assortative mating among U.S. adults. *Proceedings of the National Academy of Sciences, 111*(22), 7996–8000. https://www.pnas.org/content/pnas/111/22/7996.full.pdf

Dominguez, S., and Watkins, C. (2003). Creating networks for survival and mobility: Social capital among African-American and Latin-American low-income mothers. *Social Problems, 50*(1), 111–135.

Dorsey, S., Cornwell, C., and Macpherson, D. (1998). *Pensions and Productivity*. Upjohn Institute for Employment Research.

Drydakis, N., MacDonald, P., Chiotis, V., and Somers, L. (2018). Age discrimination in the UK labour market. Does race moderate ageism? An experimental investigation. *Applied Economic Letters, 25*(1), 1–4.

Dubay, L., Aarons, J., Brown, K.S., and Kenney, G.M. (2020). *How Risk of Exposure to the Coronavirus at Work Varies by Race and Ethnicity and How to Protect the Health and Well-Being of Workers and Their Families*. Urban Institute Research Reports. https://www.urban.org/sites/default/files/publication/103278/how-risk-of-exposure-to-the-coronavirus-at-work-varies_1.pdf

Duflo, E., and Saez, E. (2004). *Implications of Pension Plan Features, Information, and Social Interactions for Retirement Saving Decisions*. Wharton Pension Research Council Working Paper No. 429, University of Pennsylvania. https://repository.upenn.edu/cgi/viewcontent.cgi?article=1430&context=prc_papers

Duflo, E., Gale, W., Liebman, J., Orszag, P., and Saez, E. (2006). Saving incentives for low-and middle-income families: Evidence from a field experiment with H&R Block. *The Quarterly Journal of Economics, 121*(4), 1311–1346.

Duggan, M., Singleton, P., and Song, J. (2007). Aching to retire? The rise in the full retirement age and its impact on the Social Security disability rolls. *Journal of Public Economics, 91*(7–8), 1327–1350.

Duggan, M., Dushi, I., Jeong, S., and Li, G. (2021). *The Effects of Changes in Social Security's Delayed Retirement Credit: Evidence from Administrative Data*. NBER Retirement and Disability Research Center Paper No. NB19-12. https://www.nber.org/programs-projects/projects-and-centers/retirement-and-disability-research-center/center-papers/nb19-12

Dwertmann, D.J.G., Nishii, L.H., and van Knippenberg, D. (2016). Disentangling the fairness and discrimination and synergy perspectives on diversity climate: Moving the field forward. *Journal of Management, 42*(5), 1136–1168.

Dychtwald, K., Erickson, T.J. and Morison, R. (2013). *Workforce crisis: How to beat the coming shortage of skills and talent*. Harvard Business Press.

Eagly, A.H., and Kite, M.E. (1987). Are stereotypes of nationalities applied to both women and men? *Journal of Personality and Social Psychology, 53*(3), 451–462. https://psycnet.apa.org/doiLanding?doi=10.1037%2F0022-3514.53.3.451

Eagly, A.H., Wood, W., and Diekman, A.B. (2000). Social role theory of sex differences and similarities: A current appraisal. *The Developmental Social Psychology of Gender*, 123–174. Erlbaum.

Easterlin, R.A. (1980). *Birth and Fortune: The Impact of Numbers on Personal Welfare*. Basic Books.

Eaton, S.C. (2003). If you can use them: Flexibility policies, organizational commitment, and perceived performance. *Industrial Relations*, 42(2), 145–167.

Ebbinghaus, B. (2006). *Reforming Early Retirement in Europe, Japan, and the USA*. Oxford University Press. http://dx.doi.org/10.1093/0199286116.001.0001

Ebbinghaus, B., and Hofäcker, D. (2013). Reversing early retirement in advanced welfare economies: A paradigm shift to overcome push and pull factors. *Comparative Population Studies*, 38(4), 807–840.

Ebbinghaus, B., and Radl, J. (2015). Pushed out prematurely? Comparing objectively forced exits and subjective assessments of involuntary retirement across Europe. *Research in Social Stratification and Mobility*, 41, 115–130.

Ebeling, A. (2014). *Employees Are Falling for Roth 401(k)s*. Forbes article, Jersey City, NJ. https://www.forbes.com/sites/ashleaebeling/2014/08/19/employees-are-falling-for-roth-401ks

Ebenstein, A., Harrison, A.E., McMillan, M.S., and Phillips, S. (2014). Estimating the impact of trade and offshoring on American workers using the Current Population Surveys. *Review of Economics and Statistics*, 96(4), 581–595.

Eckes, T. (2002). Paternalistic and envious gender stereotypes: Testing predictions from the stereotype content model. *Sex Roles*, 47(3–4), 99–114.

Eddleston, K.A., Veiga, J.F., and Powell, G.N. (2006). Explaining sex differences in managerial career satisfier preferences: The role of gender self-schema. *Journal of Applied Psychology*, 91(2), 437–445.

Eismann, M., Henkens, K., and Kalmijn, M. (2019). Why singles prefer to retire later. *Research on Aging*, 4(10), 936–960. https://doi.org/10.1177/0164027519873537

Ekerdt, D.J., and DeViney, S. (1990). On defining persons as retired. *Journal of Aging Studies*, 4(3), 211–229.

Eliason, M., and Storrie, D. (2009). Does job loss shorten life? *Journal of Human Resources*, 44(2), 277–302.

Elder, Jr., G.H. (1985). *Life Course Dynamics: Trajectories and Transitions, 1968–1980*. Cornell University Press.

Elder, Jr., G.H. (1995). The life course paradigm: Social change and individual development. *Examining Lives in Contexts: Perspectives on the Ecology of Human Development*, 101–139. American Psychological Association.

Elder, Jr., G.H., and George, L.K. (2015). Age, cohorts, and the life course. *Handbooks of Sociology and Social Research*, 59–85. Springer.

Elder, Jr., G.H., and George, L.K. (2016). Age, cohorts, and the life course. *Handbook of the Life Course 2*, 55–89. Springer.

Elder, Jr., G.H., and Johnson, M.K. (2003). The life course and aging: Challenges, lessons, and new directions. *Invitation to the Life Course: Toward New Understandings of Later Life*, 49–81. Baywood Publishing Company.

Employee Benefit Research Institute. (2018). *Fast Facts. History of 401(k) Plans: An Update*. EBRI Report No. 318, Washington, DC. https://www.ebri.org/docs/default-source/fast-facts/ff-318-k-40year-5nov18.pdf?sfvrsn=1b773e2f_6

Engen, E.M., Gale, W.G., and Scholz, J.K. (1996). The illusory effects of saving incentives on saving. *Journal of Economic Perspectives*, 10(4), 113–138.

England, P., and McClintock, E.A. (2009). The gendered double standard of aging in U.S. marriage markets. *Population and Development Review*, 35(4), 797–816.

Eppler-Hattab, R., Meshoulam, I., and Doron, I. (2020). Conceptualizing age-friendliness in workplaces: Proposing a new multidimensional model. *Gerontologist*, 60(1), 12–21.

European Parliament. (2013). *Resolution of an Agenda for Adequate, Safe, and Sustainable Pensions*. Strasbourg, France. https://www.europarl.europa.eu/doceo/document/TA-7-2013-0204_EN.html

Evers, M., de Mooij, R., and van Vuuren, D. (2008). The wage elasticity of labor supply: A synthesis of empirical estimates. *De Economist*, 156(1), 25–43.

Fabius, C.B., Wolff, J.L., and Kasper, J.D. (2020). Race differences in characteristics and experiences of Black and White caregivers of older Americans. *Gerontologist*, 60(7), 1244–1253. http//:doi.org/10.1093/geront/gnaa042

Fadlon, I., and Deshpande, M. (2020). *Social Security Claiming and Retirement Responses to FRA Changes*. NBER Retirement and Disability Research Working Paper No. NB19-11. Cambridge, MA: National Bureau of Economic Research.

Fadlon, I., and Nielsen, T.H. (2017). *Family Labor Supply Responses to Severe Health Shocks*. NBER Working Paper Series No. #21352. Cambridge, MA: National Bureau of Economic Research.

Fahle, S., and McGarry, K. (2018). Women working longer: Labor market implications of providing family care. *Women Working Longer: Increased Employment at Older Ages*, 157–181. NBER, Cambridge: MA. University of Chicago Press. https://www.nber.org/books-and-chapters/women-working-longer-increased-employment-older-ages/women-working-longer-labor-market-implications-providing-family-care

Fair, R.C. (1994). How fast do old men slow down? *Review of Economics and Statistics*, 76(1), 103–118.

Fan, W., Moen, P., Kelly, E.L., Hammer, L.B., and Berkman, L.F. (2019). Job strain, time strain, and well-being: A longitudinal person-centered approach in two industries. *Journal of Vocational Behavior, 110*(Part A), 102–116.

Fan, W., Lam, J., Moen, P., Kelly, E.L., King, R., and McHale, S. (2015). Constrained choices? Linking employees' and spouses' work time to health behaviors. *Social Science & Medicine, 126*, 99–109.

Farber, H.S. (2004). Job loss in the United States, 1981-2001. *Research in Labor Economics, 23*(2004), 69–117.

Farber, H.S. (2015). *Job Loss in the Great Recession and its Aftermath: US Evidence from the Displaced Workers Survey*. Working Paper No. 21216, National Bureau of Economic Research.

Farber, H.S., Silverman, D., and von Wachter, T. (2016). Determinants of callbacks to job applications: An audit study. *American Economic Review, 106*(5), 314–318.

Farber, H.S., Silverman, D., and von Wachter, T. (2017). Factors determining callbacks to job applications by the unemployed. *RSF: The Russell Sage Foundation Journal of the Social Sciences, 3*(3), 168–201.

Farber, H.S., Herbst, C.M., Silverman, D., and von Wachter, T. (2019). Whom do employers want? The role of recent employment and unemployment status and age. *Journal of Labor Economics, 37*(2), 323–349.

Farmer, M.M., and Ferraro, K.F. (2005). Are racial disparities in health conditional on socioeconomic status? *Social Science & Medicine, 60*(1), 191–204.

Fasang, A.E. (2010). Retirement: Institutional pathways and individual trajectories in Britain and Germany. *Sociological Research Online, 15*(2), 1–17.

Fast, J., Keating, N., Eales, J., Kim, C., and Lee, Y. (2020). Trajectories of family care over the lifecourse: Evidence from Canada. *Ageing & Society, 41*(5), 1145–1162. https://www.cambridge.org/core/journals/ageing-and-society/article/trajectories-of-family-care-over-the-lifecourse-evidence-from-canada/55DD2050516D929AE809362A086640EE

Favreault, M.M., Mermin, G.B.T., and Steuerle, C.E. (2006). *Minimum Benefits in Social Security*. Report of The Urban Institute, Washington: DC. https://www.urban.org/sites/default/files/publication/46341/411406-Minimum-Benefits-in-Social-Security.PDF

Federal Aviation Administration. (2019). *Fair Treatment of Experienced Pilots Act (The Age 65 Law) Questions and Answers*. https://www.congress.gov/110/plaws/publ135/PLAW-110publ135.pdf

Federal Deposit Insurance Corporation. (2016). *2015 FDIC National Survey of Unbanked and Underbanked Households*. Arlington, VA. https://www.fdic.gov/householdsurvey/2015/2015report.pdf

Feldman, D.C., and Beehr, T.A. (2011). A three-phase model of retirement decision making. *American Psychologist, 66*(3), 193–203.

Ferdman, B.M. (2017). Paradoxes of inclusion: Understanding and managing the tensions of diversity and multiculturalism. *The Journal of Applied Behavioral Science, 53*(2), 235–263.

Ferguson, M. (2012). You cannot leave it at the office: Spillover and crossover of coworker incivility. *Journal of Organizational Behavior, 33*(4), 571–588.

Fernandez, R., and Fernandez-Mateo, I. (2006). Networks, race, and hiring. *American Sociological Review, 71*(1), 42–71.

Ferraro, K.F., and Shippee, T.P. (2009). Aging and cumulative inequality: How does inequality get under the skin? *Gerontologist, 49*(3), 333–343. http//:doi.org/10.1093/geront/gnp034

Feyrer, J. (2007). Demographics and productivity. *Review of Economics and Statistics, 89*(1), 100–109.

Fiedler, K., Messner, C., and Bluemke, M. (2006). Unresolved problems with the "I", the "A", and the "T": A logical and psychometric critique of the Implicit Association Test (IAT). *European Review of Social Psychology, 17*(1), 74–147.

Finke, M.S., Howe, J.S., and Huston, S.J. (2017). Old age and the decline in financial literacy. *Management Science, 63*(1), 213–230.

Finkelstein, L.M., Burke, M.J., and Raju, N.S. (1995). Age discrimination in simulated employment contexts: An integrative analysis. *Journal of Applied Psychology, 80*(6), 652–663.

Finkelstein, L.M., King, E.B., and Voyles, E.C. (2015). Age metastereotyping and cross-age workplace interactions: A meta view of age stereotypes at work. *Work, Aging and Retirement, 1*(1), 26–40.

Fisher, G.G., and Ryan, L.H. (2018). Overview of the Health and Retirement Study and introduction to the special issue. *Work, Aging, and Retirement, 4*(1), 1–9. https://academic.oup.com/workar/article/4/1/1/4762672?login=true

Fisher, G.G., Chaffee, D.S., and Sonnega, A. (2016). Retirement timing: A review and recommendations for future research. *Work, Aging, and Retirement, 2*(2), 230–261. https://doi.org/10.1093/workar/waw001

Fisher, G.G., Ryan, L.H., Sonnega, A., and Naudé, M.N. (2016). Job lock, work, and psychological well-being in the United States. *Work, Aging, and Retirement, 2*(3), 345–358. https://doi.org/10.1093/workar/waw004

Fiske, S.T. (1998). Stereotyping, prejudice, and discrimination. *Handbook of Social Psychology, Vol. 2*, 357–411. McGraw-Hill.

Fiske, S.T. (2017). Prejudices in cultural contexts: Shared stereotypes (gender, age) versus variable stereotypes (race, ethnicity, religion). *Perspectives on Psychological Science, 12*(5), 791–799.

Fiske, S.T., and North, M.S. (2014). Social psychological measures of stereotyping and prejudice. *Measures of Personality and Social Psychological Constructs*, 684–718. Elsevier/Academic Press.

Fiske, S.T., and Taylor, S. (2021). *Social Cognition: From Brains to Culture* (4th ed.). Sage.

Fiske, S.T., Bergsieker, H., Russell, A.M., and Williams, L. (2009). Images of Black Americans: Then, them and now, Obama! *DuBois Review: Social Science Research on Race, 6*(1), 83–101.

Fiske, S.T., Cuddy, A.J., Glick, P., and Xu, J. (2002). A model of (often mixed) stereotype content: Competence and warmth respectively follow from perceived status and competition. *Journal of Personality and Social Psychology, 82*(6), 878–902.

Fitzpatrick, M. (2013). Retiree health insurance for public school employees: Does it affect retirement? *National Bureau of Economic Research Working Papers*, 19524. NBER.

Fitzpatrick, M.D., and Moore, T.J. (2018). The mortality effects of retirement: Evidence from Social Security eligibility at age 62. *Journal of Public Economics, 157*(C), 121–137.

Fix, M., and Struyk, R. (1993). *Clear and Convincing Evidence: Measurement of Discrimination in America*. The Urban Institute Press.

Flippen, C.A. (2005). Minority workers and pathways to retirement. *The New Politics of Old Age Policy*, 129–157. Johns Hopkins University Press.

Flippen, C.A., and Tienda, M. (2000). Pathways to retirement: Patterns of labor force participation and labor market exit among the pre-retirement population by race, Hispanic origin, and sex. *Journals of Gerontology, Series B, 55*(1), 14–27.

Flippen, C.A., and Tienda, M. (2002). Workers of color and pathways to retirement. *Public Policy and Aging Report, 12*(3), 3–8.

Flood, S., Moen, P., and Pedtke, J.H. (2021). Derailed by the COVID-19 economy? Older adults' paid work by intersections of age, gender, race-ethnicity, and class. *Innovation in Aging, 5*(Supp. 1), 497–498.

Flores, A., and Radford, J. (2017). *Hispanic Population in the United States Statistical Portrait: Statistical Portrait of Hispanics in the United States*. Pew Research Center. https://www.pewresearch.org/hispanic/2017/09/18/2015-statistical-information-on-hispanics-in-united-states-current-data

Flynn, M. (2014). *Lessons from Japan: Helping the Older Unemployed Get Back Into Work*. The Careers Blog: The Guardian. https://www.theguardian.com/careers/careers-blog/retirement-ageing-workforce-japan-jobs

Flynn, M., Upchurch, M., Muller-Camen, M., and Schroder, H. (2013). Trade union responses to ageing workforces in the UK and Germany. *Human Relations, 66*(1), 45–64.

Foged, M., and Peri, G. (2016). Immigrants' effect on native workers: New analysis on longitudinal data. *American Economic Journal: Applied Economics, 8*(2), 1–34.

Fonseca, T., Lima, F., and Pereira, S.C. (2018). Job polarization, technological change, and routinization: Evidence for Portugal. *Labour Economics, 51*(C), 317–339.

Foote, A., Grosz, M., and Stevens, A. (2019). Locate your nearest exit: Mass layoffs and local labor market response. *Industrial and Labor Relations Review, 72*(1), 101–126.

Fossum, J.A. (2012). *Labor Relations* (12th ed.). McGraw Hill Education.

Foster, L., and Walker, A. (2015). Active and successful aging: A European policy perspective. *The Gerontologist, 55*(1), 83–90.

Frank, R.G., Glied, S.A., Marple, K., and Shields, M. (2019). *Changing Labor Markets and Mental Illness: Impacts on Work and Disability*. NBER Retirement and Disability Research Center Working Paper No. NB19-05. Cambridge, MA.

Freedman, M. (2007). *Encore: Finding Work that Matters in the Second Half of Life*. PublicAffairs.

Freedman, V.A. (2018). The demography of late-life disability. *Future Directions for the Demography of Aging: Proceedings of a Workshop*, 269–306. National Academies Press.

French, E. (2005). The effects of health, wealth, and wages on labour supply and retirement behaviour. *The Review of Economic Studies, 72*(2), 395–427.

French, E., and Jones, J.B. (2012). Public pensions and labor supply over the life cycle. *International Tax and Public Finance, 19*(2), 268–287.

French, E., and Jones, J.B. (2017). Health, health insurance, and retirement: A survey. *Annual Review of Economics, 9*(1), 383–409.

French, E., and Song, J. (2012). *The Effect of Disability Insurance Receipt on Labor Supply: A Dynamic Analysis*. Working Paper No. 2012-12, Federal Reserve Bank of Chicago.

Frey, C.B., and Osborne, M.A. (2017). The future of employment: How susceptible are jobs to computerisation? *Technological Forecasting and Social Change, 114*(C), 254–280.

Friedberg, L. (2000). The labor supply effects of the Social Security earnings test. *The Review of Economics and Statistics, 82*(1), 48–63.

Friedberg, L., and Webb, A. (2005). Retirement and the Evolution of Pension Structure. *Journal of Human Resources, 60*(2), 281–308.

Froidevaux, A., Alterman, V., and Wang, M. (2020). Leveraging aging workforce and age diversity to achieve organizational goals: A human resource management perspective. *Current and Emerging Trends in Aging and Work*, 33–58. Springer.

Fronstin, P., and Adams, N. (2012). *Employment-Based Retiree Health Benefits: Trends in Access and Coverage, 1997–2010.* Issue Brief No. 377, Employee Benefit Research Institute.

Fry, R. (2019). *Baby Boomers Are Staying in The Labor Force at Rates Not Seen in Generations For People Their Age.* Pew Research Center. https://www.pewresearch.org/fact-tank/2019/07/24/baby-boomers-us-labor-force

Furunes, T., and Mykletun, R.J. (2010). Age discrimination in the workplace: Validation of the Nordic Age Discrimination Scale. *Scandinavian Journal of Psychology*, 51, 23–30.

Gale, W.G., and John, D.C. (2017). *State-Sponsored Retirement Savings Plans: New Approaches to Boost Retirement Plan Coverage.* Working Paper No. WP2017-12, Pension Research Council, University of Pennsylvania. https://repository.upenn.edu/prc_papers/38

Galenson, D.W., and Weinberg, B.A. (2001). Creating modern art: The changing careers of painters in France from Impressionism to Cubism. *American Economic Review*, 91(4), 1063–1071.

Gallo, W.T., Bradley, E.H., Dubin, J.A., Jones, R.N., Falba, T.A., Teng, H-M., and Kasl, S.V. (2006). The persistence of depressive symptoms in older workers who experience involuntary job loss: Results from the Health and Retirement Survey. *Journals of Gerontology, Series B: Social Sciences*, 61(4), S221–S228.

Garcia, M.A., Homan, P.A., Garcia, C., and Brown, T.H. (2020). *The Color of COVID-19: Structural Racism and the Pandemic's Disproportionate Impact on Older Racial and Ethnic Minorities.* Sociology Department, Faculty Publications, 723. University of Nebraska. https://digitalcommons.unl.edu/cgi/viewcontent.cgi?article=1735&context=sociologyfacpub

Garstka, T.A., Schmitt, M.T., Branscombe, N.R., and Hummert, M.L. (2004). How young and older adults differ in their responses to perceived age discrimination. *Psychology and Aging*, 19(2), 326–335.

Gayen, K., McQuaid, R., and Raeside, R. (2010). Social networks, age cohorts, and employment. *International Journal of Sociology and Social Policy*, 30(5/6), 219–238.

Gayen, K., Raeside, R., and McQuaid, R. (2019). Social networks, accessed and mobilized social capital, and the employment status of older workers: A case study. *International Journal of Sociology and Social Policy*, 39(5), 356–375. https//:doi.org/10.1108/IJSSP-07-2018-0111

Gee, G.C., Hing, A.H., Mohammed, S., Tabor, D., and Williams, D.R. (2019). Racism and the life course: Taking time seriously. *American Journal of Public Health*, 109(Suppl. 1), S43–S47.

Gelber, A. M., Jones, D., and Sacks, D. W. (2020). Estimating adjustment frictions using nonlinear budget sets: Method and evidence from the earnings test. *American Economic Journal: Applied Economics*, 12(1), 1–31.

Gelderblom, A. (2006). *The Relationship Between Age and Productivity.* In Ageing and Employment: Identification of Good Practice to Increase Job Opportunities and Maintain Older Workers in Employment. Final Report submitted to the Commission of the European Communities DG EMPL. Warwick Institute for Employment Research, University of Warwick and Economic Research and Consulting.

Gelfand, M.J., Jackson, J.C., Pan, X., Nau, D., Pieper, D., Denison, E., Dagher, M., van Lange, P., Chiu, C., and Wang, M. (2021). The relationship between cultural tightness-looseness and COVID-19 cases and deaths: A global analysis. *The Lancet Planetary Health*, 5(3), e135–e144. https://pubmed.ncbi.nlm.nih.gov/33524310

Gettens, J., Lei, P.-P., and Henry, A. (2016). *Accounting for Geographic Variation in DI and SSI Participation.* DCR Working Paper No. 2016-03, Mathematica Policy Research.

Giandrea, M.D., Cahill, K.E., and Quinn, J.F. (2009). Bridge jobs: A comparison across cohorts. *Research on Aging*, 31(5), 549–576.

Gielen, A.C. (2009). Working hours flexibility and older workers' labor supply. *Oxford Economic Papers*, 61(2), 240–274. http://dx.doi.org/gpn035

Gielnik, M.M., Zacher, H., and Wang, M. (2018). Age in the entrepreneurial process: The role of future time perspective and prior entrepreneurial experience. *Journal of Applied Psychology*, 103(10), 1067–1085.

Gilbert, D.T., and Wilson, T.D. (2007). Prospection: Experiencing the future. *Science*, 317(5843), 1351–1354.

Glaeser, E.L. (2009). The death and life of cities. *Making Cities Work: Prospects and Policies for Urban America*, 22–62. Princeton University Press.

Glauber, R. (2011). Limited access: Gender, job composition, and flexible work scheduling. *Sociological Quarterly*, 52(3), 472–494.

Glavin, P. (2013). The impact of job insecurity and job degradation on the sense of personal control. *Work and Occupations*, 40(2), 115–142.

Göbel, C., and Zwick, T. (2012). Age and productivity: Sector differences. *De Economist*, 160(1), 35–57. https://econpapers.repec.org/article/kapdecono/v_3a160_3ay_3a2012_3ai_3a1_3ap_3a35-57.htm

Goda, G.S., Shoven, J.B., and Slavor, S.N. (2009). Removing the disincentives in Social Security for long careers. *Social Security Policy in a Changing Environment*, 21–38. University of Chicago Press.

Goda, G.S., Jackson, E., Nichols, L.H., and Stith, S.S. (2021). *The Impact of COVID-19 on Older Workers' Employment and Social Security Spillovers*. NBER Working Paper No. NB22-01. https://www.nber.org/programs-projects/projects-and-centers/retirement-and-disability-research-center/8190-nb22-01-impact-covid-19-older-workers-employment-and-social-security-spillovers?page=1&perPage=50

Goldberg, C.B., Perry, E.L., Finkelstein, L.M., and Shull, A. (2013). Antecedents and outcomes of targeting older applicants in recruitment. *European Journal of Work and Organizational Psychology, 22*(3), 265–278.

Golden, L. (2001). Flexible work schedules: Which workers get them? *American Behavioral Scientist, 44*(7), 1157–1178.

Goldin, C., and Katz, L.F. (2018a). Women working longer: Facts and some explanations. *Women Working Longer: Increased Employment at Older Ages*, 11–53. University of Chicago Press.

Goldin, C., and Katz, L.F., (Eds.) (2018b). *Women Working Longer. Increased Employment at Older Ages*. NBER, Cambridge, MA. University of Chicago Press. https://www.nber.org/books-and-chapters/women-working-longer-increased-employment-older-ages

Goldin, C., Kerr, S.P., Olivetti, C., and Barth, E. (2017). The expanding gender earnings gap: Evidence from the LEHD-2000 census. *American Economic Review: Papers and Proceedings, 107*(5), 110–114.

Goldin, C., and Mitchell, J. (2017). The new life cycle of women's employment: Disappearing humps, sagging middles, and expanding tops. *Journal of Economic Perspectives, 31*(1), 161–182.

Goldman, D.P., and Zissimopoulos, J.M. (2003). High out-of-pocket health care spending by the elderly. *Health Affairs, 22*(3), 194–202.

Gonyea, J.G., and Hudson, R.B. (2011). Promoting employment and community service among low income seniors: Successes and challenges of the Senior Community Service Employment Program. *Aging and Public Policy Report 21*, 40–47.

Gonzales, E., Gordon, S., Whetung, C., Connaught, G., Collazo, J., and Hilton, J. (2021). Acknowledging systemic discrimination in the context of a pandemic: Advancing an anti-racist and anti-ageist movement. *Journal of Gerontological Social Work, 64*(3), 223–237. https//:doi.org/10.1080/01634372.2020.1870604

Gonzales, E., Lee, Y. and Brown, C. (2017). Back to work? Not everyone. Examining the longitudinal relationships between informal caregiving and paid-work after formal retirement. *The Journals of Gerontology, Series B: Psychological Sciences and Social Sciences, 72*(3), 532–539. https//:doi.org/10.1093/geronb/gbv095

Gonzales, E., Lee, K., and Harootyan, R.A. (2019). Voices from the field: Ecological factors that promote employment and health among low-income older adults with implications for direct social work practice. *Clinical Social Work Journal, 48*(1–2), 211–222. https://link.springer.com/article/10.1007/s10615-019-00719-x

Gonzales, E., Lee, Y.J., and Marchiondo, L. (2019). Exploring the consequences of major lifetime discrimination, chronic workplace discrimination, and neighborhood conditions with health and retirement. *Journal of Applied Gerontology, 40*(2). https://journals.sagepub.com/doi/full/10.1177/0733464819892847

Gonzales, E., Lee, Y.J., and Marchiondo, L.A. (2021). Exploring the consequences of major lifetime discrimination, neighborhood conditions, chronic work, and everyday discrimination on health and retirement. *Journal of Applied Gerontology, 40*(2), 121–131.

Gonzales, E., and Nowell, W.B. (2017). Social capital and unretirement: Exploring the bonding, bridging, and linking aspects of social relationships. *Research on Aging, 39*(10), 1100–1117, https//:doi.org/10.1177/0164027516664569

Goos, M., Manning, A., and Salomons, A. (2014). Explaining job polarization: Routine-biased technological change and offshoring. *American Economic Review, 104*(8), 2509–2526.

Gordon, R.A., and Arvey, R.D. (2004). Age bias in laboratory and field settings: A meta-analytic investigation. *Journal of Applied Social Psychology, 34*(3), 468–492.

Gordon, R.J. (2016). *The Rise and Fall of American Growth: The U.S. Standard of Living since the Civil War*. Princeton University Press.

Gorodnichenko, Y., Song, J., and Stolyarov, D. (2013). *Macroeconomic Determinants of Retirement Timing*. NBER Working Paper Series No. 19638. National Bureau of Economic Research.

Gotbaum, J., and Wolfe, B. (2018). *Help People Work Longer by Phasing Retirement*. The Brookings Institution. https://www.brookings.edu/opinions/help-people-work-longer-by-phasing-retirement

Grabowski, D.C., Joyce, N.R., McGuire, T.G., and Frank, R.G. (2017). Passive enrollment of dual-eligible beneficiaries into Medicare and Medicaid managed care has not met expectations. *Health Affairs, 36*(5), 846–854.

Graf, N., Hofer, H., and Winter-Ebner, R. (2011). Labor supply effects of a subsidized old-age part-time scheme in Austria. *Zeitschrift für ArbeitsmarktForschung, 44*(217).

Granovetter, M.S. (1973). The strength of weak ties. *American Journal of Sociology, 78*(6), 1360–1380.

Granovetter, M.S. (1981). Toward a sociological theory of income differences. *Sociological Perspectives on Labor Markets*, 11–49. Academic Press.

Granovetter, M.S. (1983). The strength of weak ties: A network theory revisited. *Sociological Theory, 1*, 201–233.

Granovetter, M.S. (1995). *Getting a Job: A Study of Contacts and Careers* (2nd ed.). University of Chicago Press.

Greenwald, A.G., and Lai, C.K. (2020). Implicit social cognition. *Annual Review of Psychology, 71*, 419–445.

Greenwald, A.G., Poehlman, T.A., Uhlmann, E.L., and Banaji, M.R. (2009). Understanding and using the Implicit Association Test: III. Meta-analysis of predictive validity. *Journal of Personality and Social Psychology, 97*(1), 17–41.

Greenwald, L., Copeland, C., and VanDerhei, J. (2017). *The 2017 Retirement Confidence Survey: Many Workers Lack Retirement Confidence and Feel Stressed About Retirement Preparations*. Issue Brief No. 431, 1–29, Employee Benefit Research Institute.

Grinstein-Weiss, M., Lee, J. S., Greeson, J., Han, C., Yeo, Y., and Irish, K. (2008). Fostering low-income homeownership: A longitudinal randomized experiment on Individual Development Accounts. *Housing Policy Debate, 19*(4), 711–739. https//:doi.org/10.1080/10511482.2008.9521653

Grinstein-Weiss, M., Sherraden, M., Gale, W., Rohe, W., Schreiner, M., and Key, C. (2013). Long-term impacts of individual development accounts on homeownership among baseline renters: Follow-up evidence from a randomized experiment. *American Economic Journal: Economic Policy, 5*(1), 122–145. https//:doi.org/10.2307/23358339

Grinstein-Weiss, M., Sherraden, M., Gale, W.G., Rohe, W.M., Schreiner, M., Key, C., and Oliphant, J.E. (2015). Effects of an individual development account program on retirement saving: Follow-up evidence from a randomized experiment. *Journal of Gerontological Social Work, 58*(6), 572–589. https//:doi.org/10.1080/01634372.2015.1052174

Gruber, J. and Madrian, B.C. (1995). Health-Insurance Availability and the Retirement Decision. *American Economic Review, 85*(4), 938–948.

Gruber, J., and Madrian, B.C. (2004). Health insurance, labor supply, and job mobility: A critical review of the literature. *Health Policy and the Uninsured*, 97–178. Urban Institute Press.

Gruber, J., and Wise, D.A. (1999). *Social Security and Retirement around the World*. University of Chicago Press.

Gruber, J., and Wise, D.A. (2004). *Social Security and Retirement Around the World: Microestimation*. University of Chicago Press.

Gruber, J., and Wise, D.A. (Eds.) (2007). Social Security Programs and Retirement around the World: Fiscal Implications of Reform. NBER Books, number grub07-1, December. National Bureau of Economic Research, Inc.

Gruber, J., Milligan, K., and Wise, D.A. (2010). Introduction and summary. In J. Gruber and D.A. Wise (Eds.), *Social Security Programs and Retirement around the World: The Relationship to Youth Employment*, 1–45. University of Chicago Press.

Gu, K., and Stoyanov, A. (2019). Skills, population aging, and the pattern of international trade. *Review of International Economics, 27*(2), 499–519.

Gustafson, P. (2017). Spousal age differences and synchronized retirement. *Ageing & Society, 37*(4), 777–803.

Gustman, A.L., and Steinmeier, T.L. (1983). Minimum hours constraints and retirement behavior. *Contemporary Economic Polisy, 1*(3), 77–91.

Gustman, A.L., and Steinmeier, T.L. (2004). Social Security, pensions, and retirement behaviour within the family. *Journal of Applied Econometrics, 19*(6), 723–737.

Gustman, A.L., Steinmeier, T.L., and Tabatabai, N. (2010). *Pensions in the Health and Retirement Study*. Harvard University Press.

Gustman, A.L., Steinmeier, T.L., and Tabatabai, N. (2019). The Affordable Care Act as retiree health insurance: Implications for retirement and Social Security claiming. *Journal of Pension Economics & Finance, 18*(3), 415–449.

Gyourko, J., Mayer, C., and Sinai, T. (2013). Superstar cities. *American Economic Journal: Economic Policy, 5*(4), 167–199.

Hackmann, M.B., Kolstad, J.T., and Kowalski, A.E. (2015). Adverse selection and an individual mandate: When theory meets practice. *American Economic Review 105*(3), 1030–1066.

Hall, R.E. (1982). The importance of lifetime jobs in the U.S. economy. *American Economic Review, 72*(4), 716–724.

Hallberg, D. (2011). Economic fluctuations and retirement of older employees. *Labour, 25*(3), 287–307.

Hällsten, M., Edling, R., and Rydgren, J. (2017). Social capital, friendship networks, and youth unemployment. *Social Science Research, 61*(1), 234–250.

Haltiwanger, J.C., Lane, J.I., and Spletzer, J.R. (1999). Productivity differences across employers: The roles of employer size, age, and human capital. *American Economic Review, 89*(2), 94–98.

Halvorsen, C.J., and James, J.B. (2020). *Three Fast Facts: Self-employment Trends Among Older Americans*. Self-Employment Brief No. 1, The Center on Aging and Work at Boston College. https://dlib.bc.edu/islandora/object/bc-ir%3A108936/datastream/PDF/view

Halvorsen, C.J., and Yulikova, O. (2020a). Job training and so much more for low-income older adults: The senior community service employment program. *Clinical Social Work Journal, 48*(2), 223–229. https://link.springer.com/article/10.1007%2Fs10615-019-00734-y

Halvorsen, C.J., and Yulikova, O. (2020b). Older workers in the time of COVID-19: The senior community service employment program and implications for social work. *Journal of Gerontological Social Work, 63*(6–7), 530–541. https://www.tandfonline.com/doi/full/10.1080/01634372.2020.1774832

Hamilton, B.E., Martin, J.A., and Osterman, M.J.K. (2021). *Births: Provisional Data for 2020*. National Center for Vital Statistics Rapid Release Report No. 012. https://www.cdc.gov/nchs/data/vsrr/vsrr012-508.pdf

Han, S.-K., and Moen, P. (1999). Clocking out: Temporal patterning of retirement. *American Journal of Sociology, 105*(1), 191–236.

Hanoch, G., and Honig, M. (1983). Retirement, wages, and labor supply of the elderly. *Journal of Labor Economics, 1*(2), 131–151.

Hansson, I., Buratti, S., Thorvaldsson, V., Johansson, B., and Berg, A.I. (2018). Changes in life satisfaction in the retirement transition: Interaction effects of transition type and individual resources. *Working, Aging, and Retirement, 4*(4), 352–366. https//:doi.org/10.1093/worker/wax025

Harkonmäki, K., Rahkonen, O., Martikainen, P., Silventoinen, K., and Lahelma, E. (2006). Associations of SF-36 mental health functioning and work and family related factors with intentions to retire early among employees. *Occupational and Environmental Medicine, 63*(8), 558–563.

Haushofer, J., and Shapiro, J. (2016). The short-term impact of unconditional cash transfers to the poor: Experimental evidence from Kenya. *The Quarterly Journal of Economics, 131*(4), 1973–2042.

Hayslip, B., Fruhauf, C.A., and Dolbin-MacNab, M.L. (2019). Grandparents raising grandchildren: What have we learned over the past decade? *Gerontologist, 59*(3), e152–e163. https//:doi.org/10.1093/geront/gnx106

Hayslip, Jr., B., Glover, R.J., Harris, B.E., Miltenberger, P.B., Baird, A., and Kaminski, P.L. (2009). Perceptions of custodial grandparents among young adults. *Journal of Intergenerational Relationships, 7*(2–3), 209–224.

Hayward, M., Hardy, M.A., Lui, M. (1994). Work after retirement: The experiences of older men in the United States. *Social Sciences Research, 23*(1), 82–107. https://doi.org/10.1006/ssre.1994.1004

Hayward, M.D., Hummer, R.A., Chiu, C.T., González-González, C., and Wong, R. (2014). Does the Hispanic paradox in U.S. adult mortality extend to disability? *Population Research and Policy Review, 33*(1), 81–96.

Heckhausen, J., and Schulz, R. (1995). A life-span theory of control. *Psychological Review, 102*(2), 284–304.

Heckman, J., and Siegelman, P. (1993). The Urban Institute audit studies: Their methods and findings. *Clear and Convincing Evidence: Measurement of Discrimination in America*, 187–258. The Urban Institute Press.

Heckman, J.J., Stixrud, J., and Urzua, S. (2006). The effects of cognitive and noncognitive abilities on labor market outcomes and social behavior. *Journal of Labor Economics, 24*(3), 411–482.

Hedge, J.W., Borman, W.C., and Lammlein, S.E. (2006a). Age stereotyping and age discrimination. *The Aging Workforce: Realities, Myths, and Implications for Organizations*, 27–48. American Psychological Association.

Hedge, J.W., Borman, W.C., and Lammlein, S.E., (Eds.) (2006b). *The Aging Workforce: Realities, Myths, and Implications for Organizations*. American Psychological Association.

Heidkamp, M., and Van Horn, C. (2020). Difficult adjustments: Older workers and the contemporary labor market. *Current and Emerging Trends in Aging and Work*, 337–353. Springer Nature Switzerland.

Heim, B.T., and Lin, L. (2017). Does health reform lead to an increase in early retirement? Evidence from Massachusetts. *Industrial and Labor Relations Review, 70*(3), 704–732.

Hellerstein, J.K., and Neumark, D. (1995). Are earnings profiles steeper than productivity profiles? Evidence from Israeli firm-level data. *The Journal of Human Resources, 30*(1), 89–112.

Hellerstein, J.K., Neumark, D., and Troske, K.R. (1999). Wages, productivity, and worker characteristics: Evidence from plant-level production functions and wage equations. *Journal of Labor Economics, 17*(3), 409–446.

Hellester, M.D., Kuhn, P., and Shen, K. (2020). The age twist in employers' gender requests. *Journal of Human Resources, 55*, 428–469.

Hendley, A.A., and Bilimoria, N.F. (1999). Minorities and Social Security: An analysis of ethnic differences in the current program. *Social Security Bulletin, 62*(2), 59–64.

Hendrick, J.J., Knox, V.J., Gekoski, W.J., and Dyne, K.J. (1988). Perceived cognitive ability of young and old targets. *Canadian Journal on Aging, 7*(3), 192–203.

Henkens, K., and van Solinge, H. (2002). Spousal influences on the decision to retire. *International Journal of Sociology, 32*(2), 55–73.

Henly, J.R., and Lambert, S.J. (2014). Unpredictable work timing in retail jobs: Implications for employee work-life conflict. *Industrial & Labor Relations Review, 67*(3), 986–1016.

REFERENCES

Hennekam, S., and Ananthram, S. (2020). Involuntary and voluntary demotion: Employee reactions and outcomes. *European Journal of Work and Organizational Psychology, 29*(4), 586–600.

Henretta, J.C., Chan, C.G., and O'Rand, A.M. (1992). Retirement reason versus retirement process: Examining the reasons for retirement typology. *Journals of Gerontology, 47*(1), S1–S7.

Herd, P., Schoeni, R.F., and House, J.S. (2008). Upstream solutions: Does the Supplemental Security Income Program reduce disability in the elderly? *Milbank Quarterly, 86*(1), 5–45.

Herd, P., Favreault, M.M., Meyer, M.H., and Smeeding, T.M. (2018). A targeted minimum benefit plan: A new proposal to reduce poverty among older Social Security recipients. *RSF: The Russell Sage Foundation Journal of the Social Sciences, 42*(2), 74–90.

Herrbach, O., Mignonac, K., Vandenberghe, C., and Negrini, A. (2009). Perceived HRM practices, organizational commitment, and voluntary early retirement among late-career managers. *Human Resource Management, 48*(6), 895–915. https://onlinelibrary.wiley.com/doi/10.1002/hrm.20321

Hershey, D.A., and Henkens, K. (2014). Impact of different types of retirement transitions on perceived satisfaction with life. *Gerontologist, 54*(2), 232–244.

Hess, M., Bauknecht, J., and Pink, S. (2018). Working hours flexibility and timing of retirement: Findings from Europe. *Journal of Aging and Social Policy, 30*(5), 478–494.

Hill, M.J., Maestas, N., and Mullen, K.J. (2016). Employer accommodation and labor supply of disabled workers. *Labour Economics, 41*, 291–303.

Ho, J.H., and Raymo, J.M. (2009). Expectations and realization of joint retirement among dual-worker couples. *Research on Aging, 31*(2), 153–179.

Hofäcker, D., Hess, M., and König, S. (2016). *Delaying Retirement: Progress and Challenges of Active Ageing in Europe, the United States, and Japan*. Palgrave MacMillan.

Hofmann, W., Gawronski, B., Gschwendner, T., Le, H., and Schmitt, M. (2005). A meta-analysis on the correlation between the Implicit Association Test and explicit self-report measures. *Personality and Social Psychology Bulletin, 31*(10), 1369–1385.

Holland, J.L. (1997). *Making vocational choices: A theory of vocational personalities and work environments*, (3rd ed.). Psychological Assessment Resources.

Holzer, H., and Neumark, D. (2000). Assessing affirmative action. *Journal of Economic Literature, 39*(3), 483–568.

Homaie Rad, E.H., Rashidian, A., Arab, M., and Souri, A. (2017). Comparison the effects of poor health and low income on early retirement: A systematic review and meta-analysis. *Industrial Health, 55*(4), 306–313.

Horowitz, J.M., Igielnik, R., and Kochhar, R. (2020). *Most Americans Say There Is Too Much Economic Inequality in the U.S., But Fewer Than Half Call It a Top Priority*. Pew Research Center. https://www.pewresearch.org/social-trends/2020/01/09/most-americans-say-there-is-too-much-economic-inequality-in-the-u-s-but-fewer-than-half-call-it-a-top-priority

Hotchkiss, J.L. (2004). A closer look at the employment impact of the Americans with Disabilities Act. *Journal of Human Resources, 39*(4), 887–911.

Hotchkiss, J.L., and Rovba, L. (2003). Employment outcomes. *Labor Market Experiences of Workers with Disabilities: The ADA and Beyond*, 21–48. W.E. Upjohn Institute for Employment Research. https://research.upjohn.org/cgi/viewcontent.cgi?article=1051&context=up_press

Hou, W., and Sanzenbacher, G.T. (2020). *Measuring Racial/Ethnic Retirement Wealth Inequality*. Working Paper No. CRR WP 2020-2, Center for Retirement Research at Boston College. https://crr.bc.edu/wp-content/uploads/2020/02/wp_2020-2___.pdf

Houtenville, A.J., and Burkhauser, R.V. (2004). *Did the Employment of People with Disabilities Decline in the 1990s, and was the ADA Responsible?* Research Brief, Cornell University, Rehabilitation Research and Training Center for Economic Research on Employment Policy for Persons with Disabilities. https://ecommons.cornell.edu/bitstream/handle/1813/89903/DE43B_PDF1.pdf?sequence=1&isAllowed=y

Huang, J., Kim, Y., Sherraden, M., and Clancy, M. (2017). Heterogeneous effects of child development accounts on savings for children's education. *Journal of Policy Practice, 16*(1), 59–80. https//:doi.org/10.1080/15588742.2015.1132402

Hubbard, R.G., and Skinner, J.S. (1996). Assessing the effectiveness of saving incentives. *Journal of Economic Perspectives, 10*(4), 73–90.

Huber, M., Lechner, M., and Wunsch, C. (2013). The effect of firms' partial retirement policies on the labour market outcomes of their employees. *WWZ Discussion Paper*, No. 2013/12. University of Basel, Center of Business and Economics. http://dx.doi.org/10.5451/unibas-ep61344

Hudomiet, P., Hurd, M.D., and Rohwedder, S. (2022). Trends in health midlife and late life. *Journal of Human Capital, 16*(1), 133–156.

Hummert, M.L., Garstka, T.A., and Shaner, J.L. (1995). Beliefs about language performance: Adults' perceptions about self and elderly targets. *Journal of Language and Social Psychology, 14*(3), 235–259.

Hummert, M.L., Garstka, T.A., Shaner, J.L., and Strahm, S. (1994). Stereotypes of the elderly held by young, middle-aged, and elderly adults. *Journal of Gerontology, 49*(5), P240–P249.

Hurd, M.D., and Rohwedder, S. (2003). *The Retirement-Consumption Puzzle: Anticipated and Actual Declines in Spending at Retirement*. NBER Working Paper No. 9586. National Bureau of Economic Research. https://hrs.isr.umich.edu/publications/biblio/5538

Hurd, M.D., Reti, M., and Rohwedder, S. (2009). The effect of large capital gains or losses on retirement. *Developments in the Economics of Aging*, 127–163. University of Chicago Press.

Hurst, E. (2004). *Grasshoppers, Ants, and Pre-Retirement Wealth: A Test of Permanent Income Consumers*. Working Paper No. 2004-088. Michigan Retirement and Disability Research Center, University of Michigan. https://mrdrc.isr.umich.edu/pubs/grasshoppers-ants-and-pre-retirement-wealth-a-test-of-permanent-income-consumers

Hurst, E. (2008). *The Retirement of a Consumption Puzzle*. NBER Working Paper No. w13789. National Bureau of Economic Research. https://papers.ssrn.com/sol3/papers.cfm?abstract_id=1092817

Hyde, J.S., Honeycutt, T., and Stapleton, D. (2014). The relationship between timely delivery of vocational rehabilitation services and subsequent federal disability application and receipt. *IZA Journal of Labor Policy, 3*(15).

Iams, H.M. (2016). Married women's projected retirement benefits: An update. *Social Security Bulletin*, 76(2). https://www.ssa.gov/policy/docs/ssb/v76n2/v76n2p17.html

Ilmakunnas, P. and Ilmakunnas, S. (2006). Gradual Retirement and Lengthening of Working Life. *HECER Discussion Paper*, No. 121. http://dx.doi.org/10.2139/ssrn.937288

International Labour Organisation. (2021). ILOSTAT Explorer. https://www.ilo.org/shinyapps/bulkexplorer8/

Jackson, J. (2016). His way, her way: Retirement timing among dual-earner couples. *Advances in Life Course Research*. http://dx.doi.org/10.1016/j.alcr.2016.09.002

Jackson, L.A. (1992). *Physical Appearance and Gender: Sociological and Sociocultural Perspectives*. University of New York Press.

Jacobson, L., Lalonde, R.J., and Sullivan, D. (2005a). The impact of community college retraining on older displaced workers: Should we teach old dogs new tricks? *Industrial and Labor Relations Review, 58*(3), 398–415.

Jacobson, L.S., Lalonde, R., and Sullivan, D.G. (2005b). Is Retraining Displaced Workers a Good Investment? *Economic Perspectives, 29*(2). Federal Reserve Bank of Chicago. https://www.chicagofed.org/publications/economic-perspectives/2005/2q-jacobson-lalonde-sullivan

James, J.B., Besen, E., and Pitt-Catsouphes, M. (2011). Resilience in the workplace: Job conditions that buffer negative attitudes toward older workers. *Resilience in Aging*, 331–349. Springer.

James, J.B., Matz-Costa, C., and Smyer, M.A. (2016). Retirement security: It's not just about the money. *American Psychologist, 71*(4), 334–344.

James, J.B., Swanberg, J.E., and McKechnie, S.P. (2010). Predicting employee engagement in an age-diverse retail workforce. *Journal of Organizational Behavior. A Special Issue: Contemporary Empirical Advancements in the Study of Aging in the Workplace, 32*(2), 173–196. https//:doi.org/10.1002/job.681

James, J.B., Morrow-Howell, N., Gonzales, E., Costa, C., and Riddle-Wilder, A. (2020). Beyond the livelong workday: Is there a new face of retirement? *Current and Emerging Trends In Aging & Work*, 355–374. Springer Publishing Co.

James, J.B., Pitt-Catsouphes, M., McNamara, T., Snow, D., and Johnson, P. (2015). The relationship of work unit pressure on satisfaction with work-family balance: A new twist on negative spillover? *Research in the Sociology of Work: Work and Family in the New Economy*, 219–247. Emerald Group.

Janssens, M., and Zanoni, P. (2008). *What Makes an Organization Inclusive? Organizational Practices Favoring the Relational Inclusion of Ethnic Minorities in Operative Jobs*. Presented at the International Association for Conflict Management Annual Meeting, Chicago, IL.

Jason, K.J., Carr, D.C., Washington, T.R., Hilliard, T.S., and Mingo, C.A. (2017). Multiple chronic conditions, resilience, and workforce transitions in later life: A socio-ecological model. *The Gerontologist, 57*(2), 269–281. https://doi.org/10.1093/geront/gnv101

Johnson, E., and Sherraden, M.S. (2007). From financial literacy to financial capability among youth. *The Journal of Sociology & Social Welfare, 34*(3), 119–145. https://scholarworks.wmich.edu/jssw/vol34/iss3/7

Johnson, R.W. (2011). Phased retirement and workplace flexibility for older adults: Opportunities and challenges. *Annals of the American Academy of Political Science, 638*(1), 68–85.

Johnson, R.W. (2014). *Later Life Job Changes Before and After the Great Recession*. Draft final report to AARP. https://www.socsci.uci.edu/~dneumark/McLaughlin%20and%20Neumark%20ROA%202018.pdf

Johnson, R.W. (2020). *How Can Policymakers Close the Racial Gap in Retirement Security?* Washington, DC: Urban Institute Research Report. https://www.urban.org/research/publication/how-can-policymakers-close-racial-gap-retirement-security

Johnson, R.W. (2021). *Will Older Adults Return to the Workforce?* Urban Institute. https://www.urban.org/urban-wire/will-older-adults-return-workforce

Johnson, R.W., and Neumark, D. (1997). Age discrimination, job separations, and employment status of older workers. *Journal of Human Resources, 32*(4), 779–811.

Johnson, R.W., Butrica, B.A., and Mommaerts, C. (2010). *Work and Retirement Patterns for the G.I. Generation, Silent Generation and Early Boomers: Thirty Years of Change.* The Urban Institute.

Johnson, R.W., Kawachi, J., and Lewis, E.K. (2009). *Older Workers on the Move: Recareering in Later Life.* AARP Public Policy Institute.

Johnson, R.W., Mermin, G.B., and Uccello, C.E. (2005). *When the Nest Egg Cracks: Financial Consequences of Health Problems, Marital Status Changes, and Job Layoffs at Older Ages.* Working Paper No. WP#2005-18, Center for Retirement and Research at Boston College. https://crr.bc.edu/wp-content/uploads/2005/12/WP_2005-18-full-paper.pdf

Johnson, R.W., Mudrazija, S., and Wang, C.X. (2013). *Hispanics' Retirement Security: Past Trends and Future Prospects.* Urban Institute. https://www.urban.org/research/publication/hispanics-retirement-security/view/full_report

Jolls, C. (1996). Hands-tying and the Age Discrimination in Employment Act. *Texas Law Review, 74*(7), 1813–1816.

Jolls, C., and Prescott, J.J. (2004). *Disaggregating Employment Protection: The Case of Disability Discrimination.* Working Paper No. 10740. National Bureau of Economic Research.

Jones, B.F. (2010). Age and great invention. *Review of Economics and Statistics 92*(1), 1–14.

Jones, K.P., Sabat, I.E., King, E.B., Ahmad, A., McCausland, T.C., and Chen, T. (2017). Isms and schisms: A meta-analysis of the prejudice-discrimination relationship across racism, sexism, and ageism. *Journal of Organizational Behavior, 38*(7), 1076–1110.

Jorgensen, H., and Appelbaum, E. (2014). *Expanding Federal Family and Medical Leave Coverage: Who Benefits from Changes in Eligibility Requirements?* Center for Economic and Policy Research. https://cepr.net/documents/fmla-eligibility-2014-01.pdf

Jungmann, F., Wegge, J., Liebermann, S.C., Ries, B.C., and Schmidt, K.H. (2020). Improving team functioning and performance in age-diverse teams: Evaluation of a leadership training. *Work, Aging, and Retirement, 6*(3), 175–194.

Kaduk, A., Genadek, K., Kelly, E., and Moen, P. (2019). Involuntary vs. voluntary flexible work: Insights for scholars and stakeholders. *Community, Work, and Family, 22*(4), 412–442.

Kagan, J. (2021). *Individual Development Account.* Investopedia. https://www.investopedia.com/terms/i/ida.asp

Kahn, M.R., Rutledge, M.S., and Sanzenbacher, G.T. 2017. *Social Security and total replacement rates in disability and retirement.* Center for Retirement Research Working Paper 2017-6. Center for Retirement Research at Boston College. https://www.nber.org/sites/default/files/2020-05/NB16-05%20Khan%2C%20Rutledge%2C%20Sanzenbacher-%20Final.pdf

Kahneman, D., and Tversky. A. (1979). Prospect theory: An analysis of decision under risk. *Econometrica, 47*(2), 236–291.

Kahneman, D., and Tversky. A. (1984). Choices, values, and frames. *American Psychologist, 39*(4), 341–350.

Kail, B.L., and Warner, D.F. (2013). Leaving retirement: Age-graded relative risks of transitioning back to work or dying. *Population Research and Policy Review, 32*(2), 159–182.

Kain, J.F. (1968). Housing segregation, Negro employment, and metropolitan decentralization. *The Quarterly Journal of Economics, 82*(2), 175–197.

Kaiser Family Foundation. (2020a). *Paid Family and Sick Leave in the U.S.* https://www.kff.org/womens-health-policy/fact-sheet/paid-family-leave-and-sick-days-in-the-u-s

Kaiser Family Foundation. (2020b). *Status of State Medicaid Expansion Decisions: Interactive Map.* https://www.kff.org/medicaid/issue-brief/status-of-state-medicaid-expansion-decisions-interactive-map

Kaiser Family Foundation. (2020). Employer-Sponsored Coverage Rates for the Nonelderly by Age. https://www.kff.org/other/state-indicator/rate-by-age-2/

Kaiser, T., Lusardi, A., Menkhoff, L., and Urban, C.J. (2020). *Financial Education Affects Financial Knowledge and Downstream Behaviors.* NBER Working Paper Series No. 27057. National Bureau of Economic Research. https://www.nber.org/system/files/working_papers/w27057/w27057.pdf

Kalleberg, A.L. (2011). *Good Jobs, Bad Jobs: The Rise of Polarization and Precarious Employment Systems in the United States.* Russell Sage Foundation.

Kalleberg, A.L. (2018). *Precarious Lives: Job Insecurity and Well-Being in Rich Democracies.* Polity Press.

Kalleberg, A.L., and Dunn, M. (2016). Good jobs, bad jobs in the gig economy. *Perspectives on Work. Labor, and Employment Relations Association, 20*(10–13), 74–75.

Kamakura, W. (2009). American time-styles. *Multivariate Behavioral Research, 44*(3), 332–361. https//:doi.org/10.1080/00273170902938738

Karasek, R., and Theorell, T. (1990). *Healthy Work: Stress, Productivity, and the Reconstruction of Working Life.* Basic Books.

Katz, L.F. (2000). Technological change, computerization, and the wage structure. *Understanding the Digital Economy: Data, Tools, and Research*, 217–244. The MIT Press.

Katz, L.F., and Krueger, A.B. (2019). The rise and nature of alternative work arrangements in the United States, 1995–2015. *Industrial and Labor Relations Review, 72*(2), 382–416.

Katz, L.F., and Murphy, K.M. (1992). Changes in relative wages, 1963–1987: Supply and demand factors. *The Quarterly Journal of Economics, 107*(1), 35–78.

Keating, N., Eales, J., Fund, L., Fast, J., and Min, J. (2019). Life course trajectories of family care. *International Journal of Care and Caring, 3*(2), 147–163.

Kelly, E.L., and Moen, P. (2020). *Overload: How Good Jobs Went Bad and What We Can Do About It.* Princeton University Press.

Kelly, E.L., Moen, P., Oakes, J.M., Okechukwu, C., Davis, K., Hammer, L., Kossek, E., King, R.B., Hanson, G., Mierzwa, F., and Casper, L. (2014). Changing work and work-family conflict: Evidence from the Work, Family, and Health Network. *American Sociological Review, 79*(3), 485–516.

Kelly, E., Moen, P., and Tranby, E. (2011). Changing workplaces to reduce work-family conflict: Schedule control in a white-collar organization. *American Sociological Review, 76*(2), 265–290.

Kemmerling, A. (2016). The end of work or work without end? How people's beliefs about labour markets shape retirement policies. *Journal of Public Policy 36*, 109–138.

Khan, M.R., Rutledge, M.S., and Sanzenbacher, G.T. (2017). *Social Security and Total Replacement Rates in Disability and Retirement*. Working Paper No. 2017-6, Center for Retirement Research at Boston College. https://crr.bc.edu/working-papers/social-security-and-total-replacement-rates-in-disability-and-retirement

Kim, H., and DeVaney, S. (2005). The selection of partial or full retirement by older workers. *Journal of Family and Economic Issues, 26*(3), 371–396.

Kim, J.E., and Moen, P. (2001). Moving into retirement: Preparation and transitions in late midlife. *Handbook of Midlife Development*, 487–527. Wiley.

Kim, J.E., and Moen, P. (2002). Retirement transitions, gender, and psychological well-being: A life-course, ecological model. *Journals of Gerontology, Series B, 57*(3), P212–P222.

Kim, S. (2012). *The Labor Supply and Welfare Effects of Early Access to Medicare through Social Security Disability Insurance*. Manuscript, Ohio State University, Columbus, OH.

King, L.A., and Hicks, J.A. (2021). The science of meaning in life. *Annual Review of Psychology, 72*, 561–584.

King, S.P., and Bryant, F.B. (2016). The Workplace Intergenerational Climate Scale (WICS), A self-report instrument measuring ageism in the workplace. *Journal of Organizational Behavior, 38*(1), 124–151.

Kitagawa, E.M., and Hauser, P.M. (1973). *Differential Mortality in the United States: A Study in Socioeconomic Epidemiology*. Harvard University Press.

Kitao, S. (2014). A life-cycle model of unemployment and disability insurance. *Journal of Monetary Economics, 68*(1), 1–18.

Kite, M.E., Deaux, K., and Miele, M. (1991). Stereotypes of young and old: Does age outweigh gender? *Psychology and Aging, 6*(1), 19–27.

Kite, M.E., Stockdale, G.D., Whitley, B.E., Jr., and Johnson, B.T. (2005). Attitudes toward younger and older adults: An updated meta-analytic review. *Journal of Social Issues, 61*(2), 241–266.

Kluge, F., Zagheni, E., Loichinger, E., and Vogt, T. (2014). The advantages of demographic change after the wave: Fewer and older, but healthier, greener, and more productive? *Plos One, 9*(9), 1–11.

Knauer, N. (2016). LGBT older adults, chosen family, and caregiving. *Journal of Law and Religion, 31*(2), 150–168. https://doi.org/10.1017/jlr.2016.23

Kochan, T.A. (1980). A model of collective bargaining and industrial relations and historical development of industrial relations. *Collective Bargaining and Industrial Relations: From Theory to Policy and Practice*, 1–51. Irwin.

Kochhar, R., and Cilluffo, A. (2018). *Incomes of Whites, Blacks, Hispanics and Asians in the U.S., 1970 and 2016*. Pew Research Center. https://www.pewresearch.org/social-trends/2018/07/12/incomes-of-whites-blacks-hispanics-and-asians-in-the-u-s-1970-and-2016

Koenig, G., and Harvey, R. (2005). Utilization of the Saver's Credit: An analysis of the first year. *National Tax Journal, 58*(4), 787–806.

Kogan, D., Betesh, H., Negoita, M., Salzman, J., Paulen, L., Cuza, H., Potamites, L., Berk, J., Wolfson, C., and Cloud, P. (2012). *Evaluation of the Senior Community Service Employment Program (SCSEP)*. Progress and Outcomes Study Final Report. Mathematical Policy Research, Inc. https://wdr.doleta.gov/research/FullText_Documents/ETAOP_2013_03.pdf

Kohli, M. (2007). The institutionalization of the life course: Looking back to look ahead. *Research in Human Development, 4*(3–4), 253–271.

Kojola, E., and Moen, P. (2016). No more lock-step retirement: Boomers' shifting meanings of work and retirement. *Journal of Aging Studies, 36*, 59–70.

Kollmeyer, C., and Pichler, F. (2013). Is deindustrialization causing high unemployment in affluent countries? Evidence from 16 OECD countries, 1970–2003. *Social Forces, 91*(3), 785–812.

Kondo, A., and Shigeoka, H. (2017). The effectiveness of demand-side government intervention to promote demand-side government intervention to promote elderly employment. *Industrial and Labor Relations Review, 70*(4), 1008–1036. https://econpapers.repec.org/article/saeilrrev/v_3a70_3ay_3a2017_3ai_3a4_3ap_3a1008-1036.htm

Konrad, A.M., Ritchie, Jr., J.E., Lieb, P., and Corrigall, E. (2000). Sex differences and similarities in job attribute preferences: A meta-analysis. *Psychological Bulletin, 126*(4), 593–641.

Kooij, D.T.A.M., Jansen, P.G., Dikkers, J.S., and de Lange, A.H. (2014). Managing aging workers: A mixed methods study on bundles of HR practices for aging workers. *The International Journal of Human Resource Management, 25*(15), 2192–2212.

Kooij, D.T.A.M, Nijssen, H., Bal, P.M., and van der Kruijssen, D.T.F. (2020). Crafting an interesting job: Stimulating an active role of older workers in enhancing their daily work engagement and job performance. *Work, Aging, and Retirement, 6*(3), 165–174. https://academic.oup.com/workar/article/6/3/165/5735317

Kooij, D.T.A.M., and van de Voorde, K. (2015). Strategic HRM for older workers. *Aging Workers and the Employee-Employer Relationship,* 57–72. Springer International Publishing. https://doi.org/10.1007/978-3-319-08007-9_4

Korenman, S., and Neumark, D. (2000). Cohort crowding and youth labor markets: A cross-national analysis. *Youth Employment and Joblessness in Advanced Countries,* 57–106. University of Chicago Press.

Korff, J., Biemann, T., and Voelpel, S.C. (2017). Differentiating HR systems' impact: Moderating effects of age on the HR system—work outcome association. *Journal of Organizational Behavior, 38*(3), 415–438.

Kossek, E.E., Lautsch, B.A., and Eaton, S.C. (2006). Telecommuting, control, and boundary management: Correlates of policy use and practice, job control and work-family effectiveness. *Journal of Vocational Behavior, 68*(2), 347–367.

Kossek, E.E., Hammer, L.B., Kelly, E.L., and Moen, P. (2014). Designing organizational work, family, and health change initiatives. *Organizational Dynamics, 43*(1), 53–63.

Kotlikoff, L.J., and Gokhale, J. (1992). Estimating a firm's age-productivity profile using the present value of workers' earnings. *Quarterly Journal of Economics, 107*(4), 1215–1242.

Kotlikoff, L.J., and Wise, D. (1989). Employee retirement and a firm's pension plan. *The Economics of Aging,* 279–334. University of Chicago Press.

Kristal, T., Cohen, Y., and Navot, E. (2020). Workplace compensation practices and the rise in benefit inequality. *American Sociological Review, 85*(2), 271–297. https://doi.org/10.1177/0003122420912505

Kroft, K., Lange, F., and Notowidigdo, M.J. (2013). Duration dependence and labor market conditions: Evidence from a field experiment. *Quarterly Journal of Economics, 129*(2), 1123–1167.

Kroon, A.C., Van Selm, M., ter Hoeven, C.L., and Vliegenthart, R. (2016). Reliable and unproductive? Stereotypes of older employees in corporate and news media. *Ageing and Society, 38*(1), 166–191.

Krueger, A.B. (2017). Where have all the workers gone? An inquiry into the decline of the U.S. labor force participation rate. *Brookings Papers on Economic Activity, 2017*(2), 1–87. https://pubmed.ncbi.nlm.nih.gov/30739945

Kruse, D., and Schur, L. (2003a). Employment of people with disabilities following the ADA. *Industrial Relations, 42*(1), 31–66.

Kruse, D., and Schur, L. (2003b). Does the definition affect the outcome? Employment of people with disabilities under alternative disability definitions. *Why the Decline in Employment of People with Disabilities: A Policy Puzzle,* 279–300. W.E. Upjohn Institute for Employment Research.

Kubeck, J.E., Delp, N.D., Haslett, T.K., and McDaniel, M.A. (1996). Does job-related training performance decline with age? *Psychology and Aging, 11*(1), 92–107. https://pubmed.ncbi.nlm.nih.gov/8726375

Kuhn, A., Staubli, S., Wuellrich, J., and Zweimüller, J. (2020). Fatal attraction? Extended unemployment benefits, labor force exits, and mortality. *Journal of Public Economics, 191*(November), 10487. https://doi.org/10.1016/j.jpubeco.2019.104087

Kuhn, P., and Shen, K. (2013). Gender discrimination in job ads: Evidence from China. *Quarterly Journal of Economics, 128*(1), 287–336.

Kunze, F., Boehm, S.A., and Bruch, H. (2011). Age diversity, age discrimination climate and performance consequences—a cross organizational study. *Journal of Organizational Behavior, 32*(2), 264–290.

Kurdi, B., Seitchik, A.E., Axt, J.R., Carroll, T.J., Karapetyan, A., Kaushik, N., Tomezsko, D., Greenwald, A.G., & Banaji, M.R. (2019). Relationship between the implicit association test and intergroup behavior: A meta-analysis. *American Psychologist, 74*(5), 569–586.

Kurtulus, F.A. (2012). Affirmative action and the occupational advancement of minorities and women during 1973–2003. *Industrial Relations, 51*(2), 213–246.

Kutscher, R.E., and Walker, J.F. (1960). Comparative job performance of office workers by age. *Monthly Labor Review, 83*(1), 39–43.

Kwon, I., Milgrom, E., and Hwang, S. (2010). Cohort effects in promotions and wages: Evidence from Sweden and the United States. *The Journal of Human Resources, 45*(3), 772–808.

Lagacé, M., Firzly, N., and Zhang, A. (2020). Self-report measures of ageism in the workplace: A scoping review. *Researching Ageing: Methodological Challenges and their Empirical Background*, 41–55. Routledge.

Lahey, J.N. (2008). State age protection laws and the Age Discrimination in Employment Act. *Journal of Law and Economics, 51*(3), 433–460. https://www.nber.org/papers/w12048

Lahey, J.N. (2018). Understanding why Black women are not working longer. *Women Working Longer: Increased Employment at Older Ages*, 85–109. Chicago Press https://www.nber.org/books-and-chapters/women-working-longer-increased-employment-older-ages

Lahey, J.N., and Oxley, D.R. (2021). Discrimination at the intersection of age, race, and gender: Evidence from an eye-tracking experiment. *Journal of Policy Analysis and Management*. https://onlinelibrary.wiley.com/doi/10.1002/pam.22281

Lahey, K.E., Kim, D., and Newman, M.L. (2006). Full retirement? An examination of factors that influence the decision to return to work. *Financial Services Review 15*(1), 1.

Lahiri, K., Song, J., and Wixon, B. (2008). A model of Social Security Disability Insurance using matched SIPP/administrative data. *Journal of Econometrics, 145*(1–2), 4–20.

Laibson, D. (1997). Golden eggs and hyperbolic discounting. *The Quarterly Journal of Economics, 112*(2), 443–478.

Laitner, J., and Sonnega, A. (2013). Economic theories of retirement. *The Oxford Handbook of Retirement*, 136–151. Oxford University Press.

Laitner, J., and Stolyarov, D. (2005). *Technological Progress and Worker Productivity at Different Ages*. Michigan Retirement Research Center Research Paper No. WP2005-107. University of Michigan, Ann Arbor. https://papers.ssrn.com/sol3/papers.cfm?abstract_id=1093842

Lambert, S.J., Haley-Lock, A., and Henly, J.R. (2012). Schedule flexibility in hourly jobs: Unanticipated consequences and promising directions. *Community, Work, & Family, 15*(3), 293–315.

Lamont, R.A., Swift, H.J., and Abrams, D. (2015). A review and meta-analysis of age-based stereotype threat: Negative stereotypes, not facts, do the damage. *Psychology and Aging, 30*(1), 180–193. https://pubmed.ncbi.nlm.nih.gov/25621742

Lazear, E.P. (1979). Why is there mandatory retirement? *Journal of Political Economy, 86*(6), 1261–1284.

Lazear, E.P. (1986). Retirement from the labor force. *Handbook of Labor Economics, 1*, 305–355. Elsevier Science Publishers.

Lazear, E.P. (1995). *Personnel Economics*. The MIT Press.

Lee, M.D., Zikic, J., Noh, S., and Sargent, L. (2017). Human resource approaches to retirement: Gatekeeping, improvising, orchestrating, and partnering. *Human Resource Management, 56*(3), 455–477.

Lee, R.D. (2014). Macroeconomic consequences of population aging in the United States: Overview of a National Academy Report. *American Economic Review, 104*(5), 234–239.

Lee, R.D., and Mason, A. (2010). Some macroeconomic aspects of global population aging. *Demography, 47*(Suppl. 1), S151–S172.

Lee, T.W., Mitchell, T.R., Sablynski, C.J., Burton, J.P., and Holtom, B.C. (2004). The effects of job embeddedness on organizational citizenship, job performance, volitional absences, and voluntary turnover. *Academy of Management Journal, 47*(5), 711–722.

Lee, Z. (2020). *Returning to Work: The Role of Soft Skills and Automatability on Unretirement Decisions*. Social Science Research Network. https://papers.ssrn.com/sol3/papers.cfm?abstract_id=3878633

Lee, Z., and Angrisani, M. (2020). *Work in the Second Machine Age: Understanding the Impact of Automation on Retirement Decisions*. Unpublished paper, University of Southern California.

Lee, J., McNamara, T.K., and Pitt-Catsouphes, M. (2012). Workplace action steps for leveraging mature talent. The Sloan Center on Aging & Work at Boston College.

Levin, W.C. (1988). Age stereotyping: College student evaluations. *Research on Aging, 10*(1), 134–148.

Levy, B. (2009). Stereotype embodiment: A psychosocial approach to aging. *Current Directions in Psychological Science, 18*(6), 332–336.

Levy, H., Buchmueller, T.C., and Nikpay, S. (2018). Health reform and retirement. *The Journals of Gerontology, Series B: Psychological Sciences and Social Sciences, 73*(4), 713–722.

Lewis, E. (2011). Immigration, skill mix, and capital skill complementarity. *The Quarterly Journal of Economics, 126*(2), 1029–1069.

Li, Y., Gong, Y., Burmeister, A., Wang, M., Alterman, V., Alonso, A., and Robinson, S. (2021). Leveraging age diversity for organizational performance: An intellectual capital perspective. *Journal of Applied Psychology, 106*(1), 71–91.

Liebman, J.B. (2015). Understanding the increase in disability insurance benefit receipt in the United States. *Journal of Economic Perspectives, 29*(2), 123–150.

Lilien, D.M. (1982). Sectoral shifts and cyclical unemployment. *Journal of Political Economy, 90*(4), 777–793.

Lim, S., Cortina, L.M., and Magley, V.J. (2008). Personal and workgroup incivility: Impact on work and health outcomes. *The Journal of Applied Psychology, 93*(1), 95–107.

Lin, N., and Dumin, M. (1986). Access to occupational through social ties. *Social Networks, 8*(4), 365–385.

REFERENCES

Lin, N., Ensel, W.M., and Vaughn, J.C. (1981). Social resources and strength of ties: Structural factors in occupational status attainment. *American Sociological Review, 46*(4), 393–405.

Lindemann, B.T., and Kadue, D.D. (2003). *Age Discrimination in Employment Law*. BNA Books.

Liu, S., and Stapleton, D.C. (2011). Longitudinal statistics on work activity and use of employment supports for new Social Security Disability Insurance beneficiaries. *Social Security Bulletin, 71*(3), 35–59.

Liu, S., Huang, J., and Wang, M. (2014). Effectiveness of job search interventions: A meta-analytic review. *Psychological Bulletin, 140*(4), 1009–1041.

Lleras-Muney, A. (2005). The relationship between education and adult mortality in the United States. *The Review of Economic Studies, 72*(1), 189–221.

Lopez Garcia, I., Maestas, N., and Mullen, K. (2019). *Latent Work Capacity and Retirement Expectations*. Michigan Retirement Research Center Research Paper No. 2019-400. University of Michigan, Ann Arbor.

Loprest, P. (2007). *Strategic Assessment of the State of the Science in Research on Employment for Individuals with Disabilities*. The Urban Institute.

Loretto, W., and White, P. (2006). Employers' attitudes, practices and policies towards older workers. *Human Resource Management Journal, 16*(3), 313–330.

Lumsdaine, R.L., Stock, J.H., and Wise, D.A. (1996). Why are retirement rates so high at age 65? In D.A. Wise (Ed.), *Advances in the Economics of Aging*, 61–82. University of Chicago Press. https://scholar.harvard.edu/files/stock/files/why_are_retirement_rates_so_high_at_age_65.pdf

Lund, S., Manyika, J., Segel, L.H., Dua, A., Hancock, B., Rutherford, S., and Macon, B. (2019). *The Future of Work in America: People and Places Today and Tomorrow*. Report by McKinsey Global Institute, McKinsey and Company. https://www.mckinsey.com/featured-insights/future-of-work/the-future-of-work-in-america-people-and-places-today-and-tomorrow

Lusardi, A. (2009). U.S. household savings behavior: The role of financial literacy, information and financial education programs. *Policymaking Insights from Behavioral Economics*, 109–149. Federal Reserve Bank of Boston.

Lusardi, A., and Mitchell, O.S. (2008). Planning and financial literacy: How do women fare? *American Economic Review, 98*(2), 413–417.

Lusardi, A., and Mitchell, O.S. (2011). Financial literacy and planning: Implications for retirement well-being. *Financial Literacy: Implications for Retirement Security and the Financial Marketplace*, 17–39. Oxford University Press.

Lusardi, A., and Mitchell, O.S. (2014). The Economic Importance of Financial Literacy: Theory and Evidence. *Journal of Economic Literature, 52*(1), 5–44.

Lusardi, A., and Mitchell, O.S. (2016). *Older Women's Labor Market Attachment, Retirement Planning, and Household Debt*. NBER Working Paper Series No. 22606. National Bureau of Economic Research. https://www.nber.org/system/files/working_papers/w22606/w22606.pdf

Lusardi, A., Mitchell, O.S., and Curto, V. (2010). Financial literacy among the young. *Journal of Consumer Affairs, 44*(2), 358–380.

Lusardi, A., Mitchell, O.S., and Curto, V. (2014). Financial literacy and financial sophistication in the older population. *Journal of Pension Economics & Finance, 13*(4), 347–366.

Macunovich, D.J. (1999). The fortunes of one's birth: Relative cohort size and the youth labor market in the United States. *Journal of Population Economics, 12*(2), 215–272.

Madrian, B.C., and Beaulieu, N. (1998). Does Medicare eligibility affect retirement? *Inquiries in the Economics of Aging*, 109–131. University of Chicago Press. http://www.nber.org/chapters/c7083

Madrian, B.C., and Shea, D.F. (2001). The power of suggestion: Inertia in 401(k) participation and savings behavior. *The Quarterly Journal of Economics, 116*(4), 1149–1187.

Maestas, N. (2001). *Labor, Love, and Leisure: Complementarity and the Timing of Retirement by Working Couples*. University of California, Berkeley.

Maestas, N. (2010). Back to work: Expectations and realizations of work after retirement. *Journal of Human Resources, 45*(3), 718–748. https//:doi.org/10.1353/jhr.2010.0011

Maestas, N. (2018). *The Return to Work and Women's Employment Decisions*. NBER Working Paper Series No. 24429. National Bureau of Economic Research.

Maestas, N., and Zissimopoulos, J. (2010). How longer work lives ease the crunch of population aging. *Journal of Economic Perspectives, 24*(1), 139–160.

Maestas, N., Mullen, K.J., and Powell, D. (2013). *The Effect of Local Labor Demand Conditions on the Labor Supply Outcomes of Older Americans*. Stanford Institute for Economic Policy Research Discussion Paper No. 13-014. https://econpapers.repec.org/paper/sipdpaper/13-014.htm

Maestas, N., Mullen, K.J., and Powell, D. (2016). *The Effect of Population Aging on Economic Growth, the Labor Force, and Productivity*. NBER Working Paper No. 22452. https://www.nber.org/papers/w22452

Maestas, N., Mullen, K.J., Powell, D., von Wachter, T., and Wenge, J.B. (2017). Working conditions in the United States: Results of the 2015 American Working Conditions Survey. RAND Corporation. https://doi.org/10.7249/RR2014

Maestas, N., Mullen, K., and Rennane, S. (2019). Unmet need for workplace accommodation. *Journal of Policy Analysis and Management, 38*(4), 1004–1027.

Maestas, N., Mullen, K.J., and Strand, A. (2013). Does disability insurance receipt discourage work? Using examiner assignment to estimate causal effects of SSDI receipt. *American Economic Review 103*(5), 1797–1829.

Maestas, N., Mullen, K.J., and Strand, A. (2018). *The Effect of Economic Conditions on the Disability Insurance Program: Evidence from the Great Recession.* Working Paper No. W25338. National Bureau of Economic Research.

Maestas, N., Mullen, K.J., Powell, D., von Wachter, T., and Wenger, J.B. (2018). *The Value of Working Conditions in the United States and Implications for the Structure of Wages.* NBER Working Paper Series No. 25204. National Bureau of Economic Research.

Maghout-Juratli, S., Franklin, G.M., Mirza, S.K., Wickizer, T.M., and Fulton-Kehoe. (2006). Lumbar fusion outcomes in Washington State Workers' Compensation. *Spine, 31*(23), 2715–2723.

Malmberg, B., Lindh, T., and Halvarsson, M. (2008). Productivity consequences at the plant level of work-force ageing: Stagnation or a Horndal effect? *Population and Development Review, 34*(17), 238–256.

Mani, A., Mullainathan, S., Shafir, E., and Zhao, J. (2013). Poverty impedes cognitive function. *Science, 341*, 976–980.

Mann, A. (2011). The effect of late-life debt use on retirement decisions. *Social Science Research, 40*(6), 1623–1637. https//:doi.org/10.1016/j.ssresearch.2011.05.004

Marchiondo, L.A., Fisher, G.G., Cortina, L.M., and Matthews, R.A. (2020). Disrespect at work, distress at home: A longitudinal investigation of incivility spillover and crossover among older workers. *Work, Aging, & Retirement, 6*(3), 153–164.

Marchiondo, L.A., Gonzales, E., and Ran, S. (2016). Development and validation of the workplace age discrimination scale. *Journal of Business and Psychology, 31*(4), 493–513.

Marchiondo, L.A., Gonzales, E., and Williams, L.J. (2017). Trajectories of perceived workplace age discrimination and long-term associations with mental, self-rated, and occupational health. *Journals of Gerontology, Series B: Psychological Sciences and Social Sciences, 74*(4), 655–663.

Marcus, J., Fritzsche, B.A., Le, H., and Reeves, M.D. (2016). Validation of the work-related age-based stereotypes (WAS) scale. *Journal of Managerial Psychology, 31*(5), 989–1004.

Mark, J.A. (1957). Comparative job performance by age. *Monthly Labor Review, 80*, 1467–1471.

Marmora, P., and Ritter, M. (2015). Unemployment and the retirement decisions of older workers. *Journal of Labor Research, 36*(3), 274–290.

Marsden, P.V., and Campbell, K.E. (1984). Measuring tie strength. *Social Forces, 63*(2), 482–501.

Martens, A., Goldenberg, J.L., and Greenberg, J. (2005). A terror management perspective on ageism. *Journal of Social Issues, 61*(2), 223–239. https://doi.org/10.1111/j.1540-4560.2005.00403.x

Martin, L.G., Freedman, V.A., Schoeni, R.F., and Andreski, P.M. (2010). Trends in disability and related chronic conditions among people ages fifty to sixty-four. *Health Affairs, 29*(4), 725–731.

Martin, L.G., Schoeni, R.F., and Andreski, P.M. (2010). Trends in health of older adults in the United States: past, present, future. *Demography, 47*(Supp 1), S17–S40. https//:doi.org/10.1353/dem.2010.0003

Mason, S.E., Kuntz, C.V., and McGill, C.M. (2015). Oldsters and ngrams: Age stereotypes across time. *Psychological Reports, 116*(1), 324–329.

Mastrobuoni, G. (2009). Labor supply effects of the recent Social Security benefit cuts: Empirical estimates using cohort discontinuities. *Journal of Public Economics, 93*(11–12), 1224–1233.

Mastrobuoni, G., and Weinberg, M. (2009). Heterogeneity in intra-monthly consumption patterns, self-control, and savings at retirement. *American Economic Journal: Economic Policy, 1*(2), 163–189.

Matz-Costa, C., Besen, E., James, J.B., and Pitt-Catsouphes, M. (2014). The differential impact of multiple levels of productive activity engagement on psychological well-being in middle and later life. *The Gerontologist, 54*(2), 277–289. http://dx.doi.org/10.1093/geront/gns148

Matz-Costa, C., Carr, D.C, McNamara, T.K., and James, J.B. (2015). Physical, cognitive, social, and emotional mediators of activity involvement and health in later life. *Research on Aging, 38*(7), 791–815.

Mayer, G. (2013). *The Family and Medical Leave Act (FMLA), Policy Issues.* Congressional Research Service Report for Congress, No. 7-5700, Washington, DC.

Mazzonna, F., and Peracchi, F. (2017). Unhealthy retirement? *Journal of Human Resources, 52*(1), 128–151.

McCann, R., and Giles, H. (2002). Ageism in the workplace: A communication perspective. *Ageism: Stereotyping and Prejudice Against Older Persons*, 163–199. MIT Press.

McCllelan, M. (1998). Health events, health insurance, and labor supply: Evidence from the Health and Retirement Survey. *Frontiers in the Economics of Aging*, 301–346. University of Chicago Press.

McDonough, P., Worts, D., Corna, L.M., McMunn, A., and Sacker. A. (2017). Later-life employment trajectories and health. *Advances in Life Course Research, 34*, 22–33.

McEvoy, G.M., and Cascio, W.R. (1989). Cumulative evidence on the relationship between employee age and job performance. *Journal of Applied Psychology, 74*(1), 11–17.

McGarry, K. (1996). Factors determining participation of the elderly in Supplemental Security Income. *The Journal of Human Resources, 31*(2), 331–358.

McGarry, K. (2004). Health and retirement: Do changes in health affect retirement expectations? *Journal of Human Resources, 39*(3), 624–648.

McGonagle, A.K., Fisher, G.G., Barnes-Farrell, J.L., and Grosch, J.W. (2015). Individual and work factors related to perceived work ability and labor force outcomes. *Journal of Applied Psychology, 100*(2), 376–398.

McGuinness, S., Pouliakas, K., and Redmond, P. (2019). *Skills-Displacing Technological Change and Its Impact on Jobs: Challenging Technological Alarmism?* IZA Discussion Paper No. 12541. Institute of Labor Economics.

McInerney, M., and Simon, K. (2012). The effect of state Workers' Compensation program changes on the use of federal Social Security Disability Insurance. *Industrial Relations, 51*(1), 57–88.

McLaughlin, J.S. (2020). Falling between the cracks: Discrimination laws and older women. *Labour, 34*(2), 215–238. https://onlinelibrary.wiley.com/doi/abs/10.1111/labr.12175

McNamara, T.K., and Gonzales, E. (2011). Volunteer transitions among older adults: The role of human, social, and cultural capital in later life. *Journals of Gerontology, 66B*(4), S490–S501.

McNamara, T.K., and Pitt-Catsouphes, M. (2020). The stickiness of quality work: Exploring relationships between the quality of employment and the intent to turnover. *Current and Emerging Trends in Aging and Work*, 375–395. Springer Nature Switzerland.

McSteen, M.A. (1985). *Fifty Years of Social Security*. Commemoration of the 50th anniversary of Social Security. https://www.ssa.gov/history/50mm2.html

Medoff, J.L., and Abraham, K.G. (1980). Experience, performance, and earnings. *Quarterly Journal of Economics, 95*(4), 703–736. https://econpapers.repec.org/article/oupqjecon/v_3a95_3ay_3a1980_3ai_3a4_3ap_3a703-736..htm

Mercer and Oliver Wyman. *Twin Trends of Aging and Automation*. Marsh & McLennan Companies White Paper. https://www.mercer.com/content/dam/mercer/attachments/private/mercer-gl-2018-workforce-of-the-future-web.pdf

Mermin, G.B., Johnson, R.W., and Murphy, D.P. (2007). Why do Boomers plan to work longer? *The Journals of Gerontology, Series B: Psychological Sciences and Social Sciences, 62*(5), S286–S294.

Meyer, K., Kaiser, N., Benton, D., Fitzpatrick, S. Gassoumis, Z., Wilber, K., and California Task Force on Family Caregiving. (2018). *Picking Up the Pace of Change in California: A Report from the California Task Force on Family Caregiving*. USC Leonard Davis School of Gerontology. http://tffc.usc.edu/wp-content/uploads/2018/07/USC_CA_TFFC_Report_Digital-FINAL.pdf

Michaud, A., Moore, T.J., and Wiczer, D.G. (2019). *Understanding the Geographic Variation in Social Security Disability Insurance*. Working Paper No. DRC 18-03. NBER Disability Research Center, National Bureau of Economic Research.

Mikelson, K.S. (2017). *The Role of SCSEP in Workforce Training for Low-Income Older Workers*. The Senior Community Service Employment Program White Paper. Income and Benefits Policy Center, Urban Institute. https://www.urban.org/sites/default/files/publication/94371/2001575_scsep_white_paper_finalized_0.pdf

Miller, K. (n.d.). *The Protecting Older Workers Against Discrimination Act (POWADA)—S. 485*. https://www.aging.senate.gov/imo/media/doc/POWADA%202019%20One-Pager.pdf

Miller, M. (2020). *A Pandemic Problem for Older Workers: Will They Have to Retire Sooner?* New York Times. https://www.nytimes.com/2020/06/26/business/retirement-coronavirus.html

Mills, G., Gale, W.G., Patterson, R., and Apostolov, E. (2006). *What do Individual Development Accounts Do? Evidence from a Controlled Experiment*. Social Science Research Network. https://papers.ssrn.com/sol3/papers.cfm?abstract_id=915381

Modigliani, Franco, (1975). The life-cycle hypothesis of saving twenty years later. *Contemporary Issues in Economics*, 2–35. Manchester University Press.

Moen, P. (2007). Not so big jobs and retirements: What workers (and retirees) really want. *Generations, 31*(1), 31–36.

Moen, P. (2013). Constrained choices: The shifting institutional contexts of aging and the life course. *Perspectives on the Future of the Sociology of Aging*, 175–216. National Research Council.

Moen, P. (2016a). *Encore Adulthood: Boomers on the Edge of Risk, Renewal, and Purpose*. Oxford University Press.

Moen, P. (2016b). Work over the gendered life course. *Handbook of the Life Course, 2*, 249–275. Springer Publishing.

Moen, P. (2020). Working longer versus flexible pathways in uncertain times. *Public Policy & Aging Report, 30*(3), 124–129. https://par.nsf.gov/servlets/purl/10218803

Moen, P., and Roehling, P. (2005). *The Career Mystique: Cracks in the American Dream*. Rowman and Littlefield.

Moen, P., Fan, W., and Kelly, E.L. (2013). Team-level flexibility, work-home spillover, and health behavior. *Social Science and Medicine, 84*, 69–79.

Moen, P., Flood, S., and Wang, J. (2021). The uneven later work course: Intersectional gender, age, race, and class disparities. *Journals of Gerontology, Series B: Psychological Sciences and Social Sciences*. https://doi.org/10.1093/geronb/gbab039

Moen, P., Huang, Q., Plassmann, V., and Dentinger, E. (2006). Deciding the future: Do dual-earner couples plan together for retirement? *American Behavioral Scientist, 49*(10), 1422–1443.

Moen, P., Kelly, E., Fan, W., Lee, S., Almeida, D., Ernst Kossek, E., and Buxton, O. (2016b). Does a flexibility/support organizational initiative improve high-tech employees' well-being? Evidence from the Work, Family, and Health Network. *American Sociological Review, 81*(1), 134–164.

Moen, P., Kelly, E., and Hill, R. (2011). Does enhancing work-time control and flexibility reduce turnover? A naturally-occurring experiment. *Social Problems, 58*(1), 69–98.

Moen, P., Kelly, E., and Lam, J. (2013). Healthy work revisited: Does reducing time strain promote women's and men's well-being? *Journal of Occupational Health Psychology, 18*(2), 157–172.

Moen, P., Kelly, E.L., Lee, S.-R., Oakes, J.M., Fan, W., Bray, J., Almeida, D., Hammer, L., Hurtado, D., and Buxton, O. (2017). Can a flexibility/support initiative reduce turnover intentions and exits? Results from the Work, Family, and Health Network. *Social Problems, 64*(1), 53–85. https://doi-org.stanford.idm.oclc.org/10.1093/socpro/spw033

Moen, P., Kelly, E.L., Tranby, E., and Huang, Q. (2011). Changing work, changing health: Can real work-time flexibility promote health behaviors and well-being? *Journal of Health and Social Behavior, 52*(4), 404–429.

Moen, P., Kojola, E., Kelly, E.L., and Karakaya, Y. (2016a). Men and women expecting to work longer: Do changing work conditions matter? *Work, Aging, and Retirement, 2*(3), 321–344.

Moen, P., Pedtke, J.H., and Flood, S. (2020). Disparate disruptions: Intersectional COVID-19 employment effects by age, gender, education, and race/ethnicity. *Work, Aging, and Retirement, 6*(4), 207–228.

Moen, P., Robison, J., and Dempster-McClain, D. (1995). Caregiving and women's well-being: A life course approach. *Journal of Health and Social Behavior, 36*, 259–273.

Mokyr, J. (2014). Secular stagnation? Not in your life. *Secular Stagnation: Facts, Causes, and Cures*, 83–89. CEPR Press.

Mokyr, J., Vickers, C., and Ziebarth, N.L. (2015). The history of technological anxiety and the future of economic growth: Is this time different? *Journal of Economic Perspectives, 29*(3), 31–50.

Monahan, C., Macdonald, J., Lytle, A., Apriceno, M., and Levy, S.R. (2020). COVID-19 and ageism: How positive and negative responses impact older adults and society. *American Psychologist, 75*(7), 887–896.

Mont, D., Burton, J.F., and Reno, V. (2000). *Workers' Compensation: Benefits, Coverage, and Costs, 1997–1998: New Estimates*. National Academy of Social Insurance.

Montenegro, X., Fisher, L., and Remez, S. (2002). *Staying Ahead of the Curve: The AARP Work and Career Study, A National Survey Conducted for AARP by RoperASW*. AARP. https://assets.aarp.org/rgcenter/econ/d17773_multiwork_1.pdf

Montenovo, L., Jiang, X., Rojas, F.L., Schmutte, I.M., Simon, K.I., Weinberg, B.A., and Wing, C. (2020). *Determinants of Disparities in COVID-19 Job Losses*. NBER Working Paper No. 27132, Cambridge, MA. https://www.nber.org/system/files/working_papers/w27132/w27132.pdf

Mor Barak, M.E. (2015). Inclusion is the Key to Diversity Management, but What is Inclusion? Human Service Organizations: Management, Leadership & Governance, 39(2), 83–88.

Morelock, J.C., McNamara, T.K., and James, J.B. (2017). Workability among older adults: The role of a time and place management intervention. *Journal of Applied Gerontology, 36*(11), 1370–1392. https://scholar.google.com/citations?view_op=view_citation&hl=en&user=c50xpCwAAAAJ&citation_for_view=c50xpCwAAAAJ:WF5omc3nYNoC

Morin, L.-P. (2015). Cohort size and youth earnings: Evidence from a quasi-experiment. *Labour Economics, 32*(C), 99–111.

Morrison, M.H. (1988). Changes in the legal mandatory retirement age: Labor force participation implications. *Issues in Contemporary Retirement*, 378–405. Hoover Institute Press, Stanford University.

Morrow-Howell, N., and Gonzales, E. (2020). Recovering from coronavirus disease 2019 (COVID-19), Resisting ageism and recommitting to a productive aging perspective. *Public Policy & Aging Report, 30*(4), 133–137.

Morrow-Howell, N., and Sherraden, M.S. (2015). *Financial Capability and Asset Holding in Later Life: A Life Course Perspective*. Oxford University Press.

Morrow-Howell, N., and Sherraden, M.S., Editors. (2014). *Financial Capability and Asset Holding in Later Life: A Life Course Perspective*. Oxford University Press.

Morrow-Howell, N., Hinterlong J., and Sherraden, M.S., (Eds.). (2001). *Productive Aging: Concepts and Controversies*. Johns Hopkins University Press.

Mouw, T. (2003). Social capital and finding a job: Do contacts matter? *American Sociological Review, 68*(6), 868–898.

Mullainathan, S., and Shafir, E. (2013). Decision making and policy in contexts of poverty. *The Behavioral Foundations of Public Policy*, 281–298. Princeton University Press. https://doi.org/10.2307/j.ctv550cbm.22

Mullainathan, S., and Thaler, R. (2001). Behavioral economics. *International Encyclopedia of the Social and Behavioral Sciences, 20*, 1094–1100. Oxford University Press.

Munnell, A.H. (2015). *Falling Short: The Coming Retirement Crisis and What to Do About It.* Issue Brief No. 15-7, Center for Retirement and Research at Boston College. https://crr.bc.edu/wp-content/uploads/2015/04/IB_15-7_508.pdf

Munnell, A.H., and Chen, A. (2015). *Trends in Social Security Claiming.* Issue Brief No. 15-8, Center for Retirement Research at Boston College.

Munnell, A.H., and Sass, S.A. (2008). *Working Longer: The Solution to the Retirement Income Challenge.* The Brookings Institution.

Munnell, A.H., and Wu, A.Y. (2012). *Are Aging Boomers Squeezing Young Workers Out of Jobs?* Issue Brief No. 12-18, Center for Retirement Research at Boston College. https://crr.bc.edu/briefs/are-aging-baby-boomers-squeezing-young-workers-out-of-jobs

Munnell, A.H., Aubrey, J.-P., and Crawford, C.V. (2017). *Multiemployer Pension Plans: Current Status and Future Trends.* Special Report, Center for Retirement Research at Boston College. https://crr.bc.edu/wp-content/uploads/2017/12/multiemployer_specialreport_1_4_2018.pdf

Munnell, A.H., Chen, A., and Hou, W. (2020). *How Widespread Unemployment Might Affect Retirement Security.* Issue Brief No. 2020-11, Center for Retirement Research at Boston College. https://crr.bc.edu/briefs/how-widespread-unemployment-might-affect-retirement-security

Munnell, A.H., Hou, W., and Sanzenbacher, G.T. (2018). *Trends in Retirement Security by Race/Ethnicity.* Issue Brief No. 18-21, Center for Retirement Research at Boston College. https://crr.bc.edu/wp-content/uploads/2018/11/IB_18-21.pdf

Munnell, A.H., Meme, K.B., Cahill, K.E., and Jivan, N. (2004). Should We Raise Social Security's Earliest Eligibility Age? An Issue in Brief Series, 18. Center for Retirement Research at Boston College. https://crr.bc.edu/wp-content/uploads/2004/06/ib_18-508.pdf

Munnell, A.H., Webb, A., and Chen, A. (2018). To what extent does socioeconomic status lead people to retire too soon? *The Journal of Retirement Spring, 5*(4), 73–85. https://doi.org/10.3905/jor.2018.5.4.073

Munnell, A.H., Webb, A., and Delorme, L. (2006). *A New National Retirement Risk Index.* Issue Brief No. 48, Center for Retirement and Research at Boston College. https://citeseerx.ist.psu.edu/viewdoc/download?doi=10.1.1.962.5459&rep=rep1&type=pdf

National Academies of Sciences, Engineering, and Medicine. (2015). *The Growing Gap in Life Expectancy by Income: Implications for Federal Programs and Policy Responses.* The National Academies Press. https://doi.org/10.17226/19015

National Academies of Sciences, Engineering, and Medicine. (2017). *The Economic and Fiscal Consequences of Immigration.* The National Academies Press. https://doi.org/10.17226/23550

National Academies of Sciences, Engineering, and Medicine. (2018). *Future Directions for the Demography of Aging: Proceedings of a Workshop.* The National Academies Press. https://doi.org/10.17226/25064

National Academies of Sciences, Engineering, and Medicine. (2020). *Measuring Alternative Work Arrangements for Research and Policy.* The National Academies Press. https://doi.org/10.17226/25822

National Academies of Sciences, Engineering, and Medicine. (2021). *High and Rising Mortality Rates Among Working-Age Adults.* The National Academies Press. https://doi.org/10.17226/25976

National Center for Health Statistics. (2009). *Percent of U.S. Adults 55 and Over with Chronic Conditions.* Centers for Disease Control and Prevention. https://www.cdc.gov/nchs/health_policy/adult_chronic_conditions.htm

National Center for Health Statistics (2015). *Health, United States, 2014: With Special Feature on Adults Aged 55–64.* National Center for Health Statistics Reports Report No.: 2015-1232. National Center for Health Statistics.

National Center for Health Statistics. (2021). *Risk for COVID-19 Infection, Hospitalization, and Death by Race/Ethnicity.* https://www.cdc.gov/coronavirus/2019-ncov/covid-data/investigations-discovery/hospitalization-death-by-race-ethnicity.html

National Council on Aging. (2001). *Nine Best Practices of Highly Effective SCSEP Projects.* Arlington, VA. Prepared for the U.S. Department of Labor, Employment and Training Administration. https://www.ncoa.org/article/9-best-practices-of-highly-effective-scsep-projects

National Institute for Occupational Safety and Health. (2018). *What is Total Worker Health?* NIOSH and the Centers for Disease Control and Prevention. U.S. Department of Health and Human Services. https://www.cdc.gov/niosh/twh/totalhealth.html

National Institute of Mental Health. (2019). *Mental Illness.* NIMH. https://www.nimh.nih.gov/health/statistics/mental-illness.shtml

National Research Council. (2004). *Measuring Racial Discrimination.* National Academies Press. https://www.nap.edu/catalog/10887/measuring-racial-discrimination

Nelson, T.D. (2005). Ageism: Prejudice against our feared future selves. *Journal of Social Issues, 61*(2), 207–221.

Neufeind, M., O'Reilly, J., and Ranft, F. (2018). *Work in the Digital Age: Challenges of the Fourth Industrial Revolution.* Rowman and Littlefield.

Neuman, K. (2008). Quit your job and get healthier? The effect of retirement on health. *Journal of Labor Research, 29*(2), 177–201.

Neumark, D. (1996). Sex discrimination in restaurant hiring: An audit study. *Quarterly Journal of Economics, 111*(3), 915–941.

Neumark, D. (2009). The Age Discrimination in Employment Act and the challenge of population aging. *Research on Aging, 31*(1), 41–68.

Neumark, D. (2018). Experimental research on labor market discrimination. *Journal of Economic Literature, 56*(3), 799–866.

Neumark, D., (Ed.) (2000). *On the Job: Is Long-Term Employment a Thing of the Past?* Russell Sage Foundation.

Neumark, D., and Button, P. (2014). Did age discrimination protections help older workers weather the Great Recession? *Journal of Policy Analysis and Management, 33*(3), 566–601.

Neumark, D., and Powers, E. (2000). Welfare for the elderly: The effects of SSI on pre-retirement labor supply. *Journal of Public Economics, 78*(1–2), 51–80.

Neumark, D., and Powers, E. (2005). The effects of changes in state SSI supplements on preretirement labor supply. *Public Finance Review, 33*(1), 3–35.

Neumark, D., and Simpson, H. (2015). Place-based policies. *Handbook of Regional and Urban Economics, 5*, 1197–1287. Elsevier.

Neumark, D., and Song, J. (2013). Do stronger age discrimination laws make Social Security reforms more effective? *Journal of Public Economics, 108*, 1–16.

Neumark, D., and Stock, W.A. (1999). Age discrimination laws and labor market efficiency. *Journal of Political Economy, 107*(5), 1081–1125.

Neumark, D., and Valletta, R.G. (2012). *Worker Skills and Job Quality.* FRBSF Economic Letter, 2012-13. San Francisco: Federal Reserve Bank of San Francisco. https://www.researchgate.net/publication/254415834_Worker_skills_and_job_quality

Neumark, D., and Yen, M. (2020). Relative sizes of age cohorts and labor force participation of older workers. *Demography, 57*(1), 1–31.

Neumark, D., Burn, I., and Button, P. (2019). Is it harder for older workers to find jobs? New and improved evidence from a field experiment. *Journal of Political Economy, 127*(2), 922–970.

Neumark, D., Burn, I., Button, P., and Chehras, N. (2019). Do State Laws Protecting Older Workers from Discrimination Reduce Age Discrimination in Hiring? Evidence from a Field Experiment. *Journal of Law and Economics, 62*(2), 373–402.

Newman, K.S. (1999). *No Shame in My Game: The Working Poor in the Inner City.* Knopf and Russell Sage Foundation.

Newman, K.S., and Lennon, C. (1995). *Finding Work in the Inner City: How Hard Is It Now: How Hard Will It Be for AFDC Recipients?* Working Paper No. 76. Russell Sage Foundation.

Ng, T.W.H., and Feldman, D.C. (2008). The relationship of age to ten dimensions of job performance. *Journal of Applied Psychology, 93*(2), 392–423.

Ng, T.W.H., and Feldman, D.C. (2012). Evaluating six common stereotypes about older workers with meta-analytical data. *Personnel Psychology, 65*(4), 821–858.

Niessen, C., Swarrowsky, C., and Leiz, M. (2010). Age and adaptation to changes in the workplace. *Journal of Managerial Psychology, 25*(4), 356–383.

Nishii, L.H. (2013). The benefits of climate for inclusion for gender-diverse groups. *Academy of Management Journal, 56*(6), 1754–1774.

Nishii, L.H., and Langevin, A. (2009). Climate for inclusion: Unit predictors and outcomes. *Inclusion in organizations: Measures, HR practices, and climate.* Symposium delivered at the annual meeting of the Academy of Management, Chicago.

Nishii, L.H., Lepak, D.P., and Schneider, B. (2008). Employee attributions of the why of HR practices: Their effects on employee attitudes and behaviors, and customer satisfaction. *Personnel Psychology, 61*(3), 503–545.

Niu, X. (2014). Health insurance and self-employment: Evidence from Massachusetts. *Industrial and Labor Relations Review, 67*(4), 1235–1273.

Noe-Bustamante, L. (2019). *Key Facts About U.S. Hispanics and Their Diverse Heritage.* Pew Research Center. https://www.pewresearch.org/fact-tank/2019/09/16/key-facts-about-u-s-hispanics

North, M.S. (2019). A gate to understanding older workers: Generation, age, tenure, experience. *The Academy of Management Annals, 13*(2), 414–443.

North, M.S., and Fiske, S.T. (2012). An inconvenienced youth? Ageism and its potential intergenerational roots. *Psychological Bulletin, 138*(5), 982–997.

North, M. S., and Fiske, S.T. (2013). Act your (old) age: Prescriptive, ageist biases over succession, consumption, and identity. *Personality and Social Psychology Bulletin, 39*(6), 720–734.

North, M.S., and Fiske, S.T. (2015a). Intergenerational resource tensions in the workplace and beyond: Individual, interpersonal, institutional, international. *Research in Organizational Behavior, 35*, 159–179.

North, M. S., and Fiske, S. T. (2015b). Modern attitudes toward older adults in the aging world: A cross-cultural meta-analysis. *Psychological Bulletin, 141*(5), 993–1021.

Nosek, B.A. (2005). Moderators of the relationship between implicit and explicit evaluation. *Journal of Experimental Psychology: General, 134*(4), 565–584.

Nüß, P. (2018). *Duration Dependence as an Unemployment Stigma: Evidence from a Field Experiment in Germany*. Economics Working Paper No. 2018-06. Kiel University, Department of Economics, Kiel. http://hdl.handle.net/10419/179941

Nyberg, A.J., and Ployhart, R.E. (2013). Context-emergent turnover (CET) theory: A theory of collective turnover. *Academy of Management Review, 38*(1), 109–131.

Nyce, S., Schieber, S.J., Shoven, J.B., Slavov, S.N., and Wise, D.A. (2013). Does retiree health insurance encourage early retirement? *Journal of Public Economics 104*(C), 40–51.

OASDI Trustees. (2020). *The 2020 Annual Report of the Board of Trustees of the Federal Old-Age and Survivors Insurance and Federal Disability Insurance Trust Funds*. https://www.ssa.gov/oact/TR/2020/I_intro.html#1001487

O'Donnell, O., van Doorslaer, E., and Van Ourti, T. (2015). Health and inequality. *Handbook of Income Distribution, 2B*, 1419–1533. https://doi.org/10.1016/B978-0-444-59429-7.00018-2

O'Leary, P., Boden, L.I., Seabury, S.A., Ozonoff, A., and Scherer, E. (2012). Workplace injuries and the take-up of Social Security Disability Benefits. *Social Security Bulletin, 72*(3), 1–17.

O'Meara, D.P. (1989). *Protecting the Growing Number of Older Workers: The Age Discrimination in Employment Act*. University of Pennsylvania.

O'Neill, J., Mamun, A.A., Potamites, E., Chan, F., and da Silva Cordoso, E. (2015). Return to work of disability insurance beneficiaries who do and do not access state vocational rehabilitation agency services. *Journal of Disability Policy Studies, 26*(2), 111–123.

O'Rand, A. (1996). The precious and the precocious: Understanding cumulative disadvantage and cumulative advantage over the life course. *The Gerontologist, 36*(2), 230–238.

Olesen, S.C., Butterworth, P., and Rodgers, B. (2012). Is poor mental health a risk factor for retirement? Findings from a longitudinal population survey. *Social Psychiatry and Psychiatric Epidemiology, 47*(5), 735–744.

Ollier-Malaterre, A., McNamara, T., Matz-Costa, C., Pitt-Catsouphes, M., and Valcour, M. (2013). Looking up to regulations, out at peers or down at the bottom line: How institutional logics affect the prevalence of age-related HR practices. *Human Relations, 66*(10), 1373–1395.

Olsen, A. (2012). Mind the gap: The distributional effects of raising the early eligibility age and full retirement age. *Social Security Bulletin, 72*(4). https://www.ssa.gov/policy/docs/ssb/v72n4/v72n4p37.html

Olsen, A., and Whitman, K. (2007). Effective retirement savings programs: Design features and financial education. *Social Security Bulletin, 67*(3), 53–72.

Organisation for Economic Co-operation and Development. (2017a). *Pensions at a Glance 2017*. OECD Publishing Biennial Report. https://www.oecd-ilibrary.org/social-issues-migration-health/pensions-at-a-glance-2017_pension_glance-2017-en

Organisation for Economic Co-operation and Development. (2017b). *Preventing Ageing Unequally*. OECD Publishing. https://www.oecd.org/health/preventing-ageing-unequally-9789264279087-en.htm

Örestig, J., Strandh, M., and Stattin, M. (2013). A wish come true? A longitudinal analysis of the relationship between retirement preferences and the timing of retirement. *Population Ageing 6*(1–2), 99–118.

Oster, S.M., and Hamermesh, D.S. (1998). Aging and productivity among economists. *Review of Economics and Statistics, 80*(1), 154–156.

Ostroff, C., and Schulte, M. (2007). Multiple perspectives of fit in organizations across levels of analysis. *Perspectives on Organizational Fit*, 3–69. Lawrence Erlbaum.

Oude Mulders, J., and Henkens, K. (2019). Employers' adjustment to longer working lives. *Innovation in Aging, 3*(1), 1–10.

Oude Mulders, J., Henkens, K., and Schippers, J. (2015). Organizations' ways of employing early retirees: The role of age-based HR policies. *The Gerontologist, 55*(3), 374–383.

Ouimet, P.P., and Zarutskie, R. (2013). *Who Works for Startups? The Relation between Firm Age, Employee Age, and Growth*. Finance and Economics Discussion Series 2013-75. Board of Governors of the Federal Reserve System.

Pak, K., Kooij, T.A.M., de Lange, A., and van Veldhoven, M.J.P.M. (2018). Human resource management and the ability, motivation, and opportunity to continue working: A review of quantitative studies. *Human Resource Management Review, 29*(3), 336–352.

Papadopoulos, M., Fisher, B., Ghilarducci, T., and Radpour, S. (2020). *Over Half of Unemployed Older Workers at Risk of Involuntary Retirement*. The New School, Schwartz Center for Economic Policy Analysis. https://www.economicpolicyresearch.org/jobs-report/over-half-of-older-workers-unemployed-at-risk-of-involuntary-retirement

Papke, L.E. (1996). Quantifying the substitution of 401(k) plans for defined benefit plans: Evidence from panel data. *The Journal of Human Resources, 34*(2), 346–368.

Parent, R., Sayman, I., and Kulzer, K. (2012). *Profile of Social Security Disabled Workers and Dependents Who Have a Connection to Workers' Compensation or Public Disability Benefits*. Research and Statistics Note No. 2012-03, Social Security Administration.

Parker, K., Horowitz, J.M., and Minkin, R. (2020). *How the Coronavirus Outbreak Has—and Hasn't—Changed the Way Americans Work*. Pew Research Center. https://www.pewresearch.org/social-trends/wp-content/uploads/sites/3/2020/12/PSDT_12.09.20_covid.work_fullreport.pdf

Parker, S.K., and Andrei, D.M. (2020). Include, individualize, and integrate: Organizational meta-strategies for mature workers. *Work, Aging and Retirement, 6*(1), 1–7. https://doi.org/10.1093/workar/waz009

Parsons, D.O. (1991). The health and earnings of rejected disability insurance applicants: Comment. *American Economic Review, 81*(5), 1419–1426.

Pascoe, E.A., and Smart Richman, L. (2009). Perceived discrimination and health: A meta-analytic review. *Psychological Bulletin, 135*(4), 531–554.

Pavalko, E.K., and Artis, J.E. (1997). Women's caregiving and paid work: Causal relationships in midlife. *Journals of Gerontology, Series B: Psychological Sciences and Social Sciences, 52*(4), S170–S179.

Peiró, J.M., Tordera, N., and Potočnik, K. (2013). Retirement practices in different countries. *The Oxford Handbook of Retirement*, 510–540. Oxford University Press.

Peng, Y., Jex, S., and Wang, M. (2018). Aging and occupational health. *Aging and Work in the 21st Century*, 213–233. Psychology Press.

Peri, G. (2016). Immigrants, productivity, and labor markets. *Journal of Economic Perspectives, 30*(4), 3–30.

Perry, E.L., Kulik, C.J., and Bourhis, A.C. (1996). Moderating effects of personal and contextual factors in age discrimination. *Journal of Applied Psychology, 81*(6), 628–647.

Peterson, C.L., and Murphy, G. (2010). Transition from the labor market: Older workers and retirement. *International Journal of Health Services, 40*(4), 609–627.

Pfeffer, J. (2018). *Dying for a Paycheck*. HarperBusiness. https://jeffreypfeffer.com/books/dying-for-a-paycheck

Picchio, M. (2015). *Is Training Effective for Older Workers?* IZA World of Labor. https://wol.iza.org/articles/is-training-effective-for-older-workers/long

Picchio, M., and van Ours, J.C. (2013). Retaining through training: Even for older workers. *Economics of Education Review, 32*(C), 29–48.

Pienta, A.M., and Hayward, M.D. (2002). Who expects to continue working after age 62? The retirement plans of couples. *Journals of Gerontology, Series B: Psychological Sciences and Social Sciences, 57*(4), S199–S208.

Pingle, J.F. (2006). *Social Security's Delayed Retirement Credit and the Labor Supply of Older Men*. Working Paper No. 2006-37, Finance and Economics Discussion Series, Federal Reserve Board. https://www.federalreserve.gov/pubs/feds/2006/200637/200637pap.pdf

Pissarides, C.A. (2013). Unemployment in the Great Recession. *Economica, 80*(319), 385–403.

Piszczek, M.M. and Pimputkar, A.S. (2020). Flexible schedules across working lives: Age-specific effects on well-being and work. *Journal of Applied Psychology, 106*(12), 1907–1920. https://doi.org/10.1037/apl0000844

Pitt-Catsouphes, M., and Matz-Costa, C. (2008). The multi-generational workforce: Workplace flexibility and engagement. *Community, Work, & Family, 11*(2), 215–229.

Pitt-Catsouphes, M., Matz-Costa, C., and James, J. (2012). *Through a Different Looking Glass: The Prism of Age*. Sloan Center on Aging and Work, Boston College.

Pitt-Catsouphes, M., McNamara, T., and Sweet, S. (2015). Getting a good fit for older employees. *The Multigenerational and Aging Workforce: Challenges and Opportunities*, 383–407. Edward Elgar Publishing.

Pitts, D. (2009). Diversity management, job satisfaction, and performance: Evidence from the U.S. federal agencies. *Public Administration Review, 69*(2), 328–338. https://onlinelibrary.wiley.com/doi/full/10.1111/j.1540-6210.2008.01977.x

Plan Council Sponsor of America. (2020a). *COVID-19 Impact on 401(k) Plans*. Plan Council Sponsor of America. https://www.psca.org/sites/psca.org/files/Research/2020/401k%20Fall%20Snapshot_FINAL.pdf

Plan Council Sponsor of America. (2020b). *Impact of COVID-19 and Economic Conditions on 403(b) Plans*. Plan Council Sponsor of America. https://www.psca.org/sites/psca.org/files/Research/2020/2020403b-Snapshot_FINALreport.pdf

Pleau, R.L. (2010). Gender differences in postretirement employment. *Research on Aging, 32*(3), 267–303.

Popham, L.E., Kennison, S.M., and Bradley, K.I. (2011). Ageism, sensation-seeking, and risk-taking behavior in young adults. *Current Psychology: A Journal for Diverse Perspectives on Diverse Psychological Issues, 30*(2), 184–193. https://doi.org/10.1007/s12144-011-9107-0

Posner, R.A. (1995). *Aging and Old Age*. University of Chicago Press.

Posthuma, R.A., and Campion, M.A. (2009). Age stereotypes in the workplace: Common stereotypes, moderators, and future research directions. *Journal of Management, 35*(1), 158–188.

Portes, A. (1998). Social capital: Its origins and applications in modern sociology. *Annual Review of Sociology, 24*, 1–24. https://doi.org/10.1146/annurev.soc.24.1.1

Poterba, J.M., Venti, S.F., and Wise, D.A. (1996). How retirement saving programs increase saving. *Journal of Economic Perspectives, 10*(4), 91–112.

Powell, R., and Ferraro, S.R. (2018). The demise of the U.S. Treasury's myRA retirement program: Why it failed. *Global Journal of Accounting and Finance, 2*(1). https://go.gale.com/ps/i.do?id=GALE%7CA569113361&sid=googleScholar&v=2.1&it=r&linkaccess=abs&issn=25740474&p=AONE&sw=w&userGroupName=loyoland_main

Powers, E.T., and Neumark, D. (2003). The interaction of public retirement income programs in the United States. *American Economic Review, 93*(2), 261–265.

Pransky, G.S., Benjamin, K.L., and Savageau, J.A. (2005a). Early retirement due to occupational injury: Who is at risk? *American Journal of Industrial Medicine, 47*(4), 285–295.

Pransky, G.S., Benjamin, K.L., Savageau, J.A., Currivan, D., and Fletcher, K. (2005b). Outcomes in work-related injuries: A comparison of younger and older workers. *American Journal of Industrial Medicine, 47*(2), 104–112.

PricewaterhouseCoopers. (2015). *A Marketplace Without Boundaries? Responding to Disruption*. PWC 18th Annual Global CEO Survey. https://www.pwc.com/gx/en/ceo-survey/2015/assets/pwc-18th-annual-global-ceo-survey-jan-2015.pdf

Punnett, L., Cavallari, J.M., Henning, R.A., Nobrega, S., Dugan, A.G., and Cherniack, M.G. (2020). Defining integration for total worker health: A new proposal. *Annals of Work Exposures and Health 6*, 223–235. https//:doi.org/10.1093/annweh/wxaa003

Purdie-Vaughns, V., and Eibach, R.P. (2008). Intersectional invisibility: The distinctive advantages and disadvantages of multiple subordinate-group identities. *Sex Roles, 59*(5), 377–391.

Putnam, R. (2000). *Bowling Alone: The Collapse and Revival of American Community*. Simon and Schuster.

Quinby, L., Hou, W., Belbase, A., and Sanzenbacher, G. (2019). *Participation and Leakages in Oregon's Auto-IRA*. Working Paper No. WP2019-15, Center for Retirement Research at Boston College.

Quinn, J.F. (2010). Work, Retirement, and the Encore Career: Elders and the Future of the American Workforce. *Generations, 3*(Fall), 45–55.

Quinn, J.F., Cahill, K.E., and Giandrea, M.D. (2019). Transitions from career employment among public- and private-sector workers. *Journal of Pension Economics and Finance, 18*(4), 529–548.

Radl, J. (2013). Labour market exit and social stratification in Western Europe: The effects of social class and gender on the timing of retirement. *European Sociological Review, 29*(3), 654–668.

Rainville, C., Skufca, L., and Mehegan, L. (2016). *Family Caregiving and Out-of-Pocket Costs: 2016 Report*. American Association of Retired Persons (AARP). https://www.aarp.org/content/dam/aarp/research/surveys_statistics/ltc/2016/family-caregiving-costs. https://doi.org/10.26419-2Fres.00138.001.pdf

Rau, B.L., and Adams, G.A. (2013). Aging, retirement, and human resources management: A strategic approach. *The Oxford Handbook of Retirement*, 117–135. Oxford University Press.

Raut, L.K. (2017). Exits from the disability insurance rolls: Estimates from a competing-risks model. *Social Security Bulletin, 77*(3). https://www.ssa.gov/policy/docs/ssb/v77n3/v77n3p15.html

Raymo, J.M., and Sweeney, M.M. (2006). Work-family conflict and retirement preferences. *Journals of Gerontology, Series B: Psychological Sciences and Social Sciences, 61B*(3), S161–S169.

Raymo, J., Warren, J.R., Sweeney, M., Hauser, R., and Ho, J. (2011). Precarious employment, bad jobs, labor unions, and retirement. *Journals of Gerontology: Social Sciences, 66B*(2), 249–259.

Reinhardt, U.E. (2003). Does the aging of the population really drive the demand for health care? *Health Affairs, 22*(6), 27–39.

Reitzes, D.C., and Mutran, E.J. (2004). The transition to retirement: Stages and factors that influence retirement adjustment. *The International Journal of Aging and Human Development, 59*(1), 3–84.

Restrepo, T., and Shuford, H. (2011). *Workers Compensation and the Aging Workforce*. National Council on Compensation Insurance, Inc. Research Report. https://www.ncci.com/Articles/Pages/II_2011_Aging_Workforce_Research_Brief.pdf

Reynolds, J., and Wenger, J.B. (2010). Prelude to a RIF: Older workers, part-time hours, and unemployment. *Journal of Aging & Social Policy, 22*(2), 99–116.

Reynolds, J., and Wenger, J.B. (2012). He said, she said: The gender wage gap according to self and proxy reports in the Current Population Survey. *Social Science Research, 41*(2), 392–411.

Reznik, G.L., Weaver, D.A., and Biggs, A.G. (2009). *Social Security and Marginal Returns to Work Near Retirement*. Issue Paper No. 2009-02, Social Security Office of Retirement and Disability Policy.

Rhee, M-K., Mor Barak, M.E., and Gallo, W.T. (2015). Mechanisms of the effect of involuntary retirement on older adults' self-rated health and mental health. *Journal of Gerontological Social Work, 59*(1), 35–55. https//:doi.org/10.1080/01634372.2015.1128504

Riach, P.A., and Rich, J. (2002). Field experiments of discrimination in the market place. *The Economic Journal, 112*(483), 480–518.

Riach, P.A., and Rich, J. (2006). An Experimental Investigation of Sexual Discrimination in Hiring in the English Labor Market. *The B.E. Journal of Economic Analysis & Policy, 5*(2), 1–22.

Riach, P.A., and Rich, J. (2010). An Experimental Investigation of Age Discrimination in the English Labor Market. *Annals of Economics and Statistics, 99/100*, 169–185.

Rizzuto, T.E., Cherry, K.E., and LeDoux, J.A. (2012). The aging process and cognitive capabilities. *The Oxford Handbook of Work and Aging*, 236–255. Oxford University Press. https://doi.org/10.1093/oxfordhb/9780195385052.013.0092

Rogers, E., and Wiatrowski, W.J. (2005). Injuries, illnesses, and fatalities among older workers. *Monthly Labor Review, 128*(10), 24–30.

Rohwedder, S., and Willis, R.J. (2010). Mental retirement. *Journal of Economic Perspectives, 24*(1), 119–138.

Romero, M. (2018). *Introducing Intersectionality*. Polity Press.

Rosen, B., and Jerdee, T.H. (1976a). Influence of age stereotypes on managerial decisions. *Journal of Applied Psychology, 61*(4), 428–432.

Rosen, B., and Jerdee, T.H. (1976b). The nature of job-related age stereotypes on managerial decisions. *Journal of Applied Social Psychology, 62*, 180–183.

Rosentiel, T. (2009). *Recession Turns a Graying Office Grayer*. Pew Research Center. https://www.pewresearch.org/2009/09/03/recession-turns-a-graying-office-grayer

Rothkin, K. (2019). *Workers' Compensation Laws as of January 1, 2019*. Workers Compensation Research Institute.

Rothstein, R. (2017). *The Color of Law: A Forgotten History of How Our Government Segregated America*. Economic Policy Institute. https://www.epi.org/publication/the-color-of-law-a-forgotten-history-of-how-our-government-segregated-america

Rowe, J.W., and Kahn, R.L. (1997). Successful aging. *The Gerontologist, 37*(4), 433–440.

Rubin, J.Z., and Brown, B.R. (1975). The Social Psychology of Bargaining and Negotiation. Academic Press.

Rudolph, C.W., Rauvola, R.S., Costanza, D.P., and Zacher, H. (2020). Generations and generational differences: Debunking myths in organizational science and practice and paving new paths forward. *Journal of Business and Psychology, 36*, 945–967.

Ruffing, K. (2013). *Social Security Benefits Are Modest by International Standards*. Center on Budget and Policy Priorities. https://www.cbpp.org/blog/social-security-benefits-are-modest-by-international-standards

Ruhm, C. (1990). Bridge jobs and partial retirement. *Journal of Labor Economics, 8*(4), 482–501. https://econpapers.repec.org/article/ucpjlabec/v_3a8_3ay_3a1990_3ai_3a4_3ap_3a482-501.htm

Ruiz, N.G., Edwards, K., and Lopez, M.H. (2021). One-third of Asian Americans fear threats, physical attacks and most say violence against them is rising. Pew Research Center. https://www.pewresearch.org/fact-tank/2021/04/21/one-third-of-asian-americans-fear-threats-physical-attacks-and-most-say-violence-against-them-is-rising/

Rupp, K., Strand, A., Davies, P.S., and Sears, J. (2007). Benefit adequacy among elderly Social Security retired-worker beneficiaries and the SSI federal benefit rate. *Social Security Bulletin, 67*(3), 29–51.

Rutledge, M.S. (2018). *What Explains the Widening Gap in Retirement Ages by Education?* Issue Brief No. 18-10, Center for Retirement Research at Boston College.

Rutledge, M.S., Sass, S.A., and Ramos-Mercado, J.D. (2017). How does occupational access for older workers differ by education? *Journal of Labor Research, 38*(3), 283–305.

Ryan, B., and See, S.K. (1993). Age-based beliefs about memory changes for self and others across adulthood. *Journal of Gerontology, 48*(4), P199–P201. https://doi.org/10.1093/geronj/48.4.p199

Ryan, E.B., See, S.K., Meneer, W.B., and Trovato, D. (1992). Age-based perceptions of language performance among younger and older adults. *Communication Research, 19*(4), 423–443.

Salthouse, T.A. (2012). Consequences of age-related cognitive declines. *Annual Review of Psychology, 63*, 201–226.

Salthouse, T.A. (2018). Why is cognitive change more negative with increased age? *Neuropsychology, 32*(1), 110–120. https://doi.org/10.1037/neu0000397

Salthouse, T.A. (2019). Trajectories of normal cognitive aging. *Psychology and Aging, 34*(1), 17–24. https://doi.org/10.1037/pag0000288

Salthouse, T.A., and Maurer, T.J. (1996). Aging, job performance, and career development. *Handbook of the Psychology of Aging*, 353–364. Kluwer Academic Publishers.

Samuelson, W., and Zeckhauser, R. (1988). Status quo bias in decision making. *Journal of Risk and Uncertainty, 1*(1), 7–59.

Sanzenbacher, G.T. (2014). *What we Know About Health Reform in Massachusetts*. Issue Brief No. 14-9, Center for Retirement Research at Boston College. http://crr.bc.edu/wp-content/uploads/2014/05/IB_14-9-508.pdf

Savych, B., and Ruser, J. (2019). *How Do Claim Costs, Components of Costs, and Worker Outcomes Differ by Age?* Workers Compensation Research Institute Flash Report No. FR-19-02, Cambridge, MA.

Savych, B., Neumark, D., and Lea, R. (2019). Do opioids help injured workers recover and get back to work? The impact of opioid prescriptions on duration of temporary disability. *Industrial Relations, 58*(4):549–590.

Schaie, K.W. (2013). *Developmental Influences on Adult Intelligence: The Seattle Longitudinal Study* (2nd ed.). Oxford University Press. https://psycnet.apa.org/record/2013-04284-000

Schill, A.L., and Chosewood, L.C. (2013). The NIOSH total work health program: An overview. *Journal of Occupational and Environmental Medicine, 55*(12 Suppl.), S8–S11. https://pubmed.ncbi.nlm.nih.gov/24284752

Schmidt, D.F., and Boland, S.M. (1986). Structure of perceptions of older adults: Evidence for multiple stereotypes. *Psychology and Aging, 1*(3), 255–260.

Schneider, D. and Harknett, K. (2019). Consequences of routine work-schedule instability for worker health and well-being. *American Sociological Review, 84*(1), 82–114.

Scholz, J.K., Seshadri, A., and Khitatrakun, S. (2006). Are Americans saving optimally for retirement? *Journal of Political Economy, 114*(4), 607–643.

Schramm, J. (2018). *An Aging Labor Force and the Challenges of 65+ Jobseekers.* AARP Public Policy Institute Insight on the Issues Series No. 139. AARP Public Policy Institute. https://www.aarp.org/ppi/info-2018/an-aging-labor-force.html

Schwatka, N.V., Butler, L.M., and Rosecrance, J.C. (2012). Age in relation to worker compensation costs in the construction industry. *American Journal of Industrial Medicine, 56*(3), 356–366.

Schwerdt, G., Messer, D., Woessmann, L., and Wolter, S.C. (2012). The impact of an adult education voucher program: Evidence from a randomized field experiment. *Journal of Public Economics, 96*(7–8), 569–583.

Sciocchetti, T.E. (1991). Mandatory retirement of appointed state judges—age discrimination? *Northwestern University Law Review, 85*(3), 866–901.

Scott, J. (2021). *Availability of State Auto-IRAs Appears to Complement Private Market for Retirement Plans.* https://www.pewtrusts.org/en/research-and-analysis/articles/2021/06/17/availability-of-state-auto-iras-appears-to-complement-private-market-for-retirement-plans

Scott, J.S., Shoven, J.B., Slavov, S.N., and Watson, J.G. (2020). *Can Low Retirement Savings Be Rationalized?* NBER Working Paper No. 26784. National Bureau of Economic Research. https://www.nber.org/system/files/working_papers/w26784/w26784.pdf

Scott, K.A., Liao, Q., Fisher, G.G., Stallones, L., DiGuiseppi, C., and Tompa, E. (2018). Early labor force exit subsequent to permanently impairing occupation injury or illness among workers 50–64 years of age. *American Journal of Industrial Medicine, 61*(4), 317–325.

Sengupta, I., and Baldwin, M.L. (2015). *Workers' Compensation: Benefits, Coverage, and Costs, 2013.* National Academy of Social Insurance. https://www.nasi.org/wp-content/uploads/2018/04/NASI_Work_Comp_Year_2015.pdf

Sengupta, I., Reno, V., Burton, J.F., Jr., and Baldwin, M. (2012). *Workers' Compensation: Benefits, Coverage, and Costs, 2010.* National Academy of Social Insurance.

Settersten, Jr., R.A., and Hagestad, G.O. (1996). What's the latest? II. Cultural age deadlines for educational and work transitions. *The Gerontologist, 36*(5), 602–613.

Settersten, Jr., R.A., and Mayer, K.U. (1997). The measurement of age, age structuring, and the life course. *Annual Review of Sociology, 23*, 233–261.

Sewdas, R., Thorsen, S.V., Boot, C.R., Bjørner, J.B., and Van der Beek, A.J. (2020). Determinants of voluntary early retirement for older workers with and without chronic diseases: A Danish prospective study. *Scandinavian Journal of Public Health, 48*(2), 190–199.

Shah, A., Mullainathan, S., and Shafir, E. (2012). Some consequences of having too little. *Science, 338*(6107), 682–685.

Shanahan, M.J., Mortimer, J.T., and Johnson, M.K. (2016). *Handbook of the Life Course: Volume II (Handbooks of Sociology and Social Research),* (1st ed.). Springer.

Shapiro, J.M. (2005). Is there a daily discount rate? Evidence from the Food Stamp Nutrition Cycle. *Journal of Public Economics, 89*(2–3), 303–325.

Shefrin, H.M., and Thaler, R.H. (2004). Mental accounting, saving, and self-control. *Advances in Behavioral Economics,* 395–428. Princeton University Press.

Sherraden, M. (1991). *Assets and the Poor: A New American Welfare Policy.* M. E. Sharpe, Inc.

Sherraden, M.S., Huang, J., Frey, J.J., Birkenmaier, J., Callahan, C., Clancy, M.M., Sherraden, M. (2015). Financial capability and asset building for all. *Grand Challenges for Social Work Initiative Working Paper No. 13.* American Academy of Social Work and Social Welfare.

Shore, L.M., Cleveland, J.N., and Sanchez, D. (2018). Inclusive workplaces: A review and model. *Human Resource Management Review, 28*, 176–189.

Shoven, J.B., and Slavov, S.N. (2014). The role of retiree health insurance in the early retirement of public sector employees. *Journal of Health Economics, 38*(C), 99–108.

Shultz, K.S. (2003). Bridge employment: Work after retirement. *Retirement: Reasons, Processed, and Results*, 214–241. Springer.

Shultz, K.S., and Wang, M. (2011). Psychological perspectives on the changing nature of retirement. *American Psychologist, 66*(3), 170–179.

Shultz, K.S., Morton, K.R., and Weckerle, J.R. (1998). The influence of push and pull factors on voluntary and involuntary early retirees' retirement decision and adjustment. *Journal of Vocational Behavior, 53*(1), 45–57.

Sidanius, J., and Veniegas, R.C. (2000). Gender and race discrimination: The interactive nature of disadvantage. *Reducing prejudice and discrimination*, 47–69. Erlbaum.

Siegenthaler, J.K., and Brenner, M. (2001). Flexible work schedules, older workers, and retirement. *Journal of Aging & Social Policy*, 12(1), 19–34.

Siegrist, J., Wahrendorf, M., von dem Knesebeck, O., Jürges, H., and Börsch-Supan, A. (2007). Quality of work, well-being, and intended early retirement of older employees—baseline results from the SHARE study. *European Journal of Public Health, 17*(1), 62–68. https://academic.oup.com/eurpub/article/17/1/62/465416

Singer, M.S. (1986). Age stereotypes as a function of profession. *Journal of Social Psychology, 126*(5), 691–692.

Singh, G., and Verma, A. (2003). Work history and later-life labor force participation: Evidence from a large telecommunications firm. *Industrial and Labor Relations Review, 56*(4), 699–715.

Skirbekk, V. (2004). Age and individual productivity: A literature survey. *Vienna Yearbook of Population Research, 2*(1), 133–154. https://econpapers.repec.org/article/vidyearbk/v_3a2_3ay_3a2004_3ai_3a1_3ap_3a133-154.htm

Slack, T., and Jensen, L. (2008). Employment hardship among older workers: Does residential and gender inequality extend into older age? *The Journals of Gerontology, Series B: Psychological Sciences and Social Sciences, 63*(1), S15–S24.

Small, M.L. (2010). *Unanticipated Gains: Origins of Network Inequality in Everyday Life*. Oxford University Press.

Smeaton, D., and McKay, S. (2003). *Working After State Pension Age: Quantitative Analysis*. Research Report No. 182, Department for Work and Pensions.

Smith, K.E., Johnson, R.W., and Muller, L.A. (2004). Deferring income in employer-sponsored retirement plans: The dynamics of participant contributions. *National Tax Journal, 57*(3), 639–670.

Smith, K.E., Toder, E., and Iams, H. (2003). Lifetime distributional effects of Social Security retirement benefits. *Social Security Bulletin, 65*(1), 33–61.

Smith, P.M., and Berecki-Gisolf, J. (2014). Age, occupational demands, and the risk of serious work injury. *Occupational Medicine, 64*(8), 571–576.

Smith, P.M., Cawley, C., Williams, A., and Mustard, C. (2020). Male/female differences in the impact of caring for elderly relatives on labor market attachment and hours of work: 1997–2015. *Journals of Gerontology, Series B, 75*(3), 694–704. https://academic.oup.com/psychsocgerontology/article/75/3/694/5423973

Smith, P.M., Bielecky, A., Ibrahim, S., Mustard, C., Scott-Marshall, H., Saunders, R., and Beaton, D. (2014). How much do preexisting chronic conditions contribute to age differences in health care expenditures after a work-related musculoskeletal injury? *Medical Care, 52*(1), 71–77.

Smith, S.S. (2010). A test of sincerity: How Black and Latino service workers make decisions about making referrals. *Annals of the American Academy of Political and Social Science, 629*, 30–52.

Smith, S.S. (2017). Job-finding among the poor: Do social ties matter? *The Oxford Handbook of the Social Science of Poverty*, 438–461. Oxford, UK: Oxford University Press. https://doi.org/10.1093/oxfordhb/9780199914050.013.20

Smyer, M.A., and Pitt-Catsouphes, M. (2007). The meanings of work for older workers. *Generations, 31*(1), 23–30.

Snijders, T.A.B., van de Bunt, G.G., and Steglich, C.E.G. (2010). Introduction to stochastic actor-based models for network dynamics. *Social Networks, 32*(1), 44–60.

Social Security Technical Panel. (2015). *Report to the Social Security Advisory Board: 2015 Technical Panel on Assumptions and Methods*. Washington, DC. https://www.ssab.gov/research/report-to-the-board-2015-technical-panel-on-assumptions-and-methods/

Social Security Technical Panel. (2019). *Technical Panel on Assumptions and Methods: Report to the Social Security Advisory Board*. Washington, DC. https://www.ssab.gov/research/2019-technical-panel-on-assumptions-and-methods-a-report-to-the-board

Society for Human Resource Management. (2018). *2018 Employee Benefits: The Evolution of Benefits*. https://www.shrm.org/hr-today/trends-and-forecasting/research-and-surveys/pages/2018-employee-benefits.aspx

Sohier, I., (2019). Do involuntary longer working careers reduce well-being? *Applied Research Quality Life, 14*(1), 171–196.

Solem, P.E., Syse, A., Furunes, T., Mykletun, R.J., De Lange, A., Schaufeli, W., and Ilmarinen, J. (2014). To leave or not to leave: Retirement intentions and retirement behaviour. *Ageing & Society, 36*(2), 259–281. https://www.wilmarschaufeli.nl/publications/Schaufeli/468.pdf

Son, J., Lin, N., and George, L.K. (2008). Cross-national comparison of social support structures between Taiwan and the United States. *Journal of Health and Social Behavior*, *49*(1), 104–118. https://doi.org/10.1177/002214650804900108

Song, J., and Manchester, J. (2007). Have people delayed claiming retirement benefits: Responses to changes in Social Security rules. *Social Security Bulletin 67*(2). https://www.ssa.gov/policy/docs/ssb/v67n2/v67n2p1.html

Sonnega, A., Faul, J.D., Ofstedal, M.B., Langa, K.M., Phillips, J.W.R., and Weir, D.R. (2014). Cohort profile: The Health and Retirement Study (HRS). *International Journal of Epidemiology, 43*(2), 576–585. https://pubmed.ncbi.nlm.nih.gov/24671021

Southerton, D., and Tomlinson, M. (2005). Pressed for time—The differential impact of a time squeeze. *The Sociological Review, 53*(2), 215–239.

Stainback, K., Jason, K., and Walter, C. (2018). Organizational context and the well-being of Black workers: Does racial composition affect psychological distress? *Race, Identity, and Work, 32*, 137–164. Emerald Publishing Limited. https://doi.org/10.1108/S0277-283320180000032010

Stancanelli, E. (2017). Couples' retirement under individual pension design: A regression discontinuity study for France. *Labour Economics, 49*, 14–26.

Stango, V., and Zinman, J. (2009). Exponential growth bias and household finance. *The Journal of Finance, 64*(6), 2807–2849.

Stapleton, D., Coleman, K., Dietrich, K., and Livermore, G. (1998). Empirical analyses of DI and SSI application and award growth. *Growth in Disability Benefits: Explanations and Policy Implications*, 31–92. W.E. Upjohn Institute for Employment Research.

Stapleton, D., Mamun, A., and Page, J. (2014). Initial impacts of the Ticket to Work program: Estimates based on exogenous variation in Ticket mail months. *IZA Journal of Labor Policy, 3*(1), 1–24.

Staudinger, U.M., Finkelstein, R., Calvo, E., and Sivaramakrishnan, K. (2016). A global view on the effects of work on health in later life. *The Gerontologist, 56*(Suppl. 2), S281–S292.

Steenstra, I., Cullen, K.L., Irvin, E., Van Eerd, D., Alavinia, M., Beaton, D.E., Geary, J., Gignac, M.A., Gross, D., Mahood, Q., Macdonald, S., Puts, M., Scott-Marshall, H., and Yazdani, A. (2017). A systematic review of interventions to promote work participation in older workers. *Journal of Safety Research, 60*(93), 93–102.

Stephens, Jr., M. (2003). 3rd of tha month: Do Social Security recipients smooth consumption between checks? *American Economic Review, 93*(1), 406–422. https://www.aeaweb.org/articles?id=10.1257/000282803321455386

Stephens, Jr., M. (2006). Paycheque receipt and the timing of consumption. *The Economic Journal, 116*(513), 680–701. https://onlinelibrary.wiley.com/doi/full/10.1111/j.1468-0297.2006.01106.x

Sterns, H.L. (1986). Training and retraining adult and older adult workers. *Age, Health, and Employment*, 93–113. Prentice-Hall.

Sterns, H.L., and Doverspike, D. (1988). Training and developing the older worker: Implications for human resource management. *Fourteen Steps in Managing an Aging Workforce*, 85–96. New Lexington Press.

Sterns, H.L., and Miklos, S.M. (1995). The aging worker in a changing environment: Organizational and individual issues. *Journal of Vocational Behavior, 47*(3), 248–268. https://doi.org/10.1006/jvbe.1995.0003

Stock, J.W., and Wise, D.A. (1990). Pensions, the option value of work, and retirement. *Econometrica, 58*(5), 1151–1180. https://scholar.harvard.edu/files/stock/files/pensionsoptionvalueworkretirement.pdf

Stock, W.A., and Beegle, K. (2004). Employment protections for older workers: Do disability discrimination laws matter? *Contemporary Economic Policy, 22*(1), 111–126.

Stoiko, R.R., and Strough, J. (2019). His and her retirement: Effects of gender and familial caregiving profiles on retirement timing. *The International Journal of Aging and Human Development, 89*(2), 131–150.

Sturman, M.C. (2003). Searching for the inverted U-shaped relationship between time and performance: Meta-analyses of the experience/performance, tenure/performance, and age/performance relationships. *Journal of Management, 29*(5), 609–640.

Sudano, J.J., and Baker, D.W. (2006). Explaining US racial/ethnic disparities in health declines and mortality in late middle age: The roles of socioeconomic status, health behaviors, and health insurance. *Social Science & Medicine, 62*(4), 909–922.

Sudre, C.H., Murray, B., Varsavsky, T., Graham, M.S., Penfold, R.S., Bowyer, R.C., and Steves, C.J. (2021). Attributes and predictors of long COVID. *Nature Medicine, 27*(4), 626–631.

Sullivan, D., and von Wachter, T. (2009). Job displacement and mortality: An analysis using administrative data. *Quarterly Journal of Economics, 124*(3), 1265–1306. https//:doi.org/10.1162/qjec.2009.124.3.1265

Summers, L.H. (2014). U.S. economic prospects: Secular stagnation, hysteresis, and the zero lower bound. *Business Economics, 49*(2), 65–73.

Sung, P., Hedrich, W., and Phan, V.H. (2019). *The Twin Trends of Aging and Automation: Leveraging a Tech-Empowered Experienced Workforce*. Report by Mercer and Oliver Wyman. Marsh and McLennan Companies. https://www.oliverwyman.com/content/dam/oliver-wyman/v2/publications/2019/dec/the-twin-threats-of-aging-and-automation.pdf

Swanberg, J. E., McKechnie, S. P., Ojha, M. U., and James, J. B. (2011). Schedule control, supervisor support and work engagement: A winning combination for workers in hourly jobs? *Journal of Vocational Behavior, 79*(3), 613–624. https://doi.org/10.1016/j.jvb.2011.04.012

Swanberg, J.E., Pitt-Catsouphes, M., and Drescher-Burke, K. (2005). A question of justice: Disparities in employees' access to flexible schedule arrangements. *Journal of Family Issues, 26*(6), 866–895.

Sweeney, E.P., and Fremstad, S. (2005). *Supplemental Security Income: Supporting People with Disabilities and the Elderly Poor.* Center on Budget and Policy Priorities. https://www.cbpp.org/research/supplemental-security-income-supporting-people-with-disabilities-and-the-elderly-poor

Sweet, S., and Moen, P. (2012). Dual earners preparing for job loss: Agency, linked lives, and resilience. *Work and Occupations, 39*(1), 35–70.

Szinovacz, M.E. (2003). Contexts and pathways: Retirement as institution, process, and experience. *Retirement: Reasons, Processes, and Results,* 6–52. Springer.

Szinovacz, M.E., and Davey, A. (2005). Predictors of perceptions of involuntary retirement. *The Gerontologist, 45*(1), 36–47. https://academic.oup.com/gerontologist/article/45/1/36/631693

Szinovacz, M.E., Martin, L., and Davey, A. (2014). Recession and expected retirement age: Another look at the evidence. *The Gerontologist, 54*(2), 245–257. https//:doi.org/10.1093/geront/gnt010

Talaga, J.A., and Beehr, T.A. (1995). Are there gender differences in predicting retirement decisions? *Journal of Applied Psychology, 80*(1), 16–28.

Tali, K., Yinon, C., and Edo, N. (2018). Benefit inequality among American workers by gender, race, and ethnicity, 1982-2015. *Sociological Science, 5*(20), 461–488. https//:doi.org/10.15195/v5.a20

Tamborini, C.R., Iams, H.M., and Whitman, K. (2009). Marital history, race, and Social Security spouse and widow benefit eligibility in the United States. *Research on Aging, 31*(5), 577–605. https://doi.org/10.1177/0164027509337196

Tang, F., Choi, E., and Goode, R. (2013). Older Americans employment and retirement. *Ageing International, 38*(1), 82–94. https//:doi.org/10.1007/s12126-012-9162-3

Taubman P.J., and Sickles, R.C. (1983). *Supplemental Social Insurance and the Health of the Poor.* Working Paper No. 1062, Cambridge, MA: National Bureau of Economic Research. https://www.nber.org/system/files/working_papers/w1062/w1062.pdf

Tax Policy Center. (2020). *Briefing Book: A Citizen's Guide to the Fascinating (Though Often Complex) Elements of the Federal Tax System.* https://www.taxpolicycenter.org/sites/default/files/briefing-book/tpc_briefing_book_2020.pdf

Taylor, P., Jorgensen, B., and Watson, E. (2010). Population ageing in a globalizing labour market: Implications for older workers. *China Journal of Social Work, 3*(2–3), 259–272. https://doi.org/10.1080/17525098.2010.492651

Taylor, P., McLoughlin, C., Meyer, D., and Brooke, E. (2013). Everyday discrimination in the workplace, job satisfaction, and psychological wellbeing: Age differences and moderating variables. *Ageing and Society, 33*(7), 1105–1138.

Tett, R.P., and Burnett, D.D. (2003). A personality trait-based interactionist model of job performance. *Journal of Applied Psychology, 88*(3), 500–517.

Tett, R.P., Simonet, D.V., Walser, B., and Brown, C. (2013). Trait activation theory: Applications, developments, and implications for person-workplace fit. *Handbook of Personality at Work,* 71–100. Routledge.

Thaler, R.H. (1999). Mental accounting matters. *Journal of Behavioral Decision Making, 12*(3), 183–206.

Thaler, R.H., and Benartzi, S. (2004). Save more tomorrow: Using behavioral economics to increase employee saving. *Journal of Political Economy, 112*(S1), S164–S187.

Thompson, L.F., and Mayhorn, C.B. (2012). Aging workers and technology. *The Oxford Handbook of Work and Aging,* 341–361. Oxford University Press.

Thornton, P.H., and Ocasio, W. (2008). Institutional logics. *The Sage Handbook of Organizational Institutionalism,* 1–46. Sage.

Thumula, V., and Liu, T.-C. (2018). *Correlates of Opioid Dispensing.* Workers Compensation Research Institute.

Thumula, V., Wang, D., and Liu, T.-C. (2017). *Interstate Variations in Use of Opioids* (4th ed.). Workers Compensation Research Institute Working Paper No. WC-17-28. https://www.wcrinet.org/images/uploads/files/wcri2837.pdf

Timmons, J.C., Hall, A.C., Fesko, S.L., and Migliore, A. (2011). Retaining the older workforce: Social policy considerations for the universally designed workplace. *Journal of Aging & Social Policy, 23*(2), 119–140.

Topel, R. (1991). Specific capital, mobility, and wages: Wages rise with job seniority. *Journal of Political Economy, 99*(1), 145–176.

Trawinski, L.A. (2016a). *Disrupting Aging in the Workplace: Profiles in Intergenerational Diversity Leadership.* AARP Public Policy Institute. https://www.aarp.org/content/dam/aarp/ppi/2017/08/disrupt-aging-in-the-workforce.pdf

Trawinski, L.A. (2016b). *Leveraging the Value of an Age-Diverse Workforce.* SHRM Foundation Executive Briefing, Alexandria, VA. https://www.shrm.org/foundation/ourwork/initiatives/the-aging-workforce/documents/age-diverse%20workforce%20executive%20briefing.pdf

Tucker-Drob, E.M. (2019). Cognitive aging and dementia: A life-span perspective. *Annual Review of Developmental Psychology, 1*(1), 177–196. https://www.annualreviews.org/doi/abs/10.1146/annurev-devpsych-121318-085204

U.S. Bureau of Labor Statistics. (2020). *Table 3.3. Civilian Labor Force Participation Rates by Age, Sex, Race, and Ethnicity, 1999, 2009, 2019, and Projected 2029 (in percent)*. U.S. Bureau of Labor Statistics Employment Projections Program. https://www.bls.gov/emp/tables/civilian-labor-force-participation-rate.htm

U.S. Census Bureau. (2018). *Projected 5-Year Age Groups and Sex Composition: Main Projections Series for the United States, 2017–2060*. U.S. Census Bureau, Population Division.

U.S. Census Bureau. (2019). *Geographic Mobility: 2018 to 2019*. Table 1: General Mobility by Race and Hispanic Origin and Region, and by Sex, Age, Relationship to Householder, Educational Attainment, Marital Status, Nativity, Tenure, and Poverty Status: 2018 to 2019. https://www.census.gov/data/tables/2019/demo/geographic-mobility/cps-2019.html

U.S. Department of Commerce. (1997). *Census Brief: Disabilities Affect One-Fifth of All Americans*. Census Bureau Publication No. CENBR/97-5. https://www2.census.gov/library/publications/1997/demo/cenbr97-05.pdf

U.S. Department of Education. (2019). *Status and Trends in the Education of Racial and Ethnic Groups 2019*. NCES Working Paper No. 2019-038. National Center for Education Statistics.

U.S. Department of Health and Human Services, Office of Minority Health. (2021). *Profile: Hispanic/Latino Americans*. https://minorityhealth.hhs.gov/omh/browse.aspx?lvl=3&lvlid=64

U.S. Department of Labor. (1965). *The Older American Worker*. U.S. Government Printing Office.

U.S. Department of Labor. (2020a). *Senior Community Service Employment Program*. DOL. https://www.dol.gov/agencies/eta/seniors

U.S. Department of Labor. (2020b). *FY 2021—Department of Labor Budget in Brief*. DOL. https://www.dol.gov/sites/dolgov/files/general/budget/2021/FY2021BIB.pdf

U.S. Department of Labor. (2020c). *Customer Satisfaction Survey Results—Participant Surveys 2010-2017*. DOL. https://www.dol.gov/agencies/eta/seniors/performance

U.S. Equal Employment Opportunity Commission. (2021). *The State of Age Discrimination and Older Workers in the U.S. 50 Years After the Age Discrimination in Employment Act (ADEA)*. https://www.eeoc.gov/reports/state-age-discrimination-and-older-workers-us-50-years-after-age-discrimination-employment

U.S. Government Accountability Office. (2003). *Older Workers: Employment Assistance Focuses on Subsidized Jobs and Job Search, but Revised Performance Measures Could Improve Access to Other Services*. United States General Accounting Office Reports, GAO-03-350, Report to the Ranking Minority Member Subcommittee on Employer-Employee Relations, Committee on Education and the Workforce, House of Representatives. https://www.gao.gov/assets/gao-03-350.pdf

U.S. Government Accountability Office. (2009). *Retirement Savings: Automatic Enrollment Shows Promise for Some Workers, but Proposals to Broaden Retirement Savings for Other Workers Could Face Challenges*. Report No. GAO 10-31. https://www.gao.gov/products/gao-10-31

U.S. Office of Personnel Management. (2011). *Government-Wide Diversity and Inclusion Strategic Plan 2011*. https://www.energy.gov/sites/default/files/OPM%20Government-wide%20Diversity%20and%20Inclusion%20Strategic%20Plan%202011.pdf

U.S. Senate Special Committee on Aging. (2017). *America's Aging Workforce: Opportunities and Challenges*. https://www.aging.senate.gov/imo/media/doc/Aging%20Workforce%20Booklet_4web.pdf

U.S. Social Security Administration. (2012). *Fast Facts and Figures about Social Security*, 2012. SSA Publication No. 13-11785. https://www.ssa.gov/policy/docs/chartbooks/fast_facts/2012/fast_facts12.pdf

U.S. Social Security Administration (2019a). *Annual Statistical Supplement, 2019*.

U.S. Social Security Administration. (2019b). *Your Retirement Benefit: How It's Figured*. Social Security Administration Publication No. 05-10070. https://www.ssa.gov/pubs/EN-05-10070.pdf

U.S. Social Security Administration. (2020a). *The Faces and Facts of Disability: Facts*. https://www.ssa.gov/disabilityfacts/facts.html

U.S. Social Security Administration. (2020b). *Understanding Supplemental Security Income—2020 Edition*. 17-008, ICN 443175, Washington, DC.

U.S. Social Security Administration. (2020c). *The 2020 Annual Report of the Board of Trustees of the Federal Old-Age and Survivors Insurance and Federal Disability Insurance Trust Funds*. The 2020 OASDI Trustees Report. https://www.ssa.gov/oact/tr/2020

Valletta, R.G. (2013). House lock and structural unemployment. *Labour Economics, 25*(C), 86–97.

van Dalen, H.P., and Henkens, K. (2020). The COVID-19 pandemic: Lessons for financially fragile and aging societies. *Work, Aging, and Retirement, 6*(4), 229–232.

van Dalen, H.P., Henkens, K., and Schippers, J.J. (2009). Dealing with older workers in Europe: A comparative survey of employers' attitudes and actions. *Journal of European Social Policy, 19*(1), 47–60.

van Dalen, H.P., Henkens, K., and Schippers, J.J. (2010). Productivity of older workers: Perceptions of employers and employees. *Population and Development Review, 36*(2), 309–330.

van Dalen, H.P., Henkens, K., and Wang, M. (2015). Recharging or retiring older workers? Uncovering the age-based strategies of European employers. *The Gerontologist, 55*(5), 814–824. https://academic.oup.com/gerontologist/article/55/5/814/2605195

van der Horst, M., Lain, D., Vickerstaff, S., Clark, C., and Baumberg Geiger, B. (2017). Gender roles and employment pathways of older women and men in England. *Sage Open, 7*(4), 1–17.

van Deth, J.W. (2003). Measuring social capital: Orthodoxies and continuing controversies. *International Journal of Social Research Methodology, 6*(1), 79–92. https://doi.org/10.1080/13645570305057

van Solinge, H., and Henkens, K. (2007). Involuntary retirement: The role of restrictive circumstances, timing, and social embeddedness. *Journals of Gerontology, Series B 62*(5), S295–S303. https://doi.org/10.1093/geronb/62.5.S295

van Sonsbeek, J.-M., and Gradus, R. (2013). Estimating the effect of recent disability reforms in the Netherlands. *Oxford Economic Papers, 65*(4), 832–855.

Vanajan, A., Bültmann, U., and Henkens. K. (2020). Health-related work limitations among older workers—the role of flexible work arrangements and organizational climate. *The Gerontologist, 60*(3), 450–459.

Venkataramani, A.S., Bair, E.F., O'Brien, R.L., and Tsai, A.C. (2020). Association between automotive assembly plant closures and opioid overdose mortality in the United States: A difference-in-differences analysis. *JAMA Internal Medicine, 180*(2), 254–262. https//:doi.org/10.1001/jamainternmed.2019.5686

Veth, K.N., Korzillus, H.P.L.M., Van der Heijden, B.I.J.M., Emans, B.J.M., and De Lange, A.H. (2019). Understanding the contribution of HRM bundles for employee outcomes across the life-span. *Frontiers in Psychology*, 10(Article 2518).

Visser, M., Gesthuizen, M., Kraaykamp, G., and Wolbers, M.H. (2018). Labor market vulnerability of older workers in the Netherlands and its impact on downward mobility and reduction of working hours. *Work, Aging, and Retirement, 4*(3), 289–299.

von Bonsdorff, M.E., Zhan, Y., Song, Y., and Wang, M. (2017). Examining bridge employment from a self-employment perspective: Evidence from the Health and Retirement Study. *Work, Aging, and Retirement, 3*(3), 298–312.

von Wachter, T. (2002). *The End of Mandatory Retirement in the US: Effects on Retirement and Implicit Contracts*. Center for Labor Economics Working Paper No. 49, University of California, Berkeley.

Waid, M. (2016). *Social Security: A Key Retirement Income Source for Older Minorities*. AARP Insight on the Issues, March. Washington, DC: AARP Public Policy Institute. https://www.ncpssm.org/wp-content/uploads/2017/04/social-security-a-key-income-source-for-older-minorities-aarp-ppi.pdf

Waidmann, T.A., Choi, H., Schoeni, R.F., and Bound, J. (2020). *Recent Trends in Disability and the Implications for Use of Disability Insurance*. Michigan Retirement and Disability Research Center Working Paper No. 2020-406. University of Michigan, Ann Arbor.

Walajtys, A.R. (2007). *I Just Couldn't Sit at Home and Do Nothing: A Qualitative Analysis of Bridge Employment Experiences*. Texas State University-San Marcos. https://digital.library.txstate.edu/handle/10877/3397

Waldman, D.A., and Avolio, B.J. (1986). A meta-analysis of age differences in job performance. *Journal of Applied Psychology, 71*(1), 33–38. https://psycnet.apa.org/doiLanding?doi=10.1037%2F0021-9010.71.1.33

Wang, M. (2007). Profiling retirees in the retirement transition and adjustment process: Examining the longitudinal change patterns of retirees' psychological well-being. *Journal of Applied Psychology, 92*(2), 455–474.

Wang, M. (2015). Inaugural editorial. *Work, Aging, and Retirement, 1*(1), 1–3. https://academic.oup.com/workar/article-abstract/1/1/1/1666769?redirectedFrom=fulltext

Wang, M., and Chan, D. (2011). Mixture latent Markov modeling: Identifying and predicting unobserved heterogeneity in longitudinal qualitative status change. *Organizational Research Methods, 14*(3), 411–431.

Wang, M., and Fang, Y. (2020). Age diversity in the workplace: Facilitating opportunities with organizational practices. *Public Policy and Aging Report 30*(3), 119–123.

Wang, M., and Shi, J. (2014). Psychological research on retirement. *Annual Review of Psychology, 65*, 209–233.

Wang, M., and Shultz, K.S. (2010). Employee retirement: A review and recommendations for future investigation. *Journal of Management, 36*(1), 172–206.

Wang, M., Henkens, K., and van Solinge, H. (2011). Retirement adjustment: A review of theoretical and empirical advancements. *American Psychologist, 66*, 204–213.

Wang, M., Olson, D., and Shultz, K. (2013). *Mid and Late Career Issues: An Integrative Perspective*. Psychology Press.

Wang, M., Adams, G.A., Beehr, T.A., and Shultz, K.S. (2009). Career issues at the end of one's career: Bridge employment and retirement. *Maintaining Focus, Energy, and Options through the Life Span*, 135–162. Information Age Publishing.

Wang, M., Zhan, Y., Liu, S., and Shultz, K.S. (2008). Antecedents of bridge employment: A longitudinal investigation. *Journal of Applied Psychology, 93*(4), 818–830.

REFERENCES

Wang, M., Burlacu, G., Truxillo, D., James, K., and Yao, X. (2015). Age differences in feedback reactions: The roles of employee feedback orientation on social awareness and utility. *Journal of Applied Psychology, 100*(4), 1296–1308.

Ward, S.J., and King, L.A. (2017). Work and the good life: How work can promote meaning in life. *Research in Organizational Behavior, 37*, 59–82.

Warner, D.F., and Brown, T.H. (2011). Understanding how race/ethnicity and gender define age-trajectories of disability: An intersectionality approach. *Social Science & Medicine, 72*(8), 1236–1248.

Warner, D.F., Hayward, M.D., and Hardy, M.A. (2010). The retirement life course in America at the dawn of the twenty-first century. *Population Research and Policy Review, 29*(6), 893–919.

Warshawsky, M.J., and Marchand, R. (2015). *Modernizing the SSDI Eligibility Criteria: A Reform Proposal That Eliminates the Outdated Medical-Vocational Grid.* Mercatus Center, George Mason University. https://www.mercatus.org/publications/government-spending/modernizing-ssdi-eligibility-criteria-reform-proposal-eliminates

Weathers, R.R., and Hemmeter, J. (2011). The impact of changing financial work incentives on the earnings of Social Security Disability Insurance (SSDI) beneficiaries. *Journal of Policy Analysis and Management, 30*(4), 708–728.

Welch, F. (1979). Effects of cohort size on earnings: The Baby Boom babies' financial bust. *Journal of Political Economy, 87*(5/2), S65–S97.

Wettstein, G. (2020). Retirement lock and prescription drug insurance: Evidence from Medicare Part D. *American Economic Journal: Economic Policy, 12*(1), 389–417.

Wilensky, H.L. (1961). Orderly careers and social participation: The impact of work history on social integration in the middles mass. *American Sociological Review, 26*, 521–539.

Wilkinson, A., Dundon, T., Donaghey, J., and Freeman, R. (2014). Employee voice: Charting new terrain. *Handbook of Research on Employee Voice*, 1–15. Edward Elgar.

Williams, J.E., and Best, D.L. (1990). *Measuring Sex Stereotypes: A Multination Study.* Sage.

Willmore, L. (2007). Universal pensions for developing countries. *World Development, 35*(1), 24–51. https://econpapers.repec.org/article/eeewdevel/v_3a35_3ay_3a2007_3ai_3a1_3ap_3a24-51.htm

Willson, A.E. (2003). Race and women's income trajectories: Employment, marriage, and income security over the life course. *Social Problems, 50*(1), 87–110.

Wilson, T.D., Lindsey, S., and Schooler, T.Y. (2000). A model of dual attitudes. *Psychological Review, 107*(1), 101–126.

Wise, D.A. (2012). *Social Security and Retirement around the World: Historical Trends in Mortality and Health, Employment, and Disability Insurance Participation and Reform.* University of Chicago Press.

Witman, A. (2015). Public health insurance and disparate eligibility of spouses: The Medicare eligibility gap. *Journal of Health Economics, 40*(C), 10–25.

Wittenburg, D., Mann, D.R., and Thompkins, A. (2013). The disability system and programs to promote employment for people with disabilities. *IZA Journal of Labor Policy, 2*(4).

Wolf, M.H. (2010). *Claims Characteristics of Workers Aged 65 and Older.* National Council on Compensation Insurance, Inc. Research Brief.

Wolff, E.N. (2003). Income, wealth, and late-life inequality in the United States. *Economic Outcomes in Later Life: Public Policy, Health, and Cumulative Advantage*, 31–59. Springer.

Wright, P.M., and Nishii, L.H. (2013). Strategic HRM and organizational behavior: Integrating multiple levels of analysis. *HRM and Performance: Achievements and Challengese*, 97–110. Wiley.

Wright, R.E. (1991). Cohort size and earnings in Great Britain. *Journal of Population Economics, 4*(4), 295–305.

Wu, A.Y., and Rutledge, M.S. (2014). *Lower-Income Individuals Without Pensions: Who Misses Out and Why?* Working Paper No. 2014-2, Center for Retirement Research at Boston College. https://crr.bc.edu/wp-content/uploads/2014/03/wp_2014-2.pdf

Xu, Y.E., and Chopik, W.J. (2020). Identifying moderators in the link between workplace discrimination and health/well-being. *Frontiers in Psychology, 11*(458). https://www.frontiersin.org/articles/10.3389/fpsyg.2020.00458/full

Yakubovich, V. (2005). Weak ties, information, and influence: How workers find jobs in a local Russian labor market. *American Sociological Review, 70*(3), 408–421.

Yeatts, D.E., Folts, W.E., and Knapp, J. (1999). Older worker's adaptation to a changing workplace: Employment issues for the 21st century. *Educational Gerontology, 25*(4), 331–347. https//:doi.org/10.1080/036012799267774

Yoong, J.K., Hung, A.A., Barcellos, S.H., Carvalho, L., and Clift, J. (2019). *Disparities in Minority Retirement Savings Behavior: Survey and Experimental Evidence from a Nationally-Representative Sample of US Households.* RAND Corporation Working Paper No. WR-1331, Santa Monica, CA. https://www.rand.org/pubs/working_papers/WR1331.html

Zajacova, A., Montez, J., and Herd, P. (2014). Socioeconomic disparities in health among older adults and the implications for the retirement age debate: A brief report. *Journals of Gerontology, Series B: Psychological Sciences and Social Sciences, 69*(6), 973–978.

Zepelin, H., Sills, R.A., and Heath, M.W. (1987). Is age becoming irrelevant? An exploratory study of perceived age norms. *International Journal of Aging and Human Development, 24*, 241–256.

Zhan, Y., and Wang, M. (2015a). Bridge employment: Conceptualizations and new directions for future research. *Facing the Challenges of a Multi-Age Workforce: A Use-Inspired Approach*, 230–249. Routledge.

Zhan, Y., and Wang, M. (2015b). Retirement and bridge employment: People, context, and time. *Aging Workers and the Employee-Employer Relationship*, 203–220. Springer.

Zhan, Y., Wang, M., and Daniel, V. (2019). Lifespan perspectives on the work-to-retirement transition. *Work across the Lifespan*, 581–604. Elsevier Academic Press. https://doi.org/10.1016/B978-0-12-812756-8.00025-6

Zhan, Y., Wang, M., and Shi, J. (2015). Retirees' motivational orientations and bridge employment: Testing the moderating role of gender. *Journal of Applied Psychology, 100*(5), 1319–1331.

Zhan, Y., Wang, M., and Yao, X. (2013). Domain specific effects of commitment on bridge employment decisions: The moderating role of economic stress. *European Journal of Work and Organizational Psychology, 22*(3), 362–375.

Zinshteyn, M. (2019). *Student Loan Debt Soaring Among Older Adults Over 50*. Report by the AARP. https://www.aarp.org/money/credit-loans-debt/info-2019/student-loan-debt-report.html

Zulkarnain, A., and Rutledge, M.S. (2021). *Do Men Who Work Longer Live Longer? Evidence from the Netherlands*. Report No. 21-8, Center for Retirement Research at Boston College. https://crr.bc.edu/wp-content/uploads/2021/04/IB-21-8.pdf

Zwick, T. (2012). Training effectiveness—Differences between younger and older employees. *Working and Ageing: The Benefits of Investing in an Ageing*, 34–54. Luxembourg: Publications Office of the European Union. https://www.cedefop.europa.eu/files/3064_en.pdf

Appendix A

Meeting Agendas

**Committee on Understanding the Aging Workforce and
Employment at Older Ages
Meeting #1**

**April 8–9, 2020
Remote Conference Meeting Via Zoom**

DAY 1 – Wednesday, April 8, 2020

9:00 am – 1:30 pm	**CLOSED SESSION (Committee and Staff Only)**

OPEN SESSION

1:30 – 2:00 pm   **Welcome and Introduction to the National Academies**
        Mary Ellen O'Connell, Executive Director, DBASSE

2:00 – 3:00 pm   **Sponsor Interests and Perspectives; Discussion of Statement of Task**
        Kathleen Christensen, Alfred P. Sloan Foundation

3:00 – 3:15 pm   BREAK

OPEN SESSION ADJOURNS

3:15 – 5:00 pm   **CLOSED SESSION (Committee and Staff Only)**

DAY 2 – Thursday, April 9, 2020 – CLOSED SESSION

9:00 am – 3:00 pm   **CLOSED SESSION (Committee and Staff Only)**

**Public Workshop for The Committee on Understanding the
Aging Workforce and Employment at Older Ages
Meeting #2**

**June 9–10, 2020
Organized by the Division of Behavioral and Social Sciences and Education
Committee on Population in collaboration with the Committee on National Statistics**

Purpose of the Meeting

The purpose of this meeting is to serve as an information gathering session for the Committee to Understand the Aging Workforce and Employment at Older Ages to aid in the preparation of their report. This meeting will cover a diverse range of topics that touch on the role of individual and family characteristics, needs, and finances; workplace conditions and experiences; labor force opportunities; and public policy in the employment experiences of older workers.

DAY 1 – Tuesday, June 9, 2020

10:00 – 10:10 am	**Welcome and Introductions**
	Susan Fiske, Chair (Princeton University)
10:10 am – 12:00 pm	**Session 1: Retirement Savings and Age Discrimination**
10:10 – 10:30 am	Financial Literacy and Retirement Security
	Olivia Mitchell, University of Pennsylvania
10:30 – 10:50 am	Retirement Savings as a Rational Choice
	Eric French, University College London
10:50 – 11:10 am	Legal Aspects of Age Discrimination in the Workplace
	Laurie McCann, AARP
11:10 am – 12:00 pm	Discussion
12:00 – 12:30 pm	BREAK
12:30 – 2:30 pm	**Session 2: Technological Change, Adaptability of Older Workers, Caregiving and Transfers**
12:30 – 12:50 pm	Labor Market Effects of Technological and Organizational Change for Older Workers
	Michele Battisti, University of Glasgow

12:50 – 1:10 pm	Cognitive Aging in the Work Context
	Ursula Staudinger, Columbia University
1:10 – 1:30 pm	**Caregiving, Family Transfers, and Working at Older Ages**
	Kathleen McGarry, UCLA
1:30 – 2:30 pm	Discussion
2:30 pm	Adjourn for the day

DAY 2 – Wednesday, June 10, 2020

10:00 – 10:10 am	**Welcome and Introductions**
	Susan Fiske, Chair (Princeton University)
10:10 am – 12:00 pm	**Session 3: Nonstandard Employment, Low-Wage Workers, and Technology**
10:10 – 10:30 am	Older Workers and Nonstandard Employment
	Katharine Abraham, University of Maryland
10:30 – 10:50 am	Low-Wage Work at Older Ages
	Mary Gatta, City University of New York
10:50 – 11:10 am	Technology to Enable Working Longer
	Sara Czaja, Cornell University
11:10 am – 12:00 pm	Discussion
12:00 – 12:30 pm	BREAK
12:30 – 2:30 pm	**Session 4: Health, Workplace Diversity, and Job Displacement**
12:30 – 12:50 pm	Mental and Physical Health and Working at Older Ages
	Gwen Fisher, Colorado State University
12:50 – 1:10 pm	A GATE to Understanding Older Workers: Generation, Age, Tenure, Experience
	Michael North, New York University
1:10 – 1:30 pm	Job Displacement and Work at Older Ages
	Maria Heidkamp, Rutgers University
1:30 – 2:30 pm	Discussion
2:30 pm	Adjourn for the day

**Committee on Understanding the Aging Workforce and
Employment at Older Ages
Meeting #3**

**August 20 & 25, 2020
Remote Conference Meeting Via Zoom**

DAY 1 – Thursday, August 20, 2020

OPEN SESSION

10:00 – 10:10 am	**Welcome, Introductions**
	Susan Fiske (Committee Chair), Princeton University
	Tara Becker, Study Director
10:10 – 10:30 am	**Presentation: Technology in the Workplace**
	Joseph Coughlin, MIT
10:30 – 10:50 am	**Presentation: Workplace Experiences of Older Low-Wage Black Workers**
	Kendra Jason, UNC-Charlotte
10:50 – 11:10 am	**Presentation: Racial Disparities in Wealth Generation**
	Tyson Brown, Duke University
11:10 – 11:20 am	BREAK
11:20 am – 12:30 pm	**Committee Discussion with Presenters**
	Joseph Coughlin, MIT
	Kendra Jason, UNC-Charlotte
	Tyson Brown, Duke Univeristy
12:30 – 1:00 pm	BREAK

CLOSED SESSION (Committee and Staff Only)

1:00 – 3:15 pm	**CLOSED SESSION (Committee and Staff Only)**

DAY 2 – Tuesday, August 25, 2020 – CLOSED SESSION

10:00 am – 3:00 pm	**CLOSED SESSION (Committee and Staff Only)**

Appendix B

Committee Biosketches

SUSAN T. FISKE (*Chair*) is Eugene Higgins professor of psychology and public affairs at Princeton University. Her research covers the investigation of social cognition, especially cognitive stereotypes and emotional prejudices, at cultural, interpersonal, and neuro-scientific levels. Fiske is best known for her efforts on the stereotype content model, ambivalent sexism theory, and on the power as control theory. She is widely published, with her work appearing in over 400 publications, and she is the winner of numerous scientific awards. Fiske was elected to the National Academy of Sciences in 2013 and currently chairs the Board on Behavioral, Cognitive, and Sensory Sciences. She also serves on several other Academies' panels and boards. She has edited volumes on social cognition, nuclear war, racism, sexism, classism, social neuroscience, psychology in court, research ethics, and science making a difference, and she currently serves as editor for the *Annual Review of Psychology, PNAS,* and *Policy Insights from Behavioral and Brain Sciences*. She has a B.A. degree in social relations, and a Ph.D. in social psychology, both from Harvard University.

EMMA AGUILA is associate professor at the University of Southern California Sol Price School of Public of Policy. Her research focuses on the relationship between socioeconomic status and health, and how different designs of social insurance programs affect work and retirement behavior, saving patterns, and health and well-being of vulnerable middle-aged and older adults. She has received several awards for her work on social security systems in Mexico and she received the first prize for research in pensions from Comision Nacional del Sistema de Ahorro para el Retiro. Her work has appeared in such publications as *The Gerontologist, Proceedings of the National Academy of Sciences,* and *Review of Economics and Statistics*. Aguila has experience designing and implementing field experiments and longitudinal surveys and she currently serves as an advisor to the Mexican Health and Aging Study survey in Mexico and the Social Protection Survey in Latin America. Aguila has a B.A. degree from the Instituto Tecnológico Autónomo de Mexico, and M.A. and Ph.D. degrees in economics from University College London.

PETER B. BERG is professor of employment relations and director of the School of Human Resources and Labor Relations at Michigan State University. His research interests include the implications of an aging workforce for organizations, international comparisons of working time, and work-life flexibility policies and practices. Berg is the author of numerous articles and his work has appeared in such academic journals as *ILR Review; Human Relations;* and *Human Resource Management Review*. He is also co-author of the book *Manufacturing Advantage: Why High Performance Work Systems Pay Off.* Recently, he has conducted research on employee and firm outcomes in a number of industries, such as electronics, chemical, and hospital. Berg serves on the editorial boards of *ILR Review* and on the international advisory board of the *British Journal of Industrial Relations*. He has a Ph.D. in economics from the University of Notre Dame.

AXEL BÖRSCH-SUPAN leads the Munich Center for the Economics of Aging (MEA) at the Max Planck Institute for Social Law and Social Policy in Munich. He also holds a professorship at the Technical University of Munich, and a research associateship at the National Bureau of Economic Research (NBER). Börsch-Supan serves as the principal investigator of the Survey of Health, Ageing, and Retirement in Europe (SHARE) and as managing director of SHARE-ERIC. He is also a member of the German National Academy of Sciences Leopoldina, the Berlin-Brandenburg Academy of Sciences, a corresponding member of the Austrian Academy of Sciences, and a member of the MacArthur Foundation Aging Societies Network. Börsch-Supan has in the past provided consultant services to the Council of Advisors to the German Economics Ministry, the German Federal Government's Expert Group on Demography and German Pension Reform Commissions, and to several other ministries in Germany, as well as the Bundesbank, governments in the European Union and the United States, EU Commission, the Organisation of Economic Co-operation and Development, the World Health Organization, the World Economic Forum, and World Bank. He has a diploma in mathematics from Bonn, Germany, and a Ph.D. in economics from Massachusetts Institute of Technology.

COURTNEY C. COILE is professor of economics at Wellesley College. She is also a research associate at the National Bureau of Economic Research (NBER), where she serves as co-director of the NBER Retirement and Disability Research Center and co-director of the International Social Security project, a collaborative research project involving teams in a dozen countries. Coile is a current member of the Committee on Population at the National Academy of Sciences Division of Behavioral and Social Sciences and Education and the data monitoring committee of the Health and Retirement Study and a former member of the National Academy of Sciences' Committee on the Long-run Macroeconomic Effects of the Aging U.S. Population-Phase II. Her research focuses on the economics of aging and health, with particular focus on retirement decisions, health trends, and public programs used by older and disabled populations. Coile is the author of numerous articles and book chapters, co-author of *Reconsidering Retirement: How Losses and Layoffs Affect Older Workers*, and co-editor of the *Social Security Programs and Retirement around the World Series*. She has an AB from Harvard University and a Ph.D. in economics from MIT.

ERNEST GONZALES is associate professor in the Silver School of Social Work at New York University and a scholar in the areas of productive aging (employment, volunteering, and caregiving), health equity, and social policy. His research advances understanding of the relationships between social determinants of health (e.g., race, ethnicity, gender, education, and informal caregiving), social stratification, health, and productivity, and his work has been supported by the National Institute on Minority Health and Health Disparities, National Institute on Aging, U.S. Social Security Administration, AARP Foundation, and other public and private funders. Gonzales is widely published in leading scientific journals and serves on several editorial boards. He co-chairs the American Academy of Social Work & Social Welfare's "Grand Challenge on Advancing Long, Healthy, and Productive Lives" and is a member of the Sloan Research Network on Aging & Work, Society for Social Work and Research, and the Association for Latina/o Social Work Educators. He has a Ph.D. in social work from Washington University in St. Louis.

JACQUELYN B. JAMES is co-director of the Center on Aging & Work, and director of the Sloan Research Network on Aging & Work at Boston College. James is also research professor in the Lynch School of Education and a fellow in the Behavioral and Social Science Division of the Gerontological Society of America. Her research focuses on the meaning and experience of work, gender roles and stereotypes, adult development, perceptions of older workers, and emerging retirement issues. In 2019, she co-edited *Current and Emerging Trends in Aging and Work*. James currently serves on the editorial board of *Work, Aging, and Retirement*, and is co-editor of a special issue of *Frontiers in Psychology*, which focuses on the psychological and economic considerations in retirement decision-making. She has a Ph.D. in psychology from Boston University.

PHYLLIS E. MOEN is director of the Life Course Center at the University of Minnesota, where she also holds a McKnight presidential chair and professorship of sociology. Her research focuses on macro-structural changes—demographic, technological, economic, labor market, and social—as they intersect with health, well-being, gender, class, and race across the life course. Moen has published numerous articles on work and retirement, and is the co-author of *Overload: How Good Jobs Went Bad and What We Can Do about* It. Two of her nine other books are award-winning: *Encore Adulthood: Boomers on the Edge of Risk, Renewal, and Purpose* (2016) and *The Career Mystique: Cracks in the American Dream* (2005). Moen is a fellow of the American Association for the Advancement of Science, the National Council on Family Relations, and the Gerontological Society of America. She has a Ph.D. in sociology from the University of Minnesota.

DAVID NEUMARK is distinguished professor of economics and co-director of the Center for Population, Inequality, and Policy at the University of California-Irvine. Neumark also serves as a visiting scholar at the Federal Reserve Bank of San Francisco, and as a senior research fellow at the Workers Compensation Research Institute. He is interested in labor economics and how they intersect with public policy issues, and his work on labor market discrimination focuses on new methods of measuring discrimination. Neumark is a leading scholar on the economics of aging and age discrimination, with numerous studies on the measurement of age discrimination in labor markets and tests of alternative models of the age-earnings profile. Recently, he conducted a study on how stronger age discrimination laws complement policy reforms intended to increase labor supply of older workers, and conducted a large-scale field experiment testing for age discrimination. Neumark is actively engaged as a consultant on large, class-action discrimination lawsuits. He has M.A. and Ph.D. degrees in economics from Harvard University.

MO WANG is Lanzillotti-McKethan eminent scholar chair at the Warrington College of Business at the University of Florida. His research focuses on retirement and older worker employment, occupational health psychology, and advanced quantitative methodologies. Wang is the recipient of numerous honors, including: Academy of Management HR Division Scholarly Achievement Award; Careers Division Best Paper Award; European Commission's Erasmus Mundus Scholarship for Work, Organizational, and Personnel Psychology; and the Emerald Group's Outstanding Author Contribution Award. He currently serves as editor-in-chief of the journal *Work, Aging, and Retirement* and as associate editor of the *Journal of Applied Psychology*. He is also a fellow of the American Psychological Association, Association for Psychological Science, and Society for Industrial and Organizational Psychology, and was until recently editor of the Oxford Handbook of Retirement. Wang has a Ph.D. in industrial-organizational psychology and developmental psychology from Bowling Green State University.